GERMANY, EUROPE AND THE PERSISTENCE OF NATIONS

Germany, Europe and the Persistence of Nations

Transformation, interests and identity, 1989-1996

STEPHEN WOOD

Ashgate

Aldershot • Brookfield USA • Singapore • Sydney

Published by
Ashgate Publishing Ltd
Gower House
Croft Road
Aldershot
Hants GU11 3HR
England

Ashgate Publishing Company
Old Post Road
Brookfield
Vermont 05036
USA

British Library Cataloguing in Publication Data
Wood, Stephen
    Germany, Europe and the persistence of nations :
    transformation, interests and identity, 1989-1996
    1.Nationalism - Europe - History - 20th century 2.Germany -
    History - 1990- 3.Germany - Politics and government - 1990-
    4.Europe - Politics and government - 1989-
    I.Title
    943' .0879

Library of Congress Cataloging-in-Publication Data
Wood, Stephen
    Germany, Europe and the persistence of nations : transformation,
    interests and identity, 1989-1996 / Stephen Wood.
        p.   cm.
    Includes bibliographical references and index.
    ISBN 1-84014-444-0
    1. Germany--Politics and government--1990- 2. Europe--Politics
    and government--1989- 3. European Union. 4. Germany--Foreign
    relations--1990- 5. Europe--Foreign relations--1989- 6. Politics
    and culture--Germany. 7. Nationalism--Germany. 8. Nationalism-
    -Europe. I. Title.
    DD290.29.W66 1998   98-6527
    940,55'9--dc21   CIP

ISBN 1 84014 444 0

Printed in Great Britain by The Ipswich Book Company, Suffolk

Contents

Acknowledgments

Many thanks to: Wayne Cristaudo, John Robbins, Bob Catley, Chris White, Silke Kantimm, Olaf Mager, May Wood, Stan Wood, German Academic Exchange Service (DAAD), Ruth Plümmer-Krüger, Gert Göhs, CDU, SPD, Auswärtiges Amt, Thomas Bagger, Reinhard Meier-Walser, Dietrich Rometsch, Institut für Europäische Politik, DGAP, Eberhard Schoof, Martin Bond, Cathy Wood, Søren Kierkegaard, Pernille Tvermoes, Siegmar Schmidt, Greg O'Leary, Kristian Gerner, Nick Siegler, Hanns Maull, Knut Kirste, Simon Bulmer, Centrum für angewandte Politikforschung, Ilona Ehlert, Paul Corcoran, Ulla Holm, Peter Mayer, Helen Wood, Muckl Kantimm, Lee Kersten, Dagmar Thiel, Pat Barkass, Joan King, Eva Bohn, Sandra and Dennis, Taketsugu Tsurutani, Thomas and Kiki, The Guvnor, Chi-Ni William Wang, Paul Arnold, Terry McCann. And probably others....

List of Tables

Preface

> Let us make no mistake: in everyone's mind at this moment, circumstances
> have set up a kind of *competition* between the various political systems of
> the world. In all countries the difficulties are enormous and, in fact, similar.
> The links and connections between countries in the modern world are such
> that this could not be otherwise. Money troubles know no frontiers. The
> worries of a finance minister must be very much alike from one capital to
> another. Every nation tries to solve its problems, some by political
> innovation, others by trying to preserve their institutions. But nations watch
> each other....they draw comparisons....they compare systems and the fruits
> of those systems. There is indeed, as I have just told you, a *competition
> between political mechanisms.* It has to be determined which of them is best
> suited, in the present state of the world, to function most economically and
> with most benefit to the life of a people.[1]

In the course of European history, the period between 1989's impetus
towards German reunification and the 1996 re-negotiation of the 'bargain'
struck at Maastricht is short. Yet during these years Europe experienced
immense transformations. Some are far from completed. Adjusting to the
end of bipolarity and the retreat of the superpowers, deepening integration in
the West and expanding to incorporate the East, response to new security
threats and globalizing economic trends are among the major challenges
facing a continent purportedly moving to 'ever closer union'. As the
geographic, strategic and economic-industrial core of the new Europe, the
new Federal Republic of Germany (FRG) must simultaneously contend with
the financial costs and social adjustment of the eastern *Länder's* accession
and rehabilitation extending into the next millenium. In the coming years
whichever of Germany's presently conceivable political alliances is in
government, it faces two vast integrative tasks: an economic and social
coalescence of the formerly separate German states, over which the Federal
Republic has control, that is, national prerogative; and the political unity of
Europe, laid out in the Basic Law[2] and reiterated by politicians since, none

---

1   Paul Valéry *The Question of Universal Suffrage* (1934) in Paul Valéry *Collected
Works* v7 *History and Politics* (London: Routledge & Kegan Paul 1962) trans.
Denise Folliot & Jackson Matthews p303 Emphasis in original

2   Ulrich K. Preuss termed this an 'innovative and, at that time, unique commitment to
participation in the creation of supranational institutions and the transfer of sovereign
powers to them (article 24)' See "German Unification: Political and Constitutional
Aspects" in *United Germany and the New Europe* Ed. Heinz D. Kurz (Aldershot:

more so than Helmut Kohl. Germany has been affirmed as the nexus of a post-Cold War security structure in the northern hemisphere. From US perspectives greater expectations for 'responsibility' were placed with Germany as its foreign policy formulation and conduct took on new dimensions. Against the backdrop of a volatile political climate in Russia these 'partners in leadership' are the avant garde of NATO's proposed expansion.

While the 'federalist' or 'core Europe' views expressed by the CDU (Christian Democratic Union, the major government coalition party) parliamentary leader Wolfgang Schäuble, Kohl and others were not entirely novel, they manifested a new determination and confidence to pilot Europe towards what is variously interpreted as a tighter merger, a transference, or a ceding of state sovereignty. These strategists averred that a core group of committed states was imperative to prevent the EU unravelling and should not be hindered by 'the slowest ship'. Having incited widespread protests the call for a core was temporarily subdued. A conception of Britain as Europe's most recalcitrant member exasperated many continental politicans, especially from Germany, but it also served to camouflage a more critical divergence. An enduring rationale decreed that 'success' hinged on France— on the will of its political leadership, the overcoming of forces antipathetic to 'Europe', the capacity of its economy and adequate coherence of its society. A congenial France would provide emphatic impetus for the CDU agenda. But France was a task itself.

The old Adenauer *Bundesrepublik* of 'no experiments' is transformed and immersed in two, if not three, giant experiments[3] as policy-makers endeavour to balance domestic and international priorities with grand European visions. The discrete rather than communal nature of interest formation among the European member states soon stimulated expression of the need for Germany to recognise and define its 'national interests' amidst a new uncertainty.[4] While often in alignment or able to compromise there are also fissions between Germany and its partners. When this occurs domestic forces will direct Germany's weight in the service of what are perceived to be *German* interests with increased vigour. The 'nation', like others around it, persists and is differentiated politically from 'Europe'.

Edward Elgar 1993) pp47-58

3   *Experiment Vereinigung: ein sozialer Grossversuch* Eds. Bernd Giesen & Claus Leggewie (Berlin: Rotbuch 1991)

4   American sources were prominent, later joined by German scholars. See *Germany in a New Era* Ed. Gary L. Geipel (Indianapolis: Hudson Institute 1993); *Germany's New Position in Europe* Ed. Arnulf Baring (Oxford: Berg 1994)

Introduction

This book has theoretical and empirical components. It attempts to convey how certain identifications, boundaries, and conceptualising of interests established in nineteenth century Europe persist in the present among new forms of international organization. The pivotal actor is Germany and its progress towards becoming a 'normal nation-state' with its own culture and identity, one which preferably pursues its economic and political goals through multilateral European structures. No less essential to this analysis, however, are divergent aims and self-conceptions held by other nation-states and which often result in resistance to German objectives or preferences. Associated with, though not the same as enduring historical misgivings, this is based on perceptions that the European Union (EU) is or will evolve into a Trojan horse for predominantly German national interests with the result that others are in various ways diminished.

The book then involves exposition of several related areas and combines components which might otherwise be situated separately in the disciplines of international relations, comparative politics, history, or political theory. The theoretical framework situates 'nations' and 'Europe' in historical and current understandings and juxtaposition. The concepts of culture and identity are introduced with special regard to questions of political control and legitimacy. To develop these underpinnings I utilise the work of, among others, Anthony Smith, Ernest Gellner and Max Weber, and scholars of more recent prominence, including Ole Wæver and Philip Schlesinger. A discussion of German identity before and after 1989 precedes a more empirical focus on the transformation in Germany's political status since reunification in 1990. It responds to enquiries raised by Simon Bulmer and William Paterson in 1987. They asked 'How far will the FRG be able to build upon its status as the EC's dominant economy to become its political pacemaker as well? Is the EC about to become an international extension of West German interests, as a wider context for *Modell Deutschland* ?'.[1] In constructing a response I integrate the previous theoretical suppositions with analyses of united Germany's domestic polity and foreign affairs, aspects of French and British politics and these states' relations with Germany, and the structures and processes of the EU.

---

1   Simon Bulmer & William Paterson *The Federal Republic of Germany and the European Community* (London: Allen & Unwin 1987) pp1-2

Since 1989 the world has experienced dramatic geo-political realignments and ongoing consequences that the authors cited above, like most others, were unlikely to have foreseen. At the epicentre was the divided Germany, the 'two states, one nation' around which the Cold War order had been constructed.[2] 'History', then featured by a strange stasis, has become 'mobilised, overheating'.[3] The present, as the German President then phrased it, is 'a time with no name'.[4] It is a curious feature of this temporal—and spatial—uncertainty, that apparent progress towards European unity has been paralleled by a rise in manifestations of 'national identity' and a continued even increased reliance on the nation-state. In France and Britain politicians continue to speak in terms of 'national goals' and 'national interests'. It has also become much more 'normal' in Germany. This rhetoric is often accompanied by references to a symbiotic European interest but there is little superseding of the former in practice, though the two can often be compatible. Each political class cannot ignore the identification of a social majority (the electorate) as constituting a community of mutual responsibilities, privileges and obligations within a particular state. A combination of cultural understandings at the societal level and a locating of numerous expectations with the state at a political level remains strong. Historical experience reinforces the connection. For each population, involvement in the European Union must be transformed into tangible benefit *for it* while simultaneously maintaining the integrity of other not discernably material elements of collective identity. The European Union is not an expression of 'Post-nationalism'.[5] Rather it is a context, or theatre for another form of nationalism, or, advancing national interests by other means, filtered through and enacted by political, diplomatic and bureaucratic representatives of national populations in multilateral arrangements. This is not solely a manifestation of *states* in competition but of difference between *nations*.

---

2   *Germany and Europe in Transition* Eds. Adam Daniel Rotfield & Walther Stützle (Oxford: Oxford University Press 1991)

3   Jürgen Habermas "Citizenship and National Identity: Some reflections on the future of Europe" *Praxis International* v12 n1 1992 pp1-19

4   Roman Herzog "Die Globalisierung der deutschen Außenpolitik ist unvermeidlich" *Bulletin* 15-3-95

5   This term was coined by the eminent German scholar Karl-Dietrich Bracher in the 1970s and originally regarding West Germany. It has been employed in a wider European context and with some frequency since

Reunified Germany and Europe

The western Federal Republic had been *the* model European citizen, firmly orientated to *Westbindung* (tying itself to the West) and the leading financial sponsor of the European Community (EC). This pristine constitutional democracy rejected the symbols and the practice of past German politics. A vast corpus of academic literature has appeared on the 'new Germany', the 'new Europe', and the conjunctions between them. Challenges facing Germany after reunification, the tumult of the international environment surrounding it, and integration of the enlarged nation-state into the European Community are predominating themes.[6] The united Europe objective was pursued so that Germany could 'escape its own nation-state prison'. After forty years 'it emerged in 1989-90 at a shaft marked 'Germany' not 'Europe' and has remained there since, unable to find the 'European exit''.[7] As

---

6   Among the best accounts in English are Elizabeth Pond *Beyond the Wall: Germany's Road to Unification* (Washington: Brookings Institute 1993) featuring extensive use of interview material with key negotiators and policy-makers; Renata Fritsch-Bournazel *Europe and German Reunification* (New York: Berg 1992), a compilation of media reports, offical statements and excerpts of academic commentary; *German Unification: The Unexpected Challenge* Ed. Dieter Grosser (Oxford: Berg 1992) a volume of monographs by German scholars articulating various internal and external aspects of reunification; David Marsh *The New Germany: At the Crossroads* (London: Century 1990) both a psycho-social portrait and indicator of German economic potential; *The New Germany and the New Europe* Ed. Paul B. Stares (Washington: Brookings Institute 1992) Peter H. Merkl *German Unification in the European Context* (Pennsylvania: University Park 1993) a voluminous account presenting a 'generational analysis of German attitudes'; Timothy Garton Ash *In Europe's Name: Germany and the Divided Continent* (London: Vintage 1994) providing a penetrating insight into West German *Ostpolitik* and the "Machiavellian" capacities and strategies of Germany's post-war politicians promoting a new *Moralpolitik* or 'policy of responsibility'. *Germany's New Position in Europe* Ed. Arnulf Baring (Oxford: Berg 1994) in which most contributors argue that the 'realities' of the post-Cold War world demand a more active role for German foreign policy and clearer definition of 'national interests'. In German, Karl Kaiser *Deutschlands Vereinigung: Die Internationale Aspekt* (Bonn: Bastei Lubbe 1991) surveys the international context and assembles various related official texts; and the encyclopaedic *Handwörtebuch zur deutschen Einheit* Eds. Werner Weidenfeld & Karl-Rudolf Korte (Frankfurt a.M.:Campus 1992) encompassing abridged commentaries on numerous tangents of German unity. As evidenced by some of the titles above there is a variability in terminology regarding Germany and the events of 1990. In acknowledgment of the partly political, partly semantic debate but more so for purposes of clarity the term "reunification" shall be used throughout except where stated differently (e.g. as "unification"). On this see Dieter Mahnke "Reunification as an issue in German Politics 1949-1990" in *German Unification: The Unexpected Challenge...* pp33-54. See pp33-34

7   Edwina S. Campbell "United Germany in a Uniting Europe" in *Germany in a*

reunification came to dominate the European agenda, geo-politics impacted on an arrangement focused on economic concerns. The German leadership pressed for transference, or relinquishment, of core elements of state sovereignty to move integration beyond intergovernmentalism and its inherent capacity for deadlock. To democratize the process they favoured increased powers for the 'supranational' European Parliament. The EC's metamorphosis into a European Union followed a dramatic shift in Europe's political balance, which it was intended to contain. The resulting compromise saw the Germans placate the French by pledging to Europeanize the Deutsche Mark, but on their terms and in return for a complementary political union. Crucial tacit understandings had already dissolved.

Many accounts note French and British apprehension at the events of 1989-90 and discord surrounding the Treaty on European Union in 1992, including within the national political parties which had negotiated the agreement.[8] Discontent was exacerbated by deep acrimony over currency crises, by continuing high unemployment, a perceived 'democratic deficit', trade related issues and the abject failure of 'Europe' to resolve the Balkan conflagration.[9] The question, or spectre, of putative German domination of Europe continued to reappear.[10] However, the underlying motivation or cause

New Era Ed. Gary L. Geipel (Indianapolis: Hudson Institute 1993) pp81-89

8   Robert Picht "Deutsche-französiche Beziehungen nach dem Fall der Mauer: Angst vor 'Großdeutschland'" *Integration* n2 1990 pp47-58; Ingo Kolboom *Vom geteilten zum vereinigten Deutschland: Deutschland-Bilder in Frankreich* (Bonn: Europa Union 1991); Richard Davy "Großbritannien und die Deutsche Frage" *Europa-Archiv* n45 1990 pp139-144; See also Pond *Beyond the Wall* for an incisive analysis. Walter Goldstein "Europe after Maastricht" *Foreign Affairs* v71 n5 1993 pp117-132; Hans Arnold *Europa am Ende?* (München: Piper 1993) See also *Eurobarometer* n40 December 1993

9   Stevan K. Pavlowitch "Who is "Balkanizing" Whom? The Misunderstandings Between the Debris of Yugoslavia and an Unprepared West" *Dædelus* v123 n2 1994 pp203-223; Noel Malcolm "Bosnia and the West: A Study in Failure" *The National Interest* n39 Spring 1995 pp3-14

10   Beate Neuss "The European Community: How to Counterbalance the Germans" in *German Unification: The Unexpected Challenge* pp136-149; Andrei Markovits & Simon Reich "Deutschland New Gesicht: Über deutsches Hegemonie in Europa *Leviathan* n1 1992 pp15-63; John Laughland "The Philosophy of "Europe"" *The National Interest* Spring 1995 pp58-67. Not all interpretations of a potential German predominance are negative. See William Wallace "Deutschlands zentrale Rolle: Ein versuch, die europäische Frage neu zu definieren" *Integration* n1 1990 pp13-20. Some present it as a *fait accompli* . See Fabio Luca Cavazza & Carlo Pelanda "Maastricht: Before, During and After" *Dædelus* v123 n2 Spring 1994. See also *The Germans and their Neighbours* Eds. Dirk Verheyen & Christian Søe (Boulder: Westview 1993); transcripts from the symposium "United Germany: Stabilizing Influence or Threat?" *Partisan Review* 1995; Josef Janning "A German Europe—a European Germany? On the debate over Germany's foreign policy" *International Affairs* v72 n1 January 1996 pp9-

that prevents Europe, six years after German reunification, from becoming a political community beyond individual vetoes and detached electorates (*pace* the European Parliament) has not been systematically elucidated. Despite arguments to the contrary,[11] there is little genuinely communal European interest, somehow elevated above its component parts. When congruity appears it is the result of intergovernmental bargaining and compromise or some form of inducement leading to the success of one preference before others.[12]

A steering mechanism set on 'national interests' not only survives in present day Europe but predominates and will determine the continent's political and cultural contours in the foreseeable future. Whether the perceptions and actions of election-focused politicians, policy-makers, or populations are accurate reflections of what the 'national interest' is, is almost irresolvable and it is not a chief purpose to follow this particular avenue.[13] Suffice to say these interests might be conceived and pursued in terms of economic gain, military security, preserving a parliamentary or formal independence over policy-making, linguistic and cultural integrity, and acquiring or maintaining influence in international organizations. Adding to classical or structural realist depictions of world politics,[14] or comparative and

32; August Pradetto "After the Bipolar World: Germany and her European Neighbours" *German Monitor* n37 1996 pp167-216; Tony Judt *A Grand Illusion: An Essay on Europe* (New York: Hill & Wang 1996)

11   Cf. Michael Butler *Europe: More than a Continent* (London: Heinemann 1986); *Federal Solutions to European Issues* Eds. Bernard Burrows, Geoffrey Denton & Geoffrey Edwards (New York: St. Martins Press 1978); *Europe: Rêve-Aventure-Réalité* Ed. Henri Brugmans (Brussels: Elsevier 1987); Ernest Wistrich *The United States of Europe* (London: Routledge 1994); A mass of European Commission literature has reiterated Europe's common interests, past and destiny

12   One of the most capable proponents of this position is Andrew Moravscik. See "Negotiating the Single European Act: national interests and conventional statecraft in the European Community" *International Organization* v45 n1 1991 pp19-56 and "Preferences and Power in the European Community: A Liberal Intergovernmentalist Approach" *Journal of Common Market Studies* v31 n4 1993 pp473-519

13   The concept (and perhaps the articulation) of national interests is multifarious and often oblique. It is, however, also consequential nonetheless. It is not my intention to engage in an extended theoretical exposition of what this term means in any definitive sense, or to exhaustively catalogue the motivations behind it and examples in practice

14   Hans J. Morgenthau *Politics among Nations* Sixth Edition (New York: Knopf 1967) includes theoretical evaluations of nations, 'national character' and nationalism, and makes connections to the state and geopolitics. His conception of nationalism does not specifically entail manipulation of international institutions in a later 'interdependent' world, though it may point towards it. Kenneth Waltz *Theory of International Politics* (Reading: Addison-Welsey

institutional studies,[15] new 'societal insecurities' have extended the scope of international relations as a discipline and recent works stress the political dimensions of national cultures fearing disconnection from 'their' states.[16]

Europe is at an impasse and at the centre of a new geo-political fluidity Germany is forced to confront new realities. No amount of rhetoric about German and European unity being two sides of the same coin can expunge what, in the wider international context, German reunification impressed more than anything else: i) Germans in two states believed themselves to be a nation>despite systemic differences they have sufficient cultural unity>they sought and have a common political authority. ii) Europe is not a nation>it does not have sufficient cultural unity>it does not have a common political system.[17] Instead an *à la carte* arrangement operates. The struggle between forces in Europe's integration-fragmentation dynamics is not precisely delineated along nation-state lines but if the former prevails, one component member will most replicate its preferences. Smaller net beneficiaries lobby for assistance as a sideshow to the main competition between three visions of 'Europe': French, British and German.[18] German championing of a politically

---

1979), and Robert Gilpin *War and Change in World Politics* (Cambridge: Cambridge University Press 1981) virtually ignore the role of national identity. Somewhat more conscious of this factor is *The New European Community: Decisionmaking and Institutional Change* Eds. Robert Keohane and Stanley Hoffmann (Boulder: Westview 1991)

15 *Euro-Politics, Institutions, and Policymaking in the "New" European Community* Ed. Alberta M. Sbragia (Washington: Brookings Institute 1992)

16 Scandinavian based scholars are prominent in this area. See *Identity, Migration and the New Security Agenda in Europe*, Eds. Ole Wæver, Barry Buzan, Morten Kelstrup and Pierre Lemaitre (London: Pinter 1993); Barry Buzan *People, States and Fear: An Agenda for International Security Studies in the Post-Cold War Period* Second Edition (Brighton: Harvester Wheatsheaf 1991); *National Cultures and European Integration: Exploratory Essays on Cultural Diversity and Common Policies* Ed. Staffan Zetterholm (Oxford: Berg 1994) and Bill McSweeney "Identity and Security: Buzan and the Copenhagen school" *Review of International Studies* v22 1996 pp81-93. See also, Friedrich Kratochwil *The Return of Culture and Identity in IR Theory* (Boulder: Lynne Rienner 1996)

17 For a detailed exposition of linkages between the power of national myths and policy legitimacy in the EU see Daniela Obradovic "Policy Legitimacy and the European Union" in *Journal of Common Market Studies* v34 n2 1996

18 Cf. Ole Wæver "Three Competing Europes" *International Affairs* v66 n3 1990 pp477-493. I substitute Wæver's inclusion of a Russian Europe (along with French and German) for a British model believing it more relevant to the present EU and indeed that 'traditional' British conceptions of free trade and politically independent nation-states are in evidence. British isolationism reduces the main participants, or candidates, to France and Germany. See Ole Wæver, Ulla Holm & Henrik Larsen *The Struggle for 'Europe': French and German Concepts of State, Nation and European Union* (forthcoming). Inability to fuse their 'Europe's' ironically contributes to the continuance of a British model

integrated Europe is the internationalising of a new nationalism, less demonstrative and grandiose than the French and less stubbornly detached than the British.[19] Germany remains a nation-state because its European neighbours, not least the largest, have a different conception about Germany and Europe conflating; and because the German population are increasingly dubious about it as well. All this is traceable back to national identities overpowering the notion of a 'common European identity'.

Chapter Outlines

The first chapter is concerned with nations and nationalism which, just as they have re-emerged as an explosive political force, have also inspired a burgeoning field of scholarship. Manifestations of aggressive nationalism on Europe's eastern periphery and the Balkans; or conflict associated with the presence of 'foreigners' in the western European countries might imply that Western Europe is a unity, defining itself by what is outside: a 'fortress Europe', commonly interested in restricting the entry of non-Europeans or those from the east.[20] But in relations *between* western EU members lines of continuity can be traced for the concept 'nation' since its emergence in the late eighteenth and nineteenth centuries to its current effects on integration. While what the 'national interest' might be in specific instances or general policy directions is contestable, there is a tacit presumption that such an ideal exists.[21] A response to the ubiquitous enquiries 'what is a nation?' and 'what is nationalism?' precedes exposition of how nations and nationalism function in practice.[22] States are political shells shaped by the nations they contain and

---

19   In these external 'state' manifestations, all three could be perceived as 'liberal' or 'rational' forms of nationalism. On one hand there is cooperation or compromise where this is perceived to serve the interests of each. On the other they may pursue independent strategies, perhaps entirely rational in the national context but opposed by or damaging to others. Cf. *Nationalism and Rationality* Eds. Albert Breton, Gianluigi Galeotti, Pierre Salmon & Ronald Wintrobe (Cambridge University Press: Cambridge 1995); Yael Tami *Liberal Nationalism* (Princeton: Princeton University Press 1993); Michael Lind "In Defence of Liberal Nationalism" *Foreign Affairs* v73 n3 May/June 1994 pp87-99. This is complicated by other non-utilitarian concerns like the often intangible meanings of 'prestige', 'tradition', or 'status' in the world

20   Étienne Balibar "Es Gibt Keinen Staat in Europa: Racism and Politics in Europe Today" *New Left Review* n186 March/April 1991 pp5-19

21   Margaret Canovan has recently advanced this argument in *Nationhood and Political Theory* (Cheltenham: Edward Elgar 1996)

22   Ernst Renan, Max Weber and Ernest Gellner are among the leading thinkers on the idea of nation and its implementation. In different ways Alan Milward and Paul Taylor, among others, confirm this form of conceptualising interests and

nations denote a hierarchy of preference. The nation, whatever confusions there may be in defining it, still has relevance as an artefact of internal coherence and external differentiation.[23]

The second chapter investigates the concept of culture, its relation to nations and to a European polity. The theorising of culture as encompassing whole societies relegated previous notions to a marginalized (yet simultaneously elevated) status as 'high culture'.[24] Academic interest in its various meanings and contents continues to expand. Neither these developments nor the 'global culture' of the post-industrial age has eradicated the identification of particular cultures, especially in the form of native languages and distinctive histories, with particular nations.[25] The diffusion of a superimposed global culture has not eliminated the contingency that a political community requires sufficient cultural underpinnings. In this sense contemporary European cultures remain, not totally, but indispensably bound to nations. A cultural basis for political union, translating into 'effective Europe-wide party structures' and popular involvement with them, is chimerical. Jürgen Kocka's study on Germany's 'unification crisis' recognizes the cultural factor as a *Schwerpunkt*, and in common European terms, its absence in any substantive form. He links cultural affinity to the idea of a nation and to the functioning of political communities. While his analysis of

identities in the processes of European integration. The work of Anthony Smith provides linkages between these sets of scholarship

23   A good exposition is William Bloom *Personal Identity, National Identity and International Relations* (Cambridge: Cambridge University Press 1990) See also *Nation and Identity in Contemporary Europe* Eds. Brian Jenkins & Spyros A. Sofos (London: Routledge 1996)

24   The Frankfurt School being among the prominent precursors, followed by Raymond Williams, Stuart Hall and others

25   Max Weber *Economy and Society: An Outline of Interpretive Sociology* Eds. Guenther Roth & Claus Wittich (Berkeley: University of California Press 1978) explains the role of cultural prestige in sustaining the idea of nation. Later Ernest Gellner elaborated a theory of how culture came to the fore as denoting predominant characteristics. Intellectuals and education systems created nations, based around shared cultures. *Nations and Nationalism* (Oxford: Blackwell 1983); In *Media, State and Nation: Political Violence and Collective Identities* (London: Sage 1994) Philip Schlesinger reveals many continuities with Gellner. Cultural identifications among 'Europeans', and often connected to questions of political legitimacy, remain far closer to particular nations than they do to a common Europe. Cf. the treatments of particular nation-states by David Loosely *The Politics of Fun: Cultural Policy and Debate in Contemporary France* (Oxford: Berg 1995), and *German Cultural Studies* Ed. Rob Burns (Oxford: Oxford University Press 1995) neither of which suggests the existence of a monolithic national culture but nonetheless convey a uniqueness best described by reference to 'French' or 'German' culture. Cf. Marc Fumaroli *L'Etat culturel: Essai sur une religion moderne* (Paris: Editions de Fallois 1991)

the factors hindering the infusion of democratic legitimacy into pan-European structures is good the questions again remain insufficiently resolved.[26]

Europe's populations are concerned about exposure to the vicissitudes of interest formation, decision-making and implementation of policy in a context where control is effectively removed from the traditional political representative, the state. Globalization is reshaping national cultures but affects each differently, some being more influential or adaptable to its trends than others.[27] The EU's declared goal of political integration requires great sensitivity in cultural matters. It may involve language questions, methods of economic organization, history and the national psyche, choice of television programmes, food products, and so on. It may mean a perception about rank in the world.

1989-90 began another phase in the extensive and often torturous discussion about 'German identity' which is the theme of chapter three. In previous decades, while the political class concentrated on merging it into Europe, West German society immersed itself in economic concerns, rejected aspirations to world power, and was averse to participation in peacekeeping activity.[28] In contrast to France, the relation between territory and identity waned, even as the constitutional goal of reunification was held open. Featured by the perennial 'who is German?' and 'coping with the past', debates about defining, legitimising, or explaining 'the nation' are now conducted in a vastly changed environment.[29] For the new Germany this is a complex process. It

26   Jürgen Kocka *Vereinigungskrise: Zur Geschichte der Gegenwart* (Göttingen: Vandenhoek & Ruprecht 1995) pp167-168

27   Frederick Buell *National Culture and the New Global System* (Baltimore: Johns Hopkins University Press 1994) Montserrat Guibernau *Nationalisms: The Nation-State and Nationalism in the Twentieth Century* (Cambridge: Polity 1996), especially Chapter 7

28   Hans-Peter Schwarz *Die Gezähmten Deutschen: Von der Machtbesessenheit zur Machtvergessenheit* (Stuttgart: Deutsche Verlags-Anstalt 1985)

29   The best pre-reunification account in English is Harold James *A German Identity 1770-1990* (London: Weidenfeld & Nicholson 1989); also *Die Identität der Deutschen* Ed. Werner Weidenfeld (Bonn: 1983); Charles S. Maier *The Unmasterable Past: History, Holocaust and German National Identity* (Cambridge Ma.:Harvard University Press: 1988). Of those published in and after 1990 see *Coping with the Past: Germany and Austria after 1945* Eds. Kathy Harms, Lutz R. Reuter, Völker Dürr (Madison: University of Wisconsin 1990); Presenting arguments for a more assertive and independent Germany, *Die selbstbewußte Nation: "Anschwellende Bocksgesang" und weitere Beiträge zu einer deutschen Debatte* Eds. Heimo Schwilk & Ulrich Schacht (Frankfurt a.M. Ullstein 1994). For concentration mainly on eastern German perspectives see the *German Monitor* series (formerly *DDR Monitor*). See also Peter Schneider's picaresque survey of the year between the fall of the Berlin Wall and formal reunification *Extreme Mittelage: Eine Reise durch das deutsche Nationalgefuhl* (Reinbek: Rowohlt 1990). Overtly or tacitly Jackson Janes theme "Who is German?", is

involves three kinds of linked consciousness: a post-communist kind for the eastern *Länder*; a somewhat bewildered move to a unified national consciousness 50 years after World War Two; and the reach for a speculative 'European' consciousness. The speed at which reunification happened overwhelmed observers and participants alike. It was only later that extensive 'personal' differences between east and west Germans were manifested. One commentator summarized that 'unification has only just begun. It is a process, not a single act—a process that will take years. Two states can be unified by a legal act, two societies cannot. And two separate societies do exist in Germany.'[30] Social and economic cohesion is needed internally before 'Europe' can be built.

Some prominent figures opposed reunification and spoke out against any national self-assertion on the part of the Germans.[31] Others followed a tradition set by Willy Brandt whereby pursuing what were distinctly national goals or appealing to a national identification were quite legitimate. It was Brandt who declared that what belonged together would grow together. This legacy is continued by his wife Brigitte Seebacher-Brandt. Conservative historians like Michael Stürmer, a critic of (West) Germany's 'historyless' society, interpreted events as a 'meeting of the Germans with history', while liberals like Marion Gräfin Dönhoff wrote of being in history's 'waiting room'.[32] The anti-politics of Hans-Magnus Enzensberger portrayed the conflict of 1939-1945 as a European civil war yet he foresaw no likely appearance of a persuasive European identity.[33] While there were empirical and psychic bases for Karl-Dietrich Bracher terming West Germany a 'post-national' democracy, he was dealing then with a very different context.[34] Now,

	present in most of the above. See *History of European Ideas* v18 n2 1994 pp215-224
30	Peter Graf Kielmansegg "Germany—A Future with Two Pasts" in *German Unification: The Unexpected Challenge* pp180-195, p180
31	Günter Grass *Two States-One Nation: The Case Against German Reunification* (London: Secker & Warburg 1990); Jürgen Habermas *Die Nachholende Revolution* (Frankfurt a. M: Suhrkamp 1990)
32	Marion Gräfin Dönhoff *Im Wartesaal der Geschichte* (Stuttgart: 1993)
33	Hans-Magnus Enzensberger *Aussichten auf den Burgerkrieg* (Frankfurt: Suhrkamp 1993). His theme followed that of the controversial historian Ernst Nolte *Der europäische Bürgerkrieg 1917-1945* (Frankfurt a.M.: Ullstein 1987)
34	See Heinrich August Winkler "Rebuilding of a Nation: The Germans Before and After Unification" *Dædelus* v123 n1 1994 pp107-127

as one volume sets forth, the *Bundesrepublik* has become *Deutschland.*[35] Nations and states are more likely to be presented as essential bases.[36]

In 1989-90 East Germans' rush for Deutsche Marks and West German concerns about the currency's value provided a common object of desire. Since then scepticism about Economic and Monetary Union (EMU) has demarcated between confidence in a German symbol and the uncertainty of the 'Euro'. The CDU believe German preferences for Europe can prevail in a future European Central Bank, as they do under Bundesbank rule.[37] The public have grave doubts. The era of post-materialist politics had not eliminated material concerns, despite critics of a so-called 'Deutschmark identity' appearing from left and right of the spectrum. Now there are new and widespread worries about *who* determines these economic fortunes: that is, will it be Germans or somebody else? After Rudolf Scharping's departure, the SPD leadership attempted, through playing up doubts on EMU, to recast and grasp the 'national dynamic' for political advantage. Like the proposed transmission of a national currency into an untested European form,[38] a (re)emergent German national identity, its cultural traits, and 'normal' exercise of interests is now juxtaposed with a hypothetical pan-European identity.

Chapter four discusses the domestic polity and politics in Germany. Nation-States have persisted regardless of the growth of supranational institutions and their powers, and, in the case of the Federal Republic of Germany, despite the terminology employed to dilute or deflect the fact that it *is* a nation and a state, even though 'different' to its neighbours.[39] Variances in terminology: nation-state, republic, federal republic, constitutional monarchy, make little difference. Their foremost aim, as democracies, is to reach a balance—though just what constitutes this will inevitably be opposed by some—in the interests of one community within a larger and looser cooperative. Germany's political structures are conducive to operating on a European scale, if they can manage to move their partners to this level.

Mutual influence of *Innenpolitik* and *Aussenpolitik* (domestic and foreign policy) becomes ever more apparent. Peter Pulzer has recently summarized that 'not only is German history inseparable from German

---

35   *From Bundesrepublik to Deutschland: German Politics After Unification* Eds. Michael G. Huelshoff, Andrei Markovits & Simon Reich (Ann Arbor: University of Michigan Press 1993)

36   Karl-Rudolf Korte *Nation und National Staat: Bausteine einer europäischen Identität* (Melle: Knoth Verlag 1993)

37   David Marsh *The Bundesbank: The Bank that Rules Europe* (London: Heinemann: 1992)

38   *Stark wie die Mark* (Bonn: Finanz Ministerium 1996)

39   Peter Pulzer perceives the present Federal Republic as 'the first true nation-state in German history'. He also examines the theme of 'normalisation' in "Unified Germany: A Normal State?" *German Politics* v3 n1 1994 pp1-17

politics; foreign policy in modern Germany has been inseparable from domestic policy'.[40] Consequently, if Germany experiences crisis it will impact badly on others. Authors who argue Germany is undergoing a 'crisis',[41] point to the simultaneous costs of reunification and of pursuing European goals, a painful restructuring of the labour market, and a welfare system coming under massive strain. Early optimistic forecasts about the united German economy required reappraisal. Industry diversification is needed and dates for upswings have been deferred.[42] Unemployment has set several post-war records with no sign of when the situation might definitively improve. Immigration, asylum seekers and the presence of 'foreigners' in general remain of extreme political sensitivity as German efforts to effectively Europeanize these concerns meet reluctance by other states and their societies.[43]

Unsurprisingly, there is a considerable loathing for the implications of Europe as a 'control device'. Growing popular discontent regards European integration as (still) being excessively manipulated from elsewhere and that it is not Germans, in whom there is a greater reservoir of confidence, who are controlling their 'European destiny'. No one is sure what kind of Europe will eventuate but scepticism is palpable.[44] Many Germans want to put in to practice what other EU states already had long before: the understanding that charity begins at home. West Germany's European cloak was comfortable for two reasons: Europe was understood as a political *sine qua non*; and, as it was then constituted, it provided satisfactory results. Since 1990 it has worn thin. German society will broadly concur with the Kohl government's European vision if it delivers adequate benefit and does not estrange itself from what most Germans consider to be their 'way of life'—revolving crucially around a high material standard of living. With each subsequent election this trend can be expected to increase regardless of who is in power. After a short burst of 'Europhorie' around 1989-90 there appears scarcely any genuine enthusiasm,

40   Peter Pulzer *German Politics 1945-1995* (Oxford: Oxford University Press 1995) p12
41   David Marsh *Germany and Europe: The Crisis of Unity* (London: Mandarin 1995); Kocka *Vereinigungskrise*
42   Cf. W. R. Smyser *The Economy of United Germany: Colossus at the Crossroads* (London: Hurst 1992); *United Germany and the New Europe* Ed. Heinz D. Kurz (Aldershot: Edward Elgar 1993)
43   Klaus Bade *Ausländer, Aussiedler, Asyl in der Bundesrepublik Deutschland* (Hanover: Landeszentrale für politische Bildung 1990); *European Migration in the Late Twentieth Century: Historical Trends, Actual Patterns, and Social Implications* Eds. Heinz Fassman & Rainer Munz (Aldershot: Edward Elgar 1994); CDU/CSU Fraktion im Deutschen Bundestag "Mehr europäische Rechtstaatlichkeit" (Bonn: CDU/CSU Pressedienst June 1995)
44   Cf. Hans-Wolfgang Platzer & Walter Ruhland *Welches Deutschland in welchem Europa?: Demoskopische Analysen, politische Perspektiven, gesellschaftliche Kontroversen* (Bonn: Dietz Nachfolger 1994)

less any emotive attachment for Europe because it is perceived as not really solving difficulties and, if anything, to be doing the opposite. The 'seeds of ambivalence', as one contribution perceived in 1992, have germinated.[45]

The German electorate's mood has been characterized as one of *Politikverdrossenheit*, a disenchantment with the parties and the political process, and which finds counterparts elsewhere.[46] Through his legendary *sitzfleisch*, a capacity to outlast his problems by ignoring them, Kohl has ploughed his way through 15 years as chancellor. He is considered the least unacceptable of an uninspiring collection. Coalition partners, the liberal FDP, have suffered an alarming decline. The main opposition party, the SPD (Social Democratic Party) has been in disarray for some years. There have been signals and actual cases of dealing with the previously out of bounds PDS (Party of Democratic Socialism, the former communists). These were more indications that (West) Germany's 'tacit consensus' to keep 'extremist' parties out of the mainstream was coming to an end. The party system headed for more volatility but Kohl remained and his personal goal of unifying Europe was hauled along with him.[47]

Chapter five is concerned with German foreign policy, in which from 1949 the FRG played by ground rules firstly set by the US and USSR and then, joined in an attempt to forge post-war authority and prestige for itself, by France. Having quietly eroded as the FRG expanded towards becoming an economic superpower, the events of 1989-91 confirmed that many of the rules had been swept away. After reunification German politicians continued to stress the importance of partnerships with France, the USA and Russia, often preceded by the adjective, 'special'. A few 'keywords' found themselves in the lexicon of German foreign policy, prominent among them 'Normalization'.[48] This expression firstly inferred changing the 'culture of

45   Emil J. Kirchner "The European Community: Seeds of Ambivalence" in *Developments in German Politics* Eds. Gordon Smith, William E. Paterson, Peter H. Merkl, Stephen Padgett (Houndmills: MacMillan 1992) pp172-184

46   "Politikverdrossenheit" was Germany's 'word of the year' in 1993

47   Apart from titles already mentioned, on the party system, elections, the electorate and political issues in the 1990s see: *The New Germany Votes: Unification and the Creation of a New German Party System* Ed. Russell J. Dalton (Providence: 1993); *Das Superwahljahr* Eds. Wilhelm Bürklin & Dieter Roth (Köln: Bund-Verlag 1994); *Parties and Party Systems in the New Germany* Ed. Stephen Padgett (Brookfiled: Dartmouth 1993); *Germany's New Politics: Parties and Issues in the 1990s* Eds. David Conradt, Gerald R. Kleinfeld, George K. Rosome & Christian Søe (Providence: Berghahn 1995); Russell J. Dalton *Politics in Germany* (New York: Harper Collins 1992); Hans-Georg Betz *Postmodern Politics in Germany: The Politics of Resentment* (Houndmills: MacMillan 1991) See also the special issue of *Dædelus* v123 n1 1994

48   Philip H. Gordon "The Normalization of German Foreign Policy" *Orbis* v38 n2 1994; Peter Glotz *Die falsche Normalisierung* (Frankfurt a. M.: 1994)

reticence' regarding German security policy. But it also implied arrival at a stage where the perceived necessity to assent to unfavourable policy options is not so certain. Instead of bending, stretching or contorting the German interest to fit the European, the reverse is set to occur with greater frequency.[49] According to Timothy Garton Ash, one of the field's most perspicacious observers, 'that the German and European questions were very closely related is obvious', however

> That there was such a sublime harmony of interests is not. There are good reasons for subjecting these claims to a little closer examination. For a start, it is characteristic of most European nation-states in modern history that their representatives assert or assume a harmony, or even identity, between what they see as national interests and what they claim to be European interests. One could cite countless examples from France, Poland, Italy, Russia or Hungary over the last two centuries. It was Bismarck who observed that 'I have always found that the word "Europe" in the mouths of those politicians who wanted from other powers something they did not dare to demand in their own name...'. The all-European phenomenon acquires, however, a particular edge in the case of Germany.[50]

The importance placed by the German government on maintaining, or reaching a harmonious coherence in the sum of its foreign relations has seen frequent reference to the 'balancing act' Germany must perform. Having cherished its own stability Germany was impelled towards a role as stabilizer. US concerns about the efficacy of NATO were joined by growing aversion to embroilment in European conflicts. The Clinton administration, as Bush's before it, saw political leadership in Europe as devolving on Germany. American pressure influenced the political and constitutional decisions and a shift of the party spectrum's centre of gravity needed to undertake an extended commitment to NATO and UN missions. The conferring of a probationary term on the UN Security Council as a prelude to probable permanent membership underwrote the expectations. In response to rising demands Foreign Minister Kinkel declared that 'more responsibility calls for more influence'.[51] 'Normalization' was a two-sided coin.

---

49   *Deutschlands neue Außenpolitik*, Band 1 "Grundlagen" & Band 2 "Herausforderungen". Eds Karl Kaiser & Hans W. Maull (München: Oldenbourg 1994, 1995); Band 3 "Interessen und Strategien" Eds. Karl Kaiser & Joachim Krause (München: Oldenbourg 1996)

50   Garton Ash *In Europe's Name...* p20

51   Matthew Beard "Bonn vote backs wider role in NATO missions" *The Times* 23-7-94 p11; "Kinkel sagt UNO Bundeswehr-Soldaten für Auslands-Einsätze zu" *Die Welt* 28-9-94 p1; Tony Barber "UN role steps up German presence in world arena" *Melbourne Age* 31-12-94 p6

While a trend of assertion has been apparent in German foreign affairs, a number of shocks or disturbances have accompanied this, for Germany and its partners. Negative economic repercussions resulting from high interest rates fuelled an unpopularity which for the French was exacerbated by divergence over world trade issues. In military and security matters the Gulf War revealed a general European inefficiency and Germany's lack of experience in 'hot' foreign policy. Disintegration and war in the former Yugoslavia precipitated a near fracture of the EU itself with Germany the target of blame for having reversed its previous hesitancy.[52] A more resolute approach has been taken regarding NATO expansion and Germany has become a broker between the various security architectures preferred by the US, France, the UK and Russia. In the EU Germany wants changes in voting rules. And a thorough overhaul of the budget will occur before the current arrangements expire in 1999. With eastern states about to join, the disparity between Germany (a creditor of DM21 billion) and the nearest net contributor, the UK (DM4.2 billion), will not be sustained.

Germany is envisaged as a benefactor and gateway to the EU by states and peoples in central and eastern Europe. Strongly supported by the state, the German presence sees economic investment accompanying various cultural manifestations: language, music and literature, media and intellectual forms. This region contains much uncharted territory for scholars. What has been established is that German influence (re)appeared very quickly after November 1989 and has grown since.[53] By 1994 the volume of German trade with eastern Europe and the CIS (DM104 billion) exceeded that with the US and was on an upward trajectory.

Chapter six examines the Franco-German relationship which, while it has been the main axis of European integration,[54] also has many other tangents. Both partners realise that they need each other but there is an

---

52   Comprehensive accounts are given by Hans W. Maull "Germany in the Yugoslav Crisis" *Survival* v37 n4 1995-96 pp99-130; Beverly Crawford "Explaining Defection from International Cooperation: Germany's Unilateral Recognition of Croatia" *World Politics* v48 July 1996 pp482-521

53   Andrei S. Markovits & Simon Reich "Should Europe Fear the Germans?" *German Politics and Society* n23 1991 pp1-20; Jacques Rupnik "Central Europe or Mitteleuropa?" *Dædelus* v119 n1 1990; George Kolankiewicz "Consensus and competition in the eastern enlargement of the European Union" *International Affairs* v70 n3 1994 pp477-495; Timothy Garton Ash "Journey to the Post-Communist East" *New York Review of Books* 23-6-94 pp13-20; *Deutsche Aussenpolitik* (Bonn: Auswärtige Amt 1995)

54   Julius W. Friend *The Linchpin: French-German Relations, 1950-1990* (New York: Praeger 1991). After de Gaulle's claim that 'there is only France and Germany, the others don't matter' another author recently termed the other original members 'window dressing'. Tony Judt "Nineteen Eighty-Nine: The End of *Which* European Era?" *Dædelus* v123 n2 1994 pp1-19

unanswered question as to how privileged this dyad will remain.[55] Like it changed everything else the end of the cold war completely reorientated the respective *raisons d'etat*.[56] A phase of tension had begun with the fall of the Berlin Wall and President Mitterrand's (along with others) less than wholeheartedly enthusiastic reception. Germany is building ties to the east and along with the French connection it also has an alternative 'closest' or 'most important' relationship with the United States. Germany's two best friends have a post-war record of recurrent mutual unfriendliness, often placing German governments in an arduous dilemma. The more France proclaims itself and acts as an (exceptional) independent nation-state, the more the dilemma will pass to France.[57]

After 1945 France modernized its economy, strove to reaffirm a world power status, and pursued its universal civilising mission, all assisted through community organs that were principally French designed and administered. Geographically this occurred within a Carolingian frame itself contained and subject to the *force majeure* of international politics. Concurrently both German states were also subject to restraints. In the west these were not only imposed by bipolarity but also derived from the construction of EC Europe as a 'garden in the French style.' The key role in shaping the political structures, the configuration and decision-making procedures of the EC system was held by the 'brain of Europe', France. Considerable influence over regulatory, economic and administrative spheres filtered down from this political supremacy. As diplomatic leader and voice for the European Community in world affairs the ordering of priorities generally reflected those of France. When and wherever possible European interests should not conflict with those of France but rather be one and the same. European integration was a vehicle that delivered benefits without excessive strife. When impasse appeared insurmountable a calculation of French national interests prevailed and progress could only be rejoined at France's satisfaction. In everyday terms this disequilibrium in political weight—within which German international reticence was a critical factor—manifested itself in the institutional-cultural complexion of the EC.[58]

---

55   *France and Germany 1983-1993: The Struggle to Cooperate* Ed. Patrick McCarthy (New York: St. Martins Press 1993)

56   *Handeln für Europa: Deutsch-französische Zusammenarbeit in einer veränderten Welt* Ed. CIRAC (Opladen: Leske & Budrich 1995)

57   Hans-Peter Schwarz "Das Deutsche Dilemma" in *Deutschlands neue Außenpolitik* Band 1 pp81-97 optimistically foresees no unsolvable dilemmas in this context

58   Abram de Swaan "The Evolving European Language System: A Theory of Communication Potential and Language Competition" *International Political Science Review* v14 n3 1993 pp241-255

This drives the French strategy of binding reunified Germany to institutions within which France can exert control. By harnessing German weight there is improved capacity for advancing French global interests and maintaining a desired 'status'. Apart from the still unresolved battle over EMU, the move to 'supranationalism' was to occur *without* diluting the sovereignty of the French state. The Maastricht Treaty hastened a now unavoidable confrontation between creating a supranational union or maintaining an ongoing intergovernmental system of sovereign states. The contradictions are stark but from the French perspective, entirely logical. While leading representatives of the German government coalition made explicit reference to the obsolescence of national sovereignty, in France, 'the nation', was fused with and supported symbolically, rhetorically and practically by the state. Political and cultural forms of identification were entwined.

Germany, meanwhile, was territorially and ideologically split. In both German states reference to the 'nation' was discouraged. Whether they openly said so, most neighbours, including France, were in agreement. Strong mutually supportive connections between culture and politics were thought to revive memories, internally and externally, of the *Machtstaat* that evolved after 1871. Conducted among intellectuals, *classe politique*, and public alike, the debate about French identity features recurring themes of 'exceptionalism', the 'citoyen', the *mission civilisatrice*, the role of the state, the future of democracy, and the neighbour to the east.[59] The outcry against aspects of globalization is joined by anxieties about inability to control the direction of Europeanization. The future prestige of French culture, bound with political values and the image of France in the world, is at stake.[60] From this perspective an imminent 'end of the nation-state'—as a German 'federal Europe' and trans-European networks would entail—means the end of a certain, very cogent idea of France.[61]

---

59   See the compilation on these and other themes of French politics and society *Remaking the Hexagon: The New France in the New Europe* Ed. Gregory Flynn (Boulder: Westview 1995); and Steven Kramer *Does France Still Count?: The French Role in the New Europe* (Westport: Praeger 1994) conveying a sense of the French talent for making reactive (foreign) policy appear bold and imaginative

60   Jean-David Levitte "The Cultural Diplomacy of France" (Ambassade de France en Australie: June 1994)

61   Jean-Marie Guéhenno *The End of the Nation-State* trans. Victoria Elliott (Minneapolis: University of Minnesota Press 1995) posits a disintegration in conventional political and territorial structures, now in process, as constituting the death of politics or, in the original title *La fin de la démocratie*. It is a 'prospect that horrifies many of the French, for whom the greatness of the nation is wholly political' p55. At time of publishing the author was France's ambassador to the European Union. See also John Laughland *The Death of Politics: France under Mitterrand* (London: Michael Joseph 1994); Philip H.

Chapter seven looks at the British relationship to the EU and to Germany in particular. The British role is a curious one. On the surface it appears that the UK is Europe's 'spoiler', yet it has the best record on implementing legislation nationally which it agreed to in European forums. Some tabloid headlines and dramatic political outbursts (usually on the British side) suggest that Britons and Germans reserve a special mutual hatred. Many traditionalists still view Germany through the prism of two world wars and even among younger generations an 'us' and (or versus) 'them' is apparent. Other evidence points in an entirely different direction, that a 'silent alliance' operates between them. A short list might include: the UK rank as the largest foreign investment site in the EU with German investors leading continental Europe; many aspects of its deregulated economy are being adopted in Germany; over 50,000 Britons are working in the booming Berlin construction industry; the UK is the favoured EU destination for German university students; the worldwide influence of the English language and the capacity of many Germans to speak and read it offers advantages for exchange and joint ventures; both states insist on preserving an American military-strategic presence in Europe.

Having said that, there was resolute resistance to further dilution of the British veto. Parliamentary sovereignty remained sacred and neither EMU or the Social Charter had British participation (at least under the Conservatives). The UK opposed fusing the Western European Union (WEU) defence forces into the EC where it would come under communal competences. Approaching the 1997 general election, 'Europe' was a campaign issue. The poll-favoured Labour opposition did not declare substantive alterations and the UK appeared set to remain in semi-detachment indefinitely.[62] Its presence signified the ongoing possibility of triangular politics between it, France, and Germany, and thereby a traditional role *vis-à-vis* the continent.

Chapter eight addresses the nature of the EU itself. It is a unique aggregation whose actors include state governments and bureaucracies, citizens, 'supra-national' institutions, regions, parties, various business and labour groups, individual political mavericks and so on, some competing and some complementary. As a political conception, functioning economic and administrative entity, and one aspiring to further jurisdictions and powers, the EU accommodates several perspectives of inquiry. International relations,[63]

Gordon *A Certain Idea of France* (Princeton: Princeton University Press 1993)

62   Simon Bulmer "Britain and European Integration: Of sovereignty, slow adaption, and semi-detachment" in *Britain and the EC* Ed. Stephen George (Oxford: Oxford University Press 1992) pp1-29

63   *Theorising International Relations: Positivism and After* Eds. Steve Smith, Ken Booth & Maysia Zalewski (Cambridge: Cambridge University Press 1995); *Boundaries in Question: New Directions in in International Relations* Eds. John MacMillan and Andrew Linklater (London: Pinter 1995). See also *The New*

comparative politics,[64] and 'policy networks' or 'networks'[65] all contribute as disciplinary models of analysis. Intergovernmental, neo-functionalist or liberal-institutionalist theories are all applied its form and operation.[66]

Of these, intergovernmentalism is the most relevant. While the defined 'Community' institutions, the Commission and the Parliament, are in a position of some independence from the states, their ability to enact anything is dependent upon bargains reached by representatives of the states. This was so in forming the existing body of legislation or guiding principles to which states adhered and then transferred powers of final outcome to communal decision.[67] That effectively meant back to a majority vote among themselves. The formulation of policies in what are not areas of specified community competence (those that need unanimity) requires another round of bargaining ending in agreement or otherwise on the terms (as began in Turin in 1996). Because of how constitutional, parliamentary, and democratic processes and imperatives presently operate, states swivel from functioning as negotiators in Brussels to multifarious roles domestically:[68] as source of authority and enforcer of law and order, economic regulator, collector of taxes, provider of welfare, mediator of various internal disputes, defender against terrorism or foreign incursion, promoter of social cohesion and a more intangible sense of communal morale. All this brings the state closer to specific cultural or societal motivations as well as particular understandings of history. In democracies any executive is transient and dependent on public support. So is the state itself.

European Community: Decisionmaking and Institutional Change Eds. Keohane & Hoffmann

64 Simon Hix "The Study of the European Community: The Challenge to Comparative Politics" *West European Politics* v17 n1 1994 pp1-30

65 Hussein Kassim "Policy Networks, Networks and European Union Policy Making: A Sceptical View" *West European Politics* v17 n4 1994 pp15-27

66 *Neorealism and Neoliberalism: The Comtemporary Debate* Ed. David Baldwin (New York: Columbia University Press 1993); Ernst Haas *The Uniting of Europe: Political, Social and Economical Forces 1950-57* (London: Stevens & Sons 1958); Robert Keohane & Joseph Nye *Power and Interdependence: World Politics in Transition* (Boston: Little & Brown 1989); Keohane *International Institutions and State Power* (Boulder: Westview 1989); Helen Milner "International Theories of Cooperation Among Nations: Strengths and Weakness" *World Politics* v44 April 1992 pp489-495

67 Alan Milward *The European Rescue of the Nation State* (London: Routledge 1992) cogently argues that the forerunners of the EC institutions were created by the nation-states to strengthen themselves without any intent to transcend to a supranational Europe. Milward concentrates on economic analysis and presumes a concomitant political equilibrium

68 Simon Bulmer "Domestic Politics and European Commmunity Policy-Making" *Journal of Common Market Studies* v21 n4 1983 pp349-363. See also Bulmer & Paterson *Federal Republic*

Extrapolating from Bulmer and Paterson's earlier enquiries, the first proposition made is that *if* a practical and extensive European *Union* is achieved it will be modelled most closely and increasingly developed on German designs in accordance with German preferences. The German economy is not in the best of health but it remains by far the largest in Europe and profoundly effects all others. It also contains the potential for considerable growth once its engine is overhauled. Though such a result may be ten years away, a new *Wirtschaftswunder* would extend Germany's status as a giant among subordinates. Augmenting and bolstered by existing economic predominance Germany is exerting increased political power in, through, and outside the European Union institutions. These circumstances are accompanied by recognition of German language as an official EU working language and expansion of this linguistic presence in eastern and central Europe.

The second point is that aversion to a German ascendancy has and will emanate from France as much as the designated 'Euro-sceptic', Britain. A common aspiration for keeping the powers of the nation-state extant and separate brings French and British positions together on a fundamental level and draws a line of division between them and Germany. It coincides with a re-emergence of balance of power thinking.[69] While the strategies of the French-led and British-led factions differed, 'fear of Germany was', as Alan Milward observes, 'the cement which forced these opposed interests still to try to find common ground'.[70] This triangle and the wider European sphere have two significant undercurrents which have risen to the surface. Firstly, national populations challenge élite domination of integration processes as more decisions made at the European level affect everyday life. If Euro-policies are considered disadvantageous or in some way threatening, individual societies will, in their role as electorates, make new demands of the states then forced to retune and resell 'Europe'. This infers or accommodates potential instrumentalization of 'cultural' motivations. The other lingering anxiety, felt most among the political class in Germany, is that without continued progress to 'supranationalism', which now means decisive political breakthroughs, the show may be over and the participants will go back to their respective national

---

69   On a newly constituted balance of power between the three see Reinhard Meier-Walser "Germany, France and Britain on the Threshold to a New Europe" *Aussenpolitik* v43 n4 1992 pp334-342. On the presence of the sovereignty factor, which also serves as a synonym for 'national independence' or 'legitimacy', see R. B. J. Walker *Inside/Outside: International Relations as Political Theory* (Cambridge: Cambridge University Press 1993)

70   Alan Milward and Vibeke Sørensen "Interdependence or integration? A national choice" in *The Frontier of National Sovereignty: History and Theory 1945-1992* Eds. Alan Milward et. al. (London: Routledge 1994) pp1-32

corners preparing potentially dangerous agendas.[71] These impulses are in conflict and at this point there is no effective understanding or mechanism to overcome it.

Thomas Kielinger spelt out in early 1990, 'Somehow, what happens in the European centre is still deeply impacting on the rest of the world—for better or worse'.[72] What nobody wants to admit is that if the construction of 'Europe' is to continue and actually move beyond being as, Stanley Hoffmann put it, a 'congeries of distinctive states without distinctive will',[73] someone will have to acquiesce. As this is unlikely, the permutation 'continuity in change' will find another application in the German-European relation. Germany will not abandon Europe but impose itself politically and diplomatically, appropriating, by necessity as much as desire, the leadership previously coveted by France. Foreign policy continuity indicates that Germany's political interests remain essentially located or merged in European and Atlantic multilateral structures. Change will see a wider and more German Europe.

71   Roger Boyes "Frailty of France heightens Kohl angst about war" *The Times* 8-12-95 p12
72   Thomas Kielinger "Waking up in the new Europe — with a headache" *International Affairs* v66 n2 1990 pp249-263
73   Stanley Hoffmann "France: Keeping the Demons at Bay" *New York Review of Books* 3-3-94 pp10-16

1 Nations and Nationalism

'nation' is an elastic concept - political, cultural, psychological dimensions, reflect the intensity of national consciousness the strength of which may depend on the particular combination of political and cultural parameters in the historical experience of the respective nation. Difference in historical experience may lead to a different awareness of a nation, with respect to both its constituent elements or patterns and the intensity of this awareness.[1]

Not all nations are alike and neither are all nationalisms. Problems of definition which threaten to undermine enquiries into nations and nationalism also animate academic fascination.[2] In attempting to bring some conceptual clarity to the subject, reference to 'elasticity' or some similar terminology is a useful start. As James Coleman states, 'nationality can be seen as consisting of whatever components form the basis for the members' identity' which 'sometimes, but not always, includes a common language, a common religion, a geographic territory, ethnic consanguinity'.[3] If there is a common theme it is that a group of people conceiving of themselves as a 'nation' presumes the existence of other 'nations' and, necessarily, differences between them. Like class, gender and race, nation constitutes a political category, but

---

1   Jaroslav Krejci & Vitezslav Velimsky *Ethnic and Political Nations in Europe* (London: Croom Helm 1981) Chapter 3 "What is a Nation: The dilemma of appellation" p36

2   Ernst B. Haas "What is nationalism and why should we study it?" *International Organization* v40 n3 1986 pp707-744; John A. Hall "Nationalisms, Classified and Explained" *Dædelus* v122 n3 1993 pp1-28; For other recent attempts to illuminate the subject see Montserrat Guibernau *Nationalisms: The Nation-State and Nationalism in the Twentieth Century* (Cambridge: Polity 1996); *Notions of Nationalism* Ed. Sukumar Periwal (Budapest: Central European University Press 1995); the extensive array of interpretations offered in *Nationalism* Eds. John Hutchinson & Anthony D. Smith (Oxford: Oxford University Press 1994); and also the 22 explanatory propositions put forward by Josep Llobera in *The God of Modernity: The Development of Nationalism in Western Europe* (Oxford: Berg 1994) pp219-221

3   James S. Coleman "Rights, rationality, and nationality" in *Nationalism and Rationality* Eds. Albert Breton, Gianluigi Galeotti, Pierre Salmon & Ronald Wintrobe (Cambridge University Press: Cambridge 1995) pp1-13 See p11

one more flexible and which can incorporate the first three.[4] In the contemporary West being part of nation is not a consideration permanently at the forefront of most minds. Nonetheless, the powerful attraction of national identity, a prerequisite of nationalism, has survived communism and liberal internationalism. The transition from identification with a nation, to affirmation or endeavours on its behalf, is often imperceptible. While I am chiefly concerned with European examples, all nations pertain to one of political theory's primary concerns: the 'we' factor. How far this 'we', along with its goals, liabilities, loyalties, rights and responsibilities, extends; what restrictions there are on membership; and in what contexts, if any, this 'we' can overlap with others without dissolution, set the parameters for the constituting of a national community.

The substance of a nation is people, but not every person can be part of any nation. Qualifications, which vary as much as there are nations, apply. 'We' are those who, in Michael Ignatieff's terminology, are categorised as 'belonging'.[5] 'They' are those who do not—which does not necessarily mean they never can. In spite of its apparent relevance for political theory, Margaret Canovan has argued that the desire to belong, to possess 'nationhood', has, at least since 1945, been as ignored by this discipline as it has been embraced by some others. Behind the propensity to omit or be dismissive of nations, nationhood and nationalism, however, the nation is actually lurking as a 'tacit' assumption. These unacknowledged or phantom nations most closely correspond to that from which, in their individual cases, these theorists hail and/or themselves 'belong'. This is both a ironic form of affinity and *ipso facto* presumes other nations with other loyalties. Canovan's critique contains a recurring presumption that these theorists who refrain from conscious exploration of nations as political phenomena all possess and extol 'liberal-democratic' values. This point shall be returned to later. I continue in agreement with her claim that—where it is not explicit—the presence of nations and nationhood constitute a 'tacit premise of all contemporary political thinking'.[6]

---

4 Margaret Canovan *Nationhood and Political Theory* (Cheltenham: Edward Elgar 1996) p67 note 61

5 Michael Ignatieff *Blood and Belonging: Journeys into the New Nationalism* (New York: Farrar, Strauss & Giroux 1993)

6 Canovan *Nationhood and Political Theory* p1. Cf. Anthony D. Smith *Nationalism in the Twentieth Century* (Oxford: Martin Robertson 1979) on the assumptions behind the work of international organizations which 'are bound up with a nationalist framework which views 'societies' as 'naturally' determined by the boundaries and properties of nation-states' See p191

This assumption also applies in the statecraft of political practitioners be they engaged in the conduct of domestic or foreign policy. Political, economic or historical impulses emitting from two or more national polities are often harmonized; nationalism can be internationalized.[7] Because notions of bellicosity, isolationism, or aggressive competition are so prominent in, particularly academic, understandings of what nationalism is,[8] when precisely the same goals of nationalist activity (economic advance, political influence, cultural prestige) are achieved through peaceful means or by more than one nation simultaneously, the motivating force and process itself becomes one of 'international cooperation'. What international organizations often actually facilitate is a camouflaged nationalism. The real test of allegiances, identifications, and perceptions of interests, for politicians and publics, comes in times and events of open discord, when competition for resources intensifies, or when dramatic geo-political developments or pressures for socio-cultural change occur.[9] Pursuance or implementation of domestic or foreign policies that lead to conflict with another nation-state is then viewed as nationalistic, a 'state nationalism'. Such a perspective is especially likely from the dissenting party. However, a response from another which seeks to prevent this and impress its own preference is also nationalistic.

Interpretations of Nations

The variety of nations is matched by a variety of explanations as to their essential characteristics. For Ernst Renan, one of the earliest and still most influential authorities, nations are a category that in each case requires consensual affirmation—a nation is a nation, because it wants to be.[10] In asserting this Renan elevates the French republican conception over others

7   Cf. Smith *Nationalism in the Twentieth Century* Chapter eight "Internationalism"

8   Eric Hobsbawm *Nations and Nationalism Since 1780: Programme Myth, Reality* (New York: Cambridge University Press 1990). For some recent counterviews of nationalism see Salvador Cardus and Joan Estruch "Politically correct anti-nationalism" *International Social Science Journal* v144 June 1995 pp347-352; David Archard "Myths, Lies and Historical Truth: A Defence of Nationalism" *Political Studies* v43 1995 pp472-481; Michael Lind "In Defence of Liberal Nationalism" *Foreign Affairs* v73 n3 1994 pp87-99

9   Cf. Russel Hardin "Self-interest, group identity" in *Nationalism and Rationality* Eds. Albert Breton, Gianluigi Galeotti, Pierre Salmon & Ronald Wintrobe (Cambridge University Press: Cambridge 1995) pp14-42

10   Ernst Renan "Qu'est-ce qu'une nation?" in *Oeuvres Completes* Vol.1 (Paris: Calman Lévy 1947 [1882]) pp887-906

(allowing that fewer 'certified' nations or types of nations were then in existence). In his famous Sorbonne lecture he attempts to

> argue against the coercive limiting vision of the nation, and instead to promote a nation with a voluntary quality at its core. He wants to emphasize the nation's similarity to the individual in its personal history, and right to freedom. Nation's exist, he argued, by consent. Or at least they should.[11]

Anthony Smith's *œuvre* is permeated by the themes of nations being based on memory and on ethnicity.[12] He has written of how the ancient past 'serves to 'remake the collective personality' of the nation in each generation'.[13] This apparently brings him into direct conflict with Renan's assertion that they, or at least the 19th century western nations, were formed through 'forgetting' as a conduit or aftermath to consent. In arriving at this the crystallisation of tribes or smaller communities into a nation involves processes whereby members are influenced by at least some familiarity: understanding, acceptance or expectation of certain expressions and practices.[14] Voluntary commitment is 'meaningless in the absence of certain fundamental commonalities' felt by sufficient numbers of population. Two ingredients are treated differently by Smith and Renan, yet both are indispensable: history and culture. The memories, selective though they may be, and the symbols of a particular history and cultural code make consent and consensus far more likely. Having privileged will and forgetting over such as language, ethnicity, and geography, Renan concludes that a nation is a 'spiritual principle' which is the fusion of 'the common possession of a rich legacy of memories' *and* 'actual consent, the desire to live together, the will to continue to value the heritage that has been received in common'.[15] Nations are not solely 'political' or 'organic' but a synthesis of both phenomena.

Peter Alter's 'concept of nation' follows this combination of general similarities and specific differences, which 'represents an interlocking of objective actualities and the circumstance of subjective political will, an ever-

---

11   Michael D. Kennedy "What is 'the Nation' after Communism and Modernity?" *Polish Sociological Review* v105 n1 1994 pp47-58

12   Among others, *The Ethnic Origins of Nations* (Oxford: Blackwell 1986) & *National Identity* (London: Penguin 1991)

13   Anthony D. Smith "National identity and the idea of European unity" *International Affairs* v68 n1 1992 pp55-76 p62

14   Cf. Karl Deutsch *Nationalism and Social Communication: An Inquiry into the Foundations of Nationality* (New York 1953)

15   Renan "Qu'est-ce qu'une nation?"

changing combination whose shape is truly unique to each historical case.'[16] The issue of a broader division of European nations and nationalisms into western ('political') and eastern ('cultural') types[17] takes on a new aspect after the Cold War, not least regarding the categorization of Germany. Such a division reiterates Madame de Staël's observation of France as a state in search of a nation and Germany as a nation in search of a state. Postulating a dichotomy of *Staat* and *Kultur* nations today must contend with a situation whereby France is no less integrated by and proud of its culture than Germany is reliant on the 'state' to maintain social cohesion, public service, or conduct foreign policy. The configuration of political institutions and the specificities of their societies vary but a symbiosis of 'state' and 'cultural' elements is replicated in the two 'nations'.[18] Pure cultural nations do not exist in Europe, but there is, as Brian Singer has recently argued, 'no purely contractual nation' either.[19]

According to Liah Greenfeld, the first exemplar was the English.[20] After it emerged as a nation in the sixteenth century England became an object of jealousy and something to be emulated. It was an impression of England's now superior prestige that incited 'national feeling' amongst the French ruling strata while an English nationalism based on a broader and more developed identification was on the rise.[21] It was not until after 1789 that the distinct French model of the republican political nation came into being and this then encountered various revisionist phases and struggles between left and right through the 1800s.[22] In functional and ideal terms neither *étatism* nor *gloire* were jettisoned, they grew together. Following Napoleon's initial foray, after 1870-71 the French state centralized around Paris embarked on a bureaucratic compression of the population into a common patriotic identity. Contrary to Renan's claim that France 'never sought to obtain linguistic unity by coercive

16   Peter Alter *Nationalism* (London: Edward Arnold 1994) pp 9-10
17   See Hans Kohn *The Idea of Nationalism: A Study in its Origins and Background* (New York: MacMillan 1967)
18   Cf. Smith "National identity and the idea of European unity" p61
19   Brian C. J. Singer "Cultural versus Contractual Nations: Rethinking their Opposition" *History and Theory* v35 n3 1996 pp309-337
20   Liah Greenfeld *Nationalism: Five Roads to Modernity* (Cambridge, Ma.: Harvard University Press 1992) See Chapter 1
21   Gerald Newman *The Rise of English Nationalism: A Cultural History 1740-1830* (London: St.Martin's Press 1987)
22   See Brian Jenkins *Nationalism in France: Class and Nation since 1789* (Savage: Barnes & Noble 1990)

means',[23] political-administrative processes stemming from the *Ile-de-France* aimed at linguistic uniformity so making Burgundians, Occitans and Franks, 'French'.[24] Common language joined a defined territory. This distillation survived and evolved through the internal ideological battles of the nineteenth and twentieth century for the nation to become a *sine qua non* across the political spectrum. What was to become Germany evolved in the opposite direction, from pre-political cultural affinities, reaching the endpoint of an evolutionary phase and the beginning of another in Bismarck's unification.[25] The national liberal perspective elaborated by Friedrich Meinecke was swamped by an imperial authoritarian variant.[26]

Although considered principally a sociologist and not a specialist in the study of nations, Max Weber provides insights of continuing relevance. What he was investigating and describing, ostensibly as 'societies', were actually 'nations'. In common with Renan he ascribed a 'voluntary quality' to nations. And his 'idea of nation',[27] preceded the revelations of later twentieth century writings on the 'imagined' or 'mythical' nature of the nation.[28] Weber impressed that "'national' affiliation need not be based upon common blood'. 'Nevertheless', he continues, 'the idea of the 'nation' is apt to include the notions of common descent and of an essential, though frequently indefinite, homogeneity'.[29] Populations of present-day 'national states'[30] are not

23   Renan "Qu'est-ce qu'une nation?"

24   See on this, Eugen Weber *Peasants into Frenchmen: The Modernization of Rural France 1870-1914* (London: Chatto & Windus 1977)

25   Germany was 'the belated nation'. Helmut Plessner *Die Verspätete Nation: über die politische Verführbarkeit bürgerlichen Geistes* (Stuttgart: Kohlhammer 1974 [1959]) See also Otto Dann *Nation und Nationalismus in Deutschland 1770-1990* (München: Beck Verlag 1993)

26   Friedrich Meinecke *Weltbürgertum und Nationalstaat: Stüdien über die Genesis des deutschen Nationalstaates* (München: 1908). The subsequent degeneration towards cataclysm is well documented including by Meinicke himself in *Die Deutsche Katastrophe: Betrachtungen und Erinnerungen* (Wiesbaden: Brockhaus 1949)

27   Max Weber *Economy and Society: An Outline of Interpretive Sociology* Eds. Guenther Roth & Claus Wittich (Berkeley: University of California Press 1978)

28   J. L. Talmon *The Myth of the Nation and the Vision of Revolution* (Berkeley: University of California Press 1981); Benedict Anderson *Imagined Communities: Reflections on the Origin and Spread of Nationalism* (London: Verso 1983); Anthony D. Smith "The Nation: Invented, Imagined, Reconstructed?" *Millenium* v20 n3 1991 pp353-368; Walker Connor "The Nation and Its Myth" *International Journal of Comparative Sociology* v33 n1-2 1992 pp48-56; *Reimagining the Nation* Eds. Majorie Ringrose and Adam J. Lerner (Buckingham: Open University Press 1993)

29   Weber *Economy and Society* p923

monopolised by specifically ethnic ties but do dispose of firm congruities. National armies are one multi-ethnic example. And national football teams, the objects of among the most intense identification and support (or dislike), are composed of players often not related by ethnicity, to each other or to spectators. Successive Dutch, French and English teams are among the most notable. But these teams and their supporters in the 'mass public' have common foci, understandings and ambitions. They are representative of populations competing against others. Together, teams and supporters are 'communities of prestige', heightened as competitions become more important.

In his giant *Studien über die Deutschen*, Norbert Elias describes the meaning of prestige and power in relations between nations. He employs the state and perceptions of its 'rank' among its members as a guide or barometer of esteem:

> It may be tempting to say, 'So what? Who cares whether one's own state is a first-, or second- or third-rate centre of power?' I am not talking here about wishes and ideals. Up till now in the course of human history, it is a proven fact that the members of states and other social units which have lost their claim to a position of highest rank in the elimination struggles of their day often require a long time, even centuries to come to terms with this changed situation and the consequent lowering of their self-esteem.[31]

Nations presume the existence of other nations. Likewise national identification is not restricted to individuals feeling part of a collective. It requires that other national identities exist. Concern with prestige, from which a variety of benefits or disadvantages may flow, is symptomatic of the narcissism of nations— even if it is a 'narcissism of minor differences'.[32] Nations are concerned with their appearance and how others perceive them. These two factors become entwined, each buttressing, even perpetuating the other. When nations observe themselves they also see something of others. Comparisons in the perceived achievements, deficiencies, potentials, of other nations, as for itself, derive from and perpetuate national histories. This occurs however 'incomparable' or unique each nation considers itself. 'Information'

---

30   A term which Anthony Smith points out as more accurate than 'nation-state'

31   Norbert Elias *The Germans: Power Struggles and the Development of Habitus in the Nineteenth and Twentieth Centuries* Ed. Michael Schröter, Trans. Eric Dunning & Stephen Mennell (Cambridge: Polity 1996 [1989]) p4

32   Michael Ignatieff "Nationalism and the Narcissism of Minor Differences" *Queen's Quarterly* v102 n1 1995 pp13-25

about one's own and other nations is stored in the popular consciousness and in state databases. It becomes part of a nation-state's memory or file, on itself and on others. Some of these perspectives are or become stereotypical, some fade and some remain at the forefront. In the golden age of nationalism it became possible to exploit the idea of nation by invoking its imminent evanescence or at least its decline to a lesser rank. This point has been reiterated recently by Edward Shils. He states that 'being a nation in a subordinate status with a national state dominated by major nation is one of the causes of nationalism. It is the cause most prominent at the present time'.[33] There is remarkable prescience of 1990s Europe in the insights of Paul Valéry, who wrote in the 1920s:

> Nations are strangers to one another...they contemplate one another with curiosity and with anxiety...no matter how sincere their desire to agree and understand each other may sometimes be, *the understanding always becomes obscured and stops at a certain point*. There are insurmountable barriers to its depth and its duration...nations find motives for liking themselves best
>
> All nations have present, or past, or future reasons for thinking themselves incomparable. And moreover they are. Not one of the least difficulties of speculative politics is the impossibility of comparing these large entities which only meet and affect each other in their exterior characteristics and methods. But the essential fact which is the core and the principle of their existence, the internal bond which binds together the individuals and the generations of a nation, is not, in the various nations, of the same nature. Sometimes the race, sometimes the memories, sometimes the interests, diversely comprise the national unity of an organized human agglomeration. The basic cause of one such grouping can be quite different to that of another.[34]

Among their many curiosities nations have a capacity to fuse what appear contradictory elements. National identity can enable an instrumentalizing of emotive factors and animate emotional attitudes towards material concerns. They are rational and non-rational, and in some instances, irrational. William Pfaff gives some clues when he asserts that 'the modern western nation is a practical affair'. It comprises an organised provision of 'defense, civil order, a system of justice, an economic structure, a framework

---

33   Edward Shils "Nation, nationality, nationalism and civil society" *Nations and Nationalism* v1 n1 1995 pp93-118

34   Paul Valéry *Selected Writings* (New Directions: New York 1964) pp134-135. Section translated by Anthony Bower. Emphasis added

for industry and for commercial transactions, systems of transportation and communications, and so on.' It is also imbued with a 'national feeling', perhaps a form of subconscious gratitude for these practical provisions, but 'which is not a practical commitment but a matter of passions'.[35] This 'practical' aspect of the contemporary nation is not attainable without coherence in underlying familiarities. Common 'practical' advantages extend as far as communications, values and understandings encourage. When Raymond Aron wrote, 'the modern nation in Europe consists precisely of the conjunction of a community of culture and a desire for autonomy. Todays political units are far from achieving this conjunction uniformly', he both presaged Ernest Gellner's *Nations and Nationalism* and affirmed one of its main claims in a latter stage of European history.[36]

In Gellner's view the coming of modernity spurred romantic nationalisms which in turn created nations.[37] Operating as a political principle nationalism was imposed from above. What it needed was a 'raw material' by which to legitimate itself and spread throughout a given populous. The mass was provided by the largely agrarian societies on to which literate and powerful élites imposed a standard culture during the processes of modernization and transition to industrial society; through bureaucracies, education systems, political centralization and economic specialization.

Gellner seeks to demonstrate that there is no logically necessary link between the two elements that fused to form a nation: that is, the congruence of culture and polity that was the nation-building aim of nationalism. The 'raw material' he introduces as essential for nationalism to live off is *culture*. But he does not declare this. What Gellner wants to refute is that culture is a pre-existing component of nations, as the 'eastern' European conception attributes.[38] Of course, it undergoes radical transformations but it does *exist*, even if as a politically dormant agglomeration. Through the emergence of national consciousness cultural difference becomes politicized and more pronounced. Before culture fuses with polity, however, culture, 'in an

35   William Pfaff *The Wrath of Nations: Civilization and the Furies of Nationalism* (New York: Simon and Schuster 1993) p23
36   Raymond Aron *Peace and War: A Theory of International Relations* (English Edition) Trans. Richard Howard & Annette Baker Fox (London: Weidenfeld & Nicholson 1966) p750
37   Ernest Gellner *Nations and Nationalism* (Oxford: Blackwell 1983)
38   Cf. John Armstrong *Nations Before Nationalism* (Chapel Hill: University of North Carolina Press 1982); and on 'Eastern' nationalisms, Miroslav Hroch "National Self-Determination from a Historical Perspective" in *Notions of Nationalism...* pp65-82

anthropological sense', comes into contact with *Kultur*. 'Low' and 'high' culture meet. The 'raw material' of the politically inspired nationalists is culture of the 'high' variety which they disseminate through the nascent body politic as the substance of identification. They are aided by the physicality of other factors like territory.

Gellner argues powerfully that culture has no 'natural' place in politics nor vice versa and that nations are artificial constructs. Once imbued with a political consciousness these cultural communities have proved resistant to disconnection from structures of governance and institutions that developed from this synthesis. Even if wholesale revisions of the philosophical or ideological premises and intent were experienced, European nation-states remain characterised by the congruence of a predominant culture with a legally sovereign polity. The role of culture in European nations and relations between them shall be expanded on in the following chapter.

Sufficient cultural compatibility and the subjective qualities of will, identification and uniqueness combine to make and to sustain a nation. Cases of two or more large culturally distinct populations living under a shared political roof are exceptions rather than the rule. Switzerland is the foremost example[39] and there is case to be made that the USA fits the category. Belgium could also qualify as two cultural nations/one state yet the fractures in this case also demonstrate the strains such arrangements may come under.

The Persistence of National Identity

National identity may generate common prosperity, mutual security, great works, the development of political institutions, or a propensity for sacrifice. The triumph of national identity over class solidarity was made evident by World Wars One and Two and reaffirmed after the Cold War. At the moment of dire need, Stalin's July 1941 appeal was not to popular identification with and defence of Marxist-Leninism, but the Motherland. Socialist or Marxist programs that sought to wrest populations from national orientations

---

39 This does not mean Switzerland is not a nation, one with a particular national identity. Swiss aversion to joining the EC/EU may be interpreted as making it more nationalistic than any EU member. On the surface it might appear that Switzerland possesses to a greater degree than any other nation the prerequisites for immersion in a united Europe: it is multilingual, geographically at the centre, has both special trading requirements and financial credentials, and a history of pacifism, democracy and human rights. Nonetheless, one scholar has stated plainly that 'nationalism is at the heart of the Swiss refusal to join the EC'. See René Schwok "EC-1992 and the Swiss National Identity" *History of European Ideas* v15 n1-3 1992 pp241-247

employed, consciously or unconsciously, the same reference points. Greenfeld has noted that 'In certain conditions, socialist internationalism promised more dignity than the nation. The problem was that it transcended the nation's worth while keeping all the characteristics of the nationalisms which were the reasons for the transcendence.'[40] Other recent appraisals point in the same direction, such as, 'efforts to equip the labour movement with international consciousness' ran into 'concrete historical forces'. Internationalism of this kind (and others) could only be articulated in the form of "progressive' national values.'[41] Mitchell Cohen's summation is enlightening here: 'Marx's famous quip about modernity, that "all that's solid melts into air," would seem an appropriate metaphor for the last four years, save for one aspect of the modern world: national consciousness'.[42]

Today, athletes successful at international competitions bedeck themselves in the flags that symbolise particular nation-states. Representing a 'region' or 'section' of the EU could not carry the same significance as appearing for Italy, France or Poland. Or for spectators.[43] People take more interest in the activities or fortunes of compatriots than they do in others and national media reflect this. Belonging or loyalty to a nation may mean affinity with an idea, a myth, a construct, or simply an easily acceptable or unavoidable everyday existence. And this so not only for the average citizen but—perhaps more so—for upper echelons of policy-making.

National consciousness in a sporting context is not so far removed from politics.[44] Implausibility surrounds the potential election of a 'German'

---

40   Liah Greenfeld "Transcending the Nation's Worth" *Dædelus* v122 n3 1993 pp47-62

41   Brian Jenkins & Spyros A. Sofos "Nation and Nationalism in Contemporary Europe: A Theoretical Perspective" in *Nation and Identity in Contemporary Europe* Eds. Brian Jenkins & Spyros A. Sofos (London: Routledge 1996) pp9-32, p18

42   Mitchell Cohen "Rooted Cosmopolitanism" in *Toward A global Civil Society* Ed. Michael Walzer (Providence: Berghahn 1995) pp223-233

43   An aside here is that federal entities like Germany and Belgium are represented in such competitions as whole states while a unitary Britain, in some cases (World Cup Soccer), fields teams or individuals from England, Scotland, Wales or Northern Ireland. This presents another viewpoint on the difference between sovereignty and identity, which the predominantly 'English' governing class appear to have conflated with respect to Europe. The 'British' state and culture has, at least this century, included more representation of autonomous 'national identity' in international settings such as sporting contests, determined by political criteria; i.e state sovereignty and citizenship

44   Cf. Raymond Aron 'Is the passion with which the public supports national athletic teams a symbol of a nationalism which raises still another

as President of France, a 'Frenchman' as German Chancellor or the disappearance of both offices to be replaced by one European government.[45] British prime ministers or monarchs, German chancellors or presidents and French presidents are the bearers of offices which bestow a status as embodiment of the nation.[46] This is an aspiration of candidates and expected of incumbents. Although not a focus for complete agreement and perhaps the object of vilification for some, the president or monarch or prime minister represents a specific form of identification. In the French case the ceremonial and substantive authority of presidential endorsement confers a national mystique.[47]

Leaders are not only political representatives but part of the socio-cultural fabric which they represent. They must display membership of the nation: language, appearance, awareness of a particular history, customs, knowledge of political and social conventions, deference to certain personalities, rules and so on. These are parameters and content of identification. The rulers must be perceived, as Gellner phrased it, as 'of the majority ruled'[48] though the society as a whole may be more diverse. Let's say, hypothetically, that it could be conclusively demonstrated that financially (short and long term), in security against terrorism or aggressive states, and general governmental competence, the French or British publics would receive greater benefit through governance and administration by Europeans who happened to be (also) German, or Italian, and who utilised methods or models familiar to themselves that ensured maximum efficiency. It is presently inconceivable that French, British or other national publics would vote for this, or that their political or intellectual élites would be amenable to such a scenario. The point in question being, the promise of material prosperity and security does not necessarily outweigh the psychic attachment to a national idea or myth and its 'right' or imperative to a certain independence. Popularly elected all-European governments and leaders which render the offices of head of

---

insurmountable obstacle to block federalism?' "Old Nations, New Europe" *Dædelus* v93 n1 1964; and Ulf Hedetoft. 'In the world of European *sports*, on the other hand, nationalism has been and remains legitimate'. "The State of Sovereignty in Europe: Political Concept or Cultural Self-Image" in *National Cultures and European Integration: Exploratory Essays on Cultural Diversity and Common Policies* Ed. Staffan Zetterholm (Oxford: Berg 1994) pp13-48

45   Ernest Wistrich *The United States of Europe* (London: Routledge 1994)
46   This overrules any hereditary 'anomalies' and even ethnic or familial linkages between 'rulers' of different nations
47   Cf. Philip H. Gordon *A Certain Idea of France* (Princeton: Princeton University Press 1993)
48   Gellner *Nations and Nationalism* p1

state redundant would introduce a genuine post-national age. The chances of this are remote.

Within contemporary multilateral frameworks there is an instrumental linkage between national interest and national consciousness or sentiment, between the economic and the cultural. The means is political, the primary agent the state. This is what Canovan terms 'mediation'. It is the capacity to 'hold together various pairs of alternatives'.

> Thus, a nation is a polity that feels like a community, or conversely a cultural or ethnic community politically mobilized; it cannot exist without subjective identification, and therefore is to some extent dependent on free individual choice, but that choice is nevertheless experienced as a destiny transcending individuality; it turns political institutions into an extended family inheritance, although the kinship ties are highly metaphorical; it is a contingent historical product that feels like part of the order of nature; it links individual and community, past and present; it gives to cold institutional structures an aura of warm, intimate togetherness. In other words, nationhood is hard to define not because it is confused and nonsensical, but because it is extremely subtle, and moreover, because (as perceptive commentators have frequently observed) an element of myth is essential to it.[49]

This depicts the intersection of interests and identity, and in contemporary Europe the basic questions concern whether both still can or cannot be conceptualised nationally. De Gaulle had said that there were no friends among nations, only interests. His observation is borne out, like a daily plebiscite, as politicians, media and publics talk, write and read of this or that official 'representing Britain's or France's interests in Brussels'. Governments put national interests first and the degree of cooperative action is dependent on what the national electorate and political class have or will condone. 'Europe' is a place from which benefits are sought; not viewed as something transcendent.[50] The welfare and standing of the national polity is, and must be, a proclaimed goal of all political forces: centrist, populists, socialists who wish to nationalize industries, internationalists or xenophobes alike. Governments will not survive if the policies they pursue are perceived as debilitating the nation materially or psychically.

---

49   Canovan *Nationhood and Political Theory* p69
50   Chris Shore "Transcending the Nation-State?: The European Commission and the (Re)-Discovery of Europe" *Journal of Historical Sociology"* v9 n4 1996 pp473-496

Ulf Hedetoft has written of a 'dichotomy of loyalties' which sees a 'cost-benefit' version directed towards Europe and an 'emotional/cultural towards the nation'.[51] Material and strategic interests can be harmonized and mutual benefit derived. However, the political weight that a nation-state can bring to the shaping of this 'cost-benefit' is dependent upon the degree of domestic unity, in combination with 'objective' power factors, that a nation-state can generate. This is where the strength of cultural-historical-emotional connections count, and where they have no parallel at the European level. EU nations are not autarkic and do seek to benefit themselves through cooperative networks. But neither populations nor governing classes believe 'their nation' is better served by maintaining less rather than more control over the process. Paul Taylor has described how in the EU implementation of a federal political entity is the next 'logical' step, *but* that endogenous pressures have concurrently been created through the integration process itself with the effect of blocking this breakthrough. State élite accommodation at the hard economic-technical level gives way to reticence in the cultural-political sphere. As European integration reaches a point where core aspects of sovereignty are called into question concerns intensify that cultural underpinnings of particular polities are threatened if political authority is ceded.

> when translated to the international level the theory of consociationalism in its various aspects suggests something rather startling: that comprehensive international arrangements may in some ways challenge rather than reinforce the process of developing a transnational socio-psychological community. They may release pressures that encourage the encapsuling of nations, and the firmer definition of ethnic and cultural minorities, as well as countervailing measures towards greater community, regional decision-making. [52]

Nations and States

The European invented 'nation-state' is a fusion regarded by many scholars as purely coincidental, that the marriage of nation and state became a fixture of history and geo-politics 'because that is the form they took in the two historically significant societies, Britain and France, at the very moment when

---

51   Ulf Hedetoft "Euro-Nationalism: Or How the EC Affects the Nation-State as a Repository of Identity" in *History of European Ideas* v15 n1-3 1992 pp271-277

52   Paul Taylor *International Organization in the Modern World: The Regional and the Global Process* (London: Pinter 1993) See Chapter Four "The limits of European integration: the concepts of consociation and symbiosis", here p84 Cf. *Federalism and Nationalism* Ed. Murray Forsyth (Leicester: Leicester University Press 1989)

nationalism burst forth.'[53] History is full of accidents, and the formation of nation-states no more so. That they have survived, prospered and dominated world politics since the Westphalian universe began suggests that nation-states are not merely artificial. Engendering a harmony of 'nation' and 'state' is still a common political device, even a necessity. As an organizing principle and source of political and emotional loyalty the construct 'nation' has been successfully employed by state officialdom. Anthony Smith has noted that 'the idea of the nation is a political community only in so far as it embodies a common culture and a common social will. This is why today no state possesses legitimacy which does not also claim to represent the will of the 'nation', even where there is patently no nation for it to represent.'[54] The discipline of Inter*national* Relations was, however, quite negligent of the role and potential of nations in its world composed of states. Although the title of Hans Morgenthau's epic work[55] indicated otherwise, international relations literature did not, by and large, consider nations as primary operatives in the world system.[56] Rather, they were subordinated to the abstracted state. The two were separated with the effect that the international system was presented as a collection of state élites who were not representing or representative of nations, despite regular reference to 'national interests'.[57]

William Bloom has argued that international politics 'is not simply the relations between state structures, but it is also the relations between the *nations*...In international politics, people, government and state fuse into one image'.[58] There is a 'triangular relationship' between the 'mass national

53   Anthony D.Smith "State-making and nation-building" in *States in History* Ed. J. A. Hall (Oxford: Blackwell 1986) p230 quoted in William Wallace "Rescue or Retreat?: The Nation State in Western Europe, 1945-93" *Political Studies* v42 Special Issue 1994 pp53-76 fn23 Cf. *The Formation of National States in Western Europe* Ed. Charles Tilly (Princeton: Princeton University Press 1975)

54   Smith "National identity and the idea of European unity"

55   Hans J.Morgenthau *Politics Among Nations* Fourth Edition (New York: Knopf 1967). Morgenthau makes implicit references to national identity without referring to it as such. This is another instance of tacit presumptions about nations

56   While the discipline suffered something of a crisis during and after 1989-91, some predominantly International Relations scholars did not ignore the cultural and emotive aspects and forces of *nations* in the inter*state* system Among them Karl Deutsch, Raymond Aron, and Stanley Hoffman. See chapter eight below on states in the EU

57   The 'exception', in more than one sense, was France where this configuration was quite compatible with the vision of a French *état-nation* operating above contemporary systemic constraints in both functional and grandiose fashion

58   William Bloom *Personal Identity, National Identity and International Relations*

public', 'government foreign policy decisions' and 'images of the relationship between the nation and the international environment which threaten or provide the opportunity of enhancing national identity'. With or without state action 'the mass national public will mobilise when it perceives either that national identity is threatened, or that there is the opportunity of enhancing national identity'. The 'government *qua* state' ignores this force at its peril, not only for electoral reasons but in regard to consequences for civil order. 'Government, state and national community are entwined as one bundle of symbols representing national identity' and 'foreign policy can create a situation in which the whole national community can be perceived as sharing the same experience in relation to a foreign actor'. In this sphere governments 'may thus be dictated by internal domestic political realities as much as by the actual nature of its international relations' and 'no government can afford to ignore the pressure of such a substantial political force'. Political elites seek political gain and for this purpose the field of foreign policy generally offers opportunity for the broader mobilisation of a given polity than does a domestic context. In European institutions 'functionaries, civil servants and junior government ministers deal with the low issue areas, while prime and foreign ministers deal with the high issue areas. This occurs because all high issues can be appropriated by the domestic political competition to mobilise the national identity dynamic, whereas low issues are simply functional.'[59]

Predominant representations of globalization, or Europeanization, invoke the permeating of national frameworks yet it is entirely plausible to reverse this and view national economies, or competition between them, as both the base ingredients and ongoing infiltrators of the global or European. Economics has not vanquished politics. Rather each national state seeks resolution to its own internal and external challenges and opportunities. This involves cooperation and understandings within national structures.[60] There is still a priority 'given to the realisation of goals adopted by the nation, even though this might run counter to the maximisation of utility and efficiency in the global context...Political control of the economy...is based on the belief that

---

(Cambridge: Cambridge University Press 1990) p1

59   Bloom *Personal Identity* Chapter 4 "The National Identity Dynamic and Foreign Policy" pp76-104. For an account focusing on the British situation, see William Wallace "Foreign policy and national identity in the United Kingdom" *International Affairs* v67 n1 1991 pp65-80

60   Louis W. Pauly & Simon Reich "National Structures and Multinational Corporate Behaviour: Enduring Differences in the Age of Globalization" *International Organization* v51 n1 1997 pp1-30. See also Chapter Eight above

nationalist elites will act to protect the citizens of a state if they share a common identity.'[61]

Apart from agreements on commercial and regulatory matters, and justice and human rights codified in international law, sovereignty extends to the borders of a nation-state, within which no other has jurisdiction, and is legitimated by a distinct, bounded citizenry. This legitimacy rests on a myth of origin which provides a sense of organic foundation. However ragged or debunked, national polities still possess this mythology.[62] Most are formed of heterogeneous groups wherein one predominates. These polities pursue 'national interests' no less than more ethnically homogenous nations. Even if sub-ethnic, class or other factors were to oppose it, aims and legitimations founded on a national platform do not require the allegiance of *all* members of the polity. In fact 'national identities can outlast the defection or apathy of quite large numbers of individual members'.

> Though the vast majority of contemporary states are 'plural' in character - that is, they can have more than one ethnic community within their borders and so cannot claim to be true 'nation-states' in the strict sense - they aspire to become at least 'national states' with a common public culture open to all their citizens. Their claim to legitimacy, in other words, is based on the aspiration of a heterogeneous population to unity in terms of public culture and political community, as well as popular sovereignty.[63]

All 'national states' have domestic considerations when constructing and operating external policy. As well as economic factors they must take into account particular cultural and historical elements. Smith notes that this is as much a barrier to unity as the 'conflicting perceptions of self-interest on the part of the state actors'.[64] These differences are *part of the self-interest* of the

---

61   Brian Girvin "Nationalism, Economic Growth and Political Sovereignty" *History of European Ideas* v15 n1-3 1992 pp177-184, pp182-183. Consequences of globalizing markets include that, especially where traditional prestige or quality factors are most important, products continue to carry 'Made in America, France, or Germany' signs. Concurrently 'national' publics are encouraged to 'buy Australian, British, etc'

62   See Daniela Obradovic "Policy Legitimacy and the European Union" *Journal of Common Market Studies* v34 n2 1996 pp191-220 and Brigid Laffan "The Politics of Identity and Political Order in Europe" *Journal of Common Market Studies* v34 n1 1996 pp81-102 for good recent accounts of the relationships between national and European identities, sovereignty and political legitimacy

63   Smith "National identity and the idea of European unity" p62

64   Anthony D. Smith "A Europe of Nations—or the Nation of Europe?" *Journal of*

states. In more dramatic pronouncements it is the *nation* and/or its interests that will be diminished by the further cession of *state* sovereignty. This is then reformed back into nation, in the form of 'the Germans', 'the French' or 'the Americans'. Despite numerous destructive and self destructive actions of (nation)states and much discrediting of the form, an intangible allegiance has survived:

> One of the reasons for the power of the sovereign state — particularly when it is also a nation-state — is that no other political unit inspires such devotion and enthusiasm. Within the state most citizens feel some sentiment for the area in which they were born or the place where they live. And beyond the state people can see some value in larger groupings like NATO or the European Community. But it is difficult to see these lesser or greater allegiances providing the same sort of psychological 'high' as belonging to a nation-state. There is something peculiarly satisfying about belonging to a nation-state.[65]

This identification is then a source of power, responsibility and justification. Even when they are, ostensibly, emotive or 'non-rational', nationhood and nationalism do not function only as such but are manifested in the calculated actions of nation-states. There is no necessary, permanent contradiction between nationalism, even when sentiment, prestige, symbolism and mythologies are at work, and rationality. Thus 'to claim that nationalism is 'imagined' is not to suggest that it is meaningless'.[66] Nationalism is a bonding agent powerful enough to elicit recognition—a rational response—from leaders and publics that it can (though it may not always succeed) effectively serve communal interests.[67] But it must overcome potential divisions between official or state forms and popular feeling.

Peace Research v30 n2 1993 pp129-135

65   John C. Garnett "States, State-Centric Perspectives, and Interdependence Theory" in *Dilemmas of World Politics: International Issues in a Changing World* Eds. John Bayliss & N. J. Rengger (Oxford: Clarendon Press 1992) pp61-84. Cf. Karl Deutsch *Political Community at the International Level: Problems of Definition and Measurement* (New York: Doubleday 1954)

66   Girvin "Nationalism, Economic Growth and Political Sovereignty"

67   Haas "What is nationalism and why should we study it?" In this illuminating study Haas notes the paradox of a world constituted by 'rational nationalisms' somehow adding up to an 'inherently bellicose' whole. See also Ronald Rogowski "Causes and Varieties of Nationalism: a Rationalist Account" 87-108 in *New Nationalisms of the Developed West: Toward Explanation* Eds. Edward A. Tiryakian & Ronald Rogowski (London: Allen & Unwin 1985)

Variations on Nationalism

Nationalism has its own radius of associated terms and concepts. To underline the previous section, policy-making and direction in international affairs conceived and enacted in response to or in the interests of *primarily* one nation, or one nation before any others, constitutes 'nationalism', or, more specifically, 'state nationalism'.

For Smith or Breuilly, among others, nationalism embodies an ideology.[68] For William Pfaff nationalism is *not* an ideology but is nonetheless the 'most powerful political force of the twentieth century, which is likely to prove the most powerful of the twenty-first as well':

> ...a profound if often malign, expression of human identities, a negative force, but also a positive one. It is an expression of love as well as hate...Nationalism is not an ideology because it has no universality...(it) occupies the moral and emotional ground otherwise held by political ideology.[69]

Nationalism has generated more political force than anything else, been manifested by so many different nations, and has existed, even when perverted, manipulated or forced underground, as a component of communist, socialist, liberal or fascist regimes. Gellner has written of 'nationalists-in-the-abstract', those 'generously preaching the doctrine for all nations alike: let all nations have their own political roofs'.[70] Abstract rationality must never lose contact with the 'existential flesh and blood reality of humans in action'.[71] Edward Shils has commented that 'Human beings cannot live without collective self-consciousness focused on boundary-generating referents. Perhaps we should say that human beings want to live in a state enclosure. They need enclosure because they need community. Nationhood supplies both. This human sensitivity will never vanish.'[72] This invokes a universality that Pfaff claims nationalism lacks: a Herderesque universe of unique cultural nations, providing emotional, intellectual, and historical sustenance.

---

68   Cf. Anthony Smith "Nationalism and the Historians" *International Journal of Comparative Sociology* v33 n1-2 1992 pp58-79, 'the history of nationalism is as much a history of its interlocutors as of the ideology and movement itself' p58; John Breuilly "Reflections on Nationalism" *Philosophy of the Social Sciences* v15 1985 pp65-73

69   Pfaff *The Wrath of Nations*

70   Gellner *Nations and Nationalism* p1

71   Bloom *Personal Identity...* pix

72   Shils "Nation, nationality, nationalism and civil society" p104

Nationalism may be finessed as 'patriotism', or even patriotism and Europeanism combined.[73] Whatever the semantic distinctions, nationalism and patriotism actually have the same focus and involve the elevation, in terms of allegiance, or material or emotional ties, of one nation above others. If both are conveyed as peaceful identifications, the main difference is an etymological preference for the more maternal *natio* or (place of) 'birth', to the paternal *patria*, or 'fatherland'. Implying, however, that patriotism is an honourable phenomenon whereas nationalism is prone to violent excess is also misconceived. Warfare, or 'healthy national feeling', may occur under the auspices of either term. Making a distinction on the grounds that patriotism has a political character while nationalism is cultural or ethnic allows liberal political theorising to incorporate multi-cultures within one polity. This occurs with an apparent neutrality. But this interpretation downgrades the fact that one culture tends to predominate in most state polities, and thereby the cultural element in patriotism. It also overlooks the political element of nationalism.[74]

In his discussion of 'civic nationalism' Michael Ignatieff notes that 'most societies are not mono-ethnic, and even when they are, common ethnicity does not itself obliterate division, because nationalism is only one of many claims on an individuals loyalty...what holds a society together is not common roots but law.' The civic society 'held together by laws' certainly exists but these laws were formed, are sustained, or change for other reasons. Ignatieff indicates that the Enlightenment societies that promoted these ideals were 'ethnically homogenous or behaved as if they were'.[75] The German Federal Republic that drafted so liberal a constitution in 1949 is similar case. Social and political pressure in Germany and France for changes regarding immigration and asylum laws is pertinent.[76] In other words there are more than universalist liberal and/or democratic principles at work.[77] Neither the French *République* nor the German *Rechtsstaat* are merely objective, legal entities. Each has derived from and is the result of a specific historical experience. Each currently faces its own admixture of social and economic

---

73   Helmut Kohl "Patriotismus und europäische Gesinnung gehören untrennbar zusammen" *Bulletin* 21-6-96

74   Cf. Frank de Roose "The Politics of Patriotism" in *History of European Ideas* v15 n1-3 1992 pp55-59; Canovan *Nationhood and Political Theory* Chapter 8; Louis S. Snyder *Varieties of Nationalism: A Comparative Study* (Hinsdale: Dryden Press 1976) pp42-47

75   Ignatieff *Blood and Belonging* pp5-7

76   On the background to this see Rogers Brubaker *Citizenship and Nationhood in France and Germany* (Cambridge Ma.: Harvard University Press 1992)

77   Cf. Richard C. Sinopoli "Liberal Justice, National Community" *History of European Ideas* v15 n4-6 1992 pp519-525

pressures. Each requires the presence or absence of certain criteria before an individual can attain membership of the political community. Both not only contain particularism, they are particular.[78]

It is a concern, or fear, of profound cultural identifications that motivates Jürgen Habermas position. He also attributes an artificiality to nationalism and to national sentiment that should be replaced by abstract principles. Nationalism, he suggests, 'is the term for a specifically modern phenomenon of cultural integration...'

> a form of collective consciousness which both presupposes a reflexive appropriation of cultural traditions that have been filtered through historiography and which spreads only via the channels of modern mass communication. Both elements lend to nationalism the artificial traits of something that is to a certain extent a construct, thus rendering it by definition susceptible to manipulative misuse by political elites. [79]

But 'manipulative misuse' is not necessarily a consequence. Or if it is, it is hardly unique. One could argue with and beyond Machiavelli that 'manipulative misuse' defines not only political élites but politics. The advancement of particular 'cultural traditions' by political means cannot be invalidated *per se*, especially when enacted by democratically elected governments. If 'national consciousness, unlike political nationalism, is essentially a cultural problem'[80], the main task is not to rid Europe of nation orientated political groups. It is to create a European consciousness grounded in a common culture. The paradox is that this is something which has taken national and regional examples hundreds of years. Assigning national identities to their 'proper place' relies on an uncomplicated and unspecified displacement.[81]

Julius Friend has looked for distinctions between 'nationalism' and 'national consciousness' and applied these categories to a study of British, French and German perceptions of European integration during and after the

78   See *Nation und Emotion: Deutschland und Frankreich im Vergleich: 19 und 20 Jahrhundert* Ed. Etienne François, Hannes Siegrist & Jakob Vogel (Göttingen: 1995)

79   Jürgen Habermas "Citizenship and National Identity: Some reflections on the future of Europe" *Praxis International* v12 n1 April 1992 pp1-19

80   Julius W. Friend "Nationalism and National consciousness in France, Germany and Britain: The Year of Maastricht" *History of European Ideas* v18 n2 pp187-198 " p197

81   Jenkins & Sofos "Nation and Nationalism in Contemporary Europe: A Theoretical Perspective" p29

TEU negotiations. 'Vintage nationalism'—racial antagonism, advocation of war—is not a feature of relations between these states and societies but national rivalries remain. Friend's analysis follows Gellner in attributing a primacy of 'culture' in relation to the 'nation' and 'politics' in relation to 'nationalism'. The benign quality of 'national consciousness' is a prelude to 'nationalism' and its more pejorative connotations. According to Friend, Britain did not underestimate the 'depth of national consciousness' like politicians in France and Germany. Though they have both attacked not dissimilar British positions as insular and uncommunautaire, the upsurge in attention to the 'national' factor by the French and German political classes came in response to concerns about loss of independence and control.[82]

While Pfaff presents nationalism as potentially both positive or negative, more often than not discussions of European nationalism are analyses and descriptions of racism, a propensity for violence, destructive powers, and how the capabilities for this to occur were reached. In 1995 François Mitterrand informed the European Parliament that 'nationalism is war'.[83] Impelled by the ambitions of despotic political rulers, violence founded on ethnic and/or religious rivalries and hatreds, extending even to attempted genocide, have been the signal characteristics of the nationalisms engaged in conflict in the Balkans. Here the definition of nationalism as 'a theory of political legitimacy, which requires that ethnic boundaries should not cut across political ones' would apply.[84]

Conversely, nationalism has not been so frequently or clearly identified as a factor in relations between democratic western European states. Rogers Brubaker's collection of essays, *Nationalism Reframed* is one example which makes some minor references to the European Union or western nations while concentrating on developments in the post-communist east. The political space he describes as moving not '*beyond* but *back to* the nation-state' is not restricted to the eastern side of the former iron curtain.[85] Attempts to overcome violent nationalism, which all EU member states in their unilateral and communal declarations pronounce must be brought to an end, have been hindered by less dramatic bureaucratic-diplomatic forms of national prioritizing. The post-Maastricht period manifests discretionary *cooperative* activity between national governments, yet not so much pan-EU *integration*.

---

82   Friend "Nationalism and National Consciousness..." p187
83   This rhetorical manouevre ignores any other kind of nationalism, including, among others, Mitterrand's early 1980s version. Cf. Shore "Transcending the Nation-State?..." p491
84   Gellner *Nations and Nationalism* p1
85   Rogers Brubaker *Nationalism Reframed: Nationhood and the national question in the New Europe* (Cambridge: Cambridge University Press 1996)

Ineffectual or non-existent *common* foreign policy and impasse on critical issues have overridden any sense of Europeanness leading to common political will when this has been decisively tested. The former Yugoslavia provides the most conspicuous example. This does not mean that any of the individual nation-states responded any more effectively. They did not. They displayed their own 'democratically tamed and institutionally harnessed nationalisms'[86] as did the French insistence on nuclear testing, British opt-outs from EMU and the Social Chapter, German interest rate policy after reunification, the 'mad cow affair' and so on.

Within the EU's institutional framework, nationalism is not a demagogic force that in its manifestations appears as belligerence, insularity, xenophobia, militarism, or fear of military invasion. What has replaced outward chauvinism and bombast is more in line with 'conventional' peacetime statecraft: bargaining by politicians and technocrats, cultivation through diplomacy, positioning of resources, appeals to national unity. It also involves extensive promotion of national languages and other cultural or economic favouritism. National governments and civil services, often with media and other economic and cultural channels, conduct a sophisticated, diplomatic, inter-democratic form of nationalism. Hans-Peter Schwarz has articulated this phenomenon well

> Was als "Nationalismus" in der EU auftritt, ist der Egoismus partikulärer Wirtschaftsgesellschaften, national geprägter Kulturen und die Binnenzentrierung moderner Demokratien. Mit dem altertümlichen Nationalismus von ehedem hat dies wenig mehr gemein, auch nicht dem Tribalismus auf heutigen Balkan oder im Kaukasus.[87]

This 'official nationalism' may be challenged by the 'political nationalism of the electorate', which will occur if the latter are sufficiently dissatisfied by the direction and results of the former.[88] States then try to enforce policies at the European level to placate popular nationalisms. This introduces other tangents: two responses, positive and negative, to developments, or perceptions about developments, in Europe's political and economic evolution in the 1990s and beyond. Purveyors of the positive

---

86   Joseph S. Nye Jr. "What New World Order?" *Foreign Affairs* v71 n2 1992 p83-92; Stanley Hoffmann "Is Liberal Internationalism Dead?" *Foreign Policy* n98 Spring 1995 pp159-177

87   Hans-Peter Schwarz "Das Deutsche Dilemma" in *Deutschlands Neue Aussenpolitik* Band 1 Grundlagen Eds. Karl Kaiser & Hanns W. Maull (München: Oldenbourg 1994) pp81-97, p94

88   See Laffan "The Politics of Identity and Political Order in Europe". Here p87

approach see an opportunity to advance or preserve the interests of a particular population and various expressions of a culture (their own), and perhaps then others along with it. Adherents of the negative regard integration, having reached or heading for a certain juxtaposition of forces, as ultimately challenging to a particular (their own) culture. If the EU evolves more state-like competences each nation wants its identity *re*presented. Perceptions abide, despite insistence to the contrary, that national identity may or will be diminished through continued integration. Ole Wæver has articulated that:

> further European integration implies threats to the identity of some ethno-national societies. One threat is that societies, which have so far been privileged within the nation-states, might see their privileged situation deteriorating. They might then react against European integration, also using their states for this purpose...it is decisive that the identity formation that will have to accompany the emergence of new political structures for Europe does not take a form that is a frontal attack on national identity.[89]

Realignment of political identities to European institutions infers an end to inter*national* politics. As much as cooperation, competition is and will be a feature of relations within the European Union, whatever its foreseeable future configuration. And competition, paradoxically often aided by collaborative activity, extends beyond 'material' interests. Both besieged by and a party to the forces of globalization-Europeanization, Europe has a parallel or counter industry of political endeavour expended by individual nation-states in promoting distinctive preferences. All nations want to influence it as far as possible for the most benefit, whatever tactics they may employ: deepening, widening, isolation, fervent Euro-rhetoric, offering financial and other incentives, acceptance of payoffs in return for supporting one of the major players, and so on. As Hedetoft says, 'even in these hybrid forms, however, the national basis of European supranationalism clearly shines through', it is 'a particular official brand of nationalism'.[90] Along with changes in political and economic relations, nationalism too is transformed. Not only does it manifest in more 'traditional' forms: celebration of particular characteristics, festivals, rituals,[91] or insularity and even open aversion to

---

89   *Identity, Migration and the New Security Agenda in Europe*, Eds. Ole Wæver, Barry Buzan, Morten Kelstrup and Pierre Lemaitre (London:Pinter 1993) See Chapter 4 "Europe and its nations: political and cultural identities"
90   Hedetoft "Euro-Nationalism:..."
91   See *Revitalizing European Rituals* Ed. Jeremy Boissevain (London: Routledge 1992) especially the editor's introduction

'outsiders', it also operates in the multilateral context, aiming to capture prototype pan-European models by infusing them as far as possible—in competition to others doing the same—with the features of a national archetype. This revisits Weber's view that 'competition between nations would take place not only on the economic and political levels, but mainly in terms of the prestige or honour of a national culture'.[92] The former are now vital to the, albeit imprecise, rank of the latter.

The Imagined Communities: Europe as Nation

Anthony Smith gives an indication of the circularity confronting 'Europe' builders. While the desires of individual cultures to flourish ensures a commitment to diversity, there is no supranational organization presently capable of creating a common European culture, in effect, a European 'nation'. The lack of such an effective 'unifying authority' is explained by the 'depth of these cultural and historical differences', and, it can be added, associated elements of suspicion and rivalry that persist.[93] In dramatic terms Jacques Delors plea for continuance on the path to union declared 'what is at stake is the rise or fall of our civilization'. By this he meant European civilization. But Europe is a common civilization only up to a point. The 'European achievement was undermined in 1992-93 by the attempt to go beyond it. This occurred because the power of nationalism was not respected: the force of the individual's attachment to his *patrie*.'[94]

Each representative political class has promoted 'Europe' and each has a separate conception and intention of what this should be. It corresponds to an extension of a particular nationally conceived ideal. A united Europe means the inverse radiation of 15, 20 or 25 nations towards a common focus. It requires far-reaching political will, a European will, which must arise from, and engender, a specifically European consciousness. It means placing allegiance and trust at the European level. A Europeanization of national identities and national interests infers the formation of a 'European nation'. For champions of 'Europe', a subsequent 'European nationalism' *vis-à-vis* Asian or American trade blocs does not carry the connotations or apprehensions as do the nationalisms of individual nation-states. In the normative terms of integration, if 'Europe' pursues one interest (perhaps even

92   Ralph Schroeder *Max Weber and the Sociology of Culture* (London: Sage 1992) p119
93   Smith "A Europe of Nations—or the Nation of Europe?"
94   Pfaff *The Wrath of Nations* p221

as a 'fortress Europe') it is approved. If the whole pursues interest 'A' it is received with enthusiasm. If one nation-state pursues the same interest 'A' and the others do not it is renounced.[95] The US and Japan have large enough economies to, in the medium term at least, dominate economic confederations in the Americas or East Asia. Resident unifying factors in these polities abet much clearer distinguishing from their competitors. Global economic pressures have been the motivation for a limited and 'negative' Europeanism whereby the continent (EU) 'defines itself exclusively against other world actors',[96] while it struggles to instil or sustain enough internal agreement.[97] For Europe to compete in the 'coming battle' of world economic blocs it will need cohesion extending beyond trade agreements.[98]

It is by reference to such as its 'two inescapable Others', America and Russia,[99] that the nations of Europe move closer to conceiving of themselves as the European nation. From American, Asian or African perspectives Europe may not conjure great cultural divides existing within a geographically small faraway space. In Russian eyes these communities of the Eurasian land mass, arranged in states, take on more distinctive personas. For different nations, as either subject or object, history and geography carry an entirely different significance. It is as being somehow different from each other that the 'idea' becomes empirical. The 'nation of Europe' requires them to be somehow the same. Western Europe has reached a stage in its evolution whereby to proceed means concessions in core areas of state sovereignty. Driven by the divergent trepidations of losing distinctiveness on the one hand and being left out on the other, the politics of European unity displays 'a paradoxical assertion of separateness at the same time as a determined adhesion to the collectivity'.[100] New members will add more diversity and

---

95   An example regarding EC policy towards eastern Europe illustrates this thinking. 'If the Community were a nation-state, these goals could almost be termed imperialistic. Since it is not, they strengthen the identity of the Community, confirm the rightness of its political system and boost the ego [of] the Community's leaders'. Edelgard Mahant "Foreign Policy and European Identity" *History of European Ideas* v21 n4 pp485-498

96   Smith "National identity and the idea of European unity"

97   See the interesting treatment by Nicholas Xenos "The Natural Politics of Nation and Economy" *History of EuropeanIdeas* v20 n1-3 1995 pp383-388

98   Lester Thurow *Head to Head: The Coming Economic Battle Among Japan, Europe, and America* (St.Leonards: Allen & Unwin 1993)

99   Hervé Varenne "The Question of European Nationalism" in Thomas Wilson & M. Estellie Smith, Eds. *Cultural Change and the New Europe: Perspectives on the European Community* (Boulder: Westview 1993) pp223-240

100   Paul Taylor *International Organization in the Modern World: The Regional and the Global Process* (London:Pinter 1993) p92

severely test the capacity of unifying factors to contain the whole. Alexander Gallus noted some years ago that 'in Central Europe'

> primordially ethnocentred life is overstratified but never extinguished by an administrative level of a more sophisticated social structure...."Western European Type" national states are forced onto the area...one dominant ethnic group retains the possession of state administration, the other groups remaining "minorities"...the aim of a future reorganization must be the elimination of the "Western Type" national state. [101]

Paul Howe has underlined that 'while it is easy to imagine someone being intensely French and secondarily European, it is difficult to conceive of someone being at once intensely French and intensely European'. However, a primarily national focus of communal loyalty is not fixed. 'It is not that the people of Europe', he claims, 'are ready to will themselves to be part of a new nation, but simply that they will acquiesce as the political structures that typically precede such a development are put in place, after which the more organic phase of community-building will naturally run its course'. [102] This will be 'a gradual, almost imperceptible process'. Thus Howe elevates forgetting over will in the formation of a supranational European community. Nonetheless he acknowledges there are many 'ifs' and 'maybes'. The most significant being (and this is precisely the issue) that he cannot discount perceptions of 'the balance of power within the proposed union'. In *Paix et Guerre entre les nations* Raymond Aron predicted that Europe's economic unification may create 'embryos' of a federalism which had a 'clandestine' nature. This would ultimately prove illusory because it would not create a 'European nation' or a 'European state'.

> The system of obligations created by the institutions of Europe will surreptitiously absorb neither the authority to take decisions by which a human collectivity asserts itself in opposing others nor the power to resort to the ultima ratio; it will not create a common will among French, Germans, Italians to be henceforth autonomous as Europeans and no longer as members of historical nations...the hope that the

---

101   Alexander Gallus "Cultural Plurality and the Study of Complex Societies in Anthropology" in *Studies for a New Central Europe* Series 3 n2 1972 pp28-47

102   Paul Howe "A Community of Europeans: The Requisite Underpinnings" *Journal of Common Market Studies* v33 n1 1996 pp28-46

European federation will gradually and irresistibly emerge from the Common Market is based on a great illusion our times. [103]

Like Anthony Smith, Walker Connor stresses the roles of ethnicity and myth in the formation and sustenance of nations. Regardless of its falsities, a myth of common descent is something nations wish to preserve because it delineates them in the present. Therefore 'knowledge of contrary data and even its rational acceptance need not alter the subconscious conviction that one's nation has been ethnically hermetical. Despite the past infusion of Teutonic blood, an Englishman senses no kinship with a German.' This desire for distance is not primarily due to a perception of 'us' as *ethnically* different to 'them' but culturally and historically different. Connor adds 'it is not what is but what people perceive as is that has behavioural consequences'.[104] If we attribute mythology as an essential ingredient and follow the theoretical (and political) avenue of the individual European nations as inventions or mythical constructs, 'Europe' could only ever be the sum of (subsequently deleted) inventions.[105]

Europe is swept up in the dynamic of *transformation*—revolutionising the last decade of the millennium and set to become the 'signature of the 21st century'.[106] As stimuli for a new form of political organization, powerful historical and more recent motivations have not been lacking, along with intellectual, technical and other resources. Within this transformation, however, there is adherence to or rediscovery of old points of reference. As sources of identity, reliance, and providers of bearings, nation-states and national consciousness exert a new/old power as political ingredients in the new Europe.[107] Europeanist strategy has shifted from emphasising an obsolescence of the nation as a focus for identity to assuring its continued viability. Coming in response to popular concerns about the EU's accountability, who was controlling the agenda, and what was its direction, this

---

103   Aron *Peace and War...* See pp737-753

104   Connor "The Nation and Its Myth" p49-50

105   See *The Invention of Tradition* Eds. Eric Hobsbawm & Terence Ranger (Cambridge: Cambridge University Press 1983) and Shore "Transcending the Nation-State?..." which builds on these themes.

106   Ludwig Bress "Transformation: Die Signatur des 21. Jahrhunderts" *Deutsche Studien* Heft 125 1995 pp5-43

107   In a late 1993 survey 40% of respondents identified themselves as a particular nationality only, 45% as firstly this and European, 7% as firstly European and a nationality, and 4% as European only. *Eurobarometer* n40 December 1993 p83. In 1995 the result was 37% nationality only, 45% nationality and European, 9% European and nationality and 6% European only. *Eurobarometer* n43 Autumn 1995 p6

was to make a virtue of necessity. Martin Griffiths observes that 'although nationalism is indeed a problem for world order, it is also a solution to the problem of state legitimacy in the modern age. This paradox is unlikely to be resolved in the foreseeable future. We should learn to cope with it.'[108]

---

108   Martin Griffiths "Fear and Loathing: Nationalism versus World Order" Paper presented to Politics Department Seminar, University of Adelaide 20-9-95, p31; Theo Mechtenberg "Scheitern die Einheit Europas an den Nationalismen?: Interkulturelle Lernfähigkeit auf dem Prüfstand" *Deutsche Studien* Heft 121 1994 pp16-26

2 Culture and Politics

> Modern man is not loyal to a monarch or a land or a faith, whatever he may say, but to a culture. [1]

This chapter extends the previous discussion of nations as being the primary repositories or boundary markers of political identity, interest formation and legitimacy. Through the mediums of state organs and civil associations, nations negotiate, cooperate, exchange, compete and conflict in an interactive European framework. While (most) nations have defined territories, they are not merely uniform legal-political constructs separated by borders. What differentiates these nations, or national societies, and provides polities and economies with internal coherence, is culture.

I also examine and compare the concept of a common European culture. This is a myth, or rather the focus of an attempt to create one, whereby historical justifications are invoked as support for a contemporary political project. Reference to history actually disproves claims of a 'common cultural heritage'.[2] Some more specific and current examples: economic culture, political culture, cultural policy, and language rivalry in European institutions, also reveal shortcomings. Instead, mergers of sovereignty provoke apprehensions as culturally grounded differences compete. In addition to emotive-psychological factors, there are practical-material advantages delivered by experience of particular national models, one of which, in most cases, will come closest to replication in the broader 'European space'.[3]

---

1 Ernest Gellner *Nations and Nationalism* (Oxford: Blackwell 1983) p86

2 Cf. William Wallace *The Transformation of Western Europe* (New York: RIIA 1990) p11

3 Philip Schlesinger "Europeanness: A New Cultural Battlefield" in *Nationalism* Eds. John Hutchinson & Anthony D. Smith pp316-325 (orig. *Innovation in Social Science Research* v5 n1 1992 pp11-23)

What is Culture?

A 1996 article by Raymond Geuss opens with the suggestion that 'the attempt to say anything both general and useful about the concept of "culture" might seem doomed from the very start'. Undoubtedly it is a protean and contestable term. Nonetheless, the author soon asserts that 'members of any given human group often behave in ways that are very much alike, yet differ systematically from the ways in which members of other groups behave'. And he concludes by stating 'we can't escape acting in preferential ways, valuation, and choice, and such valuation is completely related to its social context.'[4] A culture is an integrative phenomenon which, for its bearers, entails worth and inspires affinity. Other cultures are foreign, and may be variously admired, misunderstood, sampled, learned or reviled. There are two notions of culture involved here. Firstly an 'anthropological' everyday socialisation; secondly, a 'high' culture of notable achievement in art, literature, intellectual pursuits, and historiography.[5] Both are merged in the framework in which the 'social context' is constructed and each informs the psyche of the members. Both are challenged by and may influence externalities. In the global context, the separation of these two strains of culture is secondary to the distinctiveness of the whole relative to others.[6]

The range of phenomena placed under the general rubric of 'culture' has exploded during the twentieth century. A major academic propellant is the approach of various post-structuralist or post-modern theories suggesting that culture is something detached from affiliation with *particular* populations and from politics among nations.

> That the theorization of globalization has grown out of cultural studies and communication studies is no accident. Culture avoids being located and tied down to any definable physical space. In cultural studies, the primary purpose of investigation is the examination of shifting relationships and identities — of patterns of authority and representation

4   Raymond Geuss "Kultur, Bildung, Geist" *History and Theory* v35 n2 1996 pp151-164

5   Ernest Gellner makes the claim that 'when scholars disagree about the origin of an idea, normally each claims it for his own country'. "The Roots of Cohesion" in *Culture, Identity and Politics* (Cambridge: CUP 1987) pp29-46; See also *National Histories and European History* Ed. Mary Fulbrook (Boulder: Westview 1993)

6   Cf. David Looseley's explanation of the two 'ultimately related' meanings of 'culture', specifically in the context of French cultural policy and associated debate. *The Politics of Fun: Cultural Policy and Debate in Contemporary France* (Oxford: Berg 1995) pp4-6

— and not the success or failure of people/societies to fulfil an a priori essence. [7]

Internationalization of economies, societal vicissitudes, and the growth of 'global culture' has expanded, adapted, or impinged upon national variants.[8] Changes in national cultures were internally generated and derived from immigration flows while sub-national groups asserted their uniqueness and strove for autonomy. The resulting diversity is one instance of continuity from previous eras. Another is that a distinctive cultural core persists, though its psychic and empirical ingredients have also metamorphosised. Rather than complete fragmentation of cultural identifications a core-periphery configuration provides more accurate representation.[9] In her discussion of connections between culture, nation and identity, Montserrat Guibernau suggests that the individual's search for identity is directed by 'the need to belong to a community'. National identity is the resulting 'product', defined by

---

7   Julian Saurin "The end of International Relations? The state and international theory in the age of globalization" in *Boundaries in Question: new Directions in international Relations* Eds. John MacMillan & Andrew Linklater (London: Pinter 1995) pp244-261 See p256. Similar views are reflected in Michael Ryan *Politics and Culture: Working Hypotheses for a Post-Revolutionary Society* (Houndmills: MacMillan 1989); Glenn Jordan and Chris Weedon *Cultural Politics: Class, Gender, Race and the Post-Modern World* (Oxford: Blackwell 1995) These works make scarcely, if any reference to nations and national identity but operate with the same tacit assumption about their existence as argued in the first chapter. The journal *Cultural Studies* is featured by 'fragmentation' and 'diversity' interpretations of culture as its political project. One recent article, has noted, however, 'the unchallenged epistemological boundary of the political nation-state as a 'local context' (and more problematically, the 'ultimate' local context) of cultural analysis without taking into account the increasingly uneven process of globalization...in effect reproducing the nation-state boundary'. Kuan-Hsing Chen "Not yet the Postcolonial Era: The (Super) Nation-State and Transnationalism of Cultural Studies: Response to Ang and Stratton" *Cultural Studies* v10 n1 1996 pp37-70 In other words 'cultural studies' itself retains certain 'national' connections, not least a language of composition. As Chen continues, 'I have noticed the tendency of cultural studies to be locked into the nation-state divisions; an unconscious kind of nationalism is at work'

8   Cf. Anthony D. Smith "Towards a Global Culture?" *Theory, Culture and Society* n7 1990 pp171-191; Ronald Ingelhart *Cultural Shift in Advanced Industrial Society* (Princeton: Princeton University Press 1990); Mike Featherstone *Global Culture: Nationalism, Globalization and Modernity* (London: Sage 1990); *Cultural Change and the New Europe* Eds. Thomas M. Wilson & M. Estellie Smith (Boulder: Westview 1993)

9   Edward Shils *Centre and Periphery: Essays in Macrosociology* (Chicago: University of Chicago Press 1975)

'continuity over time, and differentiation from others'. The nation is not only 'one of' these necessary communities, but constitutes a 'primary membership'. The search itself is preceded, however, by a 'community of culture and unity of meaning' which 'are the main sources that allow the construction and experience of national identity'.[10] This completes a neat circle: culture is an *a priori* component of national communities, which then continue to identify themselves by cultural referents. Comparably, Alexander Gallus has written that 'a certain measure of natural or non-conscious cohesion must operate in all group-formations (boundary systems)' and:

> contact with other modes of behaviour, which may lead to acceptance of foreign influences (acculturation) or to resistance against change, seem often explicable in terms of this "drift", which represents the organic and specific flexibility of the cultural life of a human group. According to this "model", only those values and traits are assimilated, which lay in the direction of the organic process of change (its potential and its possibilities) within a particular human group.[11]

Culture is an evolutionary process, marked, according to Clifford Geertz, by a 'symbolic and historically transmitted system of shared meanings'.[12] Concurrent with the absorption of some external influences, are predominating communicative patterns, historical and educational influences, social parameters, preferences and characteristics which combine to differentiate societies.[13] From this perspective, culture, as a fusion of 'high' and 'everyday' components, is defined as:

> 1 the total of the inherited ideas, beliefs, values, and knowledge, which constitute the shared bases of social action. 2 the total range of activities and ideas of a group of people with shared traditions, which are transmitted and reinforced by members of the group.[14]

---

10   Montserrat Guibernau *Nationalisms: The Nation-State and Nationalism in the Twentieth Century* (Cambridge: Polity 1996) See pp72-76

11   Alexander Gallus "Cultural Plurality and the Study of Complex Societies in Anthropology" in *Studies for a New Central Europe* Series 3 n2 1972 pp28-47

12   Clifford Geertz *The Interpretation of Cultures* (New York: Basic Books 1973)

13   On a global scale, cultures segmented chiefly into national units is one categorization advanced by Immanuel Wallerstein's Marxist analysis. His other interpretation is of cultural divisions within national cultures. See *Geopolitics and Geoculture: Essays on the Changing World-System* (Cambridge: Cambridge University Press 1991)

14   *Collins Dictionary of the English Language* (Sydney: Collins 1988)

Culture and Prestige

In response to the intrusive forces of modernization in the 19th century, 'everyday' culture, previously the forest unseen for the trees, became the object of partisan defence now worshipped for its special qualities, those which set it apart and made all different from each other. Culture and polity moved toward symbiosis. In postulating this interpretation, Gellner articulated the 'move from structure to culture, from fixity to fluidity, from identity through location in societal structures to identification with the whole of the society in which one circulates'.[15] Multi-culturalism in eighteenth and nineteenth century European societies was featured by a prevailing group which through superior population numbers and/or control of the state apparatus developed a 'national culture'.[16]

> They comprise especially all those who think of themselves as being the specific "partners" of a specific "culture" diffused among the members of the polity. Under the influence of these circles, the naked prestige of "power" is unavoidably transformed into other special forms of prestige and especially into the idea of the "nation." [17]

Max Weber defined 'culture' as the 'endowment of meaning', and humans as '*Kulturmenschen*'. Notes in the manuscript margins of *Economy and Society* extend Weber's theory of a close connection between the prestige of culture and the prestige of power. Political and cultural power cohere in the nation-state and internal synthesis is given external radiance. The nation 'contained the legend of a providential 'mission'' which 'can consistently be thought of 'only as a specific 'culture' mission.'

> The significance of the 'nation' is usually anchored in the superiority, or at least the irreplaceability, of the culture values that are to be preserved and developed only through the cultivation of the peculiarity of the group. It therefore goes without saying that the intellectuals, as we

---

15   *Identity, Migration and the New Security Agenda in Europe* Eds. Ole Wæver, Barry Buzan, Morten Kelstrup and Pierre Lemaitre (London: Pinter 1993) pp32-33; Gellner *Nations and Nationalism*

16   Gellner suggests that, the Enlightenment 'absolutely needed a *shared* idiom, rather than a multiplicity of in-groups jargons. It was only natural that this idiom should be that of the majority group...' "From Königsberg to Manhattan (or Hannah, Rahel, Martin and Elfriede or Thy Neighbour's Gemeinschaft)" in Gellner *Culture, Identity, and Politics* pp75-90

17   Max Weber *Economy and Society: An Outline of Interpretive Sociology* Eds. Guenther Roth & Claus Wittich (Berkeley: University of California Press 1978) p922

have in a preliminary fashion called them, are to a specific degree predestined to propagate the 'national idea', just as those who wield power in the polity provoke the idea of the state'.[18]

One can point out that Weber's writings are now the best part of a century in the past, but the linkages between political and cultural identity sustains and his work has strong resonances among eminent contemporary scholars. Anthony Smith's elucidation of nation and state as distinct components with separate functions also indicates how each has a role in the preservation or flourishing of the other. As the institutional conduit of political and legal processes, fiscal means, and military guarantee, the state has an extensive capacity to defend or to actively promote a culture, including beyond its own borders. The nation—or the idea of nation—is the primary arbiter of the state's political complexion, impossible without cultural underpinnings. The nation

> refers to a cultural and political bond which unites in a community of prestige all those who share the same myths, memories, symbols and traditions. Despite the obvious overlap between the concepts of state and nation in terms of common territory and citizenship, the idea of the nation defines and legitimates politics in cultural terms, because the nation is a political community only so far as it embodies a common culture and a common social will.[19]

Edward Shils has also investigated the connections between tangible and intangible aspects of perceived cultural welfare. He claims that while competition between nations 'might primarily be for material objects and the well-being they bring; it is at least as likely to be about matters of status, dignity and prestige. Concern about the latter are frequently reinterpreted so that they are regarded as concerns about the territorial integrity of the society and its prosperity'.[20] Liah Greenfeld has stressed the centrality of dignity in sustaining national self-conceptions and the nation itself. Even though they may be universally sought, a shared culture reinforces communication of concepts like worth, dignity and identity. Transmission in the mother tongue, especially under pressure by more dominant languages, is itself an assertion of these feelings. In Greenfeld's account, the effects of combined structural,

---

18   Weber *Economy and Society...* pp925-926. See also Ralph Schroeder *Max Weber and the Sociology of Culture* (London: Sage 1992) Here p6

19   Anthony D. Smith "National identity and the idea of European unity" *International Affairs* v68 n1 1992 pp55-76

20   Edward Shils "Nation, nationality, nationalism and civil society" *Nations and Nationalism* v1 n1 1995 pp93-118, p108

cultural, and psychological factors find expression in inter*national* politics whereby:

> Every society importing the foreign idea of the nation inevitably focused on the source of importation—an object of imitation by definition—and reacted to it. Because the model was superior to the imitator in the latter's own perception (its being a model implied that), and the contact itself more often than not served to emphasize the latter's inferiority, the reaction commonly assumed the form of *ressentiment*. [21]

The provocative element suggested here has certainly not evaporated. In contemporary Europe, as governance over the parameters of commercial activity, technical harmonization and various standards moves out of national control, and decision on political unity approaches, concerns about 'societal security' are intensifying. What this means is *cultural* security, and, despite other notions of social collectivity or 'community',[22] where this most matters 'all culture is and remains today tied to the nation'.[23] When one is compelled to adopt a method or model that has derived from the social, economic or political culture of another, sensitivities dictate that this be manufactured as a communally conceived venture. Other elements of 'foreign' intrusion will still likely follow. Former French Minister of Culture, Jack Lang, contended that in the 1980s that 'culture is a battle for the right to live freely'. It then became topical to note in the 1990s that 'the decisive questions in regard to identity arise when and if there are conflicts between different identities. It is in times of crisis that people show their identitive priorities.'[24] Helmut Schmidt's admonitions about not injuring French national pride or Italian reactions to dismissals of financial credibility may illuminate Greenfeld's comments:

---

21   Liah Greenfeld *Nationalism: Five Roads to Modernity* (Cambridge, Mass.: Harvard University Press 1992) See p15

22   Will Kymlicka *Liberalism, Community and Culture* (Oxford: Oxford University Press 1989); Antony Black "Nation and community in the international order" *Review of International Studies* v19 1993 pp81-89

23   See Schroeder *Max Weber...* p138 fn5. Following Weber, Greenfeld asserts that 'social reality is cultural reality'. *Nationalism* p18. Cf. Michael Kelly "The Hegemony of National Identity in Cultural Identities" Paper presented at the ISSEI Conference *European Identity at the Millennium* Utrecht 19/24-8-96. 'For the time being, however, national identity remains hegemonic in culture...it continues to dominate cultural activity...the expression of other identities...tend ultimately to be grounded in or harnessed in the national one'. See also Peter Marden "Geographies of dissent: globalization, identity and the nation" *Political Geography* v16 n1 1997 pp37-64

24   *Identity, Migration...* Eds. Wæver et. al. pp81-82

a society with a well-developed institutional structure and a rich legacy of cultural traditions is not likely to borrow lock, stock, and barrel from anywhere. However, since the creative process resulting from *ressentiment* is by definition a reaction to the values of others and not to one's own condition regardless of others, the new system of values that emerges is necessarily influenced by the one to which it is a reaction...Ressentiment felt by the groups that imported the idea of nation and articulated the national consciousness of their respective societies usually resulted in the selection out of their indigenous traditions of elements hostile to the original national principle and in their deliberate cultivation.[25]

The greater the perceived and unwanted challenge to some aspect of a group's culture or to the group's self-conception, the more strident the politics. Staffan Zetterholm points out that a cultural group 'can be politically threatened when another group has greater political influence, whether this is the result of the latter's conscious strategy to use the political system as an instrument for 'cultural imperialism' or only the result of a wish to influence politics in accordance with cultural values'.[26] If, as John Hutchinson argues, it is a misconception that political and cultural forms of nationalism are capable of conflation, what is the (ongoing) employment of politics which clearly aims at serving a national-cultural interest? Cultural nationalism is rarely detached from and usually backed by political nationalism. Elsewhere Hutchinson maintains that cultural nationalism is not a 'transient phenomenon, bound to fade with full modernisation'. Politics can and does serve as an agent for cultural nationalism, and has 'its own aims and politics', now not nation-*building* but nation-*sustaining*.

Cultural nationalism is forced to shift into a state-directed politics to embed its programme in the social order...if cultural nationalism elicits a formally-organised political nationalism, more capable of mustering diverse groups to gain state power, political nationalism regularly re-ignites a cultural nationalism.[27]

---

25   Greenfeld *Nationalism* p16

26   Staffan Zetterholm "Why is Cultural Diversity a Political Problem? A Discussion of Cultural Barriers to Political Integration" in *National Cultures and European Integration: Exploratory Essays on Cultural Diversity and Common Policies* Ed. Staffan Zetterholm (Oxford: Berg 1994) pp65-82. Here p68

27   John Hutchinson "Moral Innovators and the Politics of regeneration: the Distinctive Role of Cultural Nationalists in Nation-Building" *International Journal of Comparative Sociology* v33 n1-2 1992 pp101-117. Cf. on this Albert Breton & Margaret Breton "Nationalism Revisited" in *Nationalism and Rationality* pp98-115. The authors offer 'a model of cultural and political

Culture and the Dichotomy of State and Society

All societies blame their own governments for the unwanted results of policies enacted in trying to reach agreement on building 'Europe'. Yet in demanding satisfactory responses to national versus European tensions they continue to rely on the state, their own state, perpetuating the precept of 'better the devil you know'. Paul Kennedy has put it succinctly that, 'Like everyone else, Europeans are still attached to what is common and traditional.'[28] While eastern Europe adjusts to post-authoritarian regimes, western Europe is also retuning connections between state and civil society.[29] New forces are influencing what each expects, how each responds to the other, where and when the two are effectively fused. State and society are not a fixed dichotomy but have reciprocal reliance and obligation, as Smith has suggested above. Individuals are part of a civic framework, a political fabric, and in large majority a cultural fabric, psychically and practically. There are large state budgets for internal and external promotion of linguistic, literary, social, and historical elements considered representative of the core culture and its uniqueness.

Philip Schlesinger has exposed the shallowness of a united defence against Americanization in Europe's 'contradictory communicative space' and indicated a more general heightening of tensions. He outlines concerns about power and authority/ies in the realm/s of national cultures: 'Culture and polity in Europe are not congruent with one another and, at a time of uncertainty, culture takes center stage as a battleground for the elaboration of identity politics.'[30] Similarly, Ulf Hedetoft claims that 'culture and power are getting out of joint'.[31] In Schlesinger's (and Hedetoft's) view a disconnecting of state and nation is occurring and 'the unmistakeable cultural expression of this crisis has been an accentuated concern with the nation as the locus and focus of collective sentiment and interest'. The culture-nation link is indeed strong, but states are not as distant or opposed to their populations as Schlesinger suggests. He later points out the persistent strong connection, support by states of corresponding national languages, and that 'nation-states still remain the

nationalisms which integrates these two kinds' in terms of 'investments' and 'yields'

28   Paul Kennedy "Germany in Europe; Half a Hegemon" *New Perspectives Quarterly* v10 n1 1993 pp35-38
29   Elemér Hankiss "European Paradigms: East and West, 1945-1994" *Dædelus* v123 n2 1994 pp115-126
30   Philip Schlesinger "Europe's Contradictory Communicative Space" *Dædelus* v123 n2 1994 pp25-51
31   Ulf Hedetoft "The State of Sovereignty in Europe: Political Concept or Cultural Self-Image" in *National Cultures and European Integration* pp13-48

most significant spaces for political communication'. Even a speculative Europeanism in audiovisual media must wait for a 'longer term sedimentation of routine institutional practices carried across the boundaries of the nation-states.'[32] The hyphen is still relevant.[33]

Building on Gellner's assertion that 'the monopoly of legitimate education is now more important than the monopoly of legitimate violence', Michael Schudson states that 'culture is paradoxically both the most visible and most problematic force for societal integration...the modern nation-state self-consciously uses language policy, formal education, collective rituals, and mass media to integrate citizens and ensure their loyalty.'[34] When projected outwards 'British Studies' is dominated by English, the French state promotes standardized French, and the German federal state, wherein there is 'no written language apart from High German', promotes *Hochdeutsche*.[35] Schudson

32   Schlesinger "Europe's Contradictory Communicative Space" pp31, 34-35, 46. Hedetoft also goes on to note that 'politics is still a national affair in the EC' and that 'even now the message is fairly obvious; political and economic integration must stop at the point where it impinges on basic national-mental assumptions' "The State of Sovereignty in Europe..." pp30-31

33   Despite the presence of 'sub-national' languages and regional dialects, central official languages remain powerful cultural connectors of nations and states in Europe. Cf. B. de Witte "Cultural Legitimation: Back to the Language Question" in *European Identity and the Search for Legitimacy* Ed. Soledad Garcia (London: Pinter/RIIA 1993) pp154-171

34   Michael Schudson "Culture and the Integration of national societies" *International Social Science Journal* v105 n1 February 1994 pp63-79, p64 & p71. Anthems, public holidays, the symbolism of flags and official ceremony all involve a state apparatus and are all distinctly national. Their significance is attested to by the European Community appropriation of these features in an attempt to inculcate them at a European level. But scarcely anyone knows when 'Europe Day' falls (May 9) while virtually everyone knows of July 14 or that a royal wedding is occurring. Even after only six years the dates November 9 and October 3 are widely known as the fall of the Berlin Wall and *Tag der deutschen Einheit*

35   Wolfgang Zank "Cultural Diversity and the Political System: The German Experience" *National Cultures and European Integration:Exploratory Essays on Cultural Diversity and Common Policies* Ed. Staffan Zetterholm (Oxford: Berg 1994) pp83-111. Although these are three of the largest and most influential EU members (and thus may appear to have least reason to feel imperiled) they are also most concerned with their position and ensuring that prestige is justly reflected. This is another case of partnership and rivalry being coexistent, as many bi- and trilateral initiatives exist among the three states in question. A long running German bilingual education program has aimed at 'inculcating' French as the 'partner language'. The German model has been declared 'exemplary for Europe'. See Nando Mäsch "The German Model of Bilingual Education" *Language, Culture and Curriculum* v6 n3 1993 pp303-313

claims, however, that 'there is reason to doubt the centrality of culture to societal integration'. But his references to economic, social, and political 'orders', or forms of 'coordination' and communication, cannot escape the ubiquity of *cultural* influence. As he soon acknowledges 'it remains true that nation-states cannot be understood, or even defined, apart from their achievement of some degree of cultural identity'. What we are then redirected to is the, quantitatively unmeasurable, *degree* of importance. Schudson switches his enquiry from the force that 'integrates' a society, to 'what defines or identifies the boundaries of the societies to which individuals are integrated'. Having made this distinction he declares 'cultural features are essential'. Culture is then a members ticket or password *into* a society, without which questions of integration are irrelevant. The premier expression of cultural distinctiveness,—'not a neutral medium for communication but a highly charged cultural object'—language inspires spirited external promotion and partisan defence against perceived threats to autonomy. Rather than reducing the import of culture to a society Schudson's argument increases it.[36]

In common with Schlesinger's observations, Wallace remarks that Europe's 'cultural evolution has been marked by a pronounced Americanization, or globalization of popular tastes'.[37] In the rapidity of its dissemination, 'American culture' surpassed that of the 'common European', perchance for the same reason Agnes Heller suggests in the latter case—that '*it was a culture without culture.*'[38] All Europeans are exposed to and affected by this 'cultureless culture'. Unease that Americanization may be replicated from within; that is, one of Europe's cultures will move towards ascendancy, is another dimension. Schlesinger has outlined the paradoxical interplay whereby 'Europeanizing ambition confronts national resistances and to the extent that a common European audiovisual idiom exists, it is actually American'.[39] Although accusatory fingers are pointed at the US, the real concern is not Americanization; the US is not directly determining everyday European decisions and if anything is receding from European affairs. Nor is it an amorphous 'Brussels'. There is no readymade or concocted European culture to be disseminated by Euro-decree, so challenging or replacing those present.

Simultaneously they are conducting a battle for second place behind English.

36   Schudson "Culture and the Integration of national societies" pp64-65 & p70
37   Wallace *Transformation* pp3-4
38   Agnes Heller "Europe: An Epilogue?" in *The Idea of Europe: Problems of Transnational Identity* Eds. Brian Nelson, David Roberts & Walter Veit (New York: Berg 1992) pp12-25. See p22
39   Schlesinger "Europe's Contradictory Communicative Space" p46. Cf. on this Susan Emanuel "A Community of Culture?: The European Television Channel" *History of European Ideas* v21 n2 1995 pp169-176; George Wedell "Prospects for Television in Europe" *Government and Opposition* v29 n3 1994 pp315-331

Rather, underlying protestations at some political developments—or preempting them—are disquieting perceptions that 'Brussels' will facilitate the expansion of one, or more, of the *existing national cultures* to the aversion and detriment of others. While there are 'implied threats' to some identities, others may perceive a privileged situation 'deteriorating' and so precipitate reaction 'against European integration, also using their states for this purpose'.[40] Analogous to the nominal Ecu, or 'euro', as a 'basket of currencies' with the strongest in effect determining the fate of the others, various other elements may go the same way.

The shaping of 'Europe' is a contest to imbue the unknown future with features, preferences and means of communication deriving from national polities. Without an acceptable, coherent all-European formula one national-cultural expression will arrive at an ascendancy. Particular national models are already proving effective in replicating themselves. Zetterholm declares that 'National actors who can export their model to others (through common policy establishment) also have an advantage of being familiar with the model and therefore being able to use it as a power source.'[41] It is then that deep-seated attachments can lead to re-emergence of rivalries and jealousies which are not exclusively located in either the popular (societal) or élite (state) domain—'cultural differences may enter the political game and add an emotional dimension to political conflict'.

Public unrest reflects both dissatisfaction with their own governments and concern that norms of others may be imposed. Another insightful discussion by Zetterholm shows how the factors of cultural heterogeneity, structure of political influence, and legislative authority of the central government may produce combinations that incite the issue of cultural autonomy to become politically 'live'. The crucial point is the second one and it impresses the practical and even theoretical difficulties of disconnecting cultural and political instincts. It concerns political influence 'as set up by constitution and by the distribution of political resources':

> the less likely it is that the [cultural] group can control or influence government decisions to a decisive or considerable degree, the larger the perceived threat will be. The reverse is also true; the more control (by power, position or constitutional guarantees) the group can exert on government policy-making, the less likely it is that it will perceive itself to be in a culturally and existentially vulnerable position.[42]

---

40   *Identity, Migration...* Eds. Wæver et. al. See Chapter 4

41   Staffan Zetterholm "Introduction: Cultural Diversity and Common Policies" in *National Cultures and European Integration* pp1-12. See p7 and fn6

42   Zetterholm "Why is Cultural Diversity a Political Problem?..." p67

Such a scenario, especially the negative version, encourages state and society to congeal around a commonality of 'the nation' and *its* interests: economic, territorial and cultural. At grass roots level although culture is in continuous metamorphosis, it is the *pace* of change that inspires protest or fear.[43] Culture and 'freedom' are (re)linked to sovereignty and while perceptions endure that some/one could dominate the conduct and shape of the Union and others could be marginalized, the formal 'protection' of state sovereignty is clung to.[44] There is a strong resonance of Nietzsche here: politics perceived as the servant and protector of culture. Whether this is that of the nation or the good European is presently tilted towards the former. Schlesinger's characterising of 'Europeanness' as 'A New Cultural Battlefield' suggests that:

> the present salience of national identity in European politics confutes the view that the grand narratives are *passé,* and that there are no compelling tales of solidarity to tell. Both the emergent nation-states of the old East and the supranationalising European Community are heavily dependent upon convincing us that tales of solidarity within bounded communities are both plausible and desirable.[45]

Europe's 'Problem' of Unity and Diversity

> Europe does not 'melt' like the US, and so must therefore find a political unity above the great linguistic divide. The challenge for Europe is that of going toward multilingualism; we must place our hope in a polygot Europe. The challenge for Europe is finding political unity through polyglotism. Even if the decision is made to speak Esperanto at the European parliament and in airports, polyglotism will be the true unity of Europe.[46]

---

43   Cf. Anthony Smith's observation, 'Fears, like memories, are no less real for being intangible and difficult to research'. "National identity and the idea of European unity" p76 fn33

44   Cf. Hedetoft "The State of Sovereignty" p16 fn5. Interview respondent views. 'My country's political sovereignty is the central pillar in the concept of freedom...the political regime of a country cannot be dictated from without...without any political sovereignty, no freedom'

45   Schlesinger "Europeanness: A New Cultural Battlefield"

46   Umberto Eco "For a Polyglot Federation" *New Perspectives Quarterly* v10 nl Winter 1993 pp41-43

Although, as William Wallace says, 'committed 'Europeans' adjusted their definitions of European culture and identity to fit its changing institutional contours each time the Community was enlarged',[47] there are limits to how extensively and deeply this can be commonly embedded in disparate populations. Discovering and then steering a course of 'acculturation' while maintaining cultural independencies encumbers 'Europe' builders. Before the surge of commercial policy integration in the mid-1980s, the European Commission revealed that 'European unification will only be achieved if Europeans want it. Europeans will only want it if there is such a thing as a European identity. A European identity will only develop if they are adequately informed.'[48] The insights of Jacques Delors and others notwithstanding, questions of cultural identity were relegated in political importance as market integration developed a rationale of its own and preoccupied the Brussels technocracy. Basic parameters of competition were established. New challenges appeared after the international order was transformed in 1989. Moving democratic processes and decision-making in areas of core sovereignty beyond states and vetoes requires popular and élite identification at a fundamental level. 'Europe' must be accepted as one's 'way of life' and so *European culture* became the 'future good of the continent'.[49] The Commission has acknowledged the 'cultural dimension of [all] European policies', not only those specifically designated or regarded as 'Culture' itself. 'Culture' cannot be separated from other areas of integration because it is present in all.

As a political referent, 'culture' is then both a bloc, like 'defence' or 'the economy'; and multifarious elements of daily existence. It has moved to the sphere of 'high politics' but is not simply alterable through policy agreement. The integrationist dilemma is: firstly, differences manifested as diversely as retention of parliamentary sovereignty, fears for linguistic purity, preference for the colour of peas or taste of cheese, or control over monetary policy, act, *inter alia*, as barriers to political unity; secondly, there can be no political entity capable of overcoming this unless it already has a reservoir of cultural support. A profusion of assurances regarding cultural integrity were accompanied by various Commission projects, 'emblematic actions', multilingual programmes, and other initiatives intended to foster a sense of commonality.[50] High levels of interaction among younger people and the wide

47   Wallace *Transformation* pp8-9

48   *Television Without Frontiers: Green Paper on the Establishment of the Common Market for Broadcasting, Especially by Satellite and Cable* (Brussels: CEC 1984)

49   Werner Weidenfeld et.al. *Europäische Kultur: das Zukunftsgut des Kontinents* (Bertelsmann Stiftung: Gütersloh 1990)

50   See *European Community Action in Support of Culture* (Brussels 27-7-94); *The*

dissemination of English as a quasi- *lingua franca* has not established a 'European culture' that defines a way of life and network of understandings commonly practised across the continent.[51] Cross-cultural linkages and projects have a way to go as the vanguard of a 'European consciousness'.

> Even with such favourable global conditions, even with the headstart provided by Europe's cultural histories, there seems as yet a very deep and clear gulf between the aspirations for political (and economic) unity of Europe and the development of a genuine European cultural identity which can compete in popular consciousness and loyalties with deeply rooted national affiliations.[52]

If there is a sentiment that presumes an inherent sanctity of a culture it is triggered when there are perceptions that this culture is under some form of undesired challenge. Without the bearers of distinct cultures having deep attachments and sensitivities there would be no debate on unity-diversity, potential hegemonies, marginalization, and control in Europe. Decrying any 'melting pot effect', governments and think-tanks pay voluminous lip service to the positive nature of cultural diversity. Advocates aver that it can (and should) be achieved coexistent with extensive and intensive economic and political integration that presupposes considerable, evident uniformity. This is to restate the central dilemma of the European project: resolving unity *and* diversity in the same space and time. Proposals for precisely *how* are fewer and less clearly elucidated. Western Europe may not have been the first place Pierre Hassner had in mind when he wrote of a 'deeper tension between unity and diversity, which is the signature of current history', but his comments apply:

> Individual and collective selves are divided among multiple allegiances, aspirations and pressures, yet long for unity. The modern world has a powerful homogenizing influence, particularly in cultural terms, through the revolution in communications, yet the need for diversity and

---

95). The European University Institute in Florence is a pre-eminent case of the attempt to develop a 'European' educational milieu

51   Nico Wilterdink "Images of National Character" *Social Science & Modern Society* v32 n1 November/December 1994 pp43-51. This study of young, educated 'Europeans' based at the European University Institute presents a high return of belief in 'distinct national traditions' (99%) and 'personality traits different from those of other countries' (93%). The rate of agreement with national stereotypes was also pronounced, especially for such a cosmopolitan setting

52   Smith "A Europe of Nations.." p133

separation, for distinguishing among 'us', 'we' and 'the others' is felt ever more strongly.[53]

In the Rome and Maastricht treaties, political unity and cultural diversity are, respectively, ultimate goal and inviolable creed. Or, irresistible force and immovable object. Article 128 states that 'The Community shall contribute to the flowering of the cultures of the member states, while respecting their national and regional diversity and at the same time bringing the common cultural heritage to the fore'.[54] So it is with particular poignancy in the cultural field that, 'whoever wants to construct *uniformity* is as anti-European as those politicians who are still wearing their nation-state-colored spectacles while planning transnational cooperation in Brussels'.[55] Culture is the site at which enthusiastic promotion of 'ever closer union' loses authority when portrayed as a kind of manichean struggle: the momentum of integration not only as desired but imperative; and national boundaries or demarcations as a hindering a worthy ideal and ultimately dangerous. The positions are more likely reversed: 'Brussels' and its technocracy depicted as making unwanted intrusions endangering the diversity and vivacity of Europe's cultures by bland standardizations; conversely the nation-state is reaffirmed for the foreseeable future as a viable cultural-political unit. Wæver and Kelstrup put it succinctly that 'if there is one lesson learned after the various national crises about the European Union it should be: leave culture to the nations'.[56]

John Keane's vigorous argument for a federated and pluralistic European civil society, observes that 'to be a European involves recognizing and valuing the existence of a collectivity that protects and encourages diversity and thus...an ability to question the collectivity itself'.[57] Stressing that Europe's strength is its diversity is an attempt to square the circle: 'we are diverse', 'we are unified'—simultaneously. These conditions or forces are analogous to those of and fragmentation or the evolution of political authority in Europe upwards to an unspecified highest locus of governance and downwards to regional constituencies. While the second named in each of these examples suggests the preservation or empowerment of cultural identities existing in territorial units smaller than 'traditional' nation or national

53   Pierre Hassner "Beyond Nationalism and Internationalism: Ethnicity and World Order" *Survival* v35 n2 1993 pp49-65

54   Article 128 "Culture" para.1. See Richard Corbett *The Treaty of Maastricht: from conception to ratification* (Harlow: Longman Current Affairs 1993)

55   Sven Papcke"Who needs European Identity and what could it be?" in *The Idea of Europe* pp61-74, p64 Emphasis in original

56   *Identity, Migration* ... Eds. Wæver et. al. p80

57   John Keane "Questions for Europe" in *The Idea of Europe* pp55-61, 57

states, the former may, or may be perceived as, endangering them. Harmonization and institutional blending provoke misgivings about a distended 'European porridge' as nightmare Orwellian visions are invoked.[58]

Ideally, 'Europe' would be more than the sum of its parts. If it is not it still requires a solidarity, manifested politically, between cultures. Although exisiting 'multiple loyalties' (for example to München, Bayern, Germany) could add 'Europe', this does not account for situations that present conflicting tests or allegiances simultaneously.[59] Indications are that in practice one will take precedence despite the stress form Brussels on a sensible division of competencies. A variation on the multiple loyalties strategy, by route if not destination, is separation of political and cultural identifications. Populations could transfer their political allegiances from the 'empty shell' of state sovereignty to a common European level and thereby 'depoliticize' relations between themselves as bearers of differing cultures. This strategy aims at overcoming either-or scenarios of 'our' way versus another or 'their' way by splitting cultural and highest political forms of identification into national and European respectively rather than duplicating cultural-political identification with *both* national and European levels. 'Europe' would accommodate the political element with a 'republican' orientation leaving all 'cultures' protected species in their own national or regional habitats. Survival, indeed 'flourishing', of national cultures is then to be assured by this new 'political roof'.

> The real political issue...is about giving the nation that which is the nation's (that is culture, identity and those issues relevant thereto: education, a social welfare system, a cultural policy in a narrow sense)...they will increasingly have to see themselves as cultural communities reproducing primarily through cultural means.[60]

---

58   Michael Jeismann "In Zukunft: Umbesetzung: Kalt ist Europa, gemütlich die Nation" *Frankfurter Allgemeine Zeitung* 18-12-95

59   Theorising in support of transferring allegiance to 'Europe' is reliant on hopes, should be's and maybe's. Cf. Edelgard Mahant "Foreign Policy and European Identity" *History of European Ideas* v21 n4 1995 pp485-498, p489. 'The future *may* see not only a learning of multiple identities, but also a realization that political identities are not necessarily territorially based...The kind of rationality which *could* allow individuals to identify with several political units *may become possible* at a time when satellites beam information across continents...' Emphasis added. See also *European Identity and the Search for Legitimacy*

60   *Identity, Migration* .. Eds. Wæver et. al. p91

Habermas makes a similar prescriptive analysis that indicates the gulf between phrases like 'in the future' [politics and culture could be separated in the European context] and actually making such a transition.

> To date the member states have not made the legitimation of EC policy an object of controversy. By and large, the national public spheres are culturally isolated from one another. They are anchored in contexts in which political issues only gain relevance against the background of national histories and national experiences. In the future, however, differentiation could occur in a European culture between a common 'political' culture and the branching 'national' traditions of art and literature, historiography, philosophy, etc. The cultural elites and the mass media would have an important role to play...[61]

Inventing a 'Common European Culture'

> There is also talk of asserting the reality of Europe as a cultural entity of some sort...its central theme is the central theme of anthropology...and concerns the proper understanding of "culture" as it relates to human beings in any locality...the concern is with the institutional expression of this difference, its affirmation on some broader stage and its rationalisation. The concern is with "nationalism".[62]

Jean Monnet's statement 'If I should start it all over again, I would start with culture' acknowledges this mercurial factor is the most difficult to integrate into a supranational framework, and concomitantly that which is most required. The previous quotation from Varenne confirms Monnet's thoughts, and fears. Both indicate a realisation that economic progress will not suffice to sustain European integration and that common cultural underpinnings are needed. But they are not there. These foundations will have to be invented. Walter Laqueur has remarked that 'a history of European culture in the twentieth century has not been written, and it is unlikely that it will ever be written, for the simple reason that it would have to cover far too much ground and that there are not enough common themes.'[63] Europe's various cultures

---

61   Habermas "Citizenship..." p12
62   Hervé Varenne "The Question of European Nationalism" in *Cultural Change and the New Europe: Perspectives on the European Community* Eds. Thomas Wilson & M. Estellie Smith (Boulder: Westview 1993) pp223-240
63   Walter Laqueur *Europe in Our Time: A History 1945-1992* (New York: Penguin 1992) p279

have digested reciprocal influence and there are no 'purely national cultures'.[64] Assimilation of elements originating elsewhere has not led to a 'European' culture. What there may be is a European sensibility, but even this becomes diffused when a requisite 'other' is removed from the frame.

The European Commission claimed in 1985 that 'a community of culture in Europe is already an undeniable fact. Beneath a surface diversity of languages, tastes and artistic styles, there is a likeness, a kinship, a European dimension or identity based on a common cultural heritage....'.[65] These claims are questionable. The assertion of 'undeniable fact' was incorrect in 1985 and after 1992 a resolute commonality of culture remains dubious. Confusion lies between the *goal*, whether worthy or not, and the *actuality*. Exploring the pre-EU past, Agnes Heller surmises on the absence of a common cultural grounding that both plagues the 'United Europe' advocates in the EU of the 1990s and earlier led to its formation as an attempt to restrain national-cultural rivalries. '*Modernity, the creation of Europe, itself created Europe,* and this was more than a paradox...there was no *ab urbe condita* as such.' A real union requires the creation of acceptable and profound cultural and political commonalities where previously these have failed or never existed.

> The project termed 'Europe' or 'the West' requires a cultural backing, a brand new cultural mythology...(it) had never been established as a political entity that imposed certain common political duties or political obligations...the utopian idea of a United States of Europe...was quickly suppressed by vintage nationalism. Political mythologies were bound to strengthen national, rather than Western or European identity.[66]

In Heller's view 'Culture and the consciousness of culture are coexistent...(it) requires the identification of the carrier of culture, a commitment to a particular way of life and a belief in the superiority of this way of life.' In a study on the prospects of television assisting the development of a European culture, Susan Emanuel declares:

> Despite the rhetoric at many gatherings of European artists, intellectuals, and broadcasters, if one pays attention to differences in language, history and tastes in the televisions of European peoples, then arguments for a common European culture, and for the central role of culture in sustaining European political institutions and in promoting European union now become difficult to uphold.

---

64   Papcke "Who needs European Identity and what could it be?" p64
65   *The European Community and Culture* (Brussels: CEC 1985)
66   Heller "Europe: An Epilogue?..." p14

In contrast to French cultural watchdogs, Britons 'did not experience internationalization of the media as a threatening phenomena' precisely because of its 'access to the Anglophone market', that is, linguistic familiarity. Consistent with many other pursuits, 'European television audiences have been less inclined to identify with programmes that emanate from outside their national linguistic and cultural community than economic rationalists and European unionists would have wished'. Political backing encourages these divisions along national state lines.[67] Wallace has impressed that 'attempts to promote the idea of a distinctive European culture, tradition, or set of values, are thus of high political significance' and that 'shared European experience...adds an additional dimension to the bargaining over rules and conflicting interests which constitutes the agenda of multilateral intergovernmental cooperation'. This shared experience pertains to history, which constitutes an element of culture, but not of a social community, each of which tend to interpret history differently. Wallace continues that 'the idea of a distinctive European identity...is an artificial construct: an attempt to rearrange tradition and history to suit current political needs, in which historiography threatens to become a political pamphlet'. Meanwhile, real 'evidence of a set of European values...is sparser—and takes us closer to the realm of political persuasion rather than dispassionate analysis...a diffuse sense of European identity has *not* led to a transfer of loyalties from the national to the European level...'.[68] European identity is then an invention in process, reliant on 'information', will, and the imagining of a European community. 'Unity at the European level is said to be an outcome of an act of will dependent upon a prior condition: a 'European identity'...Information (culture) is therefore held to act as a homogenizer or articulator of the will...it is a thoroughly idealist and voluntarist perception of the construction of the desired social order, and a rather improbable explanation'.[69] It takes on the psychic features or persona attributed (by Renan and various successors) to nations. According to former European Parliament President Klaus Hänsch, 'reinventing Europe is the key to its success'.[70]

Invocations of a contemporary common European culture self-referentially appeal to an alleged cultural unity of previous centuries. Rhetorical employment of a 'common cultural heritage' existing long before the post-war

---

67   Emanuel "A Community of Culture?..." p171
68   Wallace *Transformation* pp30-33; Cf. *National Histories and European History* Ed. Mary Fulbrook
69   Philip Schlesinger *Media, State and Nation: Political Violence and Collective Identities* (London: Sage 1994) p139
70   Klaus Hänsch "Renewing the European Vision" *Eur-Op News* v4 n4 Winter 1995 p7

construction of 'Europe', and its desired revival, is an appeal to generate the identification necessary for political unity. To claim there was a common European culture until 'national consciousness' appeared is like asserting that all prehistoric animals were the same, until somebody discovers they were not. Culture can also be interpreted as being, in the past and present, *the* source of division. Culture and politics are linked at the pan-European level or both continue there primarily in the form of (separate) nation-states. The following diagram proposes an explanation of past, present and future connections, between culture (as borne by the majorities of individual populations) and politics (state or state supported action) in Europe.

Table 2.1   Scenarios of connections between culture and politics in Europe: past, present and future

Scenario One	Scenario Two	Scenario Three	Scenario Four
EUROPE OF THE PAST	PRESENT ORGANIZATION OF EUROPE	DUAL IDENTIFICATIONS STRATEGY FOR 'EVER CLOSER UNION'	NECESSARY RESULT (BOTH OR NEITHER)
SEPARATE CULTURES. COMMON "HIGH CULTURE" DOMINATED BY FRENCH MODEL	SEPARATE CULTURES (SOME MORE INFLUENTIAL THAN OTHERS)	ASSURE SEPARATE CULTURES WHILE ASSERTING A COMMON "EUROPEAN" HERITAGE (thus enabling a)	CONSIDERABLE DEPTH OF COMMON CULTURAL IDENTITY
SEPARATE POLITIES	SEPARATE INTERACTIVE POLITIES	UNIFIED "EUROPEAN" POLITICAL IDENTITY	UNIFIED EUROPEAN POLITY

In earlier centuries, Europe, or at least some parts of it, had a literate 'high culture' dominated initially by Latin and later appropriated by the sophisticated mores of French 'civilization'. Contemporary opposition to the EU would be reinforced if one national example was elevated, or perceived to be so, like this. If there is something of a current parallel to the French court model it is transnationalized sections (by no means all) of political, intellectual and business élites. Extensive tourism, the single market, intra-European immigration, and copious educational exchange has not instilled in the bulk of Europe's populations a belief in having derived from the same culture. Rather than any such deep resonance there may be a more general historical understanding that, for example, these 'European' peoples lived in a certain proximity and could be regarded as collectively different from African or

Asian or American peoples. Formulations like Anthony Smith's 'family of cultures' semantically inch across the gap between Europe's actual diversity and (for some) desired unity. Daniela Obradovic has argued that while 'references are also often made to an impressionistic and superficial notion of a European tradition and heritage...this concept comes up against two major problems: the indistinctiveness of Europe's boundaries and the imprecise demarcation of Europe as a cultural unity'.[71] A brief historical *tour d'horizon* does not reveal freely chosen pan-European cultural commonality as a clearly evident feature.[72]

i)The ancient Greek and Roman civilizations provide the most 'common roots of Europe'[73] and bequeathed a tradition of philosophy, principles of political organization and law, and later Christianity. While the *polis* and the Church of Rome are broad overarching models which have survived in present day European societies, knowledge of Greek philosophy or the ability to speak and read Latin did not extend much beyond ecclesiastic and intellectual élites. Belief that other peoples may have also been Christian did not mean tribes speaking different tongues would merge into one. Neither Socrates nor Saint Paul could save this 'cultural Europe' from the arrival of the Dark Ages. For smaller communities more primitive unities persisted.[74] Rather than founding and perpetuating a historic cultural unity throughout Europe, Christianity was a fragmented religion whose original form, Catholicism, 'was, after all, a product of the harsh battle for hegemony over beliefs and the collective mentality'.[75] It too was a political project.

---

71   Daniela Obradovic "Policy Legitimacy and the European Union" *Journal of Common Market Studies* v34 n2 1996 pp214-215

72   This is more accurately described as European 'civilization'. All of Western Europe and, tentatively, part of the East, or centre, comes under this rubric. Rather than making a distinction along the lines of Ferdinand Tönnies *Gemeinschaft/Gesellschaft* with the former denoting a cultural community and the latter a civilized society, 'Civilization' is a broad category which encompasses within it many cultures. But these are separate cultures not a 'communal culture'

73   Cf. Bronislaw Geremek *The Common Roots of Europe* Trans. Jan Aleksandrowicz et. al. (Cambridge: Polity 1996) whose densely documented account is delivered from a distinctly 'Eastern' perspective. Despite the title the author frequently has to acknowledge the limitations of the 'commonality'.

74   Jacques Delors is one who hoped to revitalise 'Europe' via the concept of *Christianitas*, by defining it as a Christian entity. Christianity is now neither exclusive to Europe nor a unifier of it. Could one say that Asia was a unified cultural entity because much of it was Buddhist, or Moslem?

75   Geremek *The Common Roots of Europe* p85 See also Smith "National Identity and the idea of European Unity" p69 on 'inter-Christian divides' and other

ii)Mediæval feudalism was featured by thousands of power centres and similarities have been drawn with current fragmentation or devolution towards smaller political units.[76] While for a vast pan-European majority, mediæval life was nasty, brutish and short, by and large this existence was spent in isolation from different communities doing the same. There was no widespread experience of and mutual interaction with 'foreign' neighbours. Low levels of literacy continued long after the invention of the printing press multiplied the production of written material.

iii)Formation of the state system whereby the princes and dukes of feudalism came to command larger geo-political entities. As in the previous epoch, mercenaries fought for whichever duke or prince paid them, or paid them best. Thus this arrangement was a forerunner to international capitalism. Because France was the major continental power, French language (or that of the *Ile-de-France*) and the style and mores of the Versailles court were adopted by other aristocratic centres. Frederick the Great of Prussia was a noted Francophile, at least in the realm of 'high culture', as it was then understood. This aristocratic familiarity or salon society was not replicated at the level of general populations. Although the Habsburg and Russian empires were multicultural, people identified with the language of their own community usually reinforced by common ethnicity (or vice-versa), and were held together through political-bureaucratic means underpinned by reserve military force. The lack, or alternatively the presence, of strong cultural bonding, linked and propelled by politics, emerged in the 19th century.

iv)This was the age of blooming national consciousness and the intensification of desires for political control to be congruent with distinct cultural communities. While the Austro-Hungarian empire was in process of disintegration, united Germany was ascending. The older states, Britain and France had survived, even prospered, by effective cultural homogenisation and simultaneously concretizing the focus of political and emotional loyalty. British commercial, maritime and military dominance merged with a powerful, if understated in comparison to others, identification with the nation-state. In France peasants were fashioned as Frenchmen.[77]

v)The arrival of totalitarianism then brought a new form of suppression or elimination of cultural diversity. Not only was cosmopolitanism considered a

---

problematic aspects of employing 'Christianity' as the conceptual glue with which to construct a historically grounded common European culture. Cf. Jeremy Black *Convergence or Divergence?: Britain and the Continent* (Houndmills: MacMillan 1994) p269

76   Cf. Alain Minc *Le Nouveau Moyen Age* (Paris: Editions Gallimard 1993)
77   Eugen Weber *Peasants into Frenchmen: The Modernization of Rural France 1870-1914* (London: Chatto & Windus 1977)

threat to the regime but its eradication constituted, in the case of Nazism, a *raison d'etre*. In the Soviet Union, Marxist-Leninist (Great Russian) aspirations eclipsed the political freedoms of Eurasia's multiple linguistic and ethnic populations. By 1940 the two ideologies had all but 'decultured' Europe.

vi)The 'invasion' of Americanism after 1945 constituted the single most powerful dissemination of 'common culture' across western Europe. In eastern Europe Sovietization, essentially 'Russification', extended. In the 1980s, along with erosion of the welfare states verdant in the post-war decades, liberalizing capitalism has been the dynamic to propel western European integration, assisted by geo-political bipolarity. After 1989-91 the twin, paradoxical forces of globalization and fragmentation are more pronounced. The former is based on the internationalization of economies and English as the ubiquitous language of commerce along with that of scientific and academic publications. The icons of American pop culture are prevalent. While the USA may be a multi-mutated amalgam of what were predominantly, to totalize their origins in a *geographic* sense, European cultures, this re-exportation to the old continent does not derive from a common source.

What this chronology endeavours to impress is that at no stage of historical evolution has there been a widespread, popular, *European* cultural consciousness. Great artists may be granted pan-European appreciation (though Michelangelo is claimed as first and foremost Italian, Goethe German, Shakespeare English, and Proust as French)[78] and food, drink, music and so on emanating from elsewhere in Europe are enjoyed by many. There is perhaps a sense of 'when in Rome'. All this may mean that a process of psychological Europeanization is *underway*. It has not yet made 'Europe' a genuine post-national cultural and political reality.

---

78   The artistic milieu may be Europe's most cosmopolitan and least nationalistic. But artists may be interpreted differently by other members of the national community. 'In many respects the artist is for cultural nationalists the paradigmatic figure of the national community...the source of creativity is placed not in an eternal supramundane order but in the continually evolving people itself...it is only when it is adopted by journalists and pamphleteers who translate the cultural into more concrete economic, social, and political programmes that it becomes a significant movement'   Hutchinson "Moral Innovators and the Politics of Regeneration..." p104

'European' Cultural Policy

> What philosophy of translation will dominate in Europe? In a Europe
> that from now on should avoid both the nationalistic tensions of
> linguistic difference and the violent homogenization of languages
> through the neutrality of a translating medium that would claim to be
> transparent, metalinguistic, and universal? [79]

Financial incentives for joint ventures of a cultural nature between member
nation-states or regions of different nations have grown in recent years. The
Commission has been joined in this endeavour by some political groups,
particularly the European People's Party.[80] These projects are somewhat
quarantined, having a 'safe' quality in that they do not permeate whole
cultures. Local communities are happy to accept grants to promote, restore or
otherwise engender something having a 'cultural aspect', cooperating where
necessary with other groups in doing so. As the Commission has more
recently recognised, any examination of Community texts on cultural matters
'depends on how Culture is defined...Given that it is not for an institution to
define the concept of culture, this report...has adopted a pragmatic approach.'
Culture may include 'traditional components' like the arts, literature, historical
sites and so on, 'but may also include all types of knowledge and features
which characterise a society and make it possible to understand the world.'[81]
Such an exhaustive inventory infers that *everything* a society does is Culture—
its own Culture. Everything it does not do, is not. Culture outside museums,
libraries and touring exhibitions often reacts rather differently to the appearance
of unfamiliar intrusion. Where financial carrots are not made available cross-
cultural projects are not the same success.

There are also all sorts of exceptions, exemptions, and special cases
related to culture, negotiated, with varying success, by individual member
states. 'Generally speaking aid to the cultural sector poses virtually no problem
from the competition-policy standpoint. However, the Commission has had to
oppose such aid...because the conditions under which it has been granted are
often contrary to the fundamental principles of the European Community...for
example, with aid systems contravening non-discrimination on the basis of
nationality.' In one example, the Commission 'rejected a condition imposed

79 Jacques Derrida *The Other Heading: Reflections on Today's Europe* Trans.
    Pascale-Anne Brault & Michael B. Naas (Bloomington: Indiana University
    Press 1992) p58
80 The Group of the European People's Party, "Bruges Study Days" 28-8-95/1-9-95
    produced a text of collected speeches
81 *1st Report on the Consideration of Cultural Aspects in European Community
    Action* (Brussels: CEC 17-4-96)

by the German government, under which the producer of a film receiving aid must be a German citizen or a person from a German culture'. But member states may restrict the employment of Community citizens, that is, those of other nationalities. Judgements set forth by the Court of Justice in the early 1980s determined that exceptions to anti-discrimination laws are possible in state public services 'for reasons of public order, public safety and public health' and concerns only those areas 'which includes direct or indirect participation in "the exercise of public power" or functions whose object is "to safeguard the general interests of the State" or of public authorities'. Anything could yet be extrapolated from this.[82]

Member states will try various angles to advance some particular interest or in response to a sufficiently powerful domestic lobby, often successfully shifting an issue from one area of Community policy, like Competition Policy, to another, Cultural Policy, in order to obtain a desired result: protection, autonomy, funding, and so on. Therefore 'reconciling the achievement of the objectives of the European union Treaty with the specific objectives of cultural policies has proved difficult, due to the economic and commercial nature of some cultural activities. Cultural and economic interests have had to be weighed against each other, and cultural considerations have "not always received the preferential treatment granted them in some member states".'[83] An example that illustrates this is agriculture, which despite laying outside TEU provisions on culture, 'Nevertheless, agricultural activities do have an inherent cultural nature...In Europe local or regional *savoir-faire* has generated a very wide variety of traditional products which are part of the cultural identity of the locality or region'.[84] The physical manifestations of the EU terminology, 'Cultural assets', are prominently featured by 'national treasures', though it is 'difficult, at the moment to pinpoint the criteria for determining the scope of this notion'. While there is an attempt to identify a 'common core of cultural assets', points of greatest sensitivity are swept into an 'annex' to the main 'rule and directive'. This is where the 'political compromise' presently rests and where the 'political sensitivity of the subject' requires reference to Article 100A (the veto clause).[85] As 'cultural aspects must be taken into account' in the formulation of any Community policies, *anything* could conceivably be manoeuvred under the umbrella of 'culture' in order to serve some political or financial purpose.

---

82   *1st Report...Cultural Aspects*... ptl p15
83   Draft Communication to the Parliament and the Council *European Report* n2123
      13-4-96 pp7-8
84   *1st Report...Cultural Aspects*... ptl p22
85   *1st Report...Cultural Aspects*... ptl p18

Assertions of extant cultural unity persist when, if it really was so, there would be no need to continually assert it. Community cultural policy 'cannot be confused with cultural policies conducted by the States, regions and other decentralised institutions...Cultural policy forms part of the European enterprise' and must strengthen and expand 'the influence of the "European model of society built on a set of values common to all European societies"...Community action must promote the preservation and enrichment of that which goes to make up the cultural and linguistic identities and realities of the peoples of Europe. It must allow strengthening of citizens' feeling of belonging to one and the same Community'.[86] Running the last two points into one does not disguise the potential or actual discrepancies. If Community cultural policy is intended to externally promote an 'expansion in the cultural influence of European people and of the European model [singular] of society' why is it also regarded and necessary as an 'integration factor' within the EU?

Comparison of national and 'European' cultural programmes and resource dispensation reveals in hard financial terms the relative importance attached to them. Three EU states, France, Germany and the UK, operate an extensive external cultural policy outside and within the common, and expanding, European space. Financial and technical investment on these ventures far exceeds promotion (or creation) of a common heritage. The EU Kaleidoscope program has budget estimates for 1996-2000 totalling Ecu 68million, ARIANE 34m, and Raphael 67m. Ecu 15m were to be spent in 1996-98 on the Multilingual Information Society. This is some improvement on the mere Ecu 500,000 spent on the BABEL scheme of television dubbing and sub-titling during 1988-90. Gabriel Fragniere, Principal of the College of Europe has pointed out 'that it is particularly paradoxical that everybody stresses the importance, or rather the essential importance because through this we touch on the identities of human beings themselves, of the cultural factor in European integration and yet this is the smallest and most restricted part of the budget, 0.014% enabling very limited action.'[87] By comparison, France's 1995 budget for 'cultural and linguistic cooperation' was FF2.6billion. 1300 French linguistic and educational attachés were to receive FF570million. Exterior Audiovisual Action was budgeted at FF900million. In 1993 *Auswärtige Kulturpolitik* costs of German federal ministries totalled DM3.57billion, of which the Foreign Ministry spent DM1.24billion with 1995 estimates at DM1.16billion. In 1994-95, Britain's external cultural network, the British Council, had expenditure of £427million.[88]

---

86   *1st Report...Cultural Aspects*... ptV p2
87   Gabriel Fragniere. Speech at the Group of the European People's Party "Study Days" Bruges 28-8/1-9-95
88   European Commission, British Council, French and German foreign ministries

National Languages and European Institutions

The changing circumstances of relations between European nation-states has not ended cultural-political rivalries. Rather, institutionalised European decision-making has inspired a new field, and an expansion of linguistically founded dissension is not at all unlikely.[89] Smaller states are concerned that their national languages may become marginalized and (French) suggestions to reduce linguistic transfers in European institutions to five languages are thus met with disapproval. The main issue, however, is between the larger states and their official languages. Within the EC/EU there has long been a discrepancy between the privileged status of the French language and the position of German. Linguistic trends suggested by expansion to the east exacerbate this. As in many other instances, the 'official contacts' of the east with the EU are conducted in English, which continues to thrive, or in French, a legacy of France's institutionalising of its international prestige but no longer reflecting demographic realities. This situation applied, to German disdain, even if these eastern contacts were German speakers.

> It thus often occurs that partners from eastern Europe who know German better than English or French are compelled to use English or French in any contacts with the European Union. This circumstance has already been frequently criticised by Germany, but as yet there has been no change in the situation and no secure prospect of a future change. The German government finds itself in a predicament: on the one hand it does not want to impede the further development of the European Union with quarrels over language policy, but on the other, it would like to support the international position of the German language.[90]

There is a marked difference in German and French 'logic' as applied to the concurrence of geography and economy with the political-cultural expression of the EU. Germany's prominence in eastern Europe and in motoring the EU will bring with it a cultural dimension that alters the balance of representation and relative importance in international institutions. France wants to limit transfers of executive power, while fortifying centralist features which sustain predominance of the French language in Brussels. However,

---

sources. @April 1996, Ecu1 was approximately FF6.3, DM1.8, and £0.82

89   Abram de Swaan "The Evolving European Language System: A Theory of Communication Potential and Language Competition" *International Political Science Review* v14 n3 1993 pp241-255

90   Ulrich Ammon "The German Language: Lingua Franca overshadowed by English?" *Deutschland Magazine* n2 1994 pp44-49

where France has been prominent through the incumbency of French officials in authoritative positions,[91] the direction of the EU in line with French preferences, and the status of the French language, this is changing. Germany's new polymorphous prominence includes a cultural-political dimension that is altering the balance of national representation and relative importance in international institutions:

> German proponents of the Maastricht Treaty refer to its promotion of coexisting identities at the regional, national and European levels, rather than a melting pot. But German officials also believe that they must give expression to Germany's national cultural heritage. Some commentators interpreted Kohl's December 1991 call for German to be the third EC working language as a sign of Germany's search for cultural dominance, but it should be seen more as an example of Germany's old cost-benefit calculation, made more urgent by the heightened public awareness of the EC's implications for daily life. German officials therefore, emphasize fairness, accessibility, and rationality arguments in light of the language's statistical importance, geographical scope, and bridging role to north and the east, and EC's claim to be a community for all of the people.[92]

Christian Democratic Union (CDU) resolutions from the 1992 party congress demanded that 'German must be placed on an equal footing with all other working languages in the Community's institutions.' Under the heading 'Institutional Questions' a following document on *Kulturpolitik* noted a continuing 'discrimination'. After succeeding in establishing German as a working language for the European Commission in 1993, the government sought extension to the European Council and the CFSP secretariat, still dominated by English and French.

> The political culture of the Community must be judged by the extent to which it respects the customs and traditions of its member states. National languages, which represent the foremost manifestation of cultural identity, must be handled with a particular degree of sensitivity. All national languages spoken within the Community must continue to function as official languages to be used by citizens in addressing the institutions of the EC and by the EC to publish its legislation. German

---

91   Where French nationals cannot be appointed, French speaking personnel are sought. In 1986 5,000, or 45%, of the EC's 12,000 civil servants were French speakers when approximately 30% of EC citizens were French speakers. See De Swaan "The Evolving European Language System..."

92   Lily Gardner Feldman "Germany and the EC: Realism and Responsibility" *Annals of the American Academy of Political Science* January 1994 see pp39-40

must be placed on an equal footing with all other working languages in the Community's institutions.[93]

Economic Culture

Within a 'general common culture'[94] economic and industrial cultures are prominent sub species, featuring aspects like the degree of state regulation, welfare system, business relations, corporate governance and work practices, amongst others. Economic integration has been the spearhead towards European unity and variations were accommodated and even compatible for the Community's first three decades. Even after convergence on a market economy culminated with the introduction of the Single Market in 1992, the gradualist method of homogenising the European economic space by a series of steady practical steps is challenged. This commercial space did not translate into a single economic culture. A multitude of economic and industrial cultures reduces rather than enhances competitive efficiency. Evolution towards a standard model is more likely to achieve this rather than continuing with a piecemeal composite. Such a scenario does not necessarily find favour among all parts of the sum.[95]

From a geographic and partly developed legal-institutional base, the task, for a power capable of it, is to establish other economic aspects as culturally understood and accepted. A single monetary policy and its linkage to fiscal and other elements of economic management requires the formulation of agreed common standards and procedures. While 'price stability' is the present lodestar, the supporting constellations of German, French and British economic systems have not cohered sufficiently as to produce a single economic culture, defined by Rohrlich as: 'a base of consensual knowledge of a non-factual nature, a set of values and beliefs about social economics which guides and legitimates policy-making; an autonomous variable, not derived

93   *Resolutions of the 3rd Congress of the CDU of Germany* Düsseldorf 25-10-92. Resolutions A#1, 8; CDU *Kulturpolitik* Document (Bonn: CDU Bundesgeschäftsstelle 1995)

94   See Ugo Pagano "Can Economics Explain Nationalism" in *Nationalism and Rationality* Eds. Albert Breton, Gianluigi Galeotti, Pierre Salmon & Ronald Wintrobe (Cambridge University Press: Cambridge 1995) pp173-203, here pp178-180. This general culture is applicable to and encapsulates 'more contexts '

95   See *National Diversity and Global Capitalism* Eds. Suzanne Berger & Ronald Dore (Ithaca: Cornell University Press 1996); Peter Gundelach "National Value Differences: Modernization or Institutionalization?" *International Journal of Comparative Sociology* v35 n1-2 1994 pp37-59

from the material interests of social actors but rather characterizing a whole society across social cleavages; specific to a particular time and place, representing one cultural adaption of a generic economic ideology.'[96] Instead of a new commonality, certain historically ingrained traits persist and all continue to attempt modifications affecting the underlying 'rules of the game', reflecting 'different national sensitivities towards imports and different strategies towards social and economic change', and employing 'different priorities' to both short and longer term requirements.[97]

One contributor to a recent symposium on the role of *Auswärtige Kulturpolitik* in boosting the German economy noted that 'growth presumed a cultural identity, which could only be won in productive discussion and worldwide exchange'.[98] Closely associated and high on the German agenda, 'confidence' in financial management needs to be embedded as a component of any pan-European economic culture. With reference to the US dollar, Robert Keohane noted the 'symbolic resources that go under the name of 'confidence' in discussion of international financial affairs'.[99] German political and business leaders want to institutionalize and psychologically implant this on a European scale. When the reputation of Deutsche Bank was endangered by difficulties encountered during the takeover of Postbank, concerns about external perceptions of the bank *'den namen unseres Volkes trägt'* were expressed by Kohl himself. Accordingly the health of the German economy could be reduced to: *'geht es der Deutschen Bank schlecht, leidet auch der Standort Deutschland'*.[100] It encapsulates what Antony Black, in reference to the success of Germany's post-war economic-industrial culture, termed 'a tacit agreement about ends: and, one ought to add, a tacit *Gemeinschaft* however expressed.'[101] Of the European scene a Bundesbank board member considered that 'stability must not be reduced to exchange-rate stability...a Eurocurrency must go beyond mere convergence of interests rates, deficits

---

96   Paul Egon Rohrlich "Economic culture and foreign policy: the cognitive analysis of economic policy making" *International Organization* v41 n1 1987 pp61- 92. See p71

97   Henrik Plaschke "National Economic Cultures and Economic Integration" in *National Cultures and European Integration* pp113-143

98   Gottfried Honnefelder in *Kultur, Kommerz und Außenpolitik-Ungewohnte Perspektiven, neue Kooperation* (Frankfurt a.M: Börsenverein des Deutschen Buchhandels 1996)

99   Robert Keohane "The Theory of Hegemonic Stability" in Robert Keohane *International Institutions and State Power* (Boulder: Westview 1989) p90

100   Christiane Oppermann "Primus im Zwielicht" *Die Woche* 20-10-95 p17 'The bank that carries the name of our people'. 'If the Deutsche Bank goes badly, so too does Germany'

101   Black "Nation and community in the international order" p87

and other fiscal criteria. There is also a need for an underlying consensus, a stability culture...'.[102]

Apart from a more obvious disdain for some Mediterranean members, there is a view, wider held than spoken among Germany's 'pro-Europe' élite, and less restrained elsewhere, that France may slide back into its old 'flexibility' in macro-economic management leaving Germany to keep the continent's budget and inflation rate under control. An actual or potential 'free rider' problem persists through discrepancy between economic-fiscal cultures which in turn derive from social and political practice.[103] The German love affair with Italy does not extend to underwriting the Italian budget. Nor will it extend to France. 'Complementarities' are not always possible, including in central bank practices. The treaty on monetary union was a result of international politics but in technical aspects and main criteria its 'Godfather' is *'die deutscheste aller deutschen Institutionen, die Deutsche Bundesbank'*.[104] James Sperling's account of Germany after reunification is a good demonstration of foreign policy's connections with 'economics' and 'culture'. It also spells out the choice fairly clearly.

> The Germans believe that unless all the prospective EMU member-states embrace and internalise the German economic culture, in fact become German in their outlook on macro-economic (and increasingly micro-economic) issues, and meet the existing convergence indicators, EMU will be a non-starter for Germany and Europe.[105]

Meanwhile, the Single Market continues to present a 'cultural challenge' for business managers and others. To maximise value from this political-economic agreement 'Euro-managers must learn foreign languages'

> for language embodies and reflects culture and thus offers the manager indispensable cultural insights. It also means a working knowledge and experience of the specific economic institutions that reflect and

---

102   Otmar Issing interviewed in "Germany's Role in International Stability" *International Herald Tribune* 12-7-93 p10

103   Cf. Pagano "Can Economics Explain Nationalism"

104   Ernst-Moritz Lipp und Angelika Lipp-Krull "Menschen und Märkte-Dialog über interkulturelle Erfahrungen aus Finanz- und Meinungs märkten" in *Frankreich in Europa: Ein Deutsch-Französischer Rundblick* Eds. Ingo Kolboom & Ernst Weisenfeld (Bonn: Europa Union Verlag 1993) pp263-277

105   James Sperling "German Foreign Policy after Unification: The End of Cheque Book Diplomacy?" *West European Politics* v17 n1 1994 pp73-97, p86

reinforce individual cultural patterns; and of the very different values and priorities that these institutions embody.[106]

Another study on culture as a barrier in the case of public purchasing concludes that the 'EC will never become one Single Market but will still be divided into twelve distinct and far from competitive markets.' The range of cultural discrepancies include: 'different national tastes' leading to 'preferences for certain nationally produced goods'; 'communication barriers' strongly influencing cooperation 'with our own kind'; 'distinct national ways of doing things'; and 'several culturally distinct *mental* barriers'. In a single internal market purportedly with 'no national trade policies' only 3% of public contracts are awarded to foreign suppliers.[107]

Where something approximating a European business culture has appeared, German models and practices, to which Commission procedures have grown closest, are prominent. This trend has gained some ground in France but remains 'foreign' to the individual enterprise favoured in Britain and the US. The propensity for particular national-cultural norms to endure in the integrated European market is strong. Despite being 'locked into the realm of economic forces, they have an extraordinary capacity to retain deep-rooted historical features.'[108] However, the logic of global capitalism does not recognise anything inherently sacred in this context. Rather it will demand adaptability to the most influential cultural factors, and it is then culture that 'provides criteria by which to evaluate the formulation and pursuit of economic policy.'[109] Thus while 'Anglo-American' capitalism is the prominent strain in the globalizing sweep of economic liberalism it can be successfully adapted to existing practices and characteristics, or may itself have to be adapted by its 'Anglo-American' agents.[110] One study of variations between the German and British banking industries and their cultural bases suggests a positive long-term prognosis for German institutions and a more pessimistic outlook for their British competition, whose operating methods are less appealing to continental markets.[111] If this is so British banking may have

---

106   Kenneth Dyson "Cultural Issues and the Single European Market: Barriers to Trade and Shifting Attitudes" *Political Quarterly* v64 n1 1993 pp84-97, p85

107   Poul Thøis Madsen "Is Culture a Major Barrier to a Single European market? The Case of Public Purchasing" in *National Cultures and European Integration...* pp145-160

108   Dyson "Cultural Issues" p97

109   Rohrlich "Economic culture and foreign policy" pp69-70

110   See Michael Hodges & Stephen Woolcock "Atlantic Capitalism versus European Capitalism in the European Community" *Western European Politics* v16 n3 1993 pp329-344

111   Charles J. M. R. Gullick "Cultural Values and European Financial Institutions"

to adopt some 'continental' characteristics. Even then it is predicted that 'trade within the EU in services will increase, but will reach cultural limits: British people will not want to place their money in German banks, or vice versa'.[112]

A recent incisive analysis of national structures and multinational corporate behaviour argues that 'durable national institutions and distinctive ideological traditions still seem to shape and channel crucial corporate decisions.' The authors indicate that firm connections between state and business are present, and that these are characterised by historical and cultural derivations.

> The underlying nationality of the firm remains the vitally important determinant of the nature of its adaption. That nationality is not necessarily given by the location of corporate headquarters or the addresses of principal shareholders, although it usually still is. More fundamentally, it is given by historical experience and the institutional and ideological legacies of that experience, both of which constitutute the essential structures of states.[113]

Political Culture

> The [European] community may constitute nothing less than the first truly postmodern international form.[114]

> The Greek *polis* will continue to exist at the bottom of our political culture — that is, at the bottom of the sea — for as long as we use the word "politics".[115]

When posited against one another the above quotations bring the struggle over Europe's political form into relief. The former suggests a denouement of the latter: politics, in the form of conflicts fought out and decisions reached through a legislature underpinned by a sovereign constitutional order, is to be replaced. The locus of 'politics' is that of democracy, which operates in the

in *Cultural Change and the New Europe* pp203-221

112   Hamish McRae *The World in 2020: Power, Culture and Prosperity* (Boston: Harvard Business School 1994) p227

113   Louis W. Pauly & Simon Reich "National Structures and Multinational Corporate Behaviour: Enduring Differences in the Age of Globalization" *International Organization* v51 n1 1997 pp1-30

114   John Gerald Ruggie "Territoriality and Beyond: Problematizing Modernity in International Relations" *International Organization* v47 n1 1993 pp139-174

115   Hannah Arendt "Introduction: Walter Benjamin: 1892-1940" in *Illuminations* (London: Penguin 1970) p49

nation-state context. A perceived evanescence of the latter through loss of sovereignty is equated by commentators on both left or right and variously described as nationalists or democrats, as heralding the end of democracy.

Ole Wæver and Ulla Holm have sought to blend elements of a more 'traditional' international relations approach with a discourse analysis of domestic political 'codes' regarding France<>Europe and Germany<>Europe. Their work underlines how patterns of political culture derive from and have mutual dependencies with a broader national culture. While they reject what they regard as the reactive nature of realist analyses they do not, or cannot, discard the presence of 'deep-structure' codes which constitute an element of virtual 'fixity' within their own hypothesis. Division of political cultures into 'levels' posits 'level one' as 'immensely difficult to change'.[116] This is also applicable to other features or zones of culture. By comparison, 'surface' levels of attachment in this sphere or anywhere else, are more susceptible to and easier to change. It is the deepest level referred to above that is of principal concern.

Wæver has elsewhere noted the variance in political logics at work, logics that have grown from particular histories and determine posture towards Europe.[117] The most critical mass of political will supporting integration beyond nation-state vetoes resides in Germany. Entirely rebuilt after WW2 within a European architecture it is the 'newest' political culture almost chronologically parallel to the EC/EU. German political culture still (presently) retains a level of consensus towards preferred European options that surpass France or Britain. Proposals for a federal Europe with parliamentary sovereignty and devolved power to a network of regions is favoured because it most closely replicates the German system. It does not require the sea change necessary in the French or British systems. Political systems are cultural phenomena and variance in those operating within 'Europe's' principal architects constitutes a case where two into one won't go. If the organization of political authority is to develop into a pan-European polity, France must discard unitary inclinations with something approximating the German federal model transposed for the EU. Such a wholesale transformation of the French system could not occur without a political acquiescence of staggering

---

116   Ulla Holm "The French Garden is no longer what it used to be" and Ole Wæver "Chapter One", in Ole Wæver, Ulla Holm & Henrik Larsen (Draft copy)*The Struggle for 'Europe': French and German Concepts of State, Nation and European Union* (forthcoming)

117   Ole Wæver "European Security Identities" *Journal of Common Market Studies* v34 n1 1996 pp103-132, p126

proportions.[118] Introducing the UK and others into the equation multiplies the complications.[119]

Searching for a solution in civil society reproduces the barrier faced at governmental level. A psychologically *European* public is the essential requirement, even if on an auxiliary level that is non-threatening to national identities. It is no surprise that there is no European government when there is no European public and no European political sociology.[120] For all the intellectual-political endeavours behind it, removing the (nation) state does not obviously enhance the prospects of a patchwork of affinities, identities and interests somehow adding up to a common purpose.[121] A (limited) European citizenship has not transformed the EU from a collection of diverse communities into one political community.[122] For any polity, its 'central value system must include legitimating principles that justify the existing differential distribution of economic status and political power'. The move from *Gemeinschaft* towards *Verbindungsnetzschaft*, like that towards *Gesellschaft* before it, has not extinguished all 'pre-political' links.[123] Governments are also guided by a 'principle of identity', one that is 'based on impersonal ties, remote ties, vicarious ties—all of which are mediated by a set of common symbols embedded in a certain pattern of communication'.[124] There is a duality to this exercise of cultural affinity: an understanding of this pattern of communication, *and* the acceptance of the values it communicates.

118	Robert Ladrech "Europeanization of Politics and Institutions: The Case of France" *Journal of Common Market Studies* v32 n1 1994 pp69-89; John Laughland "Apres Moi, Le Desert" *The Spectator* 11-3-95 pp9-10
119	Comparison of foreign policy-making in the UK, France and Germany indicates that research institutes directly or indirectly advising governments, are themselves part of the national political culture. William Wallace "Beyond Two Worlds: Think Tanks and Foreign Policy" in *Two Worlds of International Relations: academics, practitioners and the trade in ideas* Eds. Christopher Hill & Pamela Beshoff (London: Routledge 1994) pp139-163
120	Hans Hugo Klein "Europa-Verschiedenes gemeinsam erlebt: Es gibt kein europäisches Volk, sondern die Völker Europas" *Frankfurter Allgemeine Zeitung* 17-10-94 pp13-14
121	Cf. *Toward A global Civil Society* Ed. Michael Walzer (Providence: Berghahn 1995) See especially the contributions by Walzer, Peter Glotz, Mitchell Cohen, Didier Motchane, and Jean Bethke Elshtain
122	Lolle Nauta "Changing conceptions of citizenship" *Praxis International* v12 n1 1992 pp20-34
123	Anthony H. Richmond "Ethnic Nationalism and Post-Industrialism" in *Nationalism* Eds. John Hutchinson & Anthony D. Smith (Oxford: Oxford university Press 1994) pp289-300 (Orig. *Ethnic and Racial Studies* v7 n1 1984)
124	Ernst Haas "What is nationalism and why should we study it?" *International Organization* v40 n3 1986 pp707-744 p709

Even before western Europe has united, integrating central and eastern Europe presents a plethora of new challenges. A supranational political culture is yet to unfold, such phenomena are manifested only within the member states. With no real alliance as to the structure and distribution of competencies, it requires an initiator. A Europe-wide political culture would approximate one member more than the others, more so if the Union moved in 'variable geometries' and at variable speeds.

3 German Identity before and after Reunification

Anthony Glees has written that even if the *way* Germany is governed has not changed dramatically before and after reunification, '*what* is being governed *is* plainly different. And if the nature of Germany is changing, its politics will have to adapt accordingly...Today's reinvented Germany cannot have the same identity because it is not the same country and the world in which it lives has changed'.[1] Geo-political changes have, as Jill Stephenson states, 'permitted public debate about *German* grievances which were rarely articulated, but certainly not forgotten, in the long years of political self-denial in the west and political repression in the east.'[2] Constraints on national feeling are eased and grounds are prepared for more political assertion internationally including response to new imperatives and redress of perceived disadvantages. Irresolute or contrary attitudes towards European integration elsewhere diminishes German options weakening the appeal or prospect of a 'common European' identity and polity. Extending the emphasis given to *German* by Stephenson, this chapter evaluates psychological and/or intellectual aspects regarding German history and Germany's place in Europe, and links previous exposition of nation and culture and later domestic polity and foreign policy analyses.

Who are the Germans?

'Paradoxical' is a descriptor frequently applied to Germany. Two centuries after Goethe and Schiller imparted the national character as restive and elusive,[3] Garton Ash wrote of 'a nation in its perennial condition of

---

1   Anthony Glees *Reinventing Germany: German Political Devlopment Since 1945* (Oxford: Berg 1996) p253. Emphases in original

2   Jill Stephenson "Anniversaries, Memory and the Neighbours: The 'German Question' in Recent History" *German Politics* v5 n1 1996 pp43-57, p43. Emphasis in original

3   Goethe and Schiller's lines 'Zur Nation euch zu bilden, ihr hofft es, Deutsche, vergebens-Bildet, ihr könnt es, dafür freier zu Menschen euch aus' implies the existence of a collective group within humanity, called "Deutsche'; and to whom

becoming'.[4] Dolf Sternberger considered *'wir wissen nicht, wer wir sind. Das ist die Deutsche Frage'*, while Michael Stürmer argued that of industrialised countries the Germans were poorest in historical consciousness. In his critique of a 'historyless land', history in (West) Germany suffered from a technocratic obsession of the Right and a 'progressive choking' of the Left. A 'search for a lost history' was 'morally legitimate and politically necessary', the Federal Republic's 'inner continuity and foreign policy predictability' depended on it.[5] Even in 1995 Julius Schloep averred 'this society has no identity and it's on the way to finding that identity after the events of 1989.[6]

Although regional affinities flourished post-war national identity was cast in the shadow of 1933-45 and its, for the most part, dormant alter ego the 'German Question'.[7] Until the 'Soviet Occupation Zone' collapsed the West German 'quasi-nation' collectively experienced a common language, knowledge of war and division, 'Europe' and the Deutsche Mark, as western orientation enacted a political transformation of the population. Even as it became wealthy, stable, efficient and cosmopolitan this was a society which had lost a former cultural eminence. Now 'devoid of asperity and national celebration; it was smooth, odorless, colorless.'[8] A curious parody of the drab, real existing world of the east, the west was characterised by its 'transformation of the provincial gesture into the very style of the state at the highest symbolic level',[9] while a 'frontierless utopia of travel, consumption,

---

they transmitted their works. German identity cohered around the German language

[4] Timothy Garton Ash "Germany's Choice" *Foreign Affairs* v73 n4 July/August 1994 pp64-81

[5] See Michael Stürmer *Deutsche Fragen: oder die Suche nach der Staatsräson* (München: Piper 1988) especially "Geschichte in geschichtlosem Land" pp70-72 (orig. *Frankfurter Allgemeine Zeitung* 17-4-86)

[6] Julius Schloep, quoted in Denis Stanton "Germans war over how to celebrate peace" *Observer* 16-4-95 p18; Cf. Beate C. Gilliar *The rhetoric of (Re) Unification: Constructing Identity though East and West German Newspapers* (New York: Peter Lang 1996)

[7] *Die Identität der Deutschen* Ed. Werner Weidenfeld (Bonn: 1983); Harold James *A German Identity 1770-1990* (London: Weidenfeld & Nicholson 1989); Gordon Craig *The Germans* (Harmondsworth: Penguin 1991); Immanuel Geiss *Die deutsche Frage 1806-1990* (Mannheim: Taschenbuchverlag 1992); Charles S. Maier *Die Gegenwart der Vergangenheit: Geschichte und die nationale Identität der Deutschen* (Frankfurt: Campus Verlag 1992)

[8] Anne-Marie Le Gloannec "On German Identity" *Dædelus* v123 n1 1994 pp129-148

[9] Karl Heinz Böhrer "Why we are not a Nation—And why we should become one" in *When the Wall Came Down: Reactions to German Unification* Eds. Harold James &

and information technology'[10] kept the population 'rich, bothered and divided'.[11] The FRG did not and could not conduct a '*nationale Ellbogen-politik*' internationally.[12] It became an '*Ellbogengesellschaft*' internally,[13] one that maintained a generous social net, health care system and tertiary education lasting, on average, to thirty years of age. High trade surpluses helped West Germans became the worlds' greatest tourists, buoyed by a strong currency and six or seven weeks annual vacation. Regionalism, hedonism, materialism and environmentalism were promulgated while a taboo on national thinking was predicated on Aristotle's maxim that what has happened can happen. Abetted by reticence to define it, national identity was shaped through negative appraisal from outside and doubts amongst the establishment strata. Nathan Gardels portrayed a pseudo quality whereby 'Unable to face itself, Germany has for decades assumed an identity for the benefit of others in the hope of absolving its crimes.'

> Germany has become an alias nation, hiding its soiled soul under the bushel of NATO, the CSCE or the European Community, which above all else, institutionalizes the liberal ideal of a rational order over a national one...Teetering between guilt over a vilified past and anxiety over the menacing times to come, Germany has lost its balance in the new world order. Too terrified by memory to seek shelter in its cultural heritage, Germany clings to the only source of stability and identity it allows itself to trust: The Deutschemark.[14]

If this is a guide, Germans will carry responsibility for the past and suspicion in the future indefinitely.[15] Adopting an identity 'for the benefit of others' is unsustainable. Yet to speak or write of 'the Germans' implies a

---

Marla Stone (London: Routledge 1992) pp60-70. (orig. *Frankfurter Allgemeine Zeitung* 12-1-90)

[10] Peter Pulzer *German Politics 1945-1995* (Oxford: Oxford University Press 1995) p8

[11] David Marsh *The Germans: Rich, Bothered, and Divided* (London: Century 1989)

[12] Michael Stürmer "Deutsche Interessen" in *Deutschlands neue Außenpolitik*, Band 1 Grundlagen. Eds Karl Kaiser & Hans W. Maull (München: Oldenbourg 1994) pp39-61, p58

[13] Pulzer *German Politics 1945-1995* p20

[14] Nathan Gardels "Heimat EC: Germany as Alias Nation" *New Perspectives Quarterly* v10 n1 Winter 1993 pp1-2

[15] Cf. Marc Fisher *After the Wall: Germany, Germans and the Burdens of History* (New York: Simon & Schuster 1995); *Die haßlichen Deutschen?: Deutschland im Spiegel der westlichen und östlichen Nachbarn* Ed. Günter Trautmann (Darmstadt: Wissenschaftliche Buchgesellschaft 1991)

nation.[16] Schoenbaum and Pond perceive differently that 'after generations of presumed and authentic aberration' normality really has arrived. They depict the Germans as 'normal too in their susceptibility to the 'normal pathology' of modern life in all its variety' and that 'like any other 'normal' country, middle-class, middle-aged, export dependent Germany also faced the puzzles and vicissitudes of an ever more competitive, ever more globalized economy'.[17] A post-war work ethic has gradually reduced while interest in the acquisition of material rewards has not. Nonetheless, questionnaire respondents identified with stereotypical 'traditional German virtues',[18] even as Kohl was referring to Germany as a giant *Freizeit* park.

The German Debate on the Nation and Nationalism

Problems of interpreting or defining 'nationalist', 'nationalism' and related terms were brought to notice by Ernst Friedlaender in the 1940s. He wished to differentiate between 'liberal' nationalism and notorious imperial or ideological variants. By their extremity the latter overpowered the former in establishing a place in the European and German consciousness. Following soon after destruction wrought by the most extreme version, declaring not only the existence but the justification of any other kind was a rarity. 'When the subject of debate', Friedlaender wrote,

> is nationalism as it relates to the politics of power, which can clearly be distinguished from the 'national' without any risk to the spiritual health of the people, there is no cause to throw the national overboard...it is neither

---

16   Peter F. Merkl provides another example of both difficulty in explaining this phenomenon, and the presumption that it—a nation and an associated identity, or set of identities related to the nation—exists. He aims at constructing a 'memorable compound image of how the Germans see themselves - no fewer than *six groups of senses* of German identity, all in search of a nation in rapid change.' See "A New German Identity" in *Developments in German Politics* Eds. Gordon Smith, William E. Paterson, Peter H. Merkl, Stephen Padgett (Houndmills: MacMillan 1992) pp327-348

17   The same observers ar e bemused and frustrated by what they perceive as a mass of official and unofficial (and unnecessary) rules, laws and other intrusive or restrictive forms of etiquette and organization. David Schoenbaum & Elizabeth Pond *The German Question and Other German Questions* (Houndmills: MacMillan 1996) p52 & pp99-100; Fisher *After the Wall* pp43-65

18   Ludger Kühnhardt "Wertgrundlagen der deutschen Aussenpolitik" *Deutschlands neue Außenpolitik*, Band 1 Grundlagen. Eds Karl Kaiser & Hans W. Maull (München: Oldenbourg 1994) pp99-127, p99

good nor healthy...to be undernourished in terms not only of physiological, but also of national calories.[19]

Separation of belligerent and 'healthy' legitimate forms of nationalism remains difficult and controversial. Peter Alter relates how "Nationalism', now frequently equated with National Socialism, acquired unequivocally negative connotations.'

> As a polemical term and a term of political demarcation, it has retained these to the present day in Germany. Nationalism was seen as the opposite of devoted patriotism, which does not necessarily relate to the nation, and permits competing loyalties to exist. Nationalism was considered the antithesis of free democracy and a 'healthy' national consciousness, whatever these terms might mean.[20]

After Kurt Schumacher had directed a left nationalism against what he considered Allied despotism, terminology like 'national community' and 'national interests' was appropriated by the far Right. The era was one in which 'the question of national identity (was) kept off the national agenda by agreement among the major parties'.[21] A shift in the 1980s saw Kohl place more 'rhetorical emphasis on the German nation and national values'. Combining domestic and foreign policy strategies it was 'primarily directed towards the East' as part of keeping the reunification question alive.[22] Concurrently, academic and media spheres reached a climacteric with the *Historikerstreit*, a dispute over interpretation of the German past, centrally the singularity of Nazi crimes. In a broader context the debate was linked to the presentation and legitimation or otherwise of 'nation' and 'national identity' in German politics and society, including after reunification.[23]

---

[19]   Ernst Friedlaender "Nationalismus, 6 February 1947" in "Ernst Friedlaender: Klarung für Deutschland: Leitartikel in der Zeit 1946-1950" Eds. N. Frei & F. Friedlaender (Munich & Vienna 1982) quoted by Peter Alter "Nationalism and German politics after 1945" in *The State of Germany: The National Idea in the Making, Unmaking and Remaking of a Modern Nation-State* Ed. John Breuilly (Longman: London 1992) pp154-176. See pp161-162

[20]   Alter "Nationalism and German Politics after 1945"

[21]   Dietrich Orlow "West German Parties since 1945: Continuity and Change" *Central European History* v18 n2 1985 pp188-201

[22]   Simon Bulmer & William Paterson *The Federal Republic of Germany and the European Community* (London: Allen & Unwin 1987) p18

[23]   *Historikerstreit: Die Dokumentation der Kontroverse um die Einzigartigkeit der nationalsozialistischen Judenvernichtung* (München: Serie Piper 1987)

Related contentious issues appeared: CDU honorary chairman Alfred Dregger insisted that the conclusion of the war was a catastrophe rather than a liberation for the Germans; resituating the remains of Frederick the Great, moving the capital to Berlin, and the building, or not building, of various memorials and museums inspired their own controversies; [24] as did intermittent resurfacing of the 'boundaries of 1937' question. Members of the *Vertriebenen* carry strong identifications through active support organizations, newspapers and visits to their *Heimat*. [25] Former German regions in Poland, the Czech Republic or the 'Russian enclave' around Königsberg attract Federal, *Länder*, and private financial and political assistance. 'Buy back' schemes continue to be floated. [26]

Debate on 'the nation' and various extrapolations grew through the 1980s until the *corpus vile* revived and emerged from the earthquake of 1989-1990. The 'German Question', after being subsumed by 'other German Questions', reappeared. [27] The Germans and everyone else now had to deal with it not academically but practically. Whether the EC, the Deutsche Mark and the Atlantic alliance really would suffice as integrators and bearings was put to the test. One swift affirmation was that, merged into an international capitalist framework and logic, 'German pride in West Germany's economic accomplishments has nonetheless been a form of nationalism'. [28] So is the desire to preserve or extend these achievements through 'peaceful ways of

---

[24] Another controversy occured with the proposed construction of a supermarket on the site of the former Ravensbrück concentration camp. Eventually the builders backed down. See Fisher *After the Wall* p213

[25] Like the *Sudentendeutscher Rat*, 'representing the German nationality in the (former) CSSR', the *Kulturstiftung der Deutschen Vertriebenen*, or the *Ostpreussenblatt* newspaper which keeps its readers 'objectively informed'. Interview Sources Munich and Kiel September 1996. See also Alfred M. De Zayas *Anmerkungen zur Vertreibung der Deutschen aus dem Osten*. English translation *The German expellees: victims in war and peace* by John A. Koehler (New York: St. Martin's Press 1993)

[26] Marion Gräfin Dönhoff "Königsberg: Signal der Versöhnung" *Die Zeit* 15-11-91; Alvydas Nikzentaitis "Das Kaliningrader Gebiet im Spannungsfeld internationaler Interessen" *Osteuropa* n10 1995 pp927-935; Olaf Ihlau "Da werden Blasen geschlagen" *Der Spiegel* 17-4-95 pp68-71; Helmut Kohl "Beitrag der deutschen Heimatvertriebenen zum Wiederaufbau in Deutschland und zum Frieden in Europa" *Bulletin* 2-6-95; Emil Nagengast "Coming to terms with a 'European Identity': The Sudeten Germans between Bonn and Prague" *German Politics* v5 n1 1996 pp81-100. This constructivist approach doesn't actually resolve the core problems

[27] Schoenbaum & Pond *The German Question and Other German Questions*

[28] William Pfaff *The Wrath of Nations: Civilization and the Furies of Nationalism* (New York: Simon and Schuster 1993) p26

applying their talent and irresistible urge to excel'.[29] Now this pecuniary identity is joined by a rise in political status and a growing cultural presence. Asked if Germany was ever as powerful, the historian Saul Friedlander answered that its present economic and financial capacity made Germany stronger than ever. He added, 'One other thing can be said with certainty':

> with this unified Germany, it is easy now for a German to identify emotionally. The Federal Republic wished to be sterile; the unified Germany cannot be sterile. The unification reunites the Germans not only with the eastern parts of their country, but with their national myths.[30]

Evolution of political vocabulary has resulted in 'nation' gaining a qualified legitimacy, even if the proposition that there was more to German history than war, dictatorship and criminality is not new.[31] Martin Walser claimed that the division of Germany was a cynical exercise maintained by other states on the pretext that the Germans represented a danger. It was an absurdity that Germans 'and above all the intellectuals, should parrot this view for fear of otherwise being taken for Nazis'.[32] Other recent 'contributions to the German debate' went further in their arguments for an end to a timid international self-consciousness.[33] Germany's political maturation has been accompanied by emancipation from the 'grey provincialism' personified by Kohl in the 1980s. As Kohl internationalized himself and entered the pantheon of world statesmen, the *Bundesrepublik* became *Deutschland*,[34] or as a more national-conservative volume put it,

---

[29] Thomas Kielinger "Waking up in the new Europe - with a headache" *International Affairs* v66 n2 1990 pp249-263

[30] Yaron London interviewing Saul Friedlander "Now We Shall be Reduced to Our Due Place Within German Priorities" *When the Wall Came Down: Reactions to German Unification* Eds. Harold James & Marla Stone (London: Routledge 1992) pp295-302

[31] "Das Nationale nutzen". Interview with Wolfgang Schäuble *Der Spiegel* n38 1994 pp30-34

[32] Ian Wallace "German Intellectuals and Unification" *German Monitor* n37 1996 pp87-100

[33] *Die selbstbewußte Nation: "Anschwellende Bocksgesang" und weitere Beiträge zu einer deutschen Debatte* Eds. Heimo Schwilk & Ulrich Schacht (Frankfurt a.M.: Ullstein 1994)

[34] *From Bundesrepublik to Deutschland: German Politics After Unification* Eds. Michael G. Huelshoff, Andrei Markovits & Simon Reich (Ann Arbor: University of Michigan Press 1993)

Zurück zu Deutschland.[35] Having posed as a 'krypto-nation' in the west and a Soviet puppet in the east, a German 'national paradigm' is back on the European agenda.[36] The current question is not 'what replaces the nation'?, rather 'what *kind* of nation'?[37]

Reunification, Consensus, and After

Although a majority remained in favour of reunification, the old Federal Republic had grown used to and even comfortable with its 'incompleteness'. Continued prosperity and the guarantee of American protection against unlikely Soviet attack meant that reunification was not at the forefront of everyday concerns. Even as they reiterated the objective, politicians were peering at an unknown point in the distance. However diffuse it became, reunification and the liberation of compatriots in the 'other part of Germany' articulated a specifically national goal. One for which 'attitudinal' bases were present in both German states before the possibility came into view.[38] When Willy Brandt proposed that what belonged together was growing together he spoke of a national identity inhibited by political division.

Nations are instruments of foreign policy and, ostensibly, the beneficiaries. The metamorphosis of 'Germany' has internal and international aspects. Jürgen Kocka has written of how the East Germans expected from the West Germans what they would not ask from the English or even (*selbst*) the Austrians. What the West Germans refused the Poles they guaranteed the East Germans. 'Gerecht ist das nicht, aber national'. Although it had little to do with dangerous passions or chauvinism, 1989-90 revealed that national identity had survived in Germany, politically tenable and with supporters 'not only on the Right of the political spectrum.'[39] Regardless of what has

---

35   *Zuruck zu Deutschland: Umsturz und demokratischer Aufbruch in der DDR* Herausgegeben vom Rheinischen Merkur (Bonn: Bouvier 1990)

36   Bernd Weisbrod "German Unification and the National Paradigm" *German History* v14 n2 1996 pp193-203; Brigitte Seebacher-Brandt "Nation im vereinigten Deutschland" *Aus Politik und Zeitgeschichte* B42/94 21-10-1994 pp3-9; For a more sceptical appraisal see Götz Eisenberg "Deutschland als Prothese: Wozu nationale Identität?" *Neue Gesellschaft /Frankfurter Hefte* v8 August 1996 pp739-743

37   Heinrich August Winkler "Rebuilding of a Nation: The Germans Before and After Reunification" *Dædelus* v123 n1 pp107-127

38   See Henry Krisch "German Unification and East German Political Culture: Interaction and Change" *German Monitor* n37 1996 pp5-16

39   Jürgen Kocka *Vereinigungskrise: Zur Geschichte der Gegenwart* (Göttingen:

happened since, the west German state could not have acted as it did without popular will. In contrast to those in other communist states, dissidents in the German Democratic Republic (GDR) who wished to transform it but still retain a state separate from the FRG could not employ nation-orientated appeals and such alternatives rapidly evaporated.[40] On the new *Tag der deutschen Einheit* October 3rd 1990, President Richard von Wiezsäcker spoke of the Germans having founded a common state. But it was Renan's *plébiscite de tous les jours* which would determine what Germany became. John Breuilly interpreted the psychological effects as generally positive. 'The latent sense of national identity, that it was 'natural' for there to be a single German state, could now come to the surface, unhindered by all the political and economic considerations which had relegated the idea of unification to the realm of fantasy.'[41]

Brushing aside the 'hypochondriac effusions' of Günter Grass,[42] ideological aversions of Jürgen Habermas,[43] or the economic policy based doubts of Oscar Lafontaine, reunification epitomised the concordant *Parteienstaat* in operation. The voluminous internal Unification Treaty required agreement not only between the official representatives of the FRG and the GDR but among the major political forces within the west. Misgivings among sections of the SPD could not stop the process, which produced (another) inter-party covenant in a pluralist polity. The FRG's chief negotiator, Interior Minister, Wolfgang Schäuble, was prominent in the tuning of consensus among CDU, CSU, FDP and SPD.[44] Schäuble also had to appease a common instinct to derive some form of political capital from unfolding events. Compromise on issues of internal division ensured these were overridden by more important considerations, to the extent that it was almost a monolithic, as much as a consensual character that pervaded the process:

Vandenhoeck & Ruprecht 1995) pp22-23

[40] Jürgen Kocka "Crisis of Unification: How Germany Changes" *Dædelus* v123 n1 1994 pp173-192 p175

[41] John Breuilly "Nationalism and German Reunification" in *The State of Germany...* pp224-238. See p229

[42] Timothy Garton Ash "Germany Unbound" *New York Review of Books* 22-11-90 pp11-15

[43] Jürgen Habermas *Die Nachholende Revolution* (Frankfurt a.M: Suhrkamp 1990)

[44] See Schäuble's account *Der vertrag: Wie ich über die deutsche Einheit verhandelte* (Stuttgart: Deutsche Verlagsanstalt 1991)

In this third phase of the German unification process there was practical and purposeful co-operation between the Government on the one hand and the Bundestag and the Bundesrat on the other. Parliament and the State Governments of the West German Länder, as well as the Opposition in Bonn, were included in the unification process from the beginning, without thereby diluting the responsibilities of the executive.[45]

The success of this operation made the Federal Republic appear much like a unitary state, at least in the concentration of power and evidently pluralist interests assembled and enacted so effectively. It provided a 'shining example of the possibilities for political leadership of a 'co-ordination democracy' under less than easy conditions', and one 'due to the overriding importance of the theme of German reunification'. There were protestations against a takeover and hegemony of the west. Before long a 'wall in the head' separating east and west Germans and nostalgia for both 'old systems' appeared. However, when circumstances had most required the national dynamic, or the idea of the nation, was the determining political force. GEMSU showed that the Bundesbank was not completely autonomous. Doubts about unity on 'rational' economic-financial grounds were overwhelmed by politics; enacted in a national interest of moral-constitutional, emotive, historical, geo-strategic and cultural components. Glees argues that 'There is no real evidence that Germany is a 'post-national' state, nor any evidence that such a thing exists or could ever exist. German reunification was a clear expression of German nationalism. No serious German politician could hope to win power by seeking to rubbish nationalism, nor would they be believed, either at home or abroad, if they did so.' Although this should be modified to state that none could win power by denigrating the German nation (rather than nationalism), Glees accurately notes that in the period since, 'an element of residual submissiveness towards the international community' is not 'post-nationalism', 'but simply a current definition of Germany's national interest'.[46]

Günter Grass's plea for a *Kulturnation* without state unity is not so far from the conservative objective of merging German culture, society and economy under a European roof. It also invokes the same non-western or even anti-western, form of nation that underpinned Germany's *Sonderweg*. In practice the 'Two states, one nation' urged by Grass is ironically closer to the

---

45   Wolfgang Bergsdorf "West Germany's Political System under Stress: Decision-Making Processes in Bonn 1990" in Dieter Grosser *German Unification: The Unexpected Challenge* New York: Berg 1992) pp88-106, see p98

46   Glees *Reinventing Germany* p259

reverse.[47] Having unified on principles of common culture, ethnicity, and self-determination, for the first years of its existence united Germany is as much a *Staatsnation* after the French model. Two societies are learning to live in and with the same state. In testing circumstances of recession, tackling the 'underestimated task of social and cultural integration' between east and west Germans requires considerable 'psychological adjustments'.[48] The meeting of the Germans with history is also that of the tragic east and the ironic west.[49] One non-German put it that 'We in the West when we indulge in nostalgia, people of my generation, we buy records...West German friends told me that when they indulge in nostalgia they simply have to go to East Germany.'[50] Limitless funds are not available and the capacity for chequebook solutions is sharply curtailed. Discontent soon rose amongst the new *Landsleute*: from *Wessis* over the rise in costs expressed in outbursts against Kohl and disparaging attitudes to easterners; among *Ossis* feeling that they were second class Germans and that the promises of a new paradise were lies. The timeframe for an equalisation of living standards, which all were led to believe would be short, was revised while the vexation intensified.

In terms of positive identification both states featured economic aspects, measured by performance within their respective political blocs. While West German attachment centred on a strong currency, high export performance and the consumer comforts of material success, the GDR emphasized its efficiency and status as having the 'best socialism', referencing its (now dubious) ranking in the world's top ten industrial nations. Both were able to claim high social security, health care and education standards.[51] They were also successful in other areas of global competition, notably sporting contests like the Olympic Games and World Cup soccer. 'National pride' was missing in the search for a 'positive

---

[47]   Günter Grass *Two States-One Nation: The Case Against German Reunification* London: Secker & Warburg 1990)

[48]   Jackson Janes "Who Is German?" *History of European Ideas* v18 n2 1994 pp215-224

[49]   Michael Weck "Der ironische Westen und der tragische Osten" *Kursbuch: Deutschland, Deutschland* n109 September 1992

[50]   "Elections in the GDR: European Aspects" in *Germany and Europe in Transition...* p48; John Borneman *Belonging in the Two Berlins: Kin, state, nation* Third Edition (Cambridge: Cambridge University Press 1995)

[51]   Dieter Frey "The Unification of Germany from the Standpoint of a Social Psychologist" in *United Germany and the New Europe* Ed. Heinz D.Kurz (Aldershot: Edward Elgar 1993) pp59-72

distinctiveness' *vis-à-vis* each other and externally. National unity could not be employed as for France, the UK or the US in the international arena or for internal purposes although some West German parlance—football commentaries referring to 'Germany versus the GDR'—implied as much.[52] For all the political-ideological reasons necessary to justify itself the GDR had to create its own myth of origin and required it to suppress or invalidate much of the identity founded in history, which meant before 1933 as well as after. In attempting to saddle the old FRG with politically expressing a new imperialist Germany—the heir and locus of responsibility for the Nazi regime—the GDR also dislocated itself from what had come before.[53] Beneath the political superstructure, 'traditional' German culture probably survived more in the east than in the west.

Secured by its superior alliances and trade networks the FRG's prevalence over the GDR was confirmed by the latter's dissolution and absorption into the former. A similar feeling of inferiority among the eastern population in comparison to the West followed that of West Germany with other western democracies whereby confidence and pride in economic, industrial and technological achievements was not matched in political, cultural or historical spheres. West Germany had won the World Cup in 1954 and 1974 yet these triumphs did not spark 'normal' national celebrations. Genuine expressions of national joy appeared when the Wall fell, a transitional Germany won the World Cup again and the formalities of reunification were completed.[54]

For all the differences between the former West and former East they are closer than either is to anywhere else, if often in unmeasurable ways. The GDR could not have united with any other state and society. After the Soviet bloc collapsed other states split apart while German and German joined. Millions of visitors from the FRG entered the GDR every year. Familial contacts were retained and the western state made financial contributions for the betterment of the Germans in the east.[55] Transmissions of West German audiovisual media simply went over rather than through the concrete, wire, and armed guards. Regarding the development of a post-reunification

---

[52]   William E. Paterson & David Southern *Governing Germany* Second Edition (Oxford: Blackwell 1992) pp297-298

[53]   As the two states moved to unify, and after they had, a new phase of political, ideological, and moralistic excoriation among German intellectuals began

[54]   *Berlin im November* Eds. Anke Schwartau, Cord Schwartau & Rolf Steinberg (Berlin: Nicolai 1990)

[55]   A. James McAdams "Explaining Inter-German Cooperation in the 1980s" in *From Bundesrepublik to Deutschland* pp191-206

political culture, polls on important issues reveal a 'political agenda by and large identical in eastern and western Germany'. In 1994 75% of western Germans and 60% of eastern Germans thought NATO indispensable. About 15% of both advocated withdrawal from the EU.[56] In a 1992 poll 60% of westerners and 55% of easterners rated economic success as a reason for being proud to be German. A 1995 questionnaire on confidence in political and non-political institutions found west Germans were marginally more positive than easterners in all but one example, the Bundeswehr, which had equal approval ratings. Beginning with the inquiry 'One state, two political cultures?' the author concludes that differences are outweighed by similarities and held together by fundamental commonalities five years after reunification.[57]

Similarly Veen and Zelle consider that 'contrasts between eastern and western Germans will figure in the same way as traditional regional differences in Germany' without this 'posing a serious threat to the common German identity'.[58] Another study of continuing difference in perceptions and psychologies concludes that the most obvious can be expected to dissipate while those from the east will 'find their independent place in the context of an all-German identity' much as other regional variances. The authors impress that of 'political transformations in the central and eastern Europe the GDR is a special case'.[59]

The case of the 'ethnic' or 'Volga Germans' is another challenge. For centuries before Bismarck's unification Germans had lived in communities fragmented across Eurasia. After 1949, assistance to those elements of the 'diaspora nation' outside the boundaries of the FRG included welcome into this self-proclaimed only legitimate German state. Firstly West and now united Germany's guarantee to persons capable of proving German descent, whether in the GDR, Poland or the Soviet Union institutionalised an ethnicity

---

56   Hans-Joachim Veen & Carsten Zelle "Growing Closer Together or Drifting Apart?" *German Comments* v39 July 1995 pp54-59; Michael Mertes "Germany's Social and Political Culture: Change Through Consensus?" *Daedelus* v123 n1 1994 pp1-32

57   Jürgen W. Falter "Ein Staat, zwei Politikkulturen? Politische Einstellungsunterschiede zwischen Ost- und Westdeutschland fünf Jahre nach der Wiedervereinigung" *German Studies Review* v19 n2 May 1996 pp279-301. The author has compiled a series of informative poll and questionnaire results. Cf. Stephan Eisel "The Politics of a United Germany" *Dædelus* v123 n1 1994 pp149-171

58   Veen & Zelle "Growing Closer Together or Drifting Apart?" p59

59   Petra Bauer-Kaase & Max Kaase "Five Years of Unification: The Germans on the Path to Inner Unity?" *German Politics* v5 n1 1996 pp1-25, p22

clause. Members of German minorities have exercised this right and 'returned' to a fatherland where most have never been. After changes in asylum provisions, other commitments (A116) to *Aussiedler* with some proof of ethnic German status were retained. Among much of the far right their unpopularity rivalled that of other 'foreigners' and the system was also under challenge by the SPD. Kohl's response was that this would induce panic and precipitate a rush into Germany.

"Die D-Mark (and the Constitution) sind nicht alles"

(West) German 'liberal nationalism' was symbolised in the Deutsche Mark and fuelled the east German rush westwards. As a proponent of a stronger sense of German national identity within a European economic, political and security edifice, Schäuble expressed that Germans needed to develop beyond a D-Mark consciousness claiming 'Our communal culture and civilization counts for more...than the name of our currency. If the Mark was everything that the Germans are, that would be miserable. The D-Mark is not everything'.[60] Others have speculated on the inherent dangers of building a national identity around, or upon, the national currency. In the late 1970s Norbert Elias warned of the absence of social solidarity in the FRG, 'if one excludes the fragile pride in the 'economic miracle'.[61] Germany's 'leading playwright', Heiner Müller, was another.[62] For Harold James, 'getting rid of the notion that nationality has to have an exclusive and narrowly defined social, political and economic ideology means an important step towards a less vulnerable identity'.[63] Karl-Heinz Böhrer's critique attacked the antiseptic effects of the sublimation of the *Kulturnation* in deference to the international environment. He argued against directing allegiance and

---

[60]   Wolfgang Schäuble "Die Mark ist nicht alles" *Der Spiegel* n13 27-3-95 pp22-25. 'Unsere gemeinsame Kultur und Zivilisation zählen mehr, da bin ich sicher, als der Name unserer Währung. Wenn die Mark letztlich alles wäre, was die Deutschen eint, dann wäre das ein wenig kläglich. Die Mark ist nicht alles '

[61]   Norbert Elias "Thoughts on the Federal Republic" in *The Germans: Power Struggles and the Development of Habitus in the Nineteenth and Twentieth Centuries* Ed. Michael Schröter. Trans. Eric Dunning and Stephen Mennell (Cambridge: Polity 1996) pp405-433

[62]   Heiner Müller "What Remains of The German Essence?" *New Perspectives Quarterly* v10 n1 Winter 1993 pp16-18

[63]   James *A German Identity* p209

identification to material ends. And focusing on the constitution or Europe is no better than a fixity on the Deutsche Mark. 'The nation', he asserted,

> has not, in fact, been superseded by the idea of cross-cultural, different, new identities in Europe...even those with a very minimal knowledge of the European nations know that such a supposed European identity is nowhere to be found, if one excludes the technical-economic sector.[64]

Continuing with resonances of Jacques Delors enquiry, 'who falls in love with an inner market?', Böhrer claimed that 'the privileging of the technical-economic argument and the failure to see the deeper spiritual dimensions of national identity are themselves part of the West German loss of identity'. In the aftermath of Maastricht and recession other observers envisaged Europe going down same path as the previous *fin-de-siècle* period.[65] One of disenchantment with a mechanistic existence, a pessimism which presaged the catastrophes of the twentieth century. A new 'Iron cage of modern rationalism' was being constructed by 'Specialists without spirit, sensualists without heart' and 'this nullity imagines that it has attained a level of civilization never before achieved'.[66]

Elias Canetti has written how individuals see themselves 'in a fixed relationship to the particular symbol which has become the most important for his nation. In its periodic reappearance when the moment demands it lies the continuity of national identity. A nation's consciousness of itself changes when, and only when, its symbol changes.' [67] If, as Canetti claimed, the consciousness of a nation is so closely connected to, or even determined by its symbols, then what symbol could apply for Germany? The German government has the task of selling to the German population the necessity of 'Europeanizing' the Deutsche Mark.[68] National considerations are prerequisite to this and it is national sentiments which are opposing the currency merger.[69] In Germany the introduction of a 2DM coin featuring a likeness of

---

64   Böhrer "Why we are not a Nation..."

65   Cf. Tony Judt "Nineteen Eighty-Nine: The End of Which European Era?" *Dædelus* v123 n2 1994 pp1-19

66   Ralph Schroeder *Max Weber and the Sociology of Culture* (London: Sage 1992) p114

67   Elias Canetti *Crowds and Power* Trans. Carol Stewart (New York: Farrar Strauss Giroux 1984 [1960]) p171

68   *Stark wie die Mark* (Bonn: Finanzministerium 1996)

69   Two debates, one on the single currency and one on national identity were fused in Kenneth Clarke's pithy advocation of 'national emblems' on future Ecu notes, a

Willy Brandt was accompanied by a speech from Finance Minister Waigel covering the usual historical, political and moral references.[70] A solely 'Deutschmark Identity' will crumble, as a 'Euro Identity' would, if the economy goes off the rails. The resulting void would impact on a Germany whose 'first real test' of democracy is still ahead of it.[71]

Like Böhrer, Jürgen Habermas also pours scorn on the Deutschmark national consciousness of the Germans. Habermas goes on to argue there should be no 'nation', as such. No national symbols, no forgetting history— but more so no revering the past (to be taken as a totality, and a disastrous one at that)—no assertion in international affairs, and no excessive focus on a common cultural identity. With absence not to be filled by communal confidence, security and identification in the Deutsche Mark, it did not leave much for Germans to believe in. Originally coined by Sternberger, 'Constitutional Patriotism' became a catchphrase around which another tangent of the national identity debate was constructed.[72] As promoted by Habermas the concept was intended to, effectively, delete the nation as a focus of allegiance.

Advocacy and scepticism of 'Constitutional Patriotism' in the 1990s carry the *Historikerstreit* lineage. For some of his opponents, Habermas expresses a 'negative chiliasm' whereby *all* Germans are fixed to the 'overriding event' of German history, the Holocaust, and 'any hermeneutic of a new German self-understanding has to be developed from it'. Böhrer claims that 'to use a constitutional utopia as a substitute for the nation has one disadvantage which is becoming increasingly clear: it cannot avoid repressing entire categories of the psychic and cultural tradition which used to form part of German identity'.[73] Constitutional patriotism Habermas-style would have Germans wallow in a limbo-like condition around their own 'provisional' *Grundgesetz* until a more suitable European legal-political constitution replaces it. Such a resolution is not on the horizon. What remains then is a 'provisional patriotism'. Helmut Wagner challenges that there is a

---

kind of surface national identity on a European token of exchange. *The Times* 20-6-95 p1;.See also "1,8715 DM = 1 'Boswell'" *Die Zeit* 19-5-95 p53

70   *Bulletin* 28-7-94

71   Winkler "Rebuilding of a Nation" p127

72   Dolf Sternberger *Verfassungspatriotismus* (Frankfurt: Insel 1982)

73   Böhrer "Why we are not a nation...". One wonders if either or both interlocutors intentionally imply only 'ethnic Germans' or the multi-ethnic whole. Cf. Jürgen Habermas *The Past As Future* Trans. Max Pensky (Cambridge: Polity 1994). In 1947 Friedlaender wrote of a German *Entschuldigungsmanie* that would last long into the future. See *Die Zeit* 3-2-95 p6

dearth of positive qualities in any kind of national orientation and those 'who regard national thinking and sentiment per se, i.e. irrespective of their specific form and manifestation, as morally reprehensible and historically obsolete.' Creating a popular fealty for a set of rules rather than a simpler identification with people who live in the same community, speak the same language, have similar understandings and customs, 'requires an extremely developed ability to abstract. It suggests a makeshift, an insubstantial 'patriotism without patria'.[74] In Schäuble's interpretation:

> Some have argued that after such experiences national identity should be ignored. Instead of national sentiments or feelings of identity, Germans should develop a patriotism based on their constitution. The Basic Law, then, should be the sole target of citizens' affection. I personally believe that such a focus on the constitution would be too narrow; it would come too much from the head, and not enough from the heart. A proper feeling of identity and a feeling of togetherness could not spring from this...national identity and an historically defined national consciousness will be needed in order to prevent political instability.[75]

'Constitutional patriotism' has a role in a broader and ongoing debate comprising citizenship, national identity, multi-culturalism, immigration and ethnicity.[76] One tangent is the 'historical burden linked to the German idea of nation' built into the focus of constitutional patriotism, the *Grundgesetz*, itself. The privileging of descent as the criterion for membership of the nation may conflict with the will to belong to it. The former West Germany incorporated millions of immigrants in earlier decades. However, although

---

[74]   Helmut Wagner ""Constitutional Patriotism" as an Antidote" *Aussenpolitik* n3 1993 pp243-252, p246

[75]   Wolfgang Schäuble "The Federal Republic of Germany: Foundations and Development" in *The Federal Republic of Germany: The End of an Era* Ed. Eva Kolinsky (New York: Berg 1991) pp15-26. See pp24-25

[76]   See on this, Janes "Who is German?"; Sabine von Dirke "Mulitkulti: The German Debate on Multiculturalism" *German Studies Review* v17 n3 1994 pp513-536; Klaus J. Bade "Immigration and Social Peace in United Germany" *Dædelus* v123 n1 Winter 1994 pp85-106; Mathias Bös "Ethnisierung des Rechts?: Staatsbürgerschaft in Deutschland, Frankreich, Großbritannien und den USA" *Kölner Zeitschrift für Soziologie und Sozialpsychologie* v45 December 1993 pp619-643; E.K. Scheuch *Wie deutsch sind die Deutschen? Eine Nation wandelt ihr Gesicht* (Bergisch-Gladbach 1991); Dieter Oberndoerfer "Nation und Republik: Kollective Kultur oder kulturelle Freiheit" *Blatte für deutsche und internationale Politik* September 1994 pp1068-1081; Michael Ignatieff *Blood and Belonging: Journeys into the New Nationalism* (New York: Farrar, Strauss & Giroux 1993)

living and working in Germany these people remained 'foreigners' as did their children born there while German citizenship laws were based on a principle of *jus sanguinis*. In recognising itself as a nation the new Germany also has to come to terms with its multi-German character.[77] Immigrants of earlier decades altered the existing cultural environment without the appearance of widespread anxieties among Germans. In recent years an influx of asylum seekers coincided with reunification costs and economic recession, a volatile combination which has strained the political and social fabric and impacted negatively upon long-term foreign residents. These developments have tended to overshadow new diversity since the 1950s even as a traditional core sustained. Under these conditions it is easier for a 'pre-political notion of German identity' to become 'synonymous with a kind of national preference' whereby 'the bonds of kinship must prevail'.[78] German elites and population 'are committed to upholding democracy' but also uneasy about the prospect of Germany becoming a 'multicultural society of citizens', again undermining the idea of a 'postnational nation'.[79] Similar issues confront other societies as limitations on resources and social harmony consolidate. Nonetheless, for Germany to be considered an entirely 'ethnic', that is mono-ethnic, nation is illusory. It is more accurately 'demotic' with a core group, 'a complex and ethnically heterogeneous society'

> that is politically organised in such a way that all its members are, through special institutions, linked directly and without the mediation of subsocial units to the central authority; the integration of this society is based on democratic government and cultural homogenisation.[80]

'Cultural homogenisation' does not extend to *every* aspect of culture as applied to every individual. In the case of immigrants it is better represented as a cultural adaptability to certain communications and norms; 'those who have learned the language, put down social and economic roots, and accepted the nation's history and future as their own'.[81] Or, as Breuilly

---

77   Ludger Kühnhardt "Multi-German Germany" *Dædelus* v123 n1 1994 pp193-209

78   Le Gloannec "On Germany Identity" p143. These 'bonds of kinship' could also demarcate Germans from its EU partners

79   Mary Fulbrook "Aspects of Society and Identity in the New Germany" *Dædelus* v123 n2 1994 pp211-233, p230

80   Jaroslav Krejci & Vitezslav Velimsky *Ethnic and Political Nations in Europe* (London: Croom Helm 1981) p35

81   Janes "Who is German?" p222. See also John Tomlinson "Homogenisation and Globalisation" *History of European Ideas"* v20 n4-6 pp891-897

has written 'National identity develops at two levels—institutional and cultural. Institutionally it develops by people learning the same 'habits'...Culturally, in modern industrial societies, it develops through the construction of a 'standard national culture.'[82] This 'standard' makes national states different.

Return of the Kulturnation

> In literacy, sophistication and self-awareness, the Germans were not significantly (if at all) inferior to the French...all that nationalism needed here was to endow an existing High Culture, well suited to define a modern nation, with its political roof. A number of battles and much more diplomatic activity were required, but no other and more extreme methods were called for.[83]

Several aspects from this quotation are reconstituted in post-WW2 Europe. Through a superior standing, granted or asserted, French culture and language prevailed over German which kept a comparatively low profile. This was inextricable from Germany's division and 'semi-sovereignty'.[84] A maturing agenda after reunification is to reinvigorate German culture internationally through language promotion and in the sphere of 'high culture', where it might regain some of the vibrancy that had in large part been missing since the 1920s. Walter Laqueur has remarked that 'forty-five years after the end of the war the German cultural balance-sheet was still disappointing compared with the achievements of the late nineteenth and early twentieth centuries, when Germany had been the *Kulturnation* par excellence.'[85] Compared with other sophisticated, self-confident western European democracies centred around dazzling, cosmopolitan metropolises like Paris and London and reflected in the urbanity of their political classes, the FRG was in 'deficit'.[86] The continuity of London and Paris served as

---

[82]   John Breuilly "Nationalism and German Reunification" in *The State of Germany...* pp 224-238. See p229 & pp235-6

[83]   Ernest Gellner "Nationalism reconsidered and E.H.Carr" *Review of International Studies* v18 1992 pp285-293 p291

[84]   Peter J. Katzenstein *Policy and politics in West Germany: the growth of a semi sovereign state* (Philadelphia: Temple University Press 1987)

[85]   Walter Laqueur *Europe in Our Time: A History 1945-1992* (New York: Penguin 1992) p283

[86]   Cf. Jochen Thies "Observations on the Political Class in Germany" *Dædalus* v123

focal points in the development of the French and British nation-states and for the cultures that radiated from these cities and were reproduced under their influence.[87] Previously, West Germany had internationalised but without a national identity, something requisite between the region and Europe which extends beyond material comforts and financial interest:

> These days have shown more clearly what was less evident at the beginning of the 1970s: the objective and subjective reasons for our no longer being a nation...the Federal Republic has succumbed increasingly to the illusion that economic prosperity and pedestrian malls, the superiority of the D-Mark and a house to the north of Rome could serve as symbols of identity for an internationally orientated, happy economic bourgeoisie without political ambitions.[88]

According to Böhrer, 'almost the entirety of the cultural tradition what was once called Germany has been attacked by a notorious plague called loss of memory' and national culture and philosophy is or was 'atomized' into 'political and intellectual regionalism'. However, while Goethe, Schiller and Beethoven are proclaimed for their art, they are, in a hierarchy of 'belonging' as revered treasures, great German artists before they are European (or regional) and secondly perhaps 'Europe's' before they are the world's. Likewise, Wolf Bierman, Günter Grass or Christa Wolf are German *litérateur*, celebrities, personalities.[89] Refutations of membership in a German 'nation' are extraneous. Whatever else they are recognised for, they are identified with Germany by Germans and non-Germans alike. In 1993 SPD politician Freimut Duve expressed that Germany's aim should be to become part of the 'cultural web of the normal'.[90] Three years later Kohl

---

n1 1994 pp263-276

[87] See Elias *The Germans* pp8-9

[88] Böhrer "Why we are not a Nation"

[89] Helmut Kohl "Die Buchstadt Leipzig—ein geistig-kulturelles Zentrum in Deutschland" *Bulletin* 21-3-96. In this wide-ranging speech Kohl also mentions Brecht, Monika Maron and Martin Walser among others. Similarly the President of the Goethe Institute. 'Wenn Deutsch als Sprache von Jürgen Habermas, Niklas Luhmann, Siegfried Lenz oder Martin Walser interessant ist, dann kann uns dies in unserer Spracharbeit nur bestätigen'. Hilmar Hoffman "Rede des Präsidenten des Goethe-Instituts" *Bulletin* 12-12-95. See also *German Cultural Studies* Ed. Rob Burns (Oxford: Oxford University Press 1995)

[90] Freimut Duve "Germany and the hurricane of change" *New Perspectives Quarterly* v10 n1 Winter 1993 pp13-15; Dieter Oberndoerfer "Nation und Republik: Kollektive Kultur oder kulturelle Freiheit" *Blatte für deutsche und internationale Politik*, September 1994 pp1068-1081

stated in the Bundestag, 'Wir haben die Erfahrung, daß die Kultur für die nationale Identität von allergroßter Bedeutung ist.' [91] The imminent return of government to Berlin has great political and cultural significance. [92] Germany hosts huge international events: the annual Oktoberfest of over six million visitors, the giant Hannover Trade Fair, the world's largest, the Frankfurt Book Fair, the World Economic Summit in Berlin. Soon new French and American embassies will, with great symbolism, be in place by the Brandenburg Tor in the middle of a reinvented European capital. Along with these developments the recreation of Germany as a 'post-national' *Kulturnation* is underway. In the eastern *Länder*

> cultural high spots—the classical centre of Goethe's Weimar and the Wartburg castle where Luther translated the New Testament are being invested with a double significance: they are at once symbols of the continuity of the German *Kulturnation,* the acceptable cultural unity of the Germans and at the same time they will aid the ailing East German economy by attracting quantities of Western tourists. [93]

The CDU has been prolific in its declarations and discussion papers on *Kulturpolitik.* The party stresses that the reunified Germany is a *Kulturstaat* as indeed it was while partitioned: 'Kultur ist Ausdruck der Identität aller Deutschen...die Kultur unserer Nation muß in ihrer unverwechselbaren Eigenart erhalten werden und sich fortentwickeln'. The CDU echoes the *Einigungsvertrag* (Article 35) that it was the prime mover in sealing and much of the government's attention was directed at the eastern *Länder*. 1995 saw the introduction of the interior ministry's initiative of 'Kulturförderung von Kultureinrichtungen mit nationaler Bedeutung in den neuen Ländern im Rahmen des "Leuchtturm-Programms"'. Along with regular reference to developing a communal European cultural policy and respecting subsidiarity the CDU also focus on east-central Europe and the cultural welfare of German minorities there. Kohl spoke of soon 100 million native German speakers in the EU and postulated on people in neighbouring states enquiring, 'Germany has an important mission and plays an important

---

[91] Helmut Kohl "Rede des Bundeskanzlers vor dem Deutschen Bundestag" *Bulletin* 18-6-96

[92] See James O. Jackson "Destiny Berlin" *Time* 30-9-96 pp32-43 (Deutsche Ausgabe)

[93] Fulbrook "Aspects of Society and Identity in the New Germany" p213. One of Kohl's reiterations on the theme of (the reunified) Germany as a 'Kulturnation' is made in a speech to the tourist industry. *Bulletin* 20-10-94

role in the EU. Is it not good to learn this language?'[94] From another perspective in response to an enquiry on the relationship between politics and culture and the 'cultural implications of the German momentum', Saul Friedlander spoke of attempts for reparations for lost eastern territories that verge on irredentism, claiming 'we shall see a reinvigorated expansion of German culture, both officially—for instance through cultural agreements—and unofficially.'[95]

Nation and Europe: The End of the Past?

In the 1960s Karl Jaspers predicted that the vacuum in German political consciousness 'will not be filled by a national consciousness'.[96] A common consciousness as Germans was derived from, and belonged to, a pre-state, non-political world. Elsewhere he wrote that in political terms national orientations were inapplicable to all of Europe.[97] In France (especially) and—notwithstanding its own peculiar situation—the UK, the nation continued to characterise political cultures, along with intellectual and social *milieux*, without any particular negativity. Three decades later Manfred Görtemaker summed up the historical-psychological contrast between Germany and its two major 'partners and rivals' in the EU: 'The idea of nation-states is not actually bad as such; unlike in Germany, nationalism is not a 'dirty word' in, say, Britain or France. In fact nation-states can provide identity.'[98] 'On this theme Peter Reichel declares:

> Die frage nach unserer kollektiven Identität wird immer wieder gestellt—und ist doch noch nicht schlüssig, geschweige denn abschließend beantwortet worden. Uns beunruhigt unser zwiespältiges Image in der Welt,

[94] Helmut Kohl "Rede des Bundeskanzlers" *Bulletin* 18-6-96

[95] Yaron London interviewing Saul Friedlander "Now We Shall be Reduced to Our Due Place Within German Priorities" *When the Wall Came Down: Reactions to German Unification* (London: Routledge 1992) pp295-302

[96] Karl Jaspers *Wohin treibt die Bundesrepublik? Tatsachen, Gefahren, Chancen* (München: 1966) pp177-178

[97] Kein Nationalbewußtsein darf meines Erachtens heute in Europa noch einen politischen Charakter haben. Unser deutsches Selbstbewußtsein aber ist mit seiner Vielfachheit verwurzelt im Boden eines Jahrtausends.' Karl Jaspers *Freiheit und Wiedervereinigung* (München: Piper 1990) p44

[98] Manfred Goertemaker *Unifying Germany 1989-1990* (Houndmills: MacMillan 1994) p241

in dem sich neidvolle Bewunderung, Angst und Verachtung mischen. Im Umgang damit fehlt uns die souveräne Ignoranz der Briten, der nonchalante Nationalismus der Franzosen und die unbekümmerte Attitude der Amerikaner.[99]

In the same western European context political ramifications flowed from the German negation of (or merely tentative reference to) national identity and interests. Some effects were beneficial for the old FRG, some were restrictive or costly and may have left united Germany unprepared for the post-Cold War world. Through a well established method of operating in partnerships the historical problems of a German nationhood and its role in Europe are partly, though unquantifiably, alleviated. If 'Europe' materialises Germany will be able, 'to unfold as nation, culture and economy with less hindrance from the East-West division and from other borders.'[100] Attention on economic might and questions of geo-politics will be diluted. Having defined themselves through 'Europe', the Germans can only realise this if or as long as 'Europe' is compatible. Germany's reunification has fuelled what its political leadership expressly tried to avoid: a renationalizing of Europe even if in this age a focus or reliance on the nation is more a 'rational response to certain upheavals and frustrations, not a throwback to barbarism'.[101] Michael Bartsch expressed days after reunification that 'it would be wrong-headed to seek to transcend a German identity in a European one, before it is even halfway healed by its snap treatment'.[102] And Michael Ignatieff proposes that Germany's 'task now is not, as some liberals suppose, to pass beyond nationalism altogether and move into bland Europeanism but instead to move from the ethnic nationalism of its past to the civic nationalism of a possible future.'[103] According to Martin Walser, attempting to artificially keep national sentiment out of the public sphere and concentrate on becoming committed Europeans rather than Germans must

[99] Peter Reichel "Die haßlichen Deutschen: extrem schönheitsbedürtig und wenig politisch" in *Die haßlichen Deutschen* .pp316-333

[100] Ole Wæver "Three Competing Europes" *International Affairs* v66 n3 1990 pp477-493, p482

[101] Ernst B. Haas "What is nationalism and why should we study it?" *International Organization* v40 n3 1986 pp707-744

[102] Michael Bartsch "Der Weg zu sich selbst und zum Nachbarn: Über die Angst vor der Freiheit" *Sachsenspiegel* 12-10-90 quoted in Renata Fritsch-Bournazel *Europa and German Unification* (New York: Berg 1992) p195. Cf. Steven Muller "Democracy in Germany" *Dædelus* v123 n1 1994 pp33-56, p51

[103] Ignatieff *Blood and Belonging* p7 & p102

'appear curiously abstract to the other nations which make up Europe'. It also encourages rather than suppresses the rise of right-wing extremism through presenting a monopoly on national feeling.[104] On the one hand, to do as Kinkel says and 'find its place in Europe again' Germany must have autonomy. On the other, an ideal 'Europe' may be in Germany's interest, but there is growing scepticism about how realisable it is.[105]

There was no shortage of claims that reunification would trigger a wave of old-style and peculiarly *German* nationalism. One of the fiercest opponents was the Irish author Conor Cruise O'Brien. His—later recanted—alarmist prognostications warned of an Fourth Reich borne along by previously repressed and now unleashed nationalism.[106] Now united Germany has two distinct and distinctly unpleasant legacies. Activities of the repressive Stasi apparatus and revelations of giant spy networks both augment and in some ways abate a much longer west German 'coping with the past'.[107] In a 1992 article Reinhard Stuth summarised: 'Political thinking in western and eastern Germany is still incomparably more characterised by the second world war...than...the USA, Italy or Russia.'[108] Accordingly the 'post-war era' did not end with *Perestroika* or the fall of the Berlin Wall or on October 3 1990. Theo Sommer declared it ended with the departure of the last Russian troops from German soil: 'Der 31. August 1994 ist ein epochales Datum. Er marktiert einen tiefen Einschnitt in der deutschen, aber auch in der Europäischen Geschichte...Jetzt erst ist der Zweite Weltkrieg wirklich zu Ende gegangen...Die Schatten der Vergangenheit dürfen nicht zu Schranken vor der Zukunft werden.'[109] After the fiftieth anniversary reminder of World

---

104 Wallace "German Intellectuals and Unification" pp92-93

105 Ludger Helms "Euro-Skeptizismus—Aspekte der neueren deutschsprachigen Europa-Literatur" *Zeitschrift für Politik* v41 n3 1994 pp296-304

106 Conor Cruise o'Brien "Beware, the Reich is Reviving" *The Times* 31-10-89. Before Germany's reunification Ernest Gellner had observed O'Brien as remaining bound by the same assumption which he inferred held the German political leadership and general population captive, that 'the nation, whatever that be, is the natural political unit'. Ernest Gellner "The Sacred and the National" in *Encounters with Nationalism* (Oxford: Blackwell 1994) pp59-73. See also Conor Cruise O'Brien "Die Zukunft des Westens" *Aesthetik & Kommunikation* h84 j23 February 1994

107 *Coping with the Past: Germany and Austria after 1945* Eds. Kathy Harms, Lutz R. Reuter, Völker Dürr (Madison: University of Wisconsin 1990); Joachim Gauck *Die Stasi-Akten: Das Unheimliche Erbe der DDR* (Reinbek: Rororo 1991) & "Dealing with a Stasi Past" *Daedelus* v123 n1 1994 pp277-284

108 Reinhard Stuth "Germany's New Role in a Changing Europe" *Aussenpolitik* v43 n1 1992 pp22-32

109 Theo Sommer "Jetzt erst ist der Krieg zu Ende" *Die Zeit* 2-9-94 p1. *Die Zeit's* series

War Two's end some thought that attention may shift elsewhere, and to the development of another consciousness. One German historian forecast that 'the debate about May 8 is also a debate about Germany today. And I think its the last time there'll be a discussion here about National Socialism between 1933 and 1945. Maybe they'll look at it again in another 50 years... Debates like this are part of the process'. The article summarised that 'regardless of what kind of national identity Germany develops in the future, Germans are witnessing the end of the great national debate about the Nazi past.' [110] Regular revivals tend to contradict this.[111]

Positioning themselves 'between optimists and pessimists' Markovits and Reich present a view of the Federal Republic that will inevitably, if 'inadvertently' achieve a status of 'economic hegemon' in Europe.[112] 'Today's German question', is itself 'much more subtle, nuanced, and part of the peaceful interaction among liberal democracies'. Despite impressing the secure and integrated nature of German democracy and explicit refutation of any revival of military-based power, this discussion provoked both defence of the Germans, and the perception that it offered an insufficiently rigorous treatment of 'recent negative political-cultural events'. Bruce Goldberger produced an impressive array of evidence supporting a non-threatening, trade orientated, Europeanised Germany of devolved political power which provided, at least in part, the answer to why its western and now eastern European partners have 'allowed' such extensive penetration of their economies.[113] Moishe Postone also took up the issue and, in diametric opposition to Goldberger, he argues Markovits and Reich have not gone far enough in their summation of today's Germany as a likely hegemon, or in characterising it as a tenuous democracy. In short they have not been sufficiently negative. Postone claims that 'the possible meaning and consequences of Germany's rise to power is, however, inseparable from the Nazi past'.[114] The 'end of the post-war era' is pinpointed as beginning

---

of essays '1945 und Heute' continued to remind its readership through 1995

110 Julius Schloep, quoted in Denis Stanton "Germans war over how to celebrate peace" *Observer* 16-4-95 p18

111 Cf. Stephenson "Anniversaries, Memory and the Neighbours"

112 Andrei S. Markovits & Simon Reich "Should Europe Fear the Germans?" *German Politics and Society* n23 1991 pp1-20

113 Bruce N. Goldberger "Why Europe Should not Fear the Germans" *German Politics* v2 n2 1993 pp288-310

114 Moishe Postone "Germany's Future and Its Unmastered Past" in *From Bundesrepublik to Deutschland* pp291-299

November 9th, 1989 and presumably formalised October 3rd, 1990. This time it is in a 'refracted' form, meaning the post-war era has *not* ended.

The German transformation is still accompanied by the taint of 'otherness'. German initiatives which serve its own (and often its neighbours) interests, may be burdened by anxiety or suspicion, even if submerged, as long as the mental construct of a European 'other' persists. Michael Wolffsohn has described a 'mistrust (but not fear!) of Germany that is structurally inherent and cannot be expected to disappear in the near future'. Germany's heavily export dependent economy had to deal with factors beyond those of quality, price or availability. The 'political-psychological dimension' indicates how influential history and seemingly unconnected foreign policy decisions are in Germany's trade performance.[115] Many, though not all, American commentators were from the earliest stages of reunification generally positive. One argued 'Germany justifiably still remains on parole. But if a united Germany is ever to take its place among nations it has to be allowed to act much like any other nation. To treat it differently, to feed a German sense of victimization, would only repeat the mistakes of the past.'[116] Another sees Germany as remaining on 'international probation' indefinitely, while many among post-war generations think they should be accepted completely as 'normal members of the civilised world' possessing a 'record on individual rights and democratic respectability just as good, if not better than those of Britain, France and the U.S.'[117] Czech President Václav Havel was explicitly opposed to burdening the Germans with a 'collective guilt'. He met with German President Richard von Weizsäcker in 1990 and spoke against the dangers of a particular anti-German irrationality, that 'despising the Germans as such, condemning them simply because they are Germans or fearing them on that ground alone, is the same as being anti-Semitic.'[118]

---

[115]   Michael Wolffsohn "Fear of Germany and Security for Europe" in *German Unification: The Unexpected Challenge* Ed. Dieter Grosser (Oxford: Berg 1992) pp150-179

[116]   Richard Cohen "No Double Standard for Germany" *Washington Post* 6-12-89 quoted in Fritsch-Bournazel *Europe and German Unification* p171

[117]   Frederick S. Wyle "Europe 1990, the U.S., the U.S.S.R., Germany and all than—on Letting the Log of History Drift rather than Trying to Shove it" in *Auf der Suche nach der Gestalt Europas* Eds. Jochen Thies & Gunther van Well (Bonn: Verlag fur Internationale Politik 1990) pp163-170, here p164. The German political class, information agencies, business, and intellectual establishment appear more attuned to and concerned about American, rather than 'European', elite and public opinion on, and perceptions of, Germany

[118]   Václav Havel, Speech in Prague 15-3-90 in Fritsch-Bournazel *Europe and German*

At the centre of Kohl's political enterprise is the positive co-existence of a peaceful, confident and accepted German identity as the affiliate to a desired European identity. So there was a genuine disappointment in response to the absence of an invitation for Kohl (or any FRG representative) to the D-Day formalities in 1984. After the relationship built up in the intervening decade with Mitterrand, the sense of chagrin was amplified by a repeat performance in 1994. Maintaining such a singularity has sustained doubts on whether the 'long post-war parole' really is over. Succeeding generations and political leaders have inherited this by virtue of their 'Germanness', a historical irony which hindered an unqualified German 'return to the fold'. This form of exclusion is precisely the barrier that the political leadership want to surmount and which impedes a 'common European future'. The sense of outsider (if not outcast) in these events was made more acute by the US presence. Mitterrand later invited a German contingent to march as part of the Eurocorps down the Champs Élysée on Bastille Day, and Kohl noted that 'after a short hesitation it was agreed by a great majority of the French public, and also a majority of those who belonged to the resistance movement'.[119] In 1995 a succession of anniversaries culminated in the 50th commemoration of what was V-E for Britain. In Germany a new debate, or the reworking of an old one, arose about what May 8th, 1945 and 1995 meant and how to respond. After previous affronts it must have been a curious mix of feelings for Kohl in London as Britain relived its victory.[120]

The furore surrounding the book by Daniel Goldhagen was another recent example that the past is far from passed.[121] Only slightly less pronounced, at least tacitly connected, and due to be around for longer, was a renewed debate on the new intellectual right. In the background are the same themes of national history and national choices.[122] Also contentious is Kohl's

---

Unification p185

[119] Helmut Kohl "Aussprache über den Bundeshaushalt 1995" *Bulletin* 9-9-94

[120] Stanton "Germans war over how to celebrate peace"; Tom Schimmeck "Deutschland, erwachsen" *Die Woche* 12-5-95 p8

[121] Daniel Goldhagen *Hitler's willing executioners: ordinary Germans and the Holocaust* (New York: Knopf 1996) For a rigorous critique see Hans-Ulrich Wehler "The Goldhagen Controversy: Agonizing Problems, Scholarly Failure and the Political Dimension" *German History* v15 n1 1997 pp80-91. For other commentaries see Werner Ross "Goldhagen and German Original Sin" *German Comments* v45 January 1997 pp89-94; Fritz Stern "The Goldhagen Controversy: One Nation, One People, One Theory?" *Foreign Affairs* v76 n1 1996 pp128-137

[122] Jacob Heilbrunn "Germany's New Right" *Foreign Affairs* v76 n1 1996 pp80-98; Josef Joffe et.al. "Mr. Heilbrunn's Planet: On Which the Germans Are Back" and

persistent, though intermittently muted, desire to present the Germans and especially those in the east, as victims of Nazi rule. Waiting until after the rites, protocols and media saturation surrounding the 50th anniversary of V-E Day, Kohl reiterated this staple theme. [123] Some, like Bartsch, consider fear or distrust of the Germans and their new international 'freedom' as 'absurd', but the vestiges are perpetuated. Even Enzensberger, who urged Germany to become normal like its civilized neighbours, declares it 'morally mortgaged for an unforeseeable future'.[124] A political class and population that considers itself to be under a microscope, and whose physical landscape contains the reminders of nationalist terror, faces moral and political disadvantages. It is not difficult to regard national identifications or the 'very notion of defining the national interest [as] suspect, retrograde, even reactionary'.[125] Kohl confronts this by asking

> Warum reden wir eigentlich nicht häufiger von der Liebe zum eigenen Land, von der Vaterlandsliebe? Ich habe mich immer gegen den Versuch gewehrt, Patriotismus mit der Unterstellung zu desavouieren, die Grenzen zwischen Nationalstolz und Nationalismus seien fließend. Patriotismus deshalb zu verachten, weil dieser Wert während der NS-Zeit in verruf gebracht und mißbraucht wurde. [126]

As Germany adapts to a new authority Kohl's statements become tinged with anachronism; not because they are menacing or reactionary but because their sentiments could be questioned. If a Mitterrand, Chirac, Tony Blair, or John Major speaks of nation, national interests or national pride it is received differently than if a Kohl or Schäuble does. And all the more alarmingly if it is someone equivalent on the spectrum to a Jean-Marie Le Pen or Margaret Thatcher. The CDU resolved to further a national identity in company with its declared goals of European unity. Nation-states have not

Heilbrunn's reply *Foreign Affairs* v76 n2 1996 pp152-159 and pp160-161

123 Beitrag der deutschen Heimatvertriebenen zum Wiederaufbau in Deutschland und zum Frieden in Europa" *Bulletin* 2-6-95

124 Interview ABC (Australia) Radio 30-6-95

125 Timothy Garton Ash "Germany's Choice" *Foreign Affairs* v73 n4 1994 pp64-81

126 Helmut Kohl "Unser freiheitliches Gemeinwesen braucht Bürgersinn und Patriotismus" Speech in Munich 19-6-94 *Bulletin* 29-6-94. 'Why do we not actually speak frequently of the love of one's own country, of fatherlands love? I have always defended against the attempt (which is employed to deny patriotism) to portray the borders between national pride and nationalism as fluid. Patriotism is therefore despised, because this value was brought into disrepute and misused in the National-Socialist era.'

disappeared, it said, rather they are 'no longer capable of solving on their own the existential problems of our age'. [127] The party have attempted a 'remaking' of Germany looking to the past by invoking German history and cultural roots before the jingoism of the Wilhelmine era, and to the future towards a 'European Germany'. [128] Both left and right of the mainstream assert that the new nation is a transitional stage on the way to 'something' European. [129] A German national identity would exist with Germany, in a formal sovereign sense, again becoming a 'former country in the middle of Europe'. As Garton Ash surmised, 'the Federal Republic of (United) Germany, 1990-2000, hail and farewell?' [130] Having achieved the foreign policy aim of reunification the government moved towards abandonment of sovereignty in favour of a Europe where a 'European consciousness'—and so a European polity and government—has yet to evolve. Political processes and political identity remain for the Germans, like other Europeans, fundamentally associated with and operating within national states. And this configuration will continue for the foreseeable future.

James Sheehan has asserted that the old West Germany 'was neither the history-less, anxious neurotic its intellectuals often described, nor the sleeping, chauvinistic giant its enemies sometimes imagined'. [131] The bulk of Germans don't care about discussion on their states of mind, alleged insecurities, 'alias' identity or potential belligerence. Many wonder why they need to collectively present some form of psychological certitude or a balanced assurance that eludes other individuals, communities and nations. Through the post-reunification convulsion the commonalities between Germans turn out to be less spectacular or iniquitous than some infer: shared

---

127 Resolutions...CDU Oct 25-28 1992, #A1, Sect.2 & 3

128 Cf. Schäuble "Das Nationale nutzen"; Duve "Germany and the Hurricane of Change"

129 Oskar Lafontaine foresaw the new German state as provisional (as the old one had been) until absorption in a "United States of Europe', while Schäuble, with Renan, does 'not claim that the nation is history's final goal'. "Das Nationale als Mittel zum europäischen Zweck" *Süddeutsche Zeitung* 28-12-94. Schäuble expands on the necessity for a national identity in the present however, in *Und der Zukunft zugewandt* (Berlin: Siedler 1994). Some studies indicate that in German schools this Europeanization is proving effective. Simon Green "The European Dimension in German Schools" *German Monitor* n34 1995 pp147-155

130 Timothy Garton Ash *In Germany's Name: Germany and the Divided Continent* (London: Vintage 1994) p383

131 James Sheehan "National History and National Identity in the New Germany" in *1870/71—1989/90: German Unifications and the Change of Literary Discourse* Ed. Walter Pape (Berlin: Walter de Gruyter 1993) p31

language and other 'ordinary' cultural understandings, an array of literary and artistic giants, a desire for financial and personal security, a 'normal' dissatisfaction with politicians, a sense of *Heimat*, reflected in the popularity of the so named television show. Despite differing systemic conditions in two states some referents proved indestructable and remain quintessentially 'German.' A phrase like 'Goethe could not be divided up between Frankfurt am Main and Weimar' may be typically Kohl but it is not only he who upholds common cultural reference points as the basis of national identity.[132] Even though figures like senior Kohl advisor Michael Mertes have written of the 'irresistible need to waste energy and ink trying to solve the puzzle of what the (West) German true collective *Identität* might be' German élites still have preoccupations about Germany's image in the world.[133] And no society can be completely independent of its political and intellectual classes. The 'normality' theme encompasses and must to some extent affect all. Five year before reunification Kurt Sontheimer asked, 'Was fehlt uns?' The answer, 'der Sinn für Proportionen'; a propensity to unnecessarily press the panic button. On a mooted 'psychologische Anfälligkeit' of the Germans he put their situation in a wider perspective inclusive of social, economic and political weaknesses in the UK, Italy and France.[134] Five years after reunification two Americans wrote that Germany had been transformed to a point whereby in the company of a 'less coherent post-Cold War France, Britain and US...the Germans [finally] know who they are'—or at least no less than anybody else.[135] And this has been crucial to a new vigour and critique among public and élites regarding Germany's European role, responsibilities and benefits.

---

132   Kohl "Rede des Bundeskanzlers..." *Bulletin* 18-6-96. See also James *A German Identity* p1 on Goethe and German national pride; Cf. *Ziele und Verantwortung der Kulturpolitik* (Gütersloh: Verlag Bertelsmann Stiftung 1995)

133   Mertes "Germany's Social and Political Culture" p3

134   Kurt Sontheimer *Deutschlands Politische Kultur* (München: Serie Piper 1990) pp147-154

135   Schoenbaum & Pond *The German Question and Other German Questions* p215

4 German Domestic Polity, Politics and Economics

This chapter builds on the discussion of an evolving national confidence among the German public and political class, in particular *vis-à-vis* their European neighbours. There has been a distinct rise in dissatisfaction towards being in a European Union that perpetuates historical constraints on the Germans while expecting them to finance the enterprise. Where there are difficulties in harmonising domestic and European demands it is likely to result in the former being politically enforced. The *leitmotiv* of post-war German politics has been the ensuring of social and economic stability. As the transformations of 1989-91 impressed, stability does not equate with permanence. It is better conceived as a combination of factors engendering some sense of surety amongst change, both in the present and as much as can be instilled in prognostications for Germany and Europe. Gary Geipel targeted some premier concerns and indicated the nature and depth of the overall challenge:

> If it can create jobs by reducing the excesses of the welfare state, and if it can accept foreigners as an asset rather than a liability, the Germany that emerges from the 1990s may be one that is more humane, more competitive, and ultimately more powerful. Getting to that point, however, will strain the social and political fabric of the Federal Republic to a degree the country has never experienced.[1]

A reliance on beneficial multilateral arrangements has seen Germany utilise methods and channels that reflect the complex interdependence of a trading state. Its national interests have in the main been defined and effectively addressed through the framework of EU institutions which gave positive impetus to integration. The political levers, the perceptions, and gains or costs to parties or public are, however, local and national. A more visible international profile and high financial commitments confronted preoccupation with domestic concerns like taxes, solidarity pacts, unemployment, infrastructure, refugees and asylum seekers. On the eve of the 1996 IGC

---

1   Gary L. Geipel "The Nature and Limits of German Power" in *Germany in a New Era* Ed. Gary L. Geipel (Indianapolis: Hudson Institute 1993) pp19-48, p39

commencing in Turin, the first of the big 'ifs' that Geipel mentions above presented a scenario of escalating consternation as unemployment continued to rise beyond the post-war record reached in December 1995. The country struggled to stop job losses, meet stringent EMU criteria, and wind back its welfare apparatus (and four decades of associated mentality). Additionally, and regardless of factual inaccuracies, the presence of foreigners was connected to excessive and misdirected welfare spending and to unemployment.[2] Response (or non-response) to exigencies indicates that internal demands will be upheld before the preferences, and even at the expense, of other governments or populations. There are three main claims here:

i)Whether Germany remains a sovereign state for the foreseeable future (as is likely) or not, German *power*, or the capacity for influence, will not disappear into a supranational vacuum. Should transposition to a European configuration occur, the German political system is much more conducive than other major states. Elizabeth Pond has commented that 'a de-nationalized and decentralized Federal Republic brings far better preconditions for the new era of a supra-national Europe of the 1990s than does France or Britain, not to speak of the Soviet Union.'[3] This putative de-nationalized entity may be so in form, but not in substance. Partly because of their own uncertainties about Europe and partly because of the positions of other EU members the electorate remains a national political community. And between proposed subsidiarity and a European government—or the shifting of authority both down and up—there is no indication of when the (national) state will be replaced as the fulcrum of power even if either, or both, of these other forms of political authority reach fruition.

(ii)An enduring healthy German economy is vital for European prosperity. If achieved it means a Germany more powerful than ever before. On the other hand a Germany that struggles for buoyancy will determine a (depressed)

---

2   Several studies have shown that immigrants contributed more to the German economy than they received in publicly funded support. One calculates that without foreign workers Germany would have had 60,000 more unemployed in 1992. 'All in all, foreign residents pay about 25 billion DM more into the public purse each year than they receive in benefits'. *Ausländer und die deutsche Wirtschaft* Dokumentation n339 (Bonn: Bundesministerium für Wirtschaft 1994)

3   Elizabeth Pond "Aufbruch mit neuer Identität: Deutschland ist für das postnationale Europa gut vorbereitet" *Die Zeit* 3-8-90 in Renata Fritsch-Bournazel *Europe and German Unification* (New York: Berg 1992)p155; Cf. Ole Wæver "Three Competing Europes" *International Affairs* v66 n3 1990 pp477-493

economic and political climate for the rest of Europe.[4] Beginning with EMU and extending some way towards political union, further integration will mean German criteria has been met. If maladies worsen or other states do not meet the set guidelines, European unification will be postponed and perhaps cancelled. The national state comes first—because it has to.[5] As German unemployment rates surged upwards genuine panic was felt and unprecedented urgency convoked a *Bundnis für Arbeit*.[6] While avoiding further tax rises, and amidst continued talk about lowering them, a 50 point action plan involving around $US46billion (DM70bill) in public spending cuts was going to add up to four million jobs.[7] These exceptional pressures to assist job creation, encourage private economic interest, continue reconstruction in the east, and address expansive social demands coincided with the German model itself being 'reconsidered'.[8]

iii)A sufficient consensus within the German polity ensured that given its magnitude the initial stage of internal political-legal reunification was completed speedily and without wholesale dissent. Internal equilibrium requires effective party response to popular desires for meaningful political expression. Sustaining cohesive interdependence with the rest of the EU means delivery of policy outcomes that satisfy German voters. For the public and organized forces alike, if political authority is to be merged in the EU, Germans must have proportionate influence. Characteristics of élite direction

---

4   For excellent contributions on economic issues see *United Germany and the New Europe* Ed. Heinz D. Kurz (Aldershot: Edward Elgar 1993); and *United Germany: The First Five Years: Performance and Policy Issues* Eds. Robert Corker et.al. (Washington: IMF 1995). For other analyses on German and European political economy see Michael Kreile "The Political Economy of the New Germany" and Wolfgang H. Reinicke "Toward a New European Political Economy" in *The New Germany and the New Europe* Ed. Paul B. Stares (Washington: Brookings Institute 1992) pp55-92 & pp177-217

5   Cf. Peter Neckermann "What went wrong in Germany after the Unification?" *East European Quarterly* v26 January 1993 pp447-469 [Reunification] 'has to succeed because Europe as a whole cannot afford a Germany preoccupied with itself...unification must become a success story if it is not to undermine the larger project of European political unification'. Here p464

6   See *Deutschland Magazine* n2 April 1996 pp12-20 including the interview with Klaus Zwickel

7   Cf. "Katalog der Grausamkeiten" & "Runter mit den Steuern"*Der Spiegel* n5 29-1-96 p22-28

8   Hans-Georg Betz "The German Model Reconsidered" *German Studies Review* v19 n2 May 1996 pp303-320; Kohl makes regular appeals to broaden responsibility for fixing ills beyond the state. Ongoing difficulties would eventually be suffered by all and had to be 'communally mastered'. "Die Herausforderungen des Wandels gemeinsam meistern" *Bulletin* 29-10-96

and 'permissive consensus' identified by earlier studies are not as predictable.[9] The Kohl government has persisted with its conception that making European unification irreversible is Germany's national interest. Concurrently, policy on issues ranging from interest rates, the former Yugoslavia, EMU criteria, altering European budgetary and voting arrangements, subsidiarity, and democratising of European institutions, placed domestic opinion before external preference. A core of agreement within the trend to fragmentation and reorganization of political forces suggests that where imperatives clash German deference to other states is over. Details will differ and consensus faces many challenges but in the foreseeable future this is where it will be reconstituted.[10]

Domestic Policy-Foreign Policy and the Public: Attitudes to European Integration

Almond and Verba's famous 1963 study depicted the Germans as 'depoliticized'[11] and, after a preceding generation had been its principal stimulus, for most of the period between 1949-1989 the German public were, in a curious sense, the forgotten factor in European integration. All governments endeavour to conduct foreign policy while limiting public interference but any assumptions that post-war German foreign and domestic policy were separate realms, hermetically sealed off from influencing each other are misconceived. In their domestic policy analysis Bulmer and Paterson noted that 'national policy-making is not dominated by cohesive governments in the manner that intergovernmentalists seem to think' and that 'constitutional and electoral reasons' may constrain or otherwise influence executives.[12] They recognised that the 'externalisation' of domestic structures is as important to the study of foreign economic policies as the 'internalisation' of international relations. This can be extended to include a broad range of German foreign policy which has connections to domestic policy both closer entwined and subject to greater scrutiny than probably any other state. In previous decades the domestic covenant on 'Europe' was a profound influence on German foreign policy, or lack of it. While the European and German polities are

---

9 Simon Bulmer & William Paterson *The Federal Republic of Germany and the European Community* (London: Allen & Unwin 1987) p122
10 Cf. Michael Mertes "Germany's Social and Political Culture: Change Through Consensus?" *Dædelus* v123 n1 1994 pp1-32
11 Gabriel Almond & Sidney Verba *The Civic Culture* (Princeton: Princeton University Press 1963)
12 Bulmer and Paterson *Federal Republic* pp16-17

distinct, if German domestic and foreign policy were 'kept apart'[13] it was in functional terms—a surface separation. The illusion was maintained because the ongoing project had a strong negative component, that is, one of avoidance. The paternalism of German political leaders, exemplified by Adenauer and continued by Kohl, reiterated the 'culture of reticence', a discourse that oscillated between a secondary act on the international stage and limited parameters domestically.

Although an 'erosion at the edges of the West German consensus on the desirability of European integration', had been underway for some time, serious dissent remained beyond the horizon. The public was largely impassive even though by the early 1980s only 5% of West Germans thought their country pushed its interests more than others while 78% thought Federal Republic had done most for the EC. Parties and institutions harmonised in managing a course that revealed a 'contradiction...between communautaire rhetoric and considerable caution in concrete steps', yet accepted proposals like the Genscher-Colombo 'European Act' because they corresponded 'precisely to a public opinion which, like the British, is against financial sacrifices but, unlike the British, is in favour of rhetorical declarations'.[14] In 1990, one American commentator predicted that '"special" historical motivations may no longer serve to extract disproportionate contributions from German taxpayers'.[15] Another foresaw a Germany 'more volatile in its domestic politics' linked directly or indirectly with potential alternatives to what its western EC partners had come to expect of German foreign policy.[16] Favourable 'rhetorical declarations' now find less public resonance and the post-Maastricht downturn in support has similarities to the 'Euro-sclerosis' phase, despite some grand initiatives not present in the earlier period. While the European institutions remain the Kohl government's preferred agencies for advancing German interests internationally, the volume of domestic rumblings about the value of the EU to Germany increases. In a late 1990 poll 71% of

13   K. Michael Prince "Germany, Europe and the Dilemma of Democratic Legitimation" *Aussenpolitik* v46 n1 1995 pp3-13

14   Survey results compiled by Elisabeth Noelle-Neumann showed 32% of West Germans giving a high priority to integration in 1982 compared to 53% in 1979. 35% were in favour of a single currency in 1977, down from 52% in 1970. At the time the 'subject of Europe has not held any potential of risk...it has had no partisan colours.' Bulmer & Paterson *Federal Republic...* pp116-118. See Mertes "Germany's Social and Political Culture" p7 for a register of some prevalent terms of German political rhetoric

15   Frederick S.Wyle "Europe 1990, the U.S., the U.S.S.R., Germany and all that—on Letting the Log of History Drift rather than Trying to Shove it" in *Auf der Suche nach der Gestalt Europas* Eds. Jochen Thies & Gunther van Well (Bonn: Verlag fur Internationale Politik 1990) pp163-170

16   Gregory F. Treverton "Forces and Legacies Shaping a New Germany" in *Germany in a New Era...* pp61-78

Germans were in favour of a European federal state, for which 40% wanted a German political leader and another 40% had no particular preference.[17] By mid-1993 only 18% of west Germans and 12% in the east saw the Union as a net benefit. Prominent figures openly stated that the EC/EU had 'for too long taken advantage of German multilateralism'.[18] *Eurobarometer* polls show a steady convergence between those favouring EU membership and those considering it a 'bad thing'. In 1990 73% were positive and 8% negative. In 1994 the figures were 50% and 12% respectively. Asked whether Germany 'benefited from EU membership' the convergence was much tighter. From 61% positive versus 20% negative in 1990 to 41% and 38% in 1994.[19] Eighty per cent of another poll in that year considered that Germany should be firmly in the EU but should 'speak up more vigorously...for its own interests'.[20] In the eastern *Länder*, viewing the EU as a 'good thing' fell from 87% in 1990 to 45% in 1994.[21]

Like other peoples Germans do not want political voice and choice gained domestically closed off at the European level. A greater, though cautious, readiness to empower the European Parliament rests on not losing influence over their daily lives, future opportunities and security through European governance and, on balance, gaining from it. While Germans are in favour of democratising the EU and of referendums on integration, they are strongly against the introduction of a European citizenship.[22] As is frequently pointed out—and argued as a positive reason for Germany's EU membership—the balance sheet of trade benefits measured against EU contributions was consistently favourable. The argument carries a veiled implication that if the new Germany does not continue a high contributions-low receipts arrangement its EU markets will reduce dramatically, which in

---

17   *Süddeutsche Zeitung* 4-1-91 quoted in Fritsch-Bournazel *Europe and German Unification* p227

18   Philip H.Gordon "The Normalization of German Foreign Policy" *Orbis* v38 n2 1994 pp225-242 See p235

19   *Eurobarometer* n41 July 1994 pp14-15

20   *The Economist* 4-6-94 p47; Cf. *Financial Times* 5-12-94 pp1-2

21   "Abschied von Europa" *Die Woche* 30-6-95 p19. For comprehensive surveys and analyses on German attitudes to European integration before and after the introduction of the internal market see Hans Rattinger "Einstellungen zur europäischen Integration in der Bundesrepublik vor der Schaffung des Binnenmarktes" DFG-Projekt n2 Febuary 1993, and "Einstellungen zur Europäischen Union in Deutschland: Strukturen und Determinanten" DFG-Projekt n8 April 1995 (Bamberg: Lehrstuhl für Politikwissenschaft II, Universität Bamberg)

22   See Rattinger "Einstellungen zur Europäischen Union in Deutschland: Strukturen und Determinanten"

turn implies political intervention. Everyone wants western European markets retained yet for the average German the tangible advantages of paying for a free-trade zone Europe, which already exists, or an extensive political union in order to preserve it, are shrinking. Often overlooked is the 'lack of correspondence between the initial beneficiary (the private sector) and ultimate donor (the government)', or taxpayer.[23] Germany's net transfers to other EU states are 70% of the total or almost DM20 billion. This is four times greater than the UK at around DM4.8 billion and over six times greater than France at DM2.9 billion, when German per capita income has reduced *vis-à-vis* these states.[24] In a context of total national budgets the percentages may be small yet several billions of Marks, Pounds or Francs are hardly inconsequential, especially in the current climate.[25]

Table 4.1   Contributions to the EC Budget: Germany, France, Italy and U.K. 1991-1995

EC Budget	1991		1992		1993		1994		1995	
	Ecu bn.	%	Ecu bn. %		Ecu bn.	%	Ecu bn.	%	Ecu bn.	%
Germany	15.3	29.1	17.0	30.2	19.0	29.8	21.1	30.4	22.0	30.7
France	10.6	20.1	10.5	18.7	11.5	18.0	13.4	19.3	13.2	18.4
Italy	8.7	16.5	8.2	14.7	10.2	16.0	9.8	14.2	9.2	12.9
U.K.	4.7	9.0	6.7	11.9	7.6	11.9	8.1	11.6	10.6	14.8

A year before the late 1995 rise in unemployment, CDU foreign policy spokesman Karl Lamers expressed fears about the European resolve of the German population. The problem was not the alternative, but that people thought there was an alternative. 'The danger I see' said Lamers, 'is that Germans will say "Well, we are in a very comfortable situation, why should we work on continued European integration?" They don't have the vision to

---

23   Lily Gardner Feldman "Germany and the EC: Realism and Responsibility" *Annals of the American Academy of Political Science* January 1994 pp25-43 See fn16

24   See Gerd Langguth "Time for a New Vision" *German Comments* n42 April 1996 pp43-56; "Spoiling Shares" *The Economist* 17-6-95 pp56-57; *The Community Budget: The Facts in Figures* SEC(94) 1100 - EN (Brussels: CEC 1994) *1995 figures estimates

25   The comparison of budget contributions here does not indicate the extent of disparity because German receipts are, relative to payments, much less than the others. There is also more than money at issue, namely how the *acquis communautaire* principle behind this works in practice and for whom

see the real interests of Germany, they become egoistic, selfish.'[26] It should be no surprise that these 'real interests' of Germany are not abundantly clear to the public. Not only because obfuscation remains after the shibboleths of mutual assurance and goodwill, but because interests in any one area are so enmeshed with those from a range of other fields, each subject to domestic and international bargaining and *quids pro quo*. German and European interests are not necessarily, without a resculpting by political-diplomatic process, the same. Confusion over 'which Germany in which Europe?' has resulted in a what could be termed a *Europaverdrossenheit.*[27] 'Europe' is a widening hole of ambiguity regarding its future democratisation, common policies in areas of 'hard' sovereignty, and funding of an array of expensive projects. Many Germans regard it 'eine Frage ohne Ende' with the goal and necessity inadequately explained.[28] In straightforward fashion Hans-Peter Schwarz asserts that domestic factors and the international environment mean 'Germany will have to stop imagining that its interests can be "European"; it will have no choice but to recognize that it has national interests and to define them as such'.[29] Several contributors to a recent volume note these tensions. One points out, 'Kohl's EU treaties faced more fire from CDU nationalists and the CSU's Stoiber than the SPD (on both policies he even had to face court challenges raised by dissidents in his own coalition)'. For another, 'CDU/CSU leaders continuously tried to cater to nationalists by emphasizing the priority of national interests, at times in contradiction to the government's official European policy.'[30]

These dynamics are affecting what 'official European policy' will mean in practice and, if the EU has great influence on German fortunes, it must be assumed that German problems are in part caused by the EU. At the same time distinctions between the mutual influences of Europe and German

26 Christian Tyler "A boy who was bitten by the Eurobug" *Financial Times* 3/4-12-94 pxxiv

27 Hans-Wolfgang Platzer & Walter Ruhland *Welches Deutschland in welchem Europa?: Demoskopische Analysen, politische Perspectiven, gesellshaftliche Kontroversen* (Bonn: Dietz Nachfolger 1994)

28 Public interviews in Germany, August/September 1996. Cf. Elisabeth Noelle-Neumann "Europa hinter einem Schleier" *Frankfurter Allgemeine Zeitung* 27-9-95 p11

29 Hans-Peter Schwarz "Germany's National and European Interests" *Dædelus* v123 n2 1994 pp81-105

30 Clay Clemens "Second Wind or Last Gasp: Helmut Kohl's CDU/CSU and the Elections of 1994" & Michael Minkenberg "What's Left of the Right?: The New Right and the Superwahljahr 1994 in Perspective" in *Germany's New Politics: Parties and Issues in the 1990s* Eds. David Conradt, Gerald R. Kleinfeld, George K. Rosomer, Christian Søe (Providence: Berghahn 1995) pp131-148, p137 & pp255-271, p265

politics, economy and society; and the discrete qualities of the German polity and a 'European polity', are made more and not less apparent. Whoever wishes a share of political power in Germany must respond favourably to internal forces, actuated or supported in some critical instances by intellectual and media opinion.[31] The conjuncture has moved towards Germany determining the continent's future by political, as well as largely pre-existing economic means. Lack of further integration will result in a fragmenting of the German party system and an inevitably more national and less western European orientation. Germans had no equivalent sovereignty to that guarded and even glorified in France and the UK. It is these two 'much more nationalistic' partners who 'still face the painful loss of narrow patriotism as the European community assumes more authority'. As the fallout after Maastricht impressed, patriotism may be narrow, but it can also run deep. And while the 'social glue' of the Germans has long 'passed beyond heroic chauvinism to the more humdrum—but safer—cohesion of prosperity and national legitimacy',[32] these certitudes may no longer be assured by 'Europe'. If 'for the Germans, two deep historical chasms' really are 'reopening', one being 'German hegemony over Europe' and the other 'dictatorship over Germany', a choice may be unavoidable. The 'tendency of renationalization' has indeed encouraged 'those forces in Germany who long for "real national independence"...to blow the national horn resoundingly'.[33] For the centrist forces there would be no abandonment of Europe, rather the opposite, more attempts to speed up integration. Yet it cannot be integration on terms that German voters reject.[34] Government desires to transpose initiatives and policies to a European scale meet resistance and confrontation with external and now internal perspectives while anxiety to make European unity irreversible grows.

---

31   Peter Glotz offers an interesting treatment of the trend away from 'Europe'."Die Umfaller" *Die Woche* 23-2-96 p17

32   Elizabeth Pond "Germany in the New Europe" *Foreign Affairs* v71 n2 1992 pp114-130

33   Barthold Witte "Two Catastrophes, Two Causes, and How the Germans Dealt with them" *Dædelus* v123 n2 1994 pp235-249

34   Klaus Kinkel "Deutschland in Europa: Zu den Zielen der deutschen Präsidentschaft in der Europäischen Union" *Europa-Archiv* Folge 12/1994 pp335-342; Roman Herzog "Warum Europa?" *Bulletin* 19-11-96

A State by any other Name: 'Stable', 'Normal', 'Pivotal'

Although the old Federal Republic had been characterised as a 'stable state',[35] for most Germans it was territorially, and in a more complex psychological sense, incomplete. In international legal terms Germany is now no less a state than the U.K. or France.[36] The configuration of its parts is different but the sum is the same, or actually greater in combined weight of resources. Other European states did not sign the Treaty on European Union with several regional entities called the *Länder*. Although many challenges require the availability, if not necessarily the deployment, of considerable centralized powers, an apparent weakness of the national state has been transmitted. A certain mystification of the Federal Republic's status and its capabilities occurred for two closely entwined reasons.

Firstly to provide continuing reassurance that there could never be another episode of belligerence propelled by the integrative and productive capacities of a centralized nation-state. Under American tutelage federalism was intended to prevent the *actual* centralization of powers as had occurred during the Third Reich. Then came the fostering of a *perception* that it (centralization of political power) *could not* occur. Sustaining such a perception about Germany's scarcity of, or aversion to conventional state power was an integral component of good international relations. An aligned motivation also resulted from a belief that the necessity for extensive co-operation between existing states extends to making a higher level of political authority indispensable. Consequently states dissolve. The Kohl government's advocacy of European political union entails merging, or 'pooling' sovereignty into a federation, more or less replicating the *Bund-Länder* relation. Powers apparently surrendered to Europe are transferred to forums or institutions from which German representatives can pursue German interests, sometimes in agreement with others and sometimes not, but without the negative connotations of state power. Peter Glotz has stripped away the 'Eurocratic etiquette' that 'turns this into a taboo subject':

> everyone knows that after six or eight years of struggling to integrate its Eastern states, united Germany will once again reclaim its central position as the strongest economic power in Europe. Either it will have ceased to be a separate historical figure, a "state" measuring up to other "states", because it will have become integrated, or it will become the supreme regional power in Europe—which, given the German sense of

35   *The West German Model: Perspectives on a Stable State* Eds. Gordon Smith & William Paterson (London: Frank Cass 1981)
36   Dieter Blumenwitz *This is Germany: Germany's Legal Status after Unification* (Bonn: Kulturstiftung der Deutschen Vertriebenen 1994)

guilt, will probably lead a new and endless round of familiar confrontations (albeit in different forms) given even the best intentions of all involved (and that is hardly to be expected).[37]

Statements by Kohl and others connected with the CDU have been inconsistent on whether the nation-state should or will continue as a primary political actor or not. CDU politicians speak of both the 'empty shell' of the nation-state, to be necessarily subsumed into a federal Europe, *and* of its continued relevance. During the process of German reunification Kohl expressed 'Germany continues to grow together. State unity has moved closer. What has to be done now is to rapidly complete it.'[38] Later, at a 1994 convention he submitted the formulation 'I do not want an authoritarian state, I want a state with authority'.[39] Under the Kohl government there is maintenance of strong central influence. Through an elected executive and independent organs the federal state manages and arbitrates, calibrates the economy, negotiated and oversees the accession and integration of the east, imposes and collects various taxes and charges, controls perceived threats to the constitutional order and conducts a foreign policy growing in import. Christoph Böhr, *Fraktionschef* in Rheinland-Pfalz, is among those CDU figures acknowledging a continuance and vitality of the nation-state in Europe, arguing that these political units were 'recalled into European history' by the changes wrought in 1989-90. He claims that 'National statehood is an indispensable and necessary prerequisite for the more far-reaching second step: the extension of a cooperative and federal structure. It is thus the self-sustainable integration process, since they discernibly serve the interests of each individual national actor.'[40]

Ultimately, however, the CDU goal, which Bohr reiterates above, is a European federalism.[41] One that may advance the interests of all, but potentially impinges on or restricts one or more individual components. The configuration of German political institutions and representation exhibits a

37   Peter Glotz "Eastern European Reform and West European Integration" in *Toward a Global Civil Society* Ed. Michael Walzer (Providence: Berghahn 1995) pp211-222, p213

38   Helmut Kohl, Speech on the signing of the GEMSU Treaty 18-5-90 *Europa Archiv* n13-14 1990 D323-327 quoted in Manfred Görtemaker *Unifying Germany 1989-1990* (Houndmills: MacMillan 1994) p153

39   Clay Clemens "Second Wind or Last Gasp" p139

40   Christoph Böhr "At the End of the Post-War Order in Europe: In Search of a New Coherence of Interests and Responsibilities" *Aussenpolitik* v46 n2 1995 pp115-125; Karl-Rudolf Korte *Nation und National Staat: Bausteine einer europäischen Identität* (Melle: Knoth Verlag 1993)

41   *Wir sichern Deutschlands Zukunft: Regierungsprogramm von CDU und CSU* (Bonn: CDU Bundesgeschäftstelle 1994) A federal united Europe appears after the five most important internal goals

diffraction-contraction pattern whereby its decentralised state structure does not preclude coherence of policy choices. German federalism itself does not, for instance, prevent realisation of nationally agreed, as well as individual party or *Land* objectives, in a European system. In fact, there is a 'structural imperative' of co-operation between Federation and the *Länder* for either to function with high efficiency.[42] Greater powers in European policy formation and decision accrued by the *Länder* were arrived at through negotiation with the Federal government. Transposition of this framework to a European level is, by and large, nationally agreed. As constituent parts of a larger entity the *Länder* cannot retain *complete* political autonomy, either in the currently existing FRG or a future European structure. Subsidiarity then inverts itself. As one writer puts it 'regionalisation is more likely to reinforce than to enfeeble the nation-state.'

> Germany has been a full-blown federation for almost fifty years, yet the existence of its powerful Länder governments has in no way diminished its economic or political clout. The Basic Law may sometimes grant the Länder the last word, but Bonn is still able to decide on a policy and pursue it consistently...and no one seriously believes that were the Chancellor and his Länder to have their way and see European political integration achieved, Germany would have emasculated itself and would no longer be able to exercise influence proportionate to its size and wealth.[43]

Some *Länder* politicians contend that the Federal Republic's policies regarding the EC/EU had been, or imminently would be, transferred from the realm of foreign policy to 'European domestic policy'.[44] The *Länder* influence German foreign policy in the Council of Ministers but do not conduct their own, nor run separate monetary policies, nor possess regional defence forces. The *Bundesregierung* is pressured like other national governments. In many instances the *Länder* must convince the federal government that their claims have sufficient national importance. There is unavoidable federal government involvement in regional policy formulation, despite aversions among some

---

42   William E. Paterson & David Southern *Governing Germany* Second Edition (Oxford: Blackwell 1992) p222. See the speeches by Johannes Rau and Edmund Stoiber, the outgoing and incoming presidents of the Bundesrat, and Friedrich Bohl, chief of Kohl's chancellery. "Der Föderalismus als Ordnungsprinzip der Freheit" *Bulletin* 13-11-95

43   Alistair Bruton *A Revolution in Progress: Western Europe Since 1989* (London: Little, Brown & Co. 1996) p124

44   Andrew Scott, John Peterson & David Millar "Subsidiarity: A 'Europe of the Regions' v. the British Constitution?" *Journal of Common Market Studies* v30 n1 March 1994 pp47-67. See p56

eastern *Länder* to engage in centre-periphery bargaining in the 'traditional' West German manner, and which may have actually strengthened the position of the central government.[45] This medium then becomes the agent for expressing interests specific to a *Land* and significant enough to the next tier.[46]

In the event of a 'Europe of the Regions' based on the 'subsidiarity principle' appearing, Germany's regional units would have representation at the European level by power devolved and then directed up similar to the practice exercised through the Bundesrat.[47] German regions are already part of a larger 'unit of power', and one much more cohesive than the EU. Even if German interests actually are or are thought to be better served by presentation as regional, neighbours do not necessarily see it this way. Intra-German struggles for power are exceeded by perceptions that sixteen German *Länder* add up to one large Germany. Like the United States of America, they are components of a federation that comprises a higher political authority and a common political culture.[48] The *Länder* have internal independence and additional securities provided by a federal state, one which negotiated German reunification and (via the taxpayer) is expected to provide surety for the costs. It has raised or instituted new taxes, including for the *Länder*, as essential fiscal measures. Obversely, over 80% of regional income flows from taxes regulated by the centre.[49]

There are regular denials that more European integration means a requisite or imminent centralization of power. German reunification apparently boosted the prospects of subsidiarity yet the word 'reunification' is antithetical

---

45   Charlie Jeffrey "Failing the Challenge of Unification? The Länder and German Federalism in the 1990s" in *Contemporary Political Studies* (Political Studies Association of Great Britain) v2 Eds P.Dunleavy & J.Stanyer pp765-779; Charlie Jeffrey "The Non-Reform of the German Federal System after Unification" *West European Politics* v18 n2 1995 pp252-272

46   Charlie Jeffrey & John Yates "Unification and Maastricht: The Response of the Länder Governments" *German Politics* v1 n3 1992 pp58-81; Uwe Leonardy "Federation and Länder in German Foreign Relations: Power-sharing in Treaty-Making and European Affairs" *German Politics* v1 n3 1992 pp119-135; Arthur B. Gunlicks "German Federalism after Unification: The Legal/Constitutional Response" *Publius* v24 Spring 1994 pp81-98

47   Franz H.U. Borkenhagen "Regions in Europe" *Aussenpolitik* v44 n2 1994 pp182-188

48   Fritz W. Scharpf "Europäisches Demokratiedefizit und deutscher Föderalismus" *Staatswissenschaft und Staatspraxis* v3 n3 1992 pp293-306

49   In early 1996 an 'unholy alliance' of cross-party *Länder* chiefs attempted to prevent changes in the federally enforced tax system. The Bonn finance ministry planned to reduce the 'solidarity pact' charge, introduced as part of the reunification funding package, from 7.5% to 5.5% of incomes. The shortfall was to be made up through diverting value added tax receipts away from the *Länder* treasuries for prioritised national projects. See Tony Paterson "Tax rebels forge unholy alliance to fight Bonn" *The European* 15-2-96 p4

to it. Subsequent plans for the merging of Berlin and Brandenburg (and possibly in other instances) may serve a 'rationalisation' policy yet also head in the direction of a disavowed centralization. Closer relations with the neighbouring Polish regions were intensified to counter such a development, or more specifically any apprehension that may arise. Greater foreign policy scope then assisted an arrangement between two German regions untenable even two or three years earlier.[50] Despite the formation of a *Bürgerbund* opposing the move, more citizens of both *Länder* favoured the merger in early 1996: 51% approving versus 23% against in Berlin, and 42% in favour with 31% against in Brandenburg. The official view argued that a bigger state carried more influence and brought greater efficiency. A subsequently rejected referendum was also something of a test case of whether Germans approve of further fusion of political units in Germany (and might also on a European scale).[51] Until then the Europeanization of relations between the *Länd* governments and with the centre had 'been achieved without sacrificing or even seriously calling into question, central features of national governance'. Systemic compatibility between *Land*, Federal and European levels was not challenged by adjustments in internal German relations but does not equate with acceptance of the detail in actual EU operation.[52] A former chairman of the *Länder* European Ministers Conference has written of common positions opposing discrimination against the German language, excessive German contributions and a general lack of proportionate influence.[53] So while the influence of Europe 'has implied adaptive reactions which reinforce established characteristics of the German intergovernmental system',[54] if European integration does deepen, this reinforcement also implies a capacity and even inclination towards the reverse.

---

50   Rudolf von Thadden "Kein Preußen und kein Gloria" *Die Zeit* 7-4-95 p1; Stephen Kinzer "Berlin and Brandenburg Are to Merge" *International Herald Tribune* 28-4-95 p1

51   *Deutsche Welle* (Television News) 2-4-96

52   Klaus H. Goetz "National Governance and European Integration: Intergovernmental Relations in Germany" *Journal of Common Market Studies* v33 n1 1995 pp91-116

53   Erwin Huber "Der diplomatische Nebel muß gelichtet werden" *Frankfurter Allgemeine Zeitung* 27-7-95 p8

54   Goetz "National Governance and European Integration. "

New Challenges for Corporatism and Pluralism

While on one hand 'openness' was a purposeful objective, ambiguity was another theme employed to characterise the complex system of political relations that comprised the German polity. In the old *Bundesrepublik* pluralism and corporatism co-existed.[55] Pluralism remains evidenced by regional fiefdoms, the constitution and its lattice of checks and balances, and the changing party system. Within the federal bureaucracy an 'institutional pluralism' grants considerable autonomy for individual ministries on formulating European policy,[56] although primary responsibility is divided between the Foreign and Economics Ministries. The latter acts as an agent for German industry, or as a sectorized foreign office, at the European level.[57] These extensively autonomous actors may often reach agreement, but also may not.[58] The voluntary quality of pluralist societies is not eroded, rather, fragmentation of opinion on what constitutes Germany's principal interests in a European context was, up to the early 1990s, overshadowed by centripetal forces. An outwardly affirmative posture endured with the effect of operating as, or replacing, overt institutionalised centralisation.[59] Some projections have asserted that this centripetal quality would continue, even if the next German consensus will be different. An extensive European Commission backed

55   Cf. Kenneth Dyson "The Ambiguous Politics of Western Germany: Politicization in a 'State' Society" *European Journal of Political Research* v7 1979 pp375-396; *Organising Interests in Western Europe: Pluralism, Corporatism and the Transformation of Politics* Ed. Suzanne Berger (Cambridge: Cambridge University Press 1981); David P. Conradt *The German Polity* Third Edition (New York: Longman 1986); Gordon Smith *Politics in Western Europe* Fifth Edition (Aldershot: Dartmouth 1989); Jeffrey J. Anderson *Pluralism, Corporatism, and Economic Crisis* (Cambridge: Cambridge University Press 1992)

56   Bulmer & Paterson *Federal Republic* p17; Carl Cavanagh Hodge "The Federal Republic and the Future of Europe: A Reassessment" *German Politics* v1 n2 1992 pp223-238

57   William E. Paterson & David Southern *Governing Germany* Second Edition (Oxford: Blackwell 1992) p230

58   See Hans Keman & Paul Pennings "Managing Political and Societal Conflict in Democracies: Do Consensus and Corporatism Matter?" and Markus M. L. Crepaz & Arend Lijphart "Linking and Integrating Corporatism and Consensus Democracy: Theory, Concepts and Evidence" *British Journal of Political Science* v25 p2 1995 pp271-281 & pp281-288

59   Eberhard Schoof *EG-Ausschuss: Der Deutsche Bundestag und die Europäische Gemeinschaft* (Deutscher Bundestag: Bonn 1994) pp8-10; *Der Deutsche Bundestag und Europa* Ed. Renate Hellwig (Aktuell: München 1993) especially chapter two

study predicted a 'gradual convergence of all major political forces towards a middle-of-the road pragmatism'.[60]

Michael Huelshoff describes a psuedo-pluralism overruled by corporatist features. He states that 'one should not assume that the Germans begin each policy debate with the goal of enhancing European integration. Regardless

> the broad public support for regional integration in Germany...suggests the hypothesis that in most cases the German domestic game will result in a consensus favoring regional cooperation, although on terms consistent with German ideology and interests. In sum, the Germans are "good Europeans" in part because the state encourages cooperative decision-making that reduces the likelihood of the 'state capture' by narrow interests (more likely in pluralist domestic orders), and increases the number of mechanisms to punish defection.[61]

The critical factors here are 'German ideology and interests'. In the European context German-style corporatism contrasted with Britain and delivered much broader economic success. A capacity to reach compromise between industry and labour while minimising strikes or street violence also differed to France. A rethink and assimilation of features from 'Anglo-American' models is underway as traditional formulae are under stress. Germany's muscular but often cumbersome big business sector and a still powerful, if declining, assemblage of unions are reforming themselves and their roles as 'social partners'.[62] Still the 'virtues of *Ordnungspolitik*'[63] have not been jettisoned and evolution towards a 'new corporatism' was indicated by a round of talks in January 1996 under the banner of 'Alliance for Jobs and Germany's Future as an Industrial Location'. Following agreement between the government and the IG Metall union (from whom the SPD borrowed for their own 'ten-point plan' on unemployment), other cooperative development activities between government and non-government organizations were

60   *The European Challenges Post-1992: Shaping Factors, Shaping Actors* Eds. Alexis Jaquemin & David Wright (Aldershot: Edward Elgar 1993) See Chapter 9, p234 & pp248-9
61   Michael G. Huelshoff "Germany and European Integration: Understanding the Relationship" in *From Bundesrepublik to Deutschland: German Politics After Unification* Eds. Michael G. Huelshoff, Andrei Markovits & Simon Reich (Ann Arbor: University of Michigan Press 1993) pp301-320 Here p309
62   Rainer Hank "Signs of Erosion in the Corporative State" *German Comments* v43 July 1996 pp43-50
63   Kurt J. Lauk "Germany at the Crossroads: On the Efficiency of the German Economy" *Dædelus* v123 n1 1994 pp57-83

recommended for Germany and its European partners, as something to be anchored in the consciousness of all.[64]

Impressing this industrial culture implied that the 'state' was now there to build a European economy containing less 'state'—except when a German government determined otherwise. This will be in response to 'German society', which as Wolfgang Streeck writes, 'treats the internal life of an enterprise as a matter of public interest and subjects it to public intervention and regulation. Firms in Germany are in this way part of a politically constructed and legitimated public order...of accountable mechanisms of governance, foremost amongst them an "enabling" democratic state'.[65] With the SPD demanding priority for a national jobs strategy and the government implementing one neither centre-right nor centre-left is likely to completely abandon old models, even if they disapprove of those operating elsewhere. Like the politicians, IG Metall chief Klaus Zwickel and the president of the Federation of German Industries (BDI) agreed that ultimately the 'national economy will engulf the business economy' and reducing jobs would rebound negatively on to the latter. Whatever transpires it is only within the national context that such agreements can be reached and no other state-business-labour arrangement can match German influence in the European space:

> *some* nation states will remain the crucial actors in constructing a *political* basis of consent for the macroeconomic policies of the Community, and for their own fiscal, regulatory and industrial policies. Only at the national level can effective *distributional coalitions* be built, that is, framework agreements between the major parties and social actors about the conditions for, and necessary costs of, economic success...Parties, organized labour and employers accept the need for public and private investments in education and training.[66]

As a 'restructuring' or 'rebuilding' of the welfare state was debated,[67] change to the mentality it entrenched was agreed as necessary by a broad cross-section of the polity. Most, including the SPD and industry, have taken advantage of the system when it suited. A legal provision on early retirement

64   Carl-Dieter Spranger "Konstructive staatliche und private Zusammenarbeit für Entwicklung" *Bulletin* 21-12-95

65   Wolfgang Streeck "Lean Production in the German Automobile Industry: A Test Case for Convergence Theory" in *National Diversity and Global Capitalism* Eds. Suzanne Berger & Ronald Dore (Ithaca: Cornell University Press 1996) pp138-170

66   Thompson *The Economic Emergence of a New Europe...* p198 (Emphases in original.)

67   Irwin L. Collier Jr. "Rebuilding the German Welfare State" in *Germany's New Politics: Parties and Issues in the 1990s* Eds. David Conradt, Gerald R. Kleinfeld, George K. Rosomer, Christian Søe (Providence: Berghahn 1995) pp273-293

required the state to fund a transition period with unemployment benefits until receipt of pensions began. State shouldering of this burden meant that severance costs otherwise paid by employers were lessened. In a time of dramatic job shedding it encouraged 'an unusual alliance between unions and industry in trying to preserve the system'. Maintaining such elements of the system had enormous, and rising, costs. Social security contributions were forecast to rise from 19.2% of wages in 1996 to 19.9% in 1997.[68] Fears that pensions were not guaranteed spread, exacerbated by the proposed transference from the known and trusted Deutsche Mark to an untested euro. As proposals appeared to raise the retirement age for women from 60 to 63, reduce the parity value of vocational training from up to 7 to only 3 years, and change the payment of employer contributions from monthly to fortnightly, the SPD claimed that by the end of 1996 DM10billion of a DM16billion pension reserve fixed by law would be used. Tensions grew between ministries as the government tried to cut $US7billion just to keep pension costs under 20% of personal tax contributions.

In 1990 unemployment was 6.2% in the FRG and 2.9% in the GDR. By 1994 it had risen to 8.3% in western Germany and 14.6% in the east. West German employment growth slumped from 3% in 1990 to -1.3% in 1994 while in the east it rose from -17.1 in 1991 to 0.8 1994.[69] According to the IMF so-called 'measured unemployment' did not include 'about 1 million [in 1994] who were kept off the unemployment rolls'. And 'only a small part of the German unemployment problem is cyclical in origin' with low skilled persons likely to remain almost permanently unemployed. 'The challenge is now to find, within the framework of centralized bargaining, ways in which relatively low-productivity firms can be assured a better chance of survival...and ways in which wages at the bottom of the scale can react to the excess supply of low-productivity workers.'[70]

Worsening of the economic situation to zero growth in the third quarter of 1995 was followed by unemployment rising a full percentage point in the next quarter. Germany's crisis now matched that of France. *Die Zeit* lamented that 'Today mass unemployment burdens the national economy by DM150 billion per year. The economy has long found itself in a vicious circle: Unemployment drives social costs up, higher social burden again endangers

---

68 John Schmid "Can Germany Swallow Welfare Pill?" *International Herald Tribune* 8-2-96 p1& p6

69 Hari Vittas "Introduction" in *United Germany: The First Five Years* ... pp1-8. Here pp2-3

70 Tessa van der Willigen "Unemployment, Wages and the Wage Structure" in *United Germany: The First Five Years* ... pp21-40

workplaces. We must break out of this vicious circle'.[71] The vicious circle was, of course, easier to identify than to break out of. In February 1996 national unemployment reached 11.1%, or 4,270,000 people. *Die Woche* termed it '*die grosse Job Katastrophe*'.[72] Helmut Schmidt's 'recipe against the German sickness' urged an end to political opportunism, supporting much of the government's efforts in winding back welfare costs and warning against any SPD hindering of measures that might make available more money for job creation. This brought the former SPD chancellor closer to coalition policy at the time Finance Minister Waigel was accusing the SPD of sabotaging the government's job strategy claiming they were the work-place blocking party (*Sie sind die Arbeitsplätze blokade-Partei*). Schmidt also advocated a relaxation of the Bundesbank's money-supply fetishism (*Geldmengen-Fetischismus*), a sweeping away of excessive regulations, reductions in bureaucratic positions, development and marketing of new products, and the creation of vigorous competition among universities along with a professional management structure. The task was one for the whole nation: managers, unions, the political class, 'the Chancellor at the top', in order to keep 'our workplaces, our pensions, our social state'. Schmidt ended by stating, 'our situation is serious, but it must in no way become hopeless.'[73] These developments did not faze the government from forecasting that two million new jobs could be created by 2000. This would require growth rates of at least 5%, far above optimistic predictions of 3% or a more realistic 1.5-2%. Although August 1996 figures showed a fall to 3.9 million registered unemployed the Economics Ministry cited no real improvement in 'structural problems'.[74]

Germany contains the highest number of imported, or 'alien' workers and has the lowest rate of granting citizenship among larger European states. Presumptions and principles associated with residency and citizenship status and already debated for decades then heightened in controversy as pressure for

71   Wilfred Herz "Was zählt: Jobs, Jobs, Jobs" *Die Zeit* 19-1-96 p1 'Heute belastet die Massenarbeitslosigkeit die Volkswirtschaft mit 150 Milliarden Mark im Jahr. Längst befindet sich die Wirtschaft in einen Teufelskreis: Die Arbeitslosigkeit treibt die Sozialkosten nach oben, die höheren Soziallasten wiederum bringen weitere Arbeitsplätze in Gefahr. Aus diesem Teufelskreis müssen wir ausbrechen '

72   See *Die Woche* 1-3-96 pp14-15

73   Helmut Schmidt "Rezepte gegen die deutsche Krankheit" *Die Zeit* 12-1-96 p3 'Die manager, die Gewerkschaften, die politische klasse, der Kanzler an der Spitze, wir alle müssen eine breite Überzeugungskampagne auslösen: Wir brauchen dringend modernste technik, damit wir unsere Arbeitsplätze, unsere Renten, unseren Sozialstaat erhalten können'

74   Bundesministerium für Wirtschaft "Monatsbericht September 1996" *Bulletin* 11-10-96

constitutional changes related to the entry, exit, or stay of 'foreigners' increased.[75] While conditions underpinning citizenship laws were relaxed with new provisions introduced in 1991, polls the same year revealed high percentages of the public wanted stricter administration and policing of prospective immigrants. German politicians of all parties were anxious to find a European solution to questions of political asylum and having taken in 79% of refugees to the then EC in 1992 they were compelled towards a national response. The government introduced changes to its asylum law while other states persisted in avoiding equitable burden-sharing or mechanisms which might introduce them. With sufficient SPD support, Article 16 of the Basic Law guaranteeing right of asylum was changed in July 1993.

Geipel has highlighted a susceptibility to what he claims are factually incorrect xenophobic appeals. It was 'disconcerting' to hear Schäuble urging an end to asylum law to avert a 'state and constitutional crisis' and a delusion to think that the extreme right will be squeezed out.[76] Their potential appeal among the broader public is tempered and Schäuble and supporters have some justification if reductions in right-wing inspired violence and electoral support are criterion.[77] Since the deaths and arson attacks of 1992-3 the catastrophe some feared has not transpired. There has been a sharp reduction in such incidents and political groups most closely associated have failed to attract substantial electoral support.[78] Hundreds of thousands protested in support of immigrants and against anti-foreigner sentiments yet it was also a large silent majority that brought the constitutional change about. Belief that most claimants were economic refugees (96% in one poll) has continuing public resonance as has the rejection of persons entering Germany for these reasons. Germany is no longer thought to have a special 'moral' responsibility beyond that of its European neighbours.[79]

75   Douglas B. Klusmeyer "Aliens, Immigrants, and Citizens: The Politics of Inclusion in the Federal Republic of Germany" *Dædelus* v122 n3 1993 pp81-114; Rogers Brubaker *Citizenship and Nationhood in France and Germany* (Cambridge,Ma: Harvard University Press 1992); Sperling "(Im)migration and German Security in Post-Yalta Europe"

76   Geipel "The Nature and Limits of German Power" pp38-39

77   Cf. Ruud Koopmans "Explaining the rise of racist and extreme right violence in Western Europe: Grievances or opportunities" *European Journal of Political Research* v30 September 1996 pp185-216

78   David M. Keithly "Shadows of Germany's Authoritarian Past" *Orbis* v38 n2 1994 pp207-223

79   See Barbara Marshall "German Migration Policies" in *Developments in German Politics* Eds. Gordon Smith et. al. (Durham: Duke University Press 1992) pp 247-263. The figure of 96% resulted from only one poll but such a high percentage must entail some significance. In later years these views have resonance with 'ordinary Germans' considering that many foreigners, especially recent arrivals,

The government's aim is to decrease the onus, and attention, on Germany to provide solutions to *Europe's* immigration and refugee situation. Interdependencies between European neighbours make these responsibilities those of all and implementation of a continent-wide immigration policy is a major German objective.[80] A peak of 440,000 in 1992 brought the total number of people entering Germany and claiming refugee status to around one million in three years, several times that of the other EU states combined. In 1994 127,200 and in 1995 almost 128,000 asylum seekers entered Germany.[81] More recently Kohl referred to the 400,000 refugees from the former Yugoslavia living in Germany. His statement reiterated a presumed temporary nature of their residency as applied to earlier *Gastarbeiter*: 'We assumed this obligation without hesitation but these people should return home. Children growing up here away from their home country gradually lose their roots, and that is not good'.[82] Fear of Germany becoming a battleground for inter-ethnic rivalries brought a new round of initiatives. The government moved to speed up deportation of foreigners whose demonstrations became a security risk.[83]

The Parties and Europe

In the 1980s Bulmer and Paterson noted the 'rarified level' of agreement between German parties regarding the EC. In their view the 'bureaucratisation of policy-making [was]...linked to the absence of substantive party conflict on many economic policy issues'. The party system was characterised by a 'politics of centrality' a 'dominant economic philosophy' and 'restricted

---

are not assimilating, are ungrateful, and are either taking jobs, sending money out of the country or in other ways a drain on the economy. Interview sources in Germany 1994 and 1996. Constitutional changes were supported in principle if not in each and every detail by people such as Daniel Cohn-Bendit and Joschka Fischer, as well as the CDU/CSU and FDP. Cf. Frank Kamphaus "Unsere Fremden" & Robert Leicht "Harte Zeiten" *Die Zeit* 22-9-95 p1; Bruce Anderson "No one has a right to asylum" *The Times* 8-12-95 p18; Sarah Helm "Europe to slam door on asylum-seekers" *Independent* 22-11-95

80   CDU/CSU Fraktion im Deutschen Bundestag "Mehr europäische Rechtstaatlichkeit" (CDU/CSU Pressedienst: June 1995); See also Ole Wæver, Barry Buzan, Morten Kelstrup and Pierre Lemaitre *Identity, Migration and the New Security Agenda in Europe* (London: Pinter 1993); Sperling "(Im)migration and German Security in Post-Yalta Europe"

81   *Bulletin* 11-1-96

82   "The Chancellor of Europe" *Time* 30-9-96 pp44-46; Helmut Kohl "Aussprache über den Bundeshaushalt 1997" *Bulletin* 13-9-96

83   The Kurdish PKK was prominent and death threats against Kinkel and others did not help their cause

ideological space' which rarely questioned the fundamentals of European integration. Concurrently, there was 'no clear framework of action reflecting national interests', which were blocked by 'constitutional, political and historical-psychological factors.' Mainstream parties in the Federal Republic masked what in other polities would have been quite unexceptional expression of acceptable 'national interests' *as a national interest.* Through restraint and reassurance the FRG 'achieved the arena of co-operation...needed to establish credibility and reliability' from which economic and political development could occur.[84] Commitment to Europe was then not the subject of more aggressive manifestations of parliamentary democracy that brought German domestic politics, for better or worse, closer to the other western polities. Now, as expressed by Harold James in the wake of reunification, 'a parliamentary system with conflicts, clashes and unharmonious disputes may operate as a focus for a national legitimacy centred on institutions and the constitution.'[85] Accompanying this evolution to a more adversarial system and enhanced 'national legitimacy', for Germany to become accepted as 'normal' it had to achieve beyond 'normal' results. Challenges familiar to most western liberal democracies also exceed them. Scholars explained that 'The problems of German union, asylum-rights, and the redefinition of Germany's international role in a changing world are far greater than the normal demands placed upon political systems.'[86]

In mid-1992 President Richard von Weizsäcker warned the parties against collusion for their own interests, be they financial or simply facilitating survival, and operating as an opinion poll-driven cartel. Failure to be genuinely competitive, responsive, or offer alternatives displayed a disposition to let *Parteiverdrossenheit* drift indefinitely.[87] A government unresponsive to civil society eventually imperils both state and society.[88] Weizsäcker's critique came at a time when, according to one poll, only 21% of respondents trusted

---

84   Bulmer & Paterson *Federal Republic* pp21-22

85   Harold James *A German Identity* (London: Weidenfeld and Nicholson 1989) p209; See also Catherine McArdle Kelleher "The New Germany: A Overview" in Paul B. Stares Ed. *The New Germany and the New Europe* (Washington: Brookings Institute 1992) pp11-54; *The New Germany Votes: Unification and the Creation of a New German Party System* Ed. Russell J. Dalton (Providence: Berg 1993)

86   Russell J. Dalton & Wilhelm Buerklin "The German Party System and the Future" in *The New Germany Votes...*pp233-256, p253

87   "Wo bliebt der politische Wille des Volkes?" Richard von Weizsäcker *Die Zeit* 19-6-92 pp3-4; Cf. "Die häßlichen Enkel" *Der Spiegel* n5 31-1-94 pp36-38

88   See Tom Keating "The State and International Relations" in *World Politics: Power, Interdependence & Dependence* Eds. David G. Haglund & Michael K. Hawes (Toronto: Harcourt Brace Jovanovich 1990) pp16-37 p30

the parties, corroborating the view that Germany has reached a stage of 'crisis' in the party system.[89] The trend has frequently been underlined in local elections[90] and some observers view the parties as 'die falsche Adresse für Demokratiesucher'.[91]

The second half of the 1990s is a difficult time for hard decisions on Europe. Individual parties and interparty committees (*Europa Ausschuss*) formulating collective positions are adapting to accommodate changes in cost-benefit calculations. As budget balancing travails, unemployment rates, and immigration numbers reach new levels so too does the potential for political impact. The hour of truth had arrived.[92] The 'middle-of-the-road' is indefinite and susceptible to radicalization. 'Middle of the road pragmatism' translates into responding favourably to an electorate which has become more 'national' in its demands on the parties, reflecting a condition of *Bevormundungsverdrossenheit* rather than *Politikverdrossenheit*.[93] In recent years political parties across Europe have not hidden the 'national card'. Germany is now no different. The EU must actively win German approval, by serving the German electorate well, rather than expecting an agreeable partner.[94] Now 'above all, Germany's perspective will be shaped by the EC's self-definition, which should be clarified in the preparations for the 1996 intergovernmental conference. Germans bought into an idea when they joined the EC; the idea is still valid, but it must be resold with conviction.'[95]

In the 'professional' political culture a new volatility has emerged as all parties interpreted that changes had to occur. It may have been the last year in which Europe was not a divisive electoral issue and by 1995 it had become more openly and vigorously questioned. This has its own paradoxes. Responding to social currents, a pragmatism which (still) translates into garnering the largest possible share of power, is the propellant for the fraying of party accord. As other forces cross previously sacred parameters for political advantage and augur more so in the future, Kohl insists that only his coalition can maintain stability and keep Germany on an imperative European

---

89 Erwin Scheuch & Ute Scheuch *Cliquen, Klügel und Karrieren* (Reinbek: Rowohlt 1992); Geoffrey Roberts "The German Party System in Crisis" *Parliamentary Affairs* v48 n1 January 1995 pp125-140

90 Gunter Hoffman "Tränen für die Volksparteien" *Die Zeit* 27-10-95 p4

91 Joachim Raschke "Demokratie als Ausrede" *Der Spiegel* n4 22-1-96 pp52-53

92 "Die Stunde der Wahrheit" *Die Woche* 22-3-96 p1

93 Prince "Germany, Europe and the Dilemma of Democratic Legitimation" p6. Meaning an aversion to being spoken for, or to arrogant paternalism, rather than an exasperation with politics *per se*

94 Once instance being perceptions about EU structural aid for eastern Germany as too low (Ecu13.7 billion in 1996)

95 Feldman "Germany and the EC..." p43. Cf. Ludger Kühnhardt "Maastricht II: The German Debate" *German Comments* v43 July 1996 pp58-66

course. Actual or potential leaderships are under challenge to respond to a public dubious about aspects of Germany's commitments. But only Kohl seems capable of saying '*Vaterland*' and '*Europa*' in the same breath.[96] The CDU has dominated *Westbindung* and *Europapolitik* and reaped success through presenting itself as the 'natural party of government'. Under Adenauer and later Kohl, the CDU benefited from an ability to define the political centre, or perhaps more so, what does not. Impressing itself as the *Europapartei*, the CDU has tried to engender debate on Germany-Europe relations by means of 'discussion papers', in the parliament, in the media and in other settings. Centre parties appeared reluctant to move too far from the middle ground. Kohl's parliamentary affirmation of the more radical *Kerneuropa* paper was criticised by Scharping as advocating groups of first and second class states in Europe. In London *The Times* declared the same Kohl speech as intended to portray no concern at the 'possibility of Europe becoming an election issue'.[97]

In a 1993 article David Patton wrote of 'recent dramatic fluctuations in Chancellor Kohl's reputation as a political leader' and that 'to a casual observer, Kohl appears as a highly erratic political leader' who nonetheless 'emerged in 1990 as a great statesman...[who] would never be underestimated again.' Not long after, with criticism mounting 'for failing to address in a coherent fashion the mounting problems of unification [and] bereft of high profile foreign policy opportunities, Kohl now struggles to master the ongoing conflicts over distribution, hence his current leadership crisis'.[98] Facing adversity for most of the 1991-94 period, Kohl prevailed again, underlining that it was 'almost a cliché to say he was underestimated as a political leader'.[99] As a recent biography states, Kohl loses the questionnaires and wins the elections. He does this because voters think he will represent them 'without ifs and buts' and because 'the Germans possess a marked sense for the concrete and the real'.[100] With the election won Kohl could move from domestic manager[101] to his role as a 'European' statesman, which entailed reproducing German political, economic and security interests within less certain foreign policy co-ordinates. Whatever the complaints of sameness and

96   Helmut Kohl "Patriotismus und europäische Gesinnung gehören untrennbar zusammen" *Bulletin* 21-6-96 is fairly typical
97   Helmut Kohl "Aussprache über den Bundeshaushalt" *Bulletin* 9-9-94
98   David Patton "Social Coalitions, Political Strategies, and German Unification" *West European Politics* v16 n4 1993 pp470-91
99   George K. Rosomer "Politics, Leadership, and Coalitions in Germany, 1994" in *Germany's New Politics...*pp23-41; W. R. Smyser "Dateline Berlin: The New German Vision", *Foreign Policy* Winter 1994-95 pp140-157
100   Karl Hugo Pruys *Helmut Kohl: Die Biographie* (Berlin: edition q 1995) p526
101   Clay Clemens "The Chancellor as Manager: Helmut Kohl, the CDU and Governance in Germany" *West European Politics* v17 n4 1994 pp28-51

shortcomings, Kohl has a commanding presence on the European stage. There are no challengers within the CDU and by 1995 his continuation as chancellor in the next millennium had become a distinct possibility. A diverse *Ampel* or *Ampel*-plus coalition may be required to topple him.[102] Whoever eventually succeeds Kohl will be the single most powerful politician in Europe. Schäuble was regarded as a frontrunner and has also been a vigorous contributor to debate on the future Europe.[103] Schäuble's abilities as an organizer and strategist—'an unusually effective politician' as one commentator described him[104]—complement Kohl's own talents. A division of labour between Schäuble as superintendent of domestic affairs and development of *Europapolitik* gives Kohl greater scope in the role of statesman.[105]

For it to remain the spearhead of European integration, innovation in domestic policy became a CDU imperative and young and energetic people were sought. The appointment of Claudia Nolte, young, female and from east Germany, was one of the party's more obvious image updates, intended to raise support in three demographic categories where CDU voters and, especially, members were in low or falling numbers. Christoph Böhr belongs to a new 'post-68' group of CDU regional leaders who emerged in the early 1990s keen to ensure the party does not 'shut itself out of the future'.[106] How to achieve this brings its own disjunctions on strategy. Weakening the hold of *Die Grünen* over voters rating environmental issues as their top electoral concern is rising on the CDU agenda. German environmental laws (and lobbies) are among the world's most protective and governing parties are committed to a Green friendly orientation.[107] Faced with local difficulties in overcoming an SPD-Green coalition government, Roland Koch, CDU leader in Hessen, called for an anchoring of the *'ökologischen und sozialen Marktwirtschaft'* in the CDU program. He has challenges of a national scale in altering the 'traditional' (Green) conception of ecologically sensitive policy

102 Gunter Hoffman "Kanzler bis in nächste Jahrtausend" *Die Zeit* 20-10-95 p4; "After Kohl" *Economist* 5-10-96 pp59. All the potential candidates, even Edmund Stoiber, are said to have a 'belief in Europe'
103 Schäuble has been among the most influential members of the government and is favoured as the coalition's next chancellor candidate. According to the CDU party headquarters 'he has (the position) if he wants it'. Interview Sources, Bonn, October 1994
104 Mark Frankland "Germany lays down the law over the future of Europe" *The Observer* 19-11-95 p26
105 Gunter Hofmann "Zwei Kanzler hat die Republik" *Die Zeit* 7-4-95 p3; "More Catholic than the Pope" *The Economist* 29-7-95 p39
106 Matthias Geis "Die jungen Wilden von der Christenunion" *Die Zeit* 29-9-95 p4
107 Cf. Günter Eulefeld "Environmental Education in the Federal Republic of Germany" *History of European Ideas* v21 n1 1995 pp17-29

from one that is '*industriefeindlich*' to one that is 'responsible'.[108] The CDU has also placed firmer emphasis on self-responsibility and incentives for small and medium sized firms. On the 'guaranteed' social dimension of the federal party approach, Böhr has argued for an end to the welfare state mentality built up in both German states and based on 'paternalistic social structures' no longer sustainable.[109] The CDU still remains far more 'social' than conservatives in the UK for example, and its organizational machine has successfully sold an assurance to this without which no party will be elected to govern in Germany.[110]

Herein lie much of the SPD's difficulties. From 1982 it proved incapable of defeating the CDU/CSU in centrist politics and the temptation to widen the parameters of a 'legitimate' party spectrum increases. The SPD is undergoing a period of transition or even convulsion in the 1990s and improvement from a disastrous 33.5% in 1990 to 36.4% of the vote in 1994 was little consolation for a fourth successive *Bundeswahl* loss. In the wake of the 1994 election all parties tried to derive some comfort from the result. For some, including Scharping, this 2.9% improvement and some organizational and image related changes were presented as grounds for optimism. A year later he was replaced as party chairman. As smaller parties crowded the political space, SPD support eroded and its chances of winning singlehandedly in 1998 appeared minimal. For one commentator, on Europe and other foreign policy questions, bipartisanship and 'constructive dispute' with the CDU/CSU would serve the SPD and Germany better. The SPD's best hope may be the former 'taboo of a great coalition.'[111]

Lafontaine's failure in 1990 was sealed by his opposition to rapid reunification which excluded him from association with a powerful political dynamic. His return to the SPD leadership brought a swift indication of willingness to engage in deal-making outside established 'normal' parameters and shook the ruling coalition.[112] And although earlier SPD programs had declared the objective of creating a European currency,[113] new openings for populist politics had party figures concocting oppositionist strategies. One 'troika' member, Gerhard Schröder, expressed 'finally we social democrats

108   Geis "Die jungen Wilden..."
109   Böhr "At the End of the Post-War Order in Europe..." pp122-124
110   Heiner Geißler "Keine Verhältnisse wie in Amerika" *Die Zeit* 19-1-96 p4
111   René H. Cuperus "Gefährlicher Alleingang" *Die Zeit* 12-1-96 p8
112   Gunter Hofmann "Der richtige Mann zur rechten Zeit" and Klaus Hartung "Hoffnungen auf eine linke Mehrheit" *Die Zeit* 24-11-95 p4 & p6
113   *Grundsatzprogram der SPD* (Berlin: 1989) p36

again have a national theme'.[114] For Hans-Dietrich Genscher this was precisely the 'renationalising of thinking' that disturbs the decades of trust in Europe that CDU/CSU, SPD, and FDP had together created.[115] It had taken about five years for the social democrats to realise that many voters do not oppose politicians invoking 'the nation'.

Before the 1994 Bavarian and Federal elections the CSU adorned Munich with posters of Karl Marx containing the caption, 'Ich komme wieder'. A year later the CSU was displeased by CDU-Green contacts at the federal level. The SPD had already formed a coalition with the Greens in the Sachsen-Anhalt parliament which also involved them in legislative agreement with the PDS. Moves in this direction induced a barrage of standard 'danger to stability' rhetoric from the coalition. Kohl denounced the arrangement as a 'treasonous act' even if the real threat was to the coalition parties through absorption of PDS voters into the SPD.[116] The post-reunification period reveals the SPD controlling most *Land* governments yet not translating this nationally. Balance settled into a voter preference for CDU/CSU party government in Bonn/Berlin and SPD rule at *Länd* level. Although the SPD had attained a 'far greater say than any previous German opposition party over the contents and fate of all future bills', the configuration impressed that the federal, not *Länder* governments, possessed greatest influence on decisions at the European level.[117] The SPD was also hamstrung by divisions between its federal and *Länder Fraktionen*. While the former engaged in brinkmanship over coalition formation in the Bundestag, the SPD majority in the Bundesrat were constructing a 'peaceful coexistence' with the Kohl government. Unsurprisingly, their arrangement centred around budgets without introducing new direct taxes, fuelling speculation over rises in value-added tax (*Mehrwertsteuer*) from 15% up to 17%. A second 'solidarity pact' found common ground on raising the pension age for males to 66 and females to 63, along with changes to student and asylum-seeker policy.[118]

---

114   *Endlich haben wir Sozialdemokraten wieder ein nationales thema*' Peter Glotz "Adenauers Erbe zerrinnt" *Die Woche* 10-11-95 pp36-37. See also Ludwig Greven "Die Populisten Kommen" *Die Woche* 15-12-95 p8

115   Hans-Dietrich Genscher "Es würde kälte für uns, wenn die Währungsunion an uns scheitert" *Welt am Sonntag* 5-11-95 p9

116   On the SPD-PDS rapprochment see *Die Zeit* 1-12-95 pp1-4 especially Heinrich August Winkler "Das Trugbid von der linken Mehrheit" On SPD problems in eastern Germany after reunification and which have made it very difficult to win federal elections since see Stephen J. Silvia "Left Behind: The Social Democratic Party in Eastern Germany" *West European Politics* v16 n2 1993 pp24-49

117   See Stephen J. Silvia "The Social Democratic Party of Germany" in *Germany's New Politics...* pp149-170

118   Andreas Borchers "Keine Chance für Doppelkopf" *Die Woche* 22-3-96 p5

The FDP had traditionally been strong supporters of European unity yet serious doubts emerged about what future role they may be capable of playing. In the lead-up to the 1994 electoral campaign, speculation over the party's survival competed well for media coverage with other issues. Observers asked 'Do we still need a liberal party?'[119] An initially meteoric performance in the east was followed by plummeting voter support and an extraordinary collapse of membership. The total of members in the new *Länder* fell from 136,000 in July 1990 to 26,000 at the end of 1994. Although the accent on personal liberty appealed to those previously contained behind the wall, the FDP crash in the east is partly explained by misunderstanding about what 'liberal' actually meant in the west—a polity featured by a competitive, market economy. When confronted by some harsher realities of the liberal-democratic system, the system and the FDP seemed much less appealing to many easterners. Decline in the west was less spectacular though it accelerated after 1992. Between 1990 and December 1994 membership dropped from over 66,000 to less than 61,000.[120] The national vote of the self-proclaimed 'tax-lowering party' (*Steuer-senkungs Partei*) fell from 11% in the 1990 Bundeswahl to 6.9% in 1994. It was carried over the line by the 'tactical voting' of CDU supporters. In the 1994 campaign the struggling FDP engaged Genscher as a kind of *politicus emeritus* face on election posters. Genscher's reign as foreign minister had ended in controversy over Yugoslavia. One official tactfully put it, 'he became tired'.[121] Although the relief at scrambling over the 5% hurdle was manifest, their poor result precipitated more pressure to remove the foreign ministry from the FDP. While Kinkel retained this position he later resigned as FDP leader.

Reunification reduced the prominence of the CSU Bavarian power base on the federal scale and threatened its political leverage. However, the FDP's slump in 1994 saw the CSU move to number two in the coalition and the third party overall in voter support. Contemporaneously, and despite the prominence of Kohl's apparent ally, Theo Waigel, the CSU shifted from being the 'most European' party under Franz-Josef Strauss to one suspicious, and even opposed to the CDU's EU orientation. On occasions when outright hostility occurred it was accounted for by temporary domestic considerations. Bavarian Minister-President Edmund Stoiber's calls for a slowdown of European integration, rising in 1993, were explained by CDU headquarters as a regional manoeuvre to co-opt support for far-right groups infringing on the

---

119   Robert Leicht (pro) & Werner A. Perger (contra) "Brauchen wir noch eine liberale Partei?" *Die Zeit* 16-9-94 p38
120   See Chrisitan Søe "The Free Democratic Party: A Struggle for Survival, Influence, and Identity" in *Germany's New Politics* pp171-202
121   Interview sources, Bonn, October 1994

CSU voter base in local elections.[122] Stoiber's scepticism nonetheless undermined Kohl's Europhilia. Only days after the TEU came into effect Stoiber was claiming 'we are no longer striving for a European federal state...nation-states must maintain their dominant role'. No longer did Germans have to seek a new identity as Europeans. In response Kinkel termed the comments 'disastrous, clumsy and unpolitical'—that is, they were political.[123] Continuing friction between the CSU and the 'fairweather' FDP and the floating of Stoiber's candidacy for chancellor in 1998 also tested coalition solidarity.[124] A spell of mutual admiration with the SPD's Schröder coincided with surging disaffection for EMU[125] and was followed by a new round of charges and threats against Brussels, this time in tandem with like-minded Kurt Biedenkopf, Minister-President of Saxony.[126]

Apart from a brief incursion by the far right in late 1960s, the equilibrium of the party system was not seriously disturbed until the arrival of the Greens.[127] Regarded by some as endangering democracy, elsewhere they are claimed to have settled into a comfortable niche—from *Bürgerschreck zur Bürgerpartei geworden*.[128] Departure of *fundi* faction members has moved the *realo* dominated party closer to the middle. They have not adversely affected the European integration process to any significant degree and some evidence suggests that, in principle at least, the party and Green voters are its 'staunchest supporters.'[129] After the Greens west-east split had cost them representation in 1990 they returned as a federal force in 1994 following a series of successful *Land* elections. A return of 10.1% in the June 1994 European elections was followed by 7.3% of the vote in the October *Bundeswahl*. The continued strengthening of the Greens was highlighted by a spectacular success in the May 1995 *Nordrhein-Westfalen* election led by a return of almost 30% in central Köln for Christian Schirner.[130] Their position in the party configuration ensures environmental issues of prominence and that these concerns are pronounced in German demands of Europe.

In their 1994 election program the *Bündnis 90/Die Grünen* compact advocated a demilitarisation of Europe, opposition to participation in conflict

122   *Financial Times* 3-11-93; Interview Sources, Bonn, October 1994.
123   USIA EFS File 15-11-93 p11
124   "Üben für den Dschungel" *Der Spiegel* n19 8-5-95 pp26-27
125   Annette Ramelsberger "Marmor, Stein und Eisen" *Der Spiegel* n4 22-1-96 p37
126   Klaus-Peter Schmidt "Schimpf und Schande" *Die Zeit* 30-8-96 p1
127   Bulmer & Paterson *Federal Republic...* pp21-24
128   'From citizens terror to citizens party'. "Wir Werden Regieren" *Der Spiegel* n9 1995 pp18-19
129   Hans-Georg Betz *Postmodern Politics in Germany* (Houndmills: MacMillan 1991) pp145-148
130   Jan Bielicki "Das grüne Wunder von Köln" *Die Woche* 25-5-95 p10

outside Germany's borders and replacement by the 'construction of civil structures' based around the CSCE.[131] However, in a pre-election article Joschka Fischer conceded a necessary German participation in an all-European security system in partnership with the US and under 'transnational command structures'. He expressed no fundamental differences with his centre-spectrum opponents, or allies as the case may be, stressing virtually the same set of most important foreign policy interests: 'The breakthrough to irreversible political integration and decision structures in foreign, security, economic and monetary policy in the EU is in the primary German interest.'[132] The following year, after Bosnia, another Fischer document determined that German military action would in future be required where instances of genocide had or may occur. A 'self-declared follower of Machiavelli', Fischer is secure as leader despite now being at some variance with the Green ideal of offering a genuine alternative. He has tried to steer the party towards advocation of a pacifist society that can and will defend itself and human rights where necessary.[133] He also reiterates the Kohlspeak that 'Germany's first national interest is the European', while fearing, like Kohl, that the '[European] car is rolling backwards not forward'.[134]

John Ely has stressed the 'structural' presence of a radical right and CDU-CSU flirtation with supporters of these groups.[135] Much of his evidence relies on voting support for the *Republikaner* in the 1989 European elections, which often witness protests against bigger parties (mainly the government) in all member states. The far Right do not attain significant percentages of the national vote nor control the domestic agenda. They make periodic forays, as in the case of the *Deutsche Volks Union* (DVU) in the 1991 Bremen and 1992

131   *Frankfurter Allgemeine Zeitung* 1-9-94 p6
132   'Der Durchbruch zu irreversiblen politischen Integrations- und Entscheidungsstrukturen in der Außen-, der Sicherheits-, der Wirtschafts- und Währungspolitik in der EU liegt im obersten deutschen Interesse.' Joschka Fischer "Les Certitudes Allemandes: Grundkonstanten bundessdeutscher Aussenpolitik" *Blatte für deutsche und internationale Politik*, September 1994 pp1082-1090
133   See Hans-Georg Betz "Alliance 90/Greens: From Fundamental opposition to Black-Green" in *Germany's New Politics...* pp203-220 for a good account of the party's recent history
134   Interview ABC Television (Australia) 9-7-96; See also Joschka Fischer *Risiko Deutschland: Krise und Zukunft der deutschen Politik* (Cologne: Kiiepenheuer & Witsch 1994)
135   John D. Ely "The 'Black-Brown Hazelnut' in a Bigger Germany: The Rise of a Radical Right as a Structural Feature" *From Bundesrepublik to Deutschland...* pp235-270; Cf. Michael Schmidt ; Roberts "The German Party System in Crisis"; Michael Minkenberg "What's Left of the Right?: The New Right and the Superwahljahr 1994 in Perspective" in *Germany's New Politics...*pp255-271

Schleswig-Holstein state elections or the *Republikaner* in Baden-Würtemmberg in 1992, but have failed to sustain more than minimal support. In October 1994 the *Republikaner* attracted 1.9% of the total vote and no seats in the Bundestag. [136] This was virtually identical to their result in the first 'All-German' election of 1990. In the 1994 European elections they polled 3.9%, down from 7.1% in 1989. The following year a federal initiative against the *Republikaner* threatened to 'delist' them completely. [137] By indirect means a degree of right-wing influence is filtered through the mainstream *Parteienstaat* edifice, chiefly through the absorption and repackaging of parts of their platforms and rhetoric by the CDU-CSU. Support for implementation of moderated versions of policies advocated by parties further to the right is attempted through pressure on the middle. The Kohl government and the polity in general has moved closer to a lobby sometimes called 'revisionists' who considered Germany existed under unfair and unnatural constraints for too long and that without more assertion of national rights, interests and goals it would be susceptible indefinitely. [138] To distinguish themselves from undesirable associations with the far Right, the national identity question, which featured prominently in CDU-CSU electoral platforms in both 1987 and 1990, was married with a necessary European identity. Kohl's triumph of national unity was linked, rhetorically, constitutionally and through international institutions, from Germany's European present and future. The conservatives have not sought to detach themselves or Germany from being at the core, even constituting the core, of European integration. The CDU-CSU takeover of the Right's attempt to monopolise the reunification issue shifted the centre of the spectrum and later developments on immigration and military questions consolidated it. While Left-liberals infer that more than a few conservatives hold views further to the right than they express, the SPD was not exempt from this influence as it too came under strategic pressure to make policy alterations. [139]

Until a few months before the Bundeswahl, most analysts did not expect the PDS to gain over 5% of the vote. After garnering over 20% of the eastern German vote in the 1994 European Parliament election, the prognosis became more favourable for the PDS despite allegations of complicity in Stasi operations and other controversies surrounding leader Gregor Gysi. [140]

---

136   *Das Parlament* 21-10-94 p1
137   "The German way of democracy" *The Economist* 29-4-95 p62
138   Cf. Schäuble "Das Nationale nutzen"
139   Cf. Minkenberg "What's Left of the Right?..."
140   In May 1996 Gregor Gysi was the only leading German politician who would be photographed with Russian Communist leader Zyuganov on the latter's visit to Bonn, a contrast with Kohl, Genscher and others' enthusiasm for photo opportunities with Gorbachev

Eventually the party received 4.4% of the national vote but by means of what some considered a dangerous electoral loophole—majorities in three or more electoral districts *(Wahlkreis)*—the party was guaranteed representation in the Bundestag. The party say 'Yes to Europe, but no to Maastricht'. In its perception of the EU as a capitalist plot, the 1990s PDS was a successor to 1970s British Labour. Opposition to the TEU then brought it into a curious alignment with the Conservative Party. Both fear a German hegemonic role in Europe *(daß er Deutschland in Europa eine Vorherrschaftsrolle ermöglichen kann)*. In Gysi's opinion all Germany's established parties had the same attitudes to Maastricht while in France, England and Denmark differences of view prevailed.[141]

Now that external and internal predictability has reduced, German politics presents an intriguing array of potential coalition permutations.[142] The parliamentary survival of the PDS and the revival of the *Bündnis 90-Grünen* potentially gave each both more leverage *and* less. For the established parties, especially the centre-right, it presented a threat *and* an opportunity. The decline of the FDP elevated the prospects of the Greens, while PDS strength in the east has a counterpart in shrinkage of the SPD base. While the CSU have improved their position in the coalition the CDU remains the most powerful party. SPD decline in traditional heartlands often had a corresponding success for the Greens while the coalition linked the SPD to a forthcoming radical communist agenda by dealing with the PDS. Several possibilities could materialise: an SPD-Green alliance or the *Ampelkoalition* option that operated in Brandenburg for a period; the CDU-CSU continuing in government with the FDP; a CDU-CSU majority; or another Grand Coalition with the SPD. The possibility of a Red-Green majority in 1998 or a compact between the SPD, PDS and Greens was held open with a May 1995 poll showing combined support of 48% versus 42% for the CDU-CSU. With only 4% the FDP would fail.[143] The emergent possibility of a previously inconceivable 'Black-Green' entente further tests Kohl's skills in managing the current CDU-CSU-FDP alliance. The government has co-opted Green environmental demands into their European platform, and, while issues like the future of NATO or the role of the Bundeswehr jets may pose difficulties, after the 1994

---

141   Gregor Gysi "Ja zu Europa aber nein zu Maastricht: Der Standpunkt der PDS/Linke Liste" *Der Deutsche Bundestag und Europa*...pp190-194

142   According to one 1994 survey, only 31% of east German respondents considered democracy the best state form, down 10% from two years before. 28% thought there were better alternatives and another 41% could not decide. This does not privilege either 'right' or 'left' alternatives. 76% of west Germans stuck with democracy as the best state form. "Demokratie unattraktiver" *Münchner Merker* 1-9-94 p1

143   Manfred Bissinger "Fit für die Macht?" *Die Woche* 25-5-95 p1

election 26 of the Greens 49 Bundestag members supported 'necessary' military actions. Left-wing members of the Greens rejected coalition with the centre parties and some subsequently joined the PDS. [144]

Parties organized in opposition to the TEU appeared in many member states. In Germany the Alliance of Free Citizens (*Bund freie Bürger*) led by disaffected former Brussels technocrat Manfred Brunner did not meet with the surprise, even alarm, such a renegade group might have instigated in the past. Challenges to the treaty's validity were brought before the Federal Constitutional Court which ruled that the TEU did not supersede the Basic Law. [145] In any case the Bundestag and Bundesrat must vote on European Treaties, including EMU.

Hans Rattinger has presented some interesting findings on German attitudes to European integration and related to party affiliations. In contrast to 6% considering themselves more favourable (towards integration) than the parties, 42% of voters perceive the four main parties (which excepts the PDS and Republikaner) as being more integrationist or favouring a European government than they (the voters) are. A higher percentage is recorded for PDS and *Republikaner* supporters both of whom consider European unification to have gone too far. However, in response to whether 'united Germany has the right to play the leading role in Europe' *Republikaner* voter choices in the two most affirmative options (41%) virtually mirrored those of the CDU/CSU (40%). SPD responses on this totalled 30%. The mean average of 29% is kept down by very low PDS and low *Bündnis 90-Grünen* support. Rattinger's conclusions state that a majority 'say 'yes' to a European economic and security community, but 'no' to a common political decision-making structure.' And while supporters of the 'old' parties are most supportive of all three forms of integration their share of the vote has been decreasing for some years and a 'rise in sceptical attitudes toward European integration can be expected.' Unmistakeable supporters outnumber 'clear-cut opposition' but are in turn outnumbered by indifferent groups more likely to shift to opposition. [146] The CDU/CSU role as a stabilizing force appeared all

---

144   In March 1996 3 state elections resulted in more losses for SPD including losing its majority in Schleswig-Holstein, wins for the CDU and gains for the FDP, who now hold the balance of power in two states. The FDP remain in partnership with the SPD in Rheinland-Pfalz where new leader Gerhardt said they 'cannot go back on a pre-election agreement'. Concurrently Lafontaine was claiming the actions of the Greens in NRW had damaged the *Öko-Soziale* partnership

145   "Eurosceptic's Application for Judicial Review of Maastricht Treaty" *Guardian Weekly* 25-7-93 p1; *Europa-Archiv* n22 1993 ppD460-476

146   Hans Rattinger "Public Attitudes to European integration in Germany after Maastricht: Inventory and Typology" *Journal of Common Market Studies* v32 n4 December 1994 pp525-540

the more important after the SPD's continued demise. Combined returns of around 80-90% for the 'catch-all' parties appear past. In summary, the old political culture may not be engulfed but waves of change have arrived.

Table 4.2   **Voter Support for German political parties: October 1994 Bundeswahl and October 1995 poll results compared**

Party	All Germany		Western Länder		Eastern Länder	
	1994Wahl	Oct.1995	1994Wahl	Oct.1995	1994Wahl	Oct.1995
CDU/CSU	41.5	42.8	42.1	44.6	38.5	34.5
SPD	36.4	28.9	37.5	30.1	31.5	23.5
B90/ Grüne	7.3	13	7.9	13.3	4.3	11.6
FDP	6.9	6.4	7.7	7.1	3.5	3.5
PDS	4.4	5.8	1.0	1.7	19.8	23.8
Rep.	1.9	2.5	2.0	2.7	1.3	2.0

Source: Frankfurter Allgemeine Zeitung November 1995

The German Economy: Fading Dinosaur or Sleeping Giant?

In 1990 an IMF report presented a 'basis for optimism' which suggested that the arduous challenge of reunification could be met and negative disruption controlled.[147] Rebuilding eastern Germany's decrepit capital stock from ground up consumed vast amounts of capital and energy which the west German economy was then positioned to provide. However, mistakes made in planning the economic fusion of east and west exacerbated difficulties and major problems ensued. In essence it was an attempt to equalise conditions too fast too soon.[148] Political calculations behind economic policy chose a more

---

147   *German Unification: Economic Issues* Occasional Paper n75 Eds. Leslie Lipschitz & Donogh McDonald (Washington: IMF 1990)

148   The problems, not all unavoidable, included an exchange rate of 1.8 Ostmarks to 1 DM which should have been at least 4 to 1; a profound uncertainty about restitution of property rights which discouraged investment; a wage boom out of alignment with productivity; privatisation by the Treuhand agency when investment capital was drying up due to deficit blow-outs and a rigorous anti-inflationary policy. See Gerlinde Sinn & Hans-Werner Sinn *Jumpstart: the*

intense and, so they hoped, shorter bout of pain than a less acute but longer anguish. Within a year of German Economic Monetary and Social Union (GEMSU), production in the east had plummeted and unemployment soared while the burst of economic activity in 1990-91 also masked overdue labour market reform and restructuring in the west. Unsustainable wage demands instigated export of workplaces and financial balances in pension, health and unemployment insurance systems moved from surplus to deficit between 1990 and 1992.[149] After the state underwritten consumer boom wore off the bill remained. Total public debt was 1.6 trillion by end of 1992 of which DM621 billion was directly attributable to the federal government. Ultimately it is responsible for the rest, including DM362 billion of western *Länder* public debt. The total has been predicted to reach DM2.5 trillion by 2000.[150] More increases in expenditure came between 1994-96 to service accumulated debt and were joined by an unfactored sharp rise in unemployment costs.

Employer arguments for real reductions in labour costs had some practical effect as yearly increases in west German average hourly earnings fell from 7.3% in 1991 to 1.3% in 1994 and from 26.2% in 1992 to 8.2% in 1994 in east Germany. Unit labour costs which had risen 5.0% in 1992 were wound back to -1.1% in 1994. The eastern wage explosion, up 35% in 1990, had been reduced to 0.2% in 1994.[151] Opportunity for wholesale restructuring had been missed during the economic boom leading up to and immediately following reunification and a further chance during the recovery of 1994 was not grasped.[152] Although falling in real terms, labour market costs actuated a

---

economic unification of Germany Trans. Juli Irving-Lessmann. (Cambridge Ma: MIT Press 1992); Harald Hagemann "On Some Macroeconomic Consequences of German Unification" in *United Germany and the New Europe* ...pp89-107; Irwin J. Collier "Instant Integration and Gradual Convergence: Program Notes to the Macroeconomic Drama of German Unification" *German Studies Review* v16 n2 1993 pp311-330. The Treuhand eventually sold around 36,000 businesses and liquidated 3,600 at a cost of DM300 billion. David Schoenbaum & Elizabeth Pond *The German Question and Other German Questions* (Houndmills: MacMillan 1996) pp157-158

149 See Peter Kalmbach "On Alternative Strategies of Wage Policy in Eastern Germany" in *United Germany and the New Europe* ... pp119-133

150 David P. Conradt "Putting Germany Back Together Again: The Great Social Experiment of Unification" in *Germany in a New Era...* pp3-18; See also Vittas "Introduction" in *United Germany: the First Five Years* p2. General government expenditure rose from 42.3% of GDP in 1990 to 50.0% in 1994 after reaching 50.4% in 1993. In the same years revenue rose from 40.4% to 47.5%. Debt increased from -1.9 in 1990, to -3.3% in 1993, before improving to -2.4% in 1994. General government debt in Germany rose from 39.8% of GDP in 1990 (WG) to 51% in 1994

151 Vittas "Introduction" in *United Germany: The First Five Years* p3

152 On this see David Marsh *Germany and Europe: The Crisis of Unity* (London: Mandarin 1995) pp106-109

sustained export of workplaces as unemployment rates moved towards 12%. Correlating with public insecurities savings rates began to rise. Risk-taking, which the government wants to encourage, and lending correspondingly fell. Referencing former Kohl advisor Horst Teltschik, Schoenbaum and Pond claim that 'compliance with the multiple requirements of European and national, state and federal, economics, labor, transportation and environmental protection industries, can themselves impose supplementary costs of DM50 million on an investment of DM500 million'.[153]

It is not only workers and government who must be prepared for change. Though industry blames political factors for its lack of investment in *Standort Deutschland*, the relationship between big companies and major banks has come under increased criticism for inflexibility and insularity. In an international environment requiring rapid innovation German industry often appeared slowly reactive. While retaining a reputation for high quality products it cannot afford the luxury of concentrating on patiently building long term privileged partnerships. Loosening of bonds between German *Konzerne* and big banks and a move towards capital markets expansion is now necessary. The British *Guardian* argued that 'the scope for reaching a corporatist German consensus, traditional escape-route out of a crisis, is slim: industry now needs at least some UK-style deregulation ("flexibility") to survive in the global economy while the unions remain wedded to 1970s interventionism. Even Dr. Kohl will find it hard to fudge his way out of this conflict.'[154] At the April 1996 G7 summit in Lille, Economics Minister, Günter Rexrodt said Germany rejected US suggestions of a deregulated labor market which had created eight million American jobs in three years. Although Rexrodt claimed Germany (and the EU) would not adopt a hire and fire method he wanted greater 'flexibility' on wage differentials and work hours. The industrialised countries should 'stop fiddling and put radical proposals'. Employment Minister Blum added that the US could lead the way in services, but 'we do not have a world government' and cannot have a world economic system.[155]

As the extent of decay in the east was revealed, camouflaged problems came to the fore in western Germany. Manufacturing is undergoing a

---

153   Schoenbaum & Pond *The German Question...* p123

154   John Palmer, Mark Milner & David Gow "German woes hit single currency timetable" *Guardian Weekly* 21-1-96 p14. Cf. David Bowen "Oh, for Germany's 'deep flaws'" *Independent* 26-11-95 p21. In terms of investment flows the UK economy has been the most favoured destination and source of OECD Europe countries. See Grahame F. Thompson *The Economic Emergence of a New Europe?: The Political Economy of Cooperation and Competition in the 1990s* (Aldershot: Edward Elgar 1993) pp26-27; *World Investment Report 1995* (New York: UNCTAD 1995)

155   *Deutsche Welle* (Television News) 1-4-96

reduction of some two million workplaces through the 1990s. Many will be exported, some compensated by new jobs in the enlarged services sector, some lost forever. A survey of 8500 companies published in late 1993 reported that 30% would be shifting segments of production and jobs out of Germany. A sizeable section had already had done this.[156] In five years to late 1995, German companies invested DM173 billion outside Germany and only DM25 billion in it.[157] BMW has more than doubled its workforce since 1986 when employment outside Germany was minimal. Around 90% of this increase has been accounted for by external positions with takeover of British automobile firm Rover and a new factory in the US leading causes. By the end of 1995 the company was one of a few major concerns yet to begin large-scale job reductions internally. Of BMW's 116,000 employees, 52,000 were outside Germany. Not all firms are exporting jobs. Siemens, the largest private firm with around 373,000 employees in 1995, has scaled back external employment since 1994 having increased it for the previous decade. Chief executive Alfons Graf, a member of the SPD, embarked on ending the export of workplaces as a contribution to reversing Germany's economic and social malaise. He also cited weaker environmental protection as an additional reason to keep jobs and sites in Germany.[158] Retrenchements by the giant Bremer-Vulkan shipbuilding firm occurred as it plummeted from a US$40million profit in 1995 to insolvency and demise in 1996 and shipyards in the east came under government control. Unions resisted jobs being exported which also threatened lower wages and membership numbers in Germany. The unions and the conservative government found common ground, including raids on construction sites, in reducing numbers of itinerant foreign workers in Germany, by the mid-1990s estimated to be around 500,000. However, many from came other EU states like Portugal, Spain, and approximately 50,000 from the UK, working for less than their German counterparts and precipitating charges of 'social dumping'. Contemporaneously a survey of 25,000 businesses found that 38% wanted to reduce their workforces in the year ahead.[159]

Privatisation trends and an increasingly competitive global environment did not lessen the importance of the state's role, rather it altered the means. In broad terms the German economy will have to, and is, adopting features of 'Anglo-American' capitalism but without abandoning its reliance

156 German Chambers of Commerce Survey 8-11-93 quoted in Marsh *Germany and Europe: The Crisis of Unity* p203 fn42
157 Alan Friedman "Hidebound Capitalism, On the Cusp of Reform" *International Herald Tribune* 8-12-95 pp1 & 8
158 *Die Woche* 1-3-96
159 ibid. p14

on agreement between the 'Social Partners'.[160] A 1995 report informed that 'the industrial shakeout was mirrored in the policy debate, which began to focus on keeping Germany attractive as a location for investment'. There would also be an 'eventual privatization of the railways and the state-owned postal and telecommunications companies'.[161] The government's intentions were spelt out a few months later.[162] As some of Germany's larger companies experienced losses in profitability, scandals and bailouts, or moved jobs to foreign locations, a new governmental impetus promoted the *Mittelstand* as the engine room of employment generation. The drive to a '*schlanker Staat*' was simultaneously dependent on small and medium-sized businesses, which provided two-thirds of workplaces in Germany, as the vanguard of a 'new culture of self-responsibility.'[163]

Lester Thurow has argued that Europe was (re)writing the world's trade rules because it had the largest market, potentially larger still.[164] Another recent analysis determines that Germany is Europe's 'central analog' in a comparative study with US and Japan. The German base is 'distinctive enough and regionally dominant enough' for this purpose. 27 of the top 100 European firms are German and they hold the largest shares in industrial production, sales and 'technology-intensive sectors', where their share is rising.[165] Estimating the future European economy, two British scholars foresee 'that a lack of political solidarity and incompatible economic value systems will lead to the establishment at the EC level of a minimalist structure of regulation and corporate governance along the lines of the German model, but with some Atlanticist overtures.'[166] Geoffrey Garrett argues that the German government applied a guileful strategy in issues of protectionism

160   Cf. Helmut Kohl "Gemeinsam die Zukunft gestalten" *Gewerkschaftliche Monatshefte* n9 1994 pp553-562

161   *United Germany: The First Five Years: Performance and Policy Issues* p7

162   Wolfgang Bötsch "Liberalisierung bei Post und Telekommunikation-Perspektiven und Chancen für die Wirtschaft" *Bulletin* 21-12-95

163   Helmut Kohl "Betriebsgründungen im selbständigen Mittelstand — Schlüssel für mehr Arbeitsplätze" *Bulletin* 22-12-95; "Handwerk und mittelständische Unternehmen — Moter für Wachstum und Arbeitsplätze in Deutschland" *Bulletin* 11-1-96; "Selbständiger Mittelstand—Herzstück der Sozialen Marktwirtschaft" *Bulletin* 23-10-96

164   Lester Thurow *Head to Head: The Coming Economic Battle Among Japan, Europe, and America* (St. Leonards: Allen & Unwin 1993)

165   Louis W. Pauly & Simon Reich "National Structures and Multinational Corporate Behaviour: Enduring Differences in the Age of Globalization" *International Organization* v51 n1 1997 pp1-30

166   Michael Hodges & Stephen Woolcock "Atlantic Capitalism versus European Capitalism in the European Community" *Western European Politics* v16 n3 1993 pp329-344

versus free trade or, German interests versus EU legalities; a 'behaviour easily explained in terms of rational self-interest'. For Germany 'the portion of the economy that would be adversely affected in the short term by trade liberalization is smaller than in any other union member. Furthermore, Germany has been able effectively to insulate from EU tampering some of the most important sectors that would be hurt by free trade—such as the public utilities and the financial institutions.'[167] German economic-industrial culture with absorbed 'Atlanticist' features appears as lead candidate for a future 'European' model.

In regions like Baden-Württemberg and Bavaria where automobile and electronics industries guard their independence and success, business-labour relations, government assistance and other interventions are largely left to *Land* administrations. To sustain a buoyant national economy disparities in particular industries or regions convene a regionalized industrial policy which may occur against the spirit or letter of EU competition policy. In this respect Germany is no different to other EU states, most of which continue to provide subsidies, retain non-tariff barriers and give other assistance within national borders or to nationally based companies be they struggling or 'champions'. While studies of 'mesocorporatism' stress the importance of sectorized and regional forms of organization for explaining Germany's political economy, coordination is present at the *'meta* level'.[168] When arguing in favour of or accepting the 'European' policy or decision delivers, on balance of all associated factors, greater national benefits, this is the course followed. When domestic economic damage and political fallout is projected as too severe the government will fight the national case. Garrett indicates how, using the *Cassis de Dijon* case as the precedent in legal disputes adjudicated by the ECJ, the German government portrays a position 'whereby it could credibly claim not only that it was prepared to fight for the protection of German industry (to attract or maintain the support of the sheltered sectors of the economy) but also that it was a "good European" (because it accepted that the legal system was the appropriate arbiter in trade disputes, even when this had deleterious consequences for Germany). Garrett adds that 'one might even suggest that the Court of Justice has tended to act as a de facto agent of the German government by vigorously prosecuting the free trade cause but without extending its reach into other areas of more concern to Germany, such as financial deregulation.'[169] The *Cassis* case is a specific example of a

---

167   Geoffrey Garrett "The politics of legal integration in the European Union" *International Organization* v49 n1 Winter 1995 pp171-181, p175

168   See Christopher S. Allen "From Social Market to Mesocorporatism to European Integration: The Politics of German Economic Policy" in *From Bundesrepublik to Deutschland* pp61-76

169   Garrett "The politics of legal integration..."

government pursuing a national interest apparently contrary to European agreements and is replicated by all. The point is, to what extent will the governments of one EU member be able to do this in the future?

Since topping the world exporting table with a surplus of US$72 billion in 1989 the expanded Federal Republic confirmed itself among the top three states in global commerce. Concurrently the DM's continued appreciation through the 1990s was expected by the IMF as an 'endogenous equilibrating response to the capital needs and demands of the former east Germany' and did not in this case mean difficulties for international competitiveness. Based on data and events up to the third quarter 1994, the 'key conclusion' offered was that 'deterioration of Germany's external competitiveness suggested by some commonly used indicators of the real appreciation of the Deutsche Mark, such as those based on relative unit labor costs in manufacturing, is almost certainly exaggerated'. The report continued that 'sustaining a strong export performance into 1995 and later years will clearly be helped by a continuation of such restructuring and of labor market reforms and adjustments'.[170] Even as the German economy is under pressure as never before the Deutsche Mark continued to appreciate in 1996.[171] Helmut Schmidt claimed its foreign value had risen by 10% since 1990. He urged that in future the Bundesbank should intervene outside its normal remit in stabilizing foreign currencies to engender equilibrium and assist German competitiveness.[172] While some softening in late 1995 helped the trade surplus rise from DM8.5 billion in October to DM10.6 billion in November, firms continue to invoice in Deutsche Marks reflecting confidence in the currency but harming their own export prospects.[173]

For all the negatives there is still remarkable resilience and Germany remains the economic-industrial core on and around which Europe depends. If this is so in a depressed phase its power will be enhanced in an upswing. The IMF foresaw a brighter trade performance scenario, taking the view that 'economic activity is affected by many other factors besides fiscal policy. Monetary conditions, the international economic environment, the pace of technological innovation....as well as more general cultural and political factors'. An estimated current account balance of DM7.1billion in 1996 would

---

170   Robert A. Feldman "External Competitiveness" in *United Germany: The First Five Years...* pp9-20

171   See Schoenbaum and Pond *The German Question..*p140 fn 129. According to Hans Tietmeyer 'in the kingdom of the blind, the one-eyed man is king'

172   Schmidt "Rezepte gegen die deutsche Krankheit"

173   John Schmid "German Joblessness Hits Postwar Record" *International Herald Tribune* 9-2-96 pp1&6

rise to DM46.8bill in 2000.[174] The estimated volume of liquid assets, or
potential investment funds, in Germany at the end of 1994 was some DM7
trillion[175] and the first six months of 1995 external investment rose 60% on
the same period in the previous year.[176] There are enough signs that 'in the
long run...unification could be expected to provide for a major boom in the
German economy—perhaps leading to another Wirtschaftwunder in the
end'.[177] When and if depends on political developments.

The Deutsche Mark-EMU Debate

As Germany's reunification got underway, the Bundesbank opposed aspects
of GEMSU, none more than one for one parity of Ostmarks and Deutsche
Marks, which the bank's incumbent president Karl-Otto Pöhl termed a
'fantastical notion'.[178] When the strict terms of EMU were enforced by
German negotiators at Maastricht the main concern was for the rectitude of
economic management and budgetary discipline as practised by Germany's
European partners. This trepidation remains but with rising demands for
public expenditures it was joined by calls for more flexibility in monetary
policy. There were then two strains of opposition to EMU: one of scepticism
towards the macro-economic culture of some other EU members; and another
against the restrictions placed on management of German public finances.
These may appear contradictory: flexibility is disavowed for others but the
option should be retained at home. 'Deutschmark Nationalism' was not only
applicable to former East German desires for hard currency. The bulk of the
western German population remain resolutely attached to this symbolic and
material touchstone.[179] As the popular and populist tabloid *Bild* reflects,

174   Karl Habermeier "Fiscal Policy and Economic Growth" in *United Germany:The First five Years* table 4-8
175   Udo Perina "Zweifel am inneren Wert" *Die Zeit* 1-9-95 p26
176   Cf. the improvements cited in "Die wirtschaftliche Lage in der Bundesrepublik Deutschland" Monatsbericht Februar 1995 des Bundesministeriums für Wirtschaft. *Bulletin* 1-3-95
177   Manfred Goertemaker "Unifying Germany 1989-1990" (Houndmills: MacMillan 1994) p232; Cf. Schoenbaum and Pond *The German Question...* pp124-127
178   See Collier "Instant Integration and Gradual Convergence..."
179   From Jürgen Habermas "Der DM-Nationalismus" *Die Zeit* 30-3-90 and *Die nachholende Revolution: kleine politische Schriften VII* (Frankfurt a M: Suhrkamp 1990) to Helmut Schmidt "Deutsches Störfeuer gegen Europa" *Die Zeit* 29-9-95 p1. A 1994 survey on German youth has 47% rating the D-Mark, 40% the economic system, and 37% the social net as reasons to be proud of being German. *Der Spiegel* n38 19-9-94 pp58-63. In another poll 19% of Germans think a single currency should be called the Deutsche Mark and 40% the Euromark. *Financial Times* 5-12-94 pp1-2

Germans want *Germans* to retain control of policy over 'Unsre Schönes Geld' (Our Beautiful Money). 46% of Germans are 'very proud' of the Mark and a further 38% 'somewhat proud'. 28% advocate a European currency. A majority of another survey still thought that the Mark would be exchanged for a European currency within ten years—if German conditions are met. They also consider the whole process primarily a political (a negative compulsion), not an economic (financially positive) category.

Some observers considered that pragmatic appraisal of the political consequences as weighed against economic considerations had not been overtaken by emotive populism. Others saw things differently.[180] A organized mobilization *en masse* against EMU had not occurred, however, if several million people (and the central bank) oppose control of monetary policy being passed to 'others', this is a form of nationalism. So too is' government insistence of doing it their way in Europe: 'The German position is known. The monetary union should be built according to the image and likeness of the strong Mark. Waigel has it right if, when he looks at German taxpayers, he recognises no friends of Europe.'[181]

Amongst the economic policy élite EMU was unwanted early on and later pronouncements by officials barely disguised their aversion.[182] The more Kohl insisted that EMU was imperative and that a single currency would be as solid as the Mark the more public anxiety grew. A January 1995 poll showed only 24% of Germans supported a single currency, with 23% favouring 'closer political links' in the EU. In February 1996 the *Economist* reported 'no fewer than four out of five Germans oppose the idea of an EMU starting in 1999'. 43% wanted it scrapped altogether.[183] Public resistance has hardened as 'discussion about the single currency suddenly burst onto the streets, revealing

180   Cf. Renate Köcher "Kühle Realisten" *Frankfurter Allgemeine Zeitung* 15-11-95 p5; "People's Devotion to the Deutsche Mark Dictates White-Knuckle Sacrifice for the Rest of Europe" *International Herald Tribune* 6-12-95 p1& p8

181   Heinz-Joachim Fischer "Streit steht auf dem Programm" *Frankfurter Allgemeine Zeitung* 28-9-95 p18. 'Die deutsche Position ist bekannt: Die Währungsunion soll nach Bild und Gleichnis der starken Mark gebaut sein. Da hat Waigel recht, wenn er im Blick auf den deutschen Steuerzahler keine europäischen Freunde kennt.' Cf. David Marsh "Spaltpilz Einheitswährung" *Die Zeit* 1-3-96 p29

182   "Tietmeyer nennt die Europäische Währungsunion "Im wirtschaftlichen Sinne nicht absolut notwendig"" *Frankfurter Allegemeine Zeitung* 21-3-96 p5. Shortly after Helmut Schmidt claimed that the Bundesbank president was the 'most powerful opponent of the currency union'. "Der zweite Anlauf, die letzte Chance" *Die Zeit* 5-4-96 p4

183   "Farewell EMU?" & "EMU: What the markets tell you" *The Economist* 3-2-96 pp13-14 & pp21-22

deep fears and confusion'.[184] As the 1993 EMS crisis reverberated Kohl declared 'if it means the timetable is postponed by one or two years, what does that change?'[185] SPD intimations that EMU should be delayed began during the 1994 election campaign. Later Gerhard Schröder urged that the Mark not be 'sacrificed on the European altar'.

Kohl's will to establish EMU as the essential step to European unity is underpinned by concerns of a future alliance of neighbouring states against Germany. But there is also an implied uncertainty or distrust by German leaders about the Germans themselves, something often denied by the same political class—at least until out of office. By contrast a Deutsche Bank board member has articulated with candour that the real goal 'is to avoid Germany ever getting back to Nazism again'. Deciphering Kohl's logic leads to an either/or scenario, which in its bluntest but tacit translation says to the Germans (and indirectly other Europeans): give up the Mark and accept the euro, which we will do everything to endeavour is just as solid and dependable; or the alternative is that without associated deeper multilateralism you are susceptible to political isolation, extremism, and eventually a reversion to war.[186] Potential economic positives of EMU: removal of exchange charges, simplification of transactions, limiting the scope and dangers of currency speculation, convergence on a policy regime best able to guarantee financial security and generate prosperity—are relegated to the background. Kohl's 'negative' ploy stressing the prevention of war is not what the European Commission and others favouring currency union want to hear. The latter conducted an ambitious 'learn to love the euro' campaign. The two strategies appear at cross purposes. To employ a familiar metaphor, there are two sides to the coin. Unease *about* Germany has as its flipside an unease *of* the Germans. Increasingly they do not want German power 'sanitized' when it means maintaining a standard of living that is coming under threat. Ordinary Germans are asking, 'why are they doing this?, nobody can say why, no one asked us'.[187] An overvalued Mark is detrimental to exports yet the currency's strength indulges the German passion for holidays and second homes abroad

---

184   Oliver Schumacher "Zagen und Zaudern" *Die Zeit* 29-9-95 pp21-22; Sarah Helm "Kohl battles to curb mounting panic about loss of the mark" *The Independent* 27-11-95 p11

185   "Kohl says Union has been put back years" *The European* 13-8-93 p13

186   Helmut Schmidt is one who has 'no real confidence in the political constancy of our people'. *Handeln für Deutschland* (Hamburg: 1993) p134 Quoted in Marsh *Germany and Europe:The Crisis of Unity* p141. Schmidt appears as one of Kohl's strongest supporters in the endeavour to seal EMU. He places great stress on its political aspects and decries opponents. Next to Kohl, Stoiber or his own SPD colleagues Schröder and Spori were 'pygmies'. See "Der zweite Anlauf, die letzte Chance"

187   Public Interviews in Germany, August/September 1996

and provides a unique psychic security. Promises about European 'Esperanto money' are received with scepticism when Germans perceive that if anything goes wrong they will be the continent's underwriters. An exodus of capital to Switzerland is long underway. [188]

The German government's nominal aim is to place monetary policy under communal auspices but with so much insistence on strict convergence targets and reassurances no real loosening of German control will actually occur. Distinctions drawn between rival 'political' bank and 'independent' bank models cannot hide that the German preference for the latter is itself inherently political. It presupposes that the 'independent' bank will not operate in a way unacceptable to Germany. [189] For an audience of partners, German commitment to EMU is pitched to give the impression that the total package will contain French and Italian influence. Whatever is said publicly, there is no chance that the French, far less the Italians, will make European monetary and fiscal policy unless it concurs with what Germans want. 'The economic content of German policy is clear: it seeks to ensure that the European economy is run according to German economic precepts and wants to guarantee itself the ability to play the role of Europe's *Lehrmeister* and *Schrittmacher* even if sovereignty is eventually pooled in supranational institutions'. [190] EMU's key test is 'congruence in monetary behaviour as EMU proceeds. In particular will changes in interest rates controlled at the centre have similar effects on the financial systems of each country in the union?'

> ...The need for popular support is even more fundamental. There will be times when the actions of the central bank are judged inappropriate in particular countries. Politically, this will be all the more awkward if the bank is perceived to be far away and uninterested in the people's plight. If people are to tolerate such a regime, they must be persuaded that, on the whole it is good for them. The 'presumed core of the new regime, German'. [191]

---

188   See Perina "Zweifel am inneren Wert"

189   Thompson *The Economic Emergence of a New Europe?* pp101-106

190   James Sperling "German Foreign Policy after Unification: The End of Cheque Book Diplomacy?" *West European Politics* v17 n1 1994 pp73-97 See p92; Cf. Bundesbank director Otmar Issing "Geld stiftet noch keine Staatlichkeit" *Frankfurter Allgemeine Zeitung* 15-7-95 p13; Helmut Kohl "Die Europäische Währungsunion—ein entscheidener Schritt zum Bau des Hauses Europa" *Bulletin* 9-10-96

191   "Farewell EMU?" *Economist* 3-2-96 p13-14

If there is a European currency, whatever it is called, it will *de facto* be the Deutsche Mark and a European monetary system will *de facto* be administered by the Bundesbank under another name.[192] To keep the population, industry, financial sector, and political class assured, German representatives will impose the financial rectitude that characterised the old Federal Republic. Theo Waigel's 'stability pact' proposal would see fines levied on states whose budget deficits exceeded 3% of GDP and eventually 1% in 'times of normal growth'.[193] After a two year period to make good had expired these payments were forfeited to the EU household. The Kohl government has stuck to a longer term European conception of the national interest. This means enforcement of German economic rules across the EU and an as yet uncertain form of political union—or a continuance of separate nation-states.

---

192 David Marsh *The Bundesbank: The Bank that Rules Europe* (London: Heinemann: 1992); Alan Walters "There will be a common currency and it is called the deutschmark" *The European* 29-7-94 p9; Victor Smart "Kohl gambles on ditching the deutschmark" *The European* 26-8-94 p1; David Marsh "D-Mark für alle?" *Die Zeit* 23-9-94 p10

193 See the interview with Waigel, "No soft options on hard issues" *Financial Times* 11-12-95 p19

5 German Foreign Policy in a 'time with no name'

Focusing on German foreign policy after 1989, this chapter examines responses to forces and influences emerging from the domestic polity and from real or potential challenges and opportunities externally.[1] These include: a new assertion demonstrated in the reunification process; development of a more pragmatic and authoritative German approach within the EC/EU; policy toward central and eastern Europe where the German agenda envisages security, trade and investment, and cultural links as intertwined; and relations with the remaining superpower, the USA, and the remains of another, Russia.

Before reunification German foreign and security policy (in both states) was restricted and conditional to direction by others; afterwards it is loaded with new expectations. It has already been tested, with much negative response, apropos wars in the Persian Gulf and the former Yugoslavia and Germany may be confronted with future scenarios which challenge a tradition of pacifism.[2] Although several internal political barriers have been breached in the 1990s, military engagement retains sensitivity with many restrictions and qualifications on the deployment of German personnel and equipment. The military-security field is generally regarded as the core of Germany's 'normalization'. This process or concept is not only a response to changes in global security but the emergence of a more assertive Germany in

---

1   Many of these challenges may stem from outside Europe but impact on it, most especially Germany. Political terrorism, international crime and smuggling, spreading ecological calamity, war, famine or other disasters, further massive refugee movements all present actual or potential threats to Germany's internal security. As such they are foreign policy concerns. They are not all dealt with in depth here, rather they are considered as issues which German politicians want to 'Europeanise'. It is the difficulty in achieving a community response that is the main focus. See Hans-Georg Wieck "Transnationale Gefährdungen der Internationale Sicherheit" in *Deutschlands Neue Außenpolitik* Bd.2 "Herausforderungen" Eds. Karl Kaiser & Hanns W. Maull (München: Oldenbourg 1995) pp225-237

2   Hans-Peter Schwarz *Die Gezähmten Deutschen: Von der Machtbesessenheit zur Machtvergessenheit* (Stuttgart: Deutsche Verlags-Anstalt 1985)

general and applicable to its other external affairs.[3] Normalization is received with a degree of reluctance among some European states. Not because it encourages a dangerous hegemon but because as it occurs a broader German influence grows and 'Europe' moves in directions where German policy-makers consider it must.[4] What is, ostensibly, more 'security' for Germany and its European 'allies' in the conventional sense is accompanied by insecurity for the latter in other senses. This is paradoxical unless concerns about national identity, national independence and relative power are invoked as an explanation.[5] An indication of the sensitivities is transmitted by Kohl's statement that 'the less one says about Germany as number one in Europe, the better.'[6]

The EU (and its forerunners) and NATO have been the dominant reference points for German foreign policy. In defence dimensions the Atlantic alliance, despite occasional waverings, proved sound and cohesive enough to maintain (west) German allegiance and outlast the common foe. The viability of European integration and a simultaneous primacy of individual state actors found workable resolution through a synthesis of German and European interests. While this rhetorically scaled new heights under Helmut Kohl's leadership, the big bang of 1989-90 precipitated various crises that beset or exposed the limitations of the 'European ideal'. Familiar bearings and hierarchies were replaced by a renationalizing of the continent which altered relations between Germany and its partners, all of whom must adapt to a new context.

---

3   'Normalization' was/is at the centre of a long running debate on German history, politics, society, psychology, in fact almost anything. See, for example, *Ein ganz normaler Staat?: Perspektiven nach 40 Jahren Bundesrepublik* Eds. Wilhelm Bleek & Hans Maull (München: Piper 1989); Peter Pulzer "Unified Germany: A Normal State?" *German Politics* v3 n1 1994 pp1-17; Helmut Hubel & Bernhard May "Ein "normales" Deutschland?: Die Souveräne Bundesrepublik in der ausländischen wahrnehmung" *Arbeitspapiere zur Internationale Politik* n92 (Bonn: DGAP June 1995). On the parameters of German foreign policy before 1990 and changes since see Philip H. Gordon "The Normalization of German Foreign Policy" *Orbis* v38 n2 1994 pp225-242. Cf. Jürgen Habermas "Die zweite Lebenslüge der Bundesrepublik: Wir sind wieder 'normal' geworden" *Die Zeit* 18-12-92

4   Cf. two articles in the same edition of the *International Herald Tribune* 7-12-95 Joseph Fitchett "Germany moves to Shoulder Europe's Post-2000 Military Burden p1 & p8, and Alan Friedman "Will Europe Follow the German Map?" p8

5   Cf. another imaginative theoretical study by Ole Wæver "European Security Identities" *Journal of Common Market Studies* v34 n1 1996 pp103-132; Jill Robinson "Anniversaries, Memory and the Neighbours: The 'German Question' in Recent History" *German Politics* v5 n1 1996 pp43-57

6   See Hubel & May "Ein 'normales' Deutschland" p1

In a now widely quoted speech Roman Herzog asked "What is foreign policy, and what is the correct German foreign policy—in a time which has no name, in a Europe which becomes ever larger and a world which becomes ever smaller?'[7] His characterisation of the present as anonymous and reference to changing spatial dimensions attested to a new global fluidity. Precisely what constitutes 'interdependence', 'national interests', 'nationalism', or '*Realpolitik*', is also open to redefinition. Suspicions about German power and national prioritising have as a rule been deflected into multilateral arrangements. A harmonising of interests is everyone's preferred outcome and all governments enthusiastically advertise successes. It is also easier to desire or promote than to practically achieve.[8] Seven years after the fall of the Berlin Wall, foreign policy in Europe is neither united nor conducted by a generic class of diplomats and attachés. Even if the mass publics play little active part in particular decisions, foreign policy is the interplay of distinct national states with their own actual and presumed characteristics, interests, and histories.[9] Although the debate on German foreign policy has 'only just begun' the predominant perspective among German analysts is that 'national interests' is the necessary *Handlungsmaxim*.[10]

---

7   'Was ist Außenpolitik, und was ist richtige deutsche Außenpolitik—in einer Zeit, die noch keinen Namen hat, in einem Europa, das immer größer, und in einer Welt, die immer kleiner wird?' Roman Herzog "Die Globalisierung der deutschen Außenpolitik ist unvermeidlich" *Bulletin* 15-3-95. See also Theo Sommer "Außenpolitik mit Augenmaß" *Die Zeit* 17-3-95

8   A 1994 German Defence Ministry appraisal of foreign policy goals begins with 'the preservation of the freedom, security and welfare of Germany's citizens'. Following this come 'integration with the European democracies in the European Union'; 'the Trans-Atlantic alliance with the US'; 'a bringing in of our eastern neighbour states to Western structures and formation of a new, cooperative-security order encompassing all the states of Europe'; 'worldwide observance of human rights'. *Weißbuch* (Bundesverteidigungsministerium: 1994) quoted in David Schoenbaum & Elizabeth Pond *The German Question and Other German Questions* (Houndmills: MacMillan 1996) p219 fn 26·

9   Cf. Double-Edged Diplomacy: International Bargaining and Domestic Politics Eds. Peter Evans, Harold Jacobson & Robert Putnam (Berkeley: University of California Press 1993)

10   Timothy Garton Ash "Germany's Choice" *Foreign Affairs* v73 n4 1994 pp65-81; Cf. the series *Deutschlands neue Außenpolitik* Bd 1 "Grundlagen", Bd 2 "Herausforderungen", Eds. Karl Kaiser & Hanns W.Maull, and Bd 3 "Interessen und Strategien", Eds. Karl Kaiser & Joachim Krause (München: Oldenbourg 1994/5/6). Despite the variety of titles, the same topics and themes are repeated in all volumes and by many of the contributors. The pervading problematic, of course, is how to harmonize Germany's national interests with those of others; and how to award priority to the former when they cannot be harmonized. That this has, will and must

Strategies and Problems

Operating as the epitome of the trading nation, German export industries were well served by western European economic integration. From this base West Germany had become the 'proxy for Western Europe as a whole' by the 1970s[11] and a 'world economic power' whose inventory was dominated by intra-EU trade. This reached almost two-thirds of Germany's total by 1996. Excepting the Netherlands, a surplus has been consistently maintained with all other members.[12] In an increasingly competitive world Germany must develop this core and diversify into other regional markets. Progress in trade liberalisation and expansion of the EU to include Austria, Sweden and Finland has moved the Union in a favourable direction and continuation in both trends is desired. Acquiring mutual confidences in central and eastern Europe and elsewhere in the world[13] may be no more difficult than the assurance of congenial political relations in western Europe. German based firms retain a high external presence, second only to the US. With almost 12000 foreign affiliates they are around 80% more prevalent than French counterparts and almost four times the Japanese.[14] Regardless of its formal

---

inevitably occur is accepted nonetheless, wherever it may lead. Cf. Christian Hacke 'Manche Interessen müssen als gemeinschaftliche, andere als primär nationale definiert werden. Vor allem darf dabei Integrationspolitik nicht vordergründig idealisiert werden, als sei sie ein Prozeß, in dem nationale Macht und nationale Interessen keine Rolle mehr spielten. Das gegenteil ist der Fall: Die einzelnen Staaten versuchen sehr wohl, nationalen Einfluß auf die Politik und auf die Gemeinschaftsinstitutionen selbst auszuüben. Die Ziele der Europäischen Union mögen zunehmend trans- und supranational formuliert sein, aber Motive und Orientierungspunkte entwickeln sich aus nationalen Perspektiven.' "Nationales Interesse als Handlungsmaxime" in Bd 3. "Interessen und Strategien" pp3-28, here p7. Cf. the *Weißbuch* German text p5

11   Fred Bergsten "Economic Imbalances and World Politics" *Foreign Affairs* v65 n4 1987 pp770-794, p776

12   See Norbert Kloten "Die Bundesrepublik als Weltwirtschaftsmacht" in *Deutschlands neue Außenpolitik* Bd.1 "Grundlagen" pp63-80; Fred Bergsten "The Primacy of Economics" *Foreign Policy* n87 Summer 1992 pp3-24. *Zahlenkompaß 1996* (Wiesbaden: Statistiches Bundesamt 1996). According to one interview source in the Foreign Ministry in 1994, Germany, like the other EU members, has 'no national trade policy'. To a similar enquiry in 1996 another source replied 'well, not officially'

13   For example, next to the US, Germany is the largest trader with Latin America. See Wolf Grabendorff "Germany and Latin America" in *Europe and Latin America in the World Economy* Eds. Susan Kaufman Purcell & Francoise Simon (Boulder: Lynne Rienner 1995) pp85-112

14   See Reinhard Rode "Weltwirtschaft im Umbruch" In *Deutschlands Neue Außenpolitik* Bd. 2 "Herausforderungen" pp23-41

legal separation from the government the Bundesbank acts as an immensely powerful foreign policy instrument and EMU sharpens as a foreign policy affair. [15]

In 1992 one prominent scholar claimed that only an 'insignificant minority' considered the EC 'a device of foreign powers for constraining Germany's independence', which could now 'play a national role in co-operation with the East'. Two years later an interpretation by the same author contended that 'German official rhetoric about preferring a 'post-national' future as part of a tightly integrated Europe is a dangerous distraction from the serious task of defining Germany's real interests.' [16] No matter how much rhetoric about rendering the nation-state—or its 'mentality' [17]—obsolete, renaming or merging the political roof of a national community into a network of purported supra-national institutions does not suddenly disperse particular ties, nor its power, nor external perceptions which tend to connect these factors. It remains unlikely that further advocation of and binding into European structures 'will defuse criticisms of German "dominance" and economic "hegemony" in Europe'. German power 'will be more noticeable inside the EC than anywhere else'. [18]

Germany is confronted again by the determinants of size, both too big and not big enough, and geography. In May 1996 Foreign Minister Kinkel was still propounding phrases like 'Germany must find its place in Europe again'. Constant attention is given to fortifying the acronymic system of international relations in which German interests are preferably cultivated: the EU and NATO, the WEU as a bridge between them, the OSCE, G7, WTO, and the OECD. There is stress on the 'changed context for the definition of national interests' and the 'much more reciprocal' nature of national and international objectives and solutions. [19] Even while unable to

15   David Marsh *The Bundesbank: The Bank that Rules Europe* (London: Heinemann: 1992); Ellen Kennedy *The Bundesbank: Germany's Central Bank in the International Monetary System* (London: Pinter 1991); Michael Hennes "The Future of Europe: Monetary or Political Union" *Aussenpolitik* v48 n1 1997; Richard Medley "Keeping Monetary Union On Track" *Foreign Affairs* v75 n6 1996 pp21-26

16   Roger Morgan "Germany in the New Europe" in *Towards Greater Europe* Eds. Colin Crouch & David Marquand (Oxford: Blackwell 1992) pp105-117 and "European Integration and National Interests" Review Article, *Government and Opposition* v29 n1 Winter 1994 pp128-134, p130

17   Hans-Dietrich Genscher "The Mentality of the Nation-State has been Consigned to the Past" *The European* 11-10-91

18   Gary L. Geipel "The Nature and Limits of German Power" in *Germany in a New Era* Ed. Gary L. Geipel (Indianapolis: Hudson Institute 1993) pp19-48; Cf. Kloten "Die Bundesrepublik als Weltwirtschaftmacht' pp74-75

19   See Walter L. Bühl "Gesellschaftliche Grundlagen der Deutschen Aussenpolitik" in *Deutschlands neue Außenpolitik*, Band 1 "Grundlagen" Eds. Karl Kaiser & Hanns

achieve all its political class considers necessary, a combination of individual weight, working through multilateral structures, and hesitant or incapable alternates has steered Germany towards becoming Europe's political leader. While making references to France as a willing escort, Karl Lamers recognised as much. Yet he regarded the old problem of *großmacht* Deutschland as still apparent—lead but don't appear to: '*Wir müssen führen aber ohne daß es jemand merkt*'.[20] Required to calm anxieties while simultaneously showing leadership in crisis management, Germany is not yet beyond Scylla and Charybdis.[21]

German reunification, later exacerbated by the end phase of Soviet collapse, actuated the predicament of prioritising between deepening integration among western members and widening to include central and eastern Europe. This period was also an intermediate phase—until a future IGC would have to make definitive decisions on European political union. Up to and including the 1996 IGC this eluded communal resolution, going nowhere while German attention to relations in the east was magnified. The rest of the EU is beyond Germany's borders be they 'open' or not and European policy is still foreign policy. Josef Janning underlined the return of balance of power statecraft (not that it ever really left) as decision time on Europe's next big step—forwards, backwards or sideways—drew near.[22] The exhaustion of 'symbolic politics' threatens to leave Germany exposed as being without significant adherents to its European vision. Such a scenario may mean Germany has to live with a new 'loneliness' whereby it must learn both independence and to 'cooperate in a more amorphous and uncharted international environment'.[23]

	W. Maull (München: Oldenbourg 1994) pp175-201
20	"Oldtimer sucht Augenkontakt" *Der Spiegel* n7 13-2-95 pp26-28. 'We must lead but without anyone noticing '
21	Christopher Daase & Michael Jochum "'Partners in Leadership'?: United Germany in the Eyes of the USA" *Aussenpolitik* v43 n3 1992 pp237-245; Cf. the symposium transcripts on "United Germany: Stabilizing Influence or Threat?" especially Session Four "How Can the New Germany Defuse its Neighbours' Fears?" *Partisan Review* n4 1995 pp607-629
22	Josef Janning "A German Europe—a European Germany? On the debate over Germany's foreign policy" *International Affairs* v72 n1 1996 pp9-32
23	Christoph Bertram "The Power and the Past: Germany's New International Loneliness" in *Germany's New Position in Europe: Problems and Perspectives* Ed. Arnulf Baring (Oxford: Berg 1994) pp91-105

Germany's 'Normalization'

potsredure

For sovereign liberal democracies, 'normalization' suggests an endorsement to act in and however a government, conscious of popular desires, domestic pressures and various exigencies, determines to be in the national interest. It does not rule out the influence of international institutions or partnerships with other states on the formulation of policy, indeed for Germany it seems inconceivable that this could change. If the 'post-war era' as defined by the phrase that provided a temporal contextualization for policy-making, is, after various declarations of its end, really over, then Germany has the same options and responsibilities in setting and pursuing objectives as others. [24] There are, however, concerns about changes to an orientation that avoided friction in favour of compromise accommodation of its partners. Gary Geipel has summarised that 'some outsiders will suspect that a Germany compelled to pursue integration as the price of legitimation either doesn't have deep convictions about the process or cynically views the EC as a means of domination by proxy. On the other hand, a Germany that pursued deeper integration out of obvious self-interest would reside much further beyond question.' This type of commentary encouraged more pronouncements conflating European integration (presupposing agreement with 14 other members) with German self-interest. As Geipel continued, 'Those who remain most uncomfortable with German interests are the country's leading politicians and Germany's academic and media elite. Unfortunately, it is they who have the most direct connection to the public.' [25] This has altered as the political class, attentive to domestic demands and geo-strategic position on one hand, and divergent partners on the other, leans towards the former.

There are still doubts that German foreign policy, and with it Germany, can ever be 'normal'. One leading analyst has concluded that its 'full normalization is probably impossible', [26] indicative that any rise in

---

24   George Bush stated that 'there is no reason that a unified democratic Germany should be in any way singled out for some special status. In keeping with the Helsinki Final Act, Germany should be fully sovereign, free to choose its own alliances and security arrangements.' Speech in Washington 17-5-90. Hans Magnus Enzensberger argues that Germany should 'stop trying to be the world champions in doing good and just try to be normal like our civilized neighbours'. "Subterranean Heimat Blues" *New Perspectives Quarterly* Winter 1993 pp10-12. If, hypothetically, the sovereign state Germany were to repeal its own renunciation of possessing nuclear weapons and acquire some, thereby 'normalizing' itself in relation to France, the UK, the US and Russia, it is unlikely such a development would receive the same reaction as does the others' capabilities in this area

25   Geipel "The Nature and Limits of German Power" pp41-42

26   See Gordon "Normalization"

assertion is qualitatively different to that displayed by other leading powers. [27] This implies that the general population (and perhaps leadership) are 'abnormal' or contrary, and there is an absence of complete reliability about the Germans. French and British displeasure at German reunification and presumptions that changes in foreign, especially European, policy would follow, was signalled as concerns for Germany upsetting equilibrium and security. This was diversionary. The real concerns of the UK and France were not of a military-security nature, but chiefly economic and cultural and imbued with concerns about relative prestige. Because of these rivalries, foreign and security policy in Europe maintains a hybrid nature. There is multilateralism when suited or recognised as imperative by all and characterised by summitry and declarations of common intent. It has been unsupported by a common political will of any depth in crisis situations and usually results in stalemate or paralysis.

Compared to the French and British, Americans are more likely to urge a forthright expression of German national interests.[28] Impetus in Germany itself comes from a school of commentators many of whom are associated with the *Frankfurter Allgemeine Zeitung* and think-tanks containing various 'national conservative' elements. Usually favouring some form of, apparently contradictory, intergovernmental European federation, these sections of media, academe and politics also urged, and delivered, more German assertion and argued that it is incorrect to criticise 'national inclinations' as they were based on familiar democratic foundations.[29] There were many variants on this theme and again paradoxical elements emerged. On one hand such views transmitted a nervous perception that Germany was drifting dangerously between the former sanctuary of bipolarity and unattained anchorage in a European political union complete with the security structures so implied. There was also, however, resentment towards a Europe that primarily served a purpose of 'containment' or even as a parole officer of continuing 'rehabilitation'.

The bases of this discontent are the latent and overt continuities with Lord Ismay's 1950s summary that the purpose of NATO was to keep the Americans in, the Soviets out, and the Germans down. Andre Glucksman

---

27   There are many examples. Of the recent ones see Julian Critchley "Viertes Reich" *Die Woche* 16-2-96 p21. It may of course be others whose actions are anomalous or 'singular'

28   Cf. Ronald D. Asmus *Germany in the Eyes of the American Security Elite* (Santa Monica: RAND 1993)

29   Michael Stürmer "Deutsche Interessen" and Hans-Peter Schwarz "Das Deutsche Dilemma"in *Deutschlands neue Außenpolitik*, Band 1 Grundlagen. Eds Karl Kaiser & Hans W. Maull (München: Oldenbourg 1994) pp39-61, see p41 and pp81-97, see pp91-2

wrote some years ago that 'geo-political inferiority, whose end cannot be foreseen, is slowly being experienced as a second Versailles. The reparation demanded from the Germans, this time both in political as well as moral terms, threatens to turn into a philosophical curse, which is justifiably felt as intolerable'.[30] In an atmosphere of uncertainty over the US presence in Europe, some perceive that the EU is, or will become a veiled control device, that it 'had to degenerate into a European directorate over Germany'.[31] According to the CSU's Peter Gauweiler, the bottom line is whether the only good Germany is one without a national will.[32] Without structures geared more to community decision-making, Germany's 'normalisation' will occur as a separate nation-state, by necessity more than desire. Despite urgings to seize what may be a transient opportunity to integrate, it can only occur if partners are available and several European states have demonstrated aversions to a genuine defence, security and political community.[33] The uncomfortable but veritable reason is the perception in Paris that a 'Europeanization' not directed by France will marginalize France and allow a confident, assured Germany to predominate in central and eastern Europe while accruing more leverage in an expanded EU. In London the specific concerns and strategies vary but the intention is the same: avoidance of a situation whereby Germany becomes the proxy for the European Union.[34]

Reunification, Europe and German Pragmatism

After WW2 while Britain 'kept aloof' and France was intent on 'reestablishing its grandeur', only Germany tried for a genuine 'European

---

30   Quoted in Hans-Georg Betz *Postmodern Politics in Germany: The Politics of Resentment* (Houndmills: MacMillan 1991) p100

31   Herbert Kremp quoted in Peter Glotz "East European Reform and West European Integration" in *Toward a Global Civil Society* Ed. Michael Walzer (Providence: Berghahn 1995) pp211-222 See p214

32   'Letzten Endes geht es um die Frage, was unser Dilemma erleichtert oder kompliziert: ob ein gutes Deutschland nur ein Deutschland ohne nationalen Willen sein kann. Oder ob nur einem Deutschland, das sich nicht selbst verleugnet, ein Brükenschlag zu Europa und zur Welt gelingen kann.' Peter Gauweiler "...und über ihrem Haupt ein Kranz von zwölf Sternen" *Frankfurter Allgemeine Zeitung* 19-12-95 p11

33   Dominique Moisi "Insecurities, Old and New, Plague the Paris-Bonn Axis" *Wall Street Journal* 7-2-95

34   Jeffrey E. Garten *A Cold Peace: America, Japan, Germany, and the Struggle for Supremacy* (New York: Times Books 1993)

future'.[35] Germany and European integration were 'like twins: neither can remember an existence independent of the other'. The only area of the (West) German polity apparently 'at odds' with European integration was reunification.[36] Validated by hindsight, an almost imperceptible progression towards political leadership in Europe by the FRG had been underway since its inception as a state. German influence returned by way of prudent, gradual steps, beginning with Konrad Adenauer's reconstruction through western integration and later boosted by Ludwig Erhardt's *Wirtschaftwunder*. In a letter to Erhardt, Adenauer defined *Westbindung* as the 'necessary springboard for us to participate in foreign affairs again'.[37] Rapproachment with the GDR and the Soviet bloc through the Willy Brandt-Egon Bahr inspired *Ostpolitik* was followed by the pragmatic Helmut Schmidt's ability to engineer preferred lines of policy *vis-à-vis* his international counterparts. All had to deal with tensions between widening the bands of foreign affairs independence and political-historical constraints.[38]

Events of 1989-90 that culminated in German reunification have been well covered by a host of scholars and an extensive recapitulation is not necessary here.[39] A briefer sketch will suffice. The question of German unity

---

35   Sven Papcke "Who Needs European Identity and What could It Be?" in *The Idea of Europe: Problems of National and Transnational Identity* Eds. Brian Nelson, David Roberts and Walter Veit (New York: Berg 1992)

36   Simon Bulmer & Wiiliam Paterson *The Federal Republic of Germany and the European Community* p15 & pp6-7

37   Hanns Jürgen Küsters "West Germany's Foreign Policy in Western Europe, 1949-58: The Art of the Possible" in *Western Europe and Germany: The Beginnings of European Integration 1945-1960* Ed. Clemens Wurm (Oxford: Berg 1995) pp55-85

38   Cf. Peter H. Merkl "Politico-Cultural Restraints on West German Foreign Policy: Sense of Trust, Identity, and Agency" *Comparative Political Studies* v3 n4 1971 pp443-467; For an expansive account of *Deutschlandpolitik* in the decades leading to reunification and commentaries on various aspects of the reunification process as covered by the press, see Johannes Latsch *Die Bezeichnungen für Deutschland, seine Teile und die Deutschen* (Frankfurt a.M: Peter Lang 1994)

39   For a variety of the publications on the process, reactions and consequences of German reunification see: *Horst Teltschik 329 Tage: Innenansichten der Einigung* (Berlin: 1991); *When the Wall Came Down: Reactions to German Unification* Eds. Harold James & Marla Stone (New York: Routledge 1992); *The German Revolution of 1989: Causes and Consequences* Eds. Gert-Joachim Glaeßner & Ian Wallace (Oxford: Berg 1992); *Handwörterbuch zur deutschen Einheit* Eds. Werner Weidenfeld & Karl-Rudolf Korte (Frankfurt: Campus 1992); *German Unification: The Unexpected Challenge* Ed. Dieter Grosser (Oxford: Berg 1992); *United Germany and the New Europe* Ed. Heinz D. Kurz (Aldershot: Edward Elgar 1993); Manfred Görtemaker *Unifying Germany 1989-1990* (Houndmills: MacMillan 1994); Pekka Kalevi Hämäläinen *Uniting Germany: Actions and Reactions* (Boulder: Westview 1994); Konrad H. Jarausch *The Rush to German Unity* (New York: Oxford

was resolved through a complex series of negotiations and international legal arrangements that culminated in a political triumph for Kohl. [40] One particular aspect, the 'eastern territories-Polish border' issue, illustrates its intercontextual nature. Not only were the Poles distinctly uneasy at the prospect of German reunification they became more so by the way Kohl handled the issue risking negative international response for domestic gain. French and British leaderships tried to exploit the situation for their own ends and delay or prevent reunification. It was the US which acted as Germany's benefactor and guarantor. [41] Garton Ash has illuminated the multifarious domestic-international conjunctions and the special sensitivity of Polish-German relations. Kohl's political calculation was very much in the tradition of previous chancellors who had to operate in a more restricted manner and without the great historical-political opportunity that he was not about to relinquish. Kohl foiled domestic opponents of both right and left by presenting the successful concluding of reunification as the national interest *and* conditional on his re-election. He prevaricated in order to attract right-wing voters before having to retreat from an, in international terms, precarious position. By 'brilliant political manoeuvre' the onus was placed onto the 'nationalist-revisionists' to whom Kohl could say 'do you wish to be responsible for sabotaging the unification of Germany?'. [42] Others contested that this equivocation over the Oder-Neisse line actually prevented far-Right electoral gains. claiming such tactics were not responsible for this, that there was no evidence to support it 'but rather that unification overwhelmed their appeal'. Instead a potentially damaging foreign policy concern emerged at a time when an embryonic 'Germany' could scarcely afford it. [43] Realising things could rapidly unravel Kohl moved into assurance mode with Bundestag recognition of the existing border. But things had changed and the venture indicated there would be more challenges to what was previously

University Press 1994); Frank Elbe & Richard Kiessler *A Round Table With Sharp Corners: The Diplomatic Path to German Unity* (Baden-Baden: Nomos 1996)

40   Dieter Blumenwitz *This is Germany: Germany's Legal Status after Unification* (Bonn: Kulturstiftung der Deutschen Vertriebenen 1994)

41   See Elizabeth Pond's excellent account in *Beyond the Wall: Germany's Road to Unification* (Washington: Brookings Institution 1993) especially Chapter 14 "Meanwhile Domestic Politics"; For a later appraisal confirming the main points of the former see Josef Joffe "Amerika und Deutschland: Die Weltmacht, Der 'Sanfte Hegemon' und die natürliche Partnerschaft" in *Deutschlands neue Außenpolitik* Bd. 3 "Interessen und Strategien" pp117-122

42   Timothy Garton Ash *In Europe's Name: Germany and the Divided Continent* (London: Vintage 1994) pp230-231

43   William E. Griffith "American Views on the German Question" *Auf der Suche nach der Gestalt Europas* Eds. Jochen Thies & Günther van Well (Bonn: Verlag für internationale Politik 1990) pp115-124. See pp122-123

taboo. Ash offers a sharp insight into past practice which is, again, edifying for the future:

> If the liberal-left, as represented supremely by Willy Brandt, worked from the bases of moralism and a realism which included more than a touch of Machiavellism in foreign policy, the liberal-right, as represented by Chancellor Kohl, proceeded not only from legalism and idealism but also from a sort of Machiavellism in domestic politics - a Machiavellism which was in the real tradition of Konrad Adenauer quite as much as the desire for reconciliation with historic enemies. Some would say that without first securing their domestic power base the leaders of democracies will never have the power [to] do the right thing in foreign policy, and the reckoning paid off magnificently in the end.[44]

The reunification process and conclusion revealed a chancellor and government willing to assert a 'moral-constitutional' German national interest on a world stage amongst the heavyweight states, one that would make it 'bigger and better'.[45] While stressing multilateral and incremental features, Kohl's ten point plan was presented as a *fait accompli* and incited criticism for rushing and minimal consultation when inter-German dynamics forced an acceleration.[46] Two states becoming one Germany then precipitated transformation and convulsion in the European Community/Union. After Kohl's trade off with Mitterrand was formalised in the Maastricht TEU, a degree of symbiosis between German and European unity was maintained— until the debacle over Yugoslavia, the currency crisis, ratification problems, disagreements concerning the GATT and expansion to include central and eastern European states.

Approaching the Maastricht IGC, Germany 'supported a substantial and far-reaching relinquishment of sovereign rights'[47] in favour of a system whereby national preferences could be better presented as 'European'. Ideally, German requirements for an export-friendly trade regime, as well on immigration and refugees,[48] development policy,[49] environmental issues,[50]

---

44   Garton Ash *In Europe's Name...* pp230-231
45   Robert Gerald Livingston "United Germany: Bigger and Better" *Foreign Policy* n87 Summer 1992 pp157-174
46   See *Germany and Europe in Transition* Eds. Adam Daniel Rotfield & Walther Stützle (Oxford: Oxford University Press 1991) pp120-123 Kohl himself initially had reservations about committing to reunification
47   Reinhard Meier-Walser "Britain in Search of a 'Place at the Heart of Europe'" *Aussenpolitik* v43 n1 1994 pp10-20
48   Ursula Münch *Asylpolitik in der Bundesrepublik Deutschland* (Oplande: Leske & Budrich 1993); Cf. the contributions by Steffen Angenendt to successive volumes of *Deutschland Neue Außenpolitik*: "Migration: Herausforderung Deutscher und

peacekeeping and defence, border controls and transnational crime—especially smuggling of drugs, plutonium and other dangerous items,[51] could be channelled through a network of European institutions with expanded Qualified Majority Voting (QMV). If democratic principles of votes being allocated proportionate to population size prevailed, Germany's demographic advantages could be utilised in European forums. Behind the scenes sufficient other members, or aspiring members, could be persuaded through a combination of (mainly) carrots and (a few) sticks.[52] While retaining a strong transatlantic link, a recognition by other EU members of Germany's interests as their own would lead to the creation of a *Europäischer Bundesstaat*. Like that of an American connection, the viability and benefits of a CFSP and the dangers of existing without it are repeatedly emphasised by the governing coalition.[53] No matter how much the emphasis on common purpose, a professed philosophy and far-reaching practice of multilateralism, Germany's foreign and security policy has not become coterminous with its EU partners. Europe is still struggling in areas of intergovernmental cooperation and the *Bundesstaat* ideal has been rejected for the foreseeable future. Provision of the institutional mechanisms—meaning the political will—is sidestepped by states opposing removal of veto rights and national control over final decisions. A distinction arises between a policy of *integration*, which the German political class has in the main advocated, and one concerned with *binding*, more in line with French strategy *vis-à-vis* Germany.

German politicians want to expel 'balance of power thinking' and construct a 'European politics' beyond nation-state interactions and restrictions. Integration beyond vetoes means sovereign qualities, whatever they might be, cannot be exercised as they once were and opposition to this is based on the calculation that, if human history is any guide, the most powerful actor in the group then exerts most influence. Werner Link has shown that while European equilibrium scenarios could be antagonistic or

Europäischer Politk" Bd.2 pp 176-199 and "Nationale Interessen und Aussenpolitische Strategien in der Deutschen Migrationspolitik" Bd.3 pp231-240

49   Uwe Holtz "Entwicklungspolitik-Deutsche Interessen und Strategien" in *Deutschlands Neue Außenpolitik* Bd.2 pp221-230

50   Hans Joachim Schnellhuber & Detlef F. Sprinz "Umweltkrisen und Internationale Sicherheit" in *Deutschlands Neue Außenpolitik* Bd.2 pp239-260; Eberhard Feess & Ulrich Steger "Umwelt als Aussenpolitik und Globale Gestaltungsaufgabe" *Deutschlands Neue Außenpolitik* Bd.3 pp241-248

51   Hans Neusel "Internationale Kriminalität" in *Deutschlands Neue Außenpolitk* Bd.3 pp259-266; 'Erwarte keine Gnade' *Der Spiegel* n11 13-3-95 pp182-186

52   Cf. Josef Janning "Deutschland und die Europäische Union" in *Deutschlands neue Außenpolitik* Bd.3 pp29-54

53   Klaus Kinkel "Regierungskonferenz 1996—Europa zukunftsfähig machen" Speech to Deutsch-Amerikanischen Handelskammer, Stuttgart 27-2-96 in *Bulletin* 28-2-96

cooperative, any move away from integration means that Germany, despite it being an '*Option wider Willen*', is impelled to play the balance of power game 'nolens, volens!'[54]. Another view, often British, argues that a peaceful balance is 'one of the wisest and most profound insights into the way the European continent should operate'.[55] Inter-European relations become hazardous when 'unbalanced', when 'consensus' means, in effect, no balance. In a habitat featured by competing perspectives German international affairs are, like others, accented by the 'manipulation of interdependence'.[56] It is a question of who can do this most effectively. Requiring adroit diplomacy and a cache of inducements, Germany can turn its multiple demands to leverage by having many levers. 'Polycentric steering' and 'open polities' are favoured 'because otherwise it would lose out. Its post-war sources of power—beneficial economic cooperation and integration would be devalued and, being on the edge of an unstable post-communist area, Germany's security would actually be diminished.'[57]

With or without multilateral safeguards Germany has and will become more assertive.[58] Lily Gardner Feldman has written how 'In the past, despite the reality of systemic constraints, Germany could afford a flexible, magnanimous, relatively limitless set of policies on the EC.' The pragmatism of Adenauer and Schmidt is replaced by a new, necessarily tougher brand, one that tests not just German goals but European solidarity.

> Now, at a time of systemic fluidity, Germany has begun to face real limits in its EC policies financially and politically. Before the earthquake of 1989, Germany could paper over or ignore domestic fissures and inconsistencies in specific areas of policy toward the EC. Now Germany must squarely

---

54   Werner Link "Perspektiven der europäischen Integration" in "Die Zukunft der europäischen Integration: Folgerungen für die deutsche Politik" *Arbeitspapiere zur Internationale Politik* n78 October 1993 Eds. Karl Kaiser & Hanns W. Maull (Bonn: DGAP) pp7-26

55   John Laughland "The Philosophy of "Europe"" *The National Interest* Spring 1995 pp58-67

56   See Joseph S. Nye *Bound to Lead: The Changing Nature of American Power* (NewYork: 1990)

57   Lothar Gutjahr "Stability, integration and global responsibility: Germany's changing perspective on national interests" *Review of International Studies* v21 1995 pp310-317. Cf. CDU/CSU Fraktion im Deutschen Bundestag *Die Europäische außen- und sicherheitspolitisch handlungsfähiger machen* (Bonn: CDU Bundesgeschäftstelle 1995)

58   Cf. Harald Müller "German Foreign Policy After Unification" in *The New Germany and the New Europe* Ed. Paul B. Stares (Washington: Brookings Institute 1992) pp126-173 and the contributions to "Thema: Deutsche Außenpolitik" in *Neue Gesellschaft /Frankfurter Hefte* v8 August 1996

confront cleavages and contradictions. Divided Germany had managed to either clothe the nakedness of self-interest or, where it was obvious, not suffer suspicion about its intentions. United Germany is forced, for reasons of domestic and EC credibility, to make its objectives more transparent and then be scrutinized about its ulterior motives.[59]

This quotation impressively summarises changes in the pursuit and perceptions of Germany's interests. Firstly it is doubtful that Germany has ever been without 'suspicion about its intentions'. Why this prevails or why Germany should 'clothe' its self-interest when European partners have openly pursued their own typifies long-running double standards. Relative to the FRG's voting power in the Council of Ministers the German population is under-represented. An arrangement of one vote for every 8 million people compared with 1 *per* 5.7 million in France, Britain and Italy is unlikely to be sustained forever.[60] And Hans-Peter Schwarz predicts that

we can expect that future governments will react to harsher economic conditions by protecting Germany's own interests in the same hard-hearted, penny-pinching spirit as England did under Margaret Thatcher and as France has done for a long time. Germany can no longer indulge in a kind of generous chequebook diplomacy within the EC for the sake of advancing political integration.[61]

Adaptation to new status is characterised by blending updated versions of familiar foreign policy pronouncements with the exercise of greater assertion in actual aims and conduct. Without losing its discretionary tone Germany's 'modest profile' has changed. Kinkel claimed that 'more responsibility calls for more influence' and acknowledged that for Germany to maintain a favourable trading situation it requires 'stable international conditions'. He also made clear the large financial contributions made (in 1994) by Germany to ensure this: 8.9% of the United Nations budget, 22.8% of NATO's, 28.5% of the EU's and two thirds of aid to central and eastern Europe and states of the former Soviet Union. This exchange secured the FRG access to world markets and built its post-war prosperity. It is currently continued 'despite exceptional domestic strains', the intimation being that the absolute and relative size of German international contributions cannot be

---

59   Lily Gardner Feldman "Germany and the EC: Realism and Responsibility" *Annals of the American Academy of Political Science* January 1994 pp25-43. See pp33-34

60   R. J. Johnston "The Conflict over Qualified Majority Voting in the European Union Council of Ministers: An Analysis of the UK Negotiating Stance Using Power Indices" *British Journal of Political Science* v25 1995 pp245-288

61   Hans-Peter Schwarz "Germany's National and European Interests" *Dædelus* v123 n2 Spring 1994 pp81-105

taken for granted indefinitely. [62] A more commensurate influence in return means arriving at top echelon positions in world political, economic, and financial affairs. In the early 1990s a so-called 'French mafia' influence internationally had Frenchmen heading the European Commission, OECD, IMF, European Court of Auditors and the Bank of International Settlements among other posts. Correspondingly there was a dearth of Germans in similar positions reflected by the 'long-running and deep-seated anger and frustration of large segments of Germany's political, business and academic establishment about their country's second-tier role in the Bretton Woods institution.'

> The Americans and the French are widely perceived to have mobilised again and again the vast resources of the IFIs (international financial institutions) to promote their national economic interests around the world. As the main supporters of multilateral decision, they make the Germans feel as if they have been sold short...paymasters without adequate political clout...The Americans have the power, the French have the top jobs, and the Germans and the Japanese come up with the money.[63]

Kerneuropa or *Sonderweg*?

In 1992 the resolutions of the CDU Third Party Congress announced that 'The unity of Germany and the unification of Europe belong together. Next to the implementation of the inner unity of Germany, the unification of Europe ranks highest among the goals of the CDU. We believe that at the core of this unification should be a European Union...'[64] Academic discussions on the theme of a *Kerneuropa* reiterated the German impulse towards such a development as necessary to avoid a 'traditional' balance of power orientation. [65] Differences between potential members are deep and by 1993 most participants at one conference of experts considered that what the *Kern* implies, the beginnings of a federal European state, was no longer a

---

62   Klaus Kinkel "Deutsche Aussenpolitik in einer neuen Weltlage" Speech to the DGAP Bonn 24-8-94

63   Klaus Engelen "The mixed blessing of 50 years in Bretton Woods" *The European* 15-7-94 p19

64   *Resolutions of the 3rd Congress of the Christian Democratic Union of Germany* (Dusseldorf: October 25-28 1992) Resolution # A1 Sect. 1

65   European integration *is* a form of power balancing. Schemes like the CDU's *Kerneuropa* or the Balladur plan are proposals which seek to ensure that the originating perspective is satisifed and from which the maintainence of an overall equilibrium is conceived

'realistic objective'.[66] In the following year the EU presidency provided the opportunity, and a test, for demonstrating leadership and a capacity to set and direct an agenda. For the CDU the goal of a federal union was not consigned to the archives. In June 1994 representatives from France, Spain and Italy were invited to discuss a proposed 'communal European policy' over the course of their consecutive presidencies.[67]

Release of the *Kerneuropa* paper in September generated a controversy in German domestic politics and among various governments and media elsewhere.[68] It provoked criticism for not including Spain and Italy in the 'Kern' [69] and 'irritated' reactions came from European Parliament President Klaus Hänsch, Kinkel, Italian Prime Minister, Silvio Berlusconi, and others. The episode was criticized by some in the CDU as 'bad foreign policy'[70] and the paper's language described as 'brutal' in its directness and disregard for 'Euro-tabus'.[71] Nonetheless Kohl's Bundestag speech that followed appeared very much an endorsement with familiar intentions of repudiating German unilateralism. The Chancellor declared 'We were and we remain the motor of development in Europe...we want political union in Europe. That is our goal and is exactly what Wolfgang Schäuble wants. No more and no less is stated in this paper. Don't believe that the Germans will give up. We want the European Union.'[72]

---

66   See "Die Zukunft der europäischen Integration: Folgerungen für die deutsche Politik" *Arbeitspapiere zur Internationale Politik* n78
67   Victor Smart and Rory Watson "Germany set to begin great Union debate" *The European* 14/20-9-94 p1. The article quotes (though does not name the document) *Europa '96: Reformprogramm für die Europäische Union* Ed. Werner Weidenfeld (Gutersloh: Verlag Bertelsmann Stiftung 1994). Both the editor and a co-author, Joachim Bitterlich, are advisers to Helmut Kohl on European issues
68   CDU/CSU Fraktion des Deutschen Bundestags *Überlegungen zur europäischen Politik* (Bonn 1-9-94)
69   "Spanish Kritik am Kerneuropa-Konzept" *Frankfurter Allgemeine Zeitung* 7-9-94 p6. Relations between Italy and Germany have been under strain since with differences expanding from economic and monetary questions into foreign policy and historical issues. Tobias Piller "Zweifel an Italien" *Frankfurter Allgemeine Zeitung* 25-9-95; Heinz-Joachim Fischer "Streit steht auf dem Programm" *Frankfurter Allgemeine Zeitung* 28-9-95 p18
70   ""Kerneuropa"- Konzept führt zu Streit in der Koalition" *Süddeutscher Zeitung* 3/4-9-94 p1; "Kohl verwirft da Etikett Kerneuropa" *Süddeutsche Zeitung* 6-9-94 p2; Martin Lambeck "CDU-Spitze gegen Schäuble" *Die Welt* 5-9-94 p1; "Ein fester, aber nicht abgechlossener Kern integrationsorienterter Länder" *Frankfurter Allgemeine Zeitung* 8-9-94 p7
71   See the discussion in Hubel & May "Ein "Normales" Deutschland?" pp107-111; Theo Sommer "Wer auf alle wartet, kommt nie ans Ziel" *Die Zeit* 16-9-94 p6
72   Helmut Kohl "Aussprache über den Bundeshaushalt" *Bulletin* 9-9-94 'Wir waren und wir bleiben Motor der Entwicklung in Europa...Wir wollen die politische Union in

Kohl was temporarily placed on the defensive, charged with trying to create an elite group of some European states more equal than others. His tactic was to defend the document and its authors as a 'discussion paper' (though most observers considered it merely said what he thought). In this regard it served its purpose and sequels appeared. Initially bypassing questions relating to 'highest authorities', the CDU was pragmatic—or subtly demanding—in its methods of encouraging a greater congruence of European partners with its own conceptions of German interests. With regard to a European security architecture, the authors stated that 'without a further development of (west) European integration Germany could become required to, or through some security compulsions, attempt the stablization of eastern Europe alone and in the traditional way.'[73] A following CDU-CSU paper on foreign and security policy omitted reference to a hard core. It proposed developing a 'security policy identity' and the 'political will' enabling majority decision-making to enact an actual common policy. Germany's own lingering difficulty within the scope of a CFSP, military engagement, was provided with a convenient escape hatch whereby states could abstain from such involvement. It did not explain how situations of military crisis would be overcome if all signatories to such a proposal then exercised this option.[74] In other words the EU was highly likely to remain in square one regarding a situation like that continuing for so long in the Balkans: hopefully Britain and France (or the US) would continue to supply the actual troops while Germany would furnish diplomatic, financial, technical and logistical support. In effect, nothing would have changed. Enough ambiguity was built into the text to allow flexibility of response at a time when Franco-British relations appeared to be warming. As the *Economist* put it 'In fishing around for ways to improve European decision-making on foreign policy, Mr. Kohl's party shrank from recommending what it has in mind: a new institution whose head would in effect be Europe's foreign minister, or at

---

Europa. Das ist unser Ziel, und das will Wolfgang Schäuble genauso. Nicht mehr und nicht weniger steht auch in diesem Papier...Glaubt nicht, das die Deutschen aufgeben! Wir wollen die Europäische Union! '

73 'Ohne eine solche Weiterentwicklung der (west-)europäischen Integration könnte Deutschland aufgefordert werden oder aus eigenen Sicherheitszwängen versucht sein, die Stabilisierung des östlichen Europa allein und in der traditionellen Weise zu bewerkstelligen.' *Überlegungen* ...p3. See also Shirley Williams "Britain in the European Union: A Way Forward" *Political Quarterly* v66 n1 1995 pp5-22

74 CDU/CSU Fraktion im Deutschen Bundestag *Die Europäische Union außen-und sicherheitspolitisch handlungsfähiger machen* (Bonn: CDU Bundesgeschäftstelle June 1995)

least some foreign policy master-planner attached to the Union's Council of Ministers.'[75]

From this perspective, outright 'Euro-scepticism' or reluctance to forge communal policies can be circumvented by increasing the powers of the European Parliament, a form of foreign relations tending to diffuse confrontation between national states. France prefers strengthening the Council of Ministers, from where the French state can wield more influence, while the prevailing British position was one 'suspicious of all such ideas'.[76] Lothar Gutjahr claims that in response to aversions towards the 'F word', 'the CDU no longer talks about a European Federation'. But there is no clear alternative. Instead a 'Political Union of integrated states now is the ultimate goal—the exact political structure of which is deliberately left vague.'[77] In fact the CDU and others retain federal ideals for Europe. At its October 1995 'Party Day', more plans (or pleas) were put forward for 'effective action' in foreign and security policy by developing the 'decisive presumption' of 'political will'. This required the necessary institutional reform, along with strengthening the subsidiarity principle, improving internal affairs and justice cooperation, as well as widening the EU eastwards.[78] Pressing onwards Karl Lamers declared soon after, 'I hope that in ten years' time we will not only be striving for a European government, but we will have some kind of European government. And if we have a European state, then I hope it will be of a federal kind, and not a centralised one. We are of course strictly against a centralised government'.[79] The 'sales pitch' from Roman Herzog spelt out his version of German intentions and the barriers to it as if he were Foreign Minister. Barriers are not structural, that is, structurally insuperable, but theoretical and based on 'misunderstandings'. His optimistic prognosis is that if the Germans are 'patient' the British will realise that 'federalism is the opposite of centralism' and the French that federalism does not threaten the integrity of their fatherland.[80]

75   "Ever closer, more tactfully" *The Economist* 17-6-95 p56
76   See Paul Kennedy *Preparing for the Twenty-First Century* (London: Harper Collins 1993) pp268-272
77   Gutjahr "Stability, integration and global responsibility..." p305
78   *Beschluß des 7. Parteitages vom 16. Oktober 1995* (Bonn: CDU Bundesgeschäftstelle 1995)
79   Imre Karacs "Germany wedded to vision of unification" *Independent* 15-12-95 p8
80   Das beste deutsche Politikangebot für die politische Union Europas sind der Föderalismus und das Prinzip der Subsidiarität. Bieten wir sie geduldig an, bis unsere britischen Freunde erkannt haben, daß Föderalismus das Gegenteil von Zentralismus ist, und bis unsere französichen Freunde ein Gefühl dafür entwickeln, daß auch Vaterländer sich in einer Föderation zusammenfinden und dennoch Vaterländer bleiben können'. Herzog "Globalisierung"

Political changes throughout the twentieth century did not eliminate the present reality that although Germany may primarily be a *Zivilmacht* it is also the *Zentralmacht*. It is not only part of a Carolingian core or of a restricted trans-atlantic alliance, nor is it the 'sugar in [Europe's] tea'. [81] Garton Ash described Germany's pre-reunification condition as 'not a *Sonderweg* but a *Sonderbewußtsein*, a special consciousness'. This special consciousness, if it means being in the East and the West simultaneously, is also applicable after reunification. Despite all efforts to impress its reliability, speculation continues on what Germany will do, where its priorities lie, how demands on its attention and resources will be handled. Consecutive contributions to a 1993 publication give some indication of the uncertainties. One declares 'Germany remains a firmly western state' neither 'toying with eastern geopolitical expansion' nor 'devising an economic imperialism that will control eastern Europe'. The following appraisal predicts Germany 'will be inclined much less toward the west and much more toward the east than it was'. [82] In effect Germany does have a new *Sonderweg* but cannot permit negative connotations or anxieties to induce inertia. In a previous epoch Britain provided an external equilibrium to continental Europe. The mantle passed to US-USSR bipolarity until the system collapsed. France meanwhile dominated the agenda of integration. These states each have their own special ways and seem determined to preserve them.

The old troika of dominant German relationships, with the US, USSR and France, is now a quadriga, adding a collectively conceptualised east-central Europe. External reliance on judicious policy formation and decision-making has been placed conspicuously with Germany which occupies more space and duties as the 'balancer'. Creating a giant cohesive whole of West-East-Centre with Germany integral to all envisages greater foreign policy freedom than by being unattached to any single actor. Declaring the prosperity and security of France, Britain and the US as a national interest of Germany, Kinkel linked this amalgamation to a present

81   Hans W. Maull "Zivilmacht Bundesrepublik?: Das neue Deutschland in der internationalen Politik" *Blatte für deutsche und internationale Politik* n8 1993 pp934-948; Hans-Peter Schwarz *Zentralmacht Deutschlands: Deutschlands Rückkehr auf die Weltbühne* (Berlin: Siedler 1994); Martin Brüning "Deutschland in Europa: Zentralmacht oder Zucker im Tee?" *Neue Gesellschaft/Frankfurter Hefte* nl January 1995 pp85-87

82   Gerald R. Kleinfeld "The Integration of a Unified Germany: Update and Outlook" and Gregory F. Treverton "Forces and Legacies Shaping a New Germany" in *Germany in a New Era* pp49-60, p60 and pp61-78, p61. Questioning the sacred cow of being locked into western structures has appeared in Germany. *Westbindung: Chances und Risiken für Deutschland* Eds. Rainer Zitelmann, Karlheinz Weißmann & Michael Großheim (Berlin: 1993)

and future relationship with eastern Europe and Russia: 'Wir müssen die europäische Union nach Osten erweitern, damit auch dort Wachstum und Wohlstand die Grundlage für politsche Stabilität bieten können; wir müssen die NATO nach Osten erweitern, weil es ohne aüssere Sicherheit keine wirtschaftliche entwicklung geben kann; wir müssen das Verhältnis zu Russland und den anderen Nachfolgestaaten der Sowjetunion konstruktiv gestalten.'[83]

There are other voices countering the FRG's frequent tendency to attempt, actually or rhetorically, to be 'all things to everybody'. Quoting Frederick the Great, Zbigniew Brzezinski warned that 'he who wants to be everyone's friend has no friends in the end'.[84] And for Garton Ash 'choosing not to choose' will inevitably mean lapsing into reactive policy-making. To avoid this Germany must openly and convincingly set and follow priorities. Prone to multi-directional pulls towards the often competing interests of allies, none of which may actually be Germany's, it must not be afraid to place the preferences of France, or Russia, or the US second or third in its considerations. 'The danger is that by trying to do everything Germany will end up achieving nothing'.[85] One alternative that would not constitute a departure from *Westbindung* but would loosen 'traditional' aims of *Europapolitik,* and relieve some of its costs and tensions (if introducing others), is development of a more definitively trans-atlantic free trade orientation at the expense of a frustrated attempt at deepening European integration. Assured American interests could counter potential recklessness by an over powerful Germany or deepen a new privileged partnership.[86]

Eastern Europe and the Former Soviet Union: Cultural and other Diplomacy

The 'normalization' debate about Germany can be extended eastwards to encompass a whole region that has hardly been normal. The Kohl government's argument for taking the west to the east before it comes westwards will entail another economic shock, not least for Germany. But in the long run, apart from the various security issues it will help resolve, the

---

83   Klaus Kinkel "Eine gerechte und dauerhafte Friedensordnung für ganz Europa" *Bulletin* 16-2-95. Kinkel had by now retreated from opposition to eastwards widening

84   Zbigniew Brzezinski "A Plan for Europe" *Foreign Affairs* v74 n1 1995 pp26-42

85   See Garton Ash "Germany's Choice"

86   Cf. Wolfgang Michal "Die Vermachtung Europas unter deutschen Vorzeichen" *Neue Gesellschaft/Frankfurter Hefte* n8 August 1996 pp700-705

economic benefits are substantial. The German economy will also be invigorated and has several strategic advantages over potential competitors, not least geographic proximity and (when completed) a super-modernized communications system in its eastern *Länder*. Before reunification was sealed German negotiators were cautious about support for states in the Soviet orbit. As the communist bloc collapsed German influence soon became apparent and grew rapidly. In 1991, Markovits and Reich interpreted this presence as demonstrating 'all the necessary prerequisites for the successful institutionalization of a cultural hegemony.' Although there is a coexistent strong Anglo-American influence, their prognosis of an inevitable, if 'inadvertent', German ascendancy is at least partly substantiated. As the authors cited put it 'culture and language are among the most decisive transmitters of hegemonic rule' and with state support and business investment were propelling a re-emergent *Mitteleuropa*.[87]

Heinrich Vogel disputes that Germany has any designs on the region as a sphere of interest or that German investors have demonstrated any particular interest. Even if a vast economic potential is underplayed and great stress placed on a purported congruence of German-West European interests, the strategic necessity to stabilize its eastern borders means extensive German involvement.[88] Foundations already laid show a considerable degree of bilateral engagement. Between 1989 and 1992 German government credits to former communist states totalled DM136 billion, around 50% of international transfers.[89] Redirection of Goethe Institute and Academic Exchange Service (DAAD) resources to Eastern Europe and the retraining of former teachers of Russian has been instrumental in German becoming an 'asymmetrically dominant' language in eastern Europe. Between 1989 and 1991 *Kulturfonds* distributed there increased from DM48.6million to DM146million making it the leading recipient region, rising from 6% to 16%

87   Andrei S. Markovits & Simon Reich "Should Europe Fear the Germans?" *German Politics and Society* n23 1991 pp1-20. For Roman Herzog, by comparison, this Mitteleuropa would see German language and culture flourish without interference from politics. Roman Herzog "Über die Germanistik als Öffentliche Wissenschaft" *Bulletin* 2-10-96. See also *Mitteleuropa: History and Prospects* Ed. Peter Stirk. (Edinburgh: Edinburgh University Press 1994)
88   Heinrich Vogel "Osteuropa - Ein Schwerpunkt Deutscher Aussenpolitik" *Deutschlands neue Außenpolitik* Bd.3 pp169-174; Cf. Réka Szemerkényi "Central European Civil-Military Reforms At Risk" *Adelphi Paper* n306 (London: IISS 1996)
89   "Deutschland ist einer der grossten Zahler" F *rankfurter Allgemeine Zeitung* 1-9-94 p15; Görtemaker *Unifying Germany 1989-1990* pp157-158 & pp177-183. As the government encourages, building prosperity and civil structures in the former communist bloc is not solely a task for the state but many sections of German society. Carl-Dieter Spranger "Rolle der Nichtregierungsorganisationen bei der Armutsbekämpfung und beim Aufbau in Mittel- und Osteuropa" *Bulletin* 24-2-97

of global expenditure. According to Kinkel 'our neighbours hunger for culture' and, despite the presence of 90,000 teachers of German in eastern European schools by 1990,[90] Poland could still use another 4,000 and Hungary another 2,000 in 1996.[91] In 1992 a 'special program' promoting German language in the region was launched with 552 teachers and demand for 1000 more. Despite cutbacks in the total federal budget, by 1995 the yearly allocation for the program had risen to DM50million. For 1996 it was DM73million. Since 1992 19 new culture agreements have been concluded with east and central European and FSU states and 13 new Goethe Institutes and two DAAD bureaux were opened. 130 lecturers were educating teachers of German language and *Germanistik*. Of over 20 million people now learning German worldwide, two-thirds are in the former eastern bloc and over 6m in Russia alone.[92]

Much is contained with in the definition, offered in 1992, that stated 'External Cultural Policy fluctuates between the probably unsuccessful attempt to present who the Germans really are and the attempt to show others how we would like to be seen'.[93] Attention to foreign perceptions and the country's image abroad is matched by a desire to give expression to its cultural heritage.[94] Language programmes are joined by promotion of German literature, art and music, along with support for educational, academic, scientific and sporting activity. Enthusiastic, or relentless, proclamation of Germany as 'open to the world' and vitally interested in intellectual and cultural interactions, is the strategy for combining these goals with calculations on export, employment and international political

90   Markovits & Reich "Should Europe Fear the Germans?" p14
91   Klaus Kinkel "Kulturnation Deutschland—Partnerschaft für Kreativität" *Bulletin* 3-4-96
92   *Auswärtige Kulturpolitik 1990-1992* (Bonn: Auswärtiges Amt 1993); "Bericht der Bundesregierung zur Auswärtigen Kulturpolitik" Deutscher Bundestag 13. Wahlperiode *Drucksache* 13/3823 (20-2-96); *Deutsche Außenpolitik* (Bonn: Auswaertiges Amt 1995); Klaus Kinkel "Erklärung der Bundesregierung zur Auswärtigen Kulturpolitik" *Bulletin* 18-6-96
93   Nikolaus Werz "External Cultural Policy: Continuity or Change" *Aussenpolitik* v43 n3 1992 pp246-255, p246; Anton Pfeiffer "Ziele der auswärtigen Kulturpolitik des vereinigten Deutschland" *Bulletin* 17-1-92
94   Marc Fisher has documented this concern about international perceptions and noted Helmut Kohl's personal request for daily translations of foreign press articles related to Germany. See Marc Fisher *After the Wall: Germany, Germans and the Burdens of History* (New York: Simon & Schuster 1995) On a resurgence of political support for the nation as site of culture and identity see Wolgang Schäuble "Das Nationale nutzen", interview in *Der Spiegel* n38 1994 pp30-34; "Weitere langfristige Kulturförderung des Bundes gesichert" (Bonn: Bundesministerium des Innern 1994); "Grundlagen der CDU-Kulturpolitik" (Bonn: CDU Bundesgeschäftstelle 1995)

imperatives.[95] The external is thus a reflection or extension of the internal and provides a reciprocal invigoration of German cultural life—'internal cultural policy and cultural foreign policy belong together'.[96]

Having been eastern Europe's predominant second language before 1945, German was replaced firstly by Russian and then by English. Rapproachment with the Warsaw Pact states was accompanied by a large share of West German total expenditures on cultural diplomacy, which, in growing to a third of the foreign ministry budget, exceeded that of the US, UK, or France, with around half spent on language promotion. A sound preparation, as it turned out, for the unexpected reunification. After 1989 'official German cultural institutes were swiftly established in all countries, and there was a veritable explosion of interests in learning German. While the objects of this cultural diplomacy continued to be stated in liberal and cosmopolitan terms, there were very clearly, as in British, French or American cultural diplomacy, goals of competitive national interests as well.'[97] Geipel has noted that an 'assessment of a country's reserves of power cannot ignore the appeal and reach of its culture' and that 'even in the supposedly post-nationalistic environment of western Europe, German leaders are not beyond using language as a tool to gain political influence.'[98] Rick Fawn's analysis discerns the transformed east as a region for 'post-national' competition. 'Like Britain and France, Germany has a state programme designed to advance its language and culture in post-communist Central Europe. The same process of using state organs to create a non-state civil society that led to the influx of American 'Bohemians' is also responsible for encouraging foreign investment.'[99] Germany also remained a magnet for foreign workers whose prospects were enhanced if they spoke the language. Eastern Europeans were not learning German primarily to read Schiller and Goethe, or, in other words, 'for the children at home, father's

95   Helmut Kohl "Lebendige Demokratie—weltoffene Kulturnation" *Bulletin* 18-6-96. In the past two years President Roman Herzog has had considerable prominence in promoting cultural dialogue and related economic imperatives. See "Internationaler Bildungsaustausch verbindet Kulturen und Nationen" *Bulletin* 1-4-96; "Kultur lebt vom Dialog" *Bulletin* 17-10-96; "Für einen weltoffenen, interkulturellen Wissenschaftleraustausch" *Bulletin* 17-7-96

96   Herzog "Kultur lebt vom Dialog". Cf. *Ziele und Verantwortung der Kulturpolitik* (Gütersloh: Verlag Bertelsmann Stiftung 1995

97   Garton Ash *In Europe's Name* pp276-279

98   See Geipel "The Nature and Limits of German Power"

99   Rick Fawn "Central Europe since the revolutions of 1989: states, economies and culture in a time of flux" in *Boundaries in Question: New Directions in in International Relations* Eds. John MacMillan and Andrew Linklater (London:Pinter 1995) pp69-86

work as a window cleaner in Dortmund, not his studies on Husserl at Warsaw University, made the difference between bearable austerity and sheer deprivation.' [100]

German language promotion in Europe is regarded by some as an issue requiring more sensitivity than for English or French, including in EC institutions. [101] For Michael Clyne "the controversial question is how much Germany can push its language now that it has more political and economic supremacy in Europe if it wants to continue to regain goodwill lost through National Socialism. This sensitivity has been more strongly advocated by the SPD than by the CDU-CSU.' [102] This 'controversial question' then leads to others. If a German predominance is viewed with suspicion and Germany's military-diplomatic *Kultur der Zurückhaltung* should extend to a restraint of culture or a deference of German language to other non-local varieties like English or French, then Germany is certainly not being considered as 'normal'. Clyne goes on to mention that in eastern and central Europe 'those with right-wing political views tend to employ German as a lingua franca and those with left-wing views, English.' For Germany expectations and parameters are still apparently 'different'.

Cultural exchange, cooperation and assistance—estimated to cost DM1.2 billion in 1995—is not merely philanthropic. As its 'export world champion' status, living standards and famed *soziale Markt* system come under challenge Germany is seeking new avenues to assure prosperity and security. Herzog spoke of the connections in economic and cultural interests and their far-reaching involvement in foreign policy saying 'We need active courting of sympathy for Germany externally. That is not only a fundamental supposition for our foreign policy, rather also for worldwide economic and trade relationships. Therefore it is not only a task of politics and the cultural institutions, rather also of the German economy.' [103] Official mobilisation of this conjuncture saw a new series of initiatives including the symposium on "*Kultur, Kommerz und Außenpolitik- Ungewohnte Perspektiven, neue*

---

100   Ash *In Europe's Name...* p279
101   Helmut Schmidt is one prominent figure particularly concerned about French reactions. Assertion in linguistic matters may be 'perceived as too aggresive' and 'could stir bad feelings'. See de Swaan "The Evolving European Language System..." p253 fn 15
102   Michael Clyne *The German language in a changing Europe* (Cambridge: Cambridge University Press 1995) pp7-11
103   Roman Herzog "Globalisierung". 'Wir Brauchen aktive Sympathiewerbung für Deutschland im Ausland. Das ist nicht nur eine Grundvoraussetzung für unsere Außenpolitik, sondern auch für weltweit Wirtschafts- und Handelsbeziehungen. Deshalb ist das nicht nur eine Aufgabe der Politik und der Kulturinstitutionen, sondern auch der deutschen Wirtschaft '

Kooperation" in Frankfurt in January 1996. Kinkel's conception of a revitalized 'Germany Inc.' able to compete internationally and maintain the German standard of living determined that external cultural policy '*ist eine prioritäre Aufgabe...Wer unsere Produkte, Normen und Verfahren kennt, wird sie tendenziell auch kaufen und einsetzen.*'[104] For Kinkel, despite the EU's stress on common European identifications and interests, this is a world where competition in living standards is at its core a competition between cultures (*Standortswettberb ist im Kern Kulturwettbewerb*) Kinkel referred to multi-lingualism as a particular feature of European *Zivilisation*, not of a European culture. This was immediately followed by a ranking of German language learning among school students—number two behind English and ahead of French. In March 1996 Kinkel announced his 'ten theses for foreign cultural policy'. He continues to reiterate the imperative for an integration of Germany's cultural and commercial activity affirming that the 'culture nation and economic nation Germany are two sides of the same coin'.[105] Separation of politics, foreign trade and external cultural enterprise is a 'luxury' no longer affordable.[106] Under pressure in the high technology western marketplace, German business in partnership with the German language 'has a new chance in middle and eastern Europe.'

> The demand for German in schools and universities has explosively increased. We must use this to again build language bridges to our neighbours...language is a fundamental medium of communication. Every entrepreneur knows how important it is for one's own chances if written documents are in German. Local workers with German language knowledge are an evident advantage.[107]

---

104   *Kultur, Kommerz und Außenpolitik—UngewohntePerspektiven, neue Kooperation* (Frankfurt aM: Börsenverein des Deutschen Buchhandels 1996)

105   Klaus Kinkel "Zehn These zur Auswärtigen Politik" *Bulletin* 20-3-97; "Kulturnation Deutschland—Partnerschaft für Kreativität" *Bulletin* 3-4-96 and "Erklärung der Bundesregierung zur Auswärtigen Kulturpolitik" *Bulletin* 18-6-96. Cf. Samuel Huntington's "The Clash of Civilizations?" *Foreign Affairs* v72 n3 1993 pp22-49, which, though he mentions cultural differences in Europe early in the article, then proceeds to treat Europe's common civilization as superseding these

106   Kinkel "Erklärung der Bundesregierung zur Auswärtigen Kulturpolitik". Simultaneously, there was to be no 'instrumentalizing or commercializing' of culture, rather culture and economy were complementary factors for the 'new image of Germany in the world'. Cf. Herzog "Kultur lebt vom Dialog". 'Economy, politics and culture are equally important factors for purchase decisions...the culture of a country is not merely decorative, rather it grounds what one calls in English "good will". (Deshalb sind auch Wirtschaft, Politik und Kultur gleich wichtige Faktoren für die Kaufentscheidung...Die Kultur eines Landes ist also kein bloßer Zierat, sondern sie begründet das, was man im Englischen "good will" nennt.)

107   Klaus Kinkel in *Kultur, Kommerz und Außenpolitik* 'Die Nachfrage nach Deutsch an

Unsurprisingly, pushing the issue of eastern states entry was a priority of Germany's EU presidency and candidates were invited to 'association' meetings and the Essen summit. Having initiated a series of diplomatic and trade agreements Kinkel presided over an upgraded arrangement linking trade liberalization measures to financial assistance through the PHARE programme in 1994.[108] For one German diplomat 'the admission of other states is the tool for shaping the EU's future.'[109] Kohl reportedly told the Polish foreign minister that 'before 2000 you are in', evincing the strategy to co-ordinate EU widening with that of NATO. This date may yet prove too early and there is competition among the Visegrad states for a most-favoured status. It seems likely that at least the Czech Republic, Poland and Hungary will be admitted together.[110] In reference to the region between Germany and Russia, Herzog asserted that no state had the right to consider others as a 'security glacis'.[111] The reality is that integrating these states into the EU and/or NATO creates a buffer zone against renewed threats arising from instability in Russia. Besides more conventional security concerns, Germany requires new means to deal with a multitude of prospective immigrants. Widening the EU brings greater incentives for local populations to remain and would concurrently 'redistribute' some actual and potential German burdens. Culture related investments and programs accompany and, at least attempt to, soften traditional 'high politics' considerations.

Brzezinski has urged that 'German-Polish relations must not be subordinated to German-Russian relations', rather in the short term they must be at least equalized.[112] From German perspectives a deep and expansive

Schulen und Universitäten ist geradezu explosionsartig angestiegen. Das müssen wir nutzen, um Sprachbrücken zu unseren Nachbarn wieder aufzubauen...Sprache ist ein fundamentales Medium der Verständigung. Jeder Unternehmer weiß, wie wichtig es für die eigenen Chancen ist, wenn Ausschreibungsunterlagen in Deutsch verfaßt sind. Einheimische Mitarbeiter vor Ort mit deutschen Sprachkenntnissen sind ein evidenter Vorteil '

108   *Bulletin EU* 7/8 1994 pp74-76

109   Victor Smart "Germany courts eastern Union" *The European* 26-8-94 p10; Karl-Ludwig Günsche "Kohl lädt Staaten Osteuropas ein" *Die Welt* 1-12-95 p1

110   "Alter Traum" *Der Spiegel* n17 24-4-95 pp22-23; See also Friedbert Pflueger "Poland and the European Union" *Aussenpolitik* v46 n3 1995 pp225-231; Helmut Leipold "The Eastward Enlargement of the European Union: Opportunities and Obstacles" *Aussenpolitik* v46 n2 1995 pp126-135; Roland Freudenstein "Die Neuen Demokratien in Ostmitteleuropa und die Europäische Union" in *Deutschlands Neue Außenpolitik* Bd.2 pp103-119

111   Roman Herzog "Handel mit Mittel- und Osteuropa ein Pfeiler unserer Exportwirtschaft" *Bulletin* 10-12-96

112   See Brzezinski "A Plan for Europe"

reconciliation between Poland is vital for Europe.[113] For their part Poles must overcome fears of German irredentism and a negative image of the Germans ingrained by the school system.[114] A majority of German politicians would like to assuage persistent noises regarding the 'eastern territories' and the ethnic German populations there. In return for various German assistance, Poland granted 'special rights' to German minorities. In 1991 visa requirements for Poles travelling to Germany for up to three months were waived. Later, in his endeavours to efface the controversy caused by earlier hesitations about the German-Polish border, Kohl termed a European Union without Poland as only a 'torso'.[115] By 1995 over 20,000 Poles were living, as legal immigrants, in Berlin alone and around 125 million people now traverse the German-Polish border every year.

Germany is building another 'special relationship' with Hungary which was part of a former German speaking empire and later played a crucial role in the exit of escapees fleeing the German Democratic Republic (GDR). The Hungarian tourist trade, education system and written media all have a strong German influence. Herzog also told the Bulgarian parliament that a European Union without Bulgaria was incomplete.[116] German is used as a first language in some sections of Bulgarian and Turkish universities recalling its former predominance in scientific fields.[117] Germany is also forward in promoting relations with the Baltic states.[118] Despite a more

---

113   Roman Herzog "Für die deutsch-polnische Aussöhnung" *Bulletin* 23-3-95; Klaus Kinkel "Zur Verleihung des Deutsch-Polnischen Preises" *Bulletin* 29-11-95. Kinkel notes that Germany is Poland's most important east and central European trading partner and refers to Poland as a 'tiger' after the East Asian prototypes. At the same ceremony the following year he added youth, cultural, and academic exchange to this 'most important status'. See *Bulletin* 9-1-97

114   Richard P. Sander "The Contribution of Post-World War II Schools in Poland in Forging a Negative Image of the Germans" *East European Quarterly* v29 n2 1995 pp169-187

115   Peter O'Brien "German-Polish Migration: The Elusive Search for a German Nation-State" *International Migration Review* v26 n2 1992 pp373-387; W. R. Smyser "Dateline Berlin: Germany's New Vision" *Foreign Policy* Winter 1994-95 pp140-157 p146; See also Merkl *German Unification in the European Context* pp36-40 & p356. In general the German-Polish relationship has progressed well in recent years. 'Positive and dynamic' is how Herzog described it. "Besuch des Präsidenten der Republik Polen" *Bulletin* 18-1-96. Cf. The interview with Polish author Andrej Szczypiorski "Berlin kommt zu uns" *Der Spiegel* n4 22-1-96 pp128-132 which confirms this enthusiasm—for quite pragmatic reasons.

116   Roman Herzog "Rede vor der bulgarischen Nationalversammlung" *Bulletin* 1-4-96

117   Clyne *The German language in a changing Europe* pp13-14

118   Hans-Dieter Lucas "Prospects For Cooperation in the Baltic Sea Region" *Aussenpolitik* v46 n1 1995 pp24-33; "Fünftes Treffen des Rates der Ostseestaaten" *Bulletin* 14-8-96

problematic relationship with Germany, the Czech Republic became the pre-eminent candidate for entry into the EU and German investment and trade has played a significant role in its having the lowest unemployment rate in Europe. The two governments progressed to the signing of an open border and travel agreement in November 1994, which for Germany added another 'third country' barrier to would be immigrants.[119] German investment, constituting over 36% of the total between 1989-94 has been a major factor in the Czech Republic having the lowest unemployment rate in Europe. In 1994 this share increased to 48%. The French share dropped from 11.7% of total foreign investment after 1989 to 9% in 1994.[120] In March 1995 Kinkel announced that more than half a million Czechs were learning German. An expanded Goethe-Institute program and 13 'meeting centres' were to provide 'a great culture policy chance'.[121]

This has not been without setbacks. In support of reparations for Bavaria's 'fourth tribe', the Sudeten Germans, the CSU had blocked the Treaty on Friendly Co-operation in 1991-92. After a period of cordiality the issue of displacement or maltreatment of German minorities reappeared and a breakdown between Bonn and Prague turned the spotlight again on to 'image of the past.'[122] On the Czech side there is a contrast between the more nationalistic Prime Minister, Václav Klaus, and President Václav Havel who favours a much more conciliatory approach. Klaus was among many Czechs who believed Havel had gone too far in his apologetic response to injustices against Sudeten Germans at the end of the Second World War. On the German side the CSU, now the third largest political force, considered not far enough. Kinkel compromised by telling the Bundestag that history knew no end point.[123] Kohl's visit in January 1997 then gave some encouragement of a renewed understanding.[124]

According to German Defence Minister Volker Rühe, by mid-1993 Germany had provided DM80 billion and DM105 billion worth of aid to the

119 *Bulletin* 10-11-94
120 Schoenbaum & Pond *The German Question and Other German Questions* p139 fn119. On economic transition in the region see Bisiwajit Banerjee et.al. *Road Maps of the Transition: The Baltics. the Czech Republic, Hungary and Russia* Occassional Paper n127 (IMF: September 1995)
121 Klaus Kinkel "Zu den deutsch-tschechnischen Beziehungen" *Bulletin* 20-3-95
122 "Bittere Gefühle" *Der Spiegel* n18, 24-4-95 pp21-22; Wilfred Antusch ""Sudetendeutsch"—Überholt?" *Die Zeit* 19-5-95 p12; and the interview with former Czech foreign minister Jiri Dienstbier, "Steine über den Zaun" *Der Spiegel* n4 22-1-96 pp29-31
123 Kinkel "Zu den deutsch-tschechnischen Beziehungen"
124 "Deutsche-Tschechische Erklärung über die gegenseitigen Beziehungen und deren künftige Entwicklung" and the speeches by Kohl and Klaus *Bulletin* 24-1-97

countries of the former Soviet Union and central-eastern Europe respectively. Indicating that Germany was not striving for or capable of managing an exclusive sphere of influence he added that 'the economic revitalization of Central and Eastern Europe must not remain a predominantly German exercise. Germany alone cannot pay the bill for reforms in the East, and it cannot absorb all of the economic refugees coming from the East— functioning as a *cordon sanitaire* for the rest of Europe. What we need is a joint effort because we are faced with an issue that is vital for the whole of Europe.'[125] Echoing these sentiments, one analyst has stated that, 'ideally all nations of Western Europe ought to be as generous as the Germans. For better or worse, this is not the case'.[126] Germany is the only EU state with imports from eastern Europe growing faster than its exports. After Soviet Union's collapse, the subsequent desire for security of ex-Soviet bloc states and German economic, financial and new diplomatic power, have countered fearful perceptions of Germany among east Europeans. Whether they prefer it or not, their 'road into Europe leads through Germany'. By 1994 the volume of German trade with the eastern and central Europeans and Russians had reached DM104 billion and was on an upward trajectory with a flood of private investment expected later in the decade.[127] Herzog again highlighted this new pillar and expanding section of the German export market, growing quicker than any other region. By 1996 German trade with Poland, Hungary and the Czech Republic combined exceeded that with the USA.[128]

This cooperation manifests what Jacques Rupnik suggests is a triumph of political realism in the region, pointing to 'Poland's more classical combination of nationalism and realpolitik' outweighing the *Moralpolitik* of Václav Havel. 'National interest and the balance of power rather than a policy based on ethical values and the promise of a "new world order" are the motto of the day for Central Europe's relations with Germany.' If this is so it makes it unlikely that Germany can or will act any differently.[129] German proponents of widening must convince the German

125   Volker Rühe "Shaping Euro-Atlantic Policies: A Grand Strategy for a New Era" *Survival* v35 n2 1993 pp129-137, p134

126   Jaromir Cetoka "Barriers to European (East-West) integration" in *Transforming Economies and European Integration* Eds. Rumen Dobrinsky & Michael Landesmann (Aldershot: Edward Elgar 1995) pp32-45

127   Interview Sources, Auswärtiges Amt, Bonn; Sächsisches Ministerium des Innern, Dresden, September 1996

128   Herzog "Handel mit Mittel- und Osteuropa ein Pfeiler unserer Exportwirtschaft"

129   Jacques Rupnik "Europe's New Frontiers: Remapping Europe" *Dædelus* v123 n2 1994 pp91-115. See also Klaus Kinkel "Vorbereitung der Europäischen Union auf die Ostweiterung" *Bulletin* 3-9-96; and Istvan P. Szekely "Financial reforms and economic integration" in *Transforming Economies...* pp199-227 on a contest between

public and current EU members of its worth, or necessity, and deal with a scenario whereby prising newly gained state sovereignty from the candidates and passing it to 'Europe' may be difficult.[130] A borderless 'denationalized' Europe could alter the international legal status of Polish, Czech, or Baltic republics' sovereignty. Arrangements might even be reached with Russia. German minorities living in other states could come under some form of 'European' jurisdiction—in a 'Europe' certain to reflect greater German influence. Absorption of these states and Germany in a European Union would bring Germans outside Germany in without transgressing national political borders because these would become obsolete.[131] Like reunification itself this is German nationalism absorbed in 'Europeanism'. It could also be a 'Europeanism' that overcomes historical feuds.

The 1990s have been described as a period when 'both Germany and Russia are in the midst of sensitive and complex redefinitions'.[132] German perceptions of the absolute necessity for good relations with the former Soviet states, especially Russia, is reflected in the government's insistent stress on ensuring stability there.[133] From the moment reunification became a real possibility the Kohl government worked fervently to ensure that regression, in the form of a Soviet change of mind, or change of leadership, would not occur. In rapid response to a request for food aid Kohl asked for the immediate preparation of a 'national plan as well as an EC program—with priority to the national plan' to provide assistance. Kohl was not about to rely on his European partners in matters that needed swift action. Having been informed that between 60-100 million Soviet citizens were living on the poverty line 'the effect of German help would not only safeguard Gorbachev's position, Kohl argued, but would improve the climate for German unification as well.'[134]

Anglo-Saxon and German financal models

130   See Andreas Oldag "Wer soll das bezahlen, wer hat so viel Geld?" and Michael Frank "Die EU möge sich bitte nicht zuviel herausnehmen" *Süddeutsche Zeitung* 27-3-96 p11

131   Cf. The pre-reunification statement of current defence minister Volker Rühe. 'Anyone who wants a European peace order in which frontiers lose their political significance...must also acknowledge that only frontiers which are not politically disputed can lose their significance.' Bundestag debate quoted in Renata Fritzsch-Bournazel *Confronting the German Question: Germans on the East-West Divide* trans. Caroline Bray (Oxford: Berg 1988) See p113 & p137

132   Brzezinski "A Plan for Europe"

133   Kohl visited in February 1996. See his press conference speech "Erklärung vor der Presse in Moskau" *Bulletin* 4-3-96

134   Görtemaker *Unifying Germany 1989-1990* pp157-158. For more on loans see pp177-183

A more 'general human interest' is a written and spoken intention of German foreign policy yet it has been subordinated in favour of stable relations with the Russian government. The 1990 German-Soviet treaty on Good Neighbourliness, Partnership and Cooperation desired 'to set the final seal on the past' and 'build a new, united Europe on the basis of common values'. The contracting parties placed 'territorial integrity' high on the agenda, 'undertaking to respect without qualification' that of 'all states in Europe within their present frontiers' (A2) and 'refrain from any threat or use of force which is directed against territorial integrity or the political independence of the other side' (A3). Any potential 'threat to or violation of peace or [that which] may lead to dangerous international complications' was to result in a 'coordinating of positions'.[135] The old FRG had stipulated self-determination of the GDR population as a fundamental right and major justification for Germany's reunification. Secondly, the government (and many others in Germany) urged the recognition of the self-proclaimed Slovenian and Croatian Republics, by reference to the same principle. Having alternatively placed the desire of a nation (the Germans), the legal status of states (united Germany and the Russian Federation), and again the desires of nations without states (Croatia and Slovenia) at the forefront of its foreign policy, when faced with the Chechen bid for independence Germany acknowledged the primacy of the recognized state (Russian Federation). And this was not only for legal reasons. New Germany developed a new *Realpolitik*.

As representative of Russia's biggest trading partner and aid donor, Kohl's appeals to Boris Yeltsin for an end to bloodshed in Chechnya was joined by a veiled warning to his western partners. Kohl cautioned against what might be interpreted as abrasive or invasive responses: 'threatening gestures will achieve nothing at the moment...every destabilization of Russia is a destabilisation of Europe...territorial integrity must be respected.'[136] The memory of the 1991 attempted coup had not faded. Not only would a successful putsch have instituted a much more authoritarian regime but millions would have fled westwards. Facing calls in the Bundestag from opposition members for action or harsher condemnation of Russia, Kohl and Kinkel framed responses to the Chechen conflict within the overall German-

---

135   "German-Soviet Treaty on Good Neighbourliness, Partnership and Cooperation From 13 September 1990" in Blumenwitz *This is Germany: Germany's Legal Status after Unification* pp62-66

136   "Kohl denounces 'madness' in Chechnya" *The Australian* 9-1-94 p6; See also Boris Orlow "Europas Haltung gegenüber Rußland und der Tschetschenien-Krieg" *Osteuropa* n10 1995 pp921-926

Russian partnership, reiterating the need for the hard won friendship and trust to be secured and the reform course in Russia continued.

> Nach schwerigsten Jahren mit grosse Leid für beide Völker haben wir Deutschen zu Russland ein partnerschaftliches Verhältnis gewonnen. Das war, ist und bleibt für beide Seiten sehr wichtig. Deutschland will Partner und Freund Russlands sein und bleiben. Die Bundesregierung setzt auf die fortsetzung des Reformkurses durch die jetzige Regierung

> Die Politik der Bundesrepublik gegenüber Russland wird von unseren grundlegenden Interessen und von festen Prinzipien geleitet...Es ist unser fundamentales Interesse, dass die Entwicklung Russlands hin zu Demokratie, Rechtstaat und Marktwirtschaft nicht aufgehalten wird.[137]

A continuing enigma is the *Kaliningrader Gebiet*, home to around 20,000 *Rußlanddeutsche* and which is 'not a typical Russian territory'. Pressures for a transition of the city area to becoming an autonomous German republic keep speculation alive as to when it might become Königsberg again. [138] Attempts to develop the 'special economic zone' "Jantar'" are hindered by bureaucratic, internal political, and 'conceptual' problems. [139] Intermittent rumblings of anti-German feeling in parts of the former Soviet Union encourage German minorities to get out, while German government aid and initiatives like new Goethe Institutes at Alma-Ata in Kazakhstan and Tiflis in Georgia are intended to keep them there. [140] While there is great bilateral potential, trade with Russia has been more sluggish than with other former communist bloc states with many concerns about crime and other insecurities for investment. In May 1996 Theo Waigel met with Yeltsin in Moscow to eliminate double taxing and make German investment in Russia more attractive. Germany remains the Russian

---

137   Klaus Kinkel "Erklärung der Bundesregierung zur Lage in Tschetschenien" & Helmut Kohl " Rede des Bundeskanzlers vor dem Deutschen Bundestag" *Bulletin* 23-1-95

138   See Alvydas Nikzentaitis "Das Kalingrader Gebiet im Spannungsfeld internationaler Interessen" *Ost Europa* n10 1995 pp927-935 Olaf Ihlau "Da werden Blasen geschlagen" *Der Spiegel* 17-4-95 pp68-71

139   Heike Dörrenbächer "Die Sonderwirtschaftszone Jantar´ von Kalinigrad (Königsberg) *Arbeitspapiere zur Internationalen Politik* n81 (Bonn: DGAP 1994)

140   Klaus Kinkel "Deutsche Außenpolitk für Georgien und den Transkaukasus" *Bulletin* 6-2-96; "Deutsche-kasachische Vereinbarung über die Zusammenarbeit bei der Unterstützung der Bürger deutscher Nationalität der Republik Kasachstan" *Bulletin* 14-8-96

Federation's largest aid donor but economic aid was not enough. It may create a market economy but not necessarily a democracy.[141]

After an initial honeymoon period the relationship between the West, predominantly represented by the US and Germany, and Russia, the Soviet Union's 'legal heir', deteriorated. For many Russians if the Cold War was over and old divisions removed, why should NATO exist at all? While Germany and the USA were still engaged in internal debates on NATO widening, the 'Partnership for Peace' announced in 1994 was an interim arrangement designed to signal to eastern Europeans that they would soon be part of 'the West' while placating Russian concerns and bringing them into a common structure. Hawks in the American security establishment and the Congress became more strident while the German Defence Ministry overcame resistance by Kinkel and the Foreign Ministry. The respective hierarchies concluded that extending NATO was imperative while instability remained and even more so should a stable, but authoritarian regime come to power. In December 1994 the announcement was made.[142] Along with receiving this proposal as a threat, the Russian political and military elite also considered the treaty on disarmament of conventional weapons and troop reductions was weighted too heavily against them. Senior defence figures wanted a military build-up to balance a 'greater western alliance' and some prophesized that NATO widening would lead to the 'third world war'.[143] While on the one hand the West's vacillation in the Balkans revealed an acute lack of political will, NATO expansion made Russia even more isolated and nervous. Following the Croat counteroffensive in August 1995 amid increased speculation about a lifting of the western arms embargo, Russia removed economic sanctions on the Serbs, signalling a potential intensification.[144]

Russian political and military figures do not present the (usually) diplomatic exterior of their German counterparts. The chief of the German section in Russia's foreign ministry said he could not 'see any great competition between Germany and Russia in Central Europe'. Determining it

---

141   Michael McFaul "Why Russia's Politics Matter" *Foreign Affairs* v74 n1 1995 pp87-99; See also Hans-Hermann Hoehmann & Christian Meier "German-Russian Economic Relations—Appraisals and Perspectives" *Aussenpolitik* v46 n1 1995 pp52-5

142   See Christoph Bertram *Europe in the Balance: Securing the Peace Won in the Cold War* (Washington: Carnegie Endowment 1995)

143   "Alter Traum" *Der Spiegel* n17 24-4-95 pp22-23; "Leider hat Moskau immer noch Angst" *Der Spiegel* n15 10-4-95; Alexander Rahr & Joachim Krause "Russia's New Foreign Policy" *Arbeitspapiere zur Internationale Politik* n91 (Bonn: DGAP 1995)

144   Then came a mysterious attack on the American Embassy in Moscow and brawling in the Duma following NATO air strikes

to be a 'hypothetical question because its not a current question', he blithely concluded 'somehow we'll just have to divide it up'. German ambassador Otto von der Gablentz was more tactful claiming the world would not see 'in the last resort a German-Russian dominated Europe'. Central to his mission was informing the Russians that 'Germany is no longer the isolated nation-state they used to know'.[145] Concurrently Germany may 'understand the present problems of Russia better other European countries and because of its non-nuclear status represent no military danger'.[146]

Military Questions: The Gulf, Yugoslavia and NATO

George Bush's 'Partners in Leadership' speech set the tone for a reorganising of US priorities in Europe.[147] Divergences that appeared between the Germans and Americans as the European project revitalized during the 1980s began to narrow after 1989.[148] Common interest regrouped despite the diplomatic fracas over the Gulf War. After the Cold War Germany's ruling coalition has worked to ensure that shifts in US priorities do not cause a dealignment with German political and strategic imperatives. If, in particular regard to Germany, 'Europeans have good memories', Americans are prone to 'forgive and forget more readily'.[149] It was combined American and German statecraft that persuaded Gorbachev to facilitate reunification, marginalizing the French and British in the process.[150] Germany has and is

145   Fred Hiatt & Rick Atkinson "Europe's Giants Look Beyond the Past" *Guardian Weekly* 25-2-96 p15. Many among Russian military and political establishments do not appear to perceive Germany as primarily embedded within the EU and thus not an independent actor. Cf. A New Ostpolitik: Strategies for a United Europe Ed. Werner Weidenfeld (Gütersloh: Bertelsmann 1997) pp57-72; Helmut Hubel "Die Schwerige Partnershaft mit Russland" in *Deutschlands Neue Außenpolitik* Bd.3 pp137-141

146   Alexander Rahr "Russland in Europa" *Deutschlands Neue Außenpolitik* Bd.2 pp121-136, p135

147   George Bush, speech in Mainz 31-5-89; William E. Griffith "American Views on the German Question' in *Auf der Suche nach der Gestalt Europas* Eds. Jochen Thies & Günther van Well (Bonn: Verlag für internationale Politik 1990) pp115-123

148   W. R. Smyser *Restive Partners: Washington and Bonn Diverge* (Boulder: Westview 1990); Wolfram Hanrieder *Germany, America, Europe: Forty Years of German Foreign Policy* (New Haven: Yale University Press 1989)

149   Cf. Wolfgang Bergsdorf "West Germany's Political System under Stress: Decision-Making Processes in Bonn 1990" in Dieter Grosser *German Unification: The Unexpected Challenge* (New York: Berg 1992) pp88-106, p100 and Griffith "American Views..." p117 & p122 in *Auf der Suche nach der Gestalt Europas*

150   Philip Zelikow & Condoleeza Rice *Germany Unified and Europe Transformed: A*

198 *Germany, Europe and the Persistence of Nations*

'Americanising' as much as it is 'Europeanising'. [151] Bonn-Berlin is accepting of American economic penetration and an associated cultural presence in Europe which Paris by comparison sees as altogether undesired adjuncts to the United States' role in military security. Conversely Washington regards Germany as Europe's political, as well as economic, pacemaker. Germany's interests and Europe's are 'increasingly deemed to be the same thing'. [152] Clinton's 'America is at your side, now and forever' was the type of pronouncement German governments want to ensure in practice. The present coalition relentlessly stresses that the US remains an imperative partner for Europe. [153]

Polls consistently reveal the US to be considered Germany's most important ally especially in terms of defence and security, but also politically. In a survey published December 1994, 42% of Germans polled named the US as their country's most reliable ally with 27% citing France. [154] Many of Germany's political establishment think the same, notwithstanding the effort spent sustaining the image of a cosy Franco-German affinity. German officials working at the American Embassy in Bonn are in no doubt that the relationship with the US is the *most* crucial for Germany and is perceived as such by those who count. [155] In a typically sober analysis Josef Joffe argues that the relationship to the US is auspicious, and becoming more so, because it is devoid of historical enmities common to European nations and based on complementary interests. Without the US presence, post-war Franco-German relations would not have succeeded. [156]

United Germany's propulsion into the world of fully sovereign states brought with it criticism for early foreign policy initiatives that would

---

Study in Statecraft (Cambridge Ma.: Harvard University Press 1995)

151   *The European Challenges Post-1992: Shaping Factors, Shaping Actors* Eds. Alexis Jaquemin & David Wright (Aldershot: Edward Elgar 1993) p43

152   Victor Smart "Germany courts eastern Union" *European* 7-9-94

153   Kinkel "Deutsch-amerikanische Partnerschaft - die transatlantische Agenda 2000" *Bulletin* 24-4-95

154   David Marsh "Germans and British hold similar views on European Union" *Financial Times* 5-12-94 p2. 'Don't knows' accounted for 25%. Peter H.Merkl had previously listed 'priority in relations' among Germans as 59% for the former Soviet Union, 44% for the US and 36% for France. The top two 'priorities' are then outside Europe. See *German Unification in the European Context* p423

155   Interview sources, US embassy, Bonn, October 1994

156   Joffe "Amerika und Deutschland: Die Weltmacht, Der 'Sanfte Hegemon' und die natürliche Partnerschaft". Both Joffe and Hubel & May in "Ein 'normales' Deutschland" pp58-59, refer to the large numbers of German descended people among the American population as a significant factor in the relationship. Joffe rates Germans numerically less than the English or Irish while the other authors claim Germans, at 18%, equal English and Irish stock combined

unlikely have attracted the same response were it not a 'newcomer' to such situations and particularly were it not 'Germany'. Germans were expected to complete a massive psychological transformation and fight in an overseas war before it had registered on the 'mental maps of its politicians and citizens'. [157] Opting out of the operational theatre during the Gulf War was then followed by castigation for policy on a crumbling Yugoslavia. Being 'criticised for both abroad confirms the contradictory nature of the expectations and fears which relate to Germany'. [158] Not deploying troops in the Gulf cost the FRG DM70 billion 'compensation' and had one commentator describing it as a 'teutonic, double-headed European ostrich'. [159] Accusations of 'cheap excuses' were joined by questioning of whether Kohl had any advisers. One conference report claimed it was 'difficult for the media to find any foreign policy experts in the CDU' and went on to say 'this lack of expertise in foreign policy is true for all of the parties'. [160] This rude shock exposed the gap between parley about new responsibility and practice in a live and dangerous situation.

In the Gulf War, provision of naval vessels and logistical support was as far as German participation went. Domestic opinion and prevailing constitutional interpretations said it was not ready for more. Nonetheless Germany is expected, sooner rather than later, to be an 'equal' in all respects. The exception is national possession of nuclear weapons and that is not impossible. [161] A gravitation towards what some regard as responsibility, some as normality and others as menacing regression will see Germans develop 'more appreciation for the United States as they themselves inherit more of the American security function'. And Philip Gordon notes that it was easier to feel morally superior and make judgements when 'spared from bearing responsibility for security around the world'. Conversely the US may 'gain an appreciation of the German art of cooperative, ambiguous solutions'. An appreciation perhaps, but putting it in to practice is another thing. While ambiguity or *sowohl-als-auch*, was at the core of 'Genscherism' this has

---

157   Beate Neuss "The European Community: How to Counterbalance the Germans" in *German Unification: The Unexpected Challenge* pp136-149, p146

158   Daase & Jochum "'Partners in Leadership'?"

159   Alan Sked "Cheap Excuses" *The National Interest* n24 Summer 1991 pp51-60; On compensation costs see Theo Sommer "Der Riese Schwankt" *Die Zeit* 16-7-93 p3. Other sources range from DM15 to DM50 billion. See also Karl Kaiser & Klaus Becher *Deutschland und der Irak-Konflikt: Internationale Sicherheitsverantwortung Deutschlands und Europa nach der deutschen Vereinigung* (Bonn: DGAP 1992)

160   *German Foreign Policy after Reunification Conference Report* (Berlin: Aspen Institute 1991)

161   John Mearsheimer "Back to the Future: Instability in Europe After the Cold War" *International Security* v15 n1 1990 pp5-56

become more difficult to sustain in an 'increasingly dangerous, ambiguous, and conflict-filled world'. Ambiguity cannot forever be met with ambiguity.[162] Rühe endorsed proposed constitutional amendments 'because decisions are taken by political players not by political observers'. Expanding the context he argued that with 'no blueprint for political structures in the Euro-Atlantic area...we need to follow a practical, rather than academic, approach. We cannot afford to delay decision until perfect visions of Europe have been designed'.[163] Rühe spoke of the incongruity of the German absence in international conflicts when the nation's interests are threatened, arguing it was now untenable to expect the US or others to protect Germany's external interests when it does not do so itself. *Generalinspekteur* Klaus Naumann said Germany could no longer retain a 'special role' within its alliance structures but would if necessary have to fulfill its responsibilities beyond present limitations. Possessing a regular force restricted by law to 370,000 personnel Germany has the most well equipped and largest military among European states. After acrimonious debate the Federal Constitutional Court decreed in July 1994 that 'out of area' involvement by German units was permissible. Kinkel who had been hesitant about NATO widening and 'out of area' actions now claimed the court decision and the government's policy was a clear refutation of a German *Sonderweg*. The 'culture of reserve...only goes so far' Germany is not and could not act like '*ein impotenter Zwerg*'.[164] Both the debate on military action and the result were necessary and ultimately appropriate. If all parties had said yes immediately it would have provoked external rebuttal, just as if all persisted in saying no.

Seventy per cent of Americans polled during the mid-1995 escalation of hostilities in Bosnia were against any US troop involvement. Joint German-American military manoeuvres as part of a 'highly motivated partnership' were priming Germany for a qualitative change of its role in case of future European conflicts.[165] The Gulf experience caused a redoubling of efforts to institutionalize Europe as a vehicle by establishing a working CFSP pillar in the Maastricht Treaty. Germany has been the main advocate and link between a post-Cold War combined US and all-European defence.

---

162   Cf. Elizabeth Pond "Germany in the New Europe" *Foreign Affairs* v71 n2 1992 pp114-130; Gordon "Normalization" pp229-230; Garton Ash *In Europe's Name*
163   Volker Rühe "Shaping Euro-Atlantic Policies: A Grand Strategy for a New Era" *Survival* v35 n2 1993 pp129-137 p130 & p135
164   "Konsequenzen aus dem Urteil des Bundesverfassungsgerichts vom 12. Juli 1994" *Bulletin* 26-7-94; "Oldtimer sucht Augenkontakt" *Der Spiegel* n7 13-2-95 pp26-28
165   'Bei internationalen Kriseneinsätzen rechnen die Amerikaner jetzt fest mit der Bundeswehr als leistungsstarkem, gut ausgerüstetum und hochmotiviertem Partner.' "Völlig neues Gefühl" *Der Spiegel* n21 22-5-95 p49; "Die Maikäfer im Bomber" *Der Spiegel* n15 10-4-95 pp72-76

Envisaged as the operational embodiment of a European defence identity, the WEU, despite it's 'reactivation' in 1984 has been a white elephant.[166] Bonn has tried to employ the WEU as a bridge between the EU and NATO, as a linkage between UK and France, and of these two intergovernmentalists and states more accepting of a supranational system. On the other hand, the 'benefit' for Germany of looser European integration in the defence and security field is that it abets a continuing American role. This 'conviction that developing a fully fledged Union would be a very long-term process assured Bonn of compatibility between Europe and NATO for the foreseeable future.'[167] Rühe detailed the 'new NATO' in May 1996 and set forth his understanding of the future Bundeswehr role in a comprehensive speech in November.[168]

Hans Maull begins his comprehensive account of Germany's involvement in the break-up of Yugoslavia and its consequences with the proposal that the crisis 'may well be the defining event in the evolution of international order in the post-Cold War world'.[169] From early on conservative sections of the German media portrayed the conflict as the 'one-sided' aggression of Serbia against an 'innocent' Croatia and Slovenia,[170] while the trend of public opinion moved in favour of the latter's independence. Preferably this was to be achieved through EC channels; otherwise by Germany unilaterally. Beverly Crawford recounts that this followed the direction of elite 'bandwagoning' initiated by the *Grünen-Bündnis90*. In the course of the summer 1991 Germany's political elite switched virtually *en masse* from the EC 'statist' standpoint as 'recognition fever' spread. It meant a deviation from the primacy of state territorial integrity enshrined in the Helsinki accords to 'self-determination' and induced a still uncertain foreign policy corps to assert itself against the major

---

166   Cf. Simon Duke "The Second Death (or the Second Coming?) of the WEU" *Journal of Common Market Studies* v34 n2 1996 pp167-191; Helge Wego "Reaktivierung der WEU: Der Beitrag Deutschlands und Frankreichs" *Europäische Sicherheit* n6 1995 pp39-41

167   Mathias Jopp "The Strategic Implications of European Integration" *Adelphi Paper* n290 July 1994 p9; See also Paul R. S. Gebhard "The United States and European Security" *Adelphi Paper* n286 February 1994

168   Volker Rühe "Die Neue NATO" *Bulletin* 2-5-96 & "Deutschlands Rolle im zusammenwachsenden Europa und der Beitrag der Bundeswehr" *Bulletin* 14-11-96

169   Hans W. Maull "Germany in the Yugoslav Crisis" *Survival* v37 n4 1995-96 pp99-130; See also the account by Ljiljana Smajlovic in "United Germany: Stabilizing Influence or Threat?" pp615-620; Beverly Crawford "Explaining Defection From International Cooperation: Germany's Unilateral Recognition of Croatia" *World Politics* v48 July 1996 pp482-521

170   Philip Gordon "Die Deutsche-Französische Partnerschaft und die Atlantische Allianz" *Arbeitspapier für internationalen Politik* n82 p46

western states and Russia. [171] A further irony was that this basically *jus sanguinis* policy was driven in the domestic political arena by the party otherwise least orientated to it and which the others, for various reasons, all accepted. In Crawford's analysis, a complex combination of an evolving party system and foreign policy culture presented a 'top-down' explanation of the domestic situation in Germany. However, it is the electorate which exerts a decisive, if indirect leverage. When Kohl spoke at the first all-German CDU convention he called for a 'more forceful and independent foreign policy' in response to the situation in 'Yugoslavia'. Ultimately, domestic consensus, however formed, proved stronger than 'weak international norms'. Once this occurred the ambience within the EC became one of 'Germany' versus the others. [172]

As the camouflage of multilateralism disintegrated the crisis manifested 'European' foreign policy as the province of disparate national states. The more obvious ethno-nationalist conflict among Serbs. Croats and Bosnians was paralleled by rivalries conducted at the level of 'diplomacy', between France, Britain and Germany, all containing 'democratically tamed and institutionally harnessed nationalisms'. [173] The *New York Times* reported that the 'continued insistence by London and Paris that Bonn is to blame reflects the resurgence of historic European rivalries. When it comes to the Balkans, the European Community remains so driven by its own national and historical rivalries that it cannot offer coherent leadership or even followership.' [174] Others disputed that the policy pursued by Germany was to blame:

> Germany did not cause the war in Yugoslavia, and only forced through the recognition of Croatia and Slovenia after cities such as Dubrovnik and Vukovar had been pounded for many weeks by heavy artillery. Independence was inevitable: the idea, still cherished by Lord Carrington and others, that Croatia could have been persuaded at that stage to climb back into a Yugoslav federation was quite unreal. [175]

---

171   As related to this context the central and dramatically exposed weakness of (then) CSCE Final Act is its codification of both the 'territorial integrity' or 'statist' Principle II and ' the 'self-determination' or 'nationalist' Principle VIII

172   Cf. Crawford "Explaining Defection..." and Maull "Germany in the Yugoslav Crisis"

173   Joseph S. Nye Jr. "What New World Order?" *Foreign Affairs* v71 n2 1992 p83- 92; Stanley Hoffman "Is Liberal Internationalism Dead?" *Foreign Policy* n98 Spring 1995 pp159-177

174   David Unger "Germany is not to Blame for Bosnia" *New York Times* 7-6-93 quoted in Stjepan G. Mestrovic *The Balkanization of the West* (London: Routledge 1994) p31

175   Noel Malcolm "Bosnia and the West: A Study in Failure" *The National Interest* n39 Spring 1995 pp3-14 p13

Bonn and its EC 'partners' mishandled the situation together, or rather, apart. When Austria (and Italy) joined Germany's support of Croatia and Slovenia in opposition to France, the UK and Serbia, the alignments appeared as an ominous replica of World War Two. Some analysts regarded French and British intentions as primarily to limit the possibility of German economic and cultural influence gaining in at least the non-Serb dominated lands of the ex-Yugoslavia.[176] Stjepan Mestrovic argued that the alliance of Britain and France against Germany was based on a 'deep-seated antagonism' of the former towards the latter,[177] while Philip Gordon termed it 'extrapolating from the past'.[178] Conversely, Stevan Pavlowitch considered that the rest of the west soon followed Bonn's lead against the aggression of Serbian communism; to the extent that the actual or possible atrocities of others were less rigorously investigated or condemned.[179]

After Germany's enforcement of political muscle in 1991 its diplomacy became reserved and its military remained absent. As a defence force of German territory Bundeswehr soldiers could be German, elsewhere they would go into action under a semantic shroud as 'Europeans'. A spectacularly efficient German action in the former Yugoslavia—even acting under UN, NATO or EU auspices, could have caused as much consternation as approval.[180] Not that this was ever likely. After it became apparent that UN peacekeeping forces (without German units) embroiled in Bosnia may have to be evacuated, the German government agreed to SACEUR General Joulwan's request to provide forces conditional that there would be no ground troops among them. Six months later a squad including advanced Tornado jets and 1500 technical and medical personnel were sent to Piacenza in Italy and Split in Croatia. There were tight restrictions on the use of the Tornados and again there were to be no ground combat troops. Rühe considered that they would be 'exposed to an unacceptably high risk'. Even descriptive terminology was contentious. Rühe corrected Naumann's referral to Germany's 'combat mission' by calling it an 'enforcement of the Dayton

176   William Pfaff "Invitation to War" *Foreign Affairs* v72 n3 1993 pp97-109; Noel Malcolm *Bosnia: A Short History* (New York: New York University Press 1994) and "Bosnia and the West: A Study in Failure"
177   Mestrovic *The Balkanization of the West* See Chapter 2 "Still hunting Nazis, and losing reality"
178   Gordon "Normalization" See pp242-243
179   Stevan K. Pavlowitch "Who is "Balkanizing" Whom? The Misunderstandings Between the Debris of Yugoslavia and an Unprepared West" *Dædelus* v123 n2 1994 pp203-223
180   "Völlig neues Gefühl" *Der Spiegel* n21 22-5-95 p49 Oskar Lafontaine "Keine Tornados nach Bosnien" *Die Zeit* 17-3-95 p4

peace accord' and 'essentially a logistical task'.[181] Rühe has employed 'positive' aspects of the German military's past (a role in the wartime resistance) as a means to building acceptance as a legitimate and necessary part of the Federal Republic's existence and foreign policy presence. Kohl continues to speak against negative characterisation of German personnel and stresses the 'humanitarian' role of the Bundeswehr in external engagements.[182]

In the 1990s the original 'flexibility' built in to the NATO wording is 'coming into its own'.[183] In the absence of an all-European defence force, security provided by a coherent transatlantic alliance has been unsettled by the retreat of America leading to indecision and division.[184] Analysts impress that NATO needs decisive American leadership and convincing German support or that an 'augmented realism' is required to maintain US pre-eminence. Others called for a new concert of great powers, with the US-German partnership paramount. The Clinton administration was urged to act, with Bonn, in seizing the strategic initiative and expanding NATO sooner rather than later. Not only should Russian objections be discounted, their actions in Chechnya should be vigorously condemned.[185]

The necessity for the united Germany to be as secured within NATO as within the EU indicates not only a mutual strategic reliance with the US but that the EU is far from a political union that could transcend the need for US participation in defence of Europe, against external threat and even to ensure internal confidence. NATO was constructed as a defence against the Warsaw Pact, not for dealing with localised intra-European conflict. A

---

181   See Franz-Josef Meiers "NATO's Peacekeeping Dilemma" *Arbeitspapiere zur Internationale Politik* n94 pp61-77 and Franz-Josef Meiers "Germany: The Reluctant Power" *Survival* v37 n3 1995

182   Volker Rühe "Ethos des deutschen Widerstand als moralisches Fundament der Bundeswehr" Speech in Berlin 5-1-95, *Bulletin* 6-1-95 and "Dank an den christlichen Mentor und Fürsprecher der Bundeswehr" Speech in Bonn 29-11-94, *Bulletin* 7-12-94. Rühe conducted a February 1996 press conference in Berlin against a background of Wehrmacht resistance photographs. Protests and arrests still took place in May 1996 as Berlin witnessed the first Geman soldiers sworn in there since 1945.

183   Bertram "Europe in the Balance" p49

184   Stanley Sloan "New Designs on NATO: US Perspectives on NATO's Future" *International Affairs* v71 n2 1995 pp217-231; William D. Odom "NATO's Expansion: Why the Critics are Wrong" *The National Interest* Spring 1995 pp38-49; Anand Menon "From independence to cooperation: France, NATO and European Security" *International Affairs* v71 n1 1995 pp19-34

185   Brzezinski "A Plan for Europe"; Richard Holbrooke "America, A European Power" *Foreign Affairs* v74 n2 1995 pp38-51; William D. Odom "How to Create a True World Order" *Orbis* Spring 1995 pp155-172; Richard N. Haass "Paradigm lost" *Foreign Affairs* v74 n1 1995 p43-58

'European problem' requires an effective European military force. US rationale determines that it will provide support if Europe protects itself and extends to potential European deployments in protection of what may be predominantly US strategic interests on the basis that these are also Europe's. With all parties reducing defence spending and cutting personnel numbers [186] the logic points to more integration and sharing of resources, and variations on the 'double hatting' theme. But national perspectives make 'logic' a very relative consideration.

Interests and Responsibility

Foreign policy has one role of pursuing international interests and undertaking actions relatively independent of domestic political pressures, and another in response to specific internal motivations. Germany has tried to 'Europeanize' or 'globalize' the solutions to major challenges: masses of 'stateless' wanderers, criminal elements operating across borders, environmental hazards, creating a reliable post Cold War security architecture, assisting the development of market democracies in eastern Europe and Russia. It must deal with a reduced capacity for chequebook answers to foreign policy predicaments. International organisations intended to provide co-operative solutions often cannot do this and may exacerbate discontent within national polities and discord between governments. While the Brent Spar oil rig affair presented a gift for the government, a tougher response to greater challenges like French nuclear testing, the Chechen conflict, or backing up its diplomacy with a physical presence and active role in situations like the ex-Yugoslavia will demonstrate a more credible commitment. [187]

The 'policy of responsibility' that Germany pursued has two meanings. Firstly as 'applied to Germany', the various requirements or demands from its allies for military, diplomatic, financial and political action; secondly 'deriving from Germany', an ethic of assistance and reliability with regard to neighbours, allies and the developing world. A Kantian perspective of ethics as good intentions rather than outcomes prevails here. [188] Such normative elements of international relations are not exclusive to Germany

---

186   See Gebhard "The United States and European Security"
187   See Rick Atkinson "In foreign affairs Germany presents two faces to the world" *International Herald Tribune* 23-6-95 p5; Karl Kaiser & Joachim Krause "Deutsche Politik Gegenüber dem Balkan" in *Deutschlands Neue Außenpolitik* Bd.3 pp175-188
188   Michael Mertes "Germany's Social and Political Culture: Change Through Consensus" *Dædelus* v123 n1 1994 pp1-32. See pp17-18

by any means, but they have been pronounced. This may appear to challenge the coherence of a broader international relations theory when one large and powerful state is, still, 'different', but without clearly effecting a role of hegemon like the US. The outstanding example of difference being that the unilateral use of force, if any at all, is not a factor in the German pursuit of interests. It does not, for example, send troops to support regimes, like the US, or possess and display a nuclear capacity like France. As measures of a state's relative or absolute power, the possession of nuclear weapons and military strength were reduced in importance after the Cold War and the factors of economics and culture rose. This does not preclude cognition or employment of previously 'low politics' concerns in 'realist' terms. There is no fundamental conflict in the conception of the European states as international actors, how they are affected by and why they interact with others, how they may adapt to more immediate exigencies or longer term evolution, and the arguments elaborated by Hans Morgenthau forty years ago:

> Whatever the ultimate aims of international politics, power is always the immediate aim. Statesmen and peoples may ultimately seek freedom, security, prosperity, or power itself. They may define their goals in terms of (an) ideal...further its realization through nonpolitical means, such as technical co-operation with other nations or international organizations...the relation of nations to international politics has a dynamic quality. It changes with the vicissitudes of power...It may also change under the impact of cultural transformations, which may make a nation prefer other pursuits, for instance commerce, to those of power.[189]

Noting his reference to a proclivity for change and the necessity for states to adapt, Morgenthau's description applies to Germany in the 1990s as much as to the US or USSR in the 1950s. The difference being that what he conceived above as constituting 'power' is too narrow. Today 'commerce' is 'power', though, of course, not the only kind. Herzog referred to German aversions against pursuing interests through 'hard power', measured in terms of 'population numbers, territories, fleets and armies'. Although the FRG could not totally do away with the basis of this type of thinking—a reserve military-strategic capacity—it had advanced through 'soft power'.[190] At the onset of the EU presidency Kohl again stressed links between Germany's old cultural tradition and its newer trading culture as dual foreign policy aims.[191]

---

189   Hans J. Morgenthau *Politics Among Nations* Fourth Edition (New York: Knopf 1967) pp25-26

190   Cf. Joseph S. Nye "Soft Power" *Foreign Policy* n80 Autumn 1990 pp153-171

191   Helmut Kohl "Deutschland—ein weltoffenes Land" Speech to the Deutschen

The German *Staatsräson* has been intoned through a rhetorical convergence of the national interest (neo-realism) and co-operative multilateralism (neo-liberalism), of pragmatism and idealism, self-interest and responsibility.[192] Political units struggle to exist in the world without being substantially influenced by prevailing methods of interaction. If major states like France and Britain operate from a position of state-centric advancement of interests then it limits Germany from operating very differently. In previous decades the Federal Republic was often prepared to subordinate *Interessenpolitik* to *Verantwortungspolitik*. Without reduction in the latter, the former is now more comparable to that of others. In June 1996, while China was cancelling an official visit planned for Kinkel after a Bundestag resolution condemning Chinese policies in Tibet, Europe was shutting out refugees and Germany repatriating 120,000 people to Serbia.

In June 1994 the *Economist's* prognosis was for a German presidency 'market-minded and down to earth in economics' and less sure on immigration and foreign policy. The 'worriers' in London and Paris wonder 'how much the behaviour of sovereign Germany is to change. Their interests are not identical' and 'German politicians tend to see better than those of Britain and France the limits of trying to act alone in world affairs.' [193] While there will be a greater assertiveness 'to create or shape institutions, to initiate common policies, to place key persons in key positions, Germany will not dominate militarily, as in the past, but will exert political and economic influence'.[194] And whatever the old and the new predicaments, German foreign policy-makers have the special experience of a 'human challenge for leadership...palpably there in Germany (and palpably not in France or Britain).' [195] The period of chaperoning Germany is over, to be replaced by a foreign policy avoiding past mistakes and hoping to emulate 'American pragmatism', which rested comfortably on its status as a 'national virtue'.[196] Based as far as possible on constancy of co-ordinates in a changing global environment, *Realpolitik* in a 'highly civilised form' fairly accurately represents how Germany operates in international affairs.[197] In the mid-1990s, the Federal Republic of Germany arrived at the remarkable position of

---

Auslandshandelskammern *Bulletin* 24-6-94
192   Cf. Martin Griffiths *The Real Realism* (London: Routledge 1992)
193   "Germany's Europe" *The Economist* 11-6-94
194   Smyser "Dateline Berlin: Germany's New Vision"
195   Garton Ash "Germany's Choice"
196   Herzog "Globalisierung"
197   Garton Ash *In Europe's Name* p354

being 'stable', 'pivotal' and almost 'normal', which was enough to challenge some attitudes amongst those around it. [198]

---

198   "Germany: Nearly Normal" *The Economist* 15-4-95 p28

6 France, Germany and Europe

I consider France in all respects, and in relation to all Orders and Ranks of People which are in it; I shew plainly the great disorders of the French Government, which are such that there was perhaps never any Nation amongst those that are called Christians, so ill Governed...

The **Desolation** of **France** Demonstrated or,
Evident Proofs that one Half of the People of that Kingdom are destroyed.
Two Thirds of its Capital Stock consumed;
And the Nation Reduc'd to such a Condition that it cannot be Restored to the Flourishing State it was in *Thirty Years ago*, in less than Two hundred Years, and not then neither, except the whole Frame of their Government be new Modell'd.[1]

Thus the best account we can profitably give of the Present State of Germany, is to say, That it comes very near a System of many Sovereign States, in which one Prince or General of the League excells the rest of the Confederates, and is clothed with the Ornaments of a Sovereign Prince;

The Forces of any State may be considered as they are in themselves, or as by reason of the elegant Structure of its Form or Constitution they may be used. Forces considered in themselves, consist in *Men* and *Things*. As to the first of these, *Men, Germany* has no reason to complain that it wants numbers of them, or they Wit or Ingenuity;...so they are very constant, and have Souls very capable of Discipline and Instruction. Nor is this Nation less to be admired and commended for their Mechanick Arts and Ingenious Manufactures: And which crowns all, and tends wonderfully to the Security and Welfare of Societies, they are not at all inclined to promote Changes in their Governments...

The **Present State** of **GERMANY** or, An Account of the *Extent, Rise, Form, Wealth, Strength, Weaknesses* and *Interests* of that Empire.[2]

---

1   M. de Souligne *The Desolation of France Demonstrated* (London: John Salisbury 1697). Souligne employs the term 'nation' a century before French republican soldiers invoked it at Valmy in 1792

2   Samuel Freiherr von Pufendorf *The Present State of Germany* (London: Richard Chiswell 1690) (For this and the previous reference typography and spelling are as in the originals.)

The European Earthquake

The respective conditions of France and Germany as considered by accounts three hundred years ago had an analogue at the onset of the 1990s. The image of a triumphal united Germany exacerbated France's sudden geo-political marginalization as the Cold War system disintegrated. Added to extensive social and economic problems new forces threatened to leave France marooned without a significant role in determining the new configuration. Although many of the challenges facing France do not stem directly from its relation to Germany they can be accentuated by it and result in restrictions on the state's manoeuvrability, particularly in coming decades. Within two years of reunification Germany's position had to be revised as it joined France in the experience of recession and high unemployment. Germany will not, however, be paying for backward eastern regions indefinitely. It also has geographic, economic and linguistic advantages apropos eastern expansion of the EU. Both France and Germany face restructuring of their labour markets and social welfare systems. Both also need 'Europe', which for the present means each other. The reasons, the perceptions, the potential benefits and the extent of their mutual dependencies differ and are changing.

Ronald Tiersky has written that 'after Mitterrand no French politician who wants to become President can be against Europe'.[3] Since de Gaulle, however, none have actually rejected Europe; the aim has been to make Europe as French as possible. In the mid-1980s Mitterrand found France's options reduced after his attempt at unilateral reflation of the French economy had failed. Europe became, as in West Germany, 'an issue of (artificial) domestic consensus' with the key question 'not whether France should be at the forefront of European integration, but who was best qualified to lead the nation in this direction.' Although Mitterrand was termed the 'artisan' of European Union,[4] he retained a conception of France's 'indivisibility'. With Jacques Delors concurrently asserting himself in Brussels, Mitterrand 'forged the powerful image within the French public opinion that France's national interest coincided with the development of the EC, itself portrayed as a European extension of French leadership. Public opinion greatly appreciated the idea of a French tandem running the affairs of Europe.'[5] Through France's continuing political prominence in the EC its preferences could, to considerable extent, be transferred to a continental scale without lessening its

---

3   Ronald Tiersky "Mitterrand's Legacy" *Foreign Affairs* v74 n1 1995 pp112-121

4   Philippe Moreau-Defarges "'J'ai fait un reve...' Le president François Mitterrand, artisan de l'union europeene" *Politique Etrangere* v50 Autumn 1985 pp359-375

5   Alistair Cole *François Mitterrand: A Study in Political Leadership* (London: Routledge 1994) p128

special and inviolable status. Ulla Holm describes how 'for the French political elite there is no inherent logical contradiction in elevating the French state to the European level, since France alone among the European states possesses the political will, thanks to its political nation and its value of civilization. If this will is transferred to the EC/EU, the Community will get a French political heart, which will pulsate all over Europe.'[6] In 1989-90 this conception was overrun by events beyond France's control.

As in the post-1945 settlement, post-1990 Germany's (potential) national aspirations had to be contained by European structures. This predominantly French strategy of enmeshing Germany is accompanied or even permeated by the fear that Germany will come to dominate the continent through these communal institutions shifting it from a 'Semi-Gaullist' Europe 'toward a Gaullist Germany'.[7] Stanley Hoffmann has articulated that 'the formal anxiety about being governed from Brussels barely conceals a real anguish about being dictated to by Bonn (or Berlin)'. The 'problem' is not that one member might dominate Europe—but that it is not France, which instead finds itself 'entrapped in a Community that would be an extension of German might rather than, as was hoped originally, French power.' There is the 'gnawing fear of being caught in an enterprise that will either lead to a Federation in which the nation will lose its identity as a political unit' as political powers are dispersed and rearranged, 'manipulated above all by Germany'.[8] As this occurs, and more so afterwards, Germany will employ resources for *national* purposes that inflate its material strength along with its political weight and cultural prestige. From French perspectives precise mechanisms must be constructed that enable the *Etat-nation* to sustain its importance and self-image, and control its neighbour.[9]

---

6   Ulla Holm "The French Garden is no longer what it used to be" in Ole Wæver & Ulla Holm *The Struggle for 'Europe': French and German Concepts of State, Nation and European Union* (Draft Copy) pp14-15

7   Cf. Fritz Stern "Germany in a Semi-Gaullist Europe" *Foreign Affairs* v58 n4 1980 pp867-886; Wolfgang Krieger "Towards a Gaullist Germany? Some Lessons from the Yugoslav Crisis" *World Policy Journal* v11 n1 1994 pp26-38. Krieger indicates that Germany is not about to become 'Gaullist' because its political class does not possess the will. Regardless of any argument that diplomatic recognition of Croatia and Slovenia had resemblances to Gaullist actions, the point is why should Germany be outlawed from pursuing policies that France can and does?

8   Stanley Hoffman "Thoughts on the French Nation Today" *Dædelus* v122 n3 1993 pp63-79

9   Cf. *Remaking the Hexagon: The New France in the New Europe* Ed. Gregory Flynn (Boulder: Westview 1995); Steven Kramer *Does France Still Count?: The French Role in the New Europe* (Westport: Praeger 1994); André Brigot "Frankreich und Europa" *Aus Politik und Zeitgeschichte* B42/94 21-10-94 pp34-

Germany's complaisance as an international political actor was paralleled by French exaggeration of actual power capabilities. Despite the challenges outlined in previous chapters, Germany's *de jure* and *de facto* transformation in political status means the Franco-German partnership is manifestly between unequals. After reunification the population differential increased from around 10% to over 40%. A drop in German per capita GDP did not prevent the gap in total GDP widening from roughly 25% in 1988 to near 50% by 1992. At current prices in 1996, Germany's GDP was $US2360 billion and France's $US1548 billion.[10] Under Mitterrand France's net public debt tripled to FF3 trillion. By comparison the huge costs of German reunification are estimated to cost up to DM2 trillion. This was partially funded with international money, attracted through a monetary policy which made it unpopular with other EC/EU members. Contemporaneously the French struggled to practically apply a calculation that meeting EMU criteria was essential to avoid becoming a German satellite. Revolt in late 1995 was one consequence. Germany's rise and France's 'downward process of revision'[11] motivated some eminent commentators to reassure what they perceived as a fragile French psyche and a political elite that has to recognise it is now the junior partner in the alliance. Helmut Schmidt declared 'Nothing without France...in no event, anytime, anywhere, be it in the world, be it within the European Union, a German injuring of important French interests and feelings or of French national pride!'[12]

In contrast, French élite response to German reunification was defensive and nationalistic, ranging across the political spectrum. Jacques Morizet, Ambassador to West Germany as the Berlin Wall fell, remarked that reunification should be delayed if not prevented because it would inevitably 'give birth to a Europe dominated by Germany, which nobody, east or west, wants'. Former president Giscard d'Estaing grieved that reunification signalled the end of the Community. More shrill were Philippe Seguin (and Jacques Chirac) on the right and Jean-Pierre Chevènement on the left, while the philosopher Bernard Henri-Lévy proffered that 'Germany doubled equals

	38; Jean-Pierre Langellier & Claire Tréan "Un entretien avec Alain Juppé" *Le Monde* 2-9-93 p1 & p8
10	Eurostat *Basic Statistics of the Community* 1994 p41; OECD National Accounts (Paris: OECD 1997)
11	Adam Daniel Rotfeld "The future of Europe and of Germany" in *Germany and Europe in Transition* Eds. Adam Daniel Rotfeld & Walther Stützle (Oxford: Oxford University Press 1991). See pp84-85
12	Helmut Schmidt "Vor Alleingängen wird gewarnt" *Die Zeit* 13-1-95 p3 'Nichts ohne Frankreich...Auf keinen Fall jemals irgendwo, sei es in der Welt, sei es innerhalb der Europäischen Union, eine deutsche Verletzung wichtiger französicher Interessen und Gefühle oder französichen Nationalstolzes!'

France halved'. Mitterrand, who had to take the decisive response, stumbled through a series of stunts that were as ungracious as they were unsuccessful.[13] Having made a strategic shift Mitterrand declared in summer 1990 'after all, being a partner in a united Europe dominated by Germany is better than being part of a Europe that is un-united and still dominated by Germany'.[14] France's world political rank was disappearing more comprehensively and irreversibly than 1940[15] or 1968. 1989 began the denouement of French *grandeur*, impacting on internal economic and political developments while removing the remaining masks that represented it internationally.[16] Persisting with a European strategy now meant acceding to other—German—preferences and designs. Both systems cannot be part of the same 'united' Europe. If there is to be a genuine political union the 'whole frame of the French government must be new modell'd'. As 'general of the league' Germany will 'excel the rest of the confederates'.

The post-war Franco-German relationship has taken on new dimensions driven by geo-political, economic and generational change. Having overcome their *Erbfeindschaft*, the 'new row between an old couple' beginning as reunification became possible has yet to be patched up. In 1992 James Morgan declared the 'Franco-German relationship is at the end of its tether', with resentment against the partnership's restrictive nature, that 'when the chips are down the Germans will choose the Americans', and that French

13 Alistair Cole "Looking On: France and the New Germany" *German Politics* v2 n3 1993 pp359-376. See p371

14 Jean V. Poulard "The French Perception of German Unification" *German Monitor* n37 1996 pp157-166. On Franco-German relations in 1989-90 Mitterrand wrote of a cold atmosphere and 'la mauvaise humeur d'Helmut Kohl'. See François Mitterrand *De L'Allemagne, De La France* (Paris: Editions Odile Jacob 1996) here p153. Cf. Alain Minc *La Grande Illusion* (Paris: Grasset 1989); Georges Valence *France-Allemagne: Le Retour de Bismark* (Paris: Flammarion 1990); Jean-Pierre Chevènement *Une certaine idée de la République m'amene à...* (Paris: Albin Michel 1992) especially Chapter 4 "Le Retour de l'Allemagne"; Philippe Seguin *Discours pour la France* (Paris: Grasset 1992); Philippe Seguin *Ce que j'ai dit* (Paris: Grasset 1993); Daniel Vernet "The dilemma of French foreign policy" *International Affairs* v68 n4 1992 pp655-664. See also Jacques Attali's insider account of anxieties not only among the French political hierarchy but shared by the British. *Verbatim* vol. III *Chronique des années 1988-1991* (Paris: Fayard 1995)

15 Anthony Adamthwaite *Grandeur & Misery: France's bid for power in Europe 1914-1940* (London: Arnold 1995)

16 Cf. Richard F. Kuisel "The France We Have Lost: Social, Economic, and Cultural Discontinuities" in *Remaking the Hexagon...* pp31-48

defence of the CAP is 'highly damaging to German national interests'.[17] Another commentator summarised that 'The French know what they are but they are not sure of what they can achieve. In French eyes Germans may be too sure of what they can achieve but do not necessarily know who they are'.[18] The valence has shifted to a Germany which will be less concerned about deference to French preferences when, for younger people, 'memories of the Franco-German war are so remote as to be incomprehensible.' Dana Alin envisions that 'for these post-baby-boom Germans born after 1965, the creation of Europe cannot have the same urgency. It tends to be somewhat faddish, offering perhaps a more fashionable identity than the German national one'

> ...The challenge for future German statecraft, then, may be to make future progress in the partnership with France and Europe less dependent on fashion or ideology and more manifestly a matter of German national interest. Developing a vocabulary of German interests will be a delicate business, of course.[19]

Establishing the Relationship

The present European Union was constructed upon France and Germany's proficiency and willingness to cooperate. Ole Wæver suggests that 'any other EC member can be dispensed with, not France and Germany. Without either of them, the whole thing becomes meaningless (or at least something

17   James Morgan "Wide horizons, slender means: the scope for British influence" *International Affairs* v68 n4 1992 pp603-617, here p606

18   Adam Daniel Rotfield paraphrasing Dominique Moisï in "The Future of Europe and of Germany: conference summary" in *Germany and Europe in Transition* Eds. Adam Daniel Rotfeld & Walther Stützle (Oxford: Oxford University Press 1991) p85. French public opinion was generally favourable or at least not especially concerned by German reunification and stereotypes held by both populations had faded though not completely disappeared. Their relationship also developed a certain 'banality'. See Ingo Kolboom "Deutschlandbilder der Franzosen: Der Tod des "Dauerdeutschen" in *Die haßlichen Deutschen?* Ed. Günter Trautmann (Darmstadt: Wissenschaftliche Buchgesellschaft 1991) pp212-243

19   Dana H. Alin "Germany Looks at France" in *France-Germany 1983-1993: The Struggle to Co-operate* Ed. Patrick McCarthy (New York: St.Martins Press 1993) pp27-50, here p45. Somewhat ironically, both French and German youth seem to be more interested in Englishness and their English peers than each other. Cf. Eric Cahm "Seen from Germany: France in 1993-94—synthetic and comparative perspectives" *Modern & Contemporary France* NS4 (1) 1996 pp102-105

completely different, i.e. an intra-European alliance against the other). Core political processes have therefore been first of all French and German and Franco-German'.[20] Charles de Gaulle's autocratic style demanded independence from a US ascendancy thereby allowing, or necessitating, a French leadership in Europe. This was effected through the nascent European institutions which would service a grouping of independent nation-states, in particular combining German industrial and economic capacity with French political, diplomatic and military supremacy. Konrad Adenauer's achievements were partly dependent on and magnified by concord with de Gaulle.[21] It required the Federal Republic, now with a rapidly growing economy, to play a secondary role to France in foreign affairs and assent to French diplomatic aims. Alistair Cole impresses how 'on no account were the Germans to enjoy the same degree of independence and autonomy in foreign policy-making as the French. French policy-makers were anxious lest Germany engage in Gaullist practices in its own foreign policy.'[22] This understanding infused the Élysee Treaty signed in 1963 and the ritual of Franco-German summits continued twice per year since. Despite Adenauer and de Gaulle's close personal rapport a tension between Germany's French and American ties has sustained since.

> In stark contrast to the Germans' reticence, the French were very keen to assume the mantle of the EC's political leader from its very beginning. Fueled by visions of grandeur, the French believed that the EC provided them with the opportunity to achieve self-aggrandizing national and pan-European goals that were, if not openly challenging to the Americans, definitely perceived as being countervailing in nature. The French considered their leadership of the EC as a way of restoring their flagging continental prestige and autonomy by invigorating an independent, united Europe...[23]

In the context of this fabricated ranking arrangement, Helmut Schmidt and Valéry Giscard d'Estaing were able to deepen the relationship during the 1970s.[24] The arrival of Helmut Kohl brought to office a chancellor who

20   Ole Wæver "Introduction" in Ole Wæver & Ulla Holm *The Struggle for 'Europe'* (Draft Copy) p46
21   Adenauer was the only foreign political leader invited to de Gaulle's private residence. See Jacques Binoche *De Gaulle et les Allemands* (Bruxelles: Complexe 1990)
22   Cole "Looking On: France and the New Germany" p360
23   Andrei S. Markovits & Simon Reich "Should Europe Fear the Germans?" *German Politics and Society* n23 1991 pp1-20
24   Haig Simonian "France, Germany and Europe" *Journal of Common Market Studies* v19 n3 March 1981 pp203-219; Haig Simonian *The Privileged*

perceived himself as a spiritual as well as political successor to Adenauer and who continued the tradition of 'personal chemie' with Mitterrand. They may be the last pair of leaders to possess such an emotional attachment—in company with an assiduous pragmatism—to the idea of European unity and to a Franco-German partnership in particular.[25] In the 1980s Kohl appeared to defer, in European and international affairs, to the then more assertive and apparently capable Frenchman.[26] Kohl subsequently emerged as a world statesman, to the extent that his own vision for Europe and desired pace of implementation surpassed the ailing Mitterrand. Both were concerned with their place in history and with establishing 'Europe' at the core of their respective legacies.[27] They were largely responsible for reinvigorating the European 'idea' after the 'sclerosis' of the early 1980s, negotiating the Single European Act and pushing through the Maastricht TEU. The presentation of this period as the 'Mitterrand era' is, at least since 1990, more accurately the 'Kohl era'. The two had to deal with the often inimically opposed Margaret Thatcher, whose attitudes enhanced the closeness Kohl, especially, and Mitterrand wished to project. Despite their apparent ability to put the discordant effects of German reunification behind them, the personal and political relationship had changed. And no less than five Franco-German 'initiatives' between April 1990 and October 1991 could prevent or resolve war in the former Yugoslavia, currency turmoil, high and rising unemployment, and a general turn away from cooperative European governance as providing effective solutions.

On becoming President Jacques Chirac tried to seize the initiative with a series of 'reassertions' as if to refute that France's interlude of leadership in Europe is over. The changes in circumstance are not necessarily a negative portent for the continent. Inevitably it requires adaptation, some of

---

Partnership: Franco-German Relations in the EC 1969-1984 (Oxford: Clarendon Press 1985)

25   Cf. Julius W. Friend *The Linchpin French-German Relations, 1950-1990* (New York: Praeger 1991); Christoph Bertram "Kanzlers Händchen" *Die Zeit* 23-9-94 p8

26   Alan Clark "François Mitterand and the Idea of Europe" in *The Idea of Europe: Problems of National and Transnational Identity* Eds. Brian Nelson, David Roberts and Walter Veit (New York: Berg 1992). Following Nicholas Ridley's accusations of the French behaving as 'poodles' to the Germans, some German diplomatic sources regarded the reverse as more accurately representing the situation. See Julius W. Friend "Nationalism and National Consciousness in France, Germany and Britain: The Year of Maastricht" *History of European Ideas* v18 n2 1994 pp187-198, here p195

27   Cole *François Mitterrand: A Study in Political Leadership*; Marcus Marby "Intimations of Mortality" *Newsweek* 19-9-94 p24; Victor Smart "Kohl sees unity as his gift to history" *The European* 21-10-94 p8

which will challenge political and cultural inclination and old certainties 'dictated by the quasi-mystical reconciliation that has taken place between the French and German peoples since the war.'[28] The past six or seven years show that these are 'two friends who almost understand each other', and charades that please no-one can no longer suffice as 'solutions'.[29] As 'Maastricht Two' approached, Rudolf Augstein announced what many had been thinking: 'Nun soll ja im Jahre 1996 die nächste große europäische Regierungskonferenz stattfinden. Da mag sich denn herausstellen, ob jene französische Zeitung recht hatte, die kurz vor Maastricht schreib, Helmut Kohl sei wohl der letzte deutsche Bundeskanzler, von dem Frankreich die Berücksichtigung seiner Sonderinteressen zu erwarten habe.'[30] Germany is now far more important to France than France is to Germany. What remains in political terms is a receding historical hold.[31]

Monetary Politics and Questions of Sovereignty

The 'u-turn' on economic policy taken by the Mitterrand government in 1983 moved France closer to the German course. As the franc became dependent on Bundesbank policy, EMU and the establishment of a European Central Bank (ECB) grew as French priorities, redoubled by the events of 1989-90.[32] A 'confidential memorandum' by the French finance ministry in late 1990 forecast the short and medium term problems that Germany would face, and also the increased economic power that would result when these were overcome. It stated that 'The first paradox of unification is that it will result in the first instance in a weakening of the German economy...Once these problems are surmounted, at the end of the century Germany will be—even

---

28 Hans-Peter Schwarz "Germany's National and European Interests" *Dædelus* v123 n2 1994 pp81-105, p94

29 Daniel Vernet "Zwei Freunde, die sich fast verstehen" *Die Zeit* 14-4-95 p1

30 Rudolf Augstein "Maastricht—eine Fehlregelung?" *Der Spiegel* n13 27-3-95 p21

31 Hans-Friedrich von Poeltz, State Secretary in the German Foreign Ministry, remarked that former French Prime Minister Michel Rocard had recently asked him whether the reunified Germany needed Europe any more, to which he replied 'that is a typical French question'. "Zu aktuellen europapolitischen Fragen" *Bulletin* 3-3-97. Rocard's enquiry is another instance of substituting one's own country with 'Europe'

32 See Peter B. Kenen "The European Central Bank and monetary policy in stage three of EMU" *International Affairs* v68 n3 1992 pp457-474; David Ross Cameron "From Barre to Balladur: Economic Policy in the Era of the EMS" in *Remaking the Hexagon* pp117-157

more than today—the dominant economic power in Europe.'[33] They were correct on the first point and have since been preparing for the second. With the Deutsche Mark accounting for around 20% of world currency reserves compared to the less than 2% in French Francs, some French politicians, led by Jacques Delors, saw a federalist solution—or employing the German system—as the only way to prevent German hegemony. Welding monetary policies could serve two purposes at once: inject greater solidity into the French economy in general and compel the Franco-German alliance to consolidate. Consecutive Kohl governments decreed any future unified monetary regime to a policy of fiscal austerity, low inflation, and contained budget deficits.[34] One effect was that by 1992 gross national debt as a percentage of GDP over the previous five years had converged: 43% for Germany and 47.8% for France.[35]

Despite adherence to the *Francfort* policy for over a decade the franc has exhibited intermittent weakness in the 1990s. By merging with Europe's strongest currency France could be protected against speculative attacks. Getting there has proved difficult. The ERM calamity in July-August 1993 marked a point of particularly strained relations between Paris and Bonn. One former Kohl adviser reflected, 'they sometimes confuse our interests with theirs'.[36] It underlined how ancillary France had become relative to monetary-financial decisions made in Frankfurt or political decisions made in Bonn.[37] EMU was also reinforced as a national strategy and not a supranational ideal. The dual concerns expressed in Balladur's anxious statement, 'We can't allow a situation to continue where so much money can change hands in a very short time and threaten a nation's security', were for France and his own political future. European unity ran a distant third.[38]

| 33 | Alain Boublil "Les Consequences Economiques de l'Unification de l'Allemagne" 20-11-90. Quoted in David Marsh *The Bundesbank: The Bank that Rules Europe* (London: Heinemann: 1992) p227 |

34   Wayne Sandholtz "Choosing union: monetary politics and Maastricht" *International Organization* v47 n1 1993 pp1-20

35   See Andreas Busch "The Crisis in the EMS" *Government and Opposition* v29 n1 1994 pp80- 96. Here p85. Both national debts grew substantially in following years. Up to 62% for Germany and 57% for France at the end of 1996.

36   Lionel Barber & David Marsh "A caravan lost in the sands" *Financial Times* 8-10-93 p16; Jacques E. Le Cacheux "The Franc Fort Strategy and the EMU" in *Remaking the Hexagon...* pp69-115

37   Ross Tieman "Bundesbank will Still Rule in Paris, However France Votes" *The Times* 23-2-92; Alan Friedman "French Political Winds Cool Franc's Prospects" *International Herald Tribune* 21-11-94 pp1&11

38   John Dunn "Crisis of the Nation State?" *Political Studies* v42 Special Issue 1994 pp3-15. See pp11-12

Fundamental to his presidential election success was Chirac's promise that fighting unemployment would be his top priority. He would reinvigorate the nation and create a *France pour tous.*[39] After opposing Mitterrand's disastrous reflationary strategy in the early 1980s, in 1995 he proposed a big spending programme of his own. He also promised to reduce the national deficit, down to the specified 3% by 1997.[40] Chirac and Juppé were faced not only with a jobs versus markets decision but constructing a 'Europe' which had to be what Germans would accept. Meanwhile large numbers of both French and German publics were doubting the merits of EMU, already deferred from 1997 to 1999—at least.[41] Another round of protests in the form of French public sector strikes threatened to blunt this spearhead of integration, while scepticism among the German public impressed that it would be unwise for any government to alter present arrangements (national currencies), unless it retained and exercised a controlling influence within a new system.[42] 'Left-nationalism' from influential media transmitted a wariness of French 'trickery' and a latent 'overdraft economy'.[43]

Besides meeting the financial criteria, the other, more profound, French problem is that German agreement to EMU requires complementary political integration. The *Kerneuropa* authors declared monetary union as the 'core of the political union'.[44] Their model, however, was undesired in Paris and placed most of the *classe politique* in a dilemma. The question of sovereignty appears in all major EU developments and rescinding or retention of the unanimity rule in particular areas of legislation is the nucleus of contention. From the German perspective sovereignty has been limited; in France national sovereignty is still a shibboleth, essential to the *pacte*

---

39 Alistair Cole "La France pour tous? — The French Presidential Elections of 23 April and & May 1995" *Government and Opposition* v30 n3 1995 pp327-346

40 Craig R. Whitney "Juppé Details French Job-Creation Budget" *International Herald Tribune* 23-5-95 p5

41 Tony Barber "Is 1999 disappearing into the 21st century?" *The Independent* 8-12-95 p21

42 David Marsh "Poll shows support for vote on EU single currency" *Financial Times* 5-12-94 pp1-2

43 See Friend "Nationalism and National Consciousness..."; Augstein "Maastricht-eine Fehlregelung?"; David Marsh "D-Mark für alle?" *Die Zeit* 23-9-94 p10; Christian de Boisseur & Marie-Hélène Duprat "French Monetary policy in the light of European monetary and financial integraton" in *The Single European market and beyond: a study of the wider implications of the Single European Act* Ed. Dennis Swann (London: Routledge 1992) pp51-98

44 'weil die Währungsunion der harte Kern der Politischen Union ist'

republicain and associated notions of democracy.[45] Although the overall Franco-German relationship is more extensive and diverse, on this fundamental issue France is closer to Britain than to Germany. Where Germany wants political power and executive functions administered through supranational channels and subsidiarity, France wants intergovernmental cooperation. Whatever the stress on common interests, policies and goals a resolution to this basic difference cannot be avoided indefinitely.[46]

Mitterrand's career is a good illustration. It revealed him as a consummate politician capable of employing visions of 'Europe' for domestic purposes and visions of a European France for foreign partners. But while Mitterrand proved himself adept at Euro-rhetoric, precisely how far beyond 'anachronistic nationalism' he intended to go was uncertain. In foreign policy the European socialist appeared more Gaullist than not.[47] Tiersky has argued that Mitterrand's 'outlook which seems federalist when compared to neo-Gaullist ideas, is less so compared to German policy in the Kohl era. Mitterrand thinks this difference about whether the EU should be frankly federalist or not is a matter of deep-seated cultural and political differences between French and German traditions'.[48]

In response to charges of the EU bringing about a loss of sovereignty for the 'one and indivisible nation', the then (1992) Justice Minister Michel Vauzelle declared 'France's sovereignty indivisible'. There were to be no transfers without the will of the people which resulted in a 'self-limitation' on the 'space in which its sovereignty is exercised'.[49] The same 'self-limitation' which ultimately aims at transference of sovereignty, is included in Germany's Basic Law and carried into its *Europapolitik*. In this sense the two states are diametrically opposed: in the French example an electoral mandate is required before any *diminishing* of national sovereignty can occur; in the German case a two-thirds parliamentary majority and constitutional court

45   Philippe Seguin & Maris-France Garaud *De l'Europe en général et de la France en particulier* (Paris: Le Pré aux clercs 1992); Stanley Hoffman "Thoughts on Sovereignty and French Politics" in *Remaking the Hexagon...* pp251-258; Jean-Marie Guéhenno *The End of the Nation-State* trans. Victoria Elliott (Minneapolis: University of Minnesota Press 1995)

46   Cf. Valerie Guerin-Sendelbach ""Incertitudes françaises"?: Die Entwicklung der Europäischen Union französischer Sicht" *Zeitschrift für den deutsch-französischen Dialog* n4 1994 pp296-302; Werner Link "Integration and Balance" *German Comments* n41 January 1996 pp17-23

47   Cf. François Mitterrand *Réflexions sur la politique étrangère de la France* (Paris: Fayard 1987)

48   Tiersky "Mitterrand's Legacy" p118; Clark "François Mitterrand and the Idea of Europe"

49   *Le Monde* 7-5-92, quoted in Friend "Nationalism and National Consciousness..." pp192-93

sanction is needed to *prevent* the transference of sovereignty in the event of a European Union appearing which enables it to do so. In April 1992 the French Constitutional Council found that the TEU did not contravene French sovereignty and in June 1992 a special *congrès* gave it a political imprimatur. This was not without inserting the usual flexibility and an increased scrutiny role for the French parliament.[50] National parliaments can still legislate to overturn European Court decisions and French 'national' thinking and French political institutions have reflected each other in the structural impediments to political union. According to Dominique Bocquet 'France needs to fall into step with Europe by modifying some of its key institutions'

> The French executive has formed a wall between the Community organization and the leaders in national parliaments and local governments. The difficulty that the French government had in selling Maastricht should move it in the direction of tearing down this wall.[51]

As long as France was able to control the agenda of European integration it was able to give the appearance of being 'pro-Europe' and a driving force towards union. French governments have been no less partisan than others. Along with the UK and Denmark, France insisted on the three pillar structure of the TEU in contrast to Germany which was more favourable to the original 'federalist' Dutch draft. As a potential stimulus for activating France's European policy, the 'pyrrhic victory' of the Maastricht referendum was worse than a clear-cut result one way or the other.[52] What was for the German political class the achievement of balance through reunification was for their French counterparts the appearance of an unfavourable disequilibrium.[53] Even moderate, considered observations

---

50   Robert Ladrech "Europeanization of Domestic Politics and Institutions: The Case of France" *Journal of Common Market Studies* v32 n1 1994 pp69-87; Peter Oliver "The French Constitution and the Treaty of Maastricht" *International and Comparative Law Quarterly* v43 n1 1994 pp1-25. Under the French Constitution's Articles 55 and 88, Euro-decrees only have to be upheld in France if all other signatories do so. There are also restrictions on foreigners with European citizenship. And as Tocqueville said, the law is rigid, but the application is flexible

51   Dominique Bocquet "Democractic Deficit" *American Enterprise* May/June 1993 pp56-63

52   See Andrew Moravscik "Idealism and Interest in the European Community: The Case of the French Referendum" *French Politics and Society* v11 n1 1993 pp45-56

53   Ingo Kolboom "Dialog mit Bauchgrimmen?: Die zukunft der deutsch-französischen Beziehungen" *Europa-Archiv* Folge 9 1994 pp257-264, see pp259-260; Cole "Looking On: France and the New Germany" pp369-371

mention how 'in France, all of us, whether we are supporters or opponents of Maastricht, are afflicted with the 'German obsession'.[54] Well before a new economic miracle had appeared it was a case of how long the 'masquerade' of equality between France and Germany could continue.[55] In 1995 Moisi and Mertes reaffirmed that 'since German reunification, France can only dwell on its demographic inferiority. France's destabilizing political debates on the eve of presidential elections exacerbate its insecurity over its international standing and the rationality of its European choice'.[56] A paralysis gripped French European policy in a time of uncertainty:

> Seit dem Schock der äußerst knappen Zustimmung im Referendum kommt jedoch aus Frankreich keine einzige wichtige europapolitische Initiative mehr. Nicht daß es sich willentlich aus der internationalen Politik abgemeldet hätte. Das verbietet sein Selbstverständnis: Ein französisches ideal gilt immer auch als weltweites Ideal.[57]

The 'elusive *saut qualitif* necessary to provide a conclusive bond remains just that—elusive.[58] French intentions for political union, hitherto dominated by foreign and security policy, are for these to be operated on intergovernmental terms. Not because this method necessarily produces the best results (it often produces no results) but because it preserves a semblance of authority over Germany and maintains the formal independence essential to the identity of the *Etat-nation*. The French hope that they can seal the monetary partnership and then ignore German demands for structures and forms of representation that wean control in other areas away from the French state. But there cannot be an economic and monetary union without a parallel political union.[59] Arnulf Baring has articulated the dynamics of this *pas de deux*, stating that 'the French are trying to construct the European Union in a contradictory manner...

> they wish to use the potential of their European partners for their own benefit while maintaining French national identity and French freedom of action as far as possible. France wants to preserve her own specific resources—for example the *force de frappe* or the permanent seat in the

---

54   Vernet "French foreign policy" p658
55   Victor Smart "A German giant whose sights are set on a federal Europe" *The European* 14-10-94 p11
56   Dominique Moisi & Michael Mertes "Europe's Map, Compass, and Horizon" *Foreign Affairs* v74 n1 1995 pp122-134
57   "Die feudale Demokratie" *Die Zeit* 14-4-95, see Dossier p12
58   Martin Holland *European Community Integration* (London: Pinter 1993) p123
59   Hans Arnold ""Maastricht"—The Beginning or the end of a Development?" *Aussenpolitik* v44 n3 1993 pp271-280

Security Council—longer than any other European country, while those other countries then have to give up their resources as early as possible—for example the Germans would give up the Deutschmark and the independent Bundesbank.[60]

Josef Janning concludes a recent article by restating the fundamental problem—Europe's core 'motor' is also where it stalls. Again there is no precise recommendation as to how they should overcome this: 'Both countries need to define their common vision of Europe. Without such a decision, the uniting of Europe within the European Union will not succeed and nor will the formation of integration cores'.[61] What it actually requires, though no-one wants to say so, is an acquiescence by someone, and for integration to proceed this will have to be France.[62]

While France lodged in the minds of some among Germany's political strata as its closest partner, ally, and best example, others oppose France as a paragon. Some consider Scandinavia as providing better and others that Germany no longer needs to copy others. In 1990 Joseph Rovan claimed that in both states even 'responsible politicians' were 'with few exceptions tied to the national perspective' and reflected in general populations. According to him, 'despite the advances of European integration, nation-State thinking, and particularly the feeling of the nation-State has not disappeared in France any more than among the Germans. In times of rapid change (and changes frighten most contemporaries), the nation appears to many as a sure value in the midst of unfathomable abysses.'[63] This has, if anything, become stronger. The French position on European integration demonstrates an element of caprice not so apparent in the UK or Germany. Proclamations of the *France par l'Europe* kind abound but at decisive points there is recoil back to a clear primacy of national independence. In a 1994 interview Philippe Seguin, the influential president of the French parliament and a leading opponent of the Maastricht Treaty, indicated 'nation' would remain at the core of French politics and predicted a 'Gaullist' future in which Europe and the partnership with Germany would be viewed from this

60   Arnulf Baring "Germany, What Now?" in *Germany's New Position in Europe* Ed. Arnulf Baring (Oxford: Berg 1994) pp1-20

61   Josef Janning "A German Europe—a European Germany? On the debate over Germany's foreign policy" *International Affairs* v72 n1 1996 pp9-32, p41

62   Cf. Joachim Fest's appraisal of French intentions regarding EMU, 'Europe', and the partnership with Germany. "Europe in a Cul-de-sac" in *Germany's New Position in Europe* pp51-64

63   Joseph Rovan "Rückzug auf den Nationalstaat? Wieder einmal eine deutsch-französische Krise" *Frankfurter Allgemeine Zeitung* 8-2-90 in Renata Fritzsch-Bournazel *German Unification: The Unexpected Challenge* (New York: Berg 1992) p177

perspective.[64] Later that year the CDU-CSU parliamentary group explicitly called on France not to hesitate on making concrete commitments to union which went beyond the 'unrelinquishable sovereignty of the nation-state'.

> Es muss dann die Eindruck widerlegen, dass es zwar an seinem grundsätzlichen Willen zur europäischen Einigung keinen begrundeten Zweifel erlaubt, wohl aber immer wieder vor konkreten Integrationsschritten zögert, da die Vorstellung von der unaufgebbaren Souveränität der "Etat Nation" immer noch Gewicht hat, obwohl diese Souveränitat längst zu einer leeren Hülse geworden ist.[65]

Both French and German leaderships then avoided explanation of how this division would be surmounted. In the wake of the 'Schäuble document' *The Times* cited John Major's speech in Leiden as pointing to 'critical differences' within the continental dyad, a 'growing gulf' and 'fundamentally different views'.[66] George Brock has written, that 'no French government worthy of the name ever dreamt of surrendering any real autonomy in foreign policy to its neighbours'.[67] During France's 1995 presidency campaign the leading candidates endeavoured to sustain the contradictory aims of a *Common* Foreign Security and Policy and retaining French autonomy. This was temporarily evaded by not declaring any emphatic position. Keeping the first 'option' alive nurtured an illusion that voluntary ceding of sovereignty was a possibility. The latter preserved France as France. While regular 'initiatives' continued to be announced, they made little substantive difference. 'No one has said how a common foreign policy (which they claim to want) could be possible without a loss of sovereignty (which they claim not to want). No one has dared raise the issue of what would happen to France's jealously guarded independent nuclear deterrent once a common European defence system was set up.'[68]

Even the architect of the Balladur Plan himself claimed Europe was not the 'ultimate objective of French policy' but a 'means at the service of

---

64   "Wir haben büssen müssen": Der französiche Parlamentspräsident Philippe Seguin über die deutsch-französiche Freundschaft *Der Spiegel* n8 February 1994 pp142-145

65   CDU/CSU-Fraktion des Deutschen Bundestags *Überlegungen zur europäische Politik* Bonn 1-9-94 p7 & p9. See also Michel Korinman "Europa—die geopolitische Sicht" *Neue Gesellschaft/Frankfurter Hefte* v8 August 1996 pp695-699

66   "Our Europe: Major's good sense across the Channel" *The Times* 8-9-94

67   George Brock "Sadder and Wiser" *Times Literary Supplement* 26-11-93 p10

68   "A Conspiracy of fuzziness" *Economist* 8-4-95 p47-48; "Vor "Maastricht Zwei" eine deutsch-französische Initiative" *Frankfurter Allgemeine Zeitung* 9-10-95 p4

France's interests and permanence'.[69] European integration became more than ever dependent on German initiative and it is 'Bonn [that] remains the Mecca of European patriots'.[70] France may be 'taking a time-out'[71] but a reversion (if it ever departed) to a strong national focus also serves to legitimate the same for Germany. Whatever the entreaties, France is not an eternal *sine qua non* for German initiatives.[72] The German-American mutual perspective of the others importance sustains an old tension between Gaullism and Atlanticism and French suspicions of a transatlantic condominium. For Kohl the Europe-USA transatlantic partnership is 'besser gesagt' as 'der deutsch-amerikanischen Freundschaft'.[73] The attested closeness of the Franco-German relationship in not supported where the existence of an authority higher than the national really counts. There is no exchange of personnel in areas of primary importance; in high level security or defence posts or in foreign affairs, only lower level swaps and even this is seen by some as 'a mole in the ministry'.[74]

Divergences Apparent

When still SPD leader, Rudolf Scharping wrote of the 'deteriorated image' of Franco-German relations, of 'differing fundamental views' and the danger of 'becoming bogged down in the inertia of conventional rituals'.[75] Peter Pulzer views the partnership as 'problematical' and one in which even before 1990 French governments feared a 'greater diplomatic self-confidence on the German side' because it 'would turn France into a junior partner'. He goes on to state that 'nothing would be easier than to make a list of Franco-German disputes during and since unification' and that Europe cannot move forward without them nor against them where they agree.[76] While nothing overtly

---

69   Stanley Hoffman "France: keeping the Demons at Bay." *New York Review of Books* 3-3-94

70   Mark Frankland "A Scared Europe seeks one-way ticket to security" *The Observer* 19-6-94 p1

71   Interview Sources, Auswärtiges Amt, Bonn, November 1994

72   Klaus Bloemer "Deutschland Braucht Frankreich" *Neue Gesellschaft* v39 n12 1992 pp1065-1070

73   Helmut Kohl "Deutsch-amerikanische Freundschaft—ein Grundpfeiler unserer Außenpolitik" *Bulletin* 27-6-96

74   Interview Sources, Auswärtiges Amt, Bonn, November 1994

75   Rudolf Scharping "New Challenges for Franco-German Cooperation" *Aussenpolitik* v45 n1 1994 pp1-9

76   Peter Pulzer *German Politics 1945-1995* (Oxford: Oxford University Press 1995) pp17-18

confirms a permanent fracture, their relationship has entered a cul-de-sac. Now that the primary aims have been achieved: firstly, eliminating any conceivable prospect of war between the two; and secondly, establishing and expanding a commercial confederation, Germany has no fundamental necessity to remain as bound to France as the two have for the past forty years, which has been primarily on French terms. Each is the other's largest trading partner, neither is a military threat, and the collapse of the Warsaw Pact has sharply reduced the potential for attack from the east.

Nonetheless, the partnership was delivered sharp shocks by the inability to combine and effect an end to war in the former Yugoslavia, Maastricht referendums, the currency crisis of 1993, and by France's social unrest in late 1995. In the area of social protection the inability of France to harmonize the systems of EU members now means 'financial imperatives' will impel movement further from its own model.[77] Now the divergences are no less apparent than the convergences: in terms of visions for Europe or the means to get there; pace and depth of integration, the geographic expansion of the EU and the political action which accompanies this.[78] The strength of international relationships can really only be tested, and proved or otherwise, during a crisis. Against a background of carnage in Bosnia, when a more readily assertive Germany, represented by the Bundesbank, did not concur with French preferences on, *inter alia*, interests rates, fissures widened.[79] Continuing discord was demonstrated by the Charles Pasqua inspired opposition to a unified police network and France's reneging on the Schengen accord.[80] Territory was and is confirmed as a problem for the EU. According to Pierre Lellouche, member of the National Assembly and Chirac advisor, an internally borderless Europe was fine in theory but implausible in practice.[81] At the onset of the 1996 IGC 'communal declarations' continued with references to 'precise propositions' and 'communal ideas on further

77   Linda Hantrais "French social policy in the European context" *Modern & Contemporary France* NS3 (4) 1995 pp381-390

78   Christian Deubner "Deutschland, Frankreich und die Europäische Union: Die Interessen laufen auseinander' *Internationale Politik und Gesellschaft* n3 1994 pp210-222; Victor Smart "Cracks grow in Franco German axis" *The European* 21-10-94 pp1-2

79   Francois Renard "La Saga du SME" and "Fissures franco-allemandes" *Le Monde* 5-8-93 pp7-8; Mark Milner and Larry Elliot "Currency Dogma that cost the French Dear" *The Guardian* 31-7/1-8-93 p19

80   Lionel Barber "Hopes of wider union turn to fear of no union" *Financial Times* 9-12-94 p2; Christopher Lockwood "First battle for Euro police is to curb France" *Electronic Telegraph* 26-1-95; Jochen Hehn "Frankreich zögert bei Schengen-Abkommen" *Die Welt* 24-11-94 p5

81   "Schengen eine Katastrophe-eine gemeinsame Außenpolitik gibt es nicht" *Frankfurter Allgemeine Zeitung* 9-10-95 p4

development of foreign and security policy' while subsequently listing the problem points: qualified majority voting and the veto, relations between the European and national parliaments, a 'genuine European identity within the Atlantic Alliance'. These were 'all questions in which we must come to concrete decisions'.[82]

These later differences followed others. Because of its central role, many other components of European integration were connected to the CAP. It has been cogently argued that this constituted an 'area of conflict' where every attempt was made to assure national preferences were served.[83] From inception aspects of the CAP clashed with German preferences; for control of domestic price levels, concern over large amounts of German money going to fund it, and after 1992 the impending entry into the EU of new agricultural producers from the east.[84] French support for its aggressive farming lobby was delivered by maintaining a policy whereby Community subsidies favoured France. The CAP could not be disentangled from all the other agreements, interdependencies, obligations and so on that constituted the Franco-German relationship. Beneath the complexities lay the utilitarian accuracy of Helmut Schmidt's words; 'We Germans have known from the start that the CAP was the political price we had to pay for the founding of the Community.' As the CAP absorbed around 70% (up to 87% in 1970) of total contributions to the EC budget it was a big financial price. Between 1953 and 1968 the Federal Republic was a net contributor of $US946 million and France a net recipient of $US716 million.[85] This is why 'Germany wanted to change the rules'.[86]

When 'criticism focused on the rising costs of the CAP, to which Germany contributed a disproportionate share' German governments in the 1970s and 1980s tried by all manner of manipulations to validate the high cost of sustaining the CAP to the domestic electorate. Under Agriculture Minister Josef Ertl, the Germans constructed a policy involving the Monetary Compensatory Amount (MCA) instrument. France objected to the use of

---

82   Gemeinsamer Beitrag des deutschen und des französischen Außenministers "Unsere Vorstellungen von Europa" *Bulletin* 3-1-96

83   Gisela Hendriks *Germany and European Integration: The Common Agricultural Policy: an Area of Conflict* (New York: Berg 1991)

84   "French farmers against the world" and "Waving or drowning" *The Economist* 11-9-93 pp44-45

85   Bernard Heidelberger "La ventilation des dépenses communautaires: le juste retour" unpublished manuscript September 1968 p77. See Table 9-1 in Leon N Lindberg & Stuart A Scheingold *Europe's Would-Be Polity* (Englewood Cliffs: Prentice-Hall 1970) p300

86   Walter Grund 'Paying for the Common Farm Policy: Why Germany wants to Change the Rules" *European Community* v1 January 1969

MCA's which by the 1980s had boosted West German agricultural exports to fourth highest in the world and issued a serious challenge to France's 'traditional' role as Europe's agricultural leader.[87] By the time MCA's were dismantled in the 1990s the perception of France as an errant participant in world trade issues was widespread and French positions often constituted a difficulty for Bonn. The CAP has gradually been superseded by the global urgency of reaching cohesion on the GATT, to which France provided the major European stumbling block. Wrangling eventually witnessed Germany chose in favour of its greater international interests over loyalty to France.

A further source of friction, and indication of the importance placed on having one's own nationals in key positions, are the recurring disputes over who gets what in the distribution of Commission appointments, featured in 1994 by a Bonn-Paris struggle over the industry portfolio.[88] This and the competition brief are particularly sought after, Although the French strategic response to the Europeanization of economies conceived that a favourable industrial policy could still be employed in a larger zone, this has not been replicated as they wished. That states remain powerful in Brussels does not guarantee that the French state in particular will be able to enforce its preferences. The doctrine remains that French business should operate in the national interest and to some extent it retains the 'aura' of doing so. Much as it is still attempted, political activism or financial aid from governments to assist business towards this goal are restricted. As France loses control over what happens in the European commercial-industrial arena and the linkages between state and economy are weakened, well established understandings of democracy and national identity are threatened, more than for the Germans and even more so the British. Ultimately France 'appears weaker to a populace that continues to feel a sense of loss for the heroism of the past.'[89]

One result is prominent protectionists, for whom free trade imperils not only material interests but 'the future of France as a nation'. And the nation sustains as the focus of possibilities for 'creating a wide zone of consensus across Left and Right'. Chevènement and Seguin are pertinent examples encouraging some scholars to affirm there are still 'striking family resemblances' to old style Gaullism and any consideration that political forces

---

87   On tensions between German preferences for trade liberalisation and partial protectionism in agriculture see Stephen George *Politics and Policy-Making in the European Community* (Oxford: Oxford University Press 1992) Chapter 8

88   Rory Watson "Big two split on top EC jobs" and "Scramble for the prestige posts in Brussels" *The European* 19-8-94 p1 & p9; Klaus-Peter Schmidt "Konzert für viele Solisten" *Die Zeit* 16-9-94 p38

89   See Vivien A. Schmidt "Loosening the Ties that Bind: The Impact of European Integration on French Government and its Relationship to Business" *Journal of Common Market Studies* v34 n2 1996 pp223-253

demanding state authority will 'evaporate' is 'to underestimate the strength and resilience of the nationalist vision in modern France'.[90] A liberal market and economic networks which bypass *dirigiste* controls did not prevent strategies to sustain national champions through bail-outs like that arranged for Air France or Crédit Lyonnais among others. Despite erosion in the capacity for autarkic industrial policy, France has not abandoned these methods. As Emmanual Godin recently asserts, 'Le neo-liberalisme français est avant tout une affaire d'Etat'.[91] Another analyst suggests that in response to a situation whereby the French 'debate' on free trade and associated economic issues is 'rapidly frozen in political credos by sycophants and disparagers', a 'duty of interference' by other members states is permissible and even necessary. Otherwise Germany may catch the French malady when both are 'less able to find in the other antidotes to their own problems.'[92]

Reorganization of the EU budget is a pressing German demand. Their contributions have been paid into a household with no equivalent to the CAP favourable to France (or a rebate system extracted for the UK by Margaret Thatcher).[93] France had also been the recipient of generous Euratom and "Balance of Payments" loans.[94] Between 1990 and 1994 the contribution of each German to the Brussels treasury rose from 100 Ecu to 140 Ecu. In the same period French per capita contributions fell from 30 Ecu to 15 Ecu.[95] Germany, with DM21 billion in 1995, is a 13 times larger net payer than France, which in paying DM1.7 still ranked behind the Netherlands.[96] The issue of budgetary contributions was heading towards breakdown if, as new and poor entrants were imminent, Germany refused to maintain its levels of payment and no-one else was prepared to accept a greater share. A test of

---

90   Suzanne Berger "Trade and Identity: The Coming Protectionism?" in *Remaking the Hexagon* pp195-210

91   Emmanuel Godin "Le néo-liberalisme à la française: une exception?" *Modern & Contemporary France* NS4 (1) 1996 pp61-70; William James Adams "France and Global Competition" in *Remaking the Hexagon...* pp87-115

92   Patrick A. Messerlin "France and trade policy: is the 'French exception' passée?" *International Affairs* v72 n2 1996 pp293-309, here p308

93   Rory Watson "Germany seeks to cut its Union contributions" *The European* 15-7-94 p1; "Ghost of handbags past" *The Economist* 29-1-94 p53

94   Up to 1991, Ecu1.2 billion of a 2.8 billion total for the former and 2.6 billion, second only to Greece, of a 7 billion total for the latter. See *The Borrowing and Lending Activities of the European Communities* (Credit and Investments Directorate, CEC: Brussels 1992)

95   Andreas Oldag "Wer soll das bezahlen, wer hat so viel Geld?" *Süddeutsche Zeitung* 27-3-96 p11

96   Wolfgang Michal "Die Vermachtung Europas unter deutschen Vorzeichen" *Neue Gesellschaft/Frankfurter Hefte* v8 August 1996 pp700-705

European commitment may be placed with France which had profited handsomely in the past.

Where Germany desires to secure stability in eastern Europe, France wants greater attention and resources to combat current and potential dangers in the North African region.[97] In July 1994 the EU pledged some 382 million Ecu to central and eastern Europe for cross-border cooperation, economic reforms and infrastructure building as part of the PHARE programme. By comparison 81.4 million Ecu was granted to the Mediterranean and Middle East.[98] The following Essen summit was featured both by continuing dismay over the inadequacy of the CFSP with regard to the Bosnian crisis, and differences between France and Germany over EU expansion with the former demanding equal funds for the 'South' as a counter to Germany's 'sphere of influence' in the 'East'.[99] In June 1995 European foreign ministers agreed a compromise that determined a minimum 3.3 billion Ecus for the Mediterranean and 6.1 billion for eastern and central Europe.

Both France and Germany have established bilateral relations with states to the east in addition to arrangements under EU auspices. They have separate treaties with Poland and the creation of a special 'Euro-trio' endeavours to cement France into the eastern expansion. For all states in central and eastern Europe German trade far exceeds that of France. As an example, in the first half of 1992 Germany accounted for 45.2% of Poland's exports and 37.3% of its imports compared with 6.0% and 6.1% respectively for France.[100] German politicians may insist on Germany's diversity, regionalism, and decentralization, but from Paris Europe is still viewed as a collection of national states with relative power and influence capacities. *Ost-Erweiterung* is a project serving German (and perhaps British) national

---

97   "Nur nichts überstürtzen" *Der Spiegel* n14 1994 pp32-33; William Drozdiak "EU's Growth Strains Paris-Bonn Alliance" *International Herald Tribune* 30-10-94 p1 & p6

98   *Bulletin EU* 7/8 1994 pp72-79

99   Karl-Ludwig Günsche "Kohl lädt Staaten Osteuropas ein" *Die Welt* 1-12-95 p1; Lionel Barber & Christopher Parkes "Bosnia clouds EU summit hopes on eastern Europe" *Financial Times* 9-12-94 p1; Lionel Barber "Hopes of wider union turn to fear of no union" *Financial Times* 9-12-94 p2

100   Valerie Guerin-Sendelbach & Jacek Rulkowski ""Euro-Trio" Frankreich-Deutschland-Polen" *Aussenpolitik* v45 n2 1994 pp246-253; "Treffen der Aussenminister von Deutschland, Frankreich und Polen: Gemainsame Erklaerung der Aussenminister" *Bulletin* 20-9-94; See also the interview with Polish author Andrej Szczypiorski "Berlin kommt zu uns" *Der Spiegel* n4 22-1-96 pp128-132. His response to the enquiry whether Germany and Poland could build a relationship as close as the Franco-German one was 'How close is the relationship between Germans and French really?...this entente cordiale exists more as something sworn to (Beschwörung) than reality'. See p131

interests and only a European one from these perspectives. Conversely such developments diminish France's position, despite its involvement in tri- and multilateral ventures.[101]

French Cultural Policy

Europe has added many ironies to that occurring in 1815—'When Wellington and Blücher met, victorious, on the field of Waterloo, they greeted each other in French—the natural *lingua franca* of any educated gentleman.'[102] In the contemporary world, aversion to supporting the candidature of non-French speakers to high positions in European or global institutions persists. Sensitivities about the position of French intensify as the dominance of English—presently the official or semi-official language in over 70 states comprising around 1.4 billion people and estimated to have around 1 billion students worldwide by 2000[103]—is joined by significant increases for German. Unable to stop the EU's momentum to the east (or vice versa) France wants to establish a francophone niche in Poland. Two culture institutes and thirteen *Alliances Françaises* were opened within a few years of the *Wende*.[104] As foreign languages, however, German and English are eroding the practical importance of French in the region. In an everyday context the prevalence of the former two is joined by a conspicuous absence of the latter. By 1990 40% of Hungarian job advertisements requiring foreign languages wanted German and 37% English. In Poland, 46% English and

101   Cf. Roland Freudenstein "Deutschland, Frankreich und die Ostweiterung der Europäischen Union" and Valerie Guérin-Sendelbach & Jacek Rulkowski "Frankreich, Deutschland und Polen: Ein neues Gespann—Eine Herausforderung für die Zukunft" in *Handeln für Europa: Deutsch-französische Zusammenarbeit in einer veränderten Welt* Eds. CIRAC et.al. (Opladen: Leske & Budrich 1995) pp131-137 & pp138-157; Marie Lavigne "L'Union europeenne, toujours plus vers l'est?" and Jean-Pierre Chevenement "Un probleme d'hegemonie" *Le Monde Diplomatique* September 1994 p20 & pp20-21

102   William Wallace *The Transformation of Western Europe* (New York: RIIA 1990) p57

103   *The British Council Worldwide* (London: British Council 1995). Already in 1990 the French government had commissioned a report on the state of the French national identity including the decline of French language use and prestige. Emmanuel Le Roy Ladurie et. al. *Entre dans le XXIéme siécle: essai sur l'avenir de l'identité française* (Paris: Documentation Française 1990)

104   Guerin-Sendelbach & Rulkowski "Euro-Trio"; "Just do it" *Economist* 15-7-96 pp39-40

26% German. Figures for French were 3% and 7%.[105] In eastern and central European schools first and second foreign languages are dominated by English and German. In one survey of academics from several European countries as well as the USA and Japan, 91.3% had a knowledge of English, 65% German and 49.6% French.[106] In 1994 42% of EU citizens were able to converse fluently in English, 31% in German and 29% in French, for the first time relegating the latter to third place. German also has the largest number of native speakers, rising after Austria's membership.[107]

Since France became the first proponent of cultural diplomacy, French policy has aimed at transmitting 'not just the French language but our culture in the broadest sense of the word' and seeking to reach 'those people who influence or make decisions [who] should speak French and consider French a benchmark in the realm of ideas, art and culture, in the broadest sense of the word.'[108] Attendant to a belief that 'we are undoubtedly the country of reference for culture, ideas, and the art of living', is the conception that French ideals are universal. In this respect French 'humanism' is the export of Frenchness,[109] or an external cultural nationalism. Expressing this staple within the context of a new offensive against 'linguistic, and so, cultural, uniformity', Jacques Chirac extolled French as 'the bearer of humanism...because the concepts of *liberté* and *égalité* are expressed in French'. Besides concerns about English dominance of the Internet,[110] Chirac indicated a policy drive concentrating on Africa.[111] French political self-

105   Ulrich Ammon "The German Language: Lingua Franca overshadowed by English?" *Deutschland Magazine* n2 1994 pp44-49
106   Michael Clyne *The German language in a changing Europe* (Cambridge: Cambridge University Press 1995) pp13-18
107   *Eurobarometer* n41 July 1994 p36-37. Cf. Hilmar Hoffman "Rede des Präsidenten des Goethe-Instituts" *Bulletin* 12-12-95. 'Französisch, ehedem als Sprache von Diplomatie und Aristokratie in Osteuropa weit vor Deutsch und English, ist in unserem Jahrhundert dort auf den dritten Platz gefallen. Für die Attraktivität der Sprache wie der integralen Kultur eines Landes sind viele Faktoren verantwortlich, darunter eben auch individuelle ökonomishce Nutzenkalküle' For many people in the east this now means learning German is a necessary 'step into the future'
108   Jean-David Levitte "The Cultural Diplomacy of France" (Ambassade de France en Australie) Reprinted from *Enjeux du Monde* June 1994.
109   Michael Kelly "Humanism and Unity" *History of European Ideas* v20 n4-6 1995 pp923-928
110   Over 90% of information transmitted via the Internet is in English. The French government has sought to ensure a French language presence
111   Mary Dejevsky "Chirac spreads the word about French" *The Independent* 4-12-95 p9; See also "France Seeks a Voice in Asia" *International Herald Tribune* 30-11-94 p16

understanding remains entwined with the cultural and concern about potential or actual diminution of cultural status or 'authenticity' is palpable.[112] Thus 'the onslaught of English is a factor in the anxiety over the potential enlargement of a Union that is no longer France writ large but which amounts to a German-led trade zone supported by Britain'[113] The foreign ministry's head of cultural relations observed:

> The French language contributes to our international status the same way as our permanent seat on the Security Council. The United Nations and the European Union have only two working languages [sic] : English and French. Yet even though our language has never been so widely spoken as now *its status has never been so threatened.* A massive effort is urgently required. If we fail to act, the expanded European Union will tilt towards English, and the bases of Francophony [?]...will crumble beyond repair.[114]

France's intellectual radiance, in academe, literature, social commentary, historical analysis, or accompanying its foreign policy formulation,[115] served as a referent for a special type of national morale. This was especially pronounced immediately after the Second World War when an outwardly confident and reflexive anodyne for physical devastation, wounded pride, and compromised morality was provided by a sublime intelligentsia. The common feature of this milieu was its 'Frenchness' and its sophistication

---

112   See Fredy Gsteiger "Die Feudale Demokratie" *Die Zeit* 14-4-95 p11
113   Charles Bremner "French identity crisis fuels new drive for la gloire" *Times* 8-10-94 p16
114   Levitte "Cultural Diplomacy..." Emphasis added
115   James Cable "Foreign policy-making: Planning or reflex" in *Two Worlds of International Relations: academics, practitioners and the trade in ideas* Eds. Christopher Hill & Pamela Beshoff (London: Routledge 1994) pp93-117 Whereas British foreign policy was characterised by the 'conditioned reflex', 'Meetings with our French planners invested show business with a distinction it usually lacked. Most of our foreign colleagues were highly intelligent, but a French intellectual, on a good day, can give discussion a sharp glitter unattainable by the best minds of more stolid nations....only in Paris were we fascinated' See p107. Ruth Dudley Edwards writes that in the world of diplomacy 'the French are easily the most disliked and also the most admired...the French believe they own diplomacy' a feature intimately related to the French language tradition. Quoting Eric Clark she continues that 'French diplomats' are 'believers in the right of their own country, in the supremacy of their own culture, and are quick to take slight at any imagined offence'. See *True Brits: Inside the Foreign Office* (London: BBC Books 1994) p73

was unchallenged.[116] This leads to other curious tangents. In 1979 Stanley Hoffmann drew a link between the ostensibly separate and mutually critical strata of governing and intellectual classes. He claimed that 'France's intellectuals lost their voice at the moment when France ceased to be a pacesetter for other nations and a leader in world affairs'. Precisely when this 'moment' occurred is uncertain, however it has interesting consequences.[117] A propensity to make a virtue of apparent contradiction means the *Ministère de la Culture* can easily accommodate the avant garde of contemporary critical thought deconstructing 'traditional universal missions' to which France has been the most indefatigable claimant.[118] With considerable effect, Jacques Derrida et. al. maintain an authoritative visibility for France and French culture—language, ideas and art, at a time when 'all too often American and European educated classes seem to think French art stopped with the Impressionists and Ravel.'[119] Derrida approaches this very theme, on the one hand, to critique the 'exemplarist logic' by which 'France assigns herself this *exemplary* task' not only as the cultural avant garde but a universalizable avant garde of 'free culture itself'. Elsewhere he attacks the standard *bête noire*, English, which 'tries to erase the other language or languages...never so true. Today.' Moving between speculations on Europe's 'cultural identity' to Husserl's notion of its 'spiritual geography', Derrida chides 'one of the essential problems of European culture'; the dominance of 'Anglo-American' representing the 'tip of the European headland, in what is called the European Community, which is predominantly Mediterranean'.[120] French leaders from de Gaulle to Mitterrand[121] to Chirac could not have put it better.

Before reunification the Federal Republic effectively accepted an inflated French political and cultural superiority. France attempted to continue

---

116   See Tony Judt *Past Imperfect: French Intellectuals 1944-56* (Berkeley: University of California Press 1992) Chapter 13

117   Stanley Hoffmann "Fragments Floating in the Here and Now" *Dædelus* v108 n1 1979 pp1-26

118   Balladur put it that 'French civilization is a civilization of uniformity'

119   Levitte "Cultural Diplomacy..." 'Our objective is to reach a designated public. It is not our ambition to see everyone learn French, but rather those people who influence or make decisions. What is most important for us, for the future as it was in the past, is that the educated classes...should speak French and consider French a benchmark in the realm of ideas, art and culture, in the broadest sense of the word...'

120   Jacques Derrida *The Other Heading: Reflections on Today's Europe* (Bloomington: Indiana University Press 1992) trans. Pascale-Anne Brault & Michael B. Naas. See introduction ppxxii-xliii & p23. By 1991 indications were that Europe was not 'predominantly Mediterranean' for much longer. After 1995 it is being confirmed

121   Cole *François Mitterrand: A Study in Political Leadership* p116

the same 'civilisational missionary ideology' of the previous century by attributing a universalistic claim to itself that was nationalism in philosophical or other guise. It promoted a Jacobin strain within which the idea of France and its inherent superior qualities were conflated. As France constitutes one half of the motor on which the EU depends it is 'compelled to a growing extent to perceive itself as a nation among nations and to treat other languages and cultures as equals if it intends retaining its ability to integrate and prevent isolation'.[122] While what may be termed a 'progressive' move is occurring for the German language, the debate in France on French is permeated by a 'tradition of linguistic conservatism' which perceives the greatest threats as external.[123]

The interplay between geographic, political and economic trends and the three major European languages highlights the French dilemma: For France to gain German support in strengthening both languages *vis-à-vis* English it will have to make 'concessions' to German in central and eastern Europe—which it does not want to do. Ingo Kolboom comments that to the present, experience with France gives little encouragement and the Parisian linguistic nationalism now positions itself against a strengthening of German (*dabei sind bisherige Erfahrungen mit Frankreich wenig ermutigend, da der Pariser Sprachnationalismus sich gegen Stärkung des Deutschen stellt*). Accompanying the battle against English, France attempts to limit the rise and spread of German in the European institutions, the UN, in NATO. During 'Partnership for Peace' manoeuvres in Hungary in 1995 the French protested successfully when the daily information bulletin was produced not only in English and Hungarian, but also in German (despite France being a quasi-member of NATO). When Germany tried to establish a German speaking university for German minorities in Rumania, French diplomacy set about 'torpedoing' the venture. These are manifestations of a state-nation fearing loss of status through the declining importance of its primary cultural attribute. What it brings into relief is the 'meaning of cultural questions for the political union of Europe'. Kolboom continues to the fundamental point at issue, where the problem resurfaces again in the proposed core. 'The question is only: how much diversity does unity need? how much unity does diversity need?'.[124]

122   Helmut Wagner ""Constitutional Patriotism" as an Antidote" *Aussenpolitik* v44 n3 1993 pp243-252

123   Rodney Ball "Plus ça change...? The enduring tradition of linguistic conservatism" *French Cultural Studies* v6 p1 n16 February 1995 pp61-78

124   See Ingo Kolboom "Frankreich und Deutschland: Die Neuen Akzente" in *Deutschland's Neue Außenpolitik* Bd.3 "Interesse und Strategien" Eds. Karl Kaiser & Joachim Krause (München: Oldenbourg 1996) pp123-128

The Audiovisual Example:
'European', or French Culture Under Threat?

The European Commission has taken up the cultural cause with a certain surety of agreement when purporting to protect or further culture in a broad, and vague, 'European' sense. In this regard, 'The Commission...sees a role for European television defending both the cultural identity and economic expansion of Europe against American and Japanese rivals'.[125] When France launched 'a concerted attempt to toughen cultural controls' before the departure of Jacques Delors, its representatives tried to Europeanise the issue of culture by presenting the US as antagonist. Delors opposed compatriots, including minister for culture Jacques Toubon and the minister for budget and communications, Nicolas Sarkozy, who argued for revisions tightening the 1989 'Television without Frontiers' (within Europe) directive requiring 51% European material. In France it was 60%, of which two-thirds was to be French. French radio stations were to broadcast at least 40% French language material. Despite his later shift of priorities Delors had originally been instrumental in both ideological vision and policy implementation behind attempts at building a European media. In 1989 he had 'posed a question to our American friends: do we have the right to exist? Have we the right to preserve our traditions, our heritage, our languages?'[126] The crusade to stop invasion by English in film, television and music was legally foiled by reference to the 1789 Bill of Rights.[127] Commissioners Leon Brittan (UK) and Martin Bangemann (FRG) viewed further protectionism as 'inappropriate legislation'. Nonetheless French opposition proved the most obstinate to agreement in the GATT Uruguay Round.

Defence against extra-European intrusion is entirely different to managing intra-European concerns. The establishment of a bilateral television channel—'Arte-die real-utopische Television'[128]—had to fit French conceptions of being the premier 'guardians of European civilization' with an alternative German interpretation. Difference in systems had to be resolved; the unitary orientation of the French model and the decentralized German

---

125 Michael Schudson "Culture and the Integration of national societies" *International Social Science Journal* v105 n1 February 1994 pp63-79, here p77

126 Philip Schlesinger "Europe's Contradictory Communicative Space" *Dædelus* v123 n2 1994 pp25-51. See p31

127 "Television of Babel" *The Economist* 5-2-94; Anne-Elisabeth Mouton "French is the language of freedom not of bureaucracy" and Editorial *The European* 5-8-94 p10 & p11

128 Klaus Wenger "Kultur à la Arte: Tele-Visionen für Europa" in *Frankreich in Europa: Ein Deutsch-Französischer Rundblick* Eds. Ingo Koolboom & Ernst Weisenfeld (Bonn: Europa Union Verlag 1993) pp257-262

version. Resistance of audiences to the respective 'foreign' product and resentments among programmers displayed a good deal of rivalry, 'raised the spectre of opt-outs', and confirmed the 'negotiation of a common policy as much more difficult than Mitterrand and Kohl could have imagined when they signed their agreement the day after the re-unification of Germany'.[129] Later the Germans, along with the British, were conspicuous by their absence from the Euronews venture. The former claimed 'legal difficulties', which 'would doubtless have been overcome if Euronews had been set up in Munich rather than Lyons.'[130] At the Cannes summit the two opponents of quotas, supported by a majority of EU members, forced a French change of tack towards encouraging greater financial assistance for production of European film and television programs, especially from private sources. Nonetheless 'France had not yet shown a willingness to declare quotas dead.'[131]

Interspersed here was another debate about the merits of 'high' and 'popular' culture. For the French, 'Frenchness' transcended other considerations. Delineating the defence of French culture and cultural industries in European terms did not mean instant or lasting agreement with other EU states. Discrepancies in preferred outcomes between a more protectionist France and a Germany less concerned about cultural invasion but more disturbed by threats to free trade, impressed where the politics of preserving *patrimoine* were strongest. If Germany's cultural nationalism is a perpetual state of becoming, France's transmits a kind of reification.

> Cultural nationalism is the common ground - even when adapting to the requirements of the marriage with Germany - and so the announcement that Turner Entertainment will be broadcasting from a London-based satellite is met in France with a unanimous chorus of dismay, articulating a consensus that intelligent cultural television might be at best the least hateful form of a vulgar medium, a consensus which crosses all other division of opinion.[132]

A bilateral television channel can be claimed as a step *towards* a European culture. But if foreign presence is viewed as a potential limitation on French autonomy, growing German influence would be resisted as are excessive American or British intrusions.

---

129   Susan Emanuel "A Community of Culture?: The European Television Channel" *History of European Ideas* v21 n2 1995 pp169-176
130   "Television of Babel" *The Economist* 5-2-94
131   Tom Buerkle "France Drops Demand for TV Quotas In Europe" *International Herald Tribune* 21-6-95 p1
132   Susan Emanuel "Cultural television: current French critiques" *French Cultural Studies* v5 p2 n14 June 1994 pp139-149

Military Cooperation and the *Force de Frappe*

Franco-German security cooperation is entwined with a range of defence and foreign policy components. German aims focus on sustaining a reliable multilateral architecture within which pressures for renationalizing of German defence arrangements can be contained. Under an umbrella of 'cooperative independence' a series of Franco-German initiatives have been launched since 1990 but none have culminated in a genuine European defence force. The Eurocorps, also including Dutch, Belgian and Spanish contingents, was an originally 4200 strong brigade intended to grow into a force of 35000. It is yet to progress beyond the 'language school in uniform' it was described as being in 1993.[133] The Yugoslav crisis demonstrated how little solidarity existed among EC/EU members, most starkly between France and Germany. Although France had personnel taken hostage and suffered more deaths than any other western powers, some authors claim that 'France bears the principal blame' for the prolongation of the conflict 'since it was the one major European power in a position to act in Yugoslavia (with Germany precluded from doing so by its wartime record in the Balkans and the British government obsessed with the Ulster precedent)'. Moreover,

> It is also the one which has constantly demanded in the past that Europe take responsibility for its independent interests when these are threatened. In the event, France and the other West European powers demonstrated that they could not or would not defend the new standards of interstate conduct, legality, and political morality established in Western Europe after the Second World War.[134]

France's Cold War era 'independence' was in large part superficial but French leaders and military planners were insistent on presenting the illusion that France was self sufficient in defence terms. The objective was one of 'overcoming Yalta'. As a possible counter to French intransigence the German presence in the still chiefly symbolic Eurocorps may eventually make the latter more of an integrating rather than divisive factor between European and American defence components. When the British nuclear arsenal and conventional forces are added to the equation a coherent western alliance already has more than enough deterrent capacity. Along with the British and others French and German observers realise that the US will not provide all the necessary data and technological assistance. At the same time

---

133   David Buchan *Europe: The Strange Superpower* (Aldershot: Dartmouth 1993) Chapter 11

134   William Pfaff *The Wrath of Nations: Civilization and the Furies of Nationalism* (New York: Simon and Schuster 1993) p218. The French were galvanised into much tougher and effective action when French airmen were captured by Serbs

rivalries between the three involve 'national champions' in armaments industries. Although the French needed German money to construct and launch a 'European' spy satellite, Chirac and Lellouche were opposed to a selling of French 'crown jewels' through Germans buying into Aerospatiale, that is, Europeanising it. The 'French government' it was claimed, must 'not lose sight of the value and interests of a company that has proven its worth to the nation'.[135]

Most German politicians want a definitive partnership with the states to the country's east beginning with the Visegrad countries and joined by others at successive stages. Relinquishment of national independence to a higher authority in the form of SACEUR (or the EU) is not resisted because it has already occurred and had served the Federal Republic well for the past forty years. Maintaining a US presence in European frameworks is considered vital and NATO widening means continued American involvement for the foreseeable future. The prevailing French position has rated political independence as high or higher than military-security functions and the combined weight of the US and Germany is perceived as reducing France's international scope. Although present circumstances suggest a unified response to post-Cold War uncertainties, the 'transatlantic' network consists of states which do not all share a definitive common defence arrangement. Despite having slowly moved closer to NATO—the 1994 *Livre blanc* was another quasi-declaration; apparent rapprochement without anything conclusive[136]—France retained its special status and continued to disavow US leadership in Europe. Some analysts argued that France got what it wanted without actually relinquishing anything 'vital'.[137] In this way it could influence the efficacy of the Atlantic Alliance and confer leverage in other areas of a western security complex developing more political, rather than distinctly military-strategic functions.[138] Domestic advocates of more

---

135   Joseph Fitchett "Paris Looks to Bonn to Get and Ambitious Spy Satellite Program Off the Ground" *International Herald Tribune* 12-6-95 p13

136   *Livre Blanc sur la Défense* (Paris: La Documentation Française 1994)

137   Peter Schmidt "Germany, France and NATO" Paper for a Joint Seminar of the American Institute for Contemporary German Studies and the U.S. Army War College (June 1994). Former Prime Minister Edouard Balladur had called for participation in greater defence cooperation and a less nuclear-centric view. He did not remain around to implement it. See Hoffmann "France: keeping the Demons at Bay"; Edouard Balladur *Dictionnaire de la Reforme* (Paris: Fayard 1992). France later perpetrated another irony when the May 1997 NATO agreement—it was neither a full member of the alliance nor desired its enlargment—was signed in Paris

138   Cf. Philip H. Gordon *A Certain Idea of France: French Security Policy and the Gaullist Legacy* (Princeton: Princeton University Press 1993); Frédéric Bozo

military responsibility for Germany, including Rühe and Naumann, were disappointed at French manpower and budgetary reductions.[139] More recently Christoph Bertram has declared that the experience of Bosnia and a realisation that other EU members only want to establish a 'European defence identity' within NATO has caused a French 'Abkehr vom Sonderweg'.[140] Differing notions of Europe are still posited: as an essentially civilian power possessing a supranational defence closely bound to the US; or a military-political power of autonomous nation-states led by France.

The announcement weeks after the 1995 presidential elections that France would resume nuclear testing in the Pacific incensed populations and governments in the region. It also disturbed France's European partners. While New Zealand politicians were describing the decision as 'Gaullist-Napoleonic arrogance' French prime minister Alain Juppé was declaring that 'The higher interests of the nation deem that France continues to wield a sufficient and creditable deterrent force'. Others claimed the very future of the nation was at stake. Chiracs' declaration that after the series of tests—reduced from eight to six—all testing would end did not alter the episode being imprinted as bad foreign policy.[141] The tests were to be conducted without any apparent wider European involvement either technically or in shared security. After the initial blast other EU states were invited to send specialists to examine the site, an invitation which coincided with official protest by all but one of the other EU members. The German government, committed to the non-proliferation treaty and conscious of a strong environmental lobby made a somewhat feeble protest. This followed the indignation that greeted Chirac's appearance before the European Parliament. The EU Council had also previously declared its support of the Nuclear Non-Proliferation Treaty and intention to strengthen it by 'promoting the universality of the NPT and by extending it indefinitely and unconditionally'.[142] In 1994 Hans Blix stated that, along with China, 'France's adherences to the NPT mean that all nuclear-weapon states now firmly and formally support the objective of non-

---

"France and Security in the New Europe: Between the Gaullist Legacy and the Search for a New Model" in *Remaking the Hexagon* pp213-232

139   Fredy Gsteiger "Roßkur für die Grand Armée" *Die Zeit* 1-3-96 p13

140   Christoph Bertram "Abweher vom Sonderweg" *Die Zeit* 1-3-96 p12

141   See "Coquerico" *The Economist* 17-6-95 p55 and "Not so Pacific" *The Economist* 24-6-95 p28; Stephen Henningham "Testing Times: France's underground nuclear tests and its relations with the Asia-Pacific region" *Modern & Contemporary France* NS4 (1) 1996

142   European Commission *Official Journal* L 205, 8-8-94; Ian Black "France 'putting at risk test ban treaty'" and 'Cloud over South Pacific' *Guardian Weekly* 25-6-95 p1 & p10. 'Most of us find it hard to think of a single sound reason for the French bomb'

proliferation and the means specified in the NPT to attain it.'[143] France has jeopardised the NPT's veracity. An exercise in prestige accrual triggered the opposite as France's standing and Chirac's approval ratings plummeted. The judgement of Juppé then touted as the next President must also be questioned. Noted as a 'Europhile' and 'the man who makes (almost) no mistakes',[144] Juppé had been fiercely critical of the 'neophytes of ultra-Gaullism' belonging to former Socialist governments, claiming they were unwilling to be part of NATO reform as a step towards less insularity and more coherent forms of cooperation.[145]

The French Ambassador to Australia, Dominique Girard, reiterated that 'basically during the Cold War our policy was the same as other Western countries... the special motive was that we wanted to be independent'. He claimed that 'when General de Gaulle launched [the French nuclear defence] he was strongly criticised' but that since then the 'French public [has become] very much attached to nuclear deterrent'. For the CFSP to work it requires shared resources, responsibilities and guarantees. Provision must be made for nuclear forces as part of a communal system requiring verification of whether the French (and British) capacity is to be made available to or used on behalf of allies. Beyond institutional mechanisms EU members must be allies in trust and purpose.[146] The French action occurred when relations between major European states had been at an extended low. It also again exposed the shallow nature of the Soviet 'negative integration factor'. France did not feel threatened enough to be in NATO's integrated command structure, yet was—behind the theatrics—tacitly accepting of a US nuclear umbrella and its provision of conventional forces, serving not only as guarantor against a defined enemy in the Warsaw Pact but also animosity among western European powers.[147] While Mitterrand had called a halt to testing in the Pacific, his brand of Gaullism involved no sharing of the French nuclear force and no reduction of nuclear capability 'for any reason'.[148] To date there has been no appreciable change although Chirac himself had alluded to an

143   See "Problem der nuklearen Nichtverbreitungspolitik" *Arbeitspapiere zur Internationalen Politik* n83 (Bonn: DGAP 1994). Here, Hans Blix "Prospects of Multilateralism in the Non-Proliferation Regime" pp1-18

144   Fredy Gsteiger "Der Mann, der (fast) keine Fehler macht" *Die Zeit* 19-5-95 p8

145   Anand Menon "From Independence to Cooperation: France, NATO and European Security" *International Affairs* v71 n1 1995 pp19-34, p33

146   Cf. Harald Müller "Kernwaffen und die Europäische Union: Überlegungen zum Verhältnis der "Europäischen Option" zum Nuklearn Nichtsverbreitungsegime" in *Arbeitspapiere zur Internationalen Politik* n83 (Bonn: DGAP 1994) pp19-40

147   William D. Odom "How to Create a True World Order" *Orbis* Spring 1995 pp155-172

148   Menon "From Independence to Cooperation..." p33

extension of the French 'sanctuary' zone in the 1970s—when the US already provided one.

Since 1945 French defence policy has been permeated by an aversion to control by 'Anglo-Saxons'. French nuclear warheads have not, however, been pointed in the direction of the UK or the US, whereas for most of the last two and a half decades France has maintained a 'tactical nuclear arsenal whose range implied targeting in the Federal Republic or, later the German Democratic Republic'.[149] With INF treaty range restrictions already limiting potential targets France's upgraded home-based nuclear weapons could only land in a few places if launched after 1995. Assuming that complete nuclear disarmament is not about to be realised for some time (if ever), the most significant enquiry in this scenario is; against whom are the French *forces de dissuasion* now primarily conceived as being a deterrent? Pierre Laski spoke of a 'who's the enemy? debate' starting in France, a debate where, at that time, 'we don't know who's the enemy'. Quizzed on the 'three times in a century' theme, with the prompt 'is it Germany you fear'?, Charles Lambroschini of *Le Figaro* responded that upgrading its capacity for nuclear deterrent ensured continuation of the 'best protection against war...had we a nuclear force in 1939 or 1914 it would have stopped the invading German armies'. (He failed to mention what could have resulted if Germany had one.)[150] According to the conventional rhetoric Germany and France are best friends. At his National Press Club appearance in Canberra, Ambassador Girard, was asked about the underlying political reasons for the resumption of testing and 'concerns about a united and expansionist Germany'. His reply explained that 'our relationship with Germany is one of the most central elements of our foreign policy...[and] a basic element of European construction'. However, the decision must be 'seen in its historical perspective' which came with reiteration of his foreign minister, Herve de Charette's reference to France's necessity for independent defence capability 'having been invaded three times in a century'. However fantastic a notion the comments implied that Germany was perceived as the state posing the greatest threat to French security and consequently the most likely target of a nuclear strike.[151] Girard went on, 'tensions can come back with a different form...with a new aspect...nationalism is coming back in Europe'.

The Franco-German relationship, and by extension the whole EU, identifies itself *vis-à-vis* other external actors. Increasingly however, not less so, conceptions of the future configuration of the EU and with it the nature of its political system are embedded in national psyches. The German electorate

149   ibid. p20
150   *Lateline* ABC television (Australia) 5-9-95
151   Dominique Girard, Speech at the National Press Club, Canberra 31-8-95; Hervé
        de Charette *Lateline* ABC Television (Australia) 3-8-95

takes a strong anti-nuclear stance and Germany has disavowed possession of nuclear weapons.[152] Popular opposition was joined by upper echelon distaste for the dubious influences on French policy suggested above. In such an atmosphere the forging of a European 'defence identity' and a unified European political system is strained.[153] Even if French foreign policy and defence élites do not regard its eastern neighbour, partner and rival as remotely constituting a military threat, France's actions are sending a reminder of its nuclear capability, the traditional relativising factor to Germany's economic dominance and now increasing political and diplomatic status, a realm in which France long felt reassuredly superior. Yet realisation in Paris that France was losing an encounter—between friends—of 'Mark versus Bomb' permeated the *classe politique* before 1989 and is amplified since.[154] The relative silence from Bonn did not dispel the perception that Mururoa lies in the middle of Europe.[155]

France, Germany and the End of *Grandeur*

Gaullist impressions of *grandeur* were used to bolster an artificial construct of France's importance after WW2 had conclusively 'demonstrated that France was much too weak for the position of hegemony to which it laid claim in Europe.' [156] Although de Gaulle precipitated the myth that France had liberated itself, the unpleasant reality that it was a defeated and often collaborationist nation was reignited by revelations of Mitterrand's involvement with the Vichy regime.[157] An image of greatness or having shared in victory was critical to what France could demand in following decades. Klaus Engelen contended that into the 1990s France 'still demands and gets over-representation' in institutions like the IMF, which 'under its managing director Michel Camdessus, had deteriorated to a self-service shop for French economic and financial interests. For example, a large amount of soft financing had gone to help the French Treasury on problems of African

152   See "The Treaty on the Final Settlement with respect to Germany, 12 September 1990" (Two-plus-Four Treaty) Article 3
153   Lucas Delattre "Beim 'Widerstand' immer dabei" *Die Zeit* 7-7-95 p10
154   Dominique Moïsi "Die Mark und die Bombe" *Die Zeit* 9-12-88
155   Joachim Fritz-Vannahme "Hochmut kommt vor dem Knall" *Die Zeit* 7-7-95 p1
156   Ernst Nolte *Three Faces of Fascism* (London: Weidenfeld & Nicholson 1965) p356
157   Fredy Gsteiger "Späte Wahrheit" *Die Zeit* 9-9-94 p11; Kai U. Hartwich "Die Vergangenheit lässt nicht los: Das 'Syndrome de Vichy' bleibt virulent" *Zeitschrift für den deutsche-französische Dialog* n4 1994 pp279-280; Charles Bremner "Paris relives its liberation legend" *TheTimes* 26-8-94 p10

countries.' [158] Delors departure began an unprecedented situation where there is no French national installed as either Commission president or secretary-general. [159] Now France is overstretched and beset with internal and external problems: terrorist threats; embroilment in Africa where the Rwandan horror joined recurring crises in Algeria (to which France allocates around $US1billion per year); [160] immigration tensions; corruption scandals; the repercussions of recession and unemployment rates persisting around 12-13%. It added up to a deep political, social and spiritual 'crisis' and the panacea, if there was one, was not obvious. [161] The partly macabre, partly ironic focus on Mitterrand accentuated the paralysis. While the contestants in the 1995 presidential election promised to restore France to greatness, the campaign took on an air of apathy symptomatic of a general disillusionment with politics and politicians. For the Kohl government the sequence of favoured candidates progressively worsened. [162]

The defeat of the most pro-European integration Socialist Party (PS) in the 1993 elections followed the rise of 'anti-Maastricht' political groups. Along with *Front National* they oppose further integration, ostensibly against the terms of the TEU. The *L'Autre Europe* group led by Philippe de Villiers and James Goldsmith gained 12.3% of the vote at the 1994 European elections. *Front National* won 10.5%. Anti-integration sentiments were also expressed by 'dissident' left-wing voters totalling some 16%. In addition to divisions and wavering on independence-integration within the parties closer to the centre (at least nominally in favour of 'Europe') around 40% of French

158 Klaus Engelen "The mixed blessing of 50 years in Bretton Woods" *The European* 15-7-94 p19; Robert Gerald Livingston "United Germany: Bigger and Better" *Foreign Policy* n87 Summer 1992 pp157-174, see pp168-172; "The Trouble With Europe" *Japan Times* 14-4-93; Anne-Elisabeth Moutet "Portrait: Jacques de Larosiere" *The European* 13-8-93

159 Rory Watson "Big two split on top EC jobs" *The European* 19-8-94 p1

160 Victor Smart & Anne-Elisabeth Moutet "Paris isolated in taking on Algeria" & Claude Angeli "France's fundamental dilemma" *The European* 12-8-94 p1-2 & p9

161 Ghita Ionescu "Reading Notes, Summer 1994: Monsieur Mitterrand and French Society" *Government and Opposition* v29 n1 1994 pp546-548; Alain-Gérard Slama "Democratic Dysfunctions and Republican Obsolescence: The Demise of French Exceptionalism" in *Remaking The Hexagon* pp49-65; Patrick McCarthy "France in the Mid-1990s: Gloom but Not Doomed" *Current History* November 1994 pp364-368; Hoffmann "France: keeping the Demons at Bay"

162 Charles Bremner "Balladur resists reshuffle calls to purge odour of corruption" *The Times* 17-10-94; Charles Bremner "Chirac proclaims credentials to cure French ills" *The Times* 10-1-95 p12; Daniel Vernet "Germany doubts the French contenders" *Guardian Weekly* 1-1-95 p9; "Watching France" *The Economist* 6-5-95 pp53-54

voters chose explicitly anti-Maastricht parties.[163] Following this the presidential campaign veered to the right with Le Pen emerging as a force. In receiving 15% of first round votes he was close to Balladur (18.6%) and Chirac (20.8%).[164] What only weeks before would have been considered a good showing by the Socialist candidate Lionel Jospin was explained by fragmentation of the right vote which involved considerable personal animosity. For the second round Jospin appealed to the large working class contingent who had voted for Le Pen referring to them as 'men and women who should be with us'. As a fixture of the French political landscape the far right appeared significantly more popular and entrenched than its counterparts in Germany and was confirmed in later local elections.[165]

The conception of France as the 'brain of Europe', driving the process of integration onward was quite valid—as long as it concurred with what France preferred. France has experienced an historical lag between economic modernisation (it is the world's fourth largest exporter well ahead of Japan in per capita terms, though like elsewhere there are special problems of an economic nature) and cultural-identity issues which its political model has not transcended.[166] The reshaping of the 'world order' underlines the falsity of the great power status that France affected and the secondary role it since has little choice but to accept. One commentator declared France's impending 'political extinction' was directly connected to Mitterrand's role in the partnership with a redeemed Germany now remaking Europe in its own image.[167] The prospect, or the expectation, that German leaders would continue to bow once to the German flag and twice to the tricolor, is over and it is only with these conditions that real convergence can occur. The era has all but ended whereby 'the partnership has overcome the worst obstacles largely because the Germans, reluctant to upset their European co-builder, have usually given way in the end'.[168]

---

163   See Alain Guyomarch "The European Dynamics of Evolving Party Competition in France" *Parliamentary Affairs* v48 n1 1995 pp100-124

164   Paul Webster "Chirac faces pressure to woo far right" *The Guardian* 25-4-95; Craig R. Whitney "Chirac Campaign Takes Sharp Turn to Right" *International Herald Tribune* 27-4-95; Jonathan Steele "Chirac pipes to Le Pen's tune" *The Guardian* 26-4-95 p10

165   Paul Webster 'Toulon falls to Le Pen's National Front' *Guardian Weekly* 25-6-95 p3

166   *The European Challenges Post-1992: Shaping Factors, Shaping Actors* Eds. Alexis Jacquemin & David Wright (Aldershot: Edward Elgar 1993) pp203-233

167   John Laughland "Apres Moi, Le Desert" *Spectator* 11-3-95 pp9-10; Patrick McCarthy "France Looks at Germany, or How to Become German (and European) while Remaining French", in *France-Germany, 1983-1993.* pp51-72

168   "Watching France" *Economist* 6-5-95 pp53-54

For the Germans the vexation over Kohl's exclusion from the 1984 D-Day anniversary formalities was compounded when the perceived affront was repeated in 1994.[169] Thus the continuing, perhaps increasing, necessity of making ritual statements of the kind; 'With no other partner has Germany such a dense and confidence filled cooperation as with France'.[170] It may be dense but it is not the more reliable alliance that Germany has developed with the United States. The 'symbolic' element in the Franco-German 'connection' acquires ever more importance.[171] The fundamental difference between Paris and Bonn is just what integration means and where it ends. Political integration suffered a retrograde step with the withdrawal of Delors from the French presidential contest. The various candidates scarcely mustered anything approaching Euro-enthusiasm and certainly not a 'German-style' vision.[172] The Kohl government wants to transpose (what it sees as) the virtues, or imperatives, of the German polity: currency stability, consensual bargaining, multilateral 'security thinking', a liberal trade agenda, a formal subsidiarity of governance, and an environmental consciousness, to a European polity. They cannot do it without accomplices. According to John Laughland

> It is striking that no French politician seems to understand how badly Germany needs France in order to clothe its hegemony in Western Europe in respectability. France is the decent apparel with which German power can gird its loins, for if France were not in the hard core, then the European Union would clearly be a German empire...Germany proposes to exercise its power behind a French (or European) fig-leaf, a convenient way of not assuming its responsibilities.[173]

---

169   "Froideur, Angst or all in the mind?" *The Economist* 26-3-94 pp57-58; "Absent friends on D-Day" *European* 3-6-94 p8

170   "Rede von Bundesaussenminister Klaus Kinkel zur Stellung Deutschlands und Frankreichs in Europa, gehalten vor dem Institut Francais des Relations Internationales am 24-3-94, Paris". *Europa-Archiv* Folge 9/1994 Dokumente D316

171   This may mean a continuance of ritual German acknowlegements. For example Roman Herzog, speech in the Élysee palace "Staatsbesuch des Bundespräsidenten in der Französischen Republik" *Bulletin* 5-11-96. In response to a question why Mitterrand (or other French leader) could do things that Germans could not, an official in the Bundestag's Europa-Auschuss replied more sardonically 'because he is from the Grande Nation'. Interview sources, Bonn, October 1994

172   "A Conspiracy of fuzziness" *The Economist* 8-4-95 p47-48

173   John Laughland "The Philosophy of "Europe"" *The National Interest* Spring 1995 pp58-67

This is half-way correct. But it underestimates not only French diplomacy or French memory but French cynicism. The French political élite *do* understand this. The EU is also a competition between France and Germany. This is why France does not want a supranational CFSP, and why Chirac wants to keep a 'British card' and the possibility of an 'alliance de revers'.[174] With Britain at arms length the construction of 'Europe' devolved primarily on to France and Germany. A French Europe or a German Europe would impose a dominant political-cultural blueprint, each unacceptable to the other.[175] If such an impasse between what are 'two different cultural groups' means that 'a political choice between them must be made because they cannot both be implemented, or a compromise cannot be struck between them, then it seems to follow directly that there will be political tensions of a kind that may adversely affect the legitimacy of the regime and create demands for constitutional changes or the creation of separate political systems'.[176]

Thus not only can fifteen not go into one, neither can two. Ole Wæver has focused on this engine of integration as also where the whole process may stall and disintegrate. 'If the process of Europeanisation is registered as threatening national identity in France or Germany, this will be the most basic process that can undercut integration. It seems a safe bet that politics will continue to be cast in terms of 'Europe', even though the specific form remains open.'[177] Wæver contends that it is France, not the UK or some other state external to the proposed hard cores, that is the 'weak spot in Europe'. His prognosis is that if France's commitment to the EU fails Germany will be dragged down with it. The inference can be drawn that to avoid being unhinged (or turning east) it is Germany's responsibility to keep France on the European rails. From the German perspective it is not political dislocation *per se*, but what may stem from the psychological effects of integration grinding to a halt that is of concern. German elites have sought to pre-empt the inculcation of alternatives in the German polity and in France, where the 'danger' lies as much, if not more so, with the *classe politique*.

---

174   Cf. Moisi & Mertes "Europe's Map, Compass and Horizon"; Tiersky "Mitterrand's Legacy"

175   Ole Wæver "Three Competing Europes" *International Affairs* v66 n3 1990 pp477-493

176   Staffan Zetterholm "Why is Cultural Diversity a Political Problem? A Discussion of Cultural Barriers to Political Integration" in *National Cultures and European Integration: Exploratory Essays on Cultural Diversity and Common Policies* Ed. Staffan Zetterholm (Oxford: Berg 1994) pp65-82, here p68

177   *Identity, Migration and the New Security Agenda in Europe* Eds. Ole Wæver, Barry Buzan, Morten Kelstrup and Pierre Lemaitre (London: Pinter 1993) p64

Challenges to a European vision of France exist among the political elite, and if such challenges are not met, Germany's vision of Europe, and thereby its vision of itself will lose its force. The nationalist challengers in Germany will have the chance to fill the vacuum and German "interests" could change drastically. This interaction of domestic struggles between states over the meaning of state, nation and Europe is where the direction of the integration project will be decided. It is here that all three sides of the dynamic triangle identity, integration and security, meet. [178]

Although Delors had engineered policies intended to provide the EU with state-like qualities, Mitterrand never jettisoned Gaullist suspicions towards endowing supranational institutions with such powers. As elucidated by Ulla Holm, French political culture is based on the 'fusion of the state and nation into the nexus state-nation'. The state plays an external (global or European) role while the nation inheres of '*patriae* (a cultural and emotional concept)'. There are many connectors and 'relational filters' to other levels. The crucial point is that 'many politics are thus available so long as they do not touch the basic structure.'[179] Immigration and the politics of citizenship is a pertinent example. Social volatility associated with this has intensified in both France and Germany. As Brubaker impresses, however, 'in both cases it pivots on national self-understanding, not on state or group interests...prevailing elite self-understandings are very different'.[180] Pressures placed upon the French assimilationist model has resulted, in practice, in France moving towards the German conception of national identity and associated rights. But this itself does not contribute to an ending of French 'exceptionalism'. Rather it may impact on the extent of a present and future European citizenship, implying continued politico-legal limitations on French and Germans sharing the same 'European' polity.[181]

---

178   Ole Wæver "Identity, Integration and Security" *Journal of International Affairs* v48 n2 1995 pp389-431, p414

179   Holm "The French Garden is no longer what it used to be"; Gregory Flynn "French Identity and Cold War Europe" in *Remaking the Hexagon...* pp233-249

180   Rogers Brubaker *Citizenship and Nationhood in France and Germany* (Cambridge Ma.: Harvard University Press 1992) Here p184

181   The variance in nation types often represented by contrasting France and Germany is narrowing, without losing distinctiveness relative to each other—as was the purpose of Renan's adherents in 1882. Today both require of prospective citizens a socialization into French or German culture. Cf. Patrick Weil "Nationalities and Citizenships: The Lessons of the French experience of Germany and Europe" and Mary Fulbrook "Germany for the Germans?: Citizenship and nationality in a divided nation" in *Citizenship, Nationality and*

Contrary to the view that 'the dwindling autonomy of the nation-state has weakened the credibility of national*ism* as a political programme',[182] as integrative momentum has unravelled nationalism has returned. In France, the 'etat-nation' cannot be ignored or deprecated. 200 years after aestheticizing the notion of the political citizen and his/her reciprocity with state institutions, 'the overbearing nature of the national state and its profoundly entrenched narratives of legitimacy mean that it is all the more difficult to step out from under their shadow now that things have changed so much'.[183]

In a 1995 edited volume, articles by Pierre Hassner and Hermann Lübbe survey some of the cultural-political barriers, and dangers, present in contemporary Europe. Both refer to nationalism, atavism, old suspicions, and instability of economic and civil structures in eastern Europe. But France and Germany are also covered, internally and *vis-à-vis* each other. Both are concerned with Ingo Kolboom's theme: *'Gerade zwei so unterschiedliche Kultur- und Staatsnationen wie Deutschland und Frankreich werden in diesem Punkt Konsens finden müssen, wenn der seit "Sarajevo II" mögliche Satz, "Europas Fundament ist das Nichts", in Zukunft nicht mehr gelten soll'.*[184] Hassner outlines how the Anglo-American notion of 'nationalism' corresponds to French 'national feeling', 'identity' or national consciousness'. He also notes a renationalizing of German attitudes, yet to definitively shift in the sphere of foreign policy: *'Bei mehreren seiner Nachbarn oder Partner haben Furcht oder Mißtrauen gegenüber Deutschland bereits nationalistische Reaktionen hervorgerufen, die ihrerseits deutsche Reaktionen in derselben Richtung ermutigen könnten'.* All this is, according to Hassner, traceable to Renan and Fustel de Coulanges on one side and Strauss and Mommsen on the other—*'Von daher stammen die beiden Idealtypen französicher bzw. staatsbürgerlicher und deutscher bzw. ethnischer Konzeption, die auf die Unterscheidung zwischen jus solis und jus sanguinis...'*[185] These differences, the *'blutsorientierten deustchen*

Migration in Europe Eds. David Cesarani & Mary Fulbrook (London: Routledge 1996) pp74-87 & 88-105

182   Bryan Jenkins & Nigel Copsey "Nation, Nationalism and National Identity in France" in *Nation and Identity in Contemporary Europe* Eds. Brian Jenkins & Spyros A. Sofos (London: Routledge 1996) pp101-124. See p111 and cf. pp114-115

183   Max Silverman "The Revenge of Civil Society: State, Nation and Society in France" in *Citizenship, Nationality and Migration in Europe* pp146-158, here p157

184   Kolboom "Frankreich und Deutschland: Die Neuen Akzente". Kolboom quotes Arnulf Baring's phrase

185   Pierre Hassner "Nationalstaat-Nationalismus-Selbstbestimmung" *Die Neue Weltpolitik* Eds. Karl Kaiser & Hans-Peter Schwarz (Baden-Baden: Nomos 1995) pp91-103

Volksbegriff and '*der französische Begriff der Nation der Begriff einer politischen Einheit durch Anerkennung universeller Prinzipien*', are also invoked by Lübbe. He claims '*Der Einwand liegt auf der Hand*':

> Da ja ersichtlich auch die französische Kultur weit mehr umfaßt als die Einheit aller in Kenntnis und Anerkenntnis der Bürgerrechte und Bürgerpflichten, mußte eben Zwangs-Francisation auf Dauer nichts anderes als den Untergang alter oder auch neuer nicht-französicher Kulturen auf dem Territorium Frankreichs bedeuten. Die Frage ist, woher überhaupt der Selbstbestimmungswille seine die aktuelle internationale Politik mitbestimmende Kraft bezieht. Handelt es sich nicht um einen politischen Atavismus? Steht nicht, wie im Falle der Europäischen Union, die politische Organisation von Großraumen auf der Tagesordnung?[186]

The overt 'nationalist challengers' in Germany do not, yet, have the electoral support of those in France. In 1994 France was determined to want a 'closer embrace'. A year later the reciprocal 'Kohl hug' was not quite so welcome.[187] Daniel Vernet has cited Paul Valéry's maxim about the best alliances being between ulterior motives, as characteristic of Franco-German relations.[188] With Mitterrand's political style already characterised as a 'left-wing Gaullism'[189] and his successor the leader of the Gaullist party, 'the question is whether the moment of truth isn't approaching...?'[190] For European Union to happen it is France where change must occur. And this is the point where differences in conceptions of what constitutes 'success' are most critical: that is, what the EU's teleology, or *finalité politique*, if there is such, actually is.[191] Meanwhile French aversion, firstly among its political

---

186   Hermann Lübbe "Staatliche Souveränität, internationale Organisation und Regionalisierung" in *Die Neue Weltpolitik* pp187-195; cf. Marc Fumaroli *L'Etat culturel: Essai sur une religion moderne* (Paris: Editions de Fallois 1991) 'Il y aurait peu d'erreurs plus graves pour l'Europe que d'adopter le modèle français de l'Etat culturel, ni plus désolants pour la France. C'est cependant la pente la plus facile pour une oligarchie politico-administrative.' p300
187   "Germany's Europe" *The Economist* 11-6-94 p49-50; "Kohl opens his arms for union" *The Economist* 27-5-95 pp51-52
188   'Les seuls traités qui compteraient sont ceux qui se conclueraient entre les arrières-pensées'. See Vernet "Zwei Freunde, die sich fast verstehen"
189   Farewell to Mr Europe" *Guardian Weekly* 18-12-94 p12. See also Wayne Northcutt *Mitterrand: A Political Biography* (New York: Holmes & Meier 1992) pp341-42
190   Vernet "French Foreign Policy"; Jochen Hehn "Balladurs Europa der drei Kreise" *Die Welt* 1-12-95 p5
191   See *Le débat* n87 November-December 1995

élites, is founded in fears of a diminution of France's position and hence identity; that too much integration will compound the Germanising of Europe. [192]

---

[192]   Marie Dejevsky "France hints at looser ties with Germany' *Independent* 21-6-95 p13

7 Britain, Germany and Europe

This chapter examines British attitudes and policy towards the project and course of European unity. British endeavours to build influence while remaining distant to particular initiatives supported on the continent entailed special disadvantages. They also often deflected attention from the pursuit of divergent national interests among others. The fall of the Berlin Wall and the rapid developments that followed instilled a cognition that Germany would increasingly prescribe the terms of European political economy and eventually foreign policy. Europe would come to resemble a 'German-style' federation wherein German influence predominated. 'Sovereignty of the crown-in-parliament' and preservation of unanimity in critical EU voting procedures is thus vital to political independence and essential elements of 'Britishness'. While drama on the continent from 1989 coincided with a long period of Conservative rule there is no categorical indication that a Labour government would interpret 'the national interest' in Europe, based on certain elementary understandings of British political and cultural identity, very differently. With discontent towards the EU apparent in other member states the British insistence on intergovernmental cooperation outside of economic issues is not unique. On one hand, more common, and less coerced, positions on the Single Market and erosions of mercantilism and protectionism are developed. On the other a trend to renationalization or 'traditional' balance of power politics is encouraged and discernible.

The View from Britain

A land of settled government / a land of just and old renown / where freedom slowly broadens down / from precedent to precedent.[1]

I was always pro-Europe, but the way its been handled I'd sooner do without it.[2]

---

1   Quoted in Percy Allum *State and Society in Western Europe* (Cambridge: Polity 1995) p97
2   British cattle farmer regarding the continuing EU ban on British beef *Deutsche Welle* 20-5-96

The British posture *vis-à-vis* Europe has reflected a philosophical and political as well as geographic distance.[3] Geography though was decisive in shaping British and continental views, inhibiting the UK from attaining the levels of at least symbolic fraternity present among other EC or EU members.[4] De Gaulle said of the UK that it had 'no real European political culture' and an image of British ambivalence, as being a 'semi-detached' or 'awkward' participant has persisted.[5] After playing a constructive role as honest broker in the initial stages of Franco-German reconciliation and promoting American involvement in Europe, the British remained out of European organizations, save the WEU. This was prolonged by de Gaulle's veto after British policy changed to seeking admission to the EEC. De Gaulle's calculations took into account the resultant effects on American influence and German manoeuvrability. As a latecomer the UK had to contend with a framework set up by and favouring, most especially, France.[6] Since accession in 1973 British governments pursued economic benefits while seeking to minimise relinquishment, or transference, of controls. Apart from supporting a common commercial jurisdiction, open competition, and Britain's premier status for inward and outward direct investment, defenders of the realm gave prominence to guarding against real or imagined intrusions on British independence.

Conversely, from continental perspectives the British disposition to European integration has represented isolationist and anachronistic thinking,

3 Jeremy Black *Convergence or divergence: Britain and the Continent* (Basingstoke: Macmillan 1994)

4 Helen Wallace makes a similar point about symbolism and its reception in the UK as a rather foreign notion on which to build international political relationships. See "Britain out on a limb?" *Political Quarterly* v66 n1 1995 pp46-58. The fragility of 'symbolic alliances' in the last few years supports British government positions in this respect

5 Simon Bulmer "Britain and European Integration: Of sovereignty, slow adaptation, and semi-detachment" in *Britain and the European Community: The Politics of Semi-detachment* Ed. Stephen George (Oxford: Oxford University Press 1992) pp1-29

6 Cf. Max Beloff *The Future of British Foreign Policy* (London: Secker & Warburg 1969) p95-6 who noted in 1969 that 'the French have discovered, or believe that they have discovered, that their earlier fears of Germany were misplaced...the secular quarrel between France and Germany seems to have been buried for good....a special Franco-German relationship has grown up...through which France has exercised its hegemony within the group as a whole...every effort by the Germans to argue the case for British entry—for which they have good economic and political reasons—has run into insuperable French opposition. In the last resort the Germans have always given way. So far from the Common Market being a political community in embryo, it is simply an instrument through which France achieves its national purposes '

something which, despite victories in two world wars, has accompanied a relative decline through the twentieth century. Konrad Adenauer made a comparison between Britain and 'a rich man who has lost all his property, but does not realize it'.[7] Even as he remained an admirer of British traditions Helmut Schmidt said in the 1970s that it was 'no longer a developed nation'. A few years later, after Margaret Thatcher's abrasive attitude to what she believed existed across the channel was now broadcast, *ex officio*, as Prime Minister, he suggested other states had to 'wait for better weather' before progress might be made in making the UK more Euro-friendly. More recently SPD foreign policy spokesman Carsten Voigt claimed Britain had reached 'the end of a line of historical development'.[8] Although it has often been the odd man out, and characterised as such, British external policy is guided by a principle of national interest which in form makes it no different from other EU members. The variance is in how interests, and identity, are conceived, and presented.[9] William Wallace argued in 1991 that in defining and pursuing its foreign-European policy through an outdated conception of national identity, the vaunted British pragmatism had become ideological. Nonetheless belief in a special discreteness and 'moral authority' in relation to the continent is still present and translates into profound reasons for maintaining the UK as a distinct political community.[10]

Whether pragmatic or ideological a zero-sum calculation persists in British European policy. In its most simplistic form British opposition to deepening integration and rescinding the veto stem from a belief that other members may employ European agencies to further their preferences and interests more successfully than the UK. Thus the maximum manoeuvrability as an autonomous national state continues to be pursued, including attempts to block other groups of EU members from implementing agreed policies. The strategy relies on a combination of tensions among others to prolong an acceptable Europe *à la carte*. As conveyed by a British civil servant in 1996, negotiations in European institutions are and should be conducted as a Machiavellian poker game: 'If a point is made and secured by

---

7   See Jonathan Clarke "Repeating British Mistakes" *The National Interest* Spring 1995 pp68-77

8   *Lateline* (ABC Television) 5-5-94. Prominent Germans saying such things was not likely to be well received

9   Cf. on Britain, the national interest and Europe, two works, a generation apart, by Max Beloff *The Future of British Foreign Policy* and *Britain and European union: dialogue of the deaf* (Basingstoke: Macmillan Press 1996); and Roy Denman *Missed Chances: Britain and Europe in the Twentieth Century* (London: Casell 1996)

10   Cf. William Wallace "Foreign Policy and national identity in the United Kingdom" *International Affairs* v67 n1 1991 pp65-80

another delegation...pocket the advantage without comment of any sort and continue to pursue other UK points'.[11] In this respect the UK is not alone. While others have revealed similar concerns, they, especially the Benelux and poorer Mediterranean members, have often been more successful in addressing them. Due to a range of historical influences as well as contemporary financial and political factors their options and self-images are different.[12]

Simultaneous to a revived German nationalism being targeted as threatening and destabilizing in 1989-90, British chauvinism was more pronounced and offensive.[13] The leaked memorandum of the March 1990 summit with leading German experts became a *cause célèbre* yet it is unlikely that the meeting instilled any new conceptions for Mrs. Thatcher.[14] Followed by rejoinders from participants, the affair further damaged British-German relations as insinuations of German recidivism proliferated.[15] Sentiments like former Trade and Industry Secretary, Nicholas Ridley's outburst against a German 'takeover by economics' in July 1990 had reverberating effects,[16] betraying a realisation that indefinitely selecting from the European menu was now restricted—unless others began thinking the same. Media reports regularly adopted the position that the EU will be a vehicle for German hegemony, a network of institutions Germany intends shaping to suit itself.[17] A traitorous character was imparted to MPs advocating a more authoritative Germany or even developing the partnership. Erstwhile Conservative party chairman Norman Tebbit described the Maastricht Treaty as 'close to treason'[18] while Hurd's support

---

11   See Paul Brown "How to secure a winning hand in Brussels" *Guardian Weekly* 21-1-96 p9

12   Cf. The various interpretations and comparisons in *The Actors in Europe's Foreign Policy* Ed. Christopher Hill (London: Routledge 1996)

13   See Bernd Weisbrod "German Unification and the National Paradigm" *German History* v14 n2 1996 pp193-203

14   "Wer sind die Deutschen?" *Der Spiegel* n29 16-7-90 pp109-112

15   Charles Powell "What the PM Learnt About the Germans" and Timothy Garton Ash "The Chequers Affair" reprinted in Harold James & Marla Stone *When the Wall Came Down: Reactions to German Unification* (London: Routledge 1992) pp233-239 and pp242-246. Fritz Stern also expounded on his talk with Thatcher in the *Frankfurter Allgemeine Zeitung* 26-7-90

16   Dominic Lawson "Saying the Unsayable about the Germans" *The Spectator* 14-7-90 pp8-10. "Komplott gegen Europa" *Der Spiegel* n29 16-7-90 1990 pp108-109.

17   A German controlled European Central Bank prominent among them. See Alan Walters "Germans' stealthy plan to become bankers of Europe" *The Times* 11-4-94 p8

18   David Baker, Andrew Gamble, & Steve Ludlam "Conservative splits and European Integration" *Political Quarterly* v64 n4 1993 pp 420-434

for German rearmament and a permanent seat on the UN Security Council was berated as 'another extraordinary boost to the power and prestige of Germany'. Another Tory columnist questioned 'Why does Hurd embrace the concept of a European Union where national interest is subservient to the whole, yet encourage Germany to embark on an aggressive national foreign policy?'.[19] This stratum was a locus of support for Michael Portillo and later John Redwood.[20] Even without a coup toppling Major, the presence of rival factions arrested whatever potential there was for British participation in EMU, a CFSP or any other political union.[21] Major had to demonstrate a resoluteness on 'putting Britain first'. An unyielding veto of Jean-Luc Dehaene as Delors replacement, against the 'Franco-German cabal', was applauded by his Tory critics.[22]

While his interpretation and prescription differed Wallace also envisaged greater German influence. For him, however, the two countries are not seen as unresolvably anathematized. On the contrary, in addition to being the UK's largest trading partner, Germany is 'arguably also our most important partner in foreign policy'.[23] Likewise Garton Ash contends that there is a greater convergence of real interests between Britain and Germany than either has with France. Nonetheless there was in Germany a 'widespread belief that the Euro-sceptics are only saying out loud what others really think' and that they and the Germano-phobic press represent 'the voice of the real Britain'.[24]

Britain has not possessed the same impetus for political integration as the Federal Republic and the two have represented opposite poles regarding a European political structure, a relation apparent in the respective

---

19   John Deans & Christopher Bell "Room for one more at world's top table" *Daily Mail* 30-7-94 p2; Alistair McAlpine "Hurd is wrong and it's time for him to go" *The European* 5-8-94 p13

20   Victor Smart "Redwood shuns jingoism in foray against Europe" *The European* 15-2-96 p8

21   "With all due respect" *The Economist* 22-1-94 pp15-16

22   Donald MacIntyre & Andrew Marshall "MP's Rally to Major after his EU battle" *The Independent* 27-6-94 p1

23   Wallace "Foreign Policy and national identity in the United Kingdom" p77

24   Timothy Garton Ash "Why Britain is missing from Kohl's dream" *The Times* 20-10-94 p20; William Rees-Mogg "The final dilemma" *The Times* 20-10-94 p20. One respondent to *The European* regarded the main rift as existing between Britain and France with Germany being the chief cause. British 'pragmatism' was necessary in the EU as a counter to Franco-German 'idealism'. Letters 29-7-94; See also Robert Peston "Germanophobia rules in a day by the seaside" *Financial Times* 21-10-96 p18

national, and in the European, parliaments.[25] German political parties have not faced the same requirements to inveigle or prevaricate over 'Europe' like the British parties, those elements, that is, with a favourable view. Instead the Germans had to display their European credentials. British parties have not felt a consummate obligation to actively promote European unity. Both Labour and the Conservatives have variously been approximated to 'pro' or 'anti' Europe positions. Domestic political tactics or personal preferences have determined how a party, or faction, be it in government or opposition has acted or reacted. In the 1990s all three main British parties officially professed a pro-European outlook. But what 'pro-Europe' meant and how far it extended was obscure. According to Reinhard Meier-Walser 'most Britons do not view European integration with its inherent intensification thrust towards a supranational union as a goal *per se* .' Rather, 'in their opinion, the primary legitimation of the process of European integration are the respective benefits it can offer to Europe in general and then to the countries in particular...most Britons merely regard a cession of national sovereignty as a means to an end.[26] The 'cession of national sovereignty' is also a means to an end for Germany. And it has become increasingly obvious that other populations and governments are not in conflict with the above position. All want prosperity and security; it is the vehicle, the route and the baggage that do not concur.

While 'making European integration irreversible' is a stated intention of the Kohl government,[27] growing scepticism in the Germany and assertion of the Jacobin model in France have tended to reinforce rather than weaken national states as decision-makers. Until the 1990s 'Europe' was not an issue of significant dissent in the German context. Now tensions between national and European priorities have sharpened. Falling public enthusiasm has seen the German trajectory move towards fraying of positive consensus on European policy. This has meant becoming more like Britain, and while some British figures expressed alarm at a possible unsettling of stability in or by Germany they concur with the right to challenge what was sacred, when

---

25   This does not mean that similar wide-ranging variables of 'personality' and 'political factors' do not apply in both systems regardless of differing institutional structures. This argument allows for numerous cultural and historical influences in determining both who is elected and policy direction. See Ludger Helms "Executive Leadership in Parliamentary Democracies: The British Prime Minister and the German Chancellor Compared" in *German Politics* v5 n1 1996 pp101-120

26   Reinhard Meier-Walser "Britain in Search of a Place 'at the heart of Europe'" *Aussenpolitik* v45 n1 1994 pp10-19 p12

27   Joachim Bitterlich, CDU advisor on foreign policy. See Shirley Williams "Britain in the European Union: A Way Forward" *Political Quarterly* v66 n1 1995 pp5-22 fn5

the SPD began to question EMU for example. If William Cash, Nicholas Ridley and Lord Rees-Mogg were only saying 'out loud' what other Britons think, then Edmund Stoiber and others were building a similar status in Germany. If this keeps Europe on an intergovernmental path then without threats to the national veto in foreign policy, parliamentary authority or even EMU, the UK and Germany may reveal themselves unexpectedly compatible—and compatibility is the necessary, and sensible, objective of European integration. For instance, the 'silent alliance' in security cooperation before 1989 could be recreated on intergovernmental terms.[28]

The Conservative Party and Europe

Thatcher's failure to sufficiently adapt, even rhetorically, her position on Europe, contributed greatly to her losing the prime ministership.[29] However, her reign actually 'did more to entangle Britain with the European continent than any of her predecessors', possibly excepting only Edward Heath.[30] The implications of the Single European Act were underestimated by Thatcher after it was originally proposed in a British position paper. Her agreement was induced by the expectation that the UK would profit considerably from the creation of an internal market promising increased volume and access to free trade. The only strings attached were thought to be manageable if not inconsequential.[31] Having signed Britain into a partial erosion of its veto powers her recharged Euro-scepticism in the late 1980s was a principal factor in her removal as Conservative leader and Prime Minister. This did not stop her influence in 1992-3 as she resurfaced in the House of Lords endorsing the views of the Tory rebel faction and voting against the government.[32] Her support of cabinet members was based on a simple 'division of the political spectrum into free-market and Britain-first Dries, and free-spending pro-European Wets'. She continued to undermine John

---

28   *Die Stille Allianz: Deutsch-Britische Sicherheitskooperation* Eds. Karl Kaiser & John Roper (Bonn: Europa Union 1987)

29   Cf. Margaret Thatcher *The Downing Street Years* (London: Harper Collins 1993) and Geoffrey Howe *Conflict of Loyalty* (New York: St. Martin's Press 1994)

30   "Tweaking the European Nerve" *Political Quarterly* v66 n1 1995 pp1-4

31   See Andrew Moravscik "Negotiating the Single European Act: national interests and conventional statecraft in the European Community" *International Organization* v45 n1 1991 pp19-56

32   David Baker, Andrew Gamble, & Steve Ludlam "The Parliamentary siege of Maastricht 1993: Conservative Divisions and British Ratification" *Parliamentary Affairs* v47 n1 January 1994 pp37-59

Major as the 1997 election approached, contributing to both his and Douglas Hurd's resignations.[33]

The Conservative Party's self-conception as the 'natural party of government' merged with a role as chief promoter of national independence. One article described how 'the security, prosperity and sovereignty of the British state have been at the heart of the Conservatives' successful appeal to the mass electorate. The Maastricht rebels were able to portray the treaty as a permanent threat to all three virtues and hence involving 'matters that go to the very soul of Conservatism', as one put it.'[34] Aversion to subsuming federalism and upholding of 'unfettered sovereignty' did not change after Major became Prime Minister. While he also realised that Thatcher's posture had become antiquated, the maintenance of 'traditional British concepts of Europe' was reiterated by the 'pro-Europe' leader. The propounding of the Conservatives identity as political guardian grew even after Maastricht as Major claimed a 'game, set, match' victory from the negotiations. Following ratification of the TEU Major pronounced that 'For us the nation-state is here to stay'.[35] His foreword to the 1994 Conservative Manifesto for Europe declared 'it is for nations to build Europe, not for Europe to attempt to supersede nations.'[36]

One 1993 analysis regarded the Conservative Party in its strongest position since the 1930s—or at least it should have been. For the majority of the parliamentary Conservatives, still in a mild fashion 'pro-Europe', the chief antithetical force came not from another political party but from internal divisions. Nonetheless the authors claim that 'Without doubt, a majority in the Conservative Party would have cheerfully abandoned the Maastricht Treaty, given the opportunity.'[37] Although the intensity of the battle over Europe temporarily subsided, its potential importance for the 1997 election campaign was clear. Major pledged in January 1995 to 'block any big constitutional changes' at the 1996 IGC while his appeals for the

33   Erik Ipsen & Barry James "Deed Done, Lady Thatcher Softens Tone" *International Herald Tribune* 23-6-95 p1. Thatcher went on a tour of US media (including CNN's Larry King Live 26-6-95) to promote her book and oppose any soft line on Europe. See also Anthony Bevins "Major coup may topple Tories, rebels warned" *The Observer* 18-6-95; Philip Webster "Major Challenges his Critics" *Times* 23-6-95 p1. Cf. "John Major remet en jeu la direction du gouvernement britannique" & "La retraite de Douglas Hurd, dernier "europhile"" which described Hurd as a 'cosmopolite pro-européen et francophile'. *Le Monde* 29-6-95 p4

34   "The Parliamentary siege of Maastricht" pp46-47

35   "Major on Europe" *The Economist* 25-9-93 p19

36   *A Strong Britain in a Strong Europe: The Conservative Manifesto for Europe 1994* (London: Conservative Political Centre 1994)

37   "The Parliamentary siege of Maastricht"

rebels to come back into the fold had to be balanced by assurances to the 'pro-Europe' majority in the party. In one contemporary poll 52% of Tory voters supported immediate reinstatement of the expelled MP's who returned in April 1995.[38]

Cross-cutting axes of members opinions on more or less government intervention domestically and sovereignty-interdependence regarding Europe placed the Conservative party in four ideological quarters.[39] Under the Tories Britain promoted free enterprise, liberalization of trade and capital movement, and 'rolling back the state', on the one hand; and on the other, protection of the (national) state and its institutions, foreign policy independence, and philosophical distance.[40] By 1996 60% of British trade was with other EU members. In the UK, however, intra-European economic transactions and democratic political processes were considered distinct and as remaining so. In contrast the Germans advocated a fusion of economic and political unity and promote multilateralism in defence and security issues. In both cases 'foreign policy' is more accurately described as 'external official behaviour'. Regarding its approach to managing Britain's role in Europe and the perception via public channels, an official at the Conservative Party's European Directorate made a distinction between 'what we say and what we do'.[41] This source indicated that for domestic political purposes a national aura is maintained while behind the scenes a bureaucratic compatibility exists.

Social policy constituted the main difference between British parties on European legislation. For the Conservatives it developed into an unnecessarily large problem through a fear based on the Social Chapter's symbolic features rather than actual mechanics.[42] One ironic feature of the wrangle was that by July 1994 Britain had transposed 92% of social policy directives into national law, more than any other state, while Germany, 'the leading proponent of further legislation', had instituted only one of eleven health and safety directives. German proposals, including protection against

---

38   Philip Webster "Prime Minister is ready to use veto at European Union summit" *The Times* 9-1-95 p1; Michael White "Tory rebels welcomed back by PM" *The Guardian* 25-4-95 p1

39   See Baker, Gamble & Ludlam "Conservative splits and European Integration"

40   Will Hutton "Neo-Marxists of the right" *The Guardian Weekly* 15-5-94

41   Interview, Conservative Political Centre, European Directorate. August 1994. Cf. J.D.B.Miller *The World of States* (London: Croom Helm 1981) p45-46

42   See Dennis Swann "The Social Charter and other Issues" in *The Single European market and beyond : a study of the wider implications of the Single European Act* Ed. Dennis Swann (London: Routledge, 1992) pp214-229; Richard Corbett *The Treaty of Maastricht : from conception to ratification: a comprehensive reference guide* (Harlow: Longman Current Affairs 1993) p76

dismissal, worker privacy, wages for public holidays, collided with Michael Portillo's intractable opposition to any weakening of Britain's special status. *The Times* interpreted the Commission's 1994 White Paper on employment as a 'tactical retreat' leaving enough loopholes to instigate later assaults on the British opt-out.[43] Another curiosity was that the Germans did not originally want a binding Social charter. They were manoeuvred into it by Mitterrand—each state and head of government wanting to demonstrate an effectual turn at the EU presidency. While France and Germany came to an arrangement over a common social strategy the British government maintained its aversion. Tories complained of vetoing a federal socialist as Commission President and then nominating the same as one of Britain's Commission representatives.[44]

The UK under Labour

As the Conservatives conducted their own internecine warfare the British Labour Party presented no clear policy on the extent to which it would enmesh the UK. According to a Labour Party source Europe was 'an excuse rather than the root cause of the Conservative split',[45] yet Labour does not favour a 'federal Europe' or rescinding of national vetoes either. Chiefly through the self-immolation of the Conservatives, Labour eluded categorical, at least categorically different, positions on its own European course, with the exception of social policy.[46] Criticisms of Major zeroed in on his (mis)management of Tory dissidents rather than proposing any decisive shift in British positions.[47] In response to the inquiry 'Do you foresee a fundamental change in the British attitude under a Labour government?' an aide to the CDU's European Parliament leader Günter Rinsche foresaw

43   John Carvel "Brussels guns for UK opt-out" & "EU blue print rejects dilution of social policy" *The Guardian* 26-7-94 pp1-2; Wolfgang Muenchau "Brussels beats a tactical retreat on social policy" *The Times* 9-8-94

44   Patrick Wintour 'Kinnock wins his place in Europe' *The Guardian* 29-7-94 p1; Philip Johnston "Portillo determined to retain Britain's Maastricht opt-out" *Daily Telegraph* 28-7-94

45   Interview Sources, British Labour Party, August 1994.

46   Cf. *Make Europe work for you: Labour's Election Manifesto for the European Elections, June 1994* (London: Labour Partty 1994). The manifesto concentrates heavily on criticising the Conservatives and on social policy issues. It does mention support for 'progress towards economic and monetary union'. Convergence of 'the real economic performance' had to occur first and the 'criteria must be applied flexibly'.

47   Philip Webster "Prime Minister is ready to use veto at European Union summit" & "Major woos Euro-rebels as crucial vote looms" *The Times* 9-1-95 pp1-2

Britain 'continuing to be a problem area with Labour'.[48] To the same question an official in the German foreign ministry also did not envisage any exceptional changes. He replied that 'whoever will rid us of Portillo' would constitute a good outcome.[49]

After a prolonged absence from power the Labour Party moved, firstly under Neil Kinnock, to redefine the centre of the political spectrum. In doing so it shifted away from a previous suspicion of the EC/EU as a 'bankers plot'. Under Tony Blair Labour rhetoric was becoming cognate with the CDU. 'Social-individualism' joined *soziale markt* as his ideological overhaul of the party—to the extent that 'even the French are following Tony's lead'[50]—boosted its poll ratings and the new leader's personal popularity soared. Despite the Conservatives' unpopularity on domestic issues, a Blair leadership and his new direction were perceived by some German analysts as a essential for a Labour victory.[51] As the referendum option was urged by Euro-sceptic politicians and commentators, both Conservative and Labour parties, in contrast to the Liberals, were averse to clearly endorsing one. After hinting at the possibility Blair left his options open. 'The next stage of European progress will come through persuasion or not at all...The doubting public know they are right to pause for reflection. That is not to say they cannot be convinced; merely that they require to be so.' His first speech as leader concentrated on attacking the Tories' 'faultline on Europe', a theme 'likely to come up repeatedly' in the future. In response Major highlighted Labour's own divisions and claimed that in government it would 'slavishly follow whatever Europe says'.[52] The Tories were urged to become more aggressively political and the party's political centre advocated

---

48   However, the same source considered British antipathy to the EU to be overblown and said that when British politicians and officials went to the continent they found it much more compatible than was usually reported. Instead a positive feeling was 'like a virus'. Interview, Bonn, October 1994. An official at Labour's European Parliament office informed that around 50% of Labour voters thought that the *Sun* newspaper, known for its regular chauvinism towards Europe and Germany, was a Labour supporting newspaper. Interview, London, August 1994

49   Interview Sources, Auswärtiges Amt, Bonn, November 1994.

50   See *The Observer* 24-4-95 p1; Jill Sherman "Blair shakes off Labour image as poodle to unions" *The Times* 23-7-94 p2

51   Jürgen Kronig "Nur mit Tony Blair kann Labour noch siegen" *Neue Gesellschaft/Frankfurter Hefte* January 1995 pp6-10; Uwe Jun "Inner-Party Reforms: The SPD and Labour Party in Comparative Perspective" *German Politics* v5 n1 April 1996 pp58-80

52   Anthony Bevins & Barry Hugill "Blair to let voters rule on Europe" *The Observer* 24-7-94 p1; George Jones "Blair attempts to expose Tory rift on Europe" *Daily Telegraph* 19-10-94 p2

a more 'populist, right-wing agenda' based on research of members.[53] It did not prevent Conservative members later defecting to Labour and the Liberal Democrats.

Labour MP Dennis McShane argued that a common economy required common legal regulations, necessary for Britain to 'be changed to a 'high-skill, high-investment, high-wage' economy consciously inspired by the successful northern European states'.[54] In a May 1996 speech to the Federation of German Industry (BDI), Blair echoed the call to curb the welfare state. He also urged 'we must not do anything to undermine our national interests in the run-up to Florence...It is demeaning to my country...to be reduced to the margins of influence...behind the vision and drive of others'. One BDI member claimed the speech 'could have been made by one of us'.[55] McShane forecast that the next British general election 'will be dominated by European issues.' Whether Europe would produce unequivocal divisions between the British parties or see either of the two main ones firmly ally with those on the continent who 'share a common political lineage' was another matter.[56] Under Labour the prospect of decision-making powers over 'vital national interests' being transferred beyond British control was still unlikely, even if it joined the Social Chapter. At a conference of socialist and social-democratic parties Labour protested against and eliminated the insertion into an, intended, communal text that said 'we say no to any individual state having a right to veto further development of the union'.[57]

More recently, Anne Applebaum writes that 'Blair vigorously denies any desire to relinquish the veto on defence and foreign policy issues' and 'does not mind being "isolated" in Europe if it is in the British national interest...precisely the view that has got the Conservative Party into so much trouble in Europe.' She continues that 'in fact, on the single currency, Blair's position remains virtually identical to John Major's' one in which 'our options on a single currency should remain open, to be determined according to our national interest'.[58]

---

53   "More politics please" *Daily Telegraph* 28-7-94 p16
54   Denis MacShane "Europe's Next Challenge to British Politics" *Political Quarterly* v66 n1 1995 pp23-35
55   *Deutsche Welle* 17/18-6-96. Some Labour politicians want British adoption of aspects of the 'German model'. *The Economist* 27-5-95 pp95-96
56   McShane "Europe's Next Challenge to British Politics"
57   Christopher Parkes "Britain's Labour Party says no to 'no veto'" *Financial Times* 9-12-94 p1. Labour had already rejected the Party of European Socialists push for a 35 hour week in the 1994 European Parliament elections
58   Anne Applebaum "Tony Blair and the New Left" *Foreign Affairs* v76 n2 1997 pp45-60

The 'party of Europe', the Liberals, were also wary of alienating themselves through a perceived over-enthusiasm. According to Alan Philip, 'Historically the Liberals were the first to be *communautaire* and to support a federal Europe as part of their programme. But in their campaigning in the constituencies, and sometimes also at national level, their European commitment is often the last thing they want to discuss or to emphasise.'[59]

The 1997 election victors were to inherit a deregulated labour market and levels of investment flows that Germany has only seriously been working towards for the last three or four years. Concurrently, despite high unemployment rates, the German *soziale markt* system has not precluded discipline in monetary policy to sustain a deflationary environment. Were Labour to win government and join EMU , it may, like other candidates, be confronted by future political difficulties if it accepted the specified macroeconomic criteria. And even a gradual convergence of national budgets through greater payments into an EU household would see the UK remain a net contributor with the entry of poorer eastern European states. Nor could it expect a continuance of German transfer levels. With competitive devaluations outlawed, British budget balancing problems would have to be solved in other ways, like improving its trade balance.

British Identity

For Elias Canetti the English were a nation 'which though it does not make much public parade of its identity, undoubtedly retains the most stable national feeling in the world today.'[60] Like Germany and France, the concept of a coherent national British identity has been under challenge for some decades. Distinct Scots, Welsh and Irish communities and increasing multi-ethnicity encouraged numerous attempts at redefining 'Britishness' and questioning of how 'united' the Kingdom actually is. Nonetheless, a 'national identity' of some kind is not only presumed to exist but as being essential whatever separatist or ethno-religious challenges confront the outlook of 'little England'.[61] William Wallace declared 'no national identity,

---

59   Alan Butt Philip "Europeans First and Last: British Liberals and the European Community" *Political Quarterly* v64 n4 1993 pp447-461. On a history of federal ideas in Britain see Michael Burgess *The British tradition of federalism* (London: Leicester University Press 1995)

60   Elias Canetti *Crowds and Power* Trans. Carol Stewart (New York: Farrar Strauss Giroux 1984 [1960]) p171

61   Cf. *Patriotism: the making and unmaking of British national identity* Ed. Raphael Samuel (London: Routledge 1989); *Culture, identity and politics: ethnic minorities in Britain* Eds. Terence Ranger, Yunas Samad & Ossie Stuart (Aldershot: Avebury

no foreign policy; no foreign policy or identity, no state.' In arguing the need for a simultaneous redefinition of 'Britishness' and of Britain's foreign policy he foresaw a 'logical' movement to common interests being exercised through common frameworks of the EU. 'Defence, control of territory, maintenance of boundaries, the right to issue currency, the right to tax, the right to distinguish between citizen and aliens: the central issues of national sovereignty are to be progressively pooled within the European Union.'[62] By early 1997 none of these had departed from British to European control. Christopher Hill ended a chapter on the subject by stating, 'More profoundly, the answer is located in the fact that most policy-makers in London, and even more the political opinions behind them, still find their identity in an idea of Britain first, and Europe a distant second. Whether in this respect Britain is still significantly different from the other nation-states which make up the European Union, the next ten years should tell.'[63]

Other scholars have presented insights why Britain has been a 'very difficult country to move'. Jeremy Black portrays the British relation to continental Europe as more complex than a simple either/or dichotomy. A long history of oscillation between convergence and divergence culminated in a situation where 'Britain bought membership' of the EC or EU without buying 'the myth'. As is being revealed elsewhere in Europe, it is the 'nation-state that is most effective at eliciting and securing consent'. In Britain this is strongly influenced by identification with 'institutional, constitutional and political longevities' all of which sustain a sense of uniqueness. 'The modern British may not be a flag-waving nation; they certainly do not wave the flag of Europe.' Black concludes that 'in defending the configuration and continuity of British practices, politicians are fighting not for selfish national interests but for the living past that is such a vital component of a people's understanding, acceptance and appreciation of their own society and identity.'[64] Max Beloff depicts that the UK is presently in a quasi-federal, if malformed, political arrangement. Although methods including 'threats of commercial sanctions' might be employed to enforce

1996). Parallels with Germany are apparent in articles by Reiner Luyken "Dreigeteilt niemals?" *Die Zeit* 19-5-95 p52; David Cesarani "The Changing Character of Citizenship and Nationality in Britain" and Tony Kushner "The Spice of Life?: Ethnic Difference, politics, and culture in modern Britain" in *Citizenship, Nationality and Migration in Europe* Eds. David Cesarani & Mary Fulbrook (London: Routledge 1996) pp57-73 & 125-145

62   William Wallace "British foreign policy after the Cold War" *International Affairs* v68 n3 1992 pp423-442, see p439. Cf. Ruth Dudley Edwards *True Brits: Inside the Foreign Office* (London: BBC Books 1994) pp148-155

63   Christopher Hill "United Kingdom: Sharpening Contradictions" in *The Actors in Europe's Foreign Policy* pp68-89

64   Black *Convergence or divergence* ...pp264-270

the 'Monnet version' of a 'fully federal organisation of Europe', national identity would, it was claimed, still be preserved in the new structure. What was not admitted, was that 'part of a nation's identity might be embodied in its own inherited political and judicial institutions just as much as in its language and literature and artistic heritage.'[65]

Similar interpretations have been applied to the 'British' in the 1990s as Canetti had to the 'English' in 1960. One suggests that 'British nationalism—when it is sober and is not paraded around football stadiums— is healthy, an expression of Briton's genuine affection for their country...The British do not have any inhibitions about being British. The country's geography, undoubtedly helps. So does history. Britain has no big chunk of its past it needs to forget—unlike Japan, Germany or Italy.'[66] History still exerts powerful influences on respective British and German identities, foreign policies and raisons d'etat. In 1988 Margaret Thatcher famously asserted in Bruges that 'Europe will be stronger precisely because it has France as France, Spain as Spain, Britain as Britain, each with its own customs, traditions, and identity.' Each, it is assumed, has and will have their individual 'political roofs'. Multiple ethnic groups along with Scottish and Welsh demands for home rule were self-contained 'British' diversities not to be robotised into an 'identikit European personality'.

An anecdote involving Thatcher and Helmut Kohl indicates their respective positions regarding European integration. For some years Kohl had invited the Prime Minister to visit his homeland of Rheinland-Pfalz which, eventually, she did. While his visitor studied relics of historical interest in a cathedral crypt the Kanzler took the British German specialist, Sir Charles Powell, aside. He asked if, now that Mrs. Thatcher had met Kohl near his birthplace, by the French border, at the heart of Europe, would she finally understand that he was not foremost German, rather European, and could Powell pass on this view. Later on the plane back to London, just as Powell was about to broach the subject, Thatcher lent back in her seat, kicked off her shoes, and said quite decisively, 'My God, Helmut is so German!'.[67] This was a milder variation on her response to Kohl's jest about Germany defeating England in the 1990 World Cup—'Well, we beat you at *your* national sport twice during this century'.[68] Later, during the 1996

---

65   Beloff *Britain and European union: dialogue of the deaf* pp145-146

66   Beppe Severgnini "An Italian in London" *The Economist* 8-1-94 pp52-53

67   Quoted in Sven Papcke "Nationalismus- ein Alptraum?" *Aus Politik und Zeitgeschichte* B42/94 21-10-94 pp10-17

68   Ulf Hedetoft "The State of Sovereignty in Europe: Political Concept or Cultural Self-Image" in *National Cultures and European Integration: Exploratory Essays on Cultural Diversity and Common Policies* Ed. Staffan Zetterholm (Oxford: Berg 1994) pp13-48. In 1994 a former Labour MP published a book whose title was

European football championship, as the tabloid press went into paroxysm over the England-Germany semi-final, clichés abounded and sales of George Crosses boomed.[69] An official at the German Embassy in London mused, 'Sport should be a much more lighthearted event'.[70] Somewhat less jocose was the unveiling a few years earlier of a statue to Britain's wartime airforce commander Arthur "Bomber" Harris. In Germany Harris was considered responsible for the unnecessary destruction of Dresden and the statue a provocation. Speculation of a German 'commemoration' of the V2 rocket project was similarly received in Britain.

Sovereignty, Subsidiarity and the European Parliament

> And there assume some other horrible form, Which might deprive your sovereignty of reason. And draw you into madness—Hamlet, Act I.

Britain has been characterised as exhibiting a 'confusion between identity and sovereignty' or, the fear that relinquishing some of latter means loss of the former.[71] Along with a drive to overcome the 'democratic deficit' and the image of unaccountable elitism, devolution to the regions and 'subsidiarity' emerged as the terms to placate opponents of a 'centralised' or 'federal' political-bureaucratic entity. Divided into categories of *substantive principle* and *procedural criterion*, the subsidiarity principle was a mechanism petitioned by the Germans and agreed to by the British at Maastricht. In contrast to the constitutionally grounded and active pursuit of devolution as a political principle in Germany, as neither foreign to nor endangering of national cohesion or identity, the British favoured its inclusion in the TEU because it was perceived as a means to prevent excessive power amassing in Brussels. The government soon proved 'as unwilling to cede authority 'downwards' within the UK as it is to cede it 'upwards' to Community

---

| | enough to reflect the pessimistic thesis within. Leo Abse *Wotan My Enemy: Can Britain Live With the Germans in the European Union?* (London: Robson 1994) |

69 A combined Goethe Institut/British Council sponsored exhibition produced a collection of press cartoons giving other perspectives into the way Germans and Britons have perceived each other since the Second World War. *Coping with the Relations: Anglo-German Cartoons from the Fifties to the Nineties* Ed. Karin Hermann, Harald Husemann & Lachlan Moyle (Osnabrück: secolo Verlag 1994)

70 A few days later all sides of the European debate watched the ironic spectacle of the Queen, flanked by John Major, handing the European Championship cup to Jürgen Klinsmann.

71 See Julius W. Friend "Nationalism and National Consciousness in France, Germany and Britain: The Year of Maastricht" *History of European Ideas* v18 n2 1994 pp187-198

institutions'.[72] Norman Tebbit's outburst against a 'Europe of the regions' focused on the project as a strategy designed to inversely increase centralisation in Brussels claiming 'the only way the EU could smash the power of the nation-state was to make them switch their authority to smaller, feebler units of government. These could be more easily dominated from Brussels.'[73]

At a conference of parliamentary European Affairs Committees in Bonn in October 1994 the British delegation responded that while welcoming any reductions in EU regulations and directives, the 'broad general terms' in which the subsidiarity principle was described in the TEU, instilled 'doubt as to how effective it will prove in practice'. The report also expressed concern about the 'uncertainty as to what is meant by the areas which fall within the exclusive competence of the Community'.[74] Political obstructions have diluted subsidiarity as an effective means of European governance as it became clearer that 'subsidiarity makes sense only in the framework of a properly constituted federal union'.[75] The reasons not to commit to a union that gives external political control over British institutions involve more than economic considerations. An option which could circumvent an inevitable impasse would be to provide an escape hatch from 'irrevocable' union. Britain might enter a 'supranational' political union if it could get out again. A 'trial period' with no obligation may not be

---

72   Andrew Scott, John Peterson & David Millar "Subsidiarity: A 'Europe of the Regions' v. the British Constitution?" *Journal of Common Market Studies* v32 n1 1994 pp47-68; Several other analysts point out how differently 'subsidiarity' has been viewed and acted, or not acted upon, by the British and Germans. Keith Taylor notes how 'the British government—which certainly did play a major role in steering the whole subsidiarity debate leading up to the Maastricht intergovernmental conference—has not interpreted the subsidiarity principle in the same decentralist terms as, say, the Germans or the Belgians.' "European Union: The Challenge for Local and Regional Government" *Political Quarterly* v66 n1 1995 pp74-83; Kees van Kersbergen & Bertjan Verbeek "The Politics of Subsidiarity in the European Union" *Journal of Common Market Studies* v32 n2 1994 pp215-237 compare and contrast elements of subsidiarity as approached by 'British conservatism' and 'German federalism'. The 'basic difference' they conclude, is the 'absence of the territorial element' in the former.

73   John Carvel "Tension between hybrid members set to influence leadership struggle" *The Guardian* 7-3-94 p1

74   *XI Konferenz der Europaausschüsse der nationalen Parlamente der Mitgliedstaaten der Europäischen Union und des Europäischen Parlaments* (COCAS) Bonn 24/25-10-94 (Document 1)

75   See David Coombes "Problems of Governance in the Union" in *Maastricht and Beyond: Building the European Union* Eds. Andrew Duff, John Pinder & Roy Price (London: Routledge 1994) pp157-178

as unworkable, or as unlikely as first appears. Previous delays, opt-outs, and vetoes already have resemblances.

European Parliament elections created another set of problems. While some British conservatives were antipathetic to mere representation in the prototype federal institution, an excessively bad result endangered Major's position as leader. Approaching the 1994 EP elections the Conservative Manifesto 'strongly welcomed the Parliament's growing ability to scrutinise the Commission' as the Tories campaigned on an 'anti-federalist' theme, what one minister termed 'a straight Gaullist ticket'.[76] The British conservative presence in the EP is unlikely to provide much assistance to its ostensible allies, the European People's Party, on issues for which the EP was created: promoting Europe's political, as well as economic, unity. One section of an EPP text specifically targeted the Major government's difficulties in formulating a European policy. It stated that while it would be ideal to have all members communally engaged that was not realistic. The Major government had no room for manoeuvre with a 17 seat majority in the House of Commons and '30 hard-line anti-Europeans' in the government party.[77] The impasse over the future powers of the European Parliament extended to differing conceptions about what constituted 'democracy' in the European institutions and member state relations and how the 'deficit' was to be overcome. In Major's words, 'The European Parliament sees itself as the future democratic focus for the Union. But this is a flawed ambition...'

> The European Parliament is not the answer to the democratic deficit, as the pitiably low turn-out in this year's European elections so vividly illustrated. The upshot, sadly, has been an unrepresentative and rather incoherent range of parties in the new European Parliament in which fringe groups, protest and opposition groups are over-represented.[78]

This was a thin argument on several counts. Low turn-out's do not constitute an abrogation of democratic processes and turnouts for British elections are often barely 50%. The 'pitiably' low number of votes for

---

76   Cf. *A Strong Britain in a Strong Europe*...p38; Bagehot "Euro crunch" *The Economist* 5-2-94 p60

77   Wilfred Martens, Präsident der Europäischen Volkspartei (EVP) *Vertiefung und Erweiterung: Eine Strategie fuer die Europaeische Union* Brussels 20-9-94. 'Ideal wäre natürlich ein engagiertes gemeinsames Vorgehen aller 12 bzw. 16, aber ist das realistisch? Welchen Spielraum hat die Regierung Major vor den nächsten Unterhauswahlen im Frühjahr 1997, mit zur Zeit 17 Stimmen Mehrheit im Unterhaus und gleichzeitig mehr als 30 hard-line Anti-Europäern in der Regierung machen?'

78   John Major, speech in Leiden, quoted in *The Times* 8-9-94 p12

Conservative candidates contributed to Major's dismissive statement which undoubtedly would have been modified had the party been more successful. The 'range of parties...fringe, protest and opposition groups' could just as easily be interpreted as a healthy pluralism. There is also a contradiction in British government (and others) claims of a lack of democratic accountability in the EU while simultaneously opposing the strengthening of the EP. What this thinking does indicate, however, is that the locus for 'changing the system' lies within the nation-state polities. Attempting to construct elaborate supranational edifices and expecting continent-wide support to materialise is not likely to be a successful strategy. There is mild support in Britain for a, vaguely defined, 'European government'. The presumption is that this would be an 'intergovernmental government'. At the same time, consistent with the Conservative government's refusal to agree to the co-decision mechanism, there is low public support for the European Parliament. In 1994 only 26% advocated more power for it compared with over 50% for a common foreign policy and almost 80% for a common defence policy. Twenty-seven per cent favoured tighter integration overall and 55% a looser form.[79]

Representing British Interests

For the first seven years of the 1990s the British debate on Europe was characterised by most of the political furore occurring not between opposing parties but within one party, which was concurrently governing the country. Hostility from within regularly jeopardised the chances of successful negotiations with the 'real opposition' on the continent. For a moderate like Douglas Hurd, Tory schism and implacable Europhobia 'does not permit him to explain that EU membership is a continuous struggle for leverage conducted with shifting alliances which involve the risk that something will go wrong from time to time'. Without this minimum acceptance 'he cannot explain that Britain cannot stop its partners forming things such as a single European currency. If Tory politicians allowed Mr. Hurd to report more accurately the realities of life in the EU, he would have a better chance of shaping an agenda which fits the times.'[80] While Hurd was left as the man in

---

79   See Jim Northcott *The Future of Britain and Europe* (London: Policy Studies Institute 1995) pp297-328

80   George Brock "Hurd's spooonful of sense leaves Europe hungry for ideas" *The Times* 8-3-94 p14

the middle,[81] Sir Leon Brittan's chances to become Delors' successor were effectively obliterated by the UK stigma. Brittan had displayed his capacity as a tough negotiator and mediator of difficult international issues in finalising the GATT world trade agreement of December 1993. His role in the European Commission gave him 'vast quantities of 'centralised' powers...the sort of 'centralisation' that Mr. Hurd rather likes because it produces results of which he approves'.[82] Instead of British influence being enhanced through Brittan's appointment, a record of recalcitrance precluded it.

As Foreign Secretary, Hurd argued in favour of a consensual, meaning a unanimously agreed, Common Foreign and Security Policy against the background of an adversarial domestic political scene while the Germans pushed for a majority decision mechanism on the European level with, on this issue, a largely consensual political culture at home. Hurd proposed that 'the key to successful and coherent foreign policy cooperation is persuading your partners of the force of your arguments, not resorting to the procedural means of a vote to overrule their point of view...A policy which all can support, because all agree with it, carries far more weight than one where underlying dissent might all too easily be exposed. Countries are not going to operate successfully a foreign policy measure to which they are strongly opposed.'[83] The starting point of these individual contributions to the debate which ideally forges a 'consensual' result is still within the national polities.[84]

Displays of 'Britain versus everybody else' or opting out ensured Britain of serving as a useful 'negative integration factor'. It also indicated a continuing gulf in political cultures and the additional fervour of national representatives in conflict. From British perspectives, 'Whereas within stable "Anglo-American" democracies the norm of political conduct is not to impugn the honour and integrity of the other politicians until late in the game, in the European Community this was almost the first thing that happened when there was a dispute. In 1990 an example of this concerned

81   Cf. Douglas Hurd "Our Future in Europe" (London: Conservative Political Centre 1993); Stephen Bates et.al. "Disgruntled Hurd tells Tories: stop scratching at European wounds" *The Guardian* 26-3-94 p1
82   Brock "Hurd's spooonful of sense leaves Europe hungry for ideas"
83   Douglas Hurd "Developing the Common Foreign and Security Policy *InternationalAffairs* v70 n3 1994 pp421-428
84   Wallace "British Foreign Policy after the Cold War" p436, notes the reciprocal presence of French and German diplomats in the British foreign office. Apart from a cultural exchange it is unclear what other purpose, that is, what genuine effect on individual national policy formation or implementation this would have. Cf. Chapter 6 below fn. 74

the scandal of "mad cow disease" in Britain. Protests by the French, the Germans, the Italians, and the Luxembourgers were immediately treated in Britain as illustrations of the tendency of foreigners to cheat.'[85] This same issue exploded again in 1996 with British beef facing a Europe wide ban. Jochen Borchert, the EC agriculture minister, said that EU should help fund slaughter of British cattle, the preferred German option. The British wanted 80% of an estimated $US30 billion cost which the others refused.[86] There were calls for reciprocal sanctions. Teddy Taylor urged a ban on French wine while Jacques Santer lamented the 'anti-European atmosphere and climate' thickening in the UK, and an anti-British equivalent in the other fourteen states. As Santer told the European Parliament that a British counter ban against 'European' products had 'no place in a community built on trust', British Foreign Minister Malcolm Rifkind was saying that without a total lifting of the beef ban the situation would become the 'crisis of the EU as a whole'.

Britain has not been without allies opposing German, French, or German-French plans. Spain, Greece and Denmark have sided with it over various issues in the 1990s. Blocking changes to voting rules in 1994 plunged the UK into a renewed controversy as the 'spoiler' image intensified and Major eventually backed down with some minor concessions.[87] A possible British-Italian axis tentatively appeared after the entrance of Berlusconi's right coalition government.[88] The volatility of Italian politics rapidly made hopes of a reliable 'alliance' thoroughly implausible. European politics is fluid. Boycotts and firebombing of Shell outlets in Germany, the embarkation of a Greenpeace vessel from Germany, and pressure from Kohl over environmental risks saw a British back down in the Brent Spar oil rig issue.[89] There was, however, no official German protest at the Cannes summit against the French test resumption, despite all other EU members, save the UK, doing so. This type of expediency is a feature of the EU system.

---

85   Paul Taylor *International Organization in the Modern World: The Regional and the Global Process* (London: Pinter 1993) p88

86   *Deutsche Welle* 1-4-96

87   Tom Buerkle "EU Ministers Offer Take-It-or-Leave-It Voting plan to U.K." *International Herald Tribune* 28-3-94 pp1-2; John Carvel & Michael White "Britain Climbs down in Europe Crisis" *The Guardian Weekly* 3-4-94 p1; "Hurd woos Madrid over EU reforms" Michael Sheridan *The Independent* 21-6-95 p13

88   Victor Smart "Italy defies Kohl with attack on federalism" *The European* 15-7-94 pp1-2; Victor Smart "Consternation as Italy supports Britain over Social Chapter" *The European* 29-7-94 pp1-2

89   Nick Nutall 'Shell abandons sinking Brent Spar' *The Times* 21-6-95 p1

Rivalry between London and Frankfurt over leadership of Europe's finance industry increased as the German challenge intensified in company with political impetus behind EMU. Yet even in late 1994 a CDU foreign policy advisor expressed that long established status as a global financial centre would see a European Central Bank located in London—if Britain became a positive participant in the drive to EMU. Failing that Frankfurt would be the site, a probability which British ambivalence increased.[90] According to other sources, despite intense competition London 'seems likely to retain its position' as Europe's financial hub 'because of its socio-cultural organization; it is the centre of interpretation, of interaction and of product innovation.'[91] Following departure from the EMS in 1992, the British government, press and financial elite blamed the German Bundesbank for torpedoing the pound while the Germans invoked shortcomings in British policy and weaknesses in the British economy itself. Criticisms of British intransigence were countered by the system shattering in 1993, which appeared a sound justification for remaining outside.[92] 'What was more remarkable', according to Lippert and Stevens-Ströhmann, 'was the fact that the average house-buyer was conscious of the direct financial impact of decisions taken in Frankfurt'.[93]

From another perspective Bernard Connally argues there are sound financial reasons for Britain opting out of EMU.[94] Primarily, however, and which he acknowledges, economic and monetary union is a political issue of varying national strategies.[95] The longer term CDU agenda is to develop democratic all-European political institutions around EMU so as to, as they foresee it, prevent alliances from forming against an overly strong German nation-state. Through the 1990s this concern, justified or not, has become increasingly crucial to the underlying rationale of the entire process of European unity. Britain appears to have no such fear of itself, of self-

90   Interview sources, Bonn, October 1994. Cf. "Ivon Dawnay Looks at How the Opposition Plans to Keep London Ahead of Frankfurt" *Financial Times* 26-4-91 p1; David Marsh *The Bundesbank: The Bank that rules Europe* (London: Heinemann: 1992).
91   Scott Lash & John Urry *Economies of Signs & Space* (London: Sage 1994) See pp286-291
92   Anthony Glees "The Diplomacy of Anglo-German Relations: A Study of the ERM Crisis of September 1992" *German Politics* v3 n4 1994 pp75-90
93   Barbara Lippert & Rosalind Stevens-Ströhmann *German Unification and EC Integration: German and British Perspectives* (London: Pinter 1993) p51
94   Bernard Connally *The Rotten heart of Europe: The Dirty War for Europe's Money* (London: Faber 1995)
95   Cf. Kenneth Dyson *Elusive Union: The Process of Monetary Union in Europe* (London: Longman 1994)

274 Germany, Europe and the Persistence of Nations

destructing in a way that Kohl and others imply Europeans are susceptible if EMU does not go ahead. Some in Britain may be wallowing in a paradise lost but no-one can conceive of the nation going to war over exchange rates and market shares. Kohl's alarums are thus seen as both incomprehensible and insulting to Britain's history and the British way.[96] Former Chancellor of the Exchequer, Norman Lamont claimed it was right, and democratic for the SPD to bring into open debate the suitability of EMU for Germany and everyone else, including as an electoral theme. If Germany requires an unquestioning consensus then the edifice of assurance is meaningless. The whole ethos of the Federal Republic is undermined when war is broadcast as a possibility if a particular policy of integration is not completed. According to Lamont the scenario is one of 'fears of other countries about Germany and the fears of German leaders about Germany's past', while John Redwood claimed 'it is time to save Europe from itself'.[97] Major continued to oppose joining a single currency in 1997, calling such a move not 'remotely appropriate'. Other Tories who may have been more sympathetic to the idea had no intentions of progressing beyond it:

> No one, of course, will say that they favour monetary union because it will create political union. On the contrary, even when they do acknowledge that a single currency will entail some loss of sovereignty or political control (which is not always) the Europhiles accept this as worthwhile, in view of the influence over French and German monetary policy that will apparently be gained.[98]

British business is generally more favourable towards a single currency believing it will encourage a *laissez faire* environment. While a philosophical unity is maintained with the Conservative Party on opting out of the Social Chapter, many business leaders regarded continuing ambivalence towards European integration as distinctly unfavourable. For some British firms, a government 'reinforcing Europhobic attitudes' was not in their's or the country's interests. Government and business had to accept some European legislation that they would prefer not to in order to benefit elsewhere.[99] The chairman of British Steel interpreted political union as the

---

96   Anthony Bevins et.al. "Tory fury at Kohl's war talk" *The Observer* 4-2-96 p1
97   Norman Lamont "Gegen ein Europa aus Furcht und Gier" *Die Zeit* 1-12-95 p14; Victor Smart "Redwood shuns jingoism in foray against Europe" *The European* 15-2-96 p8
98   "All the Best Lack Conviction" Anne Applebaum *The Spectator* 18-2-95 pp12-15
99   Ian Verchere "What has to come first: the ecu or the economy?" *The European* 15-7-94 p20; "This is no way to clinch a deal" *The Economist* 2-4-94 pp53-54

price of privileged access to a lucrative free trade zone.[100] There is, however, an ongoing, if less overtly political, contest between differing forms of corporate governance which makes a 'single model of Euro-capitalism' unlikely even if EMU is implemented.[101]

With some irony, the other EU member that the Germans probably have most confidence in regarding fiscal and monetary management are the British. And a curious common cause arose between British Tories, most of whom would gladly jettison the TEU, and the mass German public, the percentage of whom opposing EMU grows by the day. Under the Conservatives, Britain would fade to irrelevance before developing an anxiety about becoming all too relevant, or before it re-entered a European monetary system regarded as being controlled from Frankfurt and Berlin. Lamont stated emphatically that 'there is an overriding case for announcing immediately' that Britain will not participate in a single currency in 1999'.[102] As disfavour grew on both sides of the channel the date for a definitive implementation of EMU regressed. The Labour Party gave no clear indication of when, or even if, it would alter the British position to one favouring a single currency.

Return of the Balance of Power

It is well documented that reunification has increased Germany's demographic, strategic, and economic potential. This is particularly so in relation to its near neighbours. London is aware that to some extent this factor relativizes anti-British attitudes and that others have expressed concerns about 'how to counterbalance the Germans.'[103] British nationalistic reactions were joined by an agitated French response and balance of power calculations were again revealed as fundamental determinants of the European agenda. Whatever the occasional vituperation between them, for

---

100   MacShane "Europe's Next Challenge to British Politics"
101   Stephen Woolcock "Competition among Forms of Corporate Governance in the European Community: The Case of Britain" in *National Diversity and Global Capitalism* Eds. Suzanne Berger & Ronald Dore (Ithaca: Cornell University Press 1996) pp179-196
102   Nicholas Wood "Lamont weighs in with ERM attack" *The Times* 23-6-95 p1
103   Cf. Beate Neuss "The European Community: How to Counterbalance the Germans" in *German Unification: The Unexpected Challenge* Ed. Dieter Grosser (Oxford: Berg 1992) pp136-149; Reinhard Meier-Walser "Germany, Britain and France on the Threshold to a New Europe" *Aussenpolitik* v43 n4 1992 pp334-344; *Germany and Europe in Transition* Eds. Adam Daniel Rotfeld & Walther Stützle (Oxford: Oxford University Press 1991)

the French political leadership the UK is an implicit counterweight to Germany. Regarding this triangle, James Morgan suggested of the Anglo-French component that 'it might seem...that relations between the two countries are bound to be mired in traditional mutual suspicion and the wider distrust that exists among the populations of Britain and France.'

> This is misleading, however. French attitudes towards Britain have never been soured by the underlying fear that exists towards Germany. Germany still suffers a negative reputation in France...and Anglo-Saxon culture enjoys a reputation in France that is not matched by Germany. The Paris-Bonn axis has never put down roots in either country. There exists at present, therefore, the potential for Britain to revert to traditional policies with regard to the European balance of power.[104]

A Europe of completely detached state actors displaying any real belligerence towards one another may never again eventuate. In the period under discussion, however, milder forms of animosity, aloofness, and genuine antagonism have featured with some frequency. And the related cultivating of alliances for some mutual interest do still persist. Moisi and Mertes indicate that 'Britain, as a midsize nuclear power with a tradition of military intervention, may be the natural strategic ally of France'. They continue that this might be 'difficult to translate into concrete measures, even if a rapprochement is perceptible between the two permanent members of the U.N. Security Council who fought next to each other in the Persian Gulf and Bosnia'.[105]

Britain has assumed a disproportionately large expenditure on defence, more than any EU member. It has continued the interventionism considered necessary to preserve world ranking. Entering the Gulf conflict impressed its credentials with the US and it continues to solidly support NATO. While it has differences with France on this issue, enough alignment in foreign policy traditions is shown by a retention of their independent nuclear power capacities, a common (and ineffectual) position on Yugoslavia, a disinclination towards investing more authority in the European parliament, and neither favour a unified European police network or what amounts to a single EU border.[106] After Chirac's presidential accession he made overtures to the British who responded in some significant instances, including support for France's nuclear tests. Distrust or

---

104   James Morgan "Wide horizons, slender means: the scope for British influence" *International Affairs* v68 n4 1992 pp603-617, see pp606-607

105   Dominique Moisi & Michael Mertes "Europe's Map, Compass, and Horizon" *Foreign Affairs* v74 n1 1995 pp122-134

106   Arthur Marshall "Britain fights to hold back Europol" *Independent* 21-6-95 p13

rapprochement among the three powers has many variations. Günter Grass's apprehensions about Germany inspired his own balance of power evaluations. 'My hope', he declared, 'rests on a strong England with a change of government after the next election' [107] A later suggestion by John Major of more Council votes for Germany was interpreted by some as 'trying to upset the French and destabilise the Franco-German alliance'. [108] The British were in favour of EU enlargement because it would in all probability dilute solidarity when decisions requiring unanimity were being taken. A new *Mitteleuropa* does not, unlike the French, instil great trepidation for the British who perceive opportunities for private enterprise. Although Moisi and Mertes conclude that Britain's 'only alternative' is more European integration 'as a key political force' they simultaneously assert that 'the European dilemma today is that one cannot deepen the EU with Britain, but one cannot without either'.

There are just as many reasons to bring the UK and Germany together, even at the risk of upsetting France. Will Hutton proposed in 1992 that for the UK 'the principal objective must be to construct a strong British-German relationship as the new fulcrum around which the EC turns'. Hutton named several areas in which 'Britain is a natural German ally' including support for 'German aims to maintain a regulated finance system' and to 'build a German-style social market economy'. Such a 'remodelling along German lines' and 'introducing German-style rules and practice', while ensuring stronger British involvement in building a European defence capacity which diluted 'mutual Franco-German distrust' would certainly propel integration. [109] It would also be near the best conceivable outcome for Germany. Both the British and Germans openly appeal to the US to remain in Europe and have the best records to do so; both agree on admitting new members from central and eastern Europe and providing financial and other aid to the region, although the British have been less forthcoming with material evidence of this than the Germans; both are for less *dirigiste* controls in the EU. The arrival of a Tony Blair government could combine

---

107   See Dennis Stanton "Forgive Me, Fatherland" *The Observer* 22-10-95 p16
108   "On the verge of Europe" *The Economist* 11-6-94 p57-58
109   Will Hutton "Britain in a cold climate: the economic aims of foreign policy in the 1990s" *International Affairs* v68 n4 1992 pp619-632. Cf. *The Future of UK Competitiveness and the Role of Industrial Policy* Ed. Kirsty Hughes (London: Policy Studies Institute 1993) including E. P. Davis "Whither Corporate Banking Relations?" pp85-107 which portrays the considerable gulf in respective British and German cultures and presents as its first recommended option a shift towards a more German orientation; and David Mayes comparison of the UK and other European economies "European Integration" pp117-133

encouragement for open markets with a social dimension more congruent with the German.

Probably more than any other single EC/EU issue, the Common Agricultural Policy has been a consistent focus of British hostility, one where 'Britain pressed with some vigour its argument that seven of the nine member states, including five more prosperous than the Community average, were net beneficiaries of the budget. In fact, the budget transferred resources from member states with relatively small agricultural sectors to those which are net exporters of agricultural products regardless of their relative prosperity. Two member states, Britain and Germany, were left to make transfers to the others.' [110] It has most audibly been British pressure, with German collusion, that has caused a gradual decline in CAP funding from near 90% in the late 1960s to about 52% and reducing in the late 1990s.

From a German perspective Thomas Kielinger has also compiled a list of common British-German interests among which he proposes: a harmony in the question of anchoring America in Europe; no 'fortress Europe' in trade policy; the 'unconditional' widening of the EU, even if Bonn does not want this to become a 'Trojan horse for watering down the European institutions'; deregulating the market and controls of the Brussels finance bureaucracy; support and coordination of multinational troops for implementing the peacekeeping arrangements agreed at Dayton. Another item that Kielinger terms, 'subsidiarity as a European core philosophy', is more questionable. Nonetheless there is a reasonable array of common ground. It contrasts with his proposal of France as the 'hinge' on which a successful German-British relation depends. His argument here is historical, invoking British assistance in bringing France and Germany together after WW2. One could just as easily invoke history to argue the opposite. [111]

The UK has one advantage in the world that is so prevalent it is almost overlooked; that of the English language. Even if the days of a special bond between 'the English speaking peoples' is faded[112] the position of

---

110   William Nicoll & Trevor C. Salmon *Understanding the European Communities* (London: Philip Allan 1990) p32

111   Thomas Kielinger "Deutsch-Britische Unterschiede: Real, Altervetraut, und doch Überbrückbar" in *Deutschlands Neue Außenpolitik* Bd.3 "Interessen und Strategien" Eds. Karl Kaiser & Joachim Krause (München: Oldenbourg 1996) pp129-136. Foreign Minister's Hurd and Kinkel published a joint article "A Strategic Vision for Europe" in the *Times* and the *Süddeutsche Zeitung* 26-4-94 which developed some of these points on NATO and EU expansion. On subsidiarity see above and cf. the COCAS Report cited at fn 54

112   It may not quite be over. In a 1990 survey on where they might otherwise like to live, 23% of the British public answered Australia, followed by Canada, the United States and New Zealand. The top four totalled 53% and all were all English

English in international organizations, in global commerce, science, academe, and in regions throughout Asia and central and eastern Europe is a significant resource for the British state, business, and general population. It is unlikely to diminish as a medium of communication in continental Europe even with an increase in the importance of German. Moreover, the two languages are likely to be of mutual assistance in the European institutions. The British attitude to eastern enlargement is influenced by this linguistic factor and by a predominantly German provision of financial aid. Also connected is the value of British diplomacy to combined EU negotiations with third countries—when the 15 are unified. On the other hand, if the UK continues to reject communal decision-making and France is also restrained by its insistence on autonomy, the gap in 'European' foreign policy may have to be filled more by Germany. A Germany whose economic power 'becomes ever more relevant to classical foreign policy issues' while Britain's relative weakness is highlighted and 'has come to bear more sharply and irresistibly on its status in the world.' [113]

This leads to another crucial factor in relations between the three main west European powers: the position and perspective of the US, both of its own interests and of the various European actors. [114] Partly due to a dislike of European politicians and politics, Margaret Thatcher tried to strengthen Britain's relationship with the US, aided by her ideological consonance with Ronald Reagan. John Major may have introduced a milder attitude to Europe but many in the post-Thatcher party wanted more attention given to an 'Atlantic alternative' [115] when the American role in Europe indicated that a special 'special relationship' with Washington was now a 'sentimental mirage'. [116] For US policy-makers Germany had secured premier status in Europe and the only way Britain could win back such a position was through the unlikely possibility of becoming Europe's political leader. [117] With this shift the Clinton administration was accused of allowing or appointing Germany as Europe's future policeman. Britain's case had not been assisted by the Conservative Party's 'foolish' offer to assist the Republicans in 1992.

---

speaking. France and Germany received 3% each. See Denman *Missed Chances: Britain and Europe in the Twentieth Century* p287

113   Christopher Hill "United Kingdom: Sharpening Contradictions" in *The Actors in Europe's Foreign Policy* pp68-89

114   On this see Max Kaase & Andrew Kohut *Estranged Friends: The Transatlantic Consequences of Societal Change* (Gütersloh: Bertelsmann 1996)

115   Bagehot "John Bull abroad and at home" *The Economist* 26-2-94 p60

116   *The New European Community: Decisionmaking and Institutional Change* Eds. Robert Keohane and Stanley Hoffmann (Boulder: Westview 1991) p33

117   "Clinton hails partnership between US and Germany" *European* 15-7-94; "On the verge of Europe" *Economist* 11-6-94 pp57-58

By contrast on a 1994 visit to Germany, Clinton's told the Germans 'America is at your side, now and forever'. [118] While the loss of a privileged status as 'Washington's proxy' in Europe is disquieting for the British, the Germans are yet to demonstrate their commitment to this responsibility while the UK was the chief American ally in the Persian Gulf. Along with France, the UK deployed militarily in the former Yugoslavia, even if like other the other Europeans, their diplomacy was a failure.

James Morgan has argued that of the G7 states, in the 1990s the UK would be placed under the least pressure to make large-scale adaptations to its foreign policy agenda, and even that 'the developing world is evolving in a manner that is peculiarly favourable to British interests'. He soon adds that 'the options that will unfold over the medium term will depend largely on the policy choices of Germany and the United States.'[119] A successful outcome implies an Anglo-German covenant in concord with the US. Jonathan Wright has suggested that 'the supranational dream is fading and that when Kohl follows Mitterrand into retirement European politics will drift back to the British way of doing things, intergovernmental, pragmatic, open to the world. It is not a disreputable concept and not all European leaders have been opposed to it.' [120] In negotiating a way through geopolitical transformation, economic recession and a new context for their relationship both Germany and the UK have opportunities and 'common discontents'. [121] After a century of very different political, social and economic experience, Germany has in many ways become what Britain was before World War One: prosperous, democratic, powerful, respected—the archetypal stable trading state. The difference is that post-war German foreign affairs methodology has emphasised the Federal Republic as part of and not apart from a politically unified Europe.

Max Beloff asserts that the 'crisis of European union was not of Britain's making, nor could Britain produce a solution'. He sees it as a much wider and deeper problem, within which the Anglo-Franco-German triangle is critical and the alignments far from decided. With some variance to

---

118   Cf. Williams "Britain in the European Union"; and the sceptical appraisals presented by Christopher Coker "Britain and the New World Order: the special relationship in the 1990s" *International Affairs* v68 n3 1992 pp407-421, and Clarke who urges the US not to slide into "Repeating British Mistakes". Alan P. Dobson *Anglo-American Relations in the Twentieth Century* (London: Routledge 1995) is more optimistic about the future relationship
119   Morgan "Wide horizons, slender means:..."
120   Jonathan Wright "The Role of Britain in West German Foreign Policy Since 1949" *German Politics* v5 n1 1996 pp26-42
121   Stephen R. Graubard "A Common Discontent: Revisiting Britain and Germany" *Foreign Affairs* v72 n3 1993 pp2-6

Kielinger, who assumes a more assured Franco-German solidarity, Beloff concludes that it is France which must 'choose between the German vision for Europe and the British vision; they could not be reconciled. The same old dilemma again, how would France choose and what would Britain do?'[122] Wolfgang Schäuble declared the predominant mutual aversion within the triangle as that between Britain and France. He claimed that 'the greatest service of friendship the United Kingdom could do for Germany is to improve relations with Paris. The better the relations between individual partners, the better the situation for the European Community.'[123] Concurrently, other observers considered the prospect of a British 'tactical alliance with France's increasingly nationalist political class' all the more possible.[124]

---

122   Beloff *Britain and European union: dialogue of the deaf* pp147-148
123   See Allan Saunderson "Soothsayer tells Britain to heed the siren call" *The European* 15-7-94 p10
124   George Brock "Major builds up image of the Enigma Man" *The Times* 8-9-94 p12

8 Europe and the Union: New Theatre, Old Actors

Even as it incorporated three new members in 1995 and retained attractions for other candidates, the European Union also lapsed into inertia, if not crisis, for much of the 1990s. This chapter examines the process and institutions, as well as some motivations and impediments to European integration and also analyses how international relations theorists have interpreted this recast political theatre: its actors, rules, clashes, scope, objectives and directions. The response of, in particular, the original six EEC members to the events of 1989-90 hurried along the move from European Community to Union. An enterprise intended to denationalize Europe politically, actually animated the opposite. It exposed limitations to European ideals while Germany's emergence imbued a drama not present in the previous forty years. Four years later Christoph Bertram remarked, 'what differences of interest exist between Germany and the rest of the Community are matters of minimal degree, but the loss of Western cohesion manifests itself in the ability to pretend that minor differences are major ones.'[1]

These 'matters of minimal degree' were fundamental to why the European nation-state survived even as new institutions, methods of organization and growing global interchange inspired predictions of the form's imminent demise.[2] Notwithstanding supranational, regional, and interest group pressures, one major lesson of post-Cold War Europe was that commercial and bureaucratic integration cannot outrun allegiances, dependencies or authority associated with the state. These become politicized when there are attempts to integrate at excessive speed, weld

---

1   Christoph Bertram "The Power and the Past: Germany's New International Loneliness" in *Germany's New Position in Europe: Problems and Perspectives* Ed. Arnulf Baring (Oxford: Berg 1994) pp91-105, here p99

2   Andrew Levine *The End of the State* (London: Verso 1987); Michael Mann *Rise and Decline of the Nation-State* (Oxford: Blackwell 1990); Martin Holland "The end of the nation-state: the EC's institutional relations" Chapter Four in *European Community Relations* (London: Pinter 1993) pp90-116; Jean-Marie Guéhenno *The End of the Nation-State* trans. Victoria Elliott (Minneapolis: University of Minnesota Press 1995)

incompatible elements or impose the demands of one or some polities on others—or even the prospect of this. Through the decade political power as critical mass remained closely aligned with (national) cultural attachments. More than a gulf between monetarists and welfareists, western and eastern Europe, or widening and deepening, this was why, in practice, the various polities of the EU had not coalesced behind a *communautaire* ideal.[3]

European Integration: A Short History (?)

In the 1960s Raymond Aron sought to discern the motivations and advantages to forming a 'homogeneous international society', whether peoples should 'out of love of peace or out of fear of war, desire such a federation or such an empire'.[4] Thirty years later an array of formal and informal European networks has rendered a repeat conflagration in western Europe virtually inconceivable. Arriving at this condition, however, also created a paradox *sui generis*. The longer peace reigns between EU states, the less convincing are the self-congratulations for not having had a war for 20 or 30 or 50 years. Expectations, often conflicting, from within and from outside have grown and negative achievements no longer have the cogency of earlier decades. If, on the other hand, it is a primarily negative compulsion that keeps 'Europe' together, the shortcomings to building a political community become obvious.

One common perspective on European integration stresses how the founders of the European Coal and Steel Community and the European Economic Community hoped to dispel national rivalries and promote cooperative and eventually communal goals, benefits, and solutions.[5] While most practical expressions of interdependence were economic, the principal impetus was political and derived from specific historical contexts. Integration progressed despite setbacks because regional cooperation and a primacy of nation- (or national) states remained compatible. Rejecting hagiographic

3   Cf. the contributions to *Governing the New Europe* Eds. Jack Hayward & Edward C. Page (Oxford: Polity 1995) and *Journal of Common Market Studies* v34 n1 1996
4   Raymond Aron *Peace and War: A Theory of International Relations* (English Edition) Trans. Richard Howard & Annette Baker Fox (London: Weidenfeld & Nicholson 1966) p736
5   See *Documents on the History of European Integration* Eds. Walter Lipgens & Wilfried Roth (Berlin: Walter de Gruyter 1990); Jean Monnet *Memoirs* Trans. Richard Mayne (London: Collins 1978); *Jean Monnet-Robert Schumann: Correspondence 1947-1953* (Lausanne: Fondation Jean Monnet par l'Europe; Centre de Recherches Europeenes 1986)

interpretations, Alan Milward's persuasive analyses focus on national economic interests as the main inducement behind formation and development of communal ventures.[6] The (geo)political dimension is, for a perspective devoid of any Euro-idealism, underplayed and Milward suggests that the 'German Question', of relevance to France in particular, was subordinated to new economic imperatives. He is quick to add that 'the ultimate goal of course remained an increase in French national security and influence in Europe and to that extent it was a foreign policy objective too.'[7] In another passage Milward directly indicates the respective political ambitions and strategies.

> The first serious studies of French post-war diplomacy made it obvious that integration was an attempt to restore France as major national force by creating an integrated area in western Europe which France would dominate politically and economically. The German Federal Republic began to be depicted as a country which espoused the cause of European integration precisely in order to establish itself as the future German nation-state.[8]

Martin Dedman acknowledges the economic propellant involved in European treaties and also highlights the specifically political aspect. Of the EDC Treaty of 1952 and the 1992 TEU, he states that although only the latter was ratified and became community law, 'nevertheless, both treaties had two things in common. They were both initially triggered by events outside the community and *both were intended to prevent, or at least delay, some political development by Germany* in contrast to other treaties, Paris 1951, Rome 1957, and the SEA 1986 which were all primarily intended to advance national economic interests.'[9] For most of its existence West Germany's EC role featured subtlety, deference and patience.[10] In 1992, two years after reunification and while the TEU was in process of ratification, the German government and Bundesbank made it clear that should national and European interests clash the former would prevail.

---

6   Alan Milward *The European Rescue of the Nation State* (London: Routledge 1992); *The Frontier of National Sovereignty: History and Theory 1945-1992* Eds. Alan Milward et. al. (London: Routledge 1994)

7   Alan Milward "Conclusions: the value of history" in *The Frontier of National Sovereignty...* pp182-201

8   Milward *European Rescue* p17

9   Martin J. Dedman *The Origins and Development of the European Union 1945-1995: A History of European Integration* (London: Routledge 1996) p132 Emphasis added

10   See *Western Europe and Germany: The Beginnings of European Integration 1945-1960* Ed. Clemens Wurm (Oxford: Berg 1995)

In the crunch the nation was more important than the continent...the reason was an all too familiar one in the annals of interstate politics. Governments do not win elections in Brussels, but at home. Their fate is determined by national rates of interest, inflation and unemployment— not by the flowering of international institutions. Integrationist virtue or the welfare of other nations...takes a back seat when national leaders have to ensure their survival in power and social peace at home.[11]

The European Union (and predecessors) has not, principally, been a determiner of events but one that reacts and sometimes evolves in response to them. As outlined by Joffe above, reunified Germany impressed the primacy of the German polity, economy, and its managers, now that certain political constraints and diplomacy of the cold war had lost their context. Although the Maastricht Treaty reimpressed the goal of 'ever closer union' it was a compromise between variable preferences that set some grandiose and some more modest objectives. Opt-out clauses were negotiated and vetoes left extensively intact. Members desiring to preserve intergovernmental competencies felt secure enough to sign an agreement flecked with declarations such as providing nominal intent to 'avoid preventing a unanimous decision where a qualified majority exists in favour of that decision.'[12] A state, or its representatives, that dissented against the majority could be presented as, or made to feel, unpopular. However, the right of veto could only be relinquished by the individual state and the heretic could reach accommodations, officially or unofficially, with the same members who decried it in other instances. Formal institutional mechanisms may have been important, but were only *one* context for the definition or pursuit of interests. Michael Greven has proposed that 'European politics, like any national politics, never embodies a general or common interest, but is inevitably the result of competition and plurality—which does not exclude the fact that some interests always dominate either European or national politics (asymmetrical pluralism).'[13] It is the latter which still dominates the former.

William Pfaff has written that 'Acknowledgment of a common European interest and moral purpose had not extinguished the divergent and sometimes conflicting practical interests and perceptions of the European states. It was possible, although difficult, to accommodate these within the

---

11   Josef Joffe "The New Europe: Yesterday's Ghosts" *Foreign Affairs* v72 n1 1993 pp29-43

12   Richard Corbett *The Treaty of Maastricht: from conception to ratification* (Harlow: Longman Current Affairs 1993) pp53-62

13   Michael Th. Greven "Political Parties Between National Identity and Eurofication" in *The Idea of Europe: Problems of National and Transnational Identity* Eds. Brian Nelson, David Roberts and Walter Veit. (New York: Berg 1992) pp75-95 fn9

European Community between 1951 and 1993 precisely because Europe remained far from political integration.' Formulas of variable geometry, concentric circles, two-speeds, and the creation of a 'European space' do not disguise that the vital ingredient of political will resides in the individual polities. Pfaff continues that 'The European Community's own development had run into the contradiction in its own ambition, to create a "union" of "sovereign" states. Europe actually had to become one or the other'.[14] This inescapable problem also, almost incidentally, raises a question as to why, if the sovereignty of the nation-state was already a chimera, states ought to give up what they no longer have? In a 'search for an optimal strategy' Wolfgang Wessels responded to what he identified as the main follow up strategies to the Treaty on European Union predicting that by mid-1995 certain developments would have made the direction clearer. 'Renationalizing' was already underway as most prominent amongst the possible outcomes nominated by Wessels.[15]

Europe and International Relations Theory

As an academic discipline, International Relations was dominated by American scholarship with a corresponding tendency to place the US or US-Soviet bipolarity at the centre of considerations. Realist theories concentrated on this frame of reference, and neo-liberalism presented analyses of regimes, organisations or institutional arrangements within which the US figured prominently.[16] Europe was principally a province of comparative politics which acquired a new focus as the iron curtain disintegrated heralding the 'new European Community'.[17] Martin Wight contended that 'in all political and historical studies the purpose of building pigeon-holes is to reassure oneself that the raw material does not fit into them. Classification becomes valuable, in humane studies, only at the point where it breaks down.'

---

14   William Pfaff *The Wrath of Nations: Civilization and the Furies of Nationalism* (New York: Simon and Schuster 1993) pp207-208 & p215

15   Wolfgang Wessels "Rationalizing Maastricht: the search for an optimal strategy of the new Europe" *International Affairs* v70 n3 1994 pp445-457

16   Stanley Hoffmann "International Relations: An American Social Science" *Daedelus* v106 n3 1977 pp41-60; Kenneth Waltz *Theory of International Politics* (Reading: Addison Wesley 1979)

17   *The New European Community: Decisionmaking and Institutional Change* (Boulder: Westview 1991) Eds. Robert Keohane and Stanley Hoffmann; *Euro-Politics, Institutions, and Policymaking in the "New" European Community* Ed. Alberta M. Sbragia (Washington: Brookings Institute 1992); John McCormick *The European Union: Politics and Policies* (Boulder: Westview 1996)

According to Wight 'the greatest political writers in international theory almost all straddle the frontiers dividing two of the traditions, and most of these writers transcend their own systems.'[18] Beyond accommodating variable perspectives, the study of European politics has encouraged interdisciplinary approaches: International relations (itself mutating into new forms), comparative policy analysis, domestic structures and sectoral interests, policy networks and new variants of functionalism.[19] Contemporaneously some statist elements are altered, some are retained. The factor 'structure' has become flexible and mobile, while the recalibrating of frictions within western Europe does not result in military power and associated 'anarchy' prevailing.[20]

The range of actors is one salient reason for the 'stop-and-go rythym' of European political development and the failure of various theories to explain this pattern.[21] Hancock and Peters have described the EU as 'both an international organization and the protogovernment for a regional political system'.[22] Christian Hacke perceived that 'the politics of the European Community has not led toward more integration and supranationality. It remains a halfway house between integration and disintegration. It is the prototypical phenomenon of a system of states in transition.'[23] As Michael Smith puts it, the role of the Union is both 'central and ambiguous' in a space

18   Martin Wight *International theory: the three traditions* Eds Gabriele Wight & Brian Porter (Leicester: Leicester Univerity Press 1991) p259, quoted in David S ·Yost "Political philosophy and the theory of international relations" *International Affairs* v70 n2 1994 pp263-90

19   See Thomas Risse-Kappen "Exploring the Nature of the Beast: International Relations Theory and Comparative Policy Analysis Meet in the European Union" *Journal of Common Market Studies* v34 n1 1996 pp53-78

20   Cf. Richard Detevak "Incomplete states: theories and practices of statecraft" in *Boundaries in Question: New Directions in in International Relations* Eds. John MacMillan and Andrew Linklater (London: Pinter 1995) pp19-39; John G. Ruggie "Territoriality and beyond: problematizing modernity in international relations" *International Organization* v47 n1 1993 pp139-174; Robert Powell "Anarchy in international relations theory: the neorealist-neoliberal debate" *International Organization* v48 n2 1994 pp313-44

21   Dorette Corbey "Dialectical functionalism: stagnation as a booster of European integration" *International Organization* v49 n2 1995 pp253-284

22   M. Donald Hancock & B. Guy Peters "The European Community" in M. Donald Hancock et.al. *Politics in Western Europe* (Houndmills: MacMillan 1993) pp461-526, here p474

23   Christian Hacke "Germany: Locomotive for European Integration or Pacemaker for Detente with Eastern Europe?" in *The European Community in the 1990s: Economics, Politics, Defense* Eds. Brian Nelson, David Roberts, and Walter Veit (New York: Berg 1992) pp62-79

consisting of 'paradoxical relationships' and 'unresolved tensions'. Boundaries in question implies that boundaries remain. So too does the 'practice of classical interstate politics' in a new setting.[24]

This 'half-way house' interpretation is reflected in a broad intersection of state-centric and institutionalist positions. Robert Keohane's work is indicative of this merging or crossover. A proponent of 'liberal-institutionalism', his concurrence with realist/neo-realist positions was such that they shared 'essentially the same ontology'.[25] Andrew Moravscik has developed this fusion with a concentration on Europe.[26] His 'intergovernmental institutionalism' merged liberal-institutionalism with a realist focus on state power and the Bulmer/Paterson stress on forces in the domestic polity. Interest groups and publics are seen as essential to the analysis of how national policies and European policies are formulated. Moravscik emphasises that despite political, geo-strategic, and economic changes the EU remains a competitive arrangement of bargaining over policy, payments, and postings.[27] Policy coordination is determined by long term factors and variables more prone to fluctuation: economic oscillations, domestic controversies and public opinion. Moravscik defines four dimensions to the process: "(1) the *geographical scope* of the regime; (2) the range of issues in which policies are co-ordinated; (3) the *institutions* of joint decision-making, implementation and enforcement; (4) the *direction and magnitude of substantive domestic policy adjustment*."[28] His explanation concludes that states are ultimately, the most important agents by which EU decisions are made. Conversely, exposure of ineffectual aspects reveals a 'partnership of states' rather than a Union which consistently speaks with one voice and acts decisively in response to crises. Intergovernmental Conferences

---

24   See Michael Smith "The European Union and a Changing Europe: Establishing the Boundaries of Order" *Journal of Common Market Studies* v34 n1 1996 pp4-28

25   *After the Cold War: International Institutions and State Strategies in Europe 1989-1991* Robert Keohane et. al. Eds. (Cambridge: Harvard University Press 1993); Robert Keohane & Joseph Nye *Power and Interdependence: World Politics in Transition*, Second Edition, (Boston: Little & Brown 1989); Robert Keohane *International Institutions and State Power* (Boulder: Westview 1989); Robert Keohane *After Hegemony: Coperation and Discord in the World Political Economy* (Princeton: Princeton University Press 1984). See also, Devetak "Incomplete states" fn 10

26   Andrew Moravscik "Negotiating the Single European Act: national interests and conventional statecraft in the European Community" *International Organization* v45 n1 1991 pp19-56

27   Andrew Moravscik "Preferences and Power in the European Community: A Liberal Intergovernmentalist Approach" *Journal of Common Market Studies* v31 n4 1993 p473-519, here p479

28   Moravscik "Preferences and Power..." p479

witness the states negotiate 'package bargains fundamental to institutional progress' which is itself subject to the 'debilitating constraints of consensus principle'. Hence the forerunner to the substantively similar Common Foreign and Security Policy, 'European Political Cooperation' was 'strong on points of secondary importance' and much less on 'issues of real crucial nature'.[29]

States may secure or advance interests through various cooperative means which can in turn refashion the parameters and the nature of those interests. This is the essence of the 'spillover' principle central to functionalist and neo-functionalist theory.[30] The flaw of neo-functionalism was to discount the vagaries of *international politics*. It did not discern that apparently rational cooperative configurations can be upset and logical trajectories of progress abandoned. Assumptions of an inexorable common movement was shaken by actors, or events, of a 'dramatic-political' nature, and also through less demonstrative means. J.D.B. Miller has summarised that 'the original Haas model was apolitical to the point of unreality. In effect, it had restricted its choice of effective political forces to those which would ensure the success of the operation'[31] The later rejection of neo-functionalism by its foremost proponent seemed to confirm this hypothesis.[32]

Constructivism adopted the neo-functionalist conviction that cooperative activity would shape the perspectives and policies of discrete actors to the point where they became communal. It added identity as an essential factor of analysis.[33] Neo-liberal or constructivist rejection of a balance of power paradigm within the EU's geo-political space still presumes the need for a united front (trade policy, common currency, a CFSP) as an instrument of leverage in a global scenario. There is recognition of a balance of power (or the need to, effectively, establish one) not between individual EU states but between a politically united Europe capable of enacting common policy, and other actors: states, blocs, or dangers associated with transnational crime, fundamentalism or terrorism. The objective is to 'move balance-of-power dynamics from within the region to outside the region'[34] Globally

29   Holland *European Community Integration* p123

30   Ernst Haas *The Uniting of Europe: Political, Social and Economical Forces 1950-57* (London: Stevens 1958)

31   J. D. B. Miller *The World of States* (London: Croom Helm 1981) pp80-81

32   Ernst Haas *The Obsolescence of Regional Integraton Theory* (Berkeley: Institute of International Studies 1975)

33   Alexander Wendt "Collective Identity Formation and the International State" *American Political Science Review* v88 n2 1994 pp384-398

34   Ole Wæver "Identity, Integration and Security: Solving the Sovereignty Puzzle in E.U. Studies" *Journal of International Affairs* v48 n2 1995 pp389-431. See pp396-399

then, if this is accepted, international relations fits a neo-realist model, while EU Europe is consistent with an interdependence model.

Wayne Sandholtz incorporates neo-functionalist and constructivist views and writes that the 'intergovernmentalist argument implies that states form their preferences via some hermetic national process, then bring those interests to Brussels.' Sandholtz is correct to suggest 'a link between international institutions and state interest formation'. He goes on to say that 'each member state tries to ensure that EC outcomes are as close as possible to its national interest, but the crucial point is that those interests are defined in the context of the EC...the national interests of EC states do not have an independent existence'. The 'crucial point' is not that which Sandholtz accents but that the national context is both the starting point of this interest formation and ultimately where governments are judged. It is states which restrict the exercise of preferences that are damaging or undesired. And even this has proven to be no guarantee. The EC/EU was not about to prevent German reunification or Germany's recognition of Croatia and Slovenia, just as it did not prevent French nuclear testing or adventurism in Africa, nor Britain's war in the Falklands. The states involved were not forced to 'define their interests in a different way as members of the EC than they would without it'.[35] And more 'Luxembourg Compromises' are always possible.

Ole Wæver expresses how 'the implicit picture of foreign policy is that it stems from inside and travels towards the outside through the medium of a decision making machinery.'[36] The 'voice of foreign policy' or 'the statesman' is then located 'inside'. Employing Henry Kissinger's *A World Restored*, Wæver posits the statesman 'neither internally, nor externally, but on the border trying to mediate two worlds' and having to 'succeed on both arenas.' He may face pressures from either 'world' and may turn in either direction to deal with them. Here 'the statesman' is portrayed as having no greater affinities, or responsibilities, to one 'world' over the other. A General de Gaulle, Margaret Thatcher or any other leader would play neutral roles with no hierarchy of loyalties in the relation of France/Europe or Britain/Europe. The analysis adopts the neo-functionalist error of ignoring national identifications among decision-makers at the state level. However, Wæver later describes the 'Kissinger/Wæver approach' as being 'about the identity and projects ascribed by the statesman to the state/nation' and that any Europe concept must be sold to a national market. For instance a 'meaningful' Europe must 'make room for a "France" which is attractive to a French

---

35   See Wayne Sandholtz "Choosing union: monetary politics and Maastricht" *International Organization* v47 n1 1993 pp1-25, see p3

36   Ole Wæver & Ulla Holm *The Struggle for 'Europe': French and German concepts of State, Nation and European Union* (forthcoming) Draft of Chapter 1B

mind' and likewise for other nations. This is the echo of Gellner's claim about loyalty to a culture.

Elsewhere Wæver has critiqued Moravscik's approach for not permitting 'interaction to shape both identity and interests'; that instead he still envisages the process as one whereby the national base determines the scope and depth of integration.[37] This seems to contradict Wæver's own recognition of the power of national motifs. Politically and culturally, the national states continue to live many lives outside the EU. For everyone's identity and interest to be synthesized with that of 'Europe' implies a homogeneity that publics and governments have demonstrated they do not want.[38] Accompanied by other crises, recession in the early 1990s strengthened the opinion that 'the 'win set' of cooperation for European integration seems to be turning into a 'lose set', as the European international regime fails to deliver enough domestic reputation benefits to offset a deteriorating domestic popularity profile...'. The mood tilted towards the latter in the pursuit of 'realistic integrative activity, while at the same time meeting the requirements of a balanced *cooperative competition.*'[39] Not a lot appeared to have changed when discussion papers intended to promote the deepening, widening and accelerating of integration were left stating the obvious:

> Europa kann nicht gegen die interessen seiner Nationen konstruiert werden...Nur wenn das europäische und das nationale Moment konstruktiv miteinander verknupft werden, steht der union das potential sowie die Akzeptanz und Legitimation zur effektiven Politikgestaltung zur Verfügung.[40]

Viewpoints stressing prominent roles for non-state actors, *Politikverflechtung*, and transnational interests, do not explain why there is no

---

37   Waever "Identity, Integration and Security" pp412-413 and fn49; Risse-Kappen "Exploring the Nature of the Beast"

38   This is not say that a geo-political space recognised by international law cannot be legally entered, profited from, lived in or partly owned by members of another cultural-political community. See Ruggie "Territoriality and beyond: problematizing modernity in international relations"

39   Grahame F. Thompson *The Economic Emergence of a New Europe?: The Political Economy of Cooperation and Competition in the 1990s* (Aldershot: Edward Elgar 1993) pp202. This combination is present in numerous areas. Kirsty Hughes and Ian Christie *UK & European Science Policy: The Role of Cooperative Research Networks* (London: Policy Studies Institute 1995) concludes that 'many issues of the appropriate roles of national and EU science policies remain to be resolved'

40   *Europa 96: Reformprogramm für die Europäische Union* Ed. Werner Weidenfeld (Gütersloh: Verlag Bertelsmann Stiftung 1994) p8

European government, no European foreign policy, no European welfare system, no European army, only a limited European citizenship, and no widespread, cogent sense of a European identity. There is also (to 1999 at least) no actual European currency. If one does come into operation then the 'Carolingian' would be a more accurate appellation than the 'euro'. For (neo)realist positions which underplay or ignore the actual content within the state shell the missing clarification concerns how and to whom governments legitimate themselves and act in foreign policy contexts. The in-between quality that gives the EU its uniqueness also means tensions and limitations involved in sustaining it or in simultaneously responding to two highest authorities. In James Caporaso's theoretical study of the EU and 'forms of state', the 'portfolio of functions performed by France, Germany and England is not duplicated by the evolving EU'. The legal dimension is one of 'norm's and values' rather than 'power and interests'. In the political sphere it is different. To take the German example, insistence on special criteria for EMU, an ECB being located in Frankfurt, and German language use or numerical representation in the Council or European Parliament all radiate more from a 'power and interests' (and identity) base no matter how much insistence there may be on the former. And this is how it is understood in France and England.[41]

Consociationalism which emerged in the 1970s looked upon EU relations and progress as managing or confining dissent. It recognises the piquancy generated by the interaction of national states that neofunctionalism overlooked, especially at elite level. According to Taylor 'the members of the Council of ministers and of the European Council did indeed behave like the members of an elite cartel in a consociational multi-party government, with enormously complex consensus-building and a marked tendency to express profound doubts about the others' intentions.'[42] For individual members, the formulation of domestic and foreign policy is influenced by being part of the Union, which in this sense, is both inside and outside the state.[43] It is, however, a question of degree and the extent to which national states have been willing to forego foreign policy autonomy remains conditioned by their

41   James Caporaso "The European Union and Forms of State: Westphalian, Regulatory or Post-Modern?" *Journal of Common Market Studies* v34 n1 1996 pp33-53

42   Arend Lijphart "Consociational Democracy" *World Politics* v21 n2 1969; Paul Taylor *International Organization in the Modern World: The Regional and the Global Process* (London: Pinter 1993) See Chapter 4

43   R.B.J. Walker *Inside/Outside: international relations as political theory* (Cambridge: Cambridge University Press 1993); Michael G. Huelshoff "Domestic Politics and Dynamic Issue Linkage: A Reformulation of Integration Theory" *International Studies Quarterly* v38 n2 1994 pp255-279

special circumstances. Moisi and Mertes's point that '2 or 3 governments of EU nations per year are being lame-ducked by national election campaigns' is itself suggestive of a dissonance between European integration and concerns on the national agendas.[44] Particularly among the big three states, agreement on major issues is hard to reach.[45]

William Wallace has observed a tendency for debate on Europe to veer 'to the realm of political persuasion rather than dispassionate analysis'.[46] Interpretations polarise or are consigned into pessimistic and optimistic camps, or, 'friends and foes'. Variations on neo-realism (or intergovernmentalists) are designated as representative of the 'foes'. Liberal, or supranational, accounts are associated with optimistic standpoints and are 'friends'. A plethora of Commission generated material has reiterated this latter position, explicitly or implicitly asserting the idea that a politically united Europe is itself 'good', and that ever closer union is imperative.[47] This side of the debate generally regards two types of appraisal as 'sceptical': that whereby the commentators themselves are *actually opposed* in some way to closer integration; and those *doubting the capacities* of the EU's institutions to surmount difficulties.

The circulation of opinion as objective information on the grounds that it promotes a 'worthy' cause because it is 'pro-Europe', or assertions of 'undeniable facts' regarding 'common European interest', have been vigorously critiqued. Depicting a for-against division has been attacked as falsely portraying doubters as being against the 'good' of the continent, and that there could not be 'rival positive goals'.[48] 'Sceptical' positions are not necessarily 'anti' current or future cooperation but may be concerned with exposure or analyses of obstacles and divergences. Milward et. al. argue that

---

44   Dominique Moisi & Michael Mertes "Europe's Map, Compass and Horizon" *Foreign Affairs* v74 n1 1995 pp122-134

45   Reinhard Meier-Walser "Germany, France and Britain on the Threshold to a New Europe" *Aussenpolitik* v43 n4 1992 pp334-342; "The Return of Triangular Diplomacy" *The Economist* 4-11-95. Where the three have concurred is in aversion to the diminution of their voting strength in the Council of Ministers and opposition to growth in the Commission's powers. See "The big countries poodle?" *The Economist* 15-7-95 p36

46   William Wallace *The Transformation of Western Europe* (New York: RIIA 1990) See Chapter Two "Europe, which Europe?"

47   See Edelgard Mahant "Foreign Policy and European Identity" *History of European Ideas* v21 n4 1995 pp485-498 fn3. 'I have here limited myself to positive evaluations...complaints of the type: Europe really ought to do more and act in a united fashion...are..hardly worth repeating or analyzing'

48   Noel Malcolm "The Case Against 'Europe'" *Foreign Affairs* v74 n2 1995 pp52-68; Philip Schlesinger *Media, State and Nation: Political Violence and Collective Identity* (London: Sage 1994) Chapters 7-9

'we have not seen the belief that a united Europe is in itself a desirable ideal as having any strong explanatory force outside its capacity to help in consensus-building in the post-war nation-state'. They also reject 'the repeated assertions that western Europe has been moving towards some form of cultural and social uniformity since 1945 and that this is the real underlying force behind European integration.'[49] The Commission itself has paid much greater attention to this after the shocks delivered by negative responses to the TEU and the process, even idea, in general.[50] Frank Vibert declares that 'even if it were possible to claim that a European political union is historically inevitable'

> it is a logical fallacy to step from an allegedly 'empirical' claim to a value judgement that a particular political union is justified...If European political union is put forward as a value in itself that has simply to be asserted in order to command respect, then, once again, the mistakes of nationalist logic are being repeated.[51]

As integration encounters the core/s of state sovereignty and demands for clarity increase, difficulties of elucidating what it is they are progressing towards and how it is to be achieved intensify. 'Integration' itself is as imprecise as other codewords. Wallace makes a distinction between *formal integration*: 'deliberate actions by authoritative policy-makers to create and adjust rules...'; and *informal integration*: or 'without the intervention of deliberate government decisions, following the dynamics of markets, technology, communications networks and social exchange...'. Beyond this he distinguishes *proactive* and *responsive* formal integration. The former 'has a deliberate and explicit political aim' the latter 'laissez faire...reacting to economic and social changes by adjusting rules and regulations'. These categories parallel, respectively, *political* and *economic and social integration*. The most significant point drawn from this is that 'Political integration is a matter of identity and loyalty' and will extend as far as this allows.[52]

---

49   Milward "Conclusions: the value of history" p185
50   In an interesting observation on Commission information dissemination one author says of EU pamphlets, 'Although they are exercises in public relations, many are packed with information and some are surprisingly honest.' See McCormick *The European Union: Politics and Policies* pp321-322 Appendix iii
51   Frank Vibert *Europe: A Constitution for the Millenium* (Aldershot: Dartmouth 1995) p53
52   Wallace *The Transformation of Western Europe* See chapter 4 "The dynamics of integration"

Resilience of the State

Arguments for relinquishment of sovereignty rest in part on a presumption that populations organised within and identified with states are susceptile to hostility against others. This danger will dissolve when, or if, Europe's publics are presented with a new form of political representation, a 'federation of free European states' which will 'preserve national identities...by eliminating...the sovereignty of the nation-state.' However, European integration has inadvertently demonstrated that state sovereignty extended beyond merely representing the 'right of a political class to make war'.[53] If the state is in crisis or heading for oblivion, 'it must in the end be a crisis not of the periphery but of the centre'.[54] Plotting the evolution of the EU reflects a more sophisticated, modernised version of the nineteenth century state system with some major differences: the elimination of war between members, constant technological advance, and an understanding that cooperative strategies will often provide the best outcomes. The transferring of some competences has not meant replacement of international legitimacy or identification of populations. Neither history, nor disillusion with political systems in the later twentieth century, have eliminated the affinity noted by Hegel. It may even be reinforced:

> Those who talk of the 'wishes' of a collection of people constituting a more or less autonomous state with its own centre, of its 'wishes' to renounce this centre and its autonomy in order to unite with others to form a new whole, have very little knowledge of the nature of a collection or of the feeling of selfhood which a nation possesses in its independence.[55]

For a new pan-European form of representation to appear and retain a democratic legitimacy, populations will have to empower it themselves and so willingly merge with what are presently other states, other polities, other peoples. Whatever happens in political, legal or territorial fusion, in economic and cultural terms some peoples are better positioned to flourish than others; or possibly have more to lose than others. All states are featured by a more or

---

53   John Keane "Questions for Europe" in *The Idea of Europe* pp55-61

54   John Dunn "Crisis of the Nation State?" *Political Studies* v42 Special Issue 1994 pp3-15

55   G.W.F. Hegel *Philosophy of Right* trans. T.M.Knox (Oxford: Oxford University Press 1942) p208. Cf. J. S. Mill *Considerations on Representative Government* (London: 1966) "...But the strongest of all is identity of political antecedents: the possession of a national history, and consequent community of recollections". Quoted in Sven Papcke "Who needs European Identity and What Could it Be?" in *The Idea of Europe* ... pp61-74, p69

less constant grumbling about the government and a type of derisive familiarity. Yet state institutions have maintained a distance from Brussels and perpetuated exclusivities. The state remains the chief protective entity, locus for political representation, provider of welfare and social services, collector of income taxes and legal determiner of criminality and sentencing. It is not dying but metamorphosing.[56] Inversely to Wight's argument that 'it would be impossible to have a society of states unless each state, while claiming sovereignty for itself, recognized that every other state had the right to claim and enjoy its own sovereignty as well',[57] it is actually impossible to have a political system of merged sovereignties unless all states agreed. Only a state, or government representing it, can voluntarily reduce its authority.[58] The 'Europeification of national policy-making' operates on an *à la carte* basis, between a federal Europe 'too utopian' in the face of national interests and cultural differences, and a loose group of states opposed by those reluctant to 'accept Germany as an uncommitted actor in Europe'. Three years after Andersen and Eliassen pronounced that 'the European village in Delors' terms and the corresponding institutions and decision-making structure of the European Union will be decided at the next intergovernmental conference in 1996/1997', the result was no particular decision.[59]

The EU's most notable success came with the introduction of the internal market. But this jewel in the crown of EU achievements did not immediately overcome a lack of uniformity in the practical implementation of 'free movement of people, goods, capital and services'.[60] Member states still

---

56   Stanley Hoffmann "Reflections on the Nation State Today" *Journal of Common Market Studies* v30 n 1982; John Lambert "The Nation-State Dies Hard" *Capital & Class* n43 Spring 1991 pp9-24; Wolfgang C. Müller & Vincent Wright "Reshaping the State in Western Europe: The Limits to Retreat" *Western European Politics* v17 n3 1994 pp1-11

57   Martin Wight *Systems of States* (Leicester: Leicester University Press 1977) p135

58   See Cynthia Weber 'Reconsidering Statehood: Examining the Sovereignty/Intervention Boundary" *Review of International Studies* v18 1992 pp199-216. Even in the most advanced integrative technologies the nation-state is at the centre of an 'internationalization of governance'. See Richard Sinnott "Theories of integration and the integration of the European database" *International Social Science Journal* v46 n4 1994 pp533-540

59   *Making Policy in Europe: The Europeification of National Policy-making* Eds. Svein S Andersen & Kjell A Eliassen (London: Sage 1993) p7 & p262

60   A seemingly prosaic item to be at the heart of a minor political crisis, bananas, precipitated what one insider termed the 'most acrimonious Council [of ministers] meeting' he had ever seen. Germany, under US pressure for Latin American producers, sided with Benelux and others against France and the UK. See Julie Wolf "Europe divided by a banana split" *Guardian Weekly* 21-1-96

employed their own methods engendering inconsistencies.[61] The Schengen agreement revealed how territory, or territorial integrity, received different emphasis from different states. Germany and several other states went ahead while Britain and Ireland opted out. France was a party to an unratified agreement and the locus of considerable antipathy to the policy. The January 1, 1993 introduction of 'free movement', originally formulated in the SEA has required several further Commission proposals, chief of which 'known as the "catch-all" Directive', is the one 'which makes the abolition of controls a reality'. The 'fixed' date for transposal was 31 December 1996, four years after internal frontiers were supposedly removed. Being based on Article 100 the new Directive must be adopted by the Council unanimously.[62]

States may not control the dynamics of the world economy but through various agencies they retain significant powers over economic policy. Some manage the business of existing in a competitive and volatile international market more effectively than others.[63] Even speculative finance requires fixed locations, stock markets, and so on to operate. Recipients of profits require 'bases' somewhere which presupposes territory.[64] Reductions in state regulation of finance and trade is not matched in the sphere of political power—the capacity to intervene as arbiter—which remains with the state. The 'global' or 'European' economy does not just happen. 'Firms' says

---

p14. If bananas are the cause of such vitriol, the controversies foreign policy, language, or security issues might incite go considerably further

61   One example central to the whole idea of integration is intra-European travel. In France and Italy motorists must pay charges to use the national highways yet in Britain or Germany they do not

62   *EU Background* (Delegation of the European Commission to Australia and New Zealand) August 1995. The nominal removal of border controls did not in practice mean passport checks were finished. In 1994 travellers from Germany or Belgium entering France were still stopped for inspection

63   Janice E. Thompson & Stephen D. Krasner "Global Transactions and the Consolidation of Sovereignty" in *Global Transactions and Theoretical Challenges* Eds. Ernst-Otto Czempiel & James N. Rosenau (Lexington: Lexington Books 1989); Gus Tyler "The Nation-State versus the Global Economy" *Challenge* v36 March/April 1993 pp26-32; Alan Murray "The Global Economy Bungled" *Foreign Affairs* v72 n1 1993 pp158-166; Will Hutton "Nova Scotia's load of baloney" *The Guardian* 18-6-95 p11. David Marsh *The Bundesbank: The Bank that rules Europe* (London: Heinemann: 1992) probably impresses more than any the ability of one national institution to determine the fortunes of other states and societies

64   William Wallace "Rescue or Retreat? The Nation State in Western Europe, 1945-93" *Political Studies* v42 Special Issue 1994 pp52-76. See pp66-68; Louis W. Pauly "Capital Mobility, State Autonomy and Political Legitimacy" *Journal of International Affairs* v48 n2 1995 pp369-388

Wolfgang Streeck, are 'embedded in and dependent on the societies in which they operate'.[65] WTO or EU competition policy agreements, are, as Peter Gourevitch argues, produced by 'political processes'. And universal rules are not agreed or adopted *in toto*. Because, 'in each country a number of forces are at work:

> culture, values, preferences, ideology, interests, international pressures and opportunities, ambition, institutions, procedures, leadership, accidents—in short the gamut of variables that influence politics. All of these influence policy by their effect on policymakers.[66]

What Gourevitch impresses is the primacy of politics, of 'who gets what, when and how'.[67] As Europe is presently constituted states remain the major boundary markers and determiners of politics. Within these states 'cultural traditions are powerful: countries have different traditions in networking, personal relationships, conception of authority, models of organizations and individuals. Macroeconomic policy is surely important. International rivalry and competition matter a great deal.'[68] Some of these political entities are simply more powerful than others. One example concerned a cornerstone of European integration, the coal industry, and witnessed a German government insistence on 'the right to subsidize its industry if it chose to', while the UK was contemporaneously closing what it deemed unprofitable mining centres. In both instances the Commission was unable to prevent them adopting their own course.[69]

In 1990 Michael Mann published the *Rise and Decline of the Nation-State*. In 1993 he wrote that 'the nation-state is thus not in any *general* decline, *anywhere*. In some ways it is still maturing.' Mann makes several points about the many transnational relations engaged in by nation-states and their less than homogenous make-up. Nonetheless they continue to function much as if they are. The EC, and now EU, 'remains fundamentally an economic planning agency', one which 'does not really cultivate a real sense of

---

65   Wolfgang Streeck "Lean Production in the German Automobile Industry: A Test Case for Convergence Theory" in *National Diversity and Global Capitalism* Eds. Suzanne Berger & Ronald Dore (Ithaca: Cornell University Press 1996) pp138-170 p154

66   Peter Gourevitch "The Macropolitics of Microinstitutional Differences in the Analysis of Comparative Capitalism" in *National Diversity and Global Capitalism* pp239-259, p258

67   Harold Lasswell *Politics: Who gets what, when, how* (New York: Meridian 1958)

68   Gourevitch "Macropolitics" p249

69   Stephen Fothergill "The Impact of Regional Alliances: The Case of the EU Coalfields" *European Urban & Regional Studies* v1 n2 1994 pp177-180

European identity or citizenship'. The 'only major "weakening" in 'strong and enduring national loyalties' is a 'substantial reduction in aggressive xenophobia'. A 'nice, gentle and civilized' European identity which 'could be mobilizable for "pan-European" politics and social purposes' is not powerful enough and so the latter are 'absent'. Important issues are those contained within national borders while 'political parties are still entirely national in organization and almost entirely national in orientation. Even referenda supposedly about Europe have tended to turn into confidence votes on the national performance of governments'. Mann concludes that 'European nation-states are neither dying nor retiring; they have merely shifted functions, and they may continue to do so in the future'.[70] Dimitris Chryssochoou's studies on the Europeanization of democratic processes suggest:

> The evidence presented so far seems to underscore the conclusion that member governments continue to possess a considerable range of possibilities open to them for both managing the process of building the great arrangements within their interactive association *and* retreating from common action when vital national interests are, or appear to be, at stake. In addition, states preserve the right to withdraw from the regional association without fear of being penalised by means of coercive action deployed by an all powerful (federal) European Leviathan.[71]

Fundamentally it is concerns about national autonomy that restrict the development of common policy and fuel governmental and popular concerns with representation quotas and appointments to EU institutions or the potential loss of privileges, such as welfare. It is 'too early to write off the nation-state [which] remains a crucial point of reference'. Individuals may fear the state, 'but they fear still more its disappearance and decomposition'.[72]

---

70   Michael Mann "Nation-States in Europe and Other Continents: Diversifying, Developing, Not Dying" *Dædelus* v122 n3 1993 pp115-140. Emphasis in original. Cf. Mann *The Rise and Decline of the Nation-State*

71   Dimitris N. Chryssochoou " Democracy and Symbiosis in the European Union: Towards a Confederal Consociation" *West European Politics* v17 n4 1994 pp1-14

72   Philip Schlesinger "Europeanness: A New Cultural Battlefield" in *Nationalism* Eds. John Hutchinson & Anthony D. Smith pp316-325 (orig. *Innovation in Social Science Research* v5 n1 1992 pp11-23)

National Affinities in a Communal Province

In a chapter entitled 'The end of the nation-state: the EC's institutional relations', Martin Holland also, unintentionally, confirms its continued authority. Failure to incorporate a goal of federalism into the Maastricht Treaty, appointments of Commissioners, the selective approach to Commission proposals and initiatives from governments, final decisions resting with the Council of Ministers and the European Council are indicative of national guidelines and prerogatives as remaining paramount. Expectation that appointees to the Commission, including Presidents, will lose national allegiances is mistaken if not naive. As Holland states, 'the metamorphosis that all Commissioners are required to undertake, from national politician to public servant, loyal exclusively to the Community, is remarkable and possibly unreasonable'. When discord between the states has occurred, having a 'Euro-loyalist' Commissioner has little impact. As an additional safeguard they can always be removed. The fate of Lord Cockfield was a 'healthy reminder of the ultimate power held by each member government'. Similarly the debates over the presidential appointee and the distribution of portfolios are decided by the states, as is the extent to which Commission proposals can be realised. Even though 'there is no strict principle of national rotation, there are clear assumptions by member states of an informal allocation of the office...the technical freedom to assign portfolios to specific individuals is, in practice, considerably restrained by national government pressures.' Holland continued that 'despite the resurgence under Delors, the Commission has become a less equal partner.'

> While constitutionally free from national interference, the success of the Commission's policy proposals is dependent on the goodwill and support of the Council: the Treaty-based legitimacy and independent political authority of the Commission is rarely a match for the intergovernmental opposition.[73]

Indeed, the protracted wrangling and often animosity that accompanies the distribution of appointments betrays any pretence that representation by one's own nationals or those considered empathetic is not pre-eminent in considerations. 'Senior appointments in the Commission are very often the result of intense lobbying' and 'the practice of 'parachuting' in a senior national official remains common if frowned upon.[74] Another

---

73   Holland *European Community Integration*. See Chapter 4 especially pp92-96
74   Geoffrey Edwards "Central Government" in *Britain and the European Community: The Politics of Semi-detachment* Ed. Stephen George (Oxford:

specialist affirms that 'their European vocation not withstanding, Commissioners, and perhaps still more their cabinets, are national champions defending national positions in the Commission.'[75] It also remains vague as to 'who' or 'what' a 'European civil servant or a 'European' foreign minister represents or are responsible to. It is from the states that the directorship and staffing of the Commission is drawn. What evolved from a 'gradual accretion of common policies and standards' is a system of bureaucratic linkages. The form of incremental integration 'by stealth' this might advance bolsters the pejorative claim of European governance becoming the province of unelected, unseen bureaucrats. Delors recognised this deficiency and image problem for the EU institutions. His declaration that the 'phase of benign despotism is now over' was in reference to the bureaucracy rather than national political elites.[76] Even a 'parliamentarization of the Brussels expertocracy' would not overcome national biases within it.[77]

Although its precedence is now diminished, France was the most successful manipulator of European institutions for national purposes. One expose of the Commission's inner workings concerned a miscellany of French technocrats, including Delors, seeking to exempt the European electronics industry from a potentially harsh free market as determined under EU competition policy. The principal reason was that major French public companies were under threat. Like other intrigues it involved a complex of interests and deal-making.[78] For Delors to advance his European vision he needed French domestic support including that of the public sector. The various cabinets, usually dominated by top level staff hailing from the same state as the Commissioner, rarely act against the national interest, however they might perceive it.[79] Following Delors' philosophical lead, the *Militantisme* and/or 'Frenchness' of his cabinet sought to impose a particular

	Oxford University Press 1992) pp64-90, p70; Rory Watson "Big two split on top EC jobs" & "Stars gather in the firmament" *The European* 19-8-94 p1 & p8
75	Peter Ludlow "The European Commission" in *The New European Community: Decisionmaking and Institutional Change* pp85-132
76	Brigitte Boyce "The Democratic deficit of the European Commission" *Parliamentary Affairs* v46 n4 1993 pp458-477; Kevin Featherstone "Jean Monnet and the 'Democratic Deficit' in the EU" *Journal of Common Market Studies* v32 n2 1994 pp149-171, p151; Dominique Bocquet "Democractic Deficit" *American Enterprise* May/June 1993 pp56-63; Hancock & Peters "The European Community" pp461-474
77	Habermas "Citizenship and National Identity" p9
78	Cf. *Privatizations in Europe* Ed. Vincent Wright (London: Pinter 1994) especially Hervé Dumez & Alain Jeunemaître "Privatizations in France (1983-1993)"
79	George Ross "Sidling into Industrial Policy: Inside the European Commission" *French Politics and Society* v11 n1 1993 pp20-44

intellectual *projet* onto Commission proceedings and its 'life' in general.[80] Concurrently, a relatively low level of French industry representation in Brussels was due to the belief that the city was, from the genesis of the European institutions, a centre for the advancement of French interests and that this would continue to occur automatically. Contrasting the French position with the British, Roy Denman notes that when Delors arrived in 1982 'the French had a major influence in the Commission. By the time he left, in 1992, they had a stranglehold.' In this period many top officials were sacked or left before being 'pushed'. 'In almost all cases their fault had been to voice reservations about Delors policies or French interests'. In 1989, in order to balance what suddenly became excessive German influence in the Directorate of External Relations, a 'new (French) Deputy Director General' for Eastern Europe was 'imported' as a *Homme de confiance*.[81] Geo-political change, later exacerbated by Delors' departure, has required a rethink about lobbying at the strategic heart of the 'European administrative environment'.[82]

The emergence of the European Court of Justice as a legal power challenging and even superseding the national courts has altered the political game—to an extent. Most of the cases in which it is called on to arbitrate are internal to one member state and the area of authority is almost entirely

---

80 George Ross "Inside the Delors Cabinet" *Journal of Common Market Studies* v32 n1 1994 pp499-523

81 Roy Denman *Missed Chances: Britain and Europe in the Twentieth Century* (London: Cassell 1996) p277-278

82 *The European Challenges Post-1992: Shaping Factors, Shaping Actors* Eds. Alexis Jaquemin & David Wright (Aldershot: Edward Elgar 1993) pp227-228. Other perspectives on Delors see him, along with Helmut Kohl and a sufficiently agreeable François Mitterrand, as having 'transformed the EEC from a bureaucratic snail to a very fast train'. See Papcke "Who Needs European Identity..?" p66. Until his withdrawal from the 1995 French presidential election, Delors had great influence over European politics. Somewhat ironically, he also personified the power of national politics despite, and even because of, his declared non-candidacy. Erstwhile socialist defence minister Jean-Pierre Chevènement termed his former colleague the 'candidate of the German CDU'. Moisi & Mertes "Europe's Map, Compass and Horizon". See also Helen Drake "Political Leadership and European Integration: The Case of Jacques Delors" *West European Politics* v18 n1 Jan 1995 pp140-160; Jacques Delors *Le Nouveau Concert Européen* (Paris: Editions Odile Jacob 1992); Vivien A. Schmidt's point about the French thinking that a phone call to Delors could solve French problems indicates both the belief in his influence on France's behalf and impresses the void now that this is no longer possible. "Loosening the Ties that Bind: The Impact of European Integration on French Government and its Relationship to Business" *Journal of Common Market Studies* v34 n2 1996 pp223-253

commercially orientated with some competences in environmental and social policy. Parochialism or partisan decision-making does not duplicate that of politicians or bureaucrats. Nonetheless 'national legal actors did not appear particularly interested in legal integration per se, indeed in interviews European lawyers and judges said they were not especially interested in the goal of promoting European integration nor did they see themselves as Community judges.' The EJC's neutrality begs the question how and when the *political power* it now apparently possessed would be used.[83] Meanwhile national ministers and bureaucrats continue to ignore various EU legislation and concoct their own.[84] Keohane confirms (even with the broadening of a European judicial space) the continued existence of a more recognised political power over vital national interests within the international system, otherwise known as state sovereignty. This particular 'legal authority', which does not exist elsewhere, is transformed into a 'bargaining resource'.[85]

For governments, domestic factors become influential at interstate level through the perceived success or otherwise of their implementation among the electorate. Potentially they determine the survival in office of the executive. These political leaders overwhelmingly, if not exclusively, belong to the cultural heritage predominating among the citizens they represent. The first point is consistent with Robert Putnam's schema of intergovernmental level bargaining being also conducted by the same political group at a domestic level and so disposing of a mutual influence.[86] The second has a more personal significance stemming from experience of a particular history and culture. This was articulated by Roman Herzog when he stated that

> everyone knows how difficult it is for the political elites of the European capitals to change their thought patterns. Everyone knows that bound with these thought patterns there is always a piece of the collective national consciousness. Everyone knows, finally, that the competition of the national capitals for influence in Brussels is sometimes also a competition of national vanities.[87]

---

83   Cf. Karen J. Alter "The European Court's Political Power" *West European Politics* v19 n3 1996 pp458-487; Mann "Nation-States in Europe and Other Continents..." p122

84   Sarah Helm "Report challenges EU's hidden deals" *Independent* 23-6-95 p13

85   Robert Keohane "Hobbes Dilemma and Institutional Change in World Politics: Sovereignty in International Society" in *Whose World Order: Uneven Globalization and the End of the Cold War* Eds. Hans-Hendrik Holm and Georg Sørensen (Boulder: Westview 1994)

86   Robert D. Putnam "Diplomacy and Domestic Politics: The Logic of Two Level Games" *International Organization* v42 n3 1988 pp427-460.

87   Roman Herzog "Die Globalisierung der deutschen Außenpolitik ist unvermeidlich" *Bulletin* 15-3-95 'Jeder weiß, wie schwer es den politischen

EMU and political unity

The three pillar structure of the TEU placed the first within the parameters of Community competence, leaving the second, the CFSP, and the third, Justice and Home Affairs, intergovernmental. The latter has been most resistant to supranational incursions and will remain so while the feasibility of successfully operating the other two under different authorities is uncertain at best. 'Pure' financial management is only part of the EMU project. The building of a supranational political structure in Europe is presently dependent on EMU as its spearhead. Introducing irrevocably fixed exchange rates specified in Stage 3 of the Delors Report will inevitably provoke dissatisfaction in the process of setting particular rates for different states, while difficulties in sticking to a timetable have been a feature of the process. Of the ERM crisis, Kohl had said it did not mean the end of the Maastricht Treaty. 'If it means the timetable is postponed by one or two years, what does that change?' he asked.[88] Rudolf Augstein later claimed 'hardly anyone half-responsible in economic and financial circles still believes in a definite date to begin the European currency union, even if those responsible in Brussels, Paris and even on the Rhine still loudly call "forwards"'.[89] The proposed 1994 date for beginning Stage 3, without British involvement, was changed to 1997. This was abandoned on the eve of the Cannes summit and moved to 1999. It may yet be postponed indefinitely. While this served the purposes of the British government, Waigel's remark that eliminating the earlier target would 'contribute to the credibility of monetary union' was also interpreted as a 'clear cut victory for Germany'.[90] Regardless of nominal agreements in proposing timetables, there has been no handover of control.[91] Hans Arnold

---

Eliten der Hauptstädte Europas fällt, ihre Denkmuster zu verändern. Jeder weiß, daß mit diesen Denkmustern auch immer ein Stück Einfluß auf das kollektive nationale Bewußtsein verbunden ist. Jeder weiß schließlich, daß der Wettbewerb der nationalen Hauptstädte um Einfluß auf Brüssel manchmal auch ein Wettbewerb der nationalen Eitelkeiten ist.'

88   "Kohl says Union has been put back Years" *The European* 13-8-93 p13
89   Rudolf Augstein "Maastricht—eine Fehlregelung?" *Der Spiegel* n13 27-3-95 p21 'Kaum jemand Halbverantwortlicher in Wirtschafts- und Finanzkreisen glaubt noch an einen fest datierbaren Beginn der Europäischen Währungsunion, mögen auch die Verantwortlichen in Brüssel, Paris und sogar am Rhein noch so laut "avanti" rufen.'; Cf. Rudi Dornbusch "Euro Fantasies" *Foreign Affairs* v75 n5 1996 pp116-124
90   Tom Buerkle "1997 Target For a Single EU Currency Is Ruled Out" *International Herald Tribune* 20-6-95 p1; George Brock & Philip Webster "Euro money is delayed by ministers" *The Times* 20-6-95 p1
91   Brian Tew "Onwards to EMU" in *The Single European Market and Beyond: A Study of the Wider Implications of the Single European Act* Ed. Dennis Swann

has noted that 'even the third stage of the EMU envisaged in the Treaty of Maastricht does not lead to an irreversible development...'

> In principle, therefore, every EC member state can pull out of the EC. Second, the EMU in particular shows that the Treaty of Maastricht cannot lead to the generally envisaged goal to the full and indissoluble integration of the twelve EC states. For it has one major shortcoming.[92]

That shortcoming being the absence of a parallel political union, necessary to legally and institutionally bolster what is intrinsically political— control over monetary affairs, which have a pervasive influence on virtually all areas of a national polity, a scenario transposed on to a European scale in the event of EMU being implemented. As Arnold continues '"Hard" restrictions on sovereignty in the foreign, security and monetary policy fields cannot be achieved selectively and gradually, but, if at all, only jointly and simultaneously, as a complete relinquishment of national sovereignty.'

> A common Western European currency with a common fiscal, money supply and exchange-rate policy, but at the same time a national *force de frappe*, national Falklands/Malvinas policy, and national social insurance system just cannot work.[93]

A common currency without a common foreign and security policy is indeed hazardous. 'European Political Cooperation' itself indicated the existence of independent actors who may, or may not, cooperate. It was a 'procedure totally dependent on consensus which regarded the communautaire method of majority voting as an anathema to national sovereignty...dictated by an intergovernmental rather than by a supranational perspective.'[94] Progressing to a CFSP was intended to strengthen the concept. Changing the wording or the acronyms has not solved the basic predicament. It remained an intergovernmental pillar separate from the revision of previous agreements and Article 224 of the Treaty of Rome still confers on the

---

(Routledge: London 1992) pp193-213; Kenneth Dyson *Elusive Union: The Process of Economic and Monetary Union in Europe* (London: Longman 1994); Sandholtz "Choosing Union..."; Wynne Godley "Derailed" *London Review of Books* 19-8-93 p9; See also transcripts of statments from *Wirtschaftstag '96* "Politische Union und Gemeinsamer Markt" at the Maritim Hotel, Bonn, 13-6-96

92   Hans Arnold ""Maastricht" - The Beginning or the end of a Development? " *Aussenpolitik* v44 n3 1993 pp271-280, p278

93   ibid. p278

94   Holland *European Community Integration* Chapter five "Creating a common foreign policy" See p119

member states authority in issues of national security. Those states favouring the *status quo ante* could not too disturbed by the Maastricht outcome.

> In the machinery in the Communities for defining and managing a common foreign policy, it was clear that what was likely to emerge for the foreseeable future was not a common European foreign policy, or, indeed, a coordinated foreign policy in the technical sense, but rather a policy made by harmonizing the various separate interests of the member states. A balance was to be struck between using membership in the Community to promote the separate interests of each individual state, as with Britain and the Commonwealth, or France and the Francophone states, or even Britain and the US, and the maintenance of the appearance of the potential for common action. It was paradoxical that the latter had to be convincing in order to preserve the capacity for individual action, and a continuing investment in the common enterprise was, therefore, necessary.[95]

Maintaining the sort of external activity deriving from the Lomé agreements and various developmental promotions had its contentions over distribution preferences but this paled in comparison to new foreign policy challenges appearing in the 1990s. Reinhard Rummel has written that 'demands on Western Europe are those of a superpower', after the Cold War it was 'an international actor exposed to the "real world" and put to the test in a fluid and demanding context.'[96] When decisive common action has been called for, breakdown and or inefficiency reveals a fairweather community with a distinct 'infirmity in matters of life and death'.[97] Apart from the Balkans, inability to prevent the Chechnyan or Moldavian disasters, and a continued reliance on the US impressed a lack of cohesion and authority. Pfaff claims that finding a 'common external policy of any consequence' for perhaps 20 or 25 member states 'is clearly impossible' and that differences in external roles, alliances and interests were the cause of EC policy regarding the former Yugoslavia ending in an 'institutionalized stalemate'. The imbroglio emphasised how unwilling foreign ministries were to disengage from other perceived national interests even though (or because) it had the effect of 'inhibiting of individual national action and rationalizing the refusal to

---

95   Taylor *International Organization in the Modern World* p95

96   Reinhardt Rummel "West European Cooperation in Foreign and Security Policy" *Annals of the American Academy of Political Science* January 1994 pp112-123

97   David Buchan *Europe. The Strange Superpower* (Aldershot: Dartmouth 1993) pp43-54

act nationally.'[98] Ponderous institutional tinkering and the use of leverage here to advance there exposed the variance between diplomacy and foreign policy. Carnage continued until the decisive response in late summer 1995. The US reimpressed itself as a supranational authority over European internal affairs, the hegemon after hegemony. It coincided with 'management' of the conflict effectively being transferred from UN auspices, with an effective EU nowhere in sight, to the US led NATO. It illuminated the prescience in Paul Valéry's 1927 assertion that 'Europe visibly aspires to be governed by an American commission. Its entire policy is directed to that end. Not knowing how to rid ourselves of our history, we will be relieved of it by a fortunate people who have almost none. They are a happy people and they will force their happiness on us.'[99]

Following the rejection of similar German initiatives some years earlier, Chirac's proposal of a foreign policy 'czar' and nomination of Giscard d'Estaing for the job as Europe's one voice in event of foreign policy crises received a lukewarm response. David Allen summarises the EU's difficulties in reaching agreement and encapsulates why institutionalists cannot discard the persistence of separate states pursuing autonomous existences, none of whom 'with the possible exceptions of Belgium and Luxembourg, is, as yet, prepared to commit suicide by agreeing to the establishment of a government, as opposed to governance, at the European level'. Therefore 'it is hard to see how the CFSP can develop beyond the ceiling that it has already reached.' Allen goes on to say 'the realists are probably wrong when they pessimistically anticipate the collapse of all the institutionalized arrangements...but it is excessively optimistic to believe that the current level of institutionalization, which allows for the parallel pursuit of national foreign policies can develop much further.'[100] And this despite most European citizens in most European states placing foreign and security policy high on the list of areas for communal action, at least as far as they understand what the latter means. Implementing a single currency while sustaining a role as a distinctly ambiguous power is not a combination to inspire confidence among governments or populations.[101]

---

98   Pfaff *The Furies of Nationalism* pp211-219. Public opinion in several EU countries had come to favour military intervention by 1992-3, including the UK 60% and France 59%. See *Financial Times* 25-5-93

99   Paul Valéry *Selected Writings* (New York: New Directions 1964) p133

100   David Allen "Conclusions: The European Rescue of national foreign policy?" in *The Actors in Europe's Foreign Policy* Ed. Christopher Hill (London: Routledge 1996) pp288-304

101   Curt Gasteyger *An Ambiguous Power: The European Union in a Changing World* (Gütersloh: Bertelsmann 1996)

A European Polity?: Federalism, Parliaments and the 'Democratic Deficit'

Some years ago Max Beloff wrote that 'No group of historic nations has ever come together voluntarily to form a federation', Switzerland, America, Canada, Australia, 'were never nations in the sense that Britain, France, Germany or Italy are nations...and the world scene is littered with federations that have collapsed.'[102] The only practical examples of federalism are those provided by recognised states. A continued 'pooling' of sovereignty, constitutes 'proactive formal integration' with its 'deliberate and explicit political aim'. It also points at evolution towards a European state. The definition of federalism at work here is that of 'classical constitutional law':

> 1. The existence of common institutional mechanisms in which the member states participate, the decisions of which are made by majority vote rather than unanimity, which could have the effect of transforming the federation into a confederation.
> 2. The transfer of a certain number of internal powers to the federal government, member states preserving the right to exercise non-transferred powers.
> 3. The exercise of the external powers of the federal state by one federal government only.[103]

Such an entity would approximate the German system more than any other member, providing a replication of the Bundestag by the European Parliament and the Bundesrat by the European Council.[104] Weeks after the publication of the CDU-CSU *Kerneuropa* paper,[105] the European Peoples Party released a document which reiterated both the expanding gap in member states' conceptions and the Schäuble-Lamers propositions to overcome this. According to EPP President Wilfred Martens *'Die Frage von Wolfgang Schäuble, aber auch meine Frage lautet: Wie können wir die Dynamik des europäischen Einigungsprozesses im Blick auf die Regierungskonferenz 1996 erhalten, wenn die Integrationsbereitschaft zwischen den Mitgliedsstaaten offentsichtlich weit auseinandergeht?'*. The paper continued that 'it is time

---

102   Max Beloff *The Future of British Foreign Policy* (London: Secker & Warburg: 1969) p111
103   Jaqueline Dutheil de la Rochère "Toward a Federal Europe" in, *The European Community in the 1990s* pp3-16
104   Cf. Fritz W. Scharpf "The Joint-Decision Trap: Lessons From German Federalism and European Integration" *Public Administration* v66 Autumn 1988 pp239-278
105   *Überlegungen zur europäischen Politik* (Bonn: CDU 1994)

dass sich die Verfechter eines föderalen Europa zu Wort melden und wieder in die Offensive gehen...wenn zum Beispiel die föderalistische Idee der Grundväter der Europäische Union in diesen Tagen für durch die Zeit überholt erklärt wird, so trifft dies auf meinen entschiedenen Widerspruch. Umständliche zwischenstaatliche Zusammenarbeit ist eine der Hauptursachen für langwierige Entscheidungsprozesse und Ineffizienz.[106]

Pressured by the *Länder* to ensure their undiminished viability, the Kohl government continued its advocacy of greater powers for the European Parliament. The increase in Germany's quota of representatives from 81 to 99 is accompanied by the tacit assumption that these members will act in the *German interest*, or are at least more likely to than any others. If they were not then why push for greater representation?[107] Through simple arithmetic such a scenario favours Germany in terms of European decision-making. Of course there is no guarantee that sufficient EP members would vote in a manner that obviously benefits Germany, or at least benefits it more than the constituencies those members represent. Nonetheless, as Ulf Hedetoft states, 'it is evident that those nations most in favour of giving further powers to the EP are those whose national interests would be best furthered in this way. Hence, Germany is in favour of giving the Parliament further powers while France is opposed. No member state, however, would dream of treating the EP as a national parliament, let alone give it corresponding powers'.[108] Unless, that is, they were confident of gaining desired results. French opposition is conditioned by perceptions that voting propensities may make many if not 'all the qualified majorities German'.[109]

106	Wilfred Martens *Vertiefung und Erweiterung: Eine Strategie fuer die Europaeische Union* Brussels 20-9-94
107	Klaus Kinkel "Deutschland in Europa: Zu den Zielen der deutschen Präsidentschaft in der Europäischen Union" *Europa-Archiv* Folge 12/1994 pp335-342
108	Ulf Hedetoft "The State of Sovereignty in Europe: Political Concept or Cultural Self-Image" in *National Cultures and European Integration: Exploratory Essays on Cultural Diversity and Common Policies* Ed. Staffan Zetterholm (Oxford: Berg 1994) pp13-48, see pp33-34. Hedetoft employs the terms 'nation' and 'national interest' as coterminus; i.e. both being formed and residing in individual national states
109	Marie-France Garaud *Le Monde* 15-4-92, quoted in Patrick McCarthy "France Looks at Germany, or How to Become German (and European) while Remaining French" in *France and Germany 1983-1993: The Struggle to Cooperate* Ed. Patrick McCarthy (New York: St.Martin's Press 1993) pp51-72, p68

Michael Greven has put it that 'like almost all other actors on the European level, the parties and their members still act as nationalists'. In the late 1980s a majority of West German EP members rated 'national egoism' as the main reason for 'intrafactional dissent.'[110] The 'pro-European' parties still promote interests of their own nation before others while domestic politics has much greater import than wider European concerns. There are strategic changes occurring. Greven continues that 'for the national political parties a clear logic of political action and judgement' had caused a 'neglect of the European dimension' but that the 'direct election of the EP forces parties...to create a European infrastructure.' The Germans, in particular, came to see the European Parliament as providing a forum which, if national parties continued to ignore it, could imperil them and so required organization on the European level. This would be unlikely to replace the primacy of national concerns but would expand the parties' involvement in Europe as a way to advance nationally. All parties must act or be perceived as acting in the interests of their constituents first and linkages between party, state and nation remain strong in the institution intended to dissolve them. And so 'democracy on a European level turns out to be a complete failure...because parties on the European level predominantly or almost exclusively act as national actors or, to put it more precisely, as actors of their respective national party systems.'[111]

Stanley Hoffmann later declared that 'there still is no European political process, if one means thereby a transnational set of parties and elections of European rather than of national delegates to a common assembly'.[112] A more intensive study by Simon Hix also demonstrates that 'national-territorial identities' among parties in the EU have still not 'transplanted transnational socio-economic identities'.[113] The relation of the three social-democratic oppositions in Britain, France and the Federal Republic to the respective government positions reflected national rather than ideological orientations. At a gathering of socialist and social-democratic parties coinciding with the December 1994 Essen summit the French socialists pushed for delaying eastern enlargement while the SPD advocated

---

110   Greven "Political Parties Between National Identity and Eurofication" fn54. The lucrative aspect and the order of importance attached to the European election by the (West) German political parties were revealed by (successful) attempts to save money from allocations through the federal budget for the 1989 European Parliament vote, for use in the 1990 national election campaign

111   Greven "Political Parties Between National Identity and Eurofication"

112   Stanley Hoffmann "Europe's Identity Crisis Revisited" *Dædelus* v123 n2 1993 pp1-23, p19

113   Simon Hix "Parties at the European Level and the Legitimacy of EU Socio-Economic Policy" *Journal of Common Market Studies* v33 n4 1995 pp527-553

precisely the opposite. Britain's Labour Party meanwhile 'vetoed' the inclusion of a non-veto clause in a draft agenda of common policy on Europe.[114]

Arguments over adjusting the representative quotas of the states to more accurately reflect population changes again exposes the frailty of a common European ideal. If MEPs are there to represent Europe as a whole, all its nations, states and regions, why should it matter from whence they came? Although all states may benefit, the EP is not a locus for a pooling of democratic sovereignty with the result that all will carry equal influence. 'What is the logic' asked Holland, 'behind having national quotas and national-based elections for the European Parliament; a federal integrated Community ought to adopt electoral characteristics that reflect the unicity (sic) of the European electorate, not reinforce the image of intergovernmentalism through national quotas and electoral laws.' The 'logic' is very simple. It's motivation is the same as having one's own nationals in important Commission positions or in other international institutions. Or in determining the direction and the pursuance of aims while incumbent in the Council Presidency, where 'depending on the political objectives of each member state...Community integration can be advanced or retarded.'[115]

Changes introduced to EP-Council relations at Maastricht meant that states opposing a proposal and outvoted by QMV could 'seek to mobilize opposition in the European Parliament in order to create a majority of members against its acceptance there'. This would require transnational agreement among MEPs when national parties want a 'towing of the party line'. Such activity 'would tend to weaken the development of European parties, despite the lip service paid to this' demonstrating 'another instance of a well-established doctrine about the development of the European Communities: that apparent concessions to supranationalism were more likely when intergovernmentalism had been bolstered'.[116] This particular situation is not as politically sensitive as greater weighting in the Council of Ministers, (or European Council) would be and for which Germany did not initially request a similar increase.[117] Imbalance in this more powerful forum suggests a more accurate population-voting power ratio is needed. If a definitive breakthrough

---

114   Christopher Parkes "Britain's Labour Party says no to 'no veto'" *Financial Times* 9-12-94 p1; In France in 1981 33% of poll respondents thought a left-right distinction was inconsequential to party platforms and individual politician's allegiances. In 1991 the figure had increased to 55%. See *The European Challenges Post-1992* p220

115   Holland *European Community Integration* p102

116   Taylor *International Organization in the Modern World* p102

117   David Spence "The European Community and German Unification" *German Politics* v1 n3 1992 pp136-163, pp143-144

to a political system satisfactory to Germany occurred this may not become a major controversy. If this does not transpire Germany has grounds to demand more votes in the Council.

With 'deep cultural forces' at work, none of the national parliaments wish to be deprived of their powers and publics remain citizens, or residents, of their respective states. Their effect on decision-making at Union level is through domestic influence on national representation.[118] Democratising Europe through increasing the powers of the European Parliament has not exceeded its rights to 'consultation', scrutiny and censure, and 'vetting of appointments'. The parliament does not supersede states in the Council nor the Council majority that of the veto employed by one state.[119] On the European level 'democratic processes that have gone hand in hand with the nation state lag hopelessly behind the supranational form taken by economic integration'.[120] What a 'transnational' form of democracy would entail is the tangible political direction over what are sovereign entities by the electors and executives of others. States whose political representatives envisage a national interest in maintaining an aura of bureaucratic remoteness around the Commission continue to do so. Thus Philippe Seguin reiterated the reproach by British conservatives against an 'undemocratic' supranationalism accumulating areas previously under state authority.[121] These expressions of aversion to Brussels' 'democratic deficit' are actually attempts to avoid transnational democratisation which threatens to impinge on state sovereignty by, in effect, claiming a monopoly of democracy. What is really opposed is increased measures of external control and so 'states may well resist any move towards the democratisation of the common regional system if such a process is perceived as entailing risks for their individual capacities to exercise their national sovereign rights'. This means then that 'the common regional

---

118   Martin Westlake "The European Parliament, the National Parliaments and the 1996 Intergovernmental Conference" *Political Quarterly* v66 n1 1995 pp59-73; *The 1996 Intergovernmental Conference: The Agenda; Democracy and Efficiency; The Role of National Parliaments* Twenty Fourth Report, Volume 1, Select Committee on European Legislation, Session 1994-95 (London: HMSO 1995)

119   See Francis Jacobs, Richard Corbett & Michael Shackelton *The European Parliament* (Harlow: Longman 1990); "Draft Interinstitutional Agreement Between the European Parliament, the Council and the Commission on The Rules for Exercising the Powers to Implement Acts Adopted jointly by the European Parliament and the Council" (Brussels: 19-4-94)

120   Jürgen Habermas "Citizenship and National Identity: Some reflections on the future of Europe" *Praxis International* v12 n1 1992 pp1-19

121   *Le Monde* 6-2-93 quoted in Kevin Featherstone "Jean Monnet and the 'Democratic Deficit' in the EU" *Journal of Common Market Studies* v32 n2 1994 pp149-171, p150

system has often come to resemble the traditional international relations model which is essentially dominated by raison d'etat and 'power politics'

> ...the main source of democratic legitimacy for EU decisions seems to be lying more in the Council of Ministers' representation of national governments—in turn based on their respective national parliamentary structures —than on the powers of the EP as the natural exponent of representative democracy at the regional level.[122]

Another commentator advised, 'Rather than staking everything on a build-up of the European Parliament's authority, it would be wiser to work for more serious treatment of European issues within the national democracies themselves.'[123] For many of the general public the cloudy European institutional system makes it difficult to decipher where 'deficits', 'control', 'responsibility' or 'democracy' lie, or who assists or deters it. Illusory or complacent assumptions held by the Commission, and backed by its own research, that national publics were in favour of continuous integration were upset[124] as it was demonstrated again that 'although nothing seems to change on the surface, the preparedness to go supranational decreases as soon as it becomes imaginable and phrased in everyday terms'.[125] The sovereign institutional focus necessary to maintain democratic underpinnings to Europeanized political structures is absent because most Europeans do not want it. Their political attachments are elsewhere.

> Given that the role of the citizen has hitherto only been institutionalized at the level of nation-states, citizens have no effective

---

122 Chryssochoou "Democracy and Symbiosis"; Cf. Karlheinz Neunreither "The Democratic Deficit of the European Union: Towards Closer Cooperation between the European Parliament and the National Parliaments" *Government and Opposition* v29 n3 1994 pp299-314

123 Dominique Bocquet "Democractic Deficit" *American Enterprise* May/June 1993 pp56-63

124 Mark Franklin, Michael Marsh & Lauren McLaren "Uncorking the Bottle: Popular Opposition to European Unification in the Wake of Maastricht" *Journal of Common Market Studies* v32 n4 1994 pp455-472; Richard C. Eichenberg & Russell J. Dalton "Europeans and the European Community: the dynamics of public support for European integration" *International Organization* v47 n4 1993 pp507-534

125 Elisabeth Noelle-Neumann "Phantom Europe: thirty years of survey research on German attitudes toward European integration" in *Contemporary Perspectives on European Integration* Ed. L. Hurwitz (Westport: Greenwood 1980) quoted in Simon Bulmer & William Paterson *The Federal Republic of Germany and the European Community* (London: Allen & Unwin 1987) p115

means of debating European decisions and influencing the decision-making processes. M. R. Lepsius terse statement sums it up: "There is no European public opinion.[126]

Regionalism has been forwarded as a means to bring Europe together by, effectively, splitting it up. The extent to which smaller regions can operate independently, potentially conducting their own political, economic-monetary, security and foreign policy regimes, is limited to say the least. Thus 'one of the arguments made by small states such as Belgium and the Netherlands for joining the EC was precisely the need to join a larger unit of power because as small, separate states they had so little control over events that influenced them.'[127] As well as extending particular hopes to 'subnational' populations, for smaller or poorer members the EU promises benefits beyond their own capabilities and has shaped their attitudes in ways different to the larger net contributors. Broadly the Benelux countries share pro-federal viewpoints and smaller states may be better able to 'define the European public good'.[128] Less influential positions means their status internationally is enhanced in a larger political system of merged sovereignties. Conversely they may be little more than satellites, amenable to larger members. Of these, the UK and France had not followed the German Federation-Länder 1993 agreement on regionally driven integration. At the time only Belgium had indicated similar intentions.[129]

Interesting cases are provided by the Dutch and Danes. The Netherlands led the rejected federalist push at Maastricht and its status as a creditor to the EU budget, its cosmopolitan liberal society, possession of a hard currency, low unemployment rates, and a favourable trade balance, including a surplus with Germany, all make it a favourable candidate for political union. Yet at a social or emotional level the relationship with its large neighbour is cordial at best. Resilient wartime memories and referents, Ruud Lubbers' opposition to German reunification and simmering feud with Kohl, a sporting rivalry extending to spectator violence, and a general disinclination

---

126   Habermas "Citizenship and National Identity" p9; Julie Smith "The 1994 European Elections: Twelve into One Won't Go" *West European Politics* v18 n3 1995 pp199-217 presents a similar view

127   Paul Kennedy "Germany in Europe; Half a Hegemon" *New Perspectives Quarterly* v10 n1 1993 pp35-38; Miriam Fendius Elman "The Foreign Policies of Small States: Challenging Neorealism in its Own Backyard" *British Journal of Political Science* v25 n2 1995 pp171-217; Teresa de Sousa "Die kleinen Länder fürchten um ihren Einfluß" *Die Zeit* 9-8-96 p8

128   *The European Challenges Post-1992* p106

129   Franz H. U. Borkenhagen "Regions in Europe" *Aussenpolitik* v45 n2 1994 pp182-188; Leopold Carrewyn "Belgium and German Policy on Europe" *Aussenpolitik* v46 n3 1995 pp220-22

to the economic ownership (or even presence) of Germans in Holland indicate that this partnership is not one of mutual affinity.[130] Denmark is the most conspicuous 'small state' proponent of national autonomy and has shown affinity with the British in opposing a Franco-German duopoly or other hegemonic tendencies. Proximity to an expanded Germany has provided a cogent stimulus to the assertion of Danish independence. Denmark remains outside the single currency provisions.[131]

A 'European polity model' had been put forward as an analytical tool in the 1970s and it was then, and still is, unable to detach itself from national loyalties and the state system.[132] Although consistent intransigence was likely

130   On German-Dutch relations see Dirk Verheyen "The Dutch and the Germans" in *The Germans and their Neighbours* Eds. Dirk Verheyen & Christian Søe (Boulder: Westview 1993); Friso Wielinga "The German Factor in Dutch Foreign Policy since 1945" in *German Monitor* n37 1996 pp133-155; Jill Robinson "Anniversaries, Memory and the Neighbours: The 'German Question' in Recent History" *German Politics* v5 n1 1996 pp43-57; Maarten van Traa "Wohlbekannt aber ungeliebt? Der deutsche Nachbar aus niederländischer Sicht" *Europa Archiv* v49 n17 1994 pp491-498

131   Danish or Denmark-based scholars and research institutions are at the forefront of a burgeoning field of inquiry into the interplay of culture-identity-politics at regional-national-European levels. See *National Cultures and European Integration: Exploratory Essays on Cultural Diversity and Common Policies* Ed. Staffan Zetterholm (Oxford: Berg 1994); *Identity, Migration and the New Security Agenda in Europe* Eds. Ole Wæver, Barry Buzan, Morten Kelstrup and Pierre Lemaitre (London: Pinter 1993); *European Integration and Denmark's Participation* Ed. Morten Kelstrup (Copenhagen: Political Studies Press 1992); Barry Buzan *People, States and Fear: An Agenda for International Security Studies in the Post-Cold War Period* Second Edition (Brighton: Harvester Wheatsheaf 1991); Ole Wæver "Identity, Integration and Security: Solving the Sovereignty Puzzle in E.U. Studies" *Journal of International Affairs* v48 n2 Winter 1995 pp389-431; Ole Wæver "European Security Identities" *Journal of Common Market Studies* v34 n1 1996 pp103-132. Here Wæver asserts that as states disconnect from nations 'culture has become security policy'. See also the critical review of this school by Bill McSweeny "Identity and Security: Buzan and the Copenhagen school" *Review of International Studies* v22 1996 pp81-93. On the Germany issue see Hedetoft "The State of Sovereignty in Europe..." pp38-41; *Identity, Migration...* Eds. Wæver et. al. p70; Barbara Lippert & Rosalind Stevens-Ströhmann *German Unification and EC Integration: German and British Perspectives* (London: Pinter 1993) pp130-133

132   Leon N. Lindberg & Stuart A. Scheingold *Europe's Would-Be Polity* (Englewood Cliffs: Prentice-Hall 1970); Martin O. Heisler & Robert B. Kravik "Patterns of European Politics: The 'European Polity' Model" in *Politics in Europe: Structure and Processes in Some Postindustrial Democracies* (New York: David McKay 1974)

reduce their ability to shape policies or a general direction, 'nation-states within the EC would almost certainly would never be excluded from the participation in the same way that interest groups might be in a single nation'.[133] Members have been encouraged to reach agreement on one issue or risk negative outcomes on others. The results of compromise bargaining may not precisely reflect the desires of any national electorate. However, it mirrors the balancing of interests necessary for political survival in western democratic polities and 'it may be that policy making in the EC oscillates between large-scale politics and small-scale increments of regulation, and that no single model is able to capture the totality of motives and processes involved in building Europe.'[134] The EU is an agglomeration of national polities of varying capacities and not a single polity. Grahame Thompson has pointed out that 'States differ massively in size, and the categories 'nation state' and 'region' have no ultimate coherence...Bavaria is a 'region' but could easily be a 'state'.' Subsidiarity may well lead to an assortment of political units more clearly delineated as weak or strong. Thompson argues 'the danger is that a 'Europe of the regions' will not emerge because of an equitable balance of power between federal, national and regional levels, but because of the reverse'.[135] Other evaluations implying that Europe is fragmenting into regions independent of central questions of defence, taxation, and foreign policy, still conclude that the 'nation-state is not going anywhere soon'.[136]

Renaud Dehousse's analysis of the EC's 1990s 'legitimacy crisis' cites several forms of 'deficit' including those of democracy, accountability, transparency, and political. And this is without leaving the 'Community pillar' for more ambitious policy fields. The root of the problem is that 'the Community is an extremely diverse gathering—it will be even more so after enlargement—in which national traditions remain very strong.'

> In a world where economic and technical transformations have strong centripetal effects, this diversity can be a precious asset, as long as it does not result in boundless competition among states. One of the

133   Hancock & Peters "The European Community" pp514-516; Moravscik "Single European Act"
134   Hancock & Peters "The European Community" p516
135   Thompson *The Economic Emergence of a New Europe?*... pp199-201; Kees van Kersbergen & Bertjan Verbeek "The Politics of Subsidiarity in the European Union" *Journal of Common Market Studies* v32 n2 1994 pp215-237; Alan James "The equality of states: contemporary manifestations of an ancient doctrine" *Review of International Studies* v18 1992 pp377-91 The author makes the points of states having 'equal status not stature' and 'equal states with unequal powers'
136   John Newhouse "Europe's Rising Regionalism" *Foreign Affairs* v76 n1 1996 pp67-84

Community's historical missions is to allow the peaceful coexistence of different national models. Moreover, states still enjoy a primary allegiance in national politics. The Community will only be able to consolidate its own authority if it shows sufficient respect for states, and for national specificities.[137]

What this indicates is that whatever the next phase of European politics, France, Britain and Germany will remain prominent as distinct political entities and relate to each other as such. How they manage it is another question.

---

137   Renaud Dehousse "Constitutional Reform in the European Community: Are there Alternatives to the Majoritarian Avenue?" *West European Politics* v18 n3 1995 pp118-36. See especially p131. 'EC' is considered here as a part of and not the entire EU although many of the problems extend past what is often an ambiguous divide, for instance when institutional competences change but personalities, governments, or nations do not

Conclusion

This book has argued that through the 1990s tensions between European integration and the preservation of national specificities and autonomy have moved towards the latter. Germany's new authority, and perceptions about it, is a critical factor in influencing these developments. Changes occuring in the decade have begun to reflect German preferences more than any other EU member state, and in all likelihood will continue to do so, even if stopping short of a supranational union. Conversely, the political class of Germany's main partner, France, is resistant to intra-European dynamics that cannot be steered by French-led institutions.

The predominant French conception of 'political Europe' contains a core contradiction in the relation between independence and integration. France is a pertinent example of nations as being not only repositories of culture but persisting as the primary loci for political allegiances in post-cold war Europe. Politics and culture remain connected in the form of nation-states because these entities provide as yet irreplaceable identifications, protective features and organization. 'Europe' does not lack administrative and technical machinery or 'institutional frameworks' to actualise itself; it lacks political will and cultural unity. A deficiency of the former exists because there is a corresponding absence of the latter. This radiates through multiple demesnes. To engage Anthony Smith, 'a common European cultural identity, if such there be, does not yet have its counterpart on the political level; to date, each state of the European Community has placed its perceived national interests and self-images above a concerted European policy based on a single presumed European interest and self-image.' An extant 'common European cultural identity' is vague and insubstantial. Its necessity as a foundation for a European political community is less ambiguous. Compared to national identification, ''Europe' is deficient both as idea and as process. Above all, it lacks...historical depth.'[1]

If Europe is to be the sum of (and more than) its parts, a European identity must develop organically from its diverse origins. It will not just appear. Counterpart to the integration of member state inputs producing various common policies, the emergence of a European identity implies the

---

1   Anthony D. Smith "National identity and the idea of European unity"
         International Affairs v68 n1 1992 pp55-76

absorption of other cultural identities into one's own. 'Europe' itself is threatening this identity-power connection. For Philip Schlesinger 'the *ultima ratio* of the current integration process'

> surely eventually points to a central source of political legitimacy in the EC, ultimately disposing of a monopoly of the means to violence. If integration continues, we are talking about the emergence of a new regime and source of sovereign authority.[2]

What sort of a regime this would be, who or what would control it, and how individuals and community are to be defined is uncertain. 'To be a 'European', Schlesinger points out, 'is obviously different from being a member of a 'European nation'. The latter, much more acutely than the former, raises an unavoidable cultural question about what the common basis of Euro-identity might be.' Schlesinger disputes the notion of a 'common cultural heritage' and, as 'Europe' builders have discovered, 'it is difficult to conceive of engineering a collective identity' which will be the result of a (long) organic process, and involve 'inclusion and exclusion'. For Europe 'to be 'us' we need those who are 'not-us'.' European unity then rests on whether 'negative' forces of extra-European 'not-us' are more powerful than the intra-European 'not-us'. Although Schlesinger claims that 'in the EC, there is no predominant cultural nation that can become the core of the would-be state's nation and hegemonic Euro-culture', competition is evident. A collective consciousness is requisite to mandate a political union. And not only in the form of 'values' such as 'democracy', a (more or less) market economy, and a commitment to human rights. As Jacques Santer realises, proclamations and institutional mechanisms will never suffice because 'A European identity is not a simple fact of life. It is based on the intuitive certainty of a joint destiny, but it is also the creation of a slow process of diplomatic negotiation...'

> this ultimate purpose of European integration: to construct a European design on a feeling of belonging to a genuine community. It is upon this feeling that the permanence of the structure depends, because it is the basis of people's willingness to stand together against the dangers which might threaten them. [3]

---

2   Philip Schlesinger "Europeanness: A New Cultural Battlefield" in *Nationalism* Eds. John Hutchinson & Anthony D. Smith (Oxford: Oxford University Press 1994) pp316-325, p319 (*Innovation in Social Science Research* v5 n1 1992 pp11-23)

3   Jacques Santer "The European Union's security and defence policy: How to avoid missing the 1996 rendez-vous" *NATO Review* November 1995 pp3-9, p3

320 Germany, Europe and the Persistence of Nations

Identifications of the kind described by Smith gave impetus to German reunification and to apprehensions or negative reactions elsewhere in Europe, some of which continue in the form of resistance to new and unfamiliar regulations and policies, or to rule from 'Brussels'. Consequently the EU's component parts operate in a new geopolitical context wherein 'Germany is back'[4] as a nation-state even if it has many challenges to surmount. Formal European structures are not preventing member states from continuing to formulate separate bodies of interest. Without effective harmonization, other factors—the power and influence to assert one's own preferences or imperatives—increasingly come to the fore. Germany will not be able to exempt itself from responding to internal and external demands in the same way.

The foreign policy of the old Federal Republic was shaped by a binary objective of recreating a united Germany in a united Europe. Establishing a political foundation located in multilateral structures provided the space and agency for the evolution of an accepted post-war identity. The historical basis for this identity, the *Kulturnation*, had not found a stable, democratic politics and had been discredited through its corruption by Nazism. Successive governments have attempted, through substantive and rhetorical means, to conflate the German interest with the European. Under Kohl the favoured technique has been to invert nationalism by decoupling the nation rhetorically and, to some uncertain degree, institutionally, from a conventional state. The nation would reappear in a new European political structure and all-European Constitution would underwrite the polity.[5] Dissolving the German state—along with its neighbours—into European structures was not intended to constrict the capacity to make decisions in German 'national' interests. Powers would not disappear into a vacuum but be enhanced. Sovereignty merged into a Europe of, eventually, one constitution and one highest authority would complete the rehabilitation of Germany. National political representation would continue within a new form wherein a numerical advantage would be conferred through a 'directly-elected all-European parliament and government' and strategic gains could be made in foreign policy. No logic supports that a political entity will aim at integration into another form which emasculates its influence.

Dilemma, paradox and uniqueness have consistently appeared in German history. The 1989-90 shift in Germany's political authority was engineered as much by changes outside the two German states as within

---

4   Gregor Schöllgen "National Interest and International Responsibility: Germany's Role in World Affairs" in *Germany's New Position in Europe* Ed. Arnulf Baring (Oxford: Berg 1994) pp35-49, p35

5   See Frank Vibert *Europe: A Constitution for the Millenium* (Aldershot: Dartmouth 1995)

them. Since the 'window of opportunity' appeared a previously reactive foreign policy has changed. Despite lapses and quandaries Germany has become more of a subject than an object, more a determiner of events than a responder to them. Official rhetoric consistently featured themes of being committed to partnerships and alliances, aware of both fears generated by the past and present and future responsibilities. Of course, the new context is not solely one of potential alliances against Germany. There are and will be others. However, all present and future EU members will find it increasingly difficult to bypass Germany, and especially German opposition, in conducting policy initiatives. Michael Huelshoff has written of German involvement in European structures as demonstrating 'all approaches to integration at work...neo-functionalism, intergovernmentalism, domestic politics'. He perceives a 'two-level model' which

> accounts for the complexity of demands that states bring to intergovernmental bargaining, suggesting the relevance of interest (the German economic needs), the ideology (the German need to win friends in Europe, support for free markets, and protection for workers), and structure (corporatism and cooperative decision-making) variables in determining these bargaining positions.[6]

All these categories constitute 'interests'. The German 'proclivity to be good Europeans' is assured as long as domestic conditions are met, which increasingly requires achievement of German goals at the European level. One synopsis of the German EU construction interprets EMU as a negotiated 'loss' borne by Germany, as one of exchanging the Deutschemark for history.[7] This will not go ahead without German parliamentary approval and there will be reiteration of the requirement for a political union. Implementation of EMU, however, will not prove that nationalism, or a predominance of 'national thinking', is overcome. A durable compatibility among European peoples without it will better demonstrate that—because it requires more than money. In circumstances when real political power has not passed to a supranational organization, Germany has already demonstrated a

---

6   Michael G. Huelshoff "Germany and European Integration: Understanding the Relationship" in *From Bundesrepublik to Deutschland: German Politics After Unification* Eds. Michael G. Huelshoff, Andrei Markovits & Simon Reich (Ann Arbor: University of Michigan Press 1993) pp301-320, here p313-314

7   Michel Korinman "Europa—die geopolitische Sicht" *Neue Gesellschaft/Frankfurter Hefte* n8 August 1996 pp695-700 'nimmt im EU-Aufbau eine deutsche Methode wahr, die Vergangenheitsbewältigung definitiv zu vollziehen: DM im Tausch gegen Zeitgeschichte. Da nützt die germanophile Gegenargumentation: Krieg an die Wand malen, historische Regression, unabänderliche Dekadenz und zuletzt ebenfalls—Kolonisierung durch Deutschland...'

'growing ability to set the rules on product regulation, trade, and monetary relations inside the EC and often on a larger scale' and 'regardless of the fate of the EC's Maastricht treaty and its progress to a common currency, Europe will be hard pressed to escape the paternalistic grip of German bankers and industrialists.'[8] Accompanying a growing economic, demographic, and cultural presence, Germany's foreign policy influence within or outside EU forums will also grow. Reinhard Rummel states that it is not yet clear what German priorities and directions will be and that it depends on other actors, especially France, the USA and Russia. This does not prevent him from censuring Garton Ash for suggesting that Germany has options, and asserting that 'in reality the room for choices in very narrow'. He continues, however, 'this does not necessarily mean that Germany will automatically adapt to other powers' wishes; others might converge around German concepts and priorities.'[9]

Despite their differences, leaderships in France and Britain were averse to outcomes that impinged on their own authority. Maintaining 'indivisibility' and preventing the 'irrevocable' element of 'ever closer union' were French and British expressions of the same disinclination. Shaping the 'European interest' or the course of European integration itself remained a 'series of compromises between national interests'. The brief 'Europhoria' of 1989-91 has not been recovered despite an improving economic climate and the addition of new members. Divergences and intransigences have blocked *communataire* motivations. The last few years have impressed the implausibility of up to fifteen national states claiming to act in the same European interest simultaneously:

> Making unilateral, national definitions of the European interest was a habit as old as the nation-states in Europe. But it was a bad habit. Unless and until there was a directly-elected all-European parliament and government, a fair definition of European interest could only be reached as a series of compromises between national interests. Moreover, if they did not define their own national interest consciously and clearly, it would be made up as they went along, in reaction to external challenges and to the pressures of public and published opinion in a television democracy.[10]

---

8   Gary L. Geipel "The Nature and Limits of German Power" in *Germany in a New Era* Ed. Gary L. Geipel (Indianapolis: Hudson Institute 1993) pp19-48, p25

9   Reinhard Rummel "Germany's Role in the CFSP: 'Normalität or 'Sonderweg'" in *The Actors in Europe's Foreign Policy*   Ed. Christopher Hill (London: Routledge 1996) pp40-67

10   Timothy Garton Ash *In Europe's Name: Germany and the Divided Continent* (London: Vintage 1994) p409

Europe's nations are not about to be seamlessly absorbed into a European community. According to Hamish McRae, 'Europe has for a thousand years been spectacularly unsuccessful at developing not just a common foreign policy, but even a modus vivendi for the different peoples who share the continent'. There will be no final constitutional form. Rather, 'the most important difference between the Europe of the 1990s and that of 2020 is that people will have realized that Europe is not progressing towards some goal of greater unity, and that the closeness of the association of European states ebbs and flows over the centuries'.[11] Claims that the 'Westphalian model of democracy...is becoming outmoded' and that 'what is emerging in Europe...is a new form of political domination and representation' have to be qualified: nothing has actually yet *replaced* the Westphalian model.[12] Within this framework Moisi and Mertes stress that Germany's 'fear of coalitions is not paranoia as long as European leaders still believe in nineteenth-century-style balance-of-power politics'. They urge that the opportunity to merge ever more German sovereignty with European partners 'should be seized...while it is available'.[13] Suggestions of discord among Germany and its partners are interpreted in the Foreign Ministry as presumptuous (and implicitly dangerous) *Feindbilder*.[14] On another level the viewpoint above makes two simultaneous presumptions: that an insufficiently integrated Germany will become (firstly economically) hegemonic and that other European states will ally against one perceived to be too powerful. When these are aggregated Germany appears as the focus of such a counter-alliance. Should such a development occur it will be self-fulfilling prophecy rather than objective necessity. The Moisi/Mertes prognosis suggests that the principle that could compel such an outcome, 'national interest', no matter how misconceived or clumsily pursued, is not only structurally embedded, but it, and not a larger and vaguer 'European interest', is the most forceful and durable determinant among EU members.

William Pfaff claimed that Germany's 'anchorage in the EC has been loosened by the Community's institutional crisis and the drift of the United States away from European commitments.'[15] Later Michael Stürmer

---

11   Hamish McRae *The World in 2020: Power, Culture and Prosperity* (Boston: Harvard Business School 1994) see pp227-231

12   Scott Lash & John Urry *Economies of Signs & Space* (London: Sage 1994) See pp281-283

13   Dominique Moisi & Michael Mertes "Europe's Map, Compass and Horizon" *Foreign Affairs* v74 n1 1995 pp122-134, pp130-131

14   Interview Sources, Auswärtiges Amt, Bonn, September 1996

15   William Pfaff *The Wrath of Nations: Civilization and the Furies of Nationalism* (New York: Simon and Schuster 1993) p225

suggested that once again the fate of Europe depends on Germany.[16] Although Germany's political leaders are faced with ensuring that the verve and now less restrained idiosyncracies of a German national dynamic do not induce its shaky European analogue to unravel this is not entirely within German control. The success of the European venture, as Hans-Peter Schwarz remarks, is dependent on how 'normally this re-united country is treated by its partners in the EU',[17] which means how *they* react as Germany's economic predominance and other forms of influence become more noticeable. In this context Peter Pulzer asks 'normal by whose standards—German or other people's?'[18] It then becomes equally noticeable that interests are coloured by particular group identifications.[19] Schwarz envisages Germans (and other Europeans) developing a national consciousness that 'no longer understands the nation in terms of an absolute value'. Instead it exists as a participant within cooperative international communities. That is, the exterior encasing is to be altered. The nation is to be transcended as the highest and 'natural' political *form* but not *content.*[20] While German federalism might well incorporate two political loyalties, and financial obligations, three is a strain.

Gregory Treverton prognosticated in 1992 that a boom would arrive in five years and so allow 'economic convergence on Germany's terms and thus a monetary union by decade's end'. This would also facilitate a German shift from 'introversion to extroversion in their approach to the neighborhood'.[21] Germany has moved from a position of division, limited sovereignty and a relatively low foreign policy profile to become the EU's 'political pacemaker'. The German political class heard, if slowly, the grass

---

16   'Wieder hängt das Schicksal Europas von Deutschland ab'. See Michael Stürmer "Deutsche Interessen" in *Deutschlands neue Außenpolitik* Band 1 Grundlagen. Eds Karl Kaiser & Hans W. Maull (München: Oldenbourg 1994) pp39-61, p40

17   Hans-Peter Schwarz "Germany's National & European Interests" *Dædelus* v123 n2 1994 pp81-105

18   Peter Pulzer "Unified Germany: A Normal State?" *German Politics* v3 n1 1994 pp1-17, p16

19   Pond and Schoenbaum quote the editor of a Zürich newspaper who 'attributes the unreasonable 'stubborn search for reasons to fear Germany' not only to history but also to envy and resentment'. David Schoenbaum & Elizabeth Pond *The German Question and Other German Questions* (Houndmills: MacMillan 1996) p219, fn 20

20   Even Schwarz's sober analysis—which is predicated on Europe's states *and* nations inevitably having differing and opposed interests in the future—does not adequately explain how 'post-modern nation-states' must 'surrender parts of their autonomy' and establish 'cooperative international communities' while simultaneously 'within them the nation retains its sovereignty'. "Germany's National and European Interests" p103

21   Gregory F. Treverton "Forces and Legacies Shaping a New Germany" in *Germany in a New Era* pp61-78, p77

roots concerns and realise a new pragmatism is required. Enough homogeneity of opinion and intent was perceived externally so that other nation-states dealt with a uniform construct of 'the Germans' rather than widely variable viewpoints. Notwithstanding claims of acting as an equal among equals (*gleicher partner unter gleichen*),[22] Germany will carry a greater degree of influence whether Europe moves closer to union—or not. The Union is being steered towards where Germans insist, even if some others are scarcely moving at all. David Marsh argues that preferences formed within the German domestic policy and based on a 'genuine belief' that they are best for all will be implemented if Germany succeeds in creating its 'Europe':

> It is evident, for example, that far from not wanting a 'German Europe', Germany wants its ideas—on social policy, on the environment, on the need to combat inflation or establish independent central banks, on the balance between 'widening' and 'deepening'—to be followed as closely as possible by its partners. This is less a question of power-play than of a curious form of political morality. The Germans genuinely believe that their ideas are in other people's (as well as their own) best interest.[23]

The problem is, so do most, if not all, of the EU's other members about *their own* ideas. As Marsh continues, however, 'Germany's economic influence, for instance as the largest contributor to the EC budget, makes it likely that its voice will be heard'. So too comes the deliverance of 'de facto political primacy' to Bonn, a 'power accumulated more by default than by design'. Perhaps so. But there was a fair measure of design nonetheless. Jeffrey Bergner has characterised unified Germany as a 'Great Power with many options'. He interpreted that as the US lessens its European commitments 'it is beginning to dawn on political leaders across the spectrum that Germany is no longer a junior partner...but will have to stand as the moral guarantor of its own policies.' Europe and the world are heading in a direction where 'the effort to craft a foreign policy that offends no one—not the French, nor the Americans, not the Russians...is becoming ever harder to sustain. Germany must and will begin to make choices...In the end there might turn out to be little difference between a European Germany and a German Europe.'[24] Repeated almost verbatim by Bundesbank chief Hans Tietmeyer,[25]

22   Interview Source, Europa-Ausschuss, Bonn, October 1994
23   David Marsh *Germany and Europe: The Crisis of Unity* (London: Mandarin 1995) p176
24   Jeffrey T. Bergner "Unified Germany: A Great Power with Many Options" in *Germany in a New Era* pp183-198, here pp185-186
25   "Gut für Deutschland" *Der Spiegel* n3 15-1-96 pp84-85

a 'senior U.S. diplomat' more recently observed that 'there are likely to be more and more occasions when German leaders, often responding to domestic pressures, decide what is good for Germany is good for Europe'. [26]

After beginning an article on the 'rebuilding' of the German nation with a reference to the owl of Minerva, Heinrich August Winkler quotes Nietzsche's claim that the Germans would be Hegelians even if Hegel had never existed. The same year Joachim Fest wrote that even if all other Germans are, he is 'not a Hegelian' but will nonetheless end his monograph 'in true Hegelian fashion'. Nothing, and especially 'Europe', will succeed 'only as a concept. In the end reality will follow.' [27] Having articulated some actual and potential countervailing forces or tendencies, and taking unforseen variables as far as possible into account, this book affirms that *if* a practical and extensive European *Union* is achieved it will most closely approximate a German design in accordance with German preferences. A broader and vibrant cultural presence will accompany *de facto* control over monetary policy and a political system resembling the Bundesrepublik model, within which German influence will more than match its population numbers and at least equate to its economic weight. Then Germany and Europe really would be two sides of the same coin.

---

26   Joseph Fitchett & Alan Friedman "Good for Germans, Good for Europe" *International Herald Tribune* 5-12-95 pp1 & 12

27   Heinrich August Winkler "Rebuilding of a Nation: The Germans Before and After Reunification" *Dædelus* v123 n1 1994 pp107-127; Joachim Fest "Europe in a Cul-de-sac" in *Germany's New Position in Europe* pp51-64

Bibliography

Books

Abse, Leo *Wotan My Enemy: Can Britain Live With the Germans in the European Union?* (London: Robson 1994)

Adamthwaite, Anthony *Grandeur & Misery: France's bid for power in Europe 1914-1940* (London: Arnold 1995)

Allum, Percy *State and Society in Western Europe* (Cambridge: Polity 1995)

Almond, Gabriel & Sidney Verba *The Civic Culture* (Princeton: Princeton University Press 1963)

Alter, Peter *Nationalism* (London: Edward Arnold 1994)

Anderson, Benedict *Imagined Communities: Reflections on the Origin and Spread of Nationalism* (London: Verso 1983)

Anderson, Jeffrey J. *Pluralism, Corporatism, and Economic Crisis* (Cambridge: Cambridge University Press 1992)

Armstrong, John *Nations Before Nationalism* (Chapel Hill: University of North Carolina Press 1982)

Arnold, Hans *Europa am Ende?* (München: Piper 1993)

Aron, Raymond *Peace and War: A Theory of International Relations* (English Edition) Trans. Richard Howard & Annette Baker Fox (London: Weidenfeld & Nicholson 1966)

Asmus, Ronald D. *Germany in the Eyes of the American Security Elite* (Santa Monica: RAND 1993)

Attali, Jacques *Verbatim* (Paris: Fayard 1995)

Bade, Klaus *Ausländer, Aussiedler, Asyl in der Bundesrepublik Deutschland* (Hanover: Landeszentrale für politische Bildung 1990)

Balladur, Edouard *Dictionnaire de la Reforme* (Paris: Fayard 1992)

Beloff, Max *The Future of British Foreign Policy* (London: Secker & Warburg 1969)

Beloff, Max *Britain and European union: dialogue of the deaf* (Basingstoke: Macmillan Press 1996)

Bertram, Christoph *Europe in the Balance: Securing the Peace Won in the Cold War* (Washington: Carnegie Endowment 1995)

Betz, Hans-Georg *Postmodern Politics in Germany: The Politics of Resentment* (Houndmills: MacMillan 1991)

Binoche, Jacques *De Gaulle et les Allemands* (Bruxelles: Complexe 1990)

Black, Jeremy *Convergence or divergence: Britain and the Continent* (Basingstoke: Macmillan 1994)

Bloom, William *Personal Identity, National Identity and International Relations* (Cambridge: Cambridge University Press 1990)

Bludau, Beatrix *Frankreich im Werk Nietzsches* (Bonn: Bouvier 1979)

Blumenwitz, Dieter *This is Germany: Germany's Legal Status after Unification* (Bonn: Kulturstiftung der Deutschen Vertriebenen 1994)

Borneman, John *Belonging in the Two Berlins: Kin, state, nation* Third Edition (Cambridge: Cambridge University Press 1995)

Brubaker, Rogers *Citizenship and Nationhood in France and Germany* (Cambridge Ma.: Harvard University Press 1992)

Brubaker, Rogers *Nationalism Reframed: Nationhood and the national question in the New Europe* (Cambridge: Cambridge University Press 1996)

Bruton, Alistair *A Revolution in Progress: Western Europe Since 1989* (London: Little, Brown & Co. 1996)

Buchan, David *Europe: The Strange Superpower* (Aldershot: Dartmouth 1993)

Buell, Frederick *National Culture and the New Global System* (Baltimore: Johns Hopkins University Press 1994)

Bulmer, Simon & William Paterson *The Federal Republic of Germany and the European Community* (London: Allen & Unwin 1987)

Burgess, Michael *The British tradition of federalism* (London: Leicester University Press 1995)

Butler, Michael *Europe: More than a Continent* (London: Heinemann 1986)

Buzan, Barry *People, States and Fear: An Agenda for International Security Studies in the Post-Cold War Period* Second Edition (Brighton: Harvester Wheatsheaf 1991)

Canetti, Elias *Crowds and Power* Trans. Carol Stewart (New York: Farrar Strauss Giroux 1984 [1960])

Canovan, Margaret *Nationhood and Political Theory* (Cheltenham: Edward Elgar 1996)

Chevènement, Jean-Pierre *Une certaine idée de la République m'amene à...* (Paris: Albin Michel 1992)

Clyne, Michael *The German language in a changing Europe* (Cambridge: Cambridge University Press 1995)

Cole, Alistair *François Mitterrand: A Study in Political Leadership* (London: Routledge 1994)

Connally, Bernard *The Rotten heart of Europe: The Dirty War for Europe's Money* (London: Faber 1995)

Conradt, David P. *The German Polity* Third Edition (New York: Longman 1986)

Corbett, Richard *The Treaty of Maastricht : from conception to ratification : a comprehensive reference guide* (Harlow: Longman Current Affairs 1993)

Craig, Gordon *The Germans* (Harmondsworth: Penguin 1991)

Dalton, Russell J. *Politics in Germany* (New York: Harper Collins 1992)

Dann, Otto *Nation und Nationalismus in Deutschland 1770-1990* (München: Beck Verlag 1993)

Dedman, Martin J. *The Origins and Development of the European Union 1945-1995: A History of European Integration* (London: Routledge 1996)

Delors, Jacques *Le Nouveau Concert Européen* (Paris: Editions Odile Jacob 1992)

Denman, Roy *Missed Chances: Britain and Europe in the Twentieth Century* (London: Casell 1996)

Derrida, Jacques *The Other Heading: Reflections on Today's Europe* Trans. Pascale-Anne Brault & Michael B. Naas (Bloomington: Indiana University Press 1992)

Deutsch, Karl *Nationalism and Social Communication: An Inquiry into the Foundations of Nationality* (New York 1953)

Deutsch, Karl *Political Community at the International Level: Problems of Definition and Measurement* (New York: Doubleday 1954)

De Zayas, Alfred M. *Anmerkungen zur Vertreibung der Deutschen aus dem Osten.* English translation *The German expellees: victims in war and peace* by John A. Koehler (New York: St. Martin's Press, 1993)

Dobson, Alan P. *Anglo-American Relations in the Twentieth Century* (London: Routledge 1995)

Dönhoff, Marion Gräfin *Im Wartesaal der Geschichte* (Stuttgart: 1993)

Dyson, Kenneth *Elusive Union: The Process of Monetary Union in Europe* (London: Longman 1994)

Edwards, Ruth Dudley *True Brits: Inside the Foreign Office* (London: BBC Books 1994)

Elbe, Frank & Richard Kiessler *A Round Table With Sharp Corners: The Diplomatic Path to German Unity* (Baden-Baden: Nomos 1996)

Elias, Norbert *The Germans: Power Struggles and the Development of Habitus in the Nineteenth and Twentieth Centuries* Ed. Michael Schröter, Trans. Eric Dunning & Stephen Mennell (Cambridge: Polity 1996 [1989])

Enzensberger, Hans-Magnus *Aussichten auf den Burgerkrieg* (Frankfurt: Suhrkamp 1993)

Featherstone, Mike *Global Culture: Nationalism, Globalization and Modernity* (London: Sage 1990)

Fischer, Joschka *Risiko Deutschland: Krise und Zukunft der deutschen Politik* (Cologne: Kiiepenheuer & Witsch 1994)

Fisher, Marc *After the Wall: Germany, Germans and the Burdens of History* (New York: Simon & Schuster 1995)

Friend, Julius W. *The Linchpin: French-German Relations, 1950-1990* (New York: Praeger 1991)

Fritsch-Bournazel, Renata *Confronting the German Question: Germans on the East-West Divide* trans. Caroline Bray (Oxford: Berg 1988)

Fritsch-Bournazel, Renata *Europe and German Unification* (New York: Berg 1992)

Fumaroli, Marc *L'Etat culturel: Essai sur une religion moderne* (Paris: Editions de Fallois 1991)

Garten, Jeffrey E. *A Cold Peace: America, Japan, Germany, and the Struggle for Supremacy* (New York: Times Books 1993)

Garton Ash, Timothy *In Europe's Name: Germany and the Divided Continent* (London: Vintage 1994)

Gasteyger, Curt *An Ambiguous Power: The European Union in a Changing World* (Gütersloh: Bertelsmann 1996)

Gauck, Joachim *Die Stasi-Akten: Das Unheimliche Erbe der DDR* (Reinbek: Rororo 1991)

Geertz, Clifford *The Interpretation of Cultures* (New York: Basic Books 1973)

Geiss, Immanuel *Die deutsche Frage 1806-1990* (Mannheim: Taschenbuchverlag 1992)

Gellner, Ernest *Nations and Nationalism* (Oxford: Blackwell 1983)

Gellner, Ernest *Culture, Identity and Politics* (Cambridge: Cambridge University Press 1987)

Gellner, Ernest *Encounters with Nationalism* (Oxford: Blackwell 1994)

George, Stephen *Politics and Policy-Making in the European Community* Second Edition (Oxford: Oxford University Press 1991)

Geremek, Bronislaw *The Common Roots of Europe* Trans. Jan Aleksandrowicz et. al. (Cambridge: Polity 1996),

Gilliar, Beate C.. *The rhetoric of (Re) Unification: Constructing Identity though East and West German Newspapers* (New York: Peter Lang 1996)

Gilpin, Robert *War and Change in World Politics* (Cambridge: Cambridge University Press 1981)

Glees, Anthony *Reinventing Germany: German Political Devlopment Since 1945* (Oxford: Berg 1996)

Glotz, Peter *Die falsche Normalisierung* (Frankfurt a. M.: 1994)

Goertemaker, Manfred *Unifying Germany 1989-1990* (Houndmills: MacMillan 1994)

Goldhagen, Daniel *Hitler's willing executioners: ordinary Germans and the Holocaust* (New York: Knopf 1996)

Gordon, Philip H. *A Certain Idea of France: French Security Policy and the Gaullist Legacy* (Princeton: Princeton University Press 1993)

Grass, Günter *Two States-One Nation: The Case Against German Reunification* (London: Secker & Warburg 1990)

Greenfeld, Liah *Nationalism: Five Roads to Modernity* (Cambridge, Ma.: Harvard University Press 1992)

Griffiths, Martin *The Real Realism* (London: Routledge 1992)

Guéhenno, Jean-Marie *The End of the Nation-State* trans. Victoria Elliott (Minneapolis: University of Minnesota Press 1995)

Guibernau, Montserrat *Nationalisms: The Nation-State and Nationalism in the Twentieth Century* (Cambridge: Polity 1996)

Haas, Ernst *The Uniting of Europe: Political, Social and Economical Forces 1950-57* (London: Stevens 1958)

Haas, Ernst *The Obsolescence of Regional Integraton Theory* (Berkeley: Institute of International Studies 1975)

Habermas, Jürgen *Die nachholende Revolution: kleine politische Schriften VII* (Frankfurt a M: Suhrkamp 1990)

Habermas, Jürgen *The Past As Future* Trans. Max Pensky (Cambridge: Polity 1994)

Hämäläinen, Pekka Kalevi *Uniting Germany: Actions and Reactions* (Boulder: Westview 1994)

Hanrieder, Wolfram *Germany, America, Europe: Forty Years of German Foreign Policy* (New Haven: Yale University Press 1989)

Hegel, G .W. F. *Philosophy of Right* trans. T.M.Knox (Oxford: Oxford University Press 1942)

Hendriks, Gisela *Germany and European Integration: The Common Agricultural Policy: an Area of Conflict* (New York: Berg 1991)

Herder, Johann Gottfried *Werke in zehn Banden* Eds. Martin Bollacher et. al. (Frankfurt a. M.: Deutscher Klassiker Verlag 1985-)

Hobsbawm, Eric *Nations and Nationalism Since 1780: Programme Myth, Reality* (New York: Cambridge University Press 1990)

Holland, Martin *European Community Integration* (London: Pinter 1993)

Howe, Geoffrey *Conflict of Loyalty* (New York: St. Martin's Press 1994)

Ignatieff, Michael *Blood and Belonging: Journeys into the New Nationalism* (New York: Farrar, Strauss & Giroux 1993)

Ingelhart, Ronald *Cultural Shift in Advanced Industrial Society* (Princeton: Princeton University Press 1990)

Jacobs Francis, Richard Corbett & Michael Shackelton *The European Parliament* (Harlow: Longman 1990)

James, Harold *A German Identity 1770-1990* (London: Weidenfeld & Nicholson 1989)

Jarausch, Konrad H. *The Rush to German Unity* (New York: Oxford University Press 1994)

Jaspers, Karl *Wohin treibt die Bundesrepublik? Tatsachen, Gefahren, Chancen* (München: Piper 1988 [1966])

Jaspers, Karl *Freiheit und Wiedervereinigung* (München: Piper 1990)

Jenkins, Brian *Nationalism in France: Class and Nation since 1789* (Savage: Barnes & Noble 1990)

Jordan, Glenn & Chris Weedon *Cultural Politics: Class, Gender, Race and the Post-Modern World* (Oxford: Blackwell 1995)

Judt, Tony *Past Imperfect: French Intellectuals 1944-56* (Berkeley: University of California Press 1992)

Judt, Tony *A Grand Illusion: An Essay on Europe* (New York: Hill & Wang 1996)

Kaase, Max & Andrew Kohut *Estranged Friends: The Transatlantic Consequences of Societal Change* (Gütersloh: Bertelsmann 1996)

Kaiser, Karl *Deutschlands Vereinigung: Die Internationale Aspekt* (Bonn: Bastei Lubbe 1991)

Katzenstein, Peter J. *Policy and politics in West Germany: the growth of a semisovereign state* (Philadelphia: Temple University Press 1987)

Kennedy, Ellen *The Bundesbank: Germany's Central Bank in the International Monetary System* (London: Pinter 1991)

Kennedy, Paul *Preparing for the Twenty-First Century* (London: Harper Collins 1993)

Keohane, Robert *After Hegemony: Coperation and Discord in the World Political Economy* (Princeton: Princeton University Press 1984)

Keohane, Robert *International Institutions and State Power* (Boulder: Westview 1989)

Keohane, Robert & Joseph Nye *Power and Interdependence: World Politics in Transition* Second Edition (Boston: Little & Brown 1989)

Kocka, Jürgen *Vereinigungskrise: Zur Geschichte der Gegenwart* (Göttingen: Vandenhoek & Ruprecht 1995)

Kohn, Hans *The Idea of Nationalism: A Study in its Origins and Background* (New York: MacMillan 1967)

Kolboom, Ingo *Vom geteilten zum vereinigten Deutschland: Deutschland-Bilder in Frankreich* (Bonn: Europa Union 1991)

Korte, Karl-Rudolf *Nation und National Staat: Bausteine einer europäischen Identität* (Melle: Knoth Verlag 1993)

Kramer, Steven *Does France Still Count?: The French Role in the New Europe* (Westport: Praeger 1994)

Kratochwil, Friedrich *The Return of Culture and Identity in IR Theory* (Boulder: Lynne Rienner 1996)

Krejci, Jaroslav & Vitezslav Velimsky *Ethnic and Political Nations in Europe* (London: Croom Helm 1981)

Kymlicka, Will *Liberalism, Community and Culture* (Oxford: Oxford University Press 1989)

Ladurie, Emmanuel Le Roy et. al. *Entre dans le XXIéme siécle: essai sur l'avenir de l'identité française* (Paris: Documentation Française 1990)

Laqueur, Walter *Europe in Our Time: A History 1945-1992* (New York: Penguin 1992)

Lash, Scott & John Urry *Economies of Signs & Space* (London: Sage 1994)

Lasswell, Harold *Politics: Who gets what, when, how* (New York: Meridian 1958)

Latsch, Johannes *Die Bezeichnungen für Deutschland, seine Teile und die Deutschen* (Frankfurt a.M: Peter Lang 1994)

Laughland, John *The Death of Politics: France under Mitterrand* (London: Michael Joseph 1994)

Levine, Andrew *The End of the State* (London: Verso 1987)

Lindberg, Leon N. & Stuart A Scheingold *Europe's Would-Be Polity* (Englewood Cliffs: Prentice-Hall 1970)

Lippert, Barbara & Rosalind Stevens-Ströhmann *German Unification and EC Integration: German and British Perspectives* (London: Pinter 1993)

Lobera, Josep L. *The God of Modernity: The Development of Nationalism in Western Europe* (Oxford: Berg 1994)

Loosely, David *The Politics of Fun: Cultural Policy and Debate in Contemporary France* (Oxford: Berg 1995)

Maier, Charles S. *The Unmasterable Past: History, Holocaust and German National Identity* (Cambridge Ma.: Harvard University Press: 1988)

Maier, Charles S. *Die Gegenwart der Vergangenheit: Geschichte und die nationale Identität der Deutschen* (Frankfurt: Campus Verlag 1992)

Malcolm, Noel *Bosnia: A Short History* (New York: New York University Press 1994)

Mann, Michael *Rise and Decline of the Nation-State* (Oxford: Blackwell 1990)

Marsh, David *The Germans: Rich, Bothered, and Divided* (London: Century 1989)

Marsh, David *The New Germany: At the Crossroads* (London: Century 1990)

Marsh, David *The Bundesbank: The Bank that Rules Europe* (London: Heinemann: 1992)

Marsh, David *Germany and Europe: The Crisis of Unity* (London: Mandarin 1995)

McCormick, John *The European Union: Politics and Policies* (Boulder: Westview 1996)

McRae, Hamish *The World in 2020: Power, Culture and Prosperity* (Boston: Harvard Business School 1994)

Meinecke, Friedrich *Weltbürgertum und Nationalstaat: Stüdien über die Genesis des deutschen Nationalstaates* (München: Oldenbourg 1928 [1908])

Meinicke, Friedrich *Die Deutsche Katastrophe: Betrachtungen und Erinnerungen* (Wiesbaden: Brockhaus 1949)

Merkl, Peter F. *German Unification in the European Context* (Pennsylvania: University Park 1993)

Mestrovic, Stjepan G. *The Balkanization of the West* (London: Routledge 1994)

Mill, J. S. *Considerations on Representative Government* (London: 1966)

Miller, J. D. B. *The World of States* (London: Croom Helm 1981)

Milward, Alan *The European Rescue of the Nation State* (London: Routledge 1992)

Minc, Alain *La Grande Illusion* (Paris: Grasset 1989)

Minc, Alain *Le Nouveau Moyen Age* (Paris: Editions Gallimard 1993)

Mitterrand, François *Réflexions sur la politique étrangère de la France* (Paris: Fayard 1987)

Mitterrand, François *De L'Allemagne, De La France* (Paris: Editions Odile Jacob 1996)

Monnet, Jean *Memoirs* Trans. Richard Mayne (London: Collins 1978)

Morgan, Roger & Caroline Bray *Partners and Rivals in Western Europe: Britain, France and Germany* (Aldershot: Gower 1986)

Morgenthau, Hans J. *Politics among Nations* Sixth Edition (New York: Knopf 1967)

Münch, Ursula *Asylpolitik in der Bundesrepublik Deutschland* (Oplande: Leske & Budrich 1993)

Newman, Gerald *The Rise of English Nationalism: A Cultural History 1740-1830* (London: St.Martin's Press 1987)

Nicoll, William & Trevor C. Salmon *Understanding the European Communities* (London: Philip Allan 1990)

Nolte, Ernst *Three Faces of Fascism* (London: Weidenfeld & Nicholson 1965)

Nolte, Ernst *Der europäische Bürgerkrieg 1917-1945* (Frankfurt a.M.: Ullstein 1987)

Northcott, Jim *The Future of Britain and Europe* (London: Policy Studies Institute 1995)

Northcutt, Wayne *Mitterrand: A Political Biography* (New York: Holmes & Meier 1992)

Nye, Joseph S. *Bound to Lead: The Changing Nature of American Power* (NewYork: 1990)

Paterson, William E. & David Southern *Governing Germany* Second Edition (Oxford: Blackwell 1992)

Pfaff, William *The Wrath of Nations: Civilization and the Furies of Nationalism* (New York: Simon and Schuster 1993)

Platzer, Hans-Wolfgang & Walter Ruhland *Welches Deutschland in welchem Europa?: Demoskopische Analysen, politische Perspektiven, gesellschaftliche Kontroversen* (Bonn: Dietz Nachfolger 1994)

Plessner, Helmut *Die Verspätete Nation: über die politische Verführbarkeit bürgerlichen Geistes* (Stuttgart: Kohlhammer 1974 [1959])

Pond, Elizabeth *Beyond the Wall: Germany's Road to Unification* (Washington: Brookings Institute 1993)

Pruys, Karl Hugo *Helmut Kohl: Die Biographie* (Berlin: edition q 1995)

Pufendorf, Freiherr Samuel von *The Present State of Germany* (London: Richard Chiswell 1690)

Pulzer, Peter *German Politics 1945-1995* (Oxford: Oxford University Press 1995)

Renan, Ernst *Oeuvres Completes* (Paris: Calman Lévy 1947)

Ryan, Michael *Politics and Culture: Working Hypotheses for a Post-Revolutionary Society* (Houndmills: MacMillan 1989)

Schäuble, Wolfgang *Der vertrag: Wie ich über die deutsche Einheit verhandelte* (Stuttgart: Deutsche Verlagsanstalt 1991)

Schäuble, Wolfgang *Und der Zukunft zugewandt* (Berlin: Siedler 1994)

Scheuch, Erwin K. *Wie deutsch sind die Deutschen? Eine Nation wandelt ihr Gesicht* (Bergisch-Gladbach 1991)

Scheuch, Erwin K. & Ute Scheuch *Cliquen, Klügel und Karrieren* (Reinbek: Rowohlt 1992)

Schlesinger, Philip *Media, State and Nation: Political Violence and Collective Identities* (London: Sage 1994)

Schmidt, Helmut *Handeln für Deutschland* (Hamburg: 1993)

Schneider, Peter *Extreme Mittelage: Eine Reise durch das deutsche Nationalgefuhl* (Reinbek: Rowohlt 1990)

Schoenbaum, David & Elizabeth Pond *The German Question and Other German Questions* (Houndmills: MacMillan 1996)

Schroeder, Ralph *Max Weber and the Sociology of Culture* (London: Sage 1992)

Schwarz, Hans-Peter *Die Gezähmten Deutschen: Von der Machtbesessenheit zur Machtvergessenheit* (Stuttgart: Deutsche Verlags-Anstalt 1985)

Schwarz, Hans-Peter *Zentralmacht Deutschlands: Deutschlands Rückkehr auf die Weltbühne* (Berlin: Siedler 1994)

Seguin, Philippe *Discours pour la France* (Paris: Grasset 1992)

Seguin, Philippe *Ce que j'ai dit* (Paris: Grasset 1993)

Seguin, Philippe & Maris-France Garaud *De l'Europe en général et de la France en particulier* (Paris: Le Pré aux clercs 1992)

Shils, Edward *Centre and Periphery: Essays in Macrosociology* (Chicago: University of Chicago Press 1975)

Simonian, Haig *The Privileged Partnership: Franco-German Relations in the EC 1969-1984* (Oxford: Clarendon Press 1985)

Sinn, Gerlinde & Hans-Werner Sinn *Jumpstart: the economic unification of Germany* Trans. Juli Irving-Lessmann. (Cambridge Ma: MIT Press 1992)

Smith, Anthony D. *Nationalism in the Twentieth Century* (Oxford: Martin Robertson 1979)

Smith, Anthony D. *The Ethnic Origins of Nations* (Oxford: Blackwell 1986)

Smith, Anthony D. *National Identity* (London: Penguin 1991)

Smith, Gordon *Politics in Western Europe* Fifth Edition (Aldershot: Dartmouth 1989)

Smyser, W. R. *Restive Partners: Washington and Bonn Diverge* (Boulder: Westview 1990)

Smyser, W. R. *The Economy of United Germany: Colossus at the Crossroads* (London: Hurst 1992)

Snyder, Louis S. *Varieties of Nationalism: A Comparative Study* (Hinsdale: Dryden Press 1976)

Sontheimer, Kurt *Deutschlands Politische Kultur* (München: Serie Piper 1990)

Souligne, M de *The Desolation of France Demonstrated* (London: John Salisbury 1697)

Sternberger, Dolf *Verfassungspatriotismus* (Frankfurt: Insel 1982)

Stürmer, Michael *Deutsche Fragen: oder die Suche nach der Staatsräson* (München: Piper 1988)

Talmon, J L. *The Myth of the Nation and the Vision of Revolution* (Berkeley: University of California Press 1981)

Tami, Yael *Liberal Nationalism* (Princeton: Princeton University Press 1993)

Taylor, Paul *International Organization in the Modern World: The Regional and the Global Process* (London: Pinter 1993)

Teltschik, Horst *329 Tage: Innenansichten der Einigung* (Berlin: Siedler 1991)

Thatcher, Margaret *The Downing Street Years* (London: Harper Collins 1993)

Thompson, Grahame F. *The Economic Emergence of a New Europe?: The Political Economy of Cooperation and Competition in the 1990s* (Aldershot: Edward Elgar 1993)

Thurow, Lester *Head to Head: The Coming Economic Battle Among Japan, Europe, and America* (St. Leonards: Allen & Unwin 1993)

Valence, Georges *France-Allemagne: Le Retour de Bismark* (Paris: Flammarion 1990)

Valéry, Paul *Collected Works* (London: Routledge & Kegan Paul 1962) trans. Denise Folliot & Jackson Matthews

Valéry, Paul *Selected Writings* (New Directions: New York 1964)

Vibert, Frank *Europe: A Constitution for the Millennium* (Aldershot: Dartmouth 1995)

Wæver, Ole, Ulla Holm & Henrik Larsen *The Struggle for 'Europe': French and German Concepts of State, Nation and European Union* (forthcoming)

Walker, R. B. J. *Inside/Outside: International Relations as Political Theory* (Cambridge: Cambridge University Press 1993)

Wallace, William *The Transformation of Western Europe* (New York: RIIA 1990)

Wallerstein, Immanuel *Geopolitics and Geoculture: Essays on the Changing World-System* (Cambridge: Cambridge University Press 1991)

Waltz, Kenneth *Theory of International Politics* (Reading: Addison-Welsey 1979)

Weber, Eugen *Peasants into Frenchmen:The Modernization of Rural France 1870-1914* (London: Chatto & Windus 1977)

Weidenfeld, Werner et. .al. *Europäische Kultur: das Zukunftsgut des Kontinents* (Bertelsmann Stiftung: Gütersloh 1990)

Wight, Martin *Systems of States* (Leicester: Leicester University Press 1977)

Wistrich, Ernest *The United States of Europe* (London: Routledge 1994)

Zelikow, Philip & Condoleeza Rice *Germany Unified and Europe Transformed: A Study in Statecraft* (Cambridge Ma.: Harvard University Press 1995)

Edited Volumes

Making Policy in Europe: The Europeification of National Policy-making Eds. Svein S Andersen & Kjell A Eliassen (London: Sage 1993)

Walter Benjamin: Illuminations Ed. Hannah Arendt (London :Penguin 1970)

Neorealism and Neoliberalism: The Comtemporary Debate Ed. David A. Baldwin (New York: Columbia University Press 1993)

Germany's New Position in Europe Ed. Arnulf Baring (Oxford: Berg 1994)

Dilemmas of World Politics: International Issues in a Changing World Eds. John Bayliss & N. J. Rengger (Oxford: Clarendon Press 1992)

Organising Interests in Western Europe: Pluralism, Corporatism and the Transformation of Politics Ed. Suzanne Berger (Cambridge: Cambridge University Press 1981)

National Diversity and Global Capitalism Eds. Suzanne Berger & Ronald Dore (Ithaca: Cornell University Press 1996)

Ein ganz normaler Staat?: Perspektiven nach 40 Jahren Bundesrepublik Eds. Wilhelm Bleek & Hans Maull (München: Piper 1989)

Revitalizing European Rituals Ed. Jeremy Boissevain (London: Routledge 1992)

Nationalism and Rationality Eds. Albert Breton, Gianluigi Galeotti, Pierre Salmon & Ronald Wintrobe (Cambridge: Cambridge University Press 1995)

The State of Germany: The National Idea in the Making, Unmaking and Remaking of a Modern Nation-State Ed. John Breuilly (Longman: London 1992)

The perils of anarchy: contemporary realism and international security Eds. Michael E. Brown, Sean M. Lynn-Jones, & Steven E. Miller (Cambridge, Ma.: MIT Press 1995)

Europe: Rêve-Aventure-Réalité Ed. Henri Brugmans (Brussels: Elsevier 1987)

Das Superwahljahr Eds. Wilhelm Bürklin & Dieter Roth (Köln: Bund-Verlag 1994)

German Cultural Studies Ed. Rob Burns (Oxford: Oxford University Press 1995)

Federal Solutions to European Issues Eds. Bernard Burrows, Geoffrey Denton & Geoffrey Edwards (New York: St. Martins Press 1978)

Citizenship, Nationality and Migration in Europe Eds. David Cesarani & Mary Fulbrook (London: Routledge 1996)

Handeln für Europa: Deutsch-französische Zusammenarbeit in einer veränderten Welt Eds. CIRAC et.al. (Opladen: Leske & Budrich 1995)

Germany's New Politics: Parties and Issues in the 1990s Eds. David Conradt, Gerald R. Kleinfeld, George K. Rosomer, Christian Søe (Providence: Berghahn 1995)

Towards Greater Europe Eds. Colin Crouch & David Marquand (Oxford: Blackwell 1992)

Global Transactions and Theoretical Challenges Eds. Ernst-Otto Czempiel & James N. Rosenau (Lexington: Lexington Books 1989)

The New Germany Votes: Unification and the Creation of a New German Party System Ed. Russell J. Dalton (Providence: Berg 1993)

Transforming Economies and European Integration Eds. Rumen Dobrinsky & Michael Landesmann (Aldershot: Edward Elgar 1995)

Maastricht and Beyond: Building the European Union Eds. Andrew Duff, John Pinder & Roy Price (London: Routledge 1994)

Double-Edged Diplomacy: International Bargaining and Domestic Politics Eds. Peter Evans, Harold Jacobson & Robert Putnam (Berkeley: University of California Press 1993)

European Migration in the Late Twentieth Century: Historical Trends, Actual Patterns, and Social Implications Eds. Heinz Fassman & Rainer Munz (Aldershot: Edward Elgar 1994)

Remaking the Hexagon: The New France in the New Europe Ed. Gregory Flynn (Boulder: Westview 1995)

Jaen Monnet-Robert Schumann: Correspondence 1947-1953 (Lausanne: Fondation Jean Monnet par l'Europe; Centre de Recherches Europeenes 1986)

Federalism and Nationalism Ed. Murray Forsyth (Leicester: Leicester University Press 1989)

Nation und Emotion: Deutschland und Frankreich im Vergleich: 19 und 20 Jahrhundert Eds. Etienne François, Hannes Siegrist & Jakob Vogel (Göttingen: Vandenhoeck & Ruprecht 1995)

European Identity and the Search for Legitimacy. Ed. Soledad Garcia (London: RIIA 1993)

Germany in a New Era Ed. Gary L. Geipel (Indianapolis: Hudson Institute 1993)

Experiment Vereinigung: ein sozialer Grossversuch Eds. Bernd Giesen & Claus Leggewie (Berlin: Rotbuch 1991)

Britain and the European Community: The Politics of Semi-detachment Ed. Stephen George (Oxford: Oxford University Press 1992)

The German Revolution of 1989: Causes and Consequences Eds. Gert-Joachim Glaeßner & Ian Wallace (Oxford: Berg 1992)

German Unification: The Unexpected Challenge Ed. Dieter Grosser (Oxford: Berg 1992)

World Politics: Power, Interdependence & Dependence Eds. David G. Haglund & Michael K. Hawes (Toronto: Harcourt Brace Jovanovich 1990)

States in History Ed. J. A.. Hall (Oxford: Blackwell 1986)

Politics in Western Europe M. Donald Hancock et.al. (Houndmills: MacMillan 1993)

Coping with the Past: Germany and Austria after 1945 Eds. Kathy Harms, Lutz R.Reuter, Völker Dürr (Madison: University of Wisconsin 1990)

Governing the New Europe Eds. Jack Hayward & Edward C. Page (Oxford: Polity 1995)

Politics in Europe: Structure and Processes in Some Postindustrial Democracies Ed. Martin O. Heisler (New York: David McKay 1974)

Der Deutsche Bundestag und Europa Ed. Renate Hellwig (München: Aktuell 1993)

Coping with the Relations: Anglo-German Cartoons from the Fifties to the Nineties Ed. Karin Hermann, Harald Husemann & Lachlan Moyle (Osnabrück: secolo Verlag 1994)

Two Worlds of International Relations: academics, practitioners and the trade in ideas Eds. Christopher Hill & Pamela Beshoff (London: Routledge 1994)

The Actors in Europe's Foreign Policy Ed. Christopher Hill (London: Routledge 1996)

Whose World Order: Uneven Globalization and the End of the Cold War Eds. Hans-Hendrik Holm and Georg Sørensen (Boulder: Westview 1994)

From Bundesrepublik to Deutschland: German Politics After Unification Eds. Michael G. Huelshoff, Andrei Markovits & Simon Reich (Ann Arbor: University of Michigan Press 1993)

The Future of UK Competitiveness and the Role of Industrial Policy Ed. Kirsty Hughes (London: Policy Studies Institute 1993)

Nationalism Eds. John Hutchinson & Anthony D. Smith (Oxford: Oxford university Press 1994)

When the Wall Came Down: Reactions to German Unification Eds. Harold James & Marla Stone (New York: Routledge 1992)

The European Challenges Post-1992: Shaping Factors, Shaping Actors Eds. Alexis Jaquemin & David Wright (Aldershot: Edward Elgar 1993)

340 *Germany, Europe and the Persistence of Nations*

Nation and Identity in Contemporary Europe Eds. Brian Jenkins & Spyros A. Sofos (London: Routledge 1996)

Die Stille Allianz: Deutsch-Britische Sicherheitskooperation Eds. Karl Kaiser & John Roper (Bonn: Europa Union 1987)

Die Neue Weltpolitik Eds. Karl Kaiser & Hans-Peter Schwarz (Baden-Baden: Nomos 1995)

Deutschlands neue Außenpolitik Band 1 "Grundlagen" and Band 2 "Herausforderungen" Eds. Karl Kaiser & Hans W. Maull; Band 3 "Interessen und Strategien" Eds. Karl Kaiser & Joachim Krause (München: Oldenbourg 1994, 1995, 1996)

European Integration and Denmark's Participation Ed. Morten Kelstrup (Copenhagen: Political Studies Press 1992)

The New European Community: Decisionmaking and Institutional Change Eds. Robert Keohane and Stanley Hoffmann (Boulder: Westview 1991)

After the Cold War: International Institutions and State Strategies in Europe 1989-1991 Eds. Robert Keohane et. al. (Cambridge: Harvard University Press 1993)

Frankreich in Europa: Ein Deutsch-Französischer Rundblick Eds. Ingo Kolboom & Ernst Weisenfeld (Bonn: Europa Union Verlag 1993)

The Federal Republic of Germany: The End of an Era Ed. Eva Kolinsky (New York: Berg 1991)

United Germany and the New Europe Ed. Heinz D. Kurz (Aldershot: Edward Elgar 1993)

Documents on the History of European Integration Eds. Walter Lipgens & Wilfried Roth (Berlin: Walter de Gruyter 1990)

Boundaries in Question: New Directions in in International Relations Eds. John MacMillan and Andrew Linklater (London: Pinter 1995)

France and Germany 1983-1993: The Struggle to Cooperate Ed. Patrick McCarthy (New York: St.Martins Press 1993)

The Frontier of National Sovereignty: History and Theory 1945-1992 Eds. Alan Milward et. al. (London: Routledge 1994)

The Idea of Europe: Problems of Transnational Identity Eds. Brian Nelson, David Roberts & Walter Veit (New York: Berg 1992)

The European Community in the 1990s: Economics, Politics, Defense Eds. Brian Nelson, David Roberts & Walter Veit (New York: Berg 1992)

Parties and Party Systems in the New Germany Ed. Stephen Padgett (Brookfield: Dartmouth 1993)

1870/71—1989/90: German Unifications and the Change of Literary Discourse Ed. Walter Pape (Berlin: Walter de Gruyter 1993)

Notions of Nationalism Ed. Sukumar Periwal (Budapest: Central European University Press 1995)

Historikerstreit: Die Dokumentation der Kontroverse um die Einzigartigkeit der nationalsozialistischen Judenvernichtung (München: Piper 1987)

Europe and Latin America in the World Economy Eds. Susan Kaufman Purcell & Francoise Simon (Boulder: Lynne Rienner 1995)

Culture, identity and politics: ethnic minorities in Britain Eds. Terence Ranger, Yunas Samad & Ossie Stuart (Aldershot: Avebury 1996)

Zuruck zu Deutschland: Umsturz und demokratischer Aufbruch in der DDR Herausgegeben vom Rheinischen Merkur (Bonn: Bouvier 1990)

Reimagining the Nation Eds. Majorie Ringrose and Adam J. Lerner (Buckingham: Open University Press 1993)

Germany and Europe in Transition Eds. Adam Daniel Rotfield & Walther Stützle (Oxford: Oxford University Press 1991)

Max Weber *Economy and Society: An Outline of Interpretive Sociology* Eds. Guenther Roth & Claus Wittich (Berkeley: University of California Press 1978)

Patriotism: the making and unmaking of British national identity Ed. Raphael Samuel (London: Routledge 1989)

Euro-Politics, Institutions, and Policymaking in the "New" European Community Ed. Alberta M. Sbragia (Washington: Brookings Institute 1992)

Berlin im November Eds. Anke Schwartau, Cord Schwartau & Rolf Steinberg (Berlin: Nicolai 1990)

Die selbstbewußte Nation: "Anschwellende Bocksgesang" und weitere Beiträge zu einer deutschen Debatte Eds. Heimo Schwilk & Ulrich Schacht (Frankfurt a.M. Ullstein 1994)

The West German Model: Perspectives on a Stable State Eds. Gordon Smith & William Paterson (London: Frank Cass 1981)

Developments in German Politics Eds. Gordon Smith, William E. Paterson, Peter H. Merk &, Stephen Padgett (Houndmills: MacMillan 1992)

Theorising International Relations: Positivism and After Eds. Steve Smith, Ken Booth & Maysia Zalewski (Cambridge: Cambridge University Press 1995)

The New Germany and the New Europe Ed. Paul B. Stares (Washington: Brookings Institute 1992)

Mitteleuropa: History and Prospects Ed. Peter Stirk (Edinburgh: Edinburgh University Press 1994)

The Single European Market and Beyond: A Study of the Wider Implications of the Single European Act Ed. Dennis Swann (Routledge: London 1992)

Auf der Suche nach der Gestalt Europas Eds. Jochen Thies & Gunther van Well (Bonn: Verlag fur Internationale Politik 1990)

The Formation of National States in Western Europe Ed. Charles Tilly (Princeton: Princeton Univesity Press 1975)

New Nationalisms of the Developed West: Toward Explanation Eds. Edward A. Tiryakian & Ronald Rogowski (London: Allen & Unwin 1985)

Die haßlichen Deutschen?: Deutschland im Spiegel der westlichen und östlichen Nachbarn Ed. Günter Trautmann (Darmstadt: Wissenschaftliche Buchgesellschaft 1991)

The Germans and their Neighbours Eds. Dirk Verheyen & Christian Søe (Boulder: Westview 1993)

Identity, Migration and the New Security Agenda in Europe Eds. Ole Wæver, Barry Buzan, Morten Kelstrup and Pierre Lemaitre (London: Pinter 1993)

Toward a Global Civil Society Ed. Michael Walzer (Providence: Berghahn 1995)

Handwörterbuch zur deutschen Einheit Eds. Werner Weidenfeld & Karl-Rudolf Korte (Frankfurt: Campus 1992)

Die Identität der Deutschen Ed. Werner Weidenfeld (Bonn: 1983)

Central and Eastern Europe on the Way into the European Union Ed. Werner Weidenfeld (Gütersloh: Bertelsmann 1996)

A New Ostpolitik: Strategies for a United Europe Ed. Werner Weidenfeld (Gütersloh: Bertelsmann 1997

Martin Wight *International theory: the three traditions* Eds Gabriele Wight & Brian Porter (Leicester: Leicester Univerity Press 1991)

Cultural Change and the New Europe Eds. Thomas M. Wilson & M.Estellie Smith (Boulder: Westview 1993)

Privatizations in Europe Ed. Vincent Wright (London: Pinter 1994)

Western Europe and Germany: The Beginnings of European Integration 1945-1960 Ed. Clemens Wurm (Oxford: Berg 1995)

National Cultures and European Integration: Exploratory Essays on Cultural Diversity and Common Policies Ed. Staffan Zetterholm (Oxford: Berg 1994)

Chapters and Articles in Edited Volumes

Adams, William James "France and Global Competition" in *Remaking the Hexagon: The New France in the New Europe* Ed. Gregory Flynn (Boulder: Westview 1995) pp87-115

Alin, Dana H. "Germany Looks at France" in *France and Germany 1983-1993: The Struggle to Cooperate* Ed. Patrick McCarthy (New York: St.Martins Press 1993) pp27-50

Allen Christopher S. "From Social Market to Mesocorporatism to European Integration: The Politics of German Economic Policy" in *From Bundesrepublik to Deutschland: German Politics After Unification* Eds. Michael G. Huelshoff, Andrei Markovits & Simon Reich (Ann Arbor: University of Michigan Press 1993) pp61-76

Allen, David "Conclusions: The European Rescue of national foreign policy?" in *The Actors in Europe's Foreign Policy* Ed. Christopher Hill (London: Routledge 1996) pp288-304

Alter, Peter "Nationalism and German politics after 1945" in *The State of Germany: The National Idea in the Making, Unmaking and Remaking of a Modern Nation-State* Ed. John Breuilly (Longman: London 1992) pp154-176.

Angenendt, Steffen "Migration: Herausforderung Deutscher und Europäischer Politk" *Deutschlands Neue Außenpolitik* Bd.2 Eds. Karl Kaiser & Hans W. Maull (München: Oldenbourg 1995) pp 176-199

Angenendt, Steffen "Nationale Interessen und Aussenpolitische Strategien in der Deutschen Migrationspolitik" *Deutschlands Neue Außenpolitik* Bd.3 Eds. Karl Kaiser & Joachim Krause München: Oldenbourg 1996) pp231-240

Arendt, Hannah "Introduction: Walter Benjamin: 1892-1940" in *Illuminations* Ed.Hannah Arendt (London: Penguin 1970)

Baring, Arnulf "Germany, What Now?" in *Germany's New Position in Europe* Ed. Arnulf Baring (Oxford: Berg 1994) pp1-20

Berger, Suzanne "Trade and Identity: The Coming Protectionism?" in *Remaking the Hexagon: The New France in the New Europe* Ed. Gregory Flynn (Boulder: Westview 1995) pp195-210

Bergner, Jeffrey T. "Unified Germany: A Great Power with Many Options" in *Germany in a New Era* Ed. Gary L. Geipel (Indianapolis: Hudson Institute 1993) pp183-198

Bergsdorf, Wolfgang "West Germany's Political System under Stress: Decision-Making Processes in Bonn 1990" in *German Unification: The Unexpected Challenge* Ed. Dieter Grosser (Oxford: Berg 1992) pp88-106

Bertram, Christoph "The Power and the Past: Germany's New International Loneliness" in *Germany's New Position in Europe* Ed. Arnulf Baring (Oxford: Berg 1994) pp91-105

Betz, Hans-Georg "Alliance 90/Greens: From Fundamental opposition to Black-Green" in *Germany's New Politics: Parties and Issues in the 1990s* Eds. David Conradt, Gerald R. Kleinfeld, George K. Rosomer, Christian Søe (Providence: Berghahn 1995) pp203-220

Böhrer, Karl-Heinz "Why we are not a Nation —And why we should become one" in *When the Wall Came Down: Reactions to German Unification* Eds. Harold James & Marla Stone (New York: Routledge 1992) pp60-70. (orig. *Frankfurter Allgemeine Zeitung* 12-1-90)

Boisseur, Christian de & Marie-Hélène Duprat "French Monetary policy in the light of European monetary and financial integraton" in *The Single European Market and Beyond: A Study of the Wider Implications of the Single European Act* Ed. Dennis Swann (Routledge: London 1992) pp51-98

Bozo, Frédéric "France and Security in the New Europe: Between the Gaullist Legacy and the Search for a New Model" in *Remaking the Hexagon: The*

New France in the New Europe Ed. Gregory Flynn (Boulder: Westview 1995) pp213-232

Breton, Albert & Margaret Breton "Nationalism Revisited" in *Nationalism and Rationality* Eds. Albert Breton, Gianluigi Galeotti, Pierre Salmon & Ronald Wintrobe (Cambridge: Cambridge University Press 1995) pp98-115

Breuilly, John "Nationalism and German Reunification" in *The State of Germany: The National Idea in the Making, Unmaking and Remaking of a Modern Nation-State* Ed. John Breuilly (Longman: London 1992) pp224-238

Bühl, Walter L. "Gesellschaftliche Grundlagen der Deutschen Aussenpolitik" in *Deutschlands Neue Außenpolitik* Bd.1 Eds. Karl Kaiser & Hanns W. Maull (München: Oldenbourg 1994) pp175-201

Bulmer, Simon "Britain and European Integration: Of sovereignty, slow adaption, and semi-detachment" in *Britain and the European Community: The Politics of Semi-detachment* Ed. Stephen George (Oxford: Oxford University Press 1992) pp1-29

Cable, James "Foreign policy-making: Planning or reflex" in *Two Worlds of International Relations: academics, practitioners and the trade in ideas* Eds. Christopher Hill & Pamela Beshoff (London: Routledge 1994) p93-117

Cameron, David Ross "From Barre to Balladur: Economic Policy in the Era of the EMS" in *Remaking the Hexagon: The New France in the New Europe* Ed. Gregory Flynn (Boulder: Westview 1995) pp117-157

Campbell Edwina S. "United Germany in a Uniting Europe" in *Germany in a New Era* Ed. Gary L. Geipel (Indianapolis: Hudson Institute 1993) pp81-89

Cesarani, David "The Changing Character of Citizenship and Nationality in Britain" in *Citizenship, Nationality and Migration in Europe* Eds. David Cesarani & Mary Fulbrook (London: Routledge 1996) pp57-73

Cetoka, Jaromir "Barriers to European (East-West) integration" in *Transforming Economies and European Integration* Eds. Rumen Dobrinsky & Michael Landesmann (Aldershot: Edward Elgar 1995) pp32-45

Clark, Alan "François Mitterand and the Idea of Europe" in *The Idea of Europe: Problems of Transnational Identity* Eds. Brian Nelson, David Roberts & Walter Veit (New York: Berg 1992) pp

Clemens, Clay "Second Wind or Last Gasp: Helmut Kohl's CDU/CSU and the Elections of 1994" *Germany's New Politics: Parties and Issues in the 1990s* Eds. David Conradt, Gerald R. Kleinfeld, George K. Rosomer, Christian Søe (Providence: Berghahn 1995) pp131-148

Cohen, Mitchell "Rooted Cosmopolitanism" in *Toward a Global Civil Society* Ed. Michael Walzer (Providence: Berghahn 1995) pp223-233

Coleman, James S. "Rights, rationality, and nationality" in *Nationalism and Rationality* Eds. Albert Breton, Gianluigi Galeotti, Pierre Salmon & Ronald Wintrobe (Cambridge: Cambridge University Press 1995) pp1-13

Collier, Irwin L. Jr. "Rebuilding the German Welfare State" in *Germany's New Politics: Parties and Issues in the 1990s* Eds. David Conradt, Gerald R.

Kleinfeld, George K. Rosomer, Christian Søe (Providence: Berghahn 1995) pp273-293

Conradt, David P. "Putting Germany Back Together Again: The Great Social Experiment of Unification" in *Germany in a New Era* Ed. Gary L. Geipel (Indianapolis: Hudson Institute 1993) pp3-18

Coombes, David "Problems of Governance in the Union" in *Maastricht and Beyond: Building the European Union* Eds. Andrew Duff, John Pinder & Roy Price (London: Routledge 1994) pp157-178

Dalton, Russell J. & Wilhelm Buerklin "The German Party System and the Future" in *The New Germany Votes: Unification and the Creation of a New German Party System* Ed. Russell J. Dalton (Providence: Berg 1993) pp233-256

Davis, E. P. "Whither Corporate Banking Relations?" in *The Future of UK Competitiveness and the Role of Industrial Policy* Ed. Kirsty Hughes (London: Policy Studies Institute 1993) pp85-107

Detevak, Richard "Incomplete states: theories and practices of statecraft" in *Boundaries in Question: New Directions in in International Relations* Eds. John MacMillan and Andrew Linklater (London: Pinter 1995) pp19-39

Dumez, Hervé & Alain Jeunemaître "Privatizations in France (1983-1993) in *Privatizations in Europe* Ed. Vincent Wright (London: Pinter 1994)

Dutheil, Jaqueline de la Rochère "Toward a Federal Europe" in *The European Community in the 1990s: Economics, Politics, Defense* Eds. Brian Nelson, David Roberts & Walter Veit (New York: Berg 1992) pp3-16

Edwards, Geoffrey "Central Government" in *Britain and the European Community: The Politics of Semi-detachment* Ed. Stephen George (Oxford: Oxford University Press 1992) pp64-90

Ely, John D. "The 'Black-Brown Hazelnut' in a Bigger Germany: The Rise of a Radical Right as a Structural Feature" *From Bundesrepublik to Deutschland: German Politics After Unification* Eds. Michael G. Huelshoff, Andrei Markovits & Simon Reich (Ann Arbor: University of Michigan Press 1993) pp235-270

Fawn, Rick "Central Europe since the revolutions of 1989: states, economies and culture in a time of flux" in *Boundaries in Question: New Directions in in International Relations* Eds. John MacMillan and Andrew Linklater (London: Pinter 1995) pp69-86

Feess, Eberhard & Ulrich Steger "Umwelt als Aussenpolitik und Globale Gestaltungsaufgabe" *Deutschlands Neue Außenpolitik* Bd.3 Eds. Karl Kaiser & Joachim Krause (München: Oldenbourg 1996) pp241-248

Fest, Joachim "Europe in a Cul-de-sac" in *Germany's New Position in Europe* Ed. Arnulf Baring (Oxford: Berg 1994) pp51-64

Flynn, Gregory "French Identity and Cold War Europe" in *Remaking the Hexagon: The New France in the New Europe* Ed. Gregory Flynn (Boulder: Westview 1995) pp233-249

Freudenstein, Roland "Deutschland, Frankreich und die Ostweiterung der Europäischen Union" in *Handeln für Europa: Deutsch-französische Zusammenarbeit in einer veränderten Welt* Eds. CIRAC et.al. (Opladen: Leske & Budrich 1995) pp131-137

Freudenstein, Roland "Die Neuen Demokratien in Ostmitteleuropa und die Europäische Union" in *Deutschlands Neue Außenpolitik* Bd.2 Eds. Karl Kaiser & Hans W. Maull (München: Oldenbourg 1995) pp103-119

Frey, Dieter "The Unification of Germany from the Standpoint of a Social Psychologist" in *United Germany and the New Europe* Ed. Heinz D. Kurz (Aldershot: Edward Elgar 1993) pp59-72

Friedlander, Saul (with Yaron London) "Now We Shall be Reduced to Our Due Place Within German Priorities" in *When the Wall Came Down: Reactions to German Unification* Eds. Harold James & Marla Stone (New York: Routledge 1992) pp295-302

Fulbrook, Mary "Germany for the Germans?: Citizenship and nationality in a divided nation" in *Citizenship, Nationality and Migration in Europe* Eds. David Cesarani & Mary Fulbrook (London: Routledge 1996) pp88-105

Garnett, John C. "States, State-Centric Perspectives, and Interdependence Theory" *Dilemmas of World Politics: International Issues in a Changing World* Eds. John Bayliss & N. J. Rengger (Oxford:Clarendon Press 1992) pp61-84

Garton Ash, Timothy "The Chequers Affair" in *When the Wall Came Down: Reactions to German Unification* Eds. Harold James & Marla Stone (New York: Routledge 1992) pp233-239

Geipel, Gary L. "The Nature and Limits of German Power" in *Germany in a New Era* Ed. Gary L. Geipel (Indianapolis: Hudson Institute 1993) pp19-48

Gellner, Ernest "The Roots of Cohesion" in Ernest Gellner *Culture, Identity and Politics Culture, Identity and Politics* (Cambridge: CUP 1987) pp29-46

Gellner, Ernest "The Sacred and the National" in Ernest Gellner *Encounters with Nationalism* (Oxford: Blackwell 1994) pp59-73

Glotz, Peter "East European Reform and West European Integration" in *Toward a Global Civil Society* Ed. Michael Walzer (Providence: Berghahn 1995) pp211-222

Gourevitch, Peter "The Macropolitics of Microinstitutional Differences in the Analysis of Comparative Capitalism" in *National Diversity and Global Capitalism* Eds. Suzanne Berger & Ronald Dore (Ithaca: Cornell University Press 1996) pp239-259

Grabendorff, Wolf "Germany and Latin America" in *Europe and Latin America in the World Economy* Eds. Susan Kaufman Purcell & Francoise Simon (Boulder: Lynne Rienner 1995) pp85-112

Greven, Michael Th. "Political Parties Between National Identity and Eurofication" in *The Idea of Europe: Problems of Transnational Identity* Eds. Brian Nelson, David Roberts & Walter Veit (New York: Berg 1992) pp75-95

Griffith William E. "American Views on the German Question" *Auf der Suche nach der Gestalt Europas* Eds. Jochen Thies & Gunther van Well (Bonn: Verlag fur Internationale Politik 1990) pp115-124

Guérin-Sendelbach, Valerie & Jacek Rulkowski "Frankreich, Deutschland und Polen: Ein neues Gespann—Eine Herausforderung für die Zukunft" in *Handeln für Europa: Deutsch-französische Zusammenarbeit in einer veränderten Welt* Eds. CIRAC et. al. (Opladen: Leske & Budrich 1995) pp138-157

Gullick, Charles J. M. R. "Cultural Values and European Financial Institutions" in *Cultural Change and the New Europe* Eds. Thomas M. Wilson & M.Estellie Smith (Boulder: Westview 1993) pp203-221

Gysi, Gregor "Ja zu Europa aber nein zu Maastricht: Der Standpunkt der PDS/Linke Liste" in *Der Deutsche Bundestag und Europa* Ed. Renate Hellwig (Aktuell: München 1993) pp190-194

Hacke, Christian "Germany: Locomotive for European Integration or Pacemaker for Detente with Eastern Europe?" in *The European Community in the 1990s: Economics, Politics, Defense* Eds. Brian Nelson, David Roberts & Walter Veit (New York: Berg 1992) pp62-79

Hacke, Christian "Nationales Interesse als Handlungsmaxime" in *Deutschlands neue Außenpolitik* Bd.3 Eds. Karl Kaiser & Joachim Krause (München: Oldenbourg 1996) pp3-28

Hagemann, Harald "On Some Macroeconomic Consequences of German Unification" in *United Germany and the New Europe* Ed. Heinz D. Kurz (Aldershot: Edward Elgar 1993) pp89-107

Hancock, M. Donald & B. Guy Peters "The European Community" in *Politics in Western Europe* M. Donald Hancock et.al. (Houndmills: MacMillan 1993) pp461-526

Hardin, Russel "Self-interest, group identity" in *Nationalism and Rationality* Eds. Albert Breton, Gianluigi Galeotti, Pierre Salmon & Ronald Wintrobe (Cambridge: Cambridge University Press 1995) pp14-42

Hassner, Pierre "Nationalstaat-Nationalismus-Selbstbestimmung" in *Die Neue Weltpolitik* Eds. Karl Kaiser & Hans-Peter Schwarz (Baden-Baden: Nomos 1995) pp91-103

Hedetoft, Ulf "The State of Sovereignty in Europe: Political Concept or Cultural Self-Image" in *National Cultures and European Integration: Exploratory Essays on Cultural Diversity and Common Policies* Ed. Staffan Zetterholm (Oxford: Berg 1994) pp13-48

Heisler, Martin O. & Robert B. Kravik "Patterns of European Politics: The 'European Polity' Model" in *Politics in Europe: Structure and Processes in Some Postindustrial Democracies* Ed. Martin O. Heisler (New York: David McKay 1974)

348 *Germany, Europe and the Persistence of Nations*

Heller, Agnes "Europe: An Epilogue?" in *The Idea of Europe: Problems of Transnational Identity* Eds. Brian Nelson, David Roberts & Walter Veit (New York: Berg 1992) pp12-25

Hill, Christopher "United Kingdom: Sharpening Contradictions" in *The Actors in Europe's Foreign Policy* Ed. Christopher Hill (London: Routledge 1996) pp68-89

Hoffman, Stanley "Thoughts on Sovereignty and French Politics" in *Remaking the Hexagon: The New France in the New Europe* Ed. Gregory Flynn (Boulder: Westview 1995) pp251-258

Holtz, Uwe "Entwicklungspolitik-Deutsche Interessen und Strategien" in *Deutschlands Neue Außenpolitik* Bd.2 Eds. Karl Kaiser & Hans W. Maull (München: Oldenbourg 1995) pp221-230

Hroch, Miroslav "National Self-Determination from a Historical Perspective" in *Notions of Nationalism* Ed. Sukumar Periwal (Budapest: Central European University Press 1995) pp65-82

Hubel, Helmut "Die Schwerige Partnershaft mit Russland" in *Deutschlands Neue Außenpolitik* Bd.3 Eds. Karl Kaiser & Joachim Krause (München: Oldenbourg 1996) pp137-141

Huelshoff, Michael G. "Germany and European Integration: Understanding the Relationship" in *From Bundesrepublik to Deutschland: German Politics After Unification* Eds. Michael G. Huelshoff, Andrei Markovits & Simon Reich (Ann Arbor: University of Michigan Press 1993) pp301-320

Janning, Josef "Deutschland und die Europäische Union" in *Deutschlands Neue Außenpolitik* Bd.3 Eds. Karl Kaiser & Joachim Krause (München: Oldenbourg 1996) pp29-54

Jenkins, Brian & Nigel Copsey "Nation, Nationalism and National Identity in France" in *Nation and Identity in Contemporary Europe* Eds. Brian Jenkins & Spyros A. Sofos (London: Routledge 1996) pp101-124

Jenkins, Brian & Spyros A. Sofos "Nation and Nationalism in Contemporary Europe: A Theoretical Perspective" in *Nation and Identity in Contemporary Europe* Eds. Brian Jenkins & Spyros A. Sofos (London: Routledge 1996) pp9-32

Joffe, Josef "Amerika und Deutschland: Die Weltmacht, Der 'Sanfte Hegemon' und die natürliche Partnerschaft" in *Deutschlands neue Außenpolitik* Bd. 3 Eds. Karl Kaiser & Joachim Krause (München: Oldenbourg 1996) pp117-122

Kaiser, Karl & Joachim Krause "Deutsche Politik Gegenüber dem Balkan" in *Deutschlands Neue Außenpolitik* Bd.3 Eds. Karl Kaiser & Joachim Krause (München: Oldenbourg 1996) pp175-188

Kalmbach, Peter "On Alternative Strategies of Wage Policy in Eastern Germany" in *United Germany and the New Europe* Ed. Heinz D. Kurz (Aldershot: Edward Elgar 1993) pp119-133

Keane, John "Questions for Europe" in *The Idea of Europe: Problems of Transnational Identity* Eds. Brian Nelson, David Roberts & Walter Veit (New York: Berg 1992) pp55-61

Keating, Tom "The State and International Relations" in *World Politics: Power, Interdependence & Dependence* Eds. David G. Haglund & Michael K. Hawes (Toronto: Harcourt Brace Jovanovich 1990) pp16-37

Keohane, Robert "Hobbes Dilemma and Institutional Change in World Politics: Sovereignty in International Society" in *Whose World Order: Uneven Globalization and the End of the Cold War* Eds. Hans-Hendrik Holm and Georg Sørensen (Boulder: Westview 1994)

Kielinger, Thomas "Deutsch-Britische Unterschiede: Real, Altervetraut, und doch Überbrückbar" in *Deutschlands Neue Außenpolitik* Bd.3 Eds. Karl Kaiser & Joachim Krause (München: Oldenbourg 1996) pp129-136

Kielmansegg, Peter Graf "Germany—A Future with Two Pasts" in *German Unification: The Unexpected Challenge* Ed. Dieter Grosser (Oxford: Berg 1992) pp180-195

Kirchner, Emil J. "The European Community: Seeds of Ambivalence" in *Developments in German Politics* Eds. Gordon Smith, William E. Paterson, Peter H. Merkl &, Stephen Padgett (Houndmills: MacMillan 1992) pp172-184

Kleinfeld, Gerald R. "The Integration of a Unified Germany: Update and Outlook" *Germany in a New Era* Ed. Gary L. Geipel (Indianapolis: Hudson Institute 1993) pp49-60

Kloten, Norbert "Die Bundesrepublik als Weltwirtschaftsmacht" in *Deutschlands Neue Außenpolitik* Bd.1 Eds. Karl Kaiser & Hanns W. Maull (München: Oldenbourg 1994) pp63-80

Kolboom, Ingo "Deutschlandbilder der Franzosen: Der Tod des "Dauerdeutschen" in *Die haßlichen Deutschen?: Deutschland im Spiegel der westlichen und östlichen Nachbarn* Ed. Günter Trautmann (Darmstadt: Wissenschaftliche Buchgesellschaft 1991) pp212-243

Kolboom, Ingo "Frankreich und Deutschland: Die Neuen Akzente" in *Deutschlands Neue Außenpolitik* Bd.3 Eds. Karl Kaiser & Joachim Krause (München: Oldenbourg 1996) pp123-128

Kreile, Michael "The Political Economy of the New Germany" in *The New Germany and the New Europe* Ed. Paul B. Stares (Washington: Brookings Institute 1992) pp55-92

Kühnhardt, Ludger "Wertgrundlagen der deutschen Aussenpolitik" *Deutschlands neue Außenpolitik* Bd1 Eds. Karl Kaiser & Hanns W. Maull (München: Oldenbourg 1994) pp99-127

Kuisel, Richard F. "The France We Have Lost: Social, Economic, and Cultural Discontinuities" in *Remaking the Hexagon: The New France in the New Europe* Ed. Gregory Flynn (Boulder: Westview 1995) pp31-48

Kushner, Tony "The Spice of Life?: Ethnic Difference, politics, and culture in modern Britain" in *Citizenship, Nationality and Migration in Europe* Eds. David Cesarani & Mary Fulbrook (London: Routledge 1996) 125-145

Küsters, Hanns Jürgen "West Germany's Foreign Policy in Western Europe, 1949-58: The Art of the Possible" in *Western Europe and Germany: The Beginnings of European Integration 1945-1960* Ed. Clemens Wurm (Oxford: Berg 1995) pp55-85

Le Cacheux, Jacques E. "The Franc Fort Strategy and the EMU" in *Remaking the Hexagon: The New France in the New Europe* Ed. Gregory Flynn (Boulder: Westview 1995) pp69-115

Lipp, Ernst-Moritz & Angelika Lipp-Krull "Menschen und Märkte - Dialog über interkulturelle Erfahrungen aus Finanz- und Meinungs märkten" in *Frankreich in Europa: Ein Deutsch-Französischer Rundblick* Eds. Ingo Kolboom & Ernst Weisenfeld (Bonn: Europa Union Verlag 1993) pp263-277

Lübbe, Hermann "Staatliche Souveranität, internationale Organisation und Regionalisierung" in *Die Neue Weltpolitik* Eds. Karl Kaiser & Hans-Peter Schwarz (Baden-Baden: Nomos 1995) pp187-195

Ludlow, Peter "The European Commission" in *The New European Community: Decisionmaking and Institutional Change* Eds. Robert Keohane and Stanley Hoffmann (Boulder: Westview 1991) pp85-132

Madsen, Poul Thøis "Is Culture a Major Barrier to a Single European market? The Case of Public Purchasing" in *National Cultures and European Integration: Exploratory Essays on Cultural Diversity and Common Policies* Ed. Staffan Zetterholm (Oxford: Berg 1994) pp145-160

Marshall, Barbara "German Migration Policies" in *Developments in German Politics* Eds. Gordon Smith, William E. Paterson, Peter H. Merk &, Stephen Padgett (Houndmills: MacMillan 1992) pp247-263

Mayes, David "European Integration" in *The Future of UK Competitiveness and the Role of Industrial Policy* Ed. Kirsty Hughes (London: Policy Studies Institute 1993) pp117-133

McAdams, A. James "Explaining Inter-German Cooperation in the 1980s" in *From Bundesrepublik to Deutschland: German Politics After Unification* Eds. Michael G. Huelshoff, Andrei Markovits & Simon Reich (Ann Arbor: University of Michigan Press 1993) pp191-206

McArdle, Catherine Kelleher "The New Germany: A Overview" in *The New Germany and the New Europe* Ed. Paul B. Stares (Washington: Brookings Institute 1992) pp11-54

McCarthy, Patrick "France Looks at Germany, or How to Become German (and European) while Remaining French" in *France and Germany 1983-1993: The Struggle to Cooperate* Ed. Patrick McCarthy (New York: St.Martins Press 1993) pp51-72

Merkl, Peter F. "A New German Identity" in *Developments in German Politics* Eds. Gordon Smith, William E. Paterson, Peter H. Merk &, Stephen Padgett (Houndmills: MacMillan 1992) pp327-348

Milward, Alan "Conclusions: the value of history" in *The Frontier of National Sovereignty: History and Theory 1945-1992* Eds. Alan Milward et. al. (London: Routledge 1994) pp182-201

Milward, Alan and Vibeke Sørensen "Interdependence or integration? A national choice" in *The Frontier of National Sovereignty: History and Theory 1945-1992* Eds. Alan Milward et. al. (London: Routledge 1994) pp1-32

Minkenberg, Michael "What's Left of the Right?: The New Right and the Superwahljahr 1994 in Perspective" in *Germany's New Politics: Parties and Issues in the 1990s* Eds. David Conradt, Gerald R. Kleinfeld, George K. Rosomer, Christian Søe (Providence: Berghahn 1995) pp255-271

Morgan, Roger "Germany in the New Europe" in *Towards Greater Europe* Eds. Colin Crouch & David Marquand (Oxford: Blackwell 1992) pp105-117

Müller, Harald "German Foreign Policy After Unification" in *The New Germany and the New Europe* Ed. Paul B. Stares (Washington: Brookings Institute 1992) pp126-173

Neusel, Hans "Internationale Kriminalität" in *Deutschlands Neue Außenpolitik* Bd.3 Eds. Karl Kaiser & Joachim Krause (München: Oldenbourg 1996) pp259-266

Neuss, Beate "The European Community: How to Counterbalance the Germans" in *German Unification: The Unexpected Challenge* Ed. Dieter Grosser (Oxford: Berg 1992) pp136-149

Pagano, Ugo "Can Economics Explain Nationalism" in *Nationalism and Rationality* Eds. Albert Breton, Gianluigi Galeotti, Pierre Salmon & Ronald Wintrobe (Cambridge: Cambridge University Press 1995) pp173-203

Papcke, Sven "Who needs European Identity and what could it be?" in *The Idea of Europe: Problems of Transnational Identity* Eds. Brian Nelson, David Roberts & Walter Veit (New York: Berg 1992) pp61-74

Plaschke, Henrik "National Economic Cultures and Economic Integration" in *National Cultures and European Integration: Exploratory Essays on Cultural Diversity and Common Policies* Ed. Staffan Zetterholm (Oxford: Berg 1994) pp113-143

Postone, Moishe "Germany's Future and Its Unmastered Past" in *From Bundesrepublik to Deutschland: German Politics After Unification* Eds. Michael G. Huelshoff, Andrei Markovits & Simon Reich (Ann Arbor: University of Michigan Press 1993) pp291-299

Powell, Charles "What the PM Learnt About the Germans" in *When the Wall Came Down: Reactions to German Unification* Eds. Harold James & Marla Stone (New York: Routledge 1992) pp242-246

Preuss, Ulrich K. "German Unification: Political and Constitutional Aspects" in *United Germany and the New Europe* Ed. Heinz D. Kurz (Aldershot: Edward Elgar 1993) pp47-58

Rahr, Alexander "Russland in Europa" *Deutschlands Neue Außenpolitik* Bd.2 Eds. Karl Kaiser & Hans W. Maull (München: Oldenbourg 1995) pp121-136

Reichel, Peter "Die haßlichen Deutschen: extrem schönheitsbedürtig und wenig politisch" in *Die haßlichen Deutschen?: Deutschland im Spiegel der westlichen und östlichen Nachbarn* Ed. Günter Trautmann (Darmstadt: Wissenschaftliche Buchgesellschaft 1991) pp316-333

Reinicke, Wolfgang H. "Toward a New European Political Economy" in *The New Germany and the New Europe* Ed. Paul B. Stares (Washington: Brookings Institute 1992) pp177-217

Richmond, Anthony H. "Ethnic Nationalism and Post-Industrialism" in *Nationalism* Eds. John Hutchinson & Anthony D. Smith (Oxford: Oxford university Press 1994) pp289-300 (Orig. *Ethnic and Racial Studies* v7 n1 1984)

Rode, Reinhard "Weltwirtschaft im Umbruch" in *Deutschlands Neue Außenpolitik* Bd.2 Eds. Karl Kaiser & Hans W. Maull (München: Oldenbourg 1995) pp23-41

Rogowski, Ronald "Causes and Varieties of Nationalism: a Rationalist Account" in *New Nationalisms of the Developed West: Toward Explanation* Eds. Edward A. Tiryakian & Ronald Rogowski (London: Allen & Unwin 1985) pp87-108

Rosomer, George K."Politics, Leadership, and Coalitions in Germany, 1994" in *Germany's New Politics: Parties and Issues in the 1990s* Eds. David Conradt, Gerald R. Kleinfeld, George K. Rosomer, Christian Søe (Providence: Berghahn 1995) pp23-41

Rotfeld, Adam Daniel "The future of Europe and of Germany" in *Germany and Europe in Transition* Eds. Adam Daniel Rotfield & Walther Stützle (Oxford: Oxford University Press 1991)

Rummel, Reinhard "Germany's Role in the CFSP: 'Normalität or 'Sonderweg'" in *The Actors in Europe's Foreign Policy* Ed. Christopher Hill (London: Routledge 1996) pp40-67

Saurin, Julian "The end of International Relations? The state and international theory in the age of globalization" in *Boundaries in Question: New Directions in in International Relations* Eds. John MacMillan and Andrew Linklater (London: Pinter 1995) pp244-261

Schäuble, Wolfgang "The Federal Republic of Germany: Foundations and Development" in *The Federal Republic of Germany: The End of an Era* Ed. Eva Kolinsky (New York: Berg 1991) pp15-26

Schlesinger, Philip "Europeanness: A New Cultural Battlefield" in *Nationalism* Eds. John Hutchinson & Anthony D. Smith (Oxford: Oxford university Press 1994) pp316-325 (orig. Innovation in Social Science Research v5 n1 1992 pp11-23)

Schnellhuber, Hans Joachim & Detlef F. Sprinz "Umweltkrisen und Internationale Sicherheit" in *Deutschlands Neue Außenpolitik* Bd.2 Eds. Karl Kaiser & Hans W. Maull (München: Oldenbourg 1995) pp239-260

Schöllgen, Gregor in *Germany's New Position in Europe* Ed. Arnulf Baring (Oxford: Berg 1994) pp35-49

Schwarz, Hans-Peter "Das Deutsche Dilemma" in *Deutschlands Neue Außenpolitik* Bd.1 Eds. Karl Kaiser & Hanns W. Maull (München: Oldenbourg 1994) pp81-97

Sheehan, James "National History and National Identity in the New Germany" in *1870/71—1989/90: German Unifications and the Change of Literary Discourse* Ed. Walter Pape (Berlin: Walter de Gruyter 1993)

Silverman, Max "The Revenge of Civil Society: State, Nation and Society in France" in *Citizenship, Nationality and Migration in Europe* Eds. David Cesarani & Mary Fulbrook (London: Routledge 1996) pp146-158

Silvia, Stephen J."The Social Democratic Party of Germany" in *Germany's New Politics: Parties and Issues in the 1990s* Eds. David Conradt, Gerald R. Kleinfeld, George K. Rosomer, Christian Søe (Providence: Berghahn 1995) pp149-170

Slama Alain-Gérard "Democratic Dysfunctions and Republican Obsolescence: The Demise of French Exceptionalism" in *Remaking the Hexagon: The New France in the New Europe* Ed. Gregory Flynn (Boulder: Westview 1995) pp49-65

Smith, Anthony D. "State-making and nation-building" in *States in History* Ed. J. A.. Hall (Oxford: Blackwell 1986)

Søe, Christian "The Free Democratic Party: A Struggle for Survival, Influence, and Identity" in *Germany's New Politics: Parties and Issues in the 1990s* Eds. David Conradt, Gerald R. Kleinfeld, George K. Rosomer, Christian Søe (Providence: Berghahn 1995) pp171-202

Streeck, Wolfgang "Lean Production in the German Automobile Industry: A Test Case for Convergence Theory" in *National Diversity and Global Capitalism* Eds. Suzanne Berger & Ronald Dore (Ithaca: Cornell University Press 1996) pp138-170

Stürmer, Michael "Deutsche Interessen" in *Deutschlands Neue Außenpolitik* Bd.1 Eds. Karl Kaiser & Hanns W. Maull (München: Oldenbourg 1994) pp39-61

Swann, Dennis "The Social Charter and other Issues" in *The Single European Market and Beyond: A Study of the Wider Implications of the Single European Act* Ed. Dennis Swann (Routledge: London 1992) pp214-229

Szekely Istvan P. "Financial reforms and economic integration" in *Transforming Economies and European Integration* Eds. Rumen Dobrinsky & Michael Landesmann (Aldershot: Edward Elgar 1995) pp199-227

Tew, Brian "Onwards to EMU" in *The Single European Market and Beyond: A Study of the Wider Implications of the Single European Act* Ed. Dennis Swann (Routledge: London 1992) pp193-213

Thompson, Janice E. & Stephen D. Krasner "Global Transactions and the Consolidation of Sovereignty" in *Global Transactions and Theoretical*

Challenges Eds. Ernst-Otto Czempiel & James N. Rosenau (Lexington: Lexington Books 1989)

Treverton, Gregory F. "Forces and Legacies Shaping a New Germany" in *Germany in a New Era* Ed. Gary L. Geipel (Indianapolis: Hudson Institute 1993) pp61-78

Varenne, Hervé "The Question of European Nationalism" in *Cultural Change and the New Europe* Eds. Thomas M. Wilson & M. Estellie Smith (Boulder: Westview 1993) pp223-240

Verheyen, Dirk "The Dutch and the Germans" in *The Germans and their Neighbours* Eds. Dirk Verheyen & Christian Søe (Boulder: Westview 1993)

Vogel, Heinrich "Osteuropa—Ein Schwerpunkt Deutscher Aussenpolitik" *Deutschlands Neue Außenpolitik* Bd.3 Eds. Karl Kaiser & Joachim Krause (München: Oldenbourg 1996) pp169-174

Wallace, William "Beyond Two Worlds: Think Tanks and Foreign Policy" in *Two Worlds of International Relations: academics, practitioners and the trade in ideas* Eds. Christopher Hill & Pamela Beshoff (London: Routledge 1994) pp139-163

Weil, Patrick "Nationalities and Citizenships: The Lessons of the French experience of Germany and Europe" in *Citizenship, Nationality and Migration in Europe* Eds. David Cesarani & Mary Fulbrook (London: Routledge 1996) pp74-87

Wenger, Klaus "Kultur à la Arte: Tele-Visionen für Europa" in *Frankreich in Europa: Ein Deutsch-Französischer Rundblick* Eds. Ingo Kolboom & Ernst Weisenfeld (Bonn: Europa Union Verlag 1993) pp257-262

Wieck, Hans-Georg "Transnationale Gefährdungen der Internationale Sicherheit" in *Deutschlands Neue Außenpolitik* Bd.2 Eds. Karl Kaiser & Hans W. Maull (München: Oldenbourg 1995) pp225-237

Witte, B. de "Cultural Legitimation: Back to the Language Question" in *European Identity and the Search for Legitimacy*. Ed. Soledad Garcia (London: RIIA 1993) pp154-171

Wolffsohn, Michael "Fear of Germany and Security for Europe" in *German Unification: The Unexpected Challenge* Ed. Dieter Grosser (Oxford: Berg 1992) pp150-179

Woolcock, Stephen "Competition among Forms of Corporate Governance in the European Community: The Case of Britain" in *National Diversity and Global Capitalism* Eds. Suzanne Berger & Ronald Dore (Ithaca: Cornell University Press 1996) pp179-196

Wyle, Frederick S. "Europe 1990, the U.S., the U.S.S.R., Germany and all that— on Letting the Log of History Drift rather than Trying to Shove it" in *Auf der Suche nach der Gestalt Europas* Eds. Jochen Thies & Gunther van Well (Bonn: Verlag fur Internationale Politik 1990) pp163-170

Zank, Wolfgang "Cultural Diversity and the Political System: The German Experience" in *National Cultures and European Integration: Exploratory*

Essays on Cultural Diversity and Common Policies Ed. Staffan Zetterholm (Oxford: Berg 1994). pp83-111

Zetterholm, Staffan "Why is Cultural Diversity a Political Problem? A Discussion of Cultural Barriers to Political Integration" in *National Cultures and European Integration: Exploratory Essays on Cultural Diversity and Common Policies* Ed. Staffan Zetterholm (Oxford: Berg 1994) pp65-82

Journal Articles

Alter, Karen J. "The European Court's Political Power" *West European Politics* v19 n3 1996 pp458-487

Ammon, Ulrich "The German Language: Lingua Franca overshadowed by English?" *Deutschland Magazine* n2 1994 pp44-49

Applebaum, Anne "Tony Blair and the New Left" *Foreign Affairs* v76 n2 1997 pp45-60

Archard, David "Myths, Lies and Historical Truth: A Defence of Nationalism" *Political Studies* v43 1995 pp472-481

Arnold, Hans ""Maastricht"—The Beginning or the end of a Development?" *Aussenpolitik* v44 n3 1993 pp271-280

Aron, Raymond "Old Nations, New Europe" *Dædelus* v93 n1 1964

Bade, Klaus J. "Immigration and Social Peace in United Germany" *Dædelus* v123 n1 1994 pp85-106

Baker David, Andrew Gamble, & Steve Ludlam "Conservative splits and European Integration" *Political Quarterly* v64 n4 1993 pp420-434

Baker David, Andrew Gamble, & Steve Ludlam "The Parliamentary siege of Maastricht 1993: Conservative Divisions and British Ratification" *Parliamentary Affairs* v47 n1 1994 pp37-59

Ball, Rodney "Plus ça change...? The enduring tradition of linguistic conservatism" *French Cultural Studies* v6 p1 n16 February 1995 pp61-78

Balibar, Étienne "Es Gibt Keinen Staat in Europa: Racism and Politics in Europe Today" *New Left Review* n186 March/April 1991 pp5-19

Bauer-Kaase, Petra & Max Kaase "Five Years of Unification: The Germans on the Path to Inner Unity?" *German Politics* v5 n1 1996 pp1-25

Bergsten, Fred "Economic Imbalances and World Politics" *Foreign Affairs* v65 n4 1987 pp770-794

Bergsten, Fred "The Primacy of Economics" *Foreign Policy* n87 Summer 1992 pp3-24

Betz, Hans-Georg "The German Model Reconsidered" *German Studies Review* v19 n2 May 1996 pp303-320

Black, Antony "Nation and community in the international order" *Review of International Studies* v19 1993 pp81-89

Bloemer, Klaus "Deutschland Braucht Frankreich" *Neue Gesellschaft* v39 n12 1992 pp1065-1070

Bocquet, Dominique "Democractic Deficit" *American Enterprise* May/June 1993 pp56-63

Böhr, Christoph "At the End of the Post-War Order in Europe: In Search of a New Coherence of Interests and Responsibilities" *Aussenpolitik* v46 n2 1995 pp115-125

Borkenhagen, Franz H. U. "Regions in Europe" *Aussenpolitik* v44 n2 1994 pp182-188

Bös, Mathias "Ethnisierung des Rechts?: Staatsbürgerschaft in Deutschland, Frankreich, Großbritannien und den USA" *Kölner Zeitschrift für Soziologie und Sozialpsychologie* v45 December 1993 pp619-643

Boyce, Brigitte "The Democratic deficit of the European Commission" *Parliamentary Affairs* v46 n4 1993 pp458-477

Bress, Ludwig "Transformation: Die Signatur des 21.Jahrhunderts" *Deutsche Studien* Heft 125 March/July 1995 pp5-43

Breuilly, John "Reflections on Nationalism" *Philosophy of the Social Sciences* v15 1985 pp65-73

Brigot, André "Frankreich und Europa" *Aus Politik und Zeitgeschichte* B42/94 21-10-94

Brock, George "Sadder and Wiser" *Times Literary Supplement* 26-11-93 p10

Brüning, Martin "Deutschland in Europa: Zentralmacht oder Zucker im Tee?" *Neue Gesellschaft/Frankfurter Hefte* n1 January 1995 pp85-87

Brzezinski, Zbigniew "A Plan for Europe" *Foreign Affairs* v74 n1 1995 pp26-42

Bulmer, Simon "Domestic Politics and European Commmunity Policy-Making" *Journal of Comon Market Studies* v21 1983 pp349-363

Busch, Andreas "The Crisis in the EMS" *Government and Opposition* v29 n1 1994 pp80-96

Butt, Alan Philip "Europeans First and Last: British Liberals and the European Community" *Political Quarterly* v64 n4 1993 pp447-461

Cahm, Eric "Seen from Germany: France in 1993-94—synthetic and comparative perspectives" *Modern & Contemporary France* NS4 (1) 1996 pp102-105

Caporaso, James "The European Union and Forms of State: Westphalian, Regulatory or Post-Modern?" *Journal of Common Market Studies* v34 n1 1996 pp33-53

Cardus, Salvador and Joan Estruch "Politically correct anti-nationalism" *International Social Science Journal* v144 June 1995 pp347-352

Carrewyn, Leopold "Belgium and German Policy on Europe" *Aussenpolitik* v46 n3 1995 pp220-227

Cavazza, Fabio Luca & Carlo Pelanda "Maastricht: Before, During and After" *Dædelus* v123 n2 1994 pp53-80

Chen, Kuan-Hsing "Not yet the Postcolonial Era: The (Super) Nation-State and Transnationalism of Cultural Studies: Response to Ang and Stratton" *Cultural Studies* v10 n1 1996 pp37-70

Chryssochoou, Dimitris N. "Democracy and Symbiosis in the European Union: Towards a Confederal Consociation" *West European Politics* v17 n4 1994 pp1-14

Clarke, Jonathan "Repeating British Mistakes" *The National Interest* Spring 1995 pp68-77

Clemens, Clay "The Chancellor as Manager: Helmut Kohl, the CDU and Governance in Germany" *West European Politics* v17 n4 1994 pp28-51

Coker, Christopher "Britain and the New World Order: the special relationship in the 1990s" *International Affairs* v68 n3 1992 pp407-421

Cole, Alistair "Looking On: France and the New Germany" *German Politics* v2 n3 1993 pp359-376

Cole, Alistair "La France pour tous? — The French Presidential Elections of 23 April and & May 1995" *Government and Opposition* v30 n3 1995 pp327-346

Collier Irwin L. "Instant Integration and Gradual Convergence: Program Notes to the Macroeconomic Drama of German Unification" *German Studies Review* v16 n2 1993 pp311-330

Connor, Walker "The Nation and Its Myth" *International Journal of Comparative Sociology* v33 n1-2 1992 pp48-56

Corbey, Dorette "Dialectical functionalism: stagnation as a booster of European integration" *International Organization* v49 n2 1995 pp253-284

Crawford, Beverly "Explaining Defection from International Cooperation: Germany's Unilateral Recognition of Croatia" *World Politics* v48 July 1996 pp482-521

Crepaz, Markus M. L. & Arend Lijphart "Linking and Integrating Corporatism and Consensus Democracy: Theory, Concepts and Evidence" *British Journal of Political Science* v25 p2 1995 pp281-288

Daase, Christopher & Michael Jochum "'Partners in Leadership'?: United Germany in the Eyes of the USA" *Aussenpolitik* v43 n3 1992 pp237-245

Davy, Richard "Großbritannien und die Deutsche Frage" *Europa-Archiv* n45 1990 pp139-144

Dehousse, Renaud "Constitutional Reform in the European Community: Are there Alternatives to the Majoritarian Avenue?" *West European Politics* v18 n3 1995 pp118-36

Deubner, Christian "Deutschland, Frankreich und die Europäische Union: Die Interessen laufen auseinander' *Internationale Politik und Gesellschaft* n3 1994 pp210-222

Dirke, Sabine von "Mulitkulti: The German Debate on Multiculturalism" *German Studies Review* v17 n3 1994 pp513-536

Dornbusch, Rudi "Euro Fantasies" *Foreign Affairs* v75 n5 1996 pp116-124

Drake, Helen "Political Leadership and European Integration: The Case of Jacques Delors" *West European Politics* v18 n1 Jan 1995 pp140-160

Duke, Simon "The Second Death (or the Second Coming?) of the WEU" *Journal of Common Market Studies* v34 n2 1996 pp167-191

Dunn, John "Crisis of the Nation State?" *Political Studies* v42 Special Issue 1994 pp3-15

Duve, Freimut "Germany and the hurricane of change" *New Perspectives Quarterly* v10 n1 1993 pp13-15

Dyson, Kenneth "The Ambiguous Politics of Western Germany: Politicization in a 'State' Society" *European Journal of Political Research* v7 1979 pp375-396

Dyson, Kenneth "Cultural Issues and the Single European Market: Barriers to Trade and Shifting Attitudes" *Political Quarterly* v64 n1 1993 pp84-97

Eco, Umberto "For a Polyglot Federation" *New Perspectives Quarterly* v10 n1 1993 pp41-43

Eichenberg, Richard C. & Russell J. Dalton "Europeans and the European Community: the dynamics of public support for European integration" *International Organization* v47 n4 1993 pp507-534

Eisel, Stephan "The Politics of a United Germany" *Dædelus* v123 n1 1994 pp149-171

Eisenberg, Götz "Deutschland als Prothese: Wozu nationale Identität?" *Neue Gesellschaft /Frankfurter Hefte* v8 August 1996 pp739-743

Emanuel, Susan "Cultural television: current French critiques" *French Cultural Studies* v5 p2 n14 June 1994 pp139-149

Emanuel, Susan "A Community of Culture?: The European Television Channel" *History of European Ideas* v21 n2 1995 pp169-176

Enzenberger, Hans Magnus "Subterranean Heimat Blues" *New Perspectives Quarterly* Winter 1993 pp10-12

Eulefeld, Günter "Environmental Education in the Federal Republic of Germany" *History of European Ideas* v21 n1 1995 pp17-29

Falter, Jürgen W. "Ein Staat, zwei Politikkulturen? Politische Einstellungsunterschiede zwischen Ost- und Westdeutschland fünf Jahre nach der Wiedervereinigung" *German Studies Review* v19 n2 May 1996 pp279-301

Featherstone, Kevin "Jean Monnet and the 'Democratic Deficit' in the EU" *Journal of Common Market Studies* v32 n2 1994 pp149-171

Feldman, Lily Gardner "Germany and the EC: Realism and Responsibility" *Annals of the American Academy of Political Science* January 1994 pp25-43

Fendius, Miriam Elman "The Foreign Policies of Small States: Challenging Neorealism in its Own Backyard" *British Journal of Political Science* v25 n2 1995 pp171-217

Fischer, Joschka "Les Certitudes Allemandes: Grundkonstanten bundessdeutscher Aussenpolitik" *Blatte für deutsche und internationale Politik*, September 1994 pp1082-1090

Fothergill, Stephen "The Impact of Regional Alliances: The Case of the EU Coalfields" *European Urban & Regional Studies* v1 n2 1994 pp177-180

Franklin, Mark, Michael Marsh & Lauren McLaren "Uncorking the Bottle: Popular Opposition to European Unification in the Wake of Maastricht" *Journal of Common Market Studies* v32 n4 1994 pp455-472

Friend, Julius W. "Nationalism and National Consciousness in France, Germany and Britain: The Year of Maastricht" *History of European Ideas* v18 n2 1994 pp187-198

Fulbrook, Mary "Aspects of Society and Identity in the New Germany" *Dædelus* v123 n2 1994 pp211-233

Gallus, Alexander "Cultural Plurality and the Study of Complex Societies in Anthropology" in *Studies for a New Central Europe* Series 3 n2 1972 pp28-47

Gardels, Nathan "Heimat EC: Germany as Alias Nation" *New Perspectives Quarterly* v10 n1 Winter 1993 pp1-2

Garrett, Geoffrey "The politics of legal integration in the European Union" *International Organization* v49 n1 Winter 1995 pp171-181

Garton, Timothy Ash "Germany Unbound" *New York Review of Books* 22-11-90 pp11-15

Garton, Timothy Ash "Germany's Choice" *Foreign Affairs* v73 n4 1994 pp65-81

Garton, Timothy Ash "Journey to the Post-Communist East" *New York Review of Books* 23-6-94 pp13-20

Gauck, Joachim "Dealing with a Stasi Past" *Daedelus* v123 n1 1994 pp277-284

Gellner, Ernest "Nationalism reconsidered and E.H.Carr" *Review of International Studies* v18 n4 1992 pp285-293

Geuss, Raymond "Kultur, Bildung, Geist" *History and Theory* v35 n2 1996 pp151-164

Girvin, Brian "Nationalism, Economic Growth and Political Sovereignty" *History of Europena Ideas* v15 n1-3 1992 pp177-184

Glees, Anthony "The Diplomacy of Anglo-German Relations: A Study of the ERM Crisis of September 1992" *German Politics* v3 n4 1994 pp75-90

Godin, Emmanuel "Le néo-liberalisme à la française: une exception?" Modern & Contemporary France NS4 (1) 1996 pp61-70

Godley, Wynne "Derailed" *London Review of Books* 19-8-93 p9

Goetz, Klaus H. "National Governance and European Integration: Intergovernmental Relations in Germany" *Journal of Common Market Studies* v33 n1 1995 pp91-116

Goldberger, Bruce N. "Why Europe Should not Fear the Germans" *German Politics* v2 n2 1993 pp288-310

Goldstein, Walter "Europe after Maastricht" *Foreign Affairs* v71 n5 Winter 1992-93 pp117-132

Gordon. Philip H. "The Normalization of German Foreign Policy" *Orbis* v38 n2 1994 pp225-242

Graubard, Stephen R. "A Common Discontent: Revisiting Britain and Germany" *Foreign Affairs* v72 n3 1993 pp2-6

Green, Simon "The European Dimension in German Schools" *German Monitor* n34 1995 pp147-155

Greenfeld, Liah "Transcending the Nation's Worth" *Dædelus* v122 n3 1993 pp47-62

Grund, Walter 'Paying for the Common Farm Policy: Why Germany wants to Change the Rules" *European Community* v1 January 1969

Guerin-Sendelbach, Valerie ""Incertitudes françaises"?: Die Entwicklung der Europäischen Union französischer Sicht" *Zeitschrift für den deutsch-französischen Dialog* n4 1994 pp296-302

Guerin-Sendelbach Valerie & Jacek Rulkowski ""Euro-Trio" Frankreich-Deutschland-Polen" *Aussenpolitik* v45 n2 1994 pp246-253

Gundelach, Peter "National Value Differences: Modernization or Institutionalization?" *International Journal of Comparative Sociology* v35 n1-2 1994 pp37-59

Gunlicks Arthur B. "German Federalism after Unification: The Legal/Constitutional Response" *Publius* v24 Spring 1994 pp81-98

Gutjahr, Lothar "Stability, integration and global responsibility: Germany's changing perspective on national interests" *Review of International Studies* v21 n3 1995 pp301-317

Guyomarch, Alain "The European Dynamics of Evolving Party Competition in France" *Parliamentary Affairs* v48 n1 1995 pp100-124

Haas, Ernst "What is nationalism and why should we study it?" *International Organization* v40 n3 1986 pp707-744

Haas, Ernst "Nationalism: An Instrumental Social Construction" *Millennium* v22 n3 1993 pp505-545

Haass, Richard N. "Paradigm lost" *Foreign Affairs* v74 n1 1995 p43-58

Habermas, Jürgen "Citizenship and National Identity: Some reflections on the future of Europe" *Praxis International* v12 n1 1992 pp1-19

Hall, John A. "Nationalisms, Classified and Explained" *Dædelus* v122 n3 1993 pp1-28

Hank, Rainer "Signs of Erosion in the Corporative State" *German Comments* v43 July 1996 pp43-50

Hankiss, Elemér "European Paradigms: East and West, 1945-1994" *Dædelus* v123 n2 1994 pp115-126

Hänsch, Klaus "Renewing the European Vision" *Eur-Op News* v4 n4 Winter 1995

Hantrais, Linda "French social policy in the European context" *Modern & Contemporary France* NS3 (4) 1995 pp381-390

Hartwich, Kai U. "Die Vergangenheit lässt nicht los: Das 'Syndrome de Vichy' bleibt virulent" *Zeitschrift für den deutsche-französiche Dialog* n4 1994 pp279-280

Hassner, Pierre "Beyond Nationalism and Internationalism: Ethnicity and World Order" *Survival* v35 n2 1993 pp49-65

Hedetoft, Ulf "Euro-Nationalism: Or How the EC Affects the Nation-State as a Repository of Identity" *History of European Ideas* v15 n1-3 1992 pp271-277

Heilbrunn, Jacob "Germany's New Right" *Foreign Affairs* v76 n1 1996 pp

Helms, Ludger "Euro-Skeptizismus—Aspekte der neueren deutschsprachigen Europa-Literatur" *Zeitschrift für Politik* v41 n3 1994 pp296-304

Helms, Ludger "Executive Leadership in Parliamentary Democracies: The British Prime Minister and the German Chancellor Compared" *German Politics* v5 n1 1996 pp101-120

Hennes, Michael "The Future of Europe: Monetary or Political Union" *Aussenpolitik* v48 n1 1997

Henningham, Stephen "Testing Times: France's underground nuclear tests and its relations with the Asia-Pacific region" *Modern & Contemporary France* NS4 (1) 1996

Hoehmann, Hans-Hermann & Christian Meier "German-Russian Economic Relations—Appraisals and Perspectives" *Aussenpolitik* v46 n1 1995 pp52-59

Hix, Simon "The Study of the European Community: The Challenge to Comparative Politics" *West European Politics* v17 n1 January 1994 pp1-30

Hix, Simon "Parties at the European Level and the Legitimacy of EU Socio-Economic Policy" *Journal of Common Market Studies* v33 n4 1995 pp527-553

Hodge, Carl Cavanagh "The Federal Republic and the Future of Europe: A Reassessment" *German Politics* v1 n2 1992 pp223-238

Hodges, Michael & Stephen Woolcock "Atlantic Capitalism versus European Capitalism in the European Community" *West European Politics* v16 n3 1993 pp329-344

Hoffmann, Stanley "International Relations: An American Social Science" *Daedelus* v106 n3 1977 pp41-60

Hoffmann, Stanley "Fragments Floating in the Here and Now" *Dædelus* v108 n1 1979 pp1-26

Hoffmann, Stanley "Reflections on the Nation State Today" *Journal of Common Market Studies* v21 n1 1982 pp21-37

Hoffmann, Stanley "Thoughts on the French Nation Today" *Dædelus* v122 n3 1993 pp63-79

Hoffmann, Stanley "Europe's Identity Crisis Revisited" *Dædelus* v123 n2 1993 pp1-23

Hoffmann, Stanley "France: Keeping the Demons at Bay" *New York Review of Books* 3-3-94 pp10-16

Hoffmann, Stanley "Is Liberal Internationalism Dead?" *Foreign Policy* n98 Spring 1995 pp159-177

Holbrooke, Richard "America, A European Power" *Foreign Affairs* v74 n2 1995 pp38-51

Howe, Paul "A Community of Europeans: The Requisite Underpinings" *Journal of Common Market Studies* v33 n1 1996 pp28-46

Huelshoff, Michael G. "Domestic Politics and Dynamic Issue Linkage: A Reformulation of Integration Theory" *International Studies Quarterly* v38 n2 1994 pp255-279

Huntington, Samuel "The Clash of Civilizations?" *Foreign Affairs* v72 n3 1993 pp22-49

Hurd, Douglas "Developing the Common Foreign and Security Policy *International Affairs* v70 n3 1994 pp421-428

Hutchinson, John "Moral Innovators and the Politics of regeneration: the Distinctive Role of Cultural Nationalists in Nation-Building" *International Journal of Comparative Sociology* v33 n1-2 1992 pp101-117

Hutton, Will "Britain in a cold climate: the economic aims of foreign policy in the 1990s" *International Affairs* v68 n4 1992 pp619-632

Ignatieff, Michael "Nationalism and the Narcissism of Minor Differences" *Queen's Quarterly* v102 n1 1995 pp13-25

Ionescu, Ghita "Reading Notes, Summer 1994: Monsieur Mitterand and French Society" *Government and Opposition* v29 n1 1994 pp546-548

James, Alan "The equality of states: contemporary manifestations of an ancient doctrine" *Review of International Studies* v18 1992 pp377-91

Janes, Jackson "Who is German?" *History of European Ideas* v18 n2 1994 pp215-224

Janning, Josef "A German Europe—a European Germany? On the debate over Germany's foreign policy" *International Affairs* v72 n1 1996 pp9-32

Jeffrey, Charlie "The Non-Reform of the German Federal System after Unification" *West European Politics* v18 n2 1995 pp252-272

Jeffrey, Charlie & John Yates "Unification and Maastricht: The Response of the Länder Governments" *German Politics* v1 n3 1992 pp58-81

Johnston, R. J. "The Conflict over Qualified Majority Voting in the European Union Council of Ministers: An Analysis of the UK Negotiating Stance Using Power Indices" *British Journal of Political Science* v25 1995 pp245-288

Joffe, Josef "The New Europe: Yesterday's Ghosts" *Foreign Affairs* v72 n1 1993 pp29-43

Joffe, Josef et.al. "Mr. Heilbrunn's Planet: On Which the Germans Are Back" *Foreign Affairs* v76 n2 1996 pp152-159

Judt, Tony "Nineteen Eighty-Nine: The End of *Which* European Era?" *Dædelus* v123 n2 1994 pp1-19

Jun, Uwe "Inner-Party Reforms: The SPD and Labour Party in Comparative Perspective" *German Politics* v5 n1 1996 pp58-80

Kassim, Hussein "Policy Networks, Networks and European Union Policy Making: A Sceptical View" *West European Politics* v17 n4 1994 pp15-27

Keithly, David M. "Shadows of Germany's Authoritarian Past" *Orbis* v38 n2 1994 pp207-223

Kelly, Michael "Humanism and Unity" *History of European Ideas* v20 n4-6 1995 pp923-928

Keman, Hans & Paul Pennings "Managing Political and Societal Conflict in Democracies: Do Consensus and Corporatism Matter?" *British Journal of Political Science* v25 p2 1995 pp271-281

Kenen, Peter B. "The European Central Bank and monetary policy in stage three of EMU" *International Affairs* v68 n3 1992 pp457-474

Kennedy, Michael D. "What is 'the Nation' after Communism and Modernity?" *Polish Sociological Review* v105 n1 1994 pp47-58

Kennedy, Paul "Germany in Europe; Half a Hegemon" *New Perspectives Quarterly* v10 n1 Winter 1993 pp35-38

Kielinger, Thomas "Waking up in the new Europe — with a headache" *International Affairs* v66 n2 1990 pp249-263

Kinkel, Klaus "Deutschland in Europa: Zu den Zielen der deutschen Präsidentschaft in der Europäischen Union" *Europa-Archiv* Folge 12/1994 pp335-342

Klusmeyer, Douglas B. "Aliens, Immigrants, and Citizens: The Politics of Inclusion in the Federal Republic of Germany" *Dædelus* v122 n3 1993 pp81-114

Kocka, Jürgen "Crisis of Unification: How Germany Changes" *Dædelus* v123 n1 1994 pp173-192 p175

Kohl, Helmut "Gemeinsam die Zukunft gestalten" *Gewerkschaftliche Monatshefte* n9 1994 pp553-562

Kolankiewicz, George "Consensus and competition in the eastern enlargement of the European Union" *International Affairs* v70 n3 1994 pp477-495

Kolboom, Ingo "Dialog mit Bauchgrimmen?: Die zukunft der deutsch-französischen Beziehungen" *Europa-Archiv* Folge 9 1994 pp257-264

Koopmans, Ruud "Explaining the rise of racist and extreme right violence in Western Europe: Grievances or opportunities" *European Journal of Political Research* v30 September 1996 pp185-216

Korinman, Michel "Europa—die geopolitische Sicht" *Neue Gesellschaft/Frankfurter Hefte* n8 August 1996 pp695-700

Krieger, Wolfgang "Towards a Gaullist Germany? Some Lessons from the Yugoslav Crisis" *World Policy Journal* v11 n1 1994 pp26-38

Krisch, Henry "German Unification and East German Political Culture: Interaction and Change" *German Monitor* n37 1996 pp5-16

Kronig, Jürgen "Nur mit Tony Blair kann Labour noch siegen" *Neue Gesellschaft/Frankfurter Hefte* January 1995 pp6-10

Kühnhardt, Ludger "Multi-German Germany" *Dædelus* v123 n1 1994 pp193-209

Kühnhardt, Ludger "Maastricht II: The German Debate" *German Comments* v43 July 1996 pp58-66

Ladrech, Robert "Europeanization of Domestic Politics and Institutions: The Case of France" *Journal of Common Market Studies* v32 n1 1994 pp69-87

Laffan, Brigid "The Politics of Identity and Political Order in Europe" *Journal of Common Market Studies* v34 n1 1996 pp81-102

Lambert, John "The Nation-State Dies Hard" *Capital & Class* n43 Spring 1991 pp9-24

Langguth, Gerd "Time for a New Vision" *German Comments* n42 April 1996 pp43-56

Laughland, John "The Philosophy of "Europe"" *The National Interest* n39 Spring 1995 pp58-67

Lauk, Kurt J. "Germany at the Crossroads: On the Efficiency of the German Economy" *Dædelus* v123 n1 1994 pp57-83

Le Gloannec, Anne-Marie "On German Identity" *Dædelus* v123 n1 1994 pp129-148

Leipold, Helmut "The Eastward Enlargement of the European Union: Opportunities and Obstacles" *Aussenpolitik* v46 n2 1995 pp126-135

Leonardy, Uwe "Federation and Länder in German Foreign Relations: Power-sharing in Treaty-Making and European Affairs" *German Politics* v1 n3 1992 pp119-135

Lijphart, Arend "Consociational Democracy" *World Politics* v21 n2 1969

Lind, Michael "In Defence of Liberal Nationalism" *Foreign Affairs* v73 n3 1994 pp87-99

Link, Werner "Integration and Balance" *German Comments* n41 January 1996 pp17-23

Livingston, Robert Gerald "United Germany: Bigger and Better" *Foreign Policy* n87 Summer 1992 pp157-174

Lucas, Hans-Dieter "Prospects For Cooperation in the Baltic Sea Region" *Aussenpolitik* v46 n1 1995 pp24-33

MacShane, Denis "Europe's Next Challenge to British Politics" *Political Quarterly* v66 n1 1995 pp23-35

Mahant, Edelgard "Foreign Policy and European Identity" *History of European Ideas* v21 n4 1995 pp485-498

Malcolm, Noel "The Case Against 'Europe'" *Foreign Affairs* v74 n2 1995 pp52-68

Malcolm, Noel "Bosnia and the West: A Study in Failure" *The National Interest* n39 Spring 1995 pp3-14

Mann, Michael "Nation-States in Europe and Other Continents: Diversifying, Developing, Not Dying" *Dædelus* v122 n3 1993 pp115-140

Marden, Peter "Geographies of dissent: globalization, identity and the nation" *Political Geography* v16 n1 1997 pp37-64

Markovits, Andrei & Simon Reich "Should Europe Fear the Germans?" *German Politics and Society* n23 1991 pp1-20

Markovits, Andrei & Simon Reich "Deutschland New Gesicht: Über deutsches Hegemonie in Europa *Leviathan* n1 1992 pp15-63

Marquand, David "Tweaking the European Nerve" *Political Quarterly* v66 n1 1995 pp1-4

Mäsch, Nando "The German Model of Bilingual Education" *Language, Culture and Curriculum* v6 n3 1993 pp303-313

Maull, Hans W. "Zivilmacht Bundesrepublik?: Das neue Deutschland in der internationalen Politik" *Blatte für deutsche und internationale Politik* n8 1993 pp934-948

Maull, Hans W. "Germany in the Yugoslav Crisis" *Survival* v37 n4 1995-96 pp99-130

McCarthy, Patrick "France in the Mid-1990s: Gloom but Not Doomed" *Current History* November 1994 pp364-368

McFaul, Michael "Why Russia's Politics Matter" *Foreign Affairs* v74 n1 1995 pp87-99

McSweeney, Bill "Identity and Security: Buzan and the Copenhagen school" *Review of International Studies* v22 1996 pp81-93

Mearsheimer, John "Back to the Future: Instability in Europe After the Cold War" *International Security* v15 n1 1990 pp5-56

Mechtenberg, Theo "Scheitern die Einheit Euopas an den Nationalismen?: Interkulturelle Lernfähigkeit auf dem Prüfstand" *Deutsche Studien* v121 1994 pp16-26

Medley, Richard "Keeping Monetary Union On Track" *Foreign Affairs* v75 n6 1996 pp21-26

Meier-Walser Reinhard "Germany, France and Britain on the Threshold to a New Europe" *Aussenpolitik* v43 n4 1992 pp334-342

Meier-Walser Reinhard "Britain in Search of a Place 'at the heart of Europe'" *Aussenpolitik* v45 n1 1994 pp10-19

Meiers, Franz-Josef "Germany: The Reluctant Power" *Survival* v37 n3 1995

Menon, Anand "Continuing politics by other means: defence policy under the French Fifth Republic" *West European Politics* v17 n4 1994 pp74-96

Menon, Anand "From Independence to Cooperation: France, NATO and European Security" *International Affairs* v71 n1 1995 pp19-34

Merkl, Peter F. "Politico-Cultural Restraints on West German Foreign Policy: Sense of Trust, Identity, and Agency" *Comparative Political Studies* v3 n4 1971 pp443-467

Mertes, Michael "Germany's Social and Political Culture: Change Through Consensus?" *Dædelus* v123 n1 1994 pp1-32

Messerlin Patrick A. "France and trade policy: is the 'French exception' passée?" *International Affairs* v72 n2 1996 pp293-309

Michal, Wolfgang "Die Vermachtung Europas unter deutschen Vorzeichen" *Neue Gesellschaft/Frankfurter Hefte* n8 August 1996 pp700-705

Milner, Helen "International Theories of Cooperation Among Nations: Strengths and Weakness" *World Politics* v44 April 1992 pp489-495

Moisi, Dominique & Michael Mertes "Europe's Map, Compass and Horizon" *Foreign Affairs* v74 n1 1995 pp122-134

Moravscik, Andrew "Negotiating the Single European Act: national interests and conventional statecraft in the European Community" *International Organization* v45 n1 1991 pp19-56

Moravscik, Andrew "Preferences and Power in the European Community: A Liberal Intergovernmentalist Approach" *Journal of Common Market Studies* v31 n4 1993 pp473-519

Moravscik, Andrew "Idealism and Interest in the European Community: The Case of the French Referendum" *French Politics and Society* v11 n1 1993 pp45-56

Moreau-Defarges, Philippe "'J'ai fait un reve...' Le president François Mitterrand, artisan de l'union europeene" *Politique Etrangere* v50 Autumn 1985 pp359-375

Morgan, James "Wide horizons, slender means: the scope for British influence" *International Affairs* v68 n4 1992 pp603-617

Morgan, Roger "European Integration and National Interests" Review Article, *Government and Opposition* v29 n1 1994 pp128-134

Müller, Heiner "What Remains of The German Essence?" *New Perspectives Quarterly* v10 n1 1993 pp16-18

Müller, Wolfgang C. & Vincent Wright "Reshaping the State in Western Europe: The Limits to Retreat" *West European Politics* v17 n3 1994 pp1-11

Muller, Steven "Democracy in Germany" *Dædelus* v123 n1 1994 pp33-56

Nagengast, Emil "Coming to terms with a 'European Identity': The Sudeten Germans between Bonn and Prague" *German Politics* v5 n1 1996 pp81-100

Nauta, Lolle "Changing conceptions of citizenship" *Praxis International* v12 n1 1992 pp20-34

Neckermann, Peter "What went wrong in Germany after the Unification?" *East European Quarterly* v26 January 1993 pp447-469

Neunreither, Karlheinz "The Democratic Deficit of the European Union: Towards Closer Cooperation between the European Parliament and the National Parliaments" *Government and Opposition* v29 n3 1994 pp299-314

Newhouse, John "Europe's Rising Regionalism" *Foreign Affairs* v76 n1 1996 pp67-84

Nikzentaitis, Alvydas "Das Kalingrader Gebiet im Spannungsfeld internationaler Interessen" *Ost Europa* n10 1995 pp927-935

Nye, Joseph S. "Soft Power" *Foreign Policy* n80 Autumn 1990 pp153-171

Nye, Joseph S. "What New World Order?" *Foreign Affairs* v71 n2 1992 p83- 92

Oberndörfer, Dieter "Nation und Republik: Kollective Kultur oder kulturelle Freiheit" *Blatte für deutsche und internationale Politik* September 1994 pp1068-1081

Obradovic, Daniela "Policy Legitimacy and the European Union" in *Journal of Common Market Studies* v34 n2 1996

O'Brien, Conor Cruise "Die Zukunft des Westens" *Aesthetik & Kommunikation* h84 j23 February 1994

O'Brien, Peter "German-Polish Migration: The Elusive Search for a German Nation-State" *International Migration Review* v26 n2 1992 pp373-387

Odom, William D. "NATO's Expansion: Why the Critics are Wrong" *The National Interest* Spring 1995 pp38-49

Odom, William D . "How to Create a True World Order" *Orbis* v39 Spring 1995 pp155-172

Oliver, Peter "The French Constitution and the Treaty of Maastricht" *International and Comparative Law Quarterly* v43 n1 1994 pp1-25

Orlow, Dietrich "West German Parties since 1945: Continuity and Change" *Central European History* v18 n2 1985 pp188-201

Patton, David "Social Coalitions, Political Strategies, and German Unification" *West European Politics* v16 n4 1993 pp470-91

Pauly, Louis W. "Capital Mobility, State Autonomy and Political Legitimacy" *Journal of International Affairs* v48 n2 1995 pp369-388

Pauly, Louis W. & Simon Reich "National Structures and Multinational Corporate Behaviour: Enduring Differences in the Age of Globalization" *International Organization* v51 n1 1997 pp1-30

Pavlowitch, Stevan "Who is "Balkanizing" Whom? The Misunderstandings Between the Debris of Yugoslavia and an Unprepared West" *Dædelus* v123 n2 1994 pp203-223

Pfaff, William "Invitation to War" *Foreign Affairs* v72 n3 1993 pp97-109

Pflueger, Friedbert "Poland and the European Union" *Aussenpolitik* v46 n3 1995 pp225-231

Picht, Robert "Deutsche-französiche Beziehungen nach dem Fall der Mauer: Angst vor 'Großdeutschland'" *Integration* n2 1990 pp47-58

Pond, Elizabeth "Germany in the New Europe" *Foreign Affairs* v71 n2 1992 pp114-130

Poulard, Jean V. "The French Perception of German Unification" *German Monitor* n37 1996 pp157-166

Powell, Robert "Anarchy in international relations theory: the neorealist-neoliberal debate" *International Organization* v48 n2 1994 pp313-44

Pradetto, August "After the Bipolar World: Germany and her European Neighbours" *German Monitor* n37 1996 pp167-216

Prince, K. Michael "Germany, Europe and the Dilemma of Democratic Legitimation" *Aussenpolitik* v46 n1 1995 pp3-13

Pulzer, Peter "Unified Germany: A Normal State?" *German Politics* v3 n1 1994 pp1-17

Putnam, Robert D. "Diplomacy and Domestic Politics: The Logic of Two Level Games" *International Organization* v42 n3 1988 pp427-460

Rattinger, Hans "Public Attitudes to European integration in Germany after Maastricht: Inventory and Typology" *Journal of Common Market Studies* v32 n4 1994 pp525-540

Risse-Kappen, Thomas "Exploring the Nature of the Beast: International Relations Theory and Comparative Policy Analysis Meet in the European Union" *Journal of Common Market Studies* v34 n1 1996 pp53-78

Roberts, Geoffrey "The German Party System in Crisis" *Parliamentary Affairs* v48 n1 1995 pp125-140

Robinson, Jill "Anniversaries, Memory and the Neighbours: The 'German Question' in Recent History" *German Politics* v5 n1 1996 pp43-57

Rohrlich, Paul Egon "Economic culture and foreign policy: the cognitive analysis of economic policy making" *International Organization* v41 n1 1987 pp61-92

Roose, Frank de "The Politics of Patriotism" in *History of European Ideas* v15 n1-3 1992 pp55-59

Ross, George "Sidling into Industrial Policy: Inside the European Commission" *French Politics and Society* v11 n1 1993 pp20-44

Ross, George "Inside the Delors Cabinet" *Journal of Common Market Studies* v32 n1 1994 pp499-523

Ross, Werner "Goldhagen and German Original Sin" *German Comments* v45 January 1997 pp89-94

Ruggie, John Gerald "Territoriality and Beyond: Problematizing Modernity in International Relations" *International Organization* v47 n1 1993 pp139-174

Rühe, Volker "Shaping Euro-Atlantic Policies: A Grand Strategy for a New Era" *Survival* v35 n2 1993 pp129-137

Rummel, Reinhardt "West European Cooperation in Foreign and Security Policy" *Annals of the American Academy of Political Science* January 1994 pp112-123

Rupnik, Jacques "Central Europe or Mitteleuropa?" *Dædelus* v119 n1 1990

Rupnik, Jacques "Europe's New Frontiers: Remapping Europe" *Dædelus* v123 n2 1994 pp91-115

Sander Richard P. "The Contribution of Post-World War II Schools in Poland in Forging a Negative Image of the Germans" *East European Quarterly* v29 n2 1995 pp169-187

Sandholtz, Wayne "Choosing union: monetary politics and Maastricht" *International Organization* v47 n1 1993 pp1-20

Santer, Jacques "The European Union's security and defence policy: How to avoid missing the 1996 rendez-vous" *NATO Review* November 1995 pp3-9

Scharpf, Fritz W. "The Joint-Decision Trap: Lessons From German Federalism and European Integration" *Public Administration* v66 Autumn 1988 pp239-278Fritz,

Scharpf, Fritz W. "Europäisches Demokratiedefizit und deutscher Föderalismus" *Staatswissenschaft und Staatspraxis* v3 n3 1992 pp293-306

Scharping, Rudolf "New Challenges for Franco-German Cooperation" *Aussenpolitik* v45 n1 1994 pp1-9

Schlesinger, Philip "Europe's Contradictory Communicative Space" *Dædelus* v123 n2 1994 pp25-51

Schmidt, Vivien A. "Loosening the Ties that Bind: The Impact of European Integration on French Government and its Relationship to Business" *Journal of Common Market Studies* v34 n2 1996 pp223-253

Schudson, Michael "Culture and the Integration of national societies" *International Social Science Journal* v105 n1 1994 pp63-79

Schwok, René "EC-1992 and the Swiss National Identity" *History of European Ideas* v15 n1-3 1992 pp241-247

Schwarz, Hans-Peter "Germany's National & European Interests" *Dædelus* v123 n2 1994 pp81-105

Scott, Andrew, John Peterson & David Millar "Subsidiarity: A 'Europe of the Regions' v. the British Constitution?" *Journal of Common Market Studies* v30 n1 1994 pp47-67

Seebacher-Brandt, Brigitte "Nation im vereinigten Deutschland" *Aus Politik und Zeitgeschichte* B42/94 21-10-1994 pp3-9

Shils, Edward "Nation, nationality, nationalism and civil society" *Nations and Nationalism* v1 n1 1995 pp93-118

Shore, Chris "Transcending the Nation-State?: The European Commission and the (Re)-Discovery of Europe" *Journal of Historical Sociology*" v9 n4 1996 pp473-496

Silvia, Stephen J. "Left Behind: The Social Democratic Party in Eastern Germany" *West European Politics* v16 n2 1993 pp24-49

Simonian, Haig "France, Germany and Europe" *Journal of Common Market Studies* v19 n3 1981 pp203-219

Singer, Brian C. J. "Cultural versus Contractual Nations: Rethinking their Opposition" *History and Theory* v35 n3 1996 pp309-337

Sinnott, Richard "Theories of integration and the integration of the European database" *International Social Science Journal* v46 n4 1994 pp533-540

Sinopoli, Richard C. "Liberal Justice, National Community" *History of European Ideas* v15 n4-6 1992 pp519-525

Sked, Alan "Cheap Excuses" *The National Interest* n24 Summer 1991 pp51-60

Sloan, Stanley "New Designs on NATO: US Perspectives on NATO's Future" *International Affairs* v71 n2 1995 pp217-231

Smith, Anthony D. "Towards a Global Culture?" *Theory, Culture and Society* 7 1990 pp171-191

Smith, Anthony D. "The Nation: Invented, Imagined, Reconstructed?" *Millennium* v20 n3 1991 pp353-368

Smith, Anthony D. "National identity and the idea of European unity" *International Affairs* v68 n1 1992 pp55-76

Smith, Anthony D. "Nationalism and the Historians" *International Journal of Comparative Sociology* v33 n1-2 1992 pp58-79

Smith, Anthony D. "A Europe of Nations—or the Nation of Europe?" *Journal of Peace Research* v30 n2 1993 pp129-135

Smith, Julie "The 1994 European Elections: Twelve into One Won't Go" *West European Politics* v18 n3 1995 pp199-217

Smith, Michael "The European Union and a Changing Europe: Establishing the Boundaries of Order" *Journal of Common Market Studies* v34 n1 1996 pp4-28

Smyser, W. R. "Dateline Berlin: The New German Vision", *Foreign Policy* Winter 1994-95 pp140-157

Special Issue *Le débat* n87 November-December 1995

Spence, David "The European Community and German Unification" *German Politics* v1 n3 1992 pp136-163

Sperling, James "German Foreign Policy after Unification: The End of Cheque Book Diplomacy?" *West European Politics* v17 n1 1994 pp73-97

Stephenson, Jill "Anniversaries, Memory and the Neighbours: The 'German Question' in Recent History" *German Politics* v5 n1 1996 pp43-57

Stern, Fritz "Germany in a Semi-Gaullist Europe" *Foreign Affairs* v58 n4 1980 pp867-886

Stern, Fritz "The Goldhagen Controversy: One Nation, One People, One Theory?" *Foreign Affairs* v76 n1 1996 pp128-137

Stuth, Reinhard "Germany's New Role in a Changing Europe" *Aussenpolitik* v43 n1 1992 pp22-32

Swaan, Abram de "The Evolving European Language System: A Theory of Communication Potential and Language Competition" *International Political Science Review* v14 n3 1993 pp241-255

Taylor, Keith "European Union: The Challenge for Local and Regional Government" *Political Quarterly* v66 n1 1995 pp74-83

Thies, Jochen "Observations on the Political Class in Germany" *Dædalus* v123 n1 1994 pp263-276

Tiersky, Ronald "Mitterrand's Legacy" *Foreign Affairs* v74 n1 1995 pp112-121

Tomlinson, John "Homogenisation and Globalisation" *History of European Ideas"* v20 n4-6 pp891-897

Tyler, Gus "The Nation-State versus the Global Economy" *Challenge* v36 March/April 1993 pp26-32

van Kersbergen, Kees & Bertjan Verbeek "The Politics of Subsidiarity in the European Union" *Journal of Common Market Studies* v32 n2 1994 pp215-237

van Traa, Maarten "Wohlbekannt aber ungeliebt? Der deutsche Nachbar aus niederländischer Sicht" *Europa Archiv* v49 n17 1994 pp491-498

Veen, Hans-Joachim & Carsten Zelle "Growing Closer Together or Drifting Apart?" *German Comments* v39 July 1995 pp54-59

Vernet, Daniel "The dilemma of French foreign policy" *International Affairs* v68 n4 1992 pp655-664

Wæver, Ole "Three Competing Europes" *International Affairs* v66 n3 1990 pp477-493

Wæver, Ole "Identity, Integration and Security: Solving the Sovereignty Puzzle in E.U. Studies" *Journal of International Affairs* v48 n2 1995 pp389-431

Wæver, Ole "European Security Identities" *Journal of Common Market Studies* v34 n1 1996 pp103-132

Wagner, Helmut ""Constitutional Patriotism" as an Antidote" *Aussenpolitik* v44 n3 1993 pp243-252

Wallace, Helen "Britain out on a limb?" *Political Quarterly* v66 n1 1995 pp46-58

Wallace, Ian "German Intellectuals and Unification" *German Monitor* n37 1996 pp87-100

Wallace, William "Deutschlands zentrale Rolle: Ein versuch, die europäische Frage neu zu definieren" *Integration* n1 1990 pp13-20

Wallace, William "Foreign Policy and national identity in the United Kingdom" *International Affairs* v67 n1 1991 pp65-80

Wallace, William "British foreign policy after the Cold War" *International Affairs* v68 n3 1992 pp423-442

Wallace, William "Rescue or Retreat?: The Nation State in Western Europe, 1945-93" *Political Studies* v42 Special Issue 1994 pp53-76

Weber, Cynthia 'Reconsidering Statehood: Examining the Sovereignty/Intervention Boundary" *Review of International Studies* v18 1992 pp199-216

Weck, Michael "Der ironische Westen und der tragische Osten" *Kursbuch: Deutschland, Deutschland* n109 September 1992

Wedell, George "Prospects for Television in Europe" *Government and Opposition* v29 n3 1994 pp315-331

Wego, Helge "Reaktivierung der WEU: Der Beitrag Deutschlands und Frankreichs" *Europäische Sicherheit* n6 1995 pp39-4

Wehler, Hans-Ulrich "The Goldhagen Controversy: Agonizing Problems, Scholarly Failure and the Political Dimension" *German History* v15 n1 1997 pp80-91

Weisbrod, Bernd "German Unification and the National Paradigm" *German History* v14 n2 1996 pp193-203

Wendt, Alexander "Collective Identity Formation and the International State" *American Political Science Review* v88 n2 1994 pp384-398

Werz, Nikolaus "External Cultural Policy: Continuity or Change" *Aussenpolitik* v43 n3 1992 pp246-255

Wessels, Wolfgang "Rationalizing Maastricht: the search for an optimal strategy of the new Europe" *International Affairs* v70 n3 1994 pp445-457

Westlake, Martin "The European Parliament, the National Parliaments and the 1996 Intergovernmental Conference" *Political Quarterly* v66 n1 1995 pp59-73

Wielinga, Friso "The German Factor in Dutch Foreign Policy since 1945" in *German Monitor* n37 1996 pp133-155

Williams, Shirley "Britain in the European Union: A Way Forward" *Political Quarterly* v66 n1 1995 pp5-22

Wilterdink, Nico "Images of National Character" *Social Science & Modern Society* v32 n1 November/December 1994 pp43-51

Winkler, Heinrich August, "Rebuilding of a Nation: The Germans Before and After Unification" *Dædelus* v123 n1 1994 pp107-127

Witte, Barthold "Two Catastrophes, Two Causes, and How the Germans Dealt with them" *Dædelus* v123 n2 1994 pp235-249

Wood, Stephen "France before the IGC: Between National Crisis and European Salvation?" in *Contemporary European Studies* (Australia) n15 May 1996 pp5-8

Wood, Stephen "Hamlet's Evolution: Decision Time for Europe" *Current Affairs Bulletin* v73 n5 January/February 1997 pp20-27

Wright, Jonathan "The Role of Britain in West German Foreign Policy Since 1949" *German Politics* v5 n1 1996 pp26-42

Xenos, Nicholas "The Natural Politics of Nation and Economy" *History of European Ideas* v20 n1-3 1995 pp383-388

Yost, David S. "Political philosophy and the theory of international relations" *International Affairs* v70 n2 1994 pp263-90

Government/Ministerial reports and other material

Auswärtige Kulturpolitik 1990-1992 (Bonn: Auswärtiges Amt 1993)

Deutsche Aussenpolitik (Bonn: Auswärtige Amt 1995)

"Weitere langfristige Kulturförderung des Bundes gesichert" (Bonn: Bundesministerium des Innern 1994)

Weißbuch (Bundesverteidigungsministerium: 1994)

Ausländer und die deutsche Wirtschaft Dokumentation n339 (Bonn: Bundesministerium für Wirtschaft 1994)

Eberhard Schoof *EG-Ausschuss: Der Deutsche Bundestag und die Europäische Gemeinschaft* (Deutscher Bundestag: Bonn 1994)

"Bericht der Bundesregierung zur Auswärtigen Kulturpolitik" Deutscher Bundestag 13. Wahlperiode *Drucksache* 13/3823 (20-2-96)

Stark wie die Mark (Bonn: Finanz Ministerium 1996)

Bulletin (Presse- und Informationsamt der Bundesregierung)

Zahlenkompaß 1994, 1995, 1996 (Wiesbaden: Statistiches Bundesamt 1994, 1995, 1996)

Livre Blanc sur la Défense (Paris: La Documentation Française 1994)

Jean-David Levitte "The Cultural Diplomacy of France" (Ambassade de France en Australie: June 1994)

The British Council Worldwide (London: British Council 1995)

The 1996 Intergovernmental Conference: The Agenda; Democracy and Efficiency; The Role of National Parliaments Twenty Fourth Report, Volume 1, Select Committee on European Legislation, Session 1994-95 (London: HMSO 1995)

European Institutions Publications

Television Without Frontiers: Green Paper on the Establishment of the Common Market for Broadcasting, Especially by Satellite and Cable (Brussels: CEC 1984)

The European Community and Culture (Brussels: CEC 1985)

The Borrowing and Lending Activities of the European Communities (Brussels: Credit and Investments Directorate CEC 1992)

The Community Budget: The Facts in Figures SEC(94) 1100 - EN (Brussels: CEC 1994)

European Community Action in Support of Culture (Brussels: CEC 27-7-94)

XI Konferenz der Europaausschüsse der nationalen Parlamente der Mitgliedstaaten der Europäischen Union und des Europäischen Parlaments (COCAS) Bonn 24/25-10-94 (Document 1)

"Draft Interinstitutional Agreement Between the European Parliament, the Council and the Commission on The Rules for Exercising the Powers to Implement Acts Adopted jointly by the European Parliament and the Council" (Brussels: 19-4-94)

Audiovisual Policy: Stimulating Dynamic Growth in the European Programme Industry (Brussels: CEC 8-2-95)

Preliminary Draft General Budget of the European Communities for the Financial Year 1996 (Brussels: CEC 15-5-95)

The Multilingual Information Society (Brussels: CEC 8-11-95)

1st Report on the Consideration of Cultural Aspects in European Community Action (Brussels: CEC 17-4-96)

"Draft Communication to the Parliament and the Council" *European Report* n2123 13-4-96

Eurobarometer

Europäische Gespräche

EC *Official Journal*

Eurostat *Basic Statistics of the Community*

European Union News (Canberra: Delegation of the European Commission to Australia and New Zealand)

EU Background (Canberra: Delegation of the European Commission to Australia and New Zealand)

Political Parties: Pamphlets, Discussion Papers, Manifestos

Resolutions of the 3rd Congress of the CDU of Germany Düsseldorf 25-10-92 (Bonn: CDU 1992)

CDU/CSU Fraktion des Deutschen Bundestags *Überlegungen zur europäischen Politik* (Bonn: CDU Bundesgeschäftstelle 1-9-94)

Wir sichern Deutschlands Zukunft: Regierungsprogramm von CDU und CSU (Bonn: CDU Bundesgeschäftstelle 1994)

CDU/CSU Fraktion im Deutschen Bundestag "Mehr europäische Rechtstaatlichkeit" (Bonn: CDU/CSU Pressedienst June 1995)

CDU/CSU Fraktion im Deutschen Bundestag *Die Europäische außen- und sicherheitspolitisch handlungsfähiger machen* (Bonn: CDU Bundesgeschäftstelle 1995)

Grundlagen der CDU-Kulturpolitik (Bonn: CDU Bundesgeschäftstelle 1995)

Kulturpolitik Document (Bonn: CDU Bundesgeschäftsstelle 1995)

Beschluß des 7. Parteitages vom 16. Oktober 1995 (Bonn: CDU Bundesgeschäftstelle 1995)

Grundsatzprogram der SPD (Berlin: 1989)

Douglas Hurd "Our Future in Europe" (London: Conservative Political Centre 1993)

A Strong Britain in a Strong Europe: The Conservative Manifesto for Europe 1994 (London: Conservative Political Centre 1994)

Make Europe work for you: Labour's Election Manifesto for the European Elections, June 1994 (London: Labour Party 1994)

Wilfred Martens (EVP) *Vertiefung und Erweiterung: Eine Strategie für die Europaeische Union* (Brussels 20-9-94)

Group of the European People's Party "Bruges Study Days" 28-8-95/1-9-95

Interview Sources

British Labour Party, London, August 1994; Conservative Party European Directorate, London, August 1994; European Parliament officials, London, August 1994 & Bonn, October 1994; Christlich Demokratische Union, Bundesgeschäftstelle, Bonn, October 1994; Sozialdemokratische Partei Deutschlands, Bonn October 1994; Auswärtiges Amt, Bonn, October/November 1994 & September 1996; Europa-Ausschuß, Bonn, October 1994; Sächsisches Ministerium des Innern, Dresden, September 1996; US Embassy, Bonn, October 1994; Public Interviews, Germany, 1994 & 1996

Conference Papers/Proceedings/Symposiums

Gerner, Kristian "A Moveable Place with a Moveable Past: Perspectives on Central Europe", Australasian Association of European Historians Conference, Adelaide, 8/11-7-97

Griffiths, Martin "Fear and Loathing: Nationalism versus World Order" Seminar paper, Politics Department, University of Adelaide 20-9-95

Jeffrey, Charlie "Failing the Challenge of Unification? The Länder and German Federalism in the 1990s" in *Contemporary Political Studies* v2 Eds P. Dunleavy & J. Stanyer (Political Studies Association of Great Britain: 1994) pp765-779

Kelly, Michael "The Hegemony of National Identity in Cultural Identities", International Society for the Study of European Ideas Conference on *European Identity at the Millennium* Utrecht 19/24-8-96

Wood, Stephen "Nation, Culture and European Identity: Prospects for Political Union", International Society for the Study of European Ideas Conference on *European Identity at the Millennium* Utrecht 19/24-8-96

Wood, Stephen "Cultural Diplomacy, Cultural Protection, and 'Ever Closer Union'", International Society for the Study of European Ideas Conference on *European Identity at the Millennium* Utrecht 19/24-8-96

Wood, Stephen "Germany's External Cultural Policy: More Politics Among Nations", Australasian Association of European Historians Conference, Adelaide, 8/11-7-97

Europa '96: Reformprogramm für die Europäische Union Ed. Werner Weidenfeld (Gütersloh: Verlag Bertelsmann Stiftung 1994)

German Foreign Policy after Reunification Conference Report (Berlin: Aspen Institute 1991)

Kultur, Kommerz und Außenpolitik—Ungewohnte Perspektiven, neue Kooperation (Frankfurt aM: Börsenverein des Deutschen Buchhandels 1996)

(Symposium) "United Germany: Stabilizing Influence or Threat?" *Partisan Review* n4 1995

Wirtschaftstag '96 "Politische Union und Gemeinsamer Markt" Maritim Hotel, Bonn, 13-6-96

Ziele und Verantwortung der Kulturpolitik (Gütersloh: Verlag Bertelsmann Stiftung 1995)

Occasional Papers/Working Papers/Unpublished Papers

German Unification: Economic Issues Occasional Paper n75 Eds. Leslie Lipschitz & Donogh McDonald (Washington: IMF 1990)

United Germany: The First Five Years: Performance and Policy Issues Eds. Robert Corker et.al. Occasional Paper n106 (Washington: IMF 1995)

Road Maps of the Transition: The Baltics. the Czech Republic, Hungary and Russia Eds. Bisiwajit Banerjee et.al. Occasional Paper n127 (Washington: IMF 1995)

Dörrenbächer, Heike "Die Sonderwirtschaftszone Jantar´ von Kalinigrad (Königsberg) *Arbeitspapiere zur Internationalen Politik* n81 (Bonn: DGAP 1994)

Gebhard, Paul R. S. "The United States and European Security" *Adelphi Paper* n286 February 1994

Gordon, Philip "Die Deutsche-Französische Partnerschaft und die Atlantische Allianz" *Arbeitspapier für internationalen Politik* n82

Hubel, Helmut & Bernhard May "Ein "normales" Deutschland?: Die Souveräne Bundesrepublik in der ausländischen wahrnehmung" *Arbeitspapiere zur Internationale Politik* n92 (Bonn: DGAP June 1995)

Jopp, Mathias "The Strategic Implications of European Integration" *Adelphi Paper* n290 July 1994

Kaiser, Karl & Klaus Becher *Deutschland und der Irak-Konflikt: Internationale Sicherheitsverantwortung Deutschlands und Europa nach der deutschen Vereinigung Arbeitspapier für internationalen Politik* n68 (Bonn: DGAP 1992

"Die Zukunft der europäischen Integration: Folgerungen für die deutsche Politik" *Arbeitspapiere zur Internationale Politik* n78 Eds. Karl Kaiser & Hanns W. Maull

Meiers, Franz-Josef "NATO's Peacekeeping Dilemma" *Arbeitspapiere zur Internationale Politik* n94 pp61-77

Rahr, Alexander & Joachim Krause "Russia's New Foreign Policy" *Arbeitspapiere zur Internationale Politik* n91 (Bonn: DGAP 1995)

Rattinger, Hans "Einstellungen zur europäischen Integration in der Bundesrepublik vor der Schaffung des Binnenmarktes" *DFG-Projekt* n2 Febuary 1993 (Bamberg: Lehrstuhl für Politikwissenschaft II, Universität Bamberg)

Rattinger, Hans "Einstellungen zur Europäischen Union in Deutschland: Strukturen und Determinanten" *DFG-Projekt* n8 April 1995 (Bamberg: Lehrstuhl für Politikwissenschaft II, Universität Bamberg)

Schmidt, Peter "Germany, France and NATO" Paper for a Joint Seminar of the American Institute for Contemporary German Studies and the U.S. Army War College (June 1994)

Szemerkényi, Réka "Central European Civil-Military Reforms At Risk" *Adelphi Paper* n306 (London: IISS 1996)

Holm, Ulla (Draft copy) "The French Garden is no longer what it used to be" in *The Struggle for 'Europe': French and German Concepts of State, Nation and European Union*

Wæver Ole (Draft copy) "Chapter One" in *The Struggle for 'Europe': French and German Concepts of State, Nation and European Union*

Newspapers and Magazines

The Age, The Australian, Deutschland Magazine, The Economist, The European, Frankfurter Allgemeine Zeitung, Le Figaro, Financial Times, Focus, General Anzeiger, The Guardian, Guardian Weekly, The Independent, International Herald Tribune, Libération, Le Monde, Le Monde Diplomatique, Merkur, Newsweek, New

York Review of Books, New York Times, The Observer, Le Point, The Spectator, Der Spiegel, Süddeutsche Zeitung, Sydney Morning Herald, Daily Telegraph, Time, The Times, Wall Street Journal, Die Welt, Welt am Sonntag, Die Woche, Die Zeit

Other

Deutsche Welle

USIA EFS File

Lateline (ABC Television, Australia)

World Investment Report 1994, 1995 1996 (New York: UNCTAD 1994, 1995, 1996)

OECD National Accounts (Paris: OECD 1995, 1996, 1997)

Index